# WORKING IN AMERICA

WORKING IN AMERICA

Continuity, Conflict, and Change

Amy S. Wharton

Washington State University

MAYFIELD PUBLISHING COMPANY
Mountain View, California
London • Toronto

Library of Congress Cataloging-in-Publication Data
Wharton, Amy S.
  Working in America : continuity, conflict, and change / Amy S. Wharton.
      p.   cm.
    ISBN 1-55934-737-6
    1. Work—Sociological aspects.   2. Work—Social aspects—United
  States   I. Title.
  HD4904.W485   1997
  306.3'6—dc21   97-16790
                                                                      CIP

Manufactured in the United States of America
10 9 8 7 6 5 4 3 2 1

Mayfield Publishing Company
1280 Villa Street
Mountain View, California 94041

Sponsoring editor, Serina Beauparlant; production, Publication Services; manuscript editor, Tom Long; art director, Jeanne M. Schreiber; text designers, Linda M. Robertson and Dorothy Evans; cover designer, Laurie Anderson; cover photo, Malcolm Piers/The Image Bank; illustrations, Publication Services; manufacturing manager, Randy Hurst. The text was set in 10/12 Book Antiqua by Publication Services and printed on 45# Ecolocote by Malloy Lithographing, Inc.

To my father, William Wharton, and the
memory of my mother, Marilyn Wharton (1921–1964)

Preface

College students today are more anxious about their futures than in the past, particularly with respect to their places in the world of work. The social contract that promised steadily increasing wages and secure employment has unraveled, leaving many uncertain about their lives and livelihoods. In these times, a sociological perspective on work is more important than ever. Analysis and understanding of the societal conditions that shape people's work lives may be the best tools for conquering their anxiety and uncertainty. To prepare for and reshape the future demands knowledge of the social forces that influenced the past and help structure the present.

The study of work is central to the discipline of sociology. From the industrial revolution to the service economy, sociologists have contributed much to our understanding of the forces shaping workers' lives and the workplace. This anthology contains a sampling of some of the best that sociologists of work have to offer. Through a variety of methods and approaches, the readings address several pertinent questions about the American workplace: What have been the most important changes in workers' lives and work organization during the twentieth century? What factors shape employment today? What does the future hold for work and workers?

By examining how sociologists have pursued answers to these questions, I hope students will acquire tools to address their own concerns and come away better equipped to make sense of their past, present, and future work experiences.

Selecting the readings for this anthology was both a challenge and a pleasure. It was challenging because my colleagues have produced such a tremendous amount of valuable research on the workplace that I could have filled several volumes easily; deciding what to exclude was a difficult task. At the same time, compiling these readings provided me with an opportunity to explore and appreciate sociologists' contributions to our knowledge about workers and work. This process reaffirmed my belief that a sociological perspective remains the best vantage point from which to understand the social world.

In the end, the readings that appear here were selected with several considerations in mind. First, I aimed for a degree of comprehensiveness in the coverage of topics. While no anthology can address everything, the anthology remains one of the best vehicles for presenting information to students on a range of topics. Second, I wanted to present the key pieces of research in a particular area. I included some classics but primarily used examples of contemporary research that have made an impact. Third, attending to gender, racial, and ethnic differentiation in the workplace was important to me. Hence, these issues are addressed throughout the anthology. Finally, I selected readings with a student audience in mind. When all is said and done, this anthology is for them.

Intellectual work is, at its best, a collective enterprise. In editing this anthology, I benefited from the valuable comments and suggestions of many colleagues around the country.

These included William Canak, Middle Tennessee State University; Samuel Cohn, Texas A&M University; Daniel Cornfield, Vanderbilt University; Barbara Thomas Coventry, The University of Toledo; Patricia Craig, Ohio State University; William Finlay, University of Georgia; Robin Leidner, University of Pennsylvania; Garth Massey, University of Wyoming; Peter Meiksins, Cleveland State University; Stephen Petterson, University of Virginia; Patricia A. Roos, Rutgers University; and Vicki Smith, University of California–Davis. At Washington State University, my friend and colleague in the English Department, Anne Maxham, cheerfully volunteered to give critical feedback on my introductions; Nathan Lauster provided crucial research assistance.

The division of labor involved in producing this book extends beyond academe to include many others' contributions. I owe tremendous thanks to Mayfield Senior Editor Serina Beauparlant, whose gentle prodding, enthusiasm, and constant positive reinforcement helped this anthology move from idea to reality in what seems like record time. Others at Mayfield, including Sara Early and April Wells-Hayes, have been equally helpful and conscientious. In fact, from the beginning to the end of this project, I have benefited from the efforts of many people who are very good at their jobs. They have my thanks and appreciation.

Contents

PART VI   Work and Society in the Twenty-First Century   445

General Introduction

The end of a century offers an opportune time to assess the past, reflect on the present, and imagine the future. As the millennium approaches, a course in the sociology of work can provide a conceptual and theoretical platform from which to explore a variety of enduring sociological issues. Though this anthology focuses mainly on the contemporary workplace, it also looks at workplaces of the past and the future through a critical, sociological lens. Work is among the most important social institutions; indeed, in the late nineteenth and early twentieth centuries, sociologists Karl Marx, Max Weber, and Emile Durkheim placed work at the center of their analyses. Contemplating the development of capitalism in the West and the burgeoning industrial revolution, these "founding fathers of sociology" understood that the organization of work helps to determine the fates of individuals as well as their societies.

Three major themes guided the selection of readings for this anthology—the first reflects a methodological concern, the second stems from an empirical observation, and the third emphasizes conceptual and theoretical issues. Each theme has continuity with past efforts to understand the American workplace, yet each also directs attention to important questions about the present and future.

The first theme is that workers' lives are shaped not only by daily life on the job but also by larger trends that are transforming work in the country and across the globe. This theme has methodological implications because it suggests that any study of work must concern itself not only with workers' experiences but also with the larger histori-

cal, economic, and social contexts within which these experiences occur. Multiple levels of analysis are thus necessary to address the important questions in the sociology of work.

The second major theme is that workers are demographically more diverse than ever, and this changing demography plays an important role in the organization and experience of work. This theme is drawn from an empirical observation: The American workplace—like the larger society—has always been composed of workers from diverse racial and ethnic backgrounds, genders, ages, religions, and sexual orientations—to name but a few characteristics. As American society moves into the next century, this demographic diversity is increasing: Most new entrants to the labor force are expected to be nonwhites, females, or immigrants (Johnston and Packer 1987). Sociologists have come to believe that we cannot fully understand work without considering the characteristics of the people who perform it.

The third theme of this book is perhaps the most significant to sociologists: Work is not strictly an instrumental activity, nor can it be understood only in economic terms. Instead, as Friedland and Robertson (1990, p. 25) explain, "Work provides identities as much as it provides bread for the table; participation in commodity and labor markets is as much an expression of who you are as what you want." Moreover, from this perspective work is not an isolated institution, closed off from the rest of society, but is profoundly interconnected with the larger social world. Not only are its boundaries permeable, making the workplace subject to influences from other institutions, but the influence of work on other aspects of society is also great. Indeed, work shapes every aspect of life—from people's conceptions of self to the degree of inequality in a society. Through the years sociologists studying work have disagreed as to which effects of work they consider most important, but there has been no dispute with the basic premise that the study of work is a vehicle for examining some of the most fundamental aspects of social life.

Linking the Micro and the Macro in Sociological Studies of Work

Like the field of sociology as a whole, teaching and scholarship in the sociology of work reflect a range of approaches, which typically have been characterized as either *micro* or *macro*. Micro-level approaches tend to focus on individuals or small groups in a particular workplace and examine processes or outcomes that operate at these levels of analysis. Though by no means all micro-level research is ethnographic, many researchers prefer qualitative methodologies that allow for close, in-depth scrutiny of particular social phenomena. Indeed, there is a long and rich tradition of micro-level ethnographic research in the sociology of work. This research has provided useful accounts of many jobs, offering the student a way to vicariously experience life as a machine shop worker, a medical student, a flight attendant, or a McDonald's employee (Roy 1959; Becker, Geer, Hughes, and Strauss 1961; Hochschild 1983; Leidner 1993).

In contrast, macro-level studies in the sociology of work tend to be less concerned with "flesh-and-blood workers" and more attentive to larger processes, trends, and outcomes (Simpson 1989, p. 565). Studies of this type typically analyze data collected from representative samples of people, jobs, or workplaces and seek to identify patterns and relationships between key variables. Macro-level research thus is often quantitative, driven by the desire to test hypotheses or produce generalizable results. The popularity of macro-level research has grown in recent years, as sociologists have borrowed concepts and theories from economists. Sociological studies of wage determination, for example, attempt to explain what factors determine the "worth" of jobs and cause some jobs to command higher wages than others (Tomaskovic-Devey 1993).

Micro and macro research traditions are often perceived as distinct, and sometimes even conflicting, approaches. Courses in the sociology of work have thus traditionally emphasized one or the other approach, but not both. Ideally, however, micro and macro studies should inform one another, as no single approach can address everything. Moreover, in my view, important sociological questions cannot be answered by only one type of study or approach but require a "division of labor" among researchers. For example, to understand the role of race in the workplace we need both fine-grained, ethnographic studies *and* more large-scale, quantitative analyses. The former can help us understand such issues as workers' experiences of discrimination and the meaning of race to employers (Kirschenman and Neckerman 1991), and the latter may address such issues as the racial gap in earnings or the consequences of corporate restructuring for the employment chances of African-Americans (Wilson 1996). This view is reflected in the selection of readings for this anthology, which incorporates studies employing diverse methodologies and approaches. By studying both the micro and the macro dimensions of work, we can begin to see how work is shaped by its social context and, conversely, how workplace dynamics may shape the larger society.

The Changing Demographics of the Workplace

Anyone who takes even a cursory look around any place of work in industrialized countries can see that workers doing the same or similar jobs tend to be of the same gender and racial and ethnic group. In a workplace in New York City—for instance, a handbag factory—a walk through the various departments might reveal that the owners and managers are white men; their secretaries and bookkeepers are white and Asian women; the order takers and data processors are African-American women; the factory hands are Hispanic men cutting pieces and Hispanic women sewing them together; African-American men are packing and loading the finished product; and non-English-speaking Eastern European women are cleaning up after everyone (Lorber 1994, p. 194).

Although the labor force is becoming increasingly diverse, jobs and workplaces continue to be highly segregated along gender, racial, and ethnic lines. The continuing association between jobs and workers of a particular gender, race, or ethnic background suggests that these social categories are as powerful in shaping life inside the workplace as they have been shown to be in shaping life in other societal institutions.

Gender, race, and ethnicity in the workplace are often studied by focusing on discrimination and inequality, and these remain important topics. Despite widespread social changes, as well as the passage of legislation and social policies designed to prevent discrimination and reduce inequality, the costs and rewards of work remain unevenly distributed across social categories. The desire to understand the sources of these work-related inequalities, the forces that perpetuate them, and the consequences of these inequalities for workers and their families has generated a tremendous amount of research in recent years. We thus know a great deal about some aspects of gender, racial, and ethnic inequality in the workplace. Changes in the organization of work brought on by a global economy and the changing demographics of workers raise new questions for analysis, however. How will these changes affect the costs and rewards of work? More important, how will the relative situations of different groups of workers be affected by the changing workplace? Will economic inequality increase or diminish as we enter the twenty-first century? Questions such as these are important topics for research and debate.

The impacts of gender, race, and ethnicity on the workplace are not confined to their roles in producing inequality and discrimination, nor do these factors affect only the personal consequences of work. Rather, sociologists argue that, at a more fundamental level, the structure and organization of work also reflect the influences of gender, race, and ethnicity. From this perspective, gender, race, and ethnicity are not just characteristics of workers but may also be considered characteristics of work roles and jobs or seen as embedded in work arrangements and technologies (Acker 1991). Understanding how the workplace is gendered and how it is imbued with racial symbolism have become important concerns in recent years. Addressing these issues requires us to examine how work structures and practices that may appear "neutral" in design or application may nevertheless contribute to the construction and maintenance of gender and racial distinctions in the workplace. Including issues pertaining to gender, race, and ethnicity throughout this anthology, instead of confining them to a section on discrimination, allows the reader to see the many ways in which these social categories shape work experience and organization.

Work and Society

Viewing work through a sociological lens enables us to consider the varied ways in which work and society are interrelated. For example, at the individual level, work shapes identity, values, and beliefs, as well as a host of other outcomes ranging from mental and physical health to political attitudes (see, e.g., Kohn and Schooler 1983; Karasek and Theorell 1990; Brint 1985). Thus, while sociologists tend to view families as the primary agents of socialization in American society, it is also important to recognize the ways in which people are socialized by their jobs and work experiences. Indeed, some argue that work is an increasingly "greedy" institution, capable of "outcompeting" other institutions for people's time, emotional energies, and commitments.

One often-overlooked feature of work is that it typically brings people into contact with others—co-workers, subordinates, supervisors, and, increasingly for many, the public. Hence, social interaction and group dynamics are just as important in the workplace as they are in other social arenas. An early, influential sociological study first called attention to the ways that the social relations of work shaped workers' reactions to their jobs (Mayo 1933). For contemporary researchers, this insight is reflected in the claim that workers are not "atomized optimizers," unaffected by their interactions with other workplace members (Baron and Pfeffer 1994). Instead, both the content and quality of these relations are seen as important for understanding the consequences and significance of work. Along these lines, some suggest that it is not so much workers' own characteristics that shape their views and behavior; rather, it is the relation between their characteristics and the characteristics of those with whom they interact. From this perspective, workplaces are settings in which both expressive and instrumental ties between people are important—not only for understanding workers' responses to their jobs, but also for understanding the broader ways in which work shapes meanings and life experience. As Marks (1994, p. 855) explains, "With the help of co-workers, ethnic statuses may get reaffirmed and enlivened, and age and gender identities may be consolidated, celebrated, reorganized, and even transformed. The same is true, of course, of worker identities."

Though the workplace has never been truly separate from other societal institutions and trends, its interdependence with the larger environment has perhaps never been greater. This point can best be illustrated by considering the relations between work and another important social institution: family life. Societal changes, such as women's rising participation in the labor force, declining birth rates, and changing gender roles, have transformed relations between families and work. In the process, new conceptual approaches have emerged, and there has been a change in the way social institutions, including work, are understood. In particular, there has been a move away from rigid dichotomies, such as public and private or impersonal and personal, that compartmentalized work and family life, toward more complex portrayals of these social institutions and those who negotiate the work-family boundary (Marks 1994). Work, family, and the relations between them are not static but rather reflect and respond to developments in the wider society.

People's lives in advanced, capitalist societies are largely dependent on forces emanating from the workplace. The organization and availability of work determine—to a great extent—the social and economic well-being of individuals, neighborhoods, cities, and societies. Work is thus among the most important social institutions, with influential consequences for just about all arenas of social life.

REFERENCES

Acker, Joan. 1991. "Hierarchies, Jobs, Bodies: A Theory of Gendered Organizations." Pp. 162–179 in *The Social Construction of Gender,* edited by Judith Lorber and Susan A. Farrell. Newbury Park, CA: Sage Publications.

Baron, James N. and Jeffrey Pfeffer. 1994. "The Social Psychology of Organizations and Inequality." *Social Psychology Quarterly* 57: 190–209.

Becker, Howard S., Blanche Geer, Everett C. Hughes, and Anselm L. Strauss. 1961. *Boys in White: Student Culture in Medical School.* Chicago: University of Chicago Press.

Brint, Steven G. 1985. "The Political Attitudes of Professionals." *Annual Review of Sociology* 11: 389–414.

Friedland, Roger and A. F. Robertson. 1990. "Beyond the Marketplace." Pp. 3–49 in *Beyond the Marketplace,* edited by Roger Friedland and A. F. Robertson. New York: Aldine de Gruyter.

Hochschild, Arlie Russell. 1983. *The Managed Heart.* Berkeley: University of California Press.

Johnston, William B. and Arnold E. Packer. 1987. *Workforce 2000: Work and Workers for the 21st Century.* Indianapolis, IN: The Hudson Institute, Inc.

Karasek, Robert and Tores Theorell. 1990. *Healthy Work: Stress, Productivity, and the Reconstruction of Working Life.* New York: Basic Books.

Kohn, Melvin L. and Carmi Schooler. 1983. *Work and Personality: An Inquiry into the Impact of Social Stratification.* Norwood, NJ: Ablex Publishing Company.

Kirschenman, Joleen and Kathryn M. Neckerman. 1991. "We'd Love to Hire Them, But . . . : The Meaning of Race for Employers." Pp. 203–232 in *The Urban Underclass,* edited by C. Jencks and P. E. Peterson. Washington, DC: The Brookings Institution.

Leidner, Robin. 1993. *Fast Food, Fast Talk: Service Work and the Routinization of Everyday Life.* Berkeley: University of California Press.

Lorber, Judith. 1994. *Paradoxes of Gender.* New Haven: Yale University Press.

Marks, Stephen R. 1994. "Intimacy in the Public Realm: The Case of Co-Workers." *Social Forces* 72: 843–858.

Mayo, Elton. 1933. *The Human Problems of an Industrial Civilization.* New York: The Macmillan Company.

Roy, Donald. 1959. " 'Banana Time': Job Satisfaction and Informal Interaction." *Human Organization* 18: 158–168.

Simpson, Ida Harper. 1989. "The Sociology of Work: Where Have the Workers Gone?" *Social Forces* 67: 563–581.

Tomaskovic-Devey, Donald. 1993. *Gender and Racial Inequality at Work.* Ithaca, NY: ILR Press.

Wilson, William Julius. 1996. *When Work Disappears: The World of the New Urban Poor.* New York: Knopf.

What is work? Is a mother preparing meals for her family "working"? What about a homeless man searching through city dumpsters for bottles and cans to recycle? A professional tennis player playing the sport she loves? People may have different answers to these questions, and, indeed, there is no single, correct response. What counts as "work" depends on how work is defined. At the same time, unless we are willing to call every expenditure of human energy "work," we must develop a sense of where the boundary between work and nonwork lies (even as we admit that the borderlands surrounding this boundary may be extensive and the boundary itself quite permeable). One aim of this introductory section is to develop such a definition.

The Meanings of Work

The first two selections in Part I, by Teresa Gowan and Marjorie DeVault, describe the "work" of scavenging for recyclables by homeless men and of feeding a family. In many people's eyes, neither activity counts as "work." There is no wage directly attached to feeding one's family, and scavenging may simply be viewed as a form of personal survival—an activity necessitated by the *absence* of paid work. In addition, neither feeding the family nor scavenging for recyclables is performed in what could be considered a conventional workplace. Families are often construed as sites of personal life, intimacy, and leisure rather than as workplaces, and sifting through city dumpsters and garbage cans—by those other than garbage collectors employed by the city gov-

ernment—may be viewed as an act of deviance motivated by economic desperation, but not "work." Furthermore, the characteristics of those engaged in these activities may be inconsistent with our conceptions of "workers." Hence, what counts as "work" may be shaped by the kinds of people who perform it. For example, traditionally female activities associated with family caretaking, such as feeding, may be less likely to be labeled "work" than activities traditionally performed by men, such as going to war. Similarly, homelessness may be inconsistent with the living situations we associate with the workforce. These issues are raised in order to provoke thought, rather than to generate easy answers. In the process, however, our taken-for-granted assumptions about work may come to light and we may begin to lay the groundwork for a definition of work.

How then should "work" be defined? How do the readings selected for this book relate to that definition? Hodson and Sullivan (1995, p. 3) provide a general definition of work that serves well: "Work is the creation of material goods or services, which may be directly consumed by the worker or sold to someone else." According to this definition, feeding a family and scavenging for recyclables *both* constitute forms of work. This definition makes no mention of compensation, and hence work is not coincident with paid labor. This point is aptly demonstrated by Marjorie DeVault, who examines the ways women organize and experience family work. Her qualitative analysis of these topics brings to light the largely invisible work of "feeding the family." In addition, DeVault cautions us against assuming that theoretical frameworks developed for studying paid work can adequately explain family work.

Nevertheless, paid labor is *one* form of work and may be the most important in certain respects. In American society, survival depends on earning a wage or receiving support from someone who does. In addition, the fate of the society is intrinsically tied to the paid economy. For these reasons, the readings selected for this anthology focus primarily on paid employment.

What makes paid work a topic worthy of study? Obvious reasons for studying paid work have already been mentioned. If work were strictly a matter of economic survival, however, economists rather than sociologists might be better suited to teach about this topic. What makes a *sociological* study of work a worthy topic? The selections by Rubin and Gowan provide some answers to this question, as they demonstrate the centrality of work in people's lives, the connections between the personal experience of work and developments in the larger society, and the salience of gender and race for understanding the meaning and experience of work.

One way to appreciate the centrality of work in people's lives is to examine the ex-periences of the unemployed. Hence, Lillian Rubin's chapter is not about work but rather is about *not working*. By exploring men's and women's experiences of unemployment, Rubin shows that work in American society is not simply a means to an end but rather—for most—is a key aspect of identity and self-worth. Rubin also allows us to consider the possible ways that the meaning and experience of work are shaped by our social locations. Historically, work has been a vehicle for expressing masculinity, and Rubin suggests that women's experiences with unemployment may thus be quite different from men's. These themes are echoed in Gowan's piece on homeless recyclers, as she describes how homeless men experience their involvement in recycling and derive meaning and dignity from this activity. Moreover, she demonstrates the connections between "the view from the street" and the "job crisis" in the broader society. Gowan's chapter thus reveals the value of bridging the divide between micro and macro in sociological research.

REFERENCE

Hodson, Randy and Teresa A. Sullivan. 1995. *The Social Organization of Work*, second edition. Belmont, CA: Wadsworth Publishing.

THE MEANINGS OF WORK

1

American Untouchables
Homeless Scavengers in San Francisco's Underground Economy

Teresa Gowan

Teresa Gowan is a graduate student in sociology at the University of California, Berkeley. Gowan writes, "Right now there is a noise of bottles rattling in the street outside my window, for in San Francisco's Mission district you can hear a recycler pushing along 24th St. every few minutes, even late into the night. Ever since I moved here these hard-working men, muscular, worn, taciturn and depressed, have reminded me of men I knew back in the north of England, factory workers, unemployed miners, 'brickies' (bricklayers). Only the recyclers were homeless, and correspondingly their miseries seemed to be several steps closer to the unimaginable. Once I got to know Sam, who became my first 'informant,' this feeling of familiarity only increased. Sam's combination of warmth with an unreachable isolation, his clunky, formal sense of humor, his heavy drinking without ever seeming to get drunk, and his refusal to give in to grief or despair—it all made me feel that 'there but for the grace of God goes me Uncle Jack.' Although I've become more and more aware of quite fundamental differences between here and there, cultural, institutional, historical, I think my feelings of connection and (often troubled) affection are the fuel for my fieldwork with the recyclers."

An early morning at Bryant Salvage, a Vietnamese recycling business, finds a variety of San Francisco's scavengers converging to sell their findings. Vehicle after vehicle enters the yard to be weighed on the huge floor scale before dumping its load in the back; ancient pick-up trucks with wooden walls, carefully loaded laundry carts, canary Cadillacs stuffed to overflow with computer paper, the shopping carts of homeless men, a 1950s ambulance carrying newspaper, and even the occasional gleaming new truck. The homeless men unload their towers of bottles and cardboard while young Latino van recyclers shout jokes across them. Middle aged Vietnamese women in jeans and padded jackets buzz around on forklifts or push around great tubs full of bottles and cans, stopping occasionally to help elderly people with their laundry carts. The van recyclers repeatedly honk their horns at the homeless guys to get out of the way. The homeless recyclers, silently methodical in their work, rarely respond.

Abridgment of "American Untouchables: Homeless Scavengers in San Francisco's Underground Economy," by Teresa Gowan, presented at the Regular Session on the Informal Economy, ASA 1995. Reprinted by permission of the author.

Equivalent scenes can be found in Jakarta, San Salvador, or Calcutta. The collection and sale of other people's trash is a common means of survival for very poor people all over the world. At the moment full-time scavenging is most prevalent in poorer countries, where a huge variety of people collect, sort out and clean rags, paper, cardboard, metals, and glass, often living on the dumps where they work. They either sell these materials for recycling, or directly recycle them into new products themselves. The United States and Western Europe have had their own share of trash pickers. The wharf rats and the tinkers, the rag and bone men, the mudlarks and the ragpickers, all lived off working the garbage of industrialization until the early twentieth century. However in these countries welfare capitalism eventually absorbed most poor people into the waged working class, leaving only the formal municipal garbage workers and an insignificant scrap economy supplied by eccentric junk lovers, school-children, and the occasional part-time cardboard or can recycler.

Trash is back. Over the last ten years the US recycling industry has mushroomed on both the formal and informal levels, taking the form of a double tiered system which relies heavily on informal labor for sorting and collection, while reprocessing is dominated by large capital enterprises. Informal labor in recycling falls into two distinct groups: the general population who sort their own household recycling for free (sometimes required by law), and those who collect and sort in order to sell. This paper is concerned with the second group. . . .

Informal Recycling in the Broader Political Economy

Homeless men are the most immediately visible group of San Francisco's recyclers, as they work in the daytime and collect from unsorted public and private trash. Making only a few dollars a load, many recyclers work more than 12 hours a day, sometimes taking in two or even three loads of 100-200 pounds each. However, the greatest volume of informal recycling is brought in by the van recyclers. Latinos and Asian Americans, many of them first generation and undocumented immigrants, use vans to collect large quantities of cardboard and bottles. Known by their competitors in the city's official recycling company as the "mosquito fleet", the van recyclers work at night and in the early morning, preempting the weekly runs of the curbside recycling program trucks or collecting the boxes and bottles put out by bars and restaurants every night. Small numbers of African American and white car-drivers specialize in computer paper and newsprint. Yet another significant group are elderly people who gather unobtrusively from public trash using plastic bags which they usually consolidate into laundry carts when they go to the recycling companies.

The increases in volume reported by the recycling business is repeated in the accounts of homeless recyclers. Clarence, who has recycled in the southern part of the SoMa district since 1991, says that there are now 25-30 men working a patch that used to only support five of them. Sam reckoned that there were five times more recyclers in the 24th Street area than when he began five years ago.

The Loss of Formal Work

The increase of informal recycling has occurred in the context of the radical transformations of the country's political economy since the 1970s. These changes include a sharp decrease in industrial jobs, especially union ones, a scaling down of formalized relationships between the state and economic enterprises, and a general decentralization of economic activity.

California suffered the effects of restructuring later than the older manufacturing regions of the United States. The state was insulated from the manufacturing collapse of the early 1980s by its disproportionate share of defense contracts, its large share of booming computer and bio-tech companies, and a real-estate frenzy financed by the spectacular but ephemeral successes of the LA based junk-bond market. The inability of these industries to really sustain the bulk of California's working class is now revealed. Working class Californians are suffering from a prolonged and severe recession, losing 1.5 million jobs in 1990-2, including 1/4 of all manufacturing jobs. Construction, always the best bet for unskilled male labor, has practically stopped—the rate of housing starts is the lowest since the second world war. Within San Francisco the very disjunction between the collapse of heavy industry and the still booming informational industries has added to the problems of blue collar workers by bringing in large numbers of younger people with high disposable incomes who are willing and able to pay increasingly fantastic rents and house prices.

The experience of the recyclers I've interviewed suggests that the rise of recycling is at least in part a direct product of this job crisis. The new full-time scavengers started recycling as a last resort, after failing to find better paid work. Victoriano, a Mexican van recycler, described how he and several other van recyclers moved to California with the idea of getting construction work, but have had to settle for recycling instead. Anita, an elderly recycler, started the work when her daughter's data entry job was cut back to 20 hours a week.

For the homeless recyclers the process of moving into recycling was more drawn out and complex, given that they only noticed this line of work after they had already become homeless. The story tends to be that the multiple economic and emo-

tional strains of long-term unemployment propelled these men on to the street. While they didn't even consider cart recycling before, once they were homeless recycling became "making the best of it", a partial solution to both extreme financial hardship and to the indignities of their condition. The stories of Bill, Jordan, and Victor are typical in this regard. Bill previously worked for PG&E as a mechanic for 17 years, but was laid off in cutbacks in the fall of 1988. Jordan had a relatively well-paid union job as a forklift operator in Oakland before his company closed down. According to both of these men, unemployment transformed a controllable alcohol habit into a major problem, their families left them, and they became homeless. Victor, a skilled carpenter who moved here from New Mexico in 1994, spent six months unsuccessfully looking for construction work before ending up sleeping under the 101 freeway and recycling.

The Contraction of Welfare Benefits

The devastating effect of the job losses on the current Californian recession are intensified by their coincidence with severe welfare cuts on both the local and federal levels. While laid-off workers in Northern and Western Europe are still at least partially protected by social democratic safety nets, Americans left unemployed by the vast job losses of the last few years have had only minimal help from the welfare system, once their unemployment eligibility has run out.

Conditions have always been harsh for Americans living on benefits. However the political and economic restructuring of the last 20 years has included a substantial reduction of the standard of living for the disabled, the unemployed, and their dependents. The US welfare system's historical principle of "less eligibility" requires that welfare benefits pay less than work, with the argument that people will only work when they can make more by working than by claiming benefits. Union-busting, capital flight, and the subsequent mushrooming of temporary work and subcontracting combined to drive the going wage for the working poor below the existing level of welfare benefits.[1] . . .

Welfare contraction has not been coupled with looser work rules for those still receiving benefits. As a result, the benefit cuts force recipients into participation in the underground economy. Elderly people without family support or private pension schemes, single adults on disability, women with children on AFDC, and above all single able-bodied adults on welfare ("General Assistance" in California), simply cannot get by without supplementing their income through other means. Mary, a woman with bad arthritis who brings in about 70 lbs. of recycling every morning, started recycling after her SSI entitlement was reduced. . . . Most homeless recyclers are only eligible for GA, which comes to $345 a month, barely enough to cover a month's rent in a welfare hotel. The welfare system therefore simultaneously requires claimants to work and forces this work underground by surveilling and penalizing any work for money in the formal economy.

The "Capital Strategy" Analysis

For working class people caught between unemployment and welfare contraction recycling has become an important subsistence strategy, attracting increasing numbers of homeless men, recent Filipino, Chinese and Latino immigrants, South-East Asian refugees on welfare, and poor elderly people.

Through which wide angle lens should we view this booming underground economy in trash? The dominant practice in the informal economy literature has been to see the growing underground economy as just one more element of the systemic offensive of capital against organized labor and government regulation. In this model, the formal and informal economies are not in competition but instead form interlocking systems which combine to maximize the profits of large capital. Castells and Portes clearly articulate this perspective when they describe the informal economy as "a new form of control characterized by the disenfranchisement of a large sector of the working class, often with the acquiescence of the state."[2] . . .

Castells and Portes' conception of informal economic activity as a capital strategy effectively explains the case of the recycling industry, where informal "production" is clearly dependent on a close relationship with large capital. The recycling collected in the informal sector eventually ends up in the hands of large corporations, as reprocessing technology is too expensive for small capital. Informal recyclers, therefore, function as essential intermediaries between consumers and capital, with thousands of informal recyclers in the Bay Area feeding perhaps a hundred small recycling companies, which in turn feed a smaller number of large buyers who export fiber, metal, and glass all over the world. In this globalized industry bottles, cans, and cardboard collected on neighborhood streets are more likely to end up in Asia or Australia than in local recycled products.[3]

Control by large capital is apparent on the local level. San Francisco's garbage giant, Norcal, dominates both the legal and the informal economies in trash. Norcal holds the city contract for both garbage collection and curbside recycling. The company also owns the two largest recycling companies in the city, both of which overwhelmingly buy from the professional scavengers of the informal economy.

It is unlikely that Norcal's official collection company would find it profitable to take over the frequent and comprehensive collection performed by informal recyclers across the city. Their weekly curbside program is too infrequent for small restaurants and bars with limited storage space, whereas the informal recyclers have a nightly circuit. In addition, the homeless and elderly recyclers get much of their material from unsorted trash which would end up as garbage. Through its recycling companies, Norcal still ends up with most of the recycling collected by the informals. "What do you say", laughs Samuel Stewart II of the city recycling department, "yes, we still make money from it!" In practice the informals provide a recycling labor force which is cheaper than the union workers of Norcal's curbside program, and greatly increases the company's volume of recycling.

The "capital strategy" implementation of San Francisco's recycling industry is therefore persuasive on the purely economic level. Rather than competing with formal industry, the informal recyclers serve as a cheap collection service for a few large companies, primarily Norcal's vertically integrated conglomerate. These companies would not have been able to rely on the efforts of the informal recyclers without so many other businesses shrinking their formal operations, creating a "fourth world" of workers permanently pushed off the bottom of the formal labor market and only partially supported by the state. Recycling is therefore both typical of capital restructuring and dependent on it at the same time.

There are however serious problems with the "capital strategy" model. The argument tends towards functionalism, jumping too quickly from what capital needs to what capital gets. I now turn to my participant observation with homeless recyclers, in hopes of showing that such an assumption strips away the living center of social life, thereby obscuring the processes by which informal

economic arrangements are sustained and reproduced from day to day.[4]

Meanings of Recycling for Homeless Men

Even for men on the street, recycling is a choice, although it is a choice made within severe constraints. Homeless people are doing all sorts of things to get by: panhandling, washing car windows or shop windows, drug dealing, selling the Street Sheet paper, doing the service agency shuffle, performing music or poetry, stealing, selling clothes or books, and turning tricks.

All these occupations vary to some extent along the lines of race and gender. The typical recycler is a man in his 30s or 40s, most often African American, but with large minorities of whites and Latinos. The racial breakdown of recyclers is therefore not noticeably dissimilar from that of the general homeless population, although there are perhaps a few more white men. Gender, on the other hand, is extremely skewed. Out of hundreds of homeless recyclers on the San Francisco scene I have encountered only four women, all classically "butch", with a muscular and taciturn self-presentation. The two I know have long histories of doing male-dominated jobs. One of them used to be a traffic cop, the other a van driver. Recycling is almost exclusively a man's job. In general there are still many more men than women on the street.[5] However the extreme scarcity of female recyclers is better explained by the gendered nature of the work. There are, after all, several homeless women who walk around with their husbands and boyfriends as they work, however they studiously ignore the process of recycling, rarely even touching the cart, let alone actually doing any dumpster diving. While recycling can be made to fit certain masculinities, it repulses women with mainstream conceptions of femininity. One woman selling clothes on the street described recycling as a filthy job which "no woman should have to do. I'd rather stand in line all day."

If anything is clear from my field work it is that even for these most socially excluded and degraded informal workers, their work couldn't be further from the analytically empty space of hand to mouth "survival". Despite the low pay, many of the homeless recyclers really get into their work with enthusiasm. They do not express the sullen resentment of people acting only out of economic compulsion—a self-presentation which is overwhelmingly in evidence in social welfare establishments. The work is inherently hard. Clarence, a very strong but not particularly obsessive recycler, works 7 or 8 hours daily, dragging two carts tied together for about nine miles and collecting 250 pounds of recycling for his average $20 receipt. Bill the Mechanic has put in at least 16 hours on the days I've spent with him, barely ever stopping for a break. His daily income of under $30 works out at about $1.80 per hour of intense physical labor. Yet recyclers often push themselves beyond reasonable goals, working obsessively fast and energetically. Keeping their carts on the road for speed they steam along, leaning hard into their loads and darting searching glances from side to side. Several recyclers I know work for 12 or more hours a day, and it's not unusual to find lonely carts full of recycling whose owners have passed out from dehydration and exhaustion.

The recyclers are also eager to display their great efforts to other people. Sam, a middle aged white man who died by the side of his recycling cart earlier this year, was always concerned with asserting the validity of his work to others. The first time I ever met him he pointedly told me a story of an argument with a "resident" the night before. "Hey, keep the noise down, I've got to *work* in the morning", the man had shouted out of a window. "What do you think I'm doing" Sam had

shouted in return. "They just don't think, you know", he said in retrospect. "They think we do this for fun or something. I work hard, I clear up the neighborhood. Don't beg, don't steal, don't deal drugs. You'd think people could be civil to me." Although Sam was unusual in his willingness to fight back at housed people, the same eagerness to impress the serious nature of their work on others is standard among the recyclers. Their physical movements themselves have elements of mime. Like the superhard stare of the gang-banger or cop, the obsessively workaholic self-presentation of many recyclers suggests how much they have to prove by *how* they do their work. We are already a long way from the simple economic self-preservation implied by the capital strategy model.

Why should the homeless recyclers be so emotionally involved in a job which is physically exhausting, low paid, and most of all, significantly stigmatized by much of the general population as not only disgusting but akin to stealing? To get at this question we need to take the experience of homelessness seriously, not only as an indication of extreme economic hardship, but as an extraordinary dehumanizing and frightening location on the American social map.

The Dominant Constructions of Homelessness

The recyclers are fighting a formidable and ancient set of discourses which set up homeless people as powerful symbols of deviance and decay. These can be simplified into two dominant strands which I call the exclusion discourse and the social welfare discourse.

The exclusion discourse sets up homelessness as a representation of fundamental and threatening outsiderness. Here homelessness is characterized by madness, the rejection of rules, and general failure or refusal to control the physical and emotional manifestations of the animal self.

The disproportionately large number of African-Americans who are homeless adds in three centuries worth of white race-think which places people with dark skin somewhere on the border between culture and nature, human and animal. Through this lens people who are not homeless intuitively attribute disgusting and irrational impulses to homeless people. In the case of recyclers, the symbolic connection of homelessness and trash is often so powerful that others don't require any rational explanation for their dumpster diving activities at all. One of the bartenders I interviewed seemed surprised at the idea of homeless recyclers selling the bottles they collect every night from his bar. "Oh yes, I suppose they do sell them—I've never really thought about it", he said.

The exclusion discourse has recently taken on a new intensity. As long as homeless people were relatively rare, they could safely symbolize intemperance, dirt, and savagery without being considered a real threat. But with the huge growth in homelessness since the early 1980s, the meaning of homeless people in public space is in the process of reinterpretation. No longer isolated *representations* of disorder, the exclusion discourse represents the "new homelessness" as a full-scale *invasion* by disruption, madness, dirt, criminality, and free-roaming idleness. Exclusive practices against homeless people have become more hostile and the use of institutional force has intensified. Local politicians, police departments, and chambers of commerce have responded to the appearance of large numbers of extremely poor people who have nowhere to disappear to by redefining public space as private space with selective access for people who don't look poor. In the same commercial strips where "consumers" are encouraged to "browse" and "linger", homeless people are moved on, cited, and arrested. In the last year, San Francisco police have issued 15,000 tickets under the "Matrix" program for "encampment", "aggressive panhandling",

"urinating in public" or "obstructing freedom of movement".

The exclusion discourse attacks homeless people as a threat to the shared values of the wider society. In contrast, the degrading practices of the welfare agencies set them up as incompetent victims. Welfare and health agencies move to analyse and tame the people outside by curing the poor of their problems and reincorporating them into housed society. In this kinder discourse, the problem of homelessness is now a pitiful state entered involuntarily, and the solution is a technical question of how to best help the vulnerable poor rehabilitate themselves. Homelessness represents not a free space but a pathetic and mundane condition. The dangerous, even visionary madness and hedonistic abandon portrayed in the exclusion discourse are contained and tamed by the social welfare discourse's mechanistic categories of involuntary mental illness, social disconnection, and substance abuse.

The American social welfare discourse is profoundly individualistic. Inability to prosper is an individual failure, stemming from personal deficiencies. For example, any analysis of a homeless person's economic activity focuses on how they consume resources, rather than how they produce value. Although agencies may recognize that a single person especially cannot live on GA alone, money-earning activity is uniformly classified as deviance rather than subsistence. By setting up "the problem of poverty" in this way the social welfare discourse draws a curtain over the self-sustaining (and self-defining) parts of poor people's lives.

Fighting Hostile Images of "The Homeless"

What both the exclusion discourse and the social welfare discourse have in common is their assertion that the state of homelessness is but an external representation of a profound internal difference from the rest of society. The response of the homeless recyclers is to argue through their work that they are neither strange nor evil nor incompetent, but just decent working men down on their luck. Rejecting both the criminality and insanity attributed to them by the exclusion discourse and the feminizing picture of pathetic incompetence and vulnerability created by the social welfare discourse, recyclers aggressively assert their normality, hard work, competence, and self-sufficiency.

Recyclers often complain of the indignities of social welfare institutions. Although few go so far as to quit the welfare system completely recyclers turn their back on their status as welfare clients and embrace an identity based on their work. Differentiating themselves strongly from "stiffs" and "winos", recyclers are not heavy users of soup kitchens or shelters, only moving inside if they get sick or the weather hits freezing. Many would agree with Jordan: "I hate the shelters, don't like being around all the bums. It's depressing. You can't keep any self-respect."

For those who have spent long years in prison, dealing with the welfare system takes on an added significance. After doing eight years inside in the 1980s, James, a white man in his early forties, has turned his back on what he calls the "poverty system" completely. "When you've been in the joint, shit, you've done your time and you don't want to do any more. I'm a citizen . . . (sigh). Dealin with the welfare and the hotels, it's like another sentence, it really is. I have to go through that any more? No. It's about time for life, real life." I asked him if recycling was real life. He laughed. "Well, that's a question. Mm. Yes, yes it is . . . it's *more* of a life anyway. You do your own thing you know." After looking life in the eye from both locations James has decided that he prefers recycling and sleeping rough to living in the hotels and spending long hours in

service agency lines. In defiance of the wider society's stigmatization of homelessness he insists that the recycling life allows him to be a man worthy of respect.

Rejecting the social welfare construction of the homeless man as a pathetic dependent, recyclers use their work to demonstrate that they are both self-sufficient and competent. Some emphasize physical strength and effort, others formal knowledge and resourcefulness. Those with technical education will often apply it to their work. Dobie is an African American recycler who works the prosperous Richmond neighborhood. He has customized a big cart, adding wheels with real tires and inner tubes. He demands respect for his work, striding along in the middle of the road, holding up traffic with imperious hand signals. Like Bill the Mechanic, Dobie applies technical concepts to the haulage aspects of recycling. Bill explains the best angle to hold your cart in relation to the road using math formulas. Dobie blinds with science in his discussions of the mechanics of weight distribution and cart design.

The recyclers are equally concerned with struggling against the exclusion discourse's representations of homelessness as criminality, madness, and disorder. Recyclers uniformly pride themselves on living as much within the law as is possible for a homeless person. Many people say explicitly that recycling is a way for them to do an honest day's work, without having to hustle or cheat. At the extreme is a person like Clarence, an African American man in his late thirties who had a desk job in the army for several years. Clarence sends in every receipt he gets to General Assistance, and will not touch the dumpsters rented out by the Norcal recycling company. Sam, who usually dropped by every couple of days, avoided me for weeks out of embarrassment over a small loan he was unable to repay.

A major priority for most recyclers is to build regular, exclusive relationships with suppliers in businesses and apartment buildings. Apart from the obvious benefits of stabilizing income, such connections are important points of pride, ways to convince themselves and others that people who are not homeless rely on their services and trust them to keep to a routine. These relationships are often referred to in formal business language: "I try not to default on my schedule", says Dobie. "I've got several long standing accounts in the Castro area", says Jordan.

Relationships with suppliers make recyclers feel that they can claim to be part of "the community", rather than outside. To be seen to get on with one another is equally important. The exclusion discourse pictures homeless people as living outside rules and social restraint, acting on impulse. Two bartenders who refused to let homeless recyclers take their bottles both explained their decisions by their wish to avoid fights. "See that would cause fights. We can't have them fighting outside the bar, it's bad for business", said one man. Neither of them had seen a fight between recyclers—but this is how they expected homeless people to behave.

Knowing that others are likely to see them in this way, recyclers strongly reject suggestions that they compete with each other for resources. Rather than fighting over scraps, recyclers treat each other as solidaristic blue collar workers. "There's no shortage, we don't need to be competing" is the accepted wisdom. It's not unusual to hear men who are only superficial acquaintances comparing their night's work after they have sold their load, telling each other where they found the best stuff. "Well, a man wouldn't just take that information and go and clean up ahead of me", Sam explained. "I mean, well, he would be embarrassed." Even Clarence, who has big plans for expanding into van recycling, and thinks of himself as an "entrepreneurial dude", puts group solidarity before financial gain.

A couple of years ago he was working the area around where he lives too intensively and some of the older men asked him to cool off a bit. "Come on Clarence, a man needs a smoke now and then." "And that was cool", says Clarence. "I don't want to be getting in anyone else's way. There's plenty out there for everyone."

Another way that the recyclers reject the anti-social characteristics attributed to them by the exclusion discourse is by forging a strict separation between work and leisure. They are acutely aware that the "unemployed" man becomes marked out from "decent" working class men when the crucial masculine work/leisure distinction blurs into the more ambiguous state of "hanging out". The recyclers' stigmatization as homeless people and their lack of privacy for leisure time combine to create a presumption of guilt—any moment of rest is liable to be interpreted by others as indication that they are a "bum". Many respond to this problem by hiding away alone in secluded space when they are not working. Others create clear spatial and temporal breaks between "work" and "leisure" by alternating vigorous work with a scheduled "breakfast break" or "lunch-hour" where they abandon their carts to socialize, eat, or drink in parks or street corners. One group of younger and more sociable African Americans in the So-Ma area regularly get together to barbecue and drink on a Friday or Saturday night. "We're single men, you know. We like to party."

Who Is Attracted to Recycling?

Men move towards recycling not just because it provides a way to demonstrate certain qualities, but also because it is the informal job they are best *able* to do. The majority of the homeless recyclers in my sample have a substantial history of stable blue-collar employment and only hit skid row life in their

30s or later. This kind of life-history tends to produce a man who is either uncomfortable or inexperienced with using his "personality" for direct economic gain. Socialized as a routinised blue collar worker, the typical recycler finds it difficult to change himself into a hustler, even an uncriminalized hustler such as a car washer or "street sheet" vendor. Victor describes himself as "an old fashioned guy. I'm not real sociable. This (recycling) suits me because, in general I mean, no one bothers you much, you can get your pay without having to bullshit about it." Victor's self-contained, taciturn masculinity was sustainable, perhaps even essential in the lower-middle class, Latino community where he spent most of his previous life. Now that he is homeless his refusal to take on a more communicative, more subordinate role has become a luxury he can afford by doing recycling.

Recycling therefore gives people an opportunity of making a living which is culturally and often spatially removed from the usual walkways of ghetto life. While this chance to make an honest buck outside of the ghetto economy is most clearly welcomed by men who feel profoundly "away from home" on skid row, recycling also appeals to cons and hustlers looking for a change. Spike spent two years stealing from cars with his best buddy Valentino, but now they are using recycling to keep straight:

> I've changed, don't want to get in trouble any more. I got one felony, I don't intend to get the other two. But I don't want to do that shit anyway. This is better. I like recycling. It's real interesting what you find out there when you put your mind to it. And you're not doin anyone any harm.

Those recyclers who work the most strenuously tend to be men who previously held long-lasting and decently paid semi-skilled or skilled jobs in the formal economy.

Many of them are white, but by no means exclusively. These mostly older men are more intense about their work, and rarely sociable with other recyclers. Clarence, who is a charitable sort of guy, says "It's not that they're alienated or anything . . . they're just doin their route, no time to chat." I disagree. My impression is that those men who have achieved some part of the American dream but then lost it find their homeless state a continual source of pain and shame. As a result they can't get much comfort from others in the same position. Only by totally immersing themselves in their recycling work can they feel that they are still men in the way they learnt to think of manhood in their formative years.

The almost obsessive effort that these recyclers put into their work becomes understandable when you realize that every heave of the cart is a blow against the ever present image of the welfare bum. This helps to explain why Bill the Mechanic, who has fallen from the prosperity of a suburban ranch house and two cars, works every waking hour; why his brother Sam worked himself to death on the job at 48.

Using Recycling to Redefine Homelessness

No matter how hard recyclers like Bill and Sam work, they cannot escape other people's perception of them as just another faceless private in the homeless army. In truth, far from proving difference from "the homeless" as constructed in mainstream discourses, doing recycling is a clear mark of the condition of homelessness, at least for work age men. These men have only got into recycling since they became homeless. In many years under the poverty line Valentino and Spike had never considered recycling, yet they instantly gravitated towards recyclers as a natural peer group within the homeless population, making their first rounds only one day after they had to move onto the street. I knew Valentino before he became homeless, and he called me a couple of days after he moved outside. "We've been sleeping in this alley down by Folsom, doin' just fine," he said. "We met some nice guys down here. Showed us the tricks of recycling." Only one of the sample had done recycling before becoming homeless, and he was using a truck to collect valuable scrap metals like copper and brass.

Recyclers respond to the close connection between homelessness and recycling in two ways. Some still try to escape a homeless identity by trying to look as un-homeless as possible in their personal appearance, and by working all the time and not socializing with other homeless people. Neither Danny nor Jordan ever use the term "homeless" at all. Still in shock, Jordan looks only to the past or the future. "I'm just waiting for something to come up", he says. "I've got a (truck-driving) license, you know . . . A man with a *license* shouldn't be in this position."

Others accept that they will be seen as homeless and consciously use their work to assert a "positive" homeless identity which contradicts the exclusion and social welfare discourses. In order to do this they often end up drawing new lines of exclusion: "Us recycling guys, well we're different from other homeless you know. We don't just bum around and do drugs."

Some of the recyclers have a more militant homeless identification. James is extremely angry about the collective abuse of the homeless by the SFPD, intensified under the current "matrix program". Using a standard American individualist conception of citizenship he argues that recyclers provide for themselves economically and they harm no-one. He therefore deserves the same presumption of innocence, the same common respect, and the same civil liberties as any other citizen.

While these approaches are radically different in their political implications, at the level of everyday self-presentation they work out much the same. All of these people work hard to present an image of competence and industry to the rest of the population, an image which contradicts the dominant meanings of homelessness.

In this way the recyclers make of their work a cultural project to transform the stigma of dumpster-diving into a public demonstration of normality and self-sufficiency. They thereby challenge the symbolic fault lines which separate homeless people from everyone else, making the implicit (and often explicit) argument that the problem of homelessness is not created by the differences and deficiencies of homeless people themselves, but is both part and product of the wider society.

> It makes me so mad when people are disrespectful. I mean, can't they see? It could have happened to them, to anybody almost, you know. I mean, you can't protect yourself against bad luck. I'm not a bad man. Can't they see?

Luther's question, "Can't they see?", is both metaphorical and literal. As he sees it, those who see *him* hard at work recycling should be able to figure out that he is an ordinary, decent man, rather than some shadowy representation of what they themselves are not.

Abstract versus Situated Labor

The capital strategy perspective emphasizes macro-structural limitations rather than the practices people develop within them. At its most extreme, it reduces the efforts of informal workers to pre-social survival by adaptation. But while objective constraints are indeed massive for the homeless recyclers, this desperately poor and socially degraded group refuse to compete aggressively or treat each other instrumentally, insisting instead on respect and solidarity as the basis of their relationships. Rather than scrabbling for survival as faceless victims of structural forces, the recyclers use their work to enact the principles they believe in: self-sufficiency, community, work ethic, "dependable" behavior.

Although they are experiencing extreme poverty and often despair, homeless recyclers don't experience their worklives as new grooves "distributed" by capital to take advantage of their desperation. Within the harsh constraints imposed by homelessness, they have taken up this particular work because it suits their needs, skills, and sense of self better than the other ways they could make money. Other people on the street have very different orientations; Valentino described his friends among the street crack dealers as *not* impressed" by his recycling. He thought it highly unlikely that any of them would try recycling, seeing as they had always been "different" from him. Most typically, recyclers welcome the opportunity to earn cash from "good honest labor" without either hustling or enacting dependency. Choosing the hard labor of recycling over the various forms of "hustling" performed by other homeless men, the recyclers tend to share a specific previous life experience—that of the male blue collar worker in a routinized workplace in the formal economy.

The move into recycling reflects not only a particular past but a particular reaction to being homeless. Without the status crisis of homelessness these proud native men would not even consider recycling, let alone invest it with such symbolic significance. However once they become homeless, recycling becomes thinkable. And once they become recyclers, that experience becomes part of what they are and what they can and cannot do, shaping their future possibilities and limitations, likes and dis-

likes. Labor is part of a life, past, present, and future.

To say that recyclers make a social world out of picking up garbage, and that they have adopted this particular form of work available to homeless people because it "suits" them does not necessarily challenge the capital strategy analysis. It does however fill it out substantially. When we do ethnography, we are forced to replace the automatons of macro-social theory with real people. In this case, qualitative fieldwork shows us the concrete ways that a group of informal workers come to "consent" to their economic activity, even making of it a centerpiece of their lives. While the capital strategy analysis may outline the origins of informal recycling, only a closer look at the social world of the recyclers explains how it is sustained and reproduced by the people who do it. . . .

In the meantime, as the recyclers say, the recycling companies are a haven, the only environment where their homelessness does not become the basis for separate and unequal treatment. The recycling staff are generally curt but fair, the rationalized economic transaction is free from the usual compulsory humiliation rituals. "No hustle, no bullshit", as Carlos puts it. Given their stigmatized social position, recyclers are choosing to concentrate their efforts on using their work to redefine themselves as people with full humanity rather than victims. In this way they not only pull themselves back into the flows of capital, but also create self-respect in a hostile world.

NOTES

1. Blau, Joel. *The Visible Poor: Homelessness in the United States.* New York: Oxford University Press, 1992, p. 49.

2. Castells, Manual and Alejandro Portes. "World Underneath: The Origins, Dynamics, and Effects of the Informal Economy." In *The Informal Economy*, p. 27.

3. *San Francisco Business Times,* September 16, 1994.

4. Since September 1994 I have used a combination of participant observation and informal interviewing to study homeless recyclers working in San Francisco. I have got to know 21 of the recyclers well, by working with them and talking as we go. I have also had occasional conversations with about 30 other men. I have also interviewed 14 bartenders about the relationship between bars and the recyclers that collect from them, four Latino van recyclers, a recycling consultant to Alameda County, an official in the San Francisco City Recycling Department, and a manager at one of the smaller recycling companies.

   I made contact with the homeless recyclers by approaching them in the street or in the recycling company yards. I focused on two yards, the largest and best-known in the city, and a smaller Vietnamese-run business. Eight of the recyclers, five white and three Latinos, are based in the Mission, a large racially and ethnically mixed neighborhood of mostly low-income people. From the Mission they travel out to the more prosperous Noe Valley and Castro neighborhoods. Another eight, six of them African American, live in the main "skid row" areas of the city—the So-Ma and Tenderloin neighborhoods—from which they have access to the hundreds of bars and restaurants surrounding the downtown area. The other members of the group each recycle in different neighborhoods of the city; the wealthy Pacific Heights and Richmond areas; the heavily touristed North Beach; the mixture of high fashion and ghetto in Hayes Valley; and the predominantly African American neighborhoods of Hunters Point and Bayview.

5. Samples taken in eight American cities in the mid-eighties ranged from 78% to 97% male composition (see Snow, David A. and Leon Anderson, *Down on Their Luck: A Study of Homeless Street People* (1993), Berkeley: University of California Press). Many homeless women may be invisible to such tracking samples, as they are approached in male-dominated places like soup lines and public parks. Yet there are good structural reasons that there should be considerably more men than women on the street, not least the differences between AFDC and GA.

2

Doing Housework
Feeding and Family Life

Marjorie L. DeVault

Marjorie L. DeVault is associate professor of sociology at Syracuse University. She describes her interests in this way: "When I became a sociologist, I was fascinated by the feminist idea that taking women's activities seriously would change our view of society. No doubt my interest in housework came, in large part, from my own socialization into this womanly activity, but my research was also driven by a desire to know what the work meant to other women. At Syracuse University, where I teach sociology and women's studies, I often notice caring work in other settings, such as classrooms, offices, and campus organizations. Like housework, it is usually unacknowledged, even though we all depend on it every day."

As recently as the turn of the century, housework was arduous and time-consuming. It required specialized skills—baking, canning, sewing, managing a wood stove—and a great deal of physical work (Strasser 1982). Now household tasks are physically easier, take less time, require fewer specialized skills, and can more easily be divided and accommodated to other activities. In spite of such changes, however, housework has not disappeared. In order to maintain small, nuclear family households, someone in each home must do the coordinative work that makes it possible for the individuals there to survive within a market economy. This coordinative work includes both the physical work of maintenance and also the work of "making meaningful patterns" of everyday life.[1] As the technical character of housework has changed, with more and more produc-

tive work (food processing, for instance) shifting to the market, the activity left in the household is increasingly the work of producing a social order, which has been largely invisible and therefore unlabeled. It has been easy to assume that there is little work left to do in most modern homes, and we are often puzzled as we struggle to get it done.

Most studies of housework have been based on common-sense definitions of the work. Oakley (1974:49), for example, identified the "six core tasks" of housework as "cleaning, shopping, cooking, washing up, washing and ironing," and Berheide et al. (1976) studied "tasks" such as "meal preparation," "laundry," and "sewing/mending." Researchers have been guided by theoretical frameworks based on the organization of paid work. . . . This kind of research has effectively called attention to previous neglect of household work. The significance attached to paid work—both in theory and in everyday life—has given force to the image of "housework as work." Ultimately, however, housework is not paid work, but a kind

Excerpt from *Families and Work,* edited by Naomi Gerstel and Harriet Engel Gross. Copyright © 1987 by Temple University. Reprinted by permission of Temple University Press.

of "family work" organized quite differently. The translation of the activities of housework into the vocabulary of a paid job—to constitute "products" and "standards," for instance—has often resulted in limited definitions of housework and analyses confined to its most obvious, mechanical parts.

I will argue here that common-sense definitions leave out important parts of housework. I will report on a study based on intensive interviewing in thirty urban U.S. households,[2] in which I began with the accounts of those who do housework and used their own words to uncover and analyze the full range of their efforts. Through close examination of the activities involved in feeding a family, I will show that beyond the material work necessary for physical maintenance, feeding involves connecting household members with the larger society and the day-to-day production of the kind of group life we know as "family."

"Work" or "Love"?

The apparently routine work that supports a household is complex and more meaningful than is typically acknowledged. We begin to see its significance in the language of those who do this work. As I talked with women (and some men) about feeding their families, they often had trouble finding words to explain their experience. They talked about feeding as something other than work in the conventional sense, trying to explain how their activities are embedded in family relations. Some, for example, talked of this work in terms of family ties. They described feeding as part of being a parent: "I feel like, you know, when I decided to have children it was a commitment, and raising them includes feeding them." Or as part of being a wife: "I like to cook for him. That's what a wife is for, right?"

Women certainly recognize that feeding requires time, effort, and skill. But it is different somehow from paid work. One young mother who had quit her job as a social worker to stay home and take care of her children explained:

> If you think of it as a job, you're not going to like it. I mean, believe me, I don't want to do this for the rest of my life. I mean, I worked before, and I enjoy working, but right now, this is something different for me.

Even though they recognize their effort, women have trouble equating their care for family members with paid employment; they describe their activity as "something different" from work.

These perceptions of housework as "not work" are reinforced by the fact that its results are somehow spoiled if it is thought of in purely instrumental terms. This effect was evident in the way that one woman talked about her mother's practices. By emphasizing the work involved in meal preparation, her mother had introduced an unpleasant "tone" into their meal:

> We had Sunday dinner at noon. Her purpose of serving it then was, quote unquote, so I can relax the rest of the day, and it kind of put that moral obligation tone on it. You know, well, now that's over with. And my mother-in-law does the same thing. She'll cook a meal and then sit down and say, "Well, now that's over with." Which makes you feel like you've really imposed on her time.

By contrast, this woman explained that for her, cooking is "a way of saying I love you." Another woman, who also talked about cooking as an expression of love for family members, explained:

> In preparing food—you know, there's a lot of work that goes into preparing

food. Therefore, for one to commit himself to the work, that's love, that's shared with those people that the food was being prepared for. I think love has a lot to do with it.

Her comment, even though it labels feeding as "love," also reveals that it is not fully described as either "love" or "work" alone. She sees her activity in terms of love precisely because "there's a lot of work that goes into preparing food."

Vocabularies of work come from the model of paid employment; there are few words with which to express the kind of effort that so many women put into their family lives. Since they have no vocabulary for their own activity, these women talk of their work at home in terms of "love." Their talk suggests that we must look beyond the theoretical categories associated with paid employment if we are to understand the full character and significance of the work they do.

Family Meals

Changes in the organization of work and home have changed typical patterns of family meals. Even a few generations ago, when more households were involved in production as well as consumption, and when work was usually closer to home, families were more likely to eat together three times daily. They had little choice because there were few other places to be fed. Now family members who work for a wage often leave home early and work far away. They may do shift work that takes them from home at different times. Many children are at school or day care all day. In addition, cooking has become less and less necessary. Many technical skills have been marketized: new products incorporate much of the work of food processing formerly done at home, and

the growth of the restaurant trade and the tremendous expansion of fast-food franchising provide new options for purchasing meals. People are no longer forced to return to a household to be fed, so that family meals become less necessary and more a volitional social form.

Typically, in contemporary households, work and school schedules cut into meal times so that very few families eat even two meals together each day. Breakfast and lunch, especially, barely survive. In the households I studied, men and women who work outside their homes eat breakfast quickly, often before the rest of the household awakens. Some purchase something to eat at work. Even when all of the family is awake, the pressure of various schedules makes an elaborate meal unlikely. In almost half the households I studied, children are fed alone in the morning while parents are busy with other work.

At lunchtime almost a third of these households are empty; in several others, only the housewife is home. Even when women are home with children and prepare lunch, the meal is an attenuated ritual. In some households women sit down to eat with their children, but in an equal number they feed the children alone and either skip lunch or eat later by themselves.

Dinner is more consistently arranged as a well-defined meal, but it too can be disrupted by the scheduling of outside activities. One man leaves the house for his night shift at 6:30, less than an hour after his wife returns from her secretarial job. Another, a professional worker, arrives home late in the evening, just as his children are going to bed. Evening activities—going to school or the gym, bowling or playing pool, working in church or community groups—may mean that men or women and their children miss dinner several times a week.

In the context of such changes, bringing a family together for any kind of regular meal requires a new kind of effort. Still, the parents I interviewed were concerned about establishing patterns of regular meals. They talked of strategizing about routines, and their comments revealed the importance of the concept "meal" as an organizer of family life. For example, the mother of an infant talked of pulling her high chair up to the dinner table so they could eat "as a family," and a single working mother explained that she has continued to cook every evening for her teenage daughter so as to provide "a dinner made by her mother." In addition, people arrange meals to mark the rhythms of family life, with regular dinners for extended family or "special" Sunday dinners designed "to enrich our family life."

Meals do more than provide sustenance; they are also social events that bring family members together. Such rituals have been recognized as critical to the internal life of families, since they serve as a basis for establishing and maintaining family culture and creating a mutual recognition of the family as a group (Bossard and Boll 1950). Producing meals, then, has increasingly become work aimed at maintaining the kind of group life we think of as constituting a family.

Producing Meals

The work of feeding a family goes on and on; food must be provided again and again, every day. But the repetitiveness of the work can be deceiving. Far from a purely mechanical task, producing meals requires coordination and interpersonal work as well as the concrete activities of preparation. When I interviewed people about feeding, I wanted to elicit detailed reports that would display both aspects of the work and go beyond my respondents' conventional assumptions about their own work (for example, the common claim "I don't really do much housework"). I therefore asked for very spe-

cific accounts of the mundane business of producing everyday meals. Respondents sometimes stopped in mid-sentence to ask, "Is this really what you want to know?" as if surprised that these everyday activities could be a topic for research. I have used these detailed accounts to analyze parts of the work of feeding that are often ignored, not only by researchers but also by those who do housework. Planning and managing meals are examples of these invisible work activities.

Planning Meals

I'll spend time in the morning thinking about what in the heck I'm going to fix.

Some women talk of planning meals as "enjoyable"; for others it is "a hassle." In any case, planning "what to put on the table" is an essential part of the work of feeding, and conceiving of a meal requires sensitivity to a variety of concerns.

The food provided for a family cannot be just any food, but must be food that will satisfy them. Family members may not eat if they do not like what is served, so women often restrict their planning to items that have been successful in the past. When I asked about typical dinners, most women responded by telling me about their families' likes and dislikes. For example:

> Like for meats, let's see—he likes so many. Well, he doesn't like pork chops.

> Let's see—well, beans are good. But my children aren't much on eating beans.

Responding to these individual preferences is not a personal favor, but a requirement of the work.

Mothers are often especially concerned that children eat the foods they need and work at devising menus that are both appropriate and appealing. Some cook special foods for their children in addition to the family's regular meal or invent techniques for encouraging children to eat, like the woman who "disguises" her daughter's meat in mashed potatoes and cuts cheese into amusing shapes.

The work of planning is rarely shared by those who only eat. In order to please family members, women must work at learning their husbands' and children's tastes. Children will sometimes respond if given a choice of foods, but husbands are typically more cryptic. Many women complained that they could not just ask their husbands what they wanted: "I'll call at the office and ask, 'Is there anything special you'd like for dinner?' And his standard answer is, 'Yes, something good.'" Women learn what their husbands like "just living with somebody," through "trial and error." They notice what gets eaten and what does not and which meals are special favorites. The active character of this learning process can be seen in one woman's comments: she explained that as a new bride she had not known what to cook for her husband, so she "started looking for things that he liked better."

When they plan meals, then, women respond to their husbands' and children's tastes. However, husbands' and children's tastes are often different, so that part of the planning must involve weighing and balancing people's contradictory desires. Again, some solve this problem by doing double cooking. Others make the balance a factor in their longer-range choices. For example:

> If we've had a particularly good meal one night, and everyone enjoyed it, and everyone ate heartily, and they've eaten well, the next day I might make something that I know everyone—other than Richard and I—they're just not going to give a lick about. And I will try to have something else on the table, that they're going to—not another entree—but a vegetable that they like, or cheese, or something that will fill them up.

Planning means making sure that everyone gets "something that will fill them up."

Those who cook must consider their own tastes as well. However, in contrast to their responsiveness to the tastes of others, most women were scrupulously careful not to give their own preferences any special weight. One spoke of her care not to be "prejudiced one way or the other," and another explained, "One of us has to compromise, and it's going to end up being me."

In addition to pleasing individual family members, meals must be culturally appropriate. Anthropologists tell us that in any society food items become part of a cultural code, expressing the structure of social relations both within a household group and between household members and outsiders (Douglas 1972). These cultural rules become part of the process of planning meals. Though not conscious of using food as a code, people talked about the essential elements in their meals (a meat entree, for example, or beans and tortillas), and the kinds of combinations of elements that make up proper meals. They spoke of rules for the combinations they can make. For example: "We Mexicans usually have rice with pork. And if you have steak, we would have, like, any kind of soup, with broth."

The importance of such categories can be seen in the fact that people referred to them as a sort of standard even when they described meals that deviated from the form that was typical for them. For example, this woman's description of a somewhat unusual dinner shows how she thinks of the meal as a set of "slots" to be filled:

> Richard had been out for a business lunch, so I knew he wasn't going to be real hungry, and I'm on another diet, so I wasn't going to be eating the regular meal, so I didn't make, like, that slot that holds potatoes or noodles or something like that.

Family members respond to meals in terms of such patterns, insisting on "meat and potatoes," or rice with every meal. Some women reported that they were trying to change their families' ideas about meals—to encourage them to eat less meat or more vegetables, for instance. But they could only succeed if they were sensitive to household members' own ideas about what a meal should be. One woman reported that when she served a quiche, her husband told her, yes, it was very good, but he didn't want "breakfast for dinner."

And even though others respond to cultural patterns, those who are served are undoubtedly not as conscious of these codes as the women who actually work at designing meals. A man who had just begun to cook for his family explained some of the requirements of planning meals, and his problem: "There has to be a vegetable. And not two starches. The trouble is, I don't know what a starch is, I can't remember what a starch is, so sometimes I end up with two starches, sometimes I don't."

Beyond pleasing family members, and designing meals so that they conform to a cultural pattern, those who cook aim at making meals varied and interesting. Variety is more important in some households than in others, and it means different things in different households, but some notion of variety seems fundamental to meal planning. The women I interviewed reported that they decided to serve a particular meal because "we hadn't had it for a while," or "it was time to have fish again."

Concern with varied menus comes partly from contemporary U.S. health discourse, which links variety and nutrition. Food producers and nutritional scientists have promoted the idea that "all food is good food" and that the safest and healthiest diet is a varied one. Many people summarized "good eating habits" with formulas like "keep the variety up, and keep the sweets to a minimum." However, women also talked of variety as a part of their craft, important to producing meals that are not just adequate but interesting as well. Many expressed concern about "getting into a rut": they reported that it was "boring" to cook the same things, and that they talk with friends about ideas for different meals: "Like, oh gosh, what am I going to do with the potato? There's only so many things you can do with it."

Making these choices about meals is like solving a puzzle. There are special requirements stemming from individuals' tastes and preferences, and relationships within the household. There is a definite form to the problem, arising from shared cultural conventions. But variety is also important, so that the puzzle must be solved in relatively novel ways each day. The intersection of these different, sometimes contradictory concerns means that planning requires continual monitoring and adjustment. Planning is based on the overall form of each meal and also the way in which it fits into a pattern of surrounding meals. By solving this puzzle each day, the person who cooks for a family is continually creating one part of the reality of household life.

Managing Meals

The details of meal patterns—the times and places that families typically eat, the formal and informal rules that govern their behavior, and the kinds of interaction that are part of the meal—vary from one household to another. To some extent people's thoughts about meals reflect idealized versions of family life. One woman described her family's typical hurried breakfast and explained apologetically, "It's not a Walton family breakfast, by any means." But even though actual events fall short of such ideals, people work at making their meals particular kinds of events. Those I interviewed reported that they tried to make meal time "a calm time," "a very social thing," or "an important getting-together time." Such goals can only be accomplished through attention to the meal and efforts to orchestrate the event.

Talk is considered an important part of most family's meals, and is something that people work at. For example: "At dinner we usually talk about the kind of day that Mark and I had. You know, you try to relate what cute thing, cute and wonderful thing the child did, and things of that nature. We try to talk during dinner." Sometimes, these norms are even more explicit: "My son will sometimes be very grumpy and grouchy, because 'the whole day went wrong,' and he's told that that's simply not an excuse for not talking." One mother with five children, worried that they did not all have a chance to participate in the dinner talk, had tried to get each child to read a news item each day and report on it at the table. The system did not work, but it reveals this mother's attention to her family's meal-time conversation.

Children's behavior at the table must also be monitored and controlled. Sometimes this is relatively simple: "Now they're getting older they aggravate each other at the table. You know, 'She did this,' 'She's doing that.' So I have to sit there and kind of watch." In more difficult situations, when children are problem eaters, managing the meal can become a "project." One woman explained: "We give her real small portions and just try to encourage her, and praise her when she is cleaning her plate. It's a project for Richard and I to get going on."

Most parents are also conscious of monitoring their own behavior at the table, since their children learn from them; meal time is time for "setting an example": "I will always take the vegetable, even though I'm not much of a vegetable-eater. I don't make a big deal about it, but so that they at least see that that sort of thing is eaten." Thus, interpersonal relations, and even one's own eat-ing, become a form of work that contributes to the production of a family meal.

I observed one family's dinner. The man who organized it clearly thought of this work of interaction as the essential part of the meal as event. After the family finished eating, the older son was to load the dishwasher; his father remained at the table, supervising him in his task. A younger son brought his book to the table, and his father looked through it, discussing the pictures with him. When they had finished, and the man had sent his older son off to do homework and was finally left alone in the kitchen, he turned to me and announced, "Well, that's dinner at our house." There was clearly more work to do—food to be put away, for example—and he went on to do it, but when the children left the room he felt the closure that marked the end of dinner as an interpersonal event.

The time and effort required to orchestrate family meals comes into focus when we examine the households in which family members do not come together for regular family meals. All of the women who reported that they rarely sat down to dinner as a group were women working outside their homes (although some working women did organize family meals). Conversely, of the women who were home full-time, only two reported that they sometimes did not eat as a family group. One woman, who works full-time as well as going to school, whose husband has two jobs, and whose teenage children are involved in their own activities, commented that sitting down to dinner every day is "just one of those luxuries that we have to give up." Thus, part of the reason for eliminating the dinner as a regular family event is the difficulty of coordinating many work schedules. However, it is also clear that arranging for family meals is itself work that takes time and energy and that is most easily accomplished when there is someone at home with time and energy to devote to the task.

One couple I interviewed talked eloquently about this problem. Their two children were seven years and seven months old at the time of the interview. Both parents had been working full-time throughout their marriage, though their jobs had changed frequently because of cutbacks and layoffs. She was going to school at night; they hoped that soon she would be able to earn enough so that he could stay home as a househusband. For the present, though, they described their routine as a "helter-skelter" one with no "set patterns." She was usually late because of school or overtime work, so they often ate at different times. In any case, supper was eaten in the living room, in front of the television. She talked of how different their life is from the one she grew up with, and her regrets:

> My mom was home. And it really makes a world of difference. She always had good meals on the table. . . . It was more of a family thing. You know, my dad got home at a certain time, and we always ate dinner after he got home. . . . Now it's like a helter-skelter routine. If we're all home, fine; if we're not then we just work around it. . . . There are a lot of times when I really regret it. I regret not having a family routine. It feels like, you know, your kids are being shuffled around, and you're being shuffled around.

It is the one thing that she would like to change about their eating habits; she says that they talk about it "all the time." Her husband described the situation in much the same way. When I asked him why they did not have "set patterns," his answer was ambiguous but reflected the time and effort involved in arranging meals:

> It doesn't make any difference. Well, it does. But you're so damn tired. It's not the time, because you could do it if you wanted to. It just gets to where you're so

tired, and fed up with the way the money situation is, and you just say, the hell with it.

In professional households, parents were more likely to work successfully at arranging family meals, even if both were employed. However, in these households, almost all the women who worked outside the home were working part-time, and they usually had jobs with flexible schedules. They had fewer obstacles to overcome in arranging a regular meal-time routine, and more time to devote to this work.

Single mothers were somewhat less likely than married women to arrange regular meals together for their families. Some of these women reported that their children ate together, but that they themselves ate alone, at another time. A mother with six children, who is home all day, explained, "I'd rather wait until it's quiet." And a single woman who works all day as a receptionist said: "We usually sit down and eat. Or I have them in here and I'll—because, you know, I've been working all day, and I might go in and sit in the living room so I'll be by myself for a while." In these situations, there is only one person to do all the family work, and no one to turn to for any relief, even help in sustaining a conversation. Like the working couple described above, these women need a respite. It is simply too much to keep working during their own meal times.

Invisible Work

The physical tasks of food preparation—essential as they are to the maintenance of individuals—are combined with another kind of coordinative work that produces group life within a market society. Those who do the work of feeding must adjust to the different schedules of household members and funnel resources from stores and service organizations into particular households for use by individuals. They plan meals, as I have shown here, so that they are appropriate for specific households and manage meals as part of a broader strategy for constructing family life. When they bring people together for meals, they are not only providing sustenance, but also producing family life itself.

The work of meal planning and management is invisible work. The meal patterns that families establish are often customary, copied from the households of the parents' own parents. Practices seem natural, like "what everybody else does," so that people fail to notice the work involved in maintaining them. And the unarticulated principles of meal planning can make the skills involved seem intuitive. Thus, a man who has just begun to cook attributes his wife's superior abilities not only to experience, but also to "personality." And a woman who has been married and cooking for over twenty years maintains that her skills are "automatic"—"sort of like instinct."

Most analysts of women's "invisible work" have used the term to describe work that women are not given credit for, like volunteer work, work on a husband's career, or behind-the-scenes work in organizations (e.g., Kahn-Hut et al. 1982: 137–43). The housework I have been discussing can be thought of as unacknowledged work in this sense; however, it is also literally invisible: much of the time, it cannot be seen. It is largely mental, spread over time and mixed in with other activities, and it can look like other things. For example, managing a meal looks like enjoying the companionship of one's family, and thinking about a menu can look like reading the newspaper, or just sitting and resting. The work is noticeable when it is not completed (when dinner is not ready on time, for instance) but disappears from view when it is done well.

Since feeding is embedded in relations with others and largely unrecognized as work, it often comes to be seen as an expression of personality and emotion. As women talked about their activities, several mentioned their "laziness": for example, "I really don't care much about making salad dressings. I think I'm a little lazy about things like that." One woman, who was running a business out of her home while caring for three children, told me that she tried to plan meals that were easy to cook: "I really am stingy with my time." And the single mother with six children, who likes to save her own dinner until they are in bed, observed: "That's a bad habit I have; I like peace and quiet."

The widespread trivialization of housework and the invisibility of its most important parts lead women to feel that they "don't really do much housework," or that the work is easy, and just "goes by pretty good." But they are often ambivalent, anxious about "making everything right," frustrated when their efforts fall short of their plans, and worried that they are not doing enough. The way they talk about housework provides clues to the kind of effort involved.

Although the work of feeding a family is not continuous, it requires attention to many different people and their needs and a continuing openness to new information of various sorts. As one woman explained, "The antennas are always out." Those who do the work spend time thinking about what they will do and strategizing about how to get it done. This thought work is squeezed into the interstices of other activities. A busy mother with young twins explained: "As soon as I get up in the morning or before I go to bed, I'm thinking of what we're going to eat tomorrow. Even though I know, but do I have this, and is this ready, and this ready?" And another woman explained that she plans her son's lunch during ten minutes of "kind of free time" before she gets out of bed in the morning. At their paid jobs, or in odd moments, people think about what to have for dinner, what they need from the store, and how to fit all of the activities of food preparation into the time available to them.

Feeding also involves attention to the needs and tastes of others. Specific tasks and routines vary, but the heart of the work is serving and pleasing others, who have learned to expect that in the family they should get what they want. The houseworker has no one upon whom to make such claims; she learns to accommodate herself to others. Deference—the submersion of a woman's own needs—becomes a way of getting the work done.

Feeding is strongly gendered and, in spite of greater male interest and participation in some tasks, continues to be women's work. In a British study, for example, Murcott (1983) found that even when men did some cooking, wives were the ones who prepared "cooked dinners," associated with home, health, and family. When adults—either men or women—were home without other family members, they tended not to cook, but to "pick at" food, or to "snack." Some—husbands more often than wives— would go to eat with relatives, where they were fed by the women of other families. This alternative was one that men felt entitled to; by contrast, when women were served by someone else, they spoke of "being spoiled."

Much writing on housework is implicitly (if not explicitly) concerned with strategies for doing away with the burdens of housework. However, limited views of the work involved have often led to the notion that housework should be given up rather easily. The work is seen as so simple that its persistence is quite puzzling. What I have shown is that feeding, though certainly necessary, is neither trivial nor simply mechanical and that much of this work is not re-

placeable by labor-saving technology or purchased goods and services. The work, though invisible, has a logic; women have learned its principles and are disturbed when it is not done. I do not claim that feeding is inevitably women's work, nor that the organization of feeding cannot or should not change. However, the work as presently constituted is at the center of family life and sociability. In order to think about changing the organization of maintenance work, we must begin to uncover and articulate the principles that have traditionally organized housework and, through it, the family.

NOTES

1. Davidoff (1976), from whom I have taken the phrase, reveals this aspect of housework in nineteenth-century households by examining upper-class homes, where the heavy work of maintenance was mostly done by paid domestic workers.

2. My study is based on interviews with those who do the work of feeding in thirty households (thirty women and three men). All of these households included children, but they were ethnically diverse and included single-parent and two-paycheck families, as well as families of different classes. Although there are important differences in the work of feeding, my analysis here focuses on those aspects of the work which were common to all households. For a more detailed discussion of methodology and sample, see DeVault 1984.

REFERENCES

Berheide, Catherine White; Sarah Fenstermaker Berk; and Richard A. Berk. 1976. "Household Work in the Suburbs: The Job and Its Participants." *Pacific Sociological Review* 19: 491–517.

Berk, Richard A., and Sarah Fenstermaker Berk. 1979. *Labor and Leisure at Home: Content and Organization of the Household Day.* Beverly Hills, Calif.: Sage.

Bossard, James H. S., and Eleanor S. Boll. 1950. *Ritual in Family Living.* Philadelphia: University of Pennsylvania Press.

Davidoff, Leonore. 1976. "The Rationalization of Housework." In Diana L. Barker and Sheila

Allen (eds.), *Dependence and Exploitation in Work and Marriage*. London: Longman.

DeVault, Marjorie L. 1984. "Women and Food: Housework and the Production of Family Life." Ph.D. dissertation, Northwestern University.

Douglas, Mary, 1972. "Deciphering a Meal." *Daedalus* 101: 61–81.

Ferber, Marianne A. 1982. "Women and Work: Issues of the 1980's." *Signs* 8: 273–95.

Kahn-Hut, Rachel; Arlene Kaplan Daniels; and Richard Colvard. 1982. *Women and Work: Problems and Perspectives*. New York: Oxford University Press.

Murcott, Anne. 1983. "'It's a Pleasure to Cook for Him': Food, Mealtimes, and Gender in Some South Wales Households." In Eva Garmarnikow, David H. J. Morgan, Jane Purvis, and Daphne Taylorson (eds.), *The Public and the Private*. London: Heinemann.

Oakley, Ann. 1974. *The Sociology of Housework*. New York: Pantheon.

Smith, Dorothy E. 1979. "A Sociology for Women." In Julia A. Sherman and Evelyn Torton Beck (eds.), *The Prism of Sex*. Madison: University of Wisconsin Press.

Strasser, Susan. 1982. *Never Done: A History of American Housework*. New York: Pantheon.

3

Families on the Fault Line

Lillian B. Rubin

Lillian Rubin is a sociologist and practicing psychotherapist in San Francisco, California. She is also senior research associate at the Institute for the Study of Social Change at the University of California, Berkeley. She writes, "Scratch the intellectual preoccupations of most writers and scholars and you'll find the personal experiences that led them there. I was born into a working-class family where I watched my mother—the only parent I had from the time I was five years old—struggle, sometimes unsuccessfully, to feed, clothe, and house our family. And I watched, too, as her life, and her very sense of herself, was deformed by the burdens she carried. It's not surprising, then, that I have devoted so much of my career to studying working-class families, trying to make them visible in a society that stigmatizes them at the same time that it refuses to acknowledge the existence of a working class."

For Larry Meecham, "downsizing" is more than a trendy word on the pages of the *Wall Street Journal* or the business section of the *New York Times*. "I was with the same company for over twelve years; I had good seniority. Then all of a sudden they laid off almost half the people who worked there, closed down whole departments, including mine," he says, his troubled brown eyes fixed on some distant point as he speaks. "One day you got a job; the next day you're out of work, just like that," he concludes, shaking his head as if he still can't believe it.

Nearly 15 percent of the men in the families I interviewed were jobless when I met them. Another 20 percent had suffered episodic bouts of unemployment—sometimes related to the recession of the early 1990s, sometimes simply because job security is fragile in the blue-collar world, especially among the younger, less experienced workers. With the latest recession, however, age and experience don't count for much; every man feels at risk.

Tenuous as the situation is for white men, it's worse for men of color, especially African-Americans. The last hired, they're likely to be the first fired. And when the axe falls, they have even fewer resources than whites to help them through the tough times. "After kicking around doing shit work for a long time, I finally got a job that paid decent," explains twenty-nine-year-old George Faucett, a black father of two who lost his factory job when the company was restructured—another word that came into vogue during the economic upheaval of the 1990s. "I worked there for two years, but I didn't have seniority, so when they started to lay guys off, I was it. We never really had a chance to catch up on all the bills before it was all over," he concludes dispiritedly.

I speak of men here partly because they're usually the biggest wage earners in intact families. Therefore, when father loses his job, it's likely to be a crushing blow to the family economy. And partly, also, it's because the issues unemployment raises are different for men and for women. For most women, identity is multifaceted, which means that the loss of a job isn't equivalent to the loss of self. No matter how invested a woman may be in her work, no matter how much her sense of self and competence are connected to it, work remains only one part of identity—a central part perhaps, especially for a professional woman, but still only a part. She's mother, wife, friend, daughter, sister—all valued facets of the self, none wholly obscuring the others. For the working-class women in this study, therefore, even those who were divorced or single mothers responsible for the support of young children, the loss of a job may have been met with pain, fear, and anxiety, but it didn't call their identity into question.

For a man, however, work is likely to be connected to the core of self. Going to work isn't just what he does, it's deeply linked to who he is. Obviously, a man is also father, husband, friend, son, brother. But these are likely to be roles he assumes, not without depth and meaning, to be sure, but not self-defining in the same way as he experiences work. Ask a man for a statement of his identity, and he'll almost always respond by telling you first what he does for a living. The same question asked of a woman brings forth a less predictable, more varied response, one that's embedded in the web of relationships that are central to her life.

Some researchers studying the impact of male unemployment have observed a sequenced series of psychological responses.[1] The first they say, is shock, followed by denial and a sense of optimism, a belief that this is temporary, a holiday, like a hiatus between jobs rather than joblessness. This period is marked by heightened activity at home, a burst of do-it-yourself projects that had been long neglected for lack of time. But soon the novelty is gone and the projects wear thin, ushering in the second phase, a time of increasing distress, when inertia trades places with activity and anxiety succeeds denial. Now a jobless man awakens every day to the reality of unemployment. And, lest he forget, the weekly trip to the unemployment office is an unpleasant reminder. In the third phase, inertia deepens into depression, fed by feelings of identity loss, inadequacy, hopelessness, a lack of self-confidence, and a general failure of self-esteem. He's tense, irritable, and feels increasingly alienated and isolated from both social and personal relationships.

This may be an apt description of what happens in normal times. But in periods of economic crisis, when losing a job isn't a singular and essentially lonely event, the predictable pattern breaks down. During the years I was interviewing families . . . millions of jobs disappeared almost overnight. Nearly everyone I met, therefore, knew someone—a family member, a neighbor, a friend—who was out of work. "My brother's been out of a job for a long time; now my bother-in-law just got laid off. It seems like every time I turn around, somebody's losing his job. I've been lucky so far, but it makes you wonder how long it'll last."

At such times, nothing cushions the reality of losing a job. When the unbelievable becomes commonplace and the unexpected is part of the mosaic of the times, denial is difficult and optimism impossible. Instead, any layoff, even if it's defined as temporary, is experienced immediately and viscerally as a potentially devastating, cataclysmic event.

It's always a shock when a person loses a job, of course. But disbelief? Denial? Not for those who have been living under a cloud of anxiety—those who leave work each night grateful for another day of safety, who wonder as they set off the next morning whether this is the day the axe will fall on them. "I tell my wife not to worry because she gets panicked about the bills. But the truth is, I stew about it plenty. The economy's gone to hell; guys are out of work all around me. I'd be nuts if I wasn't worried."

It's true that when a working-class man finds himself without a job he'll try to keep busy with projects around the house. But these aren't undertaken in the kind of holiday spirit earlier researchers describe.[2] Rather, building a fence, cleaning the garage, painting the family room, or the dozens of other tasks that might occupy him are a way of coping with his anxiety, of distracting himself from the fears that threaten to overwhelm him, of warding off the depression that lurks just below the surface of his activity. Each thrust of the saw, each blow of the hammer helps to keep the demons at bay. "Since he lost his job, he's been out there hammering away at one thing or another like a maniac," says Janet Kovacs, a white thirty-four-year-old waitress. "First it was the fence; he built the whole thing in a few days. Then it was fixing the siding on the garage. Now he's up on the roof. He didn't even stop to watch the football game last Sunday."

Her husband, Mike, a cement finisher, explains it this way: "If I don't keep busy, I feel like I'll go nuts. It's funny," he says with a caustic, ironic laugh, "before I got laid off my wife was always complaining about me watching the ball games; now she keeps nagging me to watch. What do you make of that, huh? I guess she's trying to make me feel better."

"Why didn't you watch the game last Sunday?" I ask.

"I don't know, maybe I'm kind of scared if I sit down there in front of that TV, I won't want to get up again," he replies, his shoulders hunched, his fingers raking his hair. "Besides, when I was working, I figured I had a right."

His words startled me, and I kept turning them over in my mind long after he spoke them: "When I was working, I figured I had a right." It's a sentence any of the unemployed men I met might have uttered. For it's in getting up and going to work every day that they feel they've earned the right to their manhood, to their place in the world, to the respect of their family, even the right to relax with a sporting event on TV.

It isn't that there are no gratifying moments, that getting laid off has no positive side at all. When unemployment first hits, family members usually gather around to offer support, to buoy a man's spirits and their own. Even in families where conflict is high, people tend to come together, at least at the beginning. "Considering that we weren't getting along so well before, my wife was really good about it when I got laid off," says Joe Phillips, an unemployed black truck driver. "She gave me a lot of support at first, and I appreciate it."

"You said 'at first.' Has that changed?" I ask.

"Hell, yes. It didn't last long. But maybe I can't blame it all on her. I've been no picnic to live with since I got canned."

In families with young children, there may be a period of relief—for the parents, the relief of not having to send small children off to child care every day, of knowing that one of them is there to welcome the children when they come home from school; for the children, the exhilarating novelty of having a parent, especially daddy, at home all day. "The one good thing about him not working is that there's someone home with the kids now," says twenty-five-year-old Gloria Lewis, a black hairdresser whose husband has been unemployed for just a few weeks. "That part's been a godsend. But I don't know what we'll do if he doesn't find work soon. We can't make it this way."

Teenagers, too, sometimes speak about the excitement of having father around at first. "It was great having my dad home when he first got laid off," says Kevin Sollars, a white fourteen-year-old. "We got to do things together after school sometimes. He likes to build ship models—old sailing ships. I don't know why, but he never wanted to teach me how to do it. He didn't even like it when I just wanted to watch; he'd say, 'Haven't you got something else to do?' But when he first got laid off, it was different. When I'd come home from school and he was working on a ship, he'd let me help him."

But the good times usually don't last long. "After a little while, he got really grumpy and mean, jumped on everybody over nothing," Kevin continues. "My mom used to say we had to be patient because he was so worried about money and all that. Boy, was I glad when he went back to work."

Fathers may also tell of the pleasure in getting to spend time with their children, in being a part of their daily life in ways unknown before. "There's a silver lining in every cloud, I guess. I got to know my kids like I never did before," says Kevin's father, who felt the sting of unemployment for seven months before he finally found another job. "It's just that being out of work gets old pretty fast. I ran out of stuff to do around the house; we were running out of money; and there I was sitting on my keister and stewing all day long while my wife was out working. I couldn't even enjoy building my little ships."

Once in a while, especially for a younger man, getting laid off or fired actually opens up the possibility of a new beginning. "I figured, what the hell, if I'm here, I might as well learn how to cook," says twenty-eight-year-old Darnell Jones, a black father of two who, until he was laid off, had worked steadily but always at relatively menial, low-paying jobs in which he had little interest or satisfaction. "Turned out I liked to cook, got to be real good at it, too, better than my wife," he grins proudly. "So then we talked about it and decided there was no sense in sitting around waiting for something to happen when there were no good jobs out there, especially for a black man, and we figured I should go to cooking school and learn how to do it professionally. Now I've got this job as a cook; it's only part-time, right now, but the pay's pretty good, and I think maybe I'll go full-time soon. If I could get regular work, maybe we could even save some money and I could open my own restaurant someday. That's what I really want to do."

But this outcome is rare, made possible by the fact that Darnell's wife has a middle-management position in a large corporation that pays her $38,000 a year. His willingness to try something new was a factor, of course. But that, too, was grounded in what was possible. In most young working-class families of any color or ethnic group, debts are high, savings are nonexistent, and women don't earn nearly enough to bail the family out while the men go into a training program to learn new skills. A situation that doesn't offer much encouragement for a man to dream, let alone to believe his dream could be realized.

As I have already indicated, the struggles around the division of labor shift somewhat when father loses his job. The man who's home all day while his wife goes off to work can't easily justify maintaining the traditional household gender roles. Therefore, many of the unemployed men pick up tasks that were formerly left to their wives alone. "I figure if she's working and I'm not, I ought to take up some of the slack around here. So I keep the place up, run the kids around if they need it, things like that," says twenty-nine-year-old Jim Andersen, a white unemployed electrician.

As wives feel their household burdens eased, the strains that are almost always a part of life in a two-job family are somewhat relieved. "Maybe it sounds crazy to you, but my life's so much easier since he's out of work, I wish it could stay this way," says Jim's wife, Loreen, a twenty-nine-year-old accounting clerk. "If only I could make enough money, I'd be happy for him to stay home and play Mr. Mom."

But that's only a fantasy—first because she can't make enough money; second, and equally important, because while she likes the relief from household responsibilities, she's also uneasy about such a dramatic shift in family roles. So in the next breath, Loreen says, "I worry about him, though. He doesn't feel so good about himself being unemployed and playing house."

"Is it only him you worry about? Or is there something that's hard for you, too?" I ask.

She's quiet for a moment, then acknowledges that her feelings are complicated: "I'm not sure what I think anymore. I mean, I don't think it's fair that men always have to be the support for the family; it's too hard for them sometimes. And I don't mind working; I really don't. In fact, I like it a lot better than being home with the house and the kids all the time. But I guess deep down I still have that old-fashioned idea that it's a man's job to support his family. So, yeah, then I begin to feel—I don't know how to say it—uncomfortable, right here inside me," she says, pointing to her midsection, "like maybe I won't respect him so much if he can't do that. I mean, it's okay for now," she hastens to reassure me, perhaps herself as well. "But if it goes on for a real long time like with some men, then I think I'll feel different."

Men know their wives feel this way, even when the words are never spoken, which only heightens their own anxieties about being unemployed. "Don't get me wrong; I'm glad she has her job. I don't know what we'd do if she wasn't working," says Jim. "It's just that . . . ," he hesitates, trying to frame his thoughts clearly. "I know this is going to sound pretty male, but it's my job to take care of this family. I mean, it's great that she can help out, but the responsibility is mine, not hers. She won't say so, but I know she feels the same way, and I don't blame her."

It seems, then, that no matter what the family's initial response is, whatever the good moments may be, the economic and psychological strains that attend unemployment soon overwhelm the good intentions on all sides. "It's not just the income; you lose a lot more than that," says Marvin Reed, a forty-year-old white machinist, out of work for nearly eight months. He pauses, reflects on his words, then continues. "When you get laid off, it's like you lose a part of yourself. It's terrible; something goes out of you. Then, on top of that, by staying home and not going to work and associating with people of our own level, you begin to lose the sharpness you developed at work. Everything gets slower; you move slower; your mind works slower.

"It's a real shocker to realize that about yourself, to feel like you're all slowed down and . . . ," he hesitates again, this time to find the words. "I don't know how to explain it exactly, maybe like your mind's pushing a load of mud around all the time," he concludes, his graying head bowed so as not to meet my eyes.

"Everything gets slower"—a sign of the depression that's so often the unwelcome companion of unemployment. As days turn into weeks and weeks into months, it gets harder and harder to believe in a future. "I've been working since I was fourteen," says Marvin, "and I was never out of work for more than a week or two before. Now I don't know; I don't know when I'll get work again. The jobs are gone. How do you find a job when there's none out there anymore?"

The men I talked with try to remind themselves that it's not their fault, that the layoffs at the plant have nothing to do with them or their competence, that it's all part of the economic problems of the nation. But it's hard not to doubt themselves, not to wonder whether there's something else they could have done, something they might have foreseen and planned for. "I don't know; I keep thinking I could have done something different," says Lou Coltrane, a black twenty-eight-year-old auto worker, as he looks away to hide his pain. "I know it's crazy; they closed most of the plant. But, you know, you can't help thinking, maybe this, maybe that. It keeps going round and round in my head: Maybe I should have done this; maybe I should have done that. Know what I mean?"

But even when they can accept the reality that they have no control over the situation, there's little surcease in the understanding. Instead, such thoughts increase their feelings of vulnerability and helplessness—feelings no one accepts easily. "I worked nineteen years for this damned company and how do they pay me back?" asks Eric Hueng, a forty-four-year-old unemployed Asian factory worker, as he leaves his chair and paces the room in a vain attempt to escape his torment. "They move the plant down to some godforsaken place in South America where people work for peanuts and you got no choice but to sit there and watch it happen. Even the government doesn't do a damn thing about it. They just sit back and let it happen, so how could I do anything?" he concludes, his words etched in bitterness.

For American men—men who have been nurtured and nourished in the belief that they're masters of their fate—it's almost impossible to bear such feelings of helplessness. So they find themselves in a cruel double bind. If they convince themselves that their situation is beyond their control, there's nothing left but resignation and despair. To fight their way out of the hopelessness that follows, they begin to blame themselves. But this only leaves them, as one man said, "kicking myself around the block"—kicks that, paradoxically, allow them to feel less helpless and out of control, while they also send them deeper into depression, since now it's no one's fault but their own.

"I can't believe what a fool I was," says Paul Santos, a forty-six-year-old Latino tool and die maker, his fingers drumming the table nervously as he speaks. "I was with this one company for over fifteen years, then this other job came along a couple of years ago. It seemed like a good outfit, solid, and it was a better job, more money and all. I don't know what happened; I guess they got overextended. All I know is they laid off 30 percent of the company without a day's notice. Now I feel stupid; if I had stayed where I was, I'd still be working."

Shame, too, makes an appearance, adding to the self-blame, to Paul's feeling that he did something wrong, something stupid—that if he'd somehow been better, smarter, more prescient, the outcome would be different. And the depression deepens. "I've been working all my life. Now it's like I've got nothing left," Paul explains, his eyes downcast, his voice choked with emotion. "When you work, you associate with a group of people you respect. Now you're not part of the group anymore; you don't belong anywhere. Except," he adds with disgust, "on the unemployment line."

"Now that's a sad sight, all these guys shuffling around, nobody looking at anybody else. Every time I go there, I think, *Hey, what the hell am I doing here? I don't belong here, not with these people. They're deadbeats.* Then I think, *Yeah, well you're here, so it looks like you're no better than them, doesn't it?*"

Like so many other men, Paul hasn't just lost a job; he's lost a life. For his job meant more than a living wage. It meant knowing he had an identity and a place in the world—a place where his competence was affirmed, where he had friends who respected and admired him, men with whom he could share both the frustrations and satisfactions of life on the job.

It's not just for men that the job site is a mirror in which they see themselves reflected, a mirror that reflects back an image that reassures them that they're valued contributors to the social world in which they live. It functions this way for all of us. But it's particularly important for men because when the job disappears, all this goes too, including the friendships that were so important in the validation of the self. . . .

"I don't see anybody anymore," mourns Bill Costas, a thirty-four-year-old unemployed white meat packer who had worked in the same plant for nine years. "The guys I worked with were my buddies; after all those years of working together, they were my friends. We'd go out after work and have a beer and shoot the bull. Now I don't even know what they're doing anymore."

For wives and children, it's both disturbing and frightening to watch husband and father sink even deeper into despair. "Being out of work is real hard on him; it's hard to see him like this, so sad and jumpy all the time," laments Bill's wife, Eunice, a part-time bank teller who's anxiously looking for full-time work. "He's always been a good provider, never out of work hardly a day since we got married. Then all of a sudden this happens. It's like he lost his self-respect when he lost that job."

His self-respect and also the family's medical benefits, since Eunice doesn't qualify for benefits in her part-time job. "The scariest part about Bill being out of a job is we don't have any medical insurance anymore. My daughter got pneumonia real bad last winter and I had to borrow money from my sister for the doctor bill and her medicine. Just the medicine was almost $100. The doctor wanted to put her in the hospital, but we couldn't because we don't have any health insurance."

Her husband recalls his daughter's illness, in a voice clogged with rage and grief. "Do you know what it's like listening to your kid when she can't breathe and you can't send her to the hospital because you lost your benefits when you got laid off?"

In such circumstances, some men just sit, silent, turned inward, enveloped in the gray fog of depression from which they can't rouse themselves. "I leave to go to work in the morning and he's sitting there doing nothing, and when I come home at night, it's the same thing. It's like he didn't move the whole day," worries thirty-four-year-old Deidre Limage, the wife of a black factory worker who has been jobless for over a year.

Other men defend against feeling the pain, fear, and sadness, covering them over with a flurry of activity, with angry, defensive, often irrational outbursts at wife and children—or with some combination of the two. As the financial strain of unemployment becomes crushing, everyone's fears escalate. Wives, unable to keep silent, give voice to their concerns. Their husbands, unable to tolerate what they hear as criticism and blame—spoken or not—lash out. "It seems like the more you try to pull yourself up, the more you get pushed back down," sighs Beverly Coleride, a white twenty-five-year-old cashier with two children, whose husband has worked at a variety of odd jobs in their seven-year marriage. "No matter how hard we try, we can't seem to set everything right. I don't know what we're going to do now; we don't have next month's rent. If Kenny doesn't get something steady real quick, we could be on the street." . . .

For Beverly Coleride, as for the other women and men I met, . . . no matter how much they want to obliterate the images of the homeless from consciousness, the specter haunts them, a frightening reminder of what's possible if they trip and fall. Perhaps it's because there's so much at stake now, because the unthinkable has become a reality, that anxieties escalate so quickly. So as Beverly contemplates the terror of being "on the street," she begins to blame her husband. "I keep telling myself it's not his fault, but it's real hard not to let it get you down. So then I think, well, maybe he's not trying hard enough, and I get on his case, and he gets mad, and, well, I guess you know the rest," she concludes with a harsh laugh that sounds more like a cry of pain.

She doesn't *want* to hurt her husband, but she can't tolerate feeling so helpless and out of control. If it's his fault rather than the workings of some impersonal force, then he can do something about it. For her husband, it's an impossible bind. "I keep trying, looking for something, but there's nothing out there, leastwise not for me. I don't know what to do anymore; I've tried everything, every place I know," he says disconsolately.

But he, too, can't live easily with such feelings of helplessness. His sense of his manhood, already under threat because he can't support his family, is eroded further by his wife's complaints. So he turns on her in anger: "It's hard enough being out of work, but then my wife gets on my case, yakking all the time about how we're going to be on the street if I don't get off my butt, like it's my fault or something that there's no work out there. When she starts up like that, I swear I want to hit her, anything just to shut her mouth," he says, his shoulders tensed, his fists clenched in an unconscious expression of his rage.

"And do you?" I ask.

The tension breaks; he laughs. "No, not yet. I don't know; I don't want to," he says, his hand brushing across his face. "But I get mad enough so I could. Jesus, doesn't she know I feel bad enough? Does she have to make it worse by getting on me like that? Maybe you could clue her, would you?"

"Maybe you could clue her"—a desperate plea for someone to intervene, to save him from his own rageful impulses. For Kenny Coleride isn't a violent man. But the stress and conflict in families where father loses his job can give rise to the kind of interaction described here, a dynamic that all too frequently ends in physical assaults against women and children.

Some kind of violence—sometimes against children only, more often against both women and children—is the admitted reality of life in about 14 percent of the families in this study. I say "admitted reality" because this remains one of the most closely guarded secrets in family life. So it's reasonable to assume that the proportion of families victimized by violence could be substantially higher.

Sometimes my questions about domestic violence were met with evasion: "I don't really know anything about that."

Sometimes there was outright denial, even when I could see the evidence with my own eyes: "I was visiting my sister the other day, and I tripped and fell down the steps in front of her house."

And sometimes teenage children, anguished about what they see around them, refused to participate in the cover-up. "I bet they didn't tell you that he beats my mother up, did they? Nobody's allowed to talk about it; we're supposed to pretend like it doesn't happen. I hate him; I could kill him when he does that to her. My mom, she says he can't help it; it's because he's so upset since he got fired. But that's just her excuse now. I mean, yeah, maybe it's worse than it was before, but he did it before, too. I don't understand. Why does she let him do it to her?"

"Why does she let him do it to her?" A question the children in these families are not alone in asking, one to which there are few satisfactory answers. But one thing is clear: The depression men suffer and their struggle against it significantly increase the probability of alcohol abuse, which in turn makes these kinds of eruptions more likely to occur.

"My father's really changed since he go laid off," complains Buddy Truelman, the fifteen-year-old son of an unemployed white steel worker. "It's like he's always mad about something, you know, ready to bite your head off over nothing. I mean, he's never been an at-ease guy, but now nothing you do is okay with him; he's always got something to say, like he butts in where it's none of his business, and if you don't jump to, he gets mad as hell, carries on like a crazy man." He pauses, shifts nervously in his

chair, then continues angrily, "He and my mom are always fighting, too. It's a real pain. I don't hang around here any more than I have to."

Buddy's mother, Sheila, a thirty-four-year-old telephone operator, echoes her son. "He's so touchy; you can't say anything without him getting mad. I don't mind so much if he takes it out on me, but he's terrible to the kids, especially to my son. That's when I get mad," she explains, passing a hand over her worried brow. "He's got no right to beat up on that kid the way he does."

"Do you mean he actually hits him?" I ask.

She hesitates and looks away, the torment of memory etched on her face. Finally, brushing away the tears that momentarily cloud her vision, she replies, "Yeah, he has. The last time he did it, he really hurt him—twisted his arm so bad it nearly broke—and I told him I'd leave if he ever hit Buddy again. So it's been okay for a while. But who knows? He has a few beers and it's like he goes crazy, like he can't control himself or something."

Many of the unemployed men admit turning to alcohol to relieve the anxiety, loneliness, and fear they experience as they wait day after day, week after week for, as one man put it, "something to happen." "You begin to feel as if you're going nuts, so you drink a few beers to take the edge off," explains thirty-seven-year-old Bill Anstett, a white unemployed construction worker.

It seems so easy. A few beers and he gets a respite from his unwanted feelings—fleeting, perhaps, but effective in affording some relief from the suffering they inflict. But a few beers often turn out to be enough to allow him to throw normal constraints to the wind. For getting drunk can be a way of absenting the conscious self so that it can't be held responsible for actions undertaken. Indeed, this may be as much his unconscious purpose as the need to rid himself of his discomfort. "I admit it, sometimes it's more than a few and I fall over the edge," Bill grants. "My wife, she tells me it's like I turn into somebody else, but I don't know about that because I never remember."

With enough alcohol, inhibitions can be put on hold; conscience can go underground. "It's the liquor talking," we say when we want to exempt someone from responsibility for word or deed. The responsibility for untoward behavior falls to the effects of the alcohol. The self is in the clear, absolved of any wrongdoing. So it is with domestic violence and alcohol. When a man gets drunk, the inner voice that speaks his failure and shame is momentarily stilled. Most men just relax gratefully into the relief of the internal quiet. But the man who becomes violent needs someone to blame, someone onto whom he can project the feelings that cause him such misery. Alcohol helps. It gives him license to find a target. With enough of it, the doubts and recriminations that plague him are no longer his but theirs—his wife's, his children's; "them" out there, whoever they may be. With enough of it, there's nothing to stay his hand when his helpless rage boils over. "I don't know what happens. It's like something I can't control comes over me. Then afterward I feel terrible," Peter DiAngelo, an unemployed thirty-two-year-old truck driver, says remorsefully.

One-fifth of the men in this study have a problem with alcohol, not all of them unemployed. Nor is domestic violence perfectly correlated with either alcohol abuse or unemployment. But the combination is a potentially deadly one that exponentially increases the likelihood that a man will act out his anger on the bodies of his wife and children. "My husband drinks a lot more now; I mean, he always drank some, but not like now," says Inez Reynoso, a twenty-eight-year-old Latina nurse's aide and mother of three children who is disturbed about her

husband's mistreatment of their youngest child, a three-year-old boy. "I guess he tries to drink away his troubles, but it only makes more trouble. I tell him, but he doesn't listen. He has a fiery temper, always has. But since he lost his job, it's real bad, and his drinking doesn't help it none.

"I worry about it; he treats my little boy so terrible. He's always had a little trouble with the boy because he's not one of those big, strong kids. He's not like my older kids; he's a timid one, still wakes up scared and crying a lot in the night. Before he got fired, my husband just didn't pay him much attention. But now he's always picking on him; it's like he can't stand having him around. So he makes fun of him something terrible, or he punches him around."

The mother in me recoils at Inez's story. But the psychotherapist understands at least something of what motives Ramon Reynoso's assault on his young son. For this father, this man who's supposed to be the pillar on which the family rests, who defines himself as a man by his ability to support his family, the sight of this weak and puny little boy is like holding up a mirror to his now powerless self. Unable to tolerate the feelings of self-hatred the image engenders, he projects them outward, onto the child, and rains blows down on him in an effort to distance himself from his own sense of loss and diminishment.

"Does he hit you, too?" I ask Inez.

She squirms in her chair; her fingers pick agitatedly at her jeans. I wait quietly, watching as she shakes her head no. But when she speaks, the words say something else. "He did a couple of times lately, but only when he had too many beers. He didn't mean it. It's just that he's so upset about being out of work, so then when he thinks I protect the boy too much he gets real mad."

When unemployment strikes, sex also becomes an increasingly difficult issue between wives and husbands. A recent study in Great Britain found that the number of couples seeking counseling for sexual problems increased in direct proportion to the rise in the unemployment rate.[3] Anxiety, fear, anger, depression—all emotions that commonly accompany unemployment—are not generators of sexual desire. Sometimes it's the woman whose ardor cools because she's frightened about the future: "I'm so scared all the time, I can't think about sex." Or because she's angry with her husband: "He's supposed to be supporting us and look where we are." More often it's the men who lose their libido along with their jobs—a double whammy for them since male identity rests so heavily in their sexual competence as well as in their work.

This was the one thing the men in this study couldn't talk about. I say "couldn't" because it seemed so clearly more than just "wouldn't." Psychologically, it was nearly impossible for them to formulate the words and say them aloud. They had no trouble complaining about their wives' lack of sexual appetite. But when it was they who lost interest or who become impotent, it was another matter. Then, their tongues were stilled by overwhelming feelings of shame, by the terrible threat their impotence posed to the very foundation of their masculinity.

Their wives, knowing this, are alarmed about their flagging sex lives, trying to understand what happened, wondering what they can do to be helpful. "Sex used to be a big thing for him, but since he's been out of work, he's hardly interested anymore," Dale Meecham, a white thirty-five-year-old waitress says, her anxiety palpable in the room. "Sometimes when we try to do it, he can't, and then he acts like it's the end of the world —depressed and moody, and I can't get near him. It's scary. He won't talk about it, but I can see it's eating at him. So I worry alot about it. But I don't know what to do, because if I try to, you know, seduce him and it doesn't work, then it only makes things worse."

The financial and emotional turmoil that engulfs families when a man loses his job all too frequently pushes marriages that were already fragile over the brink. Among the families in this study, 10 percent attributed their ruptured marriages directly to the strains that accompanied unemployment. "I don't know, maybe we could have made it if he hadn't lost his job," Maryanne Wallace, a twenty-eight-year-old white welfare mother, says sadly. "I mean, we had problems before, but we were managing. Then he got laid off, and he couldn't find another job, and, I don't know, it was like he went crazy. He was drinking; he hit me; he was mean to the kids. There was no talking to him, so I left, took the kids and went home to my mom's. I thought maybe I'd just give him a scare, you know, be gone for a few days. But when I came back, he was gone, just gone. Nobody's seen him for nearly a year," she says, her voice limping to a halt as if she still can't believe her own story.

Economic issues alone aren't responsible for divorce, of course, as is evident when we look at the 1930s. Then, despite the economic devastation wrought by the Great Depression, the divorce rate didn't rise. Indeed, it was probably the economic privations of that period that helped to keep marriages intact. Since it was so difficult to maintain one household, few people could consider the possibility of having to support two.

But these economic considerations exist today as well, yet recent research shows that when family income drops 25 percent, divorce rises by more than 10 percent.[4] Culture and the institutions of our times make a difference. Then, divorce was a stigma. Now, it's part of the sociology and psychology of the age, an acceptable remedy for the disappointment of our dreams.

Then, too, one-fourth of the work force was unemployed—an economic disaster that engulfed the whole nation. In such cataclysmic moments, the events outside the family tend to overtake and supersede the discontents inside. Now, unemployment is spottier, located largely in the working class, and people feel less like they're in the middle of a social catastrophe than a personal one. Under such circumstances, it's easier to act out their anger against each other.

And finally, the social safety net that came into being after the Great Depression— social security, unemployment benefits, public aid programs targeted specifically to single-parent families—combined with the increasing number of women in the work force to make divorce more feasible economically.

Are there no families, then, that stick together and get through the crisis of unemployment without all this trauma? The answer? Of course there are. But they're rare. And they manage it relatively well only if the layoff is short and the resources are long.

Almost always, these are older families where the men have a long and stable work history and where there are fewer debts, some savings, perhaps a home they can refinance. But even among these relatively privileged ones, the pressures soon begin to take their toll. "We did okay for a while, but the longer it lasts, the harder it gets," says forty-six-year-old Karen Brownstone, a white hotel desk clerk whose husband, Dan, lost his welding job nearly six months ago. "After the kids were grown, we finally managed to put some money by. Dan even did some investments, and we made some money. But we're using it up very fast, and I get real scared. What are we going to do when his unemployment runs out?"

"I tell him maybe he has to get in a different line of work because maybe they don't need so many welders anymore. But he just gets mad and tells me I don't know what I'm talking about. Then there's no point talking to him at all; he just stamps around and hollers. Or else he leaves, gets in the car and goes screeching away. But I *do* know what I'm talking about. I read in the paper about how these companies are cutting back, and they're not going to need so many workers anymore. He knows it, too; he reads the paper all the time. He just won't try something else; it's like he's too proud or something."

When I talk with Karen's husband, Dan, he leans forward in his chair and says angrily, "I can't go out and get one of those damn flunky jobs like my wife wants me to. I've been working all my life, making a decent living, too, and I got pride in what I do. I try to tell her, but she won't listen." He stops, sighs, puts his head in this hands and speaks more softly: "I'm the only one in my whole family who was doing all right; I even helped my son go to college. I was proud of that; we all were. Now what do I do? It's like I have to go back to where I started. How can you do that at my age?"

He pauses again, looks around the room with an appraising eye, and asks: "What's going to happen to us? I know my wife's scared; that's why she's on my case so much. I worry, too, but what can I do if there's no work? Even she doesn't think I should go sling hamburgers at McDonald's for some goddamn minimum wage."

"There's something between minimum wages jobs and the kind you had before you were laid off, isn't there?" I remark.

"Yeah, I know; you sound like her now," he says, his features softening into a small smile. "But I can't, not yet. I feel like I've got to be ready in case something comes up. Meanwhile, it's not like I'm just sitting around doing nothing. I've hustled up some odd jobs, building things for people, so I pick up a little extra change on the side every now and then. It's not a big deal, but it helps, especially since it doesn't get reported. I don't know, I suppose if things get bad enough, I'll have to do something else. But," he adds, his anger rising again, "dammit, why should I? The kind of jobs you're talking about pay half what I was making. How are we supposed to live on that, tell me that, will you?"

Eventually, men like Dan Brownstone who once held high-paying skilled jobs have no choice but to pocket their pride and take a step down to another kind of work, to one of the service jobs that usually pay a fraction of their former earnings—that is, if they're lucky enough to find one. It's never easy in our youth-oriented society for a man past forty to move to another job or another line of work. But it becomes doubly difficult in times of economic distress when the pool of younger workers is so large and so eager. "Either you're overqualified or you're over the hill," Ed Kruetsman, a forty-nine-year-old unemployed white factory worker, observes in a tired voice.

But young or old, when a man is forced into lower-paying, less skilled work, the move comes with heavy costs—both economic and psychological. Economically, it means a drastic reduction in the family's way of life. "Things were going great. We worked hard, but we finally got enough together so we could buy a house that had enough room for all of us," says thirty-six-year-old Nadine Materie, a white data processor in a bank clearing center. "Tina, my oldest girl, even had her own room; she was so happy about it. Then my husband lost his job, and the only thing he could find was one that pays a lot less, *a lot less*. On his salary now we just couldn't make the payments. We had no choice; we had to sell out and move. Now look at this place!" she commands, with a dismissive sweep of her hand. Then, as we surveyed the dark, cramped quarters into which this family of five is now jammed, she concludes tearfully, "I hate it, every damn inch of it; I hate it."

For Tina Materie, Nadine's fifteen-year-old daughter, her father's lost job has meant more than the loss of her room. The comforts and luxuries of the past are gone, and the way of life she once took for granted seems like a dream. For a teenager whose sense of self and place in the world is so heavily linked to peer group acceptance and to, in Tina's own words, "being like the other kids," the loss is staggering. "We can't afford anything anymore; and I mean *anything*," she announces dramatically. "I don't even go to the mall with the other kids because they've got money to buy things and I don't. I haven't bought a new record since we moved here. Now my mom says I can't get new school clothes this year; I have to wear my cousin's hand-me-downs. How am I going to go to school in those ugly things? It's bad enough being in this new school, but now . . . ," she stops, unable to find the words to express her misery.

Worst of all for the children in the Materie family, the move from house to apartment took them to a new school in a distant neighborhood, far from the friends who had been at the center of their lives. "My brother and me, we hate living here," Tina says, her eyes misting over as she speaks. "Both of us hate the kids who live around here. They're different, not as nice as the kids where we used to live. They're tough, and I'm not used to it. Sometimes I think I'll quit school and get a job and go live where I want," she concludes gloomily.

Psychologically, the loss of status can be almost as difficult to bear as the financial strain. "I used to drive a long-distance rig, but the company I worked for went broke," explains Greg Northsen, a thirty-four-year-old white man whose wife is an office worker. "I was out of work for eleven and a half months. Want to know how many days that is? Maybe how many hours? I counted every damn one," he quips acidly.

"After all that time, I was ready to take whatever I could get. So now I work as an orderly in a nursing home. Instead of cargo, I'm hauling old people around. The pay's shit and it's damn dirty work. They don't treat those old people good. Everybody's always impatient with them, ordering them around, screaming at them, talking to them like they're dumb kids or something. But with three kids to feed, I've got no choice.

He stops talking, stares wordlessly at some spot on the opposite wall for a few moments, then, his eyes clouded with unshed tears, he rakes his fingers through his hair and says hoarsely, "It's goddamn hard. This is no kind of job for a guy like me. It's not just the money; it's . . ." He hesitates, searching for the words, then, "It's like I got chopped off at the knees, like . . . aw, hell, I don't know how to say it." Finally, with a hopeless shrug, he concludes, "What's the use? It's no use talking about it. It makes no damn difference; nothing's going to make a difference. I don't understand it. What the hell's happening to this country when there's no decent jobs for men who want to work?"

Companies go bankrupt; they merge; they downsize; they restructure; they move —all reported as part of the economic indicators, the cold statistics that tell us how the economy is doing. But each such move means more loss, more suffering, more families falling victim to the despair that comes when father loses his job, more people shouting in rage and torment: "What the hell's happening to this country?"

NOTES

1. John Hill, "The Psychological Impact of Unemployment," *New Society* 43 (1978): 118–120; and Linford W. Rees, "Medical Aspects of Unemployment," *British Medical Journal* 6307 (1981): 1630–1631

2. Hill, "The Psychological Impact of Unemployment"; and Rees, "Medical Aspects of Unemployment."

3. Reported in the *San Francisco Chronicle,* February 14, 1992. The study found that in the same year that unemployment rose from 6.5 to 9.2 percent, there was a 30 percent increase in the number of couples seeking advice from marriage counselors about their waning sex lives.

4. Cited in the *San Francisco Chronicle*, October 19, 1992.

The Social Organization of Work

What factors shape the organization of work? Does work organization reflect management's interests in control? The outcome of struggles between conflicting interests? The dictates of technology? Part II addresses these issues. In the course of exploring different perspectives on the organization of work, the readings provide a glimpse of historical changes in work organization, and they introduce several key concepts that have played a role in understanding work over the past century.

Classical Sociology and the Organization of Work

Sociology in the West is a product of the industrial revolution and the rise of capitalism; thus, the history of sociology and the history of sociology of work are closely intertwined. Readings by Karl Marx, Emile Durkheim, and Max Weber are therefore an appropriate starting point for a historical survey of work organization. The selections by these three sociological theorists have more, however, than historical value. As classics, they have a "privileged status" in the discipline, meaning that "contemporary [sociologists] . . . believe they can learn as much about their field through understanding this earlier work as they can from the work of their own contemporaries" (Alexander 1987). Although their views diverge in important respects, Marx, Durkheim, and Weber each were highly critical of the industrial, capitalist society emerging during their lifetimes. As Watson (1987, p. 3) explains, "The founding fathers of sociology can be seen as striving to make

sense of the dislocations of their age. Their attempts to make sense of their situation are invaluable to us because these men, in a historical location more marginal than our own, were better able to look at the industrial capitalist world in light of conceptions of alternatives. This is their humanistic significance."

Marx's theory of capitalism has shaped sociologists' views on work for more than a century. Adherents and critics alike continue to discuss and debate Marx's ideas about private property, social class, and capitalist society. The reading that leads off this section, titled "Alienated Labour," may be one of Marx's most well known writings, especially among sociologists of work. Marx's analysis of alienation is important for two primary reasons. First, the concept of alienation is important in its own right as an expression of Marx's critique of capitalist society. No other concept in sociology conveys the dehumanizing potential of industrial work as effectively. Second, in addition to developing this concept, Marx demonstrates the connections between the experience of work and the conditions under which work is performed. Although contemporary sociologists sometimes portray alienation as a purely subjective state, Marx viewed alienation as a product of the social organization of work.

The next two selections, by Emile Durkheim and Max Weber, also show the intersections between sociological classics and the sociology of work. The reading by Durkheim, "The Social and Political Role of the Occupational Groups," is drawn from his famous study, *The Division of Labor in Society* (1893). In this work Durkheim examined the transition from a traditional social order to an industrial economy, paying particular attention to the forms of moral regulation that characterized each type of society. Durkheim believed that the changes associated with industrialization engendered new moral understandings, a transformation he captured with his distinction between "mechanical" and "organic" solidarity. The moral underpinnings of industrial society, which included cooperation, interdependence, and individuation, originated in the division of labor. "Organic solidarity thus consists in the ties of cooperation between individuals or groups of individuals which derive from their occupational interdependence within the differentiated division of labor" (Giddens 1972, p. 8). Despite these views, Durkheim was critical of the "incompletely developed" division of labor he observed at the end of the nineteenth century. These criticisms are contained in his discussions of "anomie" and the "forced division of labor"; they provide an interesting contrast with Marx's critique of capitalism.

Like his counterparts Marx and Durkheim, Weber was concerned with the transition to an industrial, capitalist economy and sought to develop a narrative that would capture the totality of this change. Thus emerged the concept of "rationalization," an orientation and a process that Weber saw as the dominant feature of the modern capitalist world. In his view, a rationalized society is dominated by concerns for efficiency, productivity, and the ability to subject life to rational calculation. For Weber, bureaucracy represented the epitome of rational organization. His discussion of this concept, contained in Reading 6, is the foundation of all subsequent sociological analyses of bureaucracy.

Though Marx, Durkheim, and Weber each saw aspects of progress in the development of an industrial capitalist society, none

considered this transformation to be wholly desirable for individuals or society. Marx believed that capitalism was inherently exploitative of workers and would eventually be transformed. Perhaps the least critical of the three, Durkheim nevertheless critiqued the "incompletely developed" nineteenth-century division of labor. Weber argued that rationalization and its embodiment in bureaucratic work organization were inevitable features of modern life, but they left people trapped in an "iron cage" that diminished their creativity, autonomy, and humanity. Sociologists for over a century have debated the merits of these sociologists' views, but their abilities to critically examine the organization of work in their own societies established Marx, Weber, and Durkheim as the first sociologists of work. It remains to be seen whether they will have as much influence in the twenty-first century.

Historical Perspectives on the American Workplace

In the next set of readings we move from the work of classical sociologists of Europe to the work of social scientists in the United States. The chapters in this section span most of the twentieth century, beginning with the writings of Frederick Taylor in the early 1900s and ending with a selection from Richard Edwards's book, *Contested Terrain* (1979). Although these authors may not be as well known as Marx, Durkheim, and Weber, they have been influential in shaping sociologists' conceptions of work organization.

Frederick Taylor (1856–1915) is best known as the "Father of Scientific Management" (Merkle 1980, p. 10) and in Reading 7, he outlines the fundamentals of his system. As Taylor's discussion reveals, Scientific Management (or Taylorism, as it is sometimes called) was much more than a set of techniques for improving workplace efficiency.

Taylor combined technical, organizational, and ideological elements into an integrated system as a solution to the problems of modern industrial society. The legacy of Scientific Management thus derives from its vision of work organization. According to Merkle (1980, p. 82), three elements were central to this vision: "the systematic application of science (and especially quantified) methods of study to industrial problems," "the invention of a new profession modeled on the role of the engineer for organizational design and maintenance," and "the use of machines for social control." As later selections in this anthology reveal, Taylor's legacy has continued to shape the organization of work.

Taylor's belief that scientific methods could be used to understand workers' behavior was shared by others during the first half of the twentieth century. Studies by Elton Mayo and his colleagues, conducted during the 1930s and 1940s at the Western Electric factory in Chicago, represent the most well known example of such research. In his detailed description of the famous "Hawthorne Experiment," Mayo lays the foundation for what would become another influential view of work organization: the Human Relations Movement. In contrast to Taylor's conception of workers as machines or beasts of burden, Mayo and his colleagues argued that workers were social beings and that the workplace thus must be understood as a social system. These studies and those following in the human relations tradition were scathingly labeled "cow sociology" by critics who viewed sociological interest in workers' morale as merely attempts to help managers achieve control and higher productivity (Whyte 1987). Nevertheless, studies by Mayo and his colleagues also inspired an ongoing tradition of sociological research on occupational cultures, groups, and the social relations of work (Whyte 1987; Simpson 1989).

In the 1960s and 1970s the sociology of work became heavily influenced by the field of economics. Rising levels of industrial conflict, as well as social movements and change outside the workplace, provided a context for more critical conceptions of work organization. The two remaining selections in this section are examples of these views. Harry Braverman's study, *Labor and Monopoly Capitalism* (1974), is among the most influential books on the workplace in the twentieth century. Paying particular attention to the relations between the division of labor, skills, and technology, Braverman echoed Marx's critique of work in a capitalist society. Braverman described the degradation, deskilling, and managerial control that he viewed as inevitable consequences of work organization under capitalism. Though later sociologists have faulted Braverman for his lack of attention to workers and their resistance to management's initiatives, Braverman inspired numerous followers. Studies exploring the "labor process" and the effects of technological change on skill levels are just two examples of his legacy.

Whereas Braverman focused on the forces that were "homogenizing" workers, sociologists of work in the late 1970s and 1980s began to examine the ways that the organization of work divided (or "segmented") groups of workers from one another. This research produced concepts such as *dual economy, dual labor market,* and *labor market segmentation.* For Richard Edwards and others, these divisions derived from differences between industries, between firms, and between jobs within firms. Edwards suggests that three labor market segments, each with a different type of control system, emerged in the latter half of the twentieth century. The jobs of Maureen, Fred, and Stanley, described in the first part of Reading 10, are examples of these three forms of control.

Technological Change and the Organization of Work

The final section in Part II is devoted to technological change. Although this topic has come up in previous readings, technology is important in its own right as a factor shaping work organization. This is not to suggest that technology is an independent force, with a will and logic of its own; the technological and the social are linked in workplaces, as they are in other arenas of life. As Thomas (1994, p. 204) states, "organizations—more precisely, people in organizations—exercise influence over the choice between technologies and within technologies and over the manner of technology's use." Because, however, there may be multiple interests guiding these choices, we must closely examine the processes through which technological changes are introduced and their consequences for work and workers.

The readings in this section offer several vantage points from which to consider technological change. The first reading in the section, drawn from Shoshana Zuboff's book, *In the Age of the Smart Machine* (1988), describes the experiences of pulp and paper mill workers as their jobs undergo computerization. Zuboff is particularly interested in the impact of computerization on workers' skills. Rather than focus simply on the gain or loss of skill, Zuboff suggests that computerization potentially alters the *types* of skills required by pulp and paper mill workers. Whether this potential is deployed to expand workers' control and responsibilities or to restrict them depends on how the technology is introduced and used. Zuboff shows that computers can have powerful effects on how workers conceive of and perform their jobs, but these effects depend on organizational and social factors as much as on the technological capabilities of the machines.

The next two readings adopt a more macrohistorical view of workplace technologies. In his reading, "Capital, Labor, and New Technology," Steven Vallas examines technological change at AT&T. Like Zuboff, Vallas is particularly interested in how technological change affects workers' skill levels and experiences. He shows that the issues are not simple, as technology's impacts varied among people of different occupations and genders. In addition, Vallas's analysis reveals complex interrelations between technological change, occupational restructuring, and workers' power. Ruth Milkman's reading shifts the focus from telecommunications to the automobile industry, where technological change has coincided with increased international competition. Milkman reveals the challenges both factors pose for organized labor and examines how labor and management have coped with a rapidly changing automobile industry. Her reading illustrates that technological change has the potential to not only alter jobs but to transform relations between workers and between workers and management. Moreover, Milkman shows how technological change in the American automobile industry is linked to other factors, such as international competition, that are transforming the industry.

Does technology have different impacts in white-collar settings? Though computers have been introduced into many workplaces, they have had a particularly profound impact in the office. Barbara Garson examines this impact from the perspectives of those most affected: clerical workers and managers in computerized offices. Recalling Taylor's ideas about improving efficiency in the workplace through tighter management control, Garson suggests that the computerized office may have much in common with the factory of the past. In addition, she discusses ways in which the introduction of technology may have unintended consequences for the social organization of work. Garson shows how the spread of computers and sophisticated word-processing programs has altered the gendered social relations of the traditional office. As secretaries were replaced by word processors, bosses lost the personal services and deference provided by (typically) female assistants. Although many of the male managers Garson studied lamented the loss of their personal secretaries, this change was not always viewed negatively by the female clerical staff.

REFERENCES

Alexander, Jeffrey C. 1987. "The Centrality of the Classics." Pp. 11–57 in *Social Theory Today*, edited by Anthony Giddens and Jonathon H. Turner. Stanford, CA: Stanford University Press.

Braverman, Harry. 1974. *Labor and Monopoly Capitalism*. New York: Monthly Review Press.

Edwards, Richard. 1978. *Contested Terrain: The Transformation of the Workplace in the Twentieth Century*. New York: Basic Books.

Giddens, Anthony. 1972. *Emile Durkheim: Selected Writings*. Cambridge: Cambridge University Press.

Mayo, Elton. 1933. *The Human Problems of an Industrial Civilization*. New York: The Macmillan Company.

Merkle, Judith A. 1980. *Management and Ideology: The Legacy of the International Scientific Management Movement*. Berkeley: University of California Press.

Simpson, Ida Harper. 1989. "The Sociology of Work: Where Have the Workers Gone?" *Social Forces* 67: 563–581.

Thomas, Robert J. 1994. *What Machines Can't Do: Politics and Technology in the Industrial Enterprise*. Berkeley: University of California Press.

Thompson, Paul. 1989. *The Nature of Work*. London: Macmillan.

Watson, Tony J. 1987. *Sociology, Work, and Industry*. London: Routledge and Kegan Paul.

Whyte, William Foote. 1987. "From Human Relations to Organizational Behavior: Reflections on the Changing Scene." *Industrial and Labor Relations Review* 40: 487–490.

Zuboff, Shoshana. 1988. *In the Age of the Smart Machine*. New York: Basic Books.

CLASSICAL SOCIOLOGY AND THE ORGANIZATION OF WORK

4

Alienated Labour

Karl Marx

Karl Marx (1818–1883) was born in Germany but spent much of his life in France and England. Along with Weber and Durkheim, he is recognized as one of the most important theorists in sociology. This reading draws from Marx's early writings.

W̲e started from the presuppositions of political economy. We accepted its vocabulary and its laws. We presupposed private property, the separation of labour, capital, and land, and likewise of wages, profit, and ground rent; also division of labour; competition; the concept of exchange value, etc. Using the very words of political economy we have demonstrated that the worker is degraded to the most miserable sort of commodity; that the misery of the worker is in inverse proportion to the power and size of his production; that the necessary result of competition is the accumulation of capital in a few hands, and thus a more terrible restoration of monopoly; and that finally the distinction between capitalist and landlord, and that between peasant and industrial worker disappears and the whole of society must fall apart into the two classes of the property owners and the propertyless workers.

Political economy starts with the fact of private property, it does not explain it to us. It conceives of the material process that private property goes through in reality in general abstract formulas which then have for it a value of laws. It does not understand these laws, i.e. it does not demonstrate how they arise from the nature of private property. Political economy does not afford us any explanation of the reason for the separation of labour and capital, of capital and land. When, for example, political economy defines the relationship of wages to profit from capital, the interest of the capitalist is the ultimate court of appeal, that is, it presupposes what should be its result. In the same way competition enters the argument everywhere. It is explained by exterior circumstances. But political economy tells us nothing about how far these exterior, apparently fortuitous circumstances are merely the expression of a necessary development. We have seen how it regards exchange itself as something fortuitous. The only wheels that political economy sets in motion are greed and war among the greedy, competition.

It is just because political economy has not grasped the connections in the movement that new contradictions have arisen in its doctrines, for example, between that of monopoly and that of competition, freedom of craft and corporations, division of landed property and large estates. For competition, free trade, and the division of landed prop-

Reprinted from "Alienated Labour," in *Karl Marx: Selected Writings*, edited by David McLellan, by permission of Oxford University Press. © David McLellan 1977.

erty were only seen as fortuitous circumstances created by will and force, not developed and comprehended as necessary, inevitable, and natural results of monopoly, corporations, and feudal property.

So what we have to understand now is the essential connection of private property, selfishness, the separation of labour, capital, and landed property, of exchange and competition, of the value and degradation of man, of monopoly and competition, etc.—the connection of all this alienation with the money system.

Let us not be like the political economist who, when he wishes to explain something, puts himself in an imaginary original state of affairs. Such an original stage of affairs explains nothing. He simply pushes the question back into a grey and nebulous distance. He presupposes as a fact and an event what he ought to be deducing, namely the necessary connection between the two things, for example, between the division of labour and exchange. Similarly, the theologian explains the origin of evil through the fall, i.e. he presupposes as an historical fact what he should be explaining.

We start with a contemporary fact of political economy:

The worker becomes poorer the richer is his production, the more it increases in power and scope. The worker becomes a commodity that is all the cheaper the more commodities he creates. The depreciation of the human world progresses in direct proportion to the increase in value of the world of things. Labour does not only produce commodities; it produces itself and the labourer as a commodity and that to the extent to which it produces commodities in general.

What this fact expresses is merely this: the object that labour produces, its product, confronts it as an alien being, as a power independent of the producer. The product of labour is labour that has solidified itself into an object, made itself into a thing, the objectification of labour. The realization of labour is its objectification. In political economy this realization of labour appears as a loss of reality for the worker, objectification as a loss of the object of slavery to it, and appropriation as alienation, as externalization.

The realization of labour appears as a loss of reality to an extent that the worker loses his reality by dying of starvation. Objectification appears as a loss of the object to such an extent that the worker is robbed not only of the objects necessary for his life but also of the objects of his work. Indeed, labour itself becomes an object he can only have in his power with the greatest of efforts and at irregular intervals. The appropriation of the object appears as alienation to such an extent that the more objects the worker produces, the less he can possess and the more he falls under the domination of his product, capital.

All these consequences follow from the fact that the worker relates to the product of his labour as to an alien object. For it is evident from this presupposition that the more the worker externalizes himself in his work, the more powerful becomes the alien, objective world that he creates opposite himself, the poorer he becomes himself in his inner life and the less he can call his own. It is just the same in religion. The more man puts into God, the less he retains in himself. The worker puts his life into the object and this means that it no longer belongs to him but to the object. So the greater this activity, the more the worker is without an object. What the product of his labour is, that he is not. So the greater this product the less he is himself. The externalization of the worker in his product implies not only that his labour becomes an object, an exterior existence but also that it exists outside him, independent and alien, and becomes a self-sufficient power opposite him, that the life that he has lent to the object affronts him, hostile and alien.

Let us now deal in more detail with objectification, the production of the worker, and the alienation, the loss of the object, his product, which is involved in it.

The worker can create nothing without nature, the sensuous exterior world. It is the matter in which his labour realizes itself, in which it is active, out of which and through which it produces.

But as nature affords the means of life for labour in the sense that labour cannot live without objects on which it exercises itself, so it affords a means of life in the narrower sense, namely the means for the physical subsistence of the worker himself.

Thus the more the worker appropriates the exterior world of sensuous nature by his labour, the more he doubly deprives himself of the means of subsistence, firstly since the exterior sensuous world increasingly ceases to be an object belonging to his work, a means of subsistence for his labour; secondly, since it increasingly ceases to be a means of subsistence in the direct sense, a means for the physical subsistence of the worker.

Thus in these two ways the worker becomes a slave to his object: firstly he receives an object of labour, that is he receives labour, and secondly, he receives the means of subsistence. Thus it is his object that permits him to exist first as a worker and secondly as a physical subject. The climax of this slavery is that only as a worker can he maintain himself as a physical subject and it is only as a physical subject that he is a worker.

(According to the laws of political economy the alienation of the worker in his object is expressed as follows: the more the worker produces the less he has to consume, the more values he creates the more valueless and worthless he becomes, the more formed the product the more deformed the worker, the more civilized the product, the more barbaric the worker, the more powerful the work the more powerless becomes the worker, the more cultured the work the more philistine the worker becomes and more of a slave to nature.)

Political economy hides the alienation in the essence of labour by not considering the immediate relationship between the worker (labour) and production. Labour produces works of wonder for the rich, but nakedness for the worker. It produces palaces, but only hovels for the worker; it produces beauty, but cripples the worker; it replaces labour by machines but throws a part of the workers back to a barbaric labour and turns the other part into machines. It produces culture, but also imbecility and cretinism for the worker.

The immediate relationship of labour to its products is the relationship of the worker to the objects of his production. The relationship of the man of means to the objects of production and to production itself is only a consequence of this first relationship. And it confirms it. We shall examine this other aspect later.

So when we ask the question: what relationship is essential to labour, we are asking about the relationship of the worker to production.

Up to now we have considered only one aspect of the alienation or externalization of the worker, his relationship to the products of his labour. But alienation shows itself not only in the result, but also in the act of production, inside productive activity itself. How would the worker be able to affront the product of his work as an alien being if he did not alienate himself in the act of production itself? For the product is merely the summary of the activity of production. So if the product of labour is externalization, production itself must be active externalization, the externalization of activity, the activity of externalization. The alienation of the object of labour is only the résumé of the alienation, the externalization in the activity of labour itself.

What does the externalization of labour consist of then?

Firstly, that labour is exterior to the worker, that is, it does not belong to his essence. Therefore he does not confirm himself in his work, he denies himself, feels miserable instead of happy, deploys no free physical and intellectual energy, but mortifies his body and ruins his mind. Thus the worker only feels a stranger. He is at home when he is not working and when he works he is not at home. His labour is therefore not voluntary but compulsory, forced labour. It is therefore not the satisfaction of a need but only a means to satisfy needs outside itself. How alien it really is is very evident from the fact that when there is no physical or other compulsion, labour is avoided like the plague. External labour, labour in which man externalizes himself, is a labour of self-sacrifice and mortification. Finally, the external character of labour for the worker shows itself in the fact that it is not his own but someone else's, that it does not belong to him, that he does not belong to himself in his labour but to someone else. As in religion the human imagination's own activity, the activity of man's head and his heart, reacts independently on the individual as an alien activity of gods or devils, so the activity of the worker is not his own spontaneous activity. It belongs to another and is the loss of himself.

The result we arrive at then is that man (the worker) only feels himself freely active in his animal functions of eating, drinking, and procreating, at most also in his dwelling and dress, and feels himself an animal in his human functions.

Eating, drinking, procreating, etc. are indeed truly human functions. But in the abstraction that separates them from the other round of human activity and makes them into final and exclusive ends they become animal.

We have treated the act of alienation of practical human activity, labour, from two aspects. (1) The relationship of the worker to the product of his labour as an alien object that has power over him. This relationship is at the same time the relationship to the sensuous exterior world and to natural objects as to an alien and hostile world opposed to him. (2) The relationship of labour to the act of production inside labour. This relationship is the relationship of the worker to his own activity as something that is alien and does not belong to him; it is activity that is passivity, power that is weakness, procreation that is castration, the worker's own physical and intellectual energy, his personal life (for what is life except activity?) as an activity directed against himself, independent of him and not belonging to him. It is self-alienation, as above it was the alienation of the object.

We now have to draw a third characteristic of alienated labour from the two previous ones.

Man is a species-being not only in that practically and theoretically he makes both his own and other species into his objects, but also, and this is only another way of putting the same thing, he relates to himself as to the present, living species, in that he relates to himself as to a universal and therefore free being.

Both with man and with animals the species-life consists physically in the fact that man (like animals) lives from inorganic nature, and the more universal man is than animals the more universal is the area of inorganic nature from which he lives. From the theoretical point of view, plants, animals, stones, air, light, etc. form part of human consciousness, partly as objects of natural science, partly as objects of art; they are his intellectual inorganic nature, his intellectual means of subsistence, which he must first prepare before he can enjoy and assimilate them. From the practical point of view, too, they form a part of human life and activity. Physically man lives solely from these products of nature, whether they appear as food, heating, clothing, habitation, etc. The universality of man appears in practice precisely in the universality that makes the whole of nature into his inorganic body in that it is both (i) his immediate means of subsistence and also (ii) the material object and tool of his vital activity. Nature is the inorganic body of a man, that is, in so far as it is not itself a human body. That man lives from nature means that nature is his body with which he must maintain a constant interchange so as not to die. That man's physical and intellectual life depends on nature merely means that nature depends on itself, for man is part of nature.

While alienated labour alienates (1) nature from man, and (2) man from himself, his own active function, his vital activity, it also alienates the species from man; it turns his species-life into a means towards his individual life. Firstly it alienates species-life and individual life, and secondly in its abstraction it makes the latter into the aim of the former which is also conceived of in its abstract and alien form. For firstly, work, vital activity, and productive life itself appear to man only as a means to the satisfaction of a need, the need to preserve his physical existence. But productive life is species-life. It is life producing life. The whole character of a species, its generic character, is contained in its manner of vital activity, and free conscious activity is the species-characteristic of man. Life itself appears merely as a means to life.

The animal is immediately one with its vital activity. It is not distinct from it. They are identical. Man makes his vital activity itself into an object of his will and consciousness. He has a conscious vital activity. He is not immediately identical to any of his characterizations. Conscious vital activity differentiates man immediately from animal vital activity. It is this and this alone that makes man a species-being. He is only a conscious

being, that is, his own life is an object to him, precisely because he is a species-being. This is the only reason for his activity being free activity. Alienated labour reverses the relationship so that, just because he is a conscious being, man makes his vital activity and essence a mere means to his existence.

The practical creation of an objective world, the working-over of inorganic nature, is the confirmation of man as a conscious species-being, that is, as a being that relates to the species as to himself and to himself as to the species. It is true that the animal, too, produces. It builds itself a nest, a dwelling, like the bee, the beaver, the ant, etc. But it only produces what it needs immediately for itself or its offspring; it produces one-sidedly whereas man produces universally; it produces only under the pressure of immediate physical need, whereas man produces freely from physical need and only truly produces when he is thus free; it produces only itself whereas man reproduces the whole of nature. Its product belongs immediately to its physical body whereas man can freely separate himself from his product. The animal only fashions things according to the standards and needs of the species it belongs to, whereas man knows how to produce according to the measure of every species and knows everywhere how to apply its inherent standard to the object; thus man also fashions things according to the laws of beauty.

Thus it is in the working over of the objective world that man first really affirms himself as a species-being. This production is his active species-life. Through it nature appears as his work and his reality. The object of work is therefore the objectification of the species-life of man; for he duplicates himself not only intellectually, in his mind, but also actively in reality and thus can look at his image in a world he has created. Therefore when alienated labour tears from man the object of his production, it also tears from him his species-life, the real objectivity of his species and turns the advantage he has over animals into a disadvantage in that his inorganic body, nature, is torn from him.

Similarly, in that alienated labour degrades man's own free activity to a means, it turns the species-life of man into a means for his physical existence.

Thus consciousness, which man derives from his species, changes itself through alienation so that species-life becomes a means for him.

Therefore alienated labor:

(3) makes the species-being of man, both nature and the intellectual faculties of his species, into a being that is alien to him, into a means for his individual existence. It alienates from man his own body, nature exterior to him, and his intellectual being, his human essence.

(4) An immediate consequence of man's alienation from the product of his work, his vital activity and his species-being, is the alienation of man from man. When man is opposed to himself, it is another man that is opposed to him. What is valid for the relationship of a man to his work, of the product of his work and himself, is also valid for the relationship of man to other men and of their labour and the objects of their labour.

In general, the statement that man is alienated from his species-being, means that one man is alienated from another as each of them is alienated from the human essence.

The alienation of man and in general of every relationship in which man stands to himself is first realized and expressed in the relationship with which man stands to other men.

Thus in the situation of alienated labour each man measures his relationship to other men by the relationship in which he finds himself placed as a worker.

We began with a fact of political economy, the alienation of the worker and his production. We have expressed this fact in conceptual terms: alienated, externalized labour. We have analysed this concept and thus analysed a purely economic fact.

Let us now see further how the concept of alienated, externalized labour must express and represent itself in reality.

If the product of work is alien to me, opposes me as an alien power, whom does it belong to then?

If my own activity does not belong to me and is an alien, forced activity to whom does it belong then?

To another being than myself.

Who is this being?

The gods? Of course in the beginning of history the chief production, as for example, the building of temples etc. in Egypt, India, and Mexico was both in the service of the gods and also belonged to them. But the gods alone were never the masters of the work. And nature just as little. And what a paradox it would be if, the more man mastered nature through his work and the more the miracles of the gods were rendered superfluous by the miracles of industry, the more man had to give up his pleasure in producing and the enjoyment in his product for the sake of these powers.

The alien being to whom the labour and the product of the labour belongs, whom the labour serves and who enjoys its product, can only be man himself. If the product of labour does not belong to the worker but stands over against him as an alien power, this is only possible in that it belongs to another man apart from the worker.

If his activity torments him it must be a joy and a pleasure to someone else. This alien power above man can be neither the gods nor nature, only man himself.

Consider further the above sentence that the relationship of man to himself first becomes objective and real to him through his relationship to other men. So if he relates to the product of his labour, his objectified labour, as to an object that is alien, hostile, powerful, and independent of him, this relationship implies that another man is the alien, hostile, powerful, and independent master of this object. If he relates to his own activity as to something unfree, it is a relationship to an activity that is under the domination, oppression, and yoke of another man.

Every self-alienation of man from himself and nature appears in the relationship in which he places himself and nature to other men distinct from himself. Therefore religious self-alienation necessarily appears in the relationship of layman to priest, or, because here we are dealing with a spiritual world, to a mediator, etc. In the practical, real world, the self-alienation can only appear through the practical, real relationship to other men. The means through which alienation makes progress are themselves practical. Through alienated labour, then, man creates not only his relationship to the object and act of production as to alien and hostile men; he creates too the relationship in which other men stand to his production and his product and the relationship in which he stands to these other men. Just as he turns his production into his own loss of reality and punishment and his own product into a loss, a product that does not belong to him, so he creates the domination of the man who does not produce over the production and the product. As he alienates his activity from himself, so he hands over to an alien person an activity that does not belong to him.

Up till now we have considered the relationship only from the side of the worker and we will later consider it from the side of the non-worker.

Thus through alienated, externalized labour the worker creates the relationship to this labour of a man who is alien to it and remains exterior to it. The relationship of the worker to his labour creates the relationship to it of the capitalist, or whatever else one wishes to call the master of the labour. Private property is thus the product, result, and necessary consequence of externalized labour, of the exterior relationship of the worker to nature and to himself.

Thus private property is the result of the analysis of the concept of externalized labour, i.e. externalized man, alienated work, alienated life, alienated man.

We have, of course, obtained the concept of externalized labour (externalized life) from political economy as the result of the movement of private property. But it is evident from the analysis of this concept that, although private property appears to be the ground and reason for externalized labour, it is rather a consequence of it, just as the gods are originally not the cause but the effect of the aberration of the human mind, although later this relationship reverses itself.

It is only in the final culmination of the development of private property that these hidden characteristics come once more to the fore, in that firstly it is the product of externalized labour and secondly it is the means through which labour externalizes itself, the realization of this externalization.

5

The Social and Political Role of the Occupational Groups
Emile Durkheim

Emile Durkheim (1858–1917), a French sociologist, wrote *The Division of Labor* in 1893. This reading is an excerpt from that classic study.

The absence of corporative institutions . . . creates in the organisation of a society like ours a void whose importance it is difficult to exaggerate. What is lacking is a complete system of agencies necessary to the functioning of social life. This structural defect is evidently not a localised failure, limited to one part of society; it is a malady *totius substantiae,* affecting the whole organism. Consequently, any attempt to put an end to it cannot fail to produce the most far-reaching consequences. It is the general health of the social body which is in question here.

That does not mean to say, however, that the corporation is a sort of panacea for everything. The crisis which we are experiencing is not to be traced to any one specific cause. In order to overcome it, it is not enough to establish some sort of regulation where it is needed. This regulation must be just. Now, as we shall say further on "as long as there are rich and poor at birth, there cannot be just contract", nor an equitable distribution of social goods. But while corporative reform must be accompanied by other reforms, it is the primary condition for these others to be effective. Let us imagine that the primordial state of ideal justice were achieved; let us

suppose that men enter life in a state of perfect economic equality, which is to say, that wealth has completely ceased to be hereditary. The problems with which we are now struggling would not thereby be solved. Evidently there will always be an economic apparatus, and various agencies co-operating in its functioning. It will still be necessary to determine their rights and duties for each form of industry. In each occupation a body of rules will have to be established which fix the quantity of work expected, equitable rates of payment for different workers, their duties toward each other and toward the community, etc. We shall face a *tabula rasa,* just as now. Because wealth will not be inherited any longer, as it is today, it does not follow that the state of anarchy will disappear, for it is not a question of the ownership of wealth, but of the regulation of the activity to which this wealth gives rise. It will not regulate itself by magic, as soon as it is necessary, if the forces which can generate this regulation have not been previously aroused and organised. . .

Since a body of rules is the specific form which is assumed by spontaneously established relations between social functions in the course of time, we can say, *a priori,* that the state of *anomie* is impossible wherever interdependent organs are sufficiently in contact and sufficiently extensive. If they are close to each other, they are readily aware, in every situation, of the need which they have

Excerpt from *Emile Durkheim: Selected Writings,* edited, translated, and with an introduction by Anthony Giddens. Reprinted with the permission of Cambridge University Press.

of one-another, and consequently they have an active and permanent feeling of mutual dependence. For the same reason that exchanges take place among them easily, they take place frequently; being habitual, they regularise themselves accordingly, and in time become consolidated. As the smallest reaction is transmitted from one part to another, the rules which are thus created express this directly: that is to say, they embody and fix, in detail, the conditions of equilibrium. But if, on the other hand, they are not clearly visible to each other, then only stimuli of a certain intensity can be communicated from one organ to another. The relationships being infrequent, they are not repeated often enough to become fixed; they must be established anew each time. The channels cut by the streams of movement cannot deepen because the streams themselves are too intermittent. If a few rules, at least, do come into existence, they are nevertheless too abstract and diffuse, for under these conditions it is only the most general outline of the phenomena that can become fixed. The same thing will be the case if the contiguity, although sufficient, is too recent or has not existed for long enough.

In a general way, this condition is realised in the nature of things. A function can be divided between two or several parts of an organism only if these parts are fairly close to each other. Moreover, once labour is divided, since these elements are dependent upon one-another, they naturally tend to lessen the distance separating them. That is why as one goes up the evolutionary scale, one sees organs coming together, and, as Spencer says, being introduced in the spaces between one another. But, in unusual circumstances, a different situation can be brought about.

This is what happens in the cases we are discussing. In so far as the segmental type is strongly marked, there are nearly as many economic markets as there are different segments. Consequently, each of them is very limited. Producers, being near consumers, can easily calculate the range of needs to be satisfied. Equilibrium is established without any difficulty and production regulates itself. On the other hand, as the organised type develops, the fusion of different segments draws the markets together into a single market which embraces almost all society. This event extends further, and tends to become universal, for the frontiers which separate peoples break down at the same time as those which separate the segments of each of them. The result is that each industry produces for consumers spread over the whole surface of the country or even of the entire world. Here the contact is broken; the producer can no longer take in the market at a glance, or even conceptualise it. He can no longer have an idea of its limits, since it is, so to speak, limitless. Accordingly, production becomes unchecked and unregulated. It can only operate haphazardly, and in the course of these gropings, it is inevitable that it will be out of proportion, either in one direction or the other. From this come the crises which periodically dislocate economic life. The growth of local, restricted crises—or business failures—is in all likelihood an effect of the same cause.

As the market extends, large-scale industry appears. This has the effect of changing the relations between employers and workers. An increasing fatigue of the nervous system joined to the contagious influence of large concentrations of population increase the needs of the workers. Machines replace men; manufacturing replaces handwork. The worker is regimented, separated from his family throughout the day. He always lives apart from his employer, etc. These new conditions of industrial life naturally demand a new organisation, but as these changes have been accomplished with extreme rapidity, the interests in conflict have not yet had the time to become equilibrated. . .

An occupational activity can be effectively regulated only by a group close enough to it to know how it operates, what its needs are, and how it is likely to change. The only one that meets all these conditions is the one which might be formed by all the agents of the same industry united and organised into a single body. This is what we call the "corporation" or "occupational group".

Now, in the economic order, the occupational group does not exist any more than occupational ethics. Since the eighteenth century suppressed the old corporations, *not without reason*, only fragmentary and inadequate attempts have been made to reestablish them upon new foundations. To be sure, individuals working at the same trade have contacts with one-another, because of their similar occupation. Their very competition puts them in relationship. But these relationships are not permanent; they depend upon chance meetings, and have, very often, an entirely personal aspect. A particular industrial worker is found in contact with a colleague; this does not result from the industrial body of this or that speciality united for common action. In rare cases, the members of the same occupation come together as a group to discuss some question of general interest, but these meetings are only temporary. They do not survive the particular circumstances which bring them into being, and consequently the collective life which they stimulate more or less disappears with them.

The only groups which have a certain permanence today are the unions, composed of either employers or workmen. Certainly there is here the beginning of occupational organisation, but still quite formless and rudimentary. For, first, a union is a private association, without legal authority, and consequently without any regulatory power.

Moreover, the number of unions is theoretically limitless, even within the same industrial category; and as each of them is independent of the others, if they do not federate or unify there is nothing intrinsic in them expressing the unity of the occupation in its entirety. Finally, not only are the employers' union and the employees' unions distinct from each other, which is *legitimate and necessary*, but there is no regular contact between them. There exists no common organisation which brings them together, where they can develop common forms of regulation which will determine the relationships between them in an authoritative fashion, without either of them losing their own autonomy. Consequently, it is always the rule of the strongest which settles conflicts, and the state of war is continuous. Save for those of their actions which are governed by common moral codes, employers and workers are, in relation to each other, in the same situation as two autonomous states, but of unequal power. They can form contracts, as nations do through the medium of their governments, but these contracts express only the respective state of their military forces. They sanction it as a condition of reality; they cannot make it legally valid.

In order to establish occupational morality and law in the different economic occupations, the corporation, instead of remaining a diffuse, disorganised aggregate, must become—or rather, must again become—a defined, organised group; in a word, a public institution. . .

What the experience of the past proves, above all, is that the framework of the occupational group must always be related to the framework of economic life; it is because of this dislocation that the corporative regime disappeared. Since the market, formerly localised in the town, has become national and international, the corporation must expand to the same degree. Instead of being limited only to the artisans within one town, it must grow in such a way as to include all the members of the occupation throughout the country, for in whatever area they are found, whether they live in the town or country, they are all interdependent, and participate in a common activity. Since this common activity is, in certain respects, independent of any territorial basis, the appropriate agency must be created that expresses and stabilises its operation. Because of the extensiveness of those dimensions, such an agency would necessarily be in direct contact with the central agency of collective life; for events which are important enough to interest a whole category of industrial enterprises in a country necessarily have very general implications, which the state cannot ignore. This leads it to intervene. Thus, it is not without reason that royal power tended instinctively not to allow large-scale industry to operate outside its control when it first appeared. It was impossible for it not to be concerned with a form of activity which, by its very nature, can always be capable of influencing the whole of society. But while this regulatory action is necessary, it must not degenerate into direct subordination, as happened in the seventeenth and eighteenth centuries. The two related agencies must remain distinct and autonomous; each of them has its function, which it alone can execute. While the function of formulating general principles of industrial legislation belongs to the governmental assemblies, they are not able to diversify them according to the different forms of industry. It is this diversification which is the proper task of the corporation. This unitary organisation, representing the whole country, in no way excludes the formation of secondary agencies, comprising workers of the same region or locality, whose role would be to further specify the occupational regulation demanded by local or regional conditions. Economic life would thus be regulated and determined without losing any of its diversity.

For that very reason, the corporative system would be preserved from the tendency towards stagnation that it has often been criticised for in the past, for this was a defect rooted in the narrowly communal character of the corporation. As long as it was limited to the town, it was inevitable that it become a prisoner of tradition, like the town itself. In so restricted a group the conditions of life are almost invariable, habit has complete control over people and things, and anything new comes to be feared. The traditionalism of the corporations was thus only an aspect of the traditionalism of the local community, and showed the same properties. Once it had become ingrained in the mores, it survived the factors which had produced and originally justified it. This is why, when the material and moral centralisation of the country, and large-scale industry which followed from it, had opened up new wants, awakened new deeds, introduced into tastes and fashions a changeability heretofore unknown, the corporation, which was obstinately attached to its established customs, was unable to satisfy these new demands. But national corporations, in virtue of their dimension and complexity, would not be exposed to this danger. Too many different men would be involved to lead to a situation of unchanging uniformity. In a group formed of numerous and varied elements, new combinations are always being produced. There would then be nothing rigid about such an organisation, and it would consequently be adapted to the changing equilibrium of needs and ideas.

6

Bureaucracy

Max Weber

Max Weber (1864–1920) was a German scholar whose writings have influenced sociologists for a century. Weber's analysis of bureaucracy, excerpted here, is among his
most important work.

I: Characteristics of Bureaucracy

Modern officialdom functions in the following specific manner:

I. There is the principle of fixed and official jurisdictional areas, which are generally
ordered by rules, that is, by laws or administrative regulations.

1. The regular activities required for the
purposes of the bureaucratically governed
structure are distributed in a fixed way as
official duties.

2. The authority to give the commands
required for the discharge of these duties is
distributed in a stable way and is strictly delimited by rules concerning the coercive
means, physical, sacerdotal, or otherwise,
which may be placed at the disposal of officials.

3. Methodical provision is made for the
regular and continuous fulfillment of these
duties and for the execution of the corresponding rights; only persons who have the
generally regulated qualifications to serve
are employed.

In public and lawful government these
three elements constitute "bureaucratic
authority." In private economic domination, they constitute bureaucratic "man-

agement." Bureaucracy, thus understood,
is fully developed in political and ecclesi-
astical communities only in the modern
state, and, in the private economy, only in
the most advanced institutions of capitalism. Permanent and public office authority,
with fixed jurisdiction, is not the historical
rule but rather the exception. This is so
even in large political structures such as
those of the ancient Orient, the Germanic
and Mongolian empires of conquest, or of
many feudal structures of state. In all these
cases, the ruler executes the most important measures through personal trustees,
table-companions, or court-servants. Their
commissions and authority are not precisely delimited and are temporarily called
into being for each case.

II. The principles of office hierarchy and
of levels of graded authority mean a firmly
ordered system of super- and subordination
in which there is a supervision of the lower
offices by the higher ones. Such a system offers the governed the possibility of appealing the decision of a lower office to its
higher authority, in a definitely regulated
manner. With the full development of the
bureaucratic type, the office hierarchy is
monocratically organized. The principle of
hierarchical office authority is found in all
bureaucratic structures: in state and ecclesi-
astical structures as well as in large party organizations and private enterprises. It does
not matter for the character of bureaucracy

whether its authority is called "private" or "public."

When the principle of jurisdictional "competency" is fully carried through, hierarchical subordination—at least in public office—does not mean that the "higher" authority is simply authorized to take over the business of the "lower." Indeed, the opposite is the rule. Once established and having fulfilled its task, an office tends to continue in existence and be held by another incumbent.

III. The management of the modern office is based upon written documents ("the files"), which are preserved in their original or draught form. There is, therefore, a staff of subaltern officials and scribes of all sorts. The body of officials actively engaged in a "public" office, along with the respective apparatus of material implements and the files, make up a "bureau." In private enterprise, "the bureau" is often called "the office."

In principle, the modern organization of the civil service separates the bureau from the private domicile of the official, and, in general, bureaucracy segregates official activity as something distinct from the sphere of private life. Public monies and equipment are divorced from the private property of the official. This condition is everywhere the product of a long development. Nowadays, it is found in public as well as in private enterprises; in the latter, the principle extends even to the leading entrepreneur. In principle, the executive office is separated from the household, business from private correspondence, and business assets from private fortune. The more consistently the modern type of business management had been carried through the more are these separations the case. The beginnings of this process are to be found as early as the Middle Ages.

It is the peculiarity of the modern entrepreneur that he conducts himself as the "first official" of his enterprise, in the very same way in which the ruler of a specifically modern bureaucratic state spoke of himself as "the first servant" of the state. The idea that the bureau activities of the state are intrinsically different in character from the management of private economic offices is a continental European notion and, by way of contrast, is totally foreign to the American way.

IV. Office management, at least all specialized office management—and such management is distinctly modern—usually presupposes thorough and expert training. This increasingly holds for the modern executive and employee of private enterprises, in the same manner as it holds for the state official.

V. When the office is fully developed, official activity demands the full working capacity of the official, irrespective of the fact that his obligatory time in the bureau may be firmly delimited. In the normal case, this is only the product of a long development, in the public as well as in the private office. Formerly, in all cases, the normal state of affairs was reversed: official business was discharged as a secondary activity.

VI. The management of the office follows general rules, which are more or less stable, more or less exhaustive, and which can be learned. Knowledge of these rules represents a special technical learning which the officials possess. It involves jurisprudence, or administrative or business management.

The reduction of modern office management to rules is deeply embedded in its very nature. The theory of modern public administration, for instance, assumes that the authority to order certain matters by decree—which has been legally granted to public authorities—does not entitle the bureau to regulate the matter by commands given for each case, but only to regulate the matter abstractly. This stands in extreme contrast to the regulation of all relationships through individual privileges and bestowals of favor, which is absolutely dominant in patrimonialism, at least in so far as such relationships are not fixed by sacred tradition.

2: The Position of the Official

All this results in the following for the internal and external position of the official:

I. Office holding is a "vocation." This is shown, first, in the requirement of a firmly prescribed course of training, which demands the entire capacity for work for a long period of time, and in the generally prescribed and special examinations which are prerequisites of employment. Furthermore, the position of the official is in the nature of a duty. This determines the internal structure of his relations, in the following manner: Legally and actually, office holding is not considered a source to be exploited for rents or emoluments, as was normally the case during the Middle Ages and frequently up to the threshold of recent times. Nor is office holding considered a usual exchange of services for equivalents, as is the case with free labor contracts. Entrance into an office, including one in the private economy, is considered an acceptance of a specific obligation of faithful management in return for a secure existence. It is decisive for the specific nature of modern loyalty to an office that, in the pure type, it does not establish a relationship to a *person*, like the vassal's or disciple's faith in feudal or in patrimonial relations of authority. Modern loyalty is devoted to impersonal and functional purposes. Behind the functional purposes, of course, "ideas of culture-values" usually stand. These are *ersatz* for the earthly or supra-mundane personal master: ideas such as "state," "church," "community," "party," or "enterprise" are thought of as being realized in a community; they provide an ideological halo for the master.

The political official—at least in the fully developed modern state—is not considered the personal servant of a ruler. Today, the bishop, the priest, and the preacher are in fact no longer, as in early Christian times, holders of purely personal charisma. The supra-mundane and sacred values which they offer are given to everybody who seems to be worthy of them and who asks for them. In former times, such leaders acted upon the personal command of their master; in principle, they were responsible only to him. Nowadays, in spite of the partial survival of the old theory, such religious leaders are officials in the service of a functional purpose, which in the present-day "church" has become routinized and, in turn, ideologically hallowed.

II. The personal position of the official is patterned in the following way:

1. Whether he is in a private office or a public bureau, the modern official always strives and usually enjoys a distinct *social esteem* as compared with the governed. His social position is guaranteed by the prescriptive rules of rank order and, for the political official, by special definitions of the criminal code against "insults of officials" and "contempt" of state and church authorities.

The actual social position of the official is normally highest where, as in old civilized countries, the following conditions prevail: a strong demand for administration by trained experts; a strong and stable social differentiation, where the official predominantly derives from socially and economically privileged strata because of the social distribution of power; or where the costliness of the required training and status conventions are binding upon him. The possession of educational certificates—to be discussed elsewhere—are usually linked with qualification for office. Naturally, such certificates or patents enhance the "status element" in the social position of the official. For the rest this status factor in individual cases is explicitly and impassively acknowledged; for example, in the prescription that the acceptance or rejection of an aspirant to an official career depends upon the consent ("election") of the members of the official body. This is the case in the German army with the officer corps. Similar phenomena, which promote this guild-like closure of officialdom, are typically found in patrimonial and, particularly, in prebendal officialdoms of the past. The desire to resurrect such phenomena in changed forms is by no means infrequent among modern bureaucrats. For instance, they have played a role among the demands of the quite proletarian and expert officials (the *tretyj* element) during the Russian revolution.

Usually the social esteem of the officials as such is especially low where the demand for expert administration and the dominance of status conventions are weak. This is especially the case in the United States; it is often the case in new settlements by virtue of their wide fields for profit-making and the great instability of their social stratification.

2. The pure type of bureaucratic official is *appointed* by a superior authority. An official elected by the governed is not a purely bureaucratic figure. Of course, the formal existence of an election does not by itself mean that no appointment hides behind the election—in the state, especially, appointment by party chiefs. Whether or not this is the case does not depend upon legal statutes but upon the way in which the party mechanism functions. Once firmly organized, the parties can turn a formally free election into the mere acclamation of a candidate designated by the party chief. As a rule, however, a formally free election is turned into a fight, conducted according to definite rules, for votes in favor of one of two designed candidates.

In all circumstances, the designation of officials by means of an election among the governed modifies the strictness of hierarchical subordination. In principle, an official who is so elected has an autonomous position opposite the superordinate official. The elected official does not derive his position "from above" but "from below," or at least not from a superior authority of the official hierarchy but from powerful party men ("bosses"), who also determine his further career. The career of the elected official is not, or at least not primarily, dependent upon his chief in the administration. The official who is not elected but appointed by a chief normally functions more exactly, from a technical point of view, because, all other circumstances being equal, it is more likely that purely functional points of consideration and qualities will determine his selection and career. As laymen, the governed can become acquainted with the extent to which a candidate is expertly qualified for office only in terms of experience, and hence only after his service. Moreover, in every sort of selection of officials by election, parties quite naturally give decisive weight not to expert considerations but to the services a follower renders to the party boss. This holds for all kinds of procurement of officials by elections, for the designation of formally free, elected officials by party bosses when they determine the slate of candidates, or the free appointment by a chief who has himself been elected. The contrast, however, is relative: substantially similar conditions hold where legitimate monarchs and their subordinates appoint officials, except that the influence of the followings are then less controllable.

Where the demand for administration by trained experts is considerable, and the party followings have to recognize an intellectually developed, educated, and freely moving "public opinion," the use of unqualified officials falls back upon the party in power at the next election. Naturally, this is more likely to happen when the officials are appointed by the chief. The demand for a trained administration now exists in the United States, but in the large cities, where immigrant votes are "corralled," there is, of course, no educated public opinion. Therefore, popular elections of the administrative chief and also of his subordinate officials usually endanger the expert qualification of the official as well as the precise functioning of the bureaucratic mechanism. It also weakens the dependence of the officials upon the hierarchy. This holds at least for the large administrative bodies that are difficult to supervise. The superior qualification and integrity of federal judges, appointed by the President, as over against elected judges in the United States is well known, although both types of officials have been selected primarily in terms of party considerations. The great changes in American metropolitan administrations demanded by reformers have proceeded essentially from elected mayors working with an apparatus of officials who were appointed by them. These reforms have thus come about in a "Caesarist" fashion. Viewed technically, as an organized form of authority, the efficiency of "Caesarism," which often grows out of democracy, rests in general upon the position of the "Caesar" as a free trustee of the masses (of the army or of the citizenry), who is unfettered by tradition. The "Caesar" is thus the unrestrained master of a body of highly qualified military officers and officials whom he selects freely and personally without regard to tradition or to any other considerations. This "rule of the personal genius," however, stands in contradiction to the formally "democratic" principle of a universally elected officialdom.

3. Normally, the position of the official is held for life, at least in public bureaucracies; and this is increasingly the case for all similar structures. As a factual rule, *tenure for life* is presupposed, even where the giving of notice or periodic reappointment occurs. In contrast to the worker in a private enterprise, the official normally holds tenure. Legal or actual life-tenure, however, is not recognized as the official's right to the possession of office, as was the case with many structures of authority in the past. Where legal guarantees against arbitrary dismissal or transfer are developed, they merely serve to guarantee a strictly objective discharge of specific office duties free from all personal considerations. In Germany, this is the case for all juridical and, increasingly, for all administrative officials.

Within the bureaucracy, therefore, the measure of "independence," legally guaranteed by tenure is not always a source of increased status for the official whose position is thus secured. Indeed, often the reverse holds, especially in old cultures and communities that are highly differentiated. In such communities, the stricter the subordination under the arbitrary rule of the master, the more it guarantees the maintenance of the conventional seigneurial style of living for the official. Because of the very absence of these legal guarantees of tenure, the conventional esteem for the official may rise in the same way as, during the Middle Ages, the esteem of the nobility of office rose at the expense of esteem for the freemen, and as the king's judge surpassed that of the people's judge. In Germany, the military officer or the administrative official can be removed from office at any time, or at least far more readily that the "independent judge," who never pays with loss of his office for even the grossest offense against the "code of honor" or against social conventions of the salon. For this very reason, if other things are equal, in the eyes of the master stratum the judge is considered less qualified for the social intercourse than are officers and administrative officials, whose greater dependence on the master is a greater guarantee of their conformity with status conventions. Of course, the average official strives for a civil-service law, which would materially secure his old age and provide increased guarantees against his arbitrary removal from office. This striving, however, has its limits. A very strong development of the "right to the office" naturally makes it more difficult to staff them with regard to technical efficiency, for such a development decreases the career-opportunities of ambitious candidates for office. This makes for the fact that officials, on the whole, do not feel their dependency upon those at the top. This lack of a feeling of dependency, however, rests primarily upon the inclination to depend upon one's equals rather than upon the socially inferior and governed strata. The present conservative movement among the Badenia clergy, occasioned by the anxiety of a presumably threatening separation of church and state, has been expressly determined by the desire not to be turned "from a master into a servant of the parish."

4. The official receives the regular *pecuniary* compensation of a normally fixed *salary* and the old age security provided by a pension. The salary is not measured like a wage in terms of work done, but according to "status," that is, according to the kind of function (the "rank") and, in addition, possibly, according to the length of service. The relatively great security of the official's income, as well as the rewards of social esteem, make the office a sought-after position, especially in countries which no longer provide opportunities for colonial profits. In such countries, this situation permits relatively low salaries for officials.

5. The official is set for a *"career"* within the hierarchical order of the public service. He moves from the lower, less important, and lower paid to the higher positions. The average official naturally desires a mechanical fixing of the conditions of promotion: if not the offices, as least of the salary levels. He wants these conditions fixed in terms of "seniority," or possibly according to grades achieved in a developed system of expert examinations. Here and there, such examinations actually form a character *indelebilis* of the official and have lifelong effects on his career. To this is joined the desire to qualify the right to office and the increasing tendency toward status group closure and economic security. All of this makes for a tendency to consider the offices as "prebends" of those who are qualified by educational certificates. The necessity of taking general personal and intellectual qualifications into consideration, irrespective of the often subaltern character of the educational certificate, has led to a condition in which the highest political offices, especially the positions of "ministers," are principally filled without reference to such certificates.

HISTORICAL PERSPECTIVES ON THE AMERICAN WORKPLACE

7

Fundamentals of Scientific Management

Frederick Winslow Taylor

Frederick Winslow Taylor (1856–1915) was an engineer credited with developing the theory and practice of Scientific Management. Although Taylor's system was not widely applied during his lifetime, his views on management, control, and the organization of work remain influential.

The principal object of management should be to secure the maximum prosperity for the employer, coupled with the maximum prosperity for each employé.

The words "maximum prosperity" are used, in their broad sense, to mean not only large dividends for the company or owner, but the development of every branch of the business to its highest state of excellence, so that the prosperity may be permanent.

In the same way maximum prosperity for each employé means not only higher wages than are usually received by men of his class, but, of more importance still, it also means the development of each man to his state of maximum efficiency, so that he may be able to do, generally speaking, the highest grade of work for which his natural abilities fit him, and it further means giving him, when possible, this class of work to do.

It would seem to be so self-evident that maximum prosperity for the employer, coupled with maximum prosperity for the employé, ought to be the two leading objects of management, that even to state this fact

should be unnecessary. And yet there is no question that, throughout the industrial world, a large part of the organization of employers, as well as employés, is for war rather than for peace, and that perhaps the majority on either side do not believe that it is possible so to arrange their mutual relations that their interests become identical.

The majority of these men believe that the fundamental interests of employés and employers are necessarily antagonistic. Scientific management, on the contrary, has for its very foundation the firm conviction that the true interests of the two are one and the same; that prosperity for the employer cannot exist through a long term of years unless it is accompanied by prosperity for the employé, and *vice versa*; and that it is possible to give the workman what he most wants—high wages—and the employer what he wants—a low labor cost—for his manufactures.

It is hoped that some at least of those who do not sympathize with each of these objects may be led to modify their views; that some employers, whose attitude toward their workmen has been that of trying to get the largest amount of work out of them for the smallest possible wages, may

From Taylor, Frederick Winslow, *The Principles of Scientific Management*. New York: Harper & Brothers, 1911.

be led to see that a more liberal policy toward their men will pay them better; and that some of those workmen who begrudge a fair and even a large profit to their employers, and who feel that all of the fruits of their labor should belong to them, and that those for whom they work and the capital invested in the business are entitled to little or nothing, may be led to modify these views.

No one can be found who will deny that in the case of any single individual the greatest prosperity can exist only when that individual has reached his highest state of efficiency; that is, when he is turning out his largest daily output.

The truth of this fact is also perfectly clear in the case of two men working together. To illustrate: if you and your workman have become so skilful that you and he together are making two pairs of shoes in a day, while your competitor and his workman are making only one pair, it is clear that after selling your two pairs of shoes you can pay your workman much higher wages than your competitor who produces only one pair of shoes is able to pay his man, and that there will still be enough money left over for you to have a larger profit than your competitor.

In the case of a more complicated manufacturing establishment, it should also be perfectly clear that the greatest permanent prosperity for the workman, coupled with the greatest prosperity for the employer, can be brought about only when the work of the establishment is done with the smallest combined expenditure of human effort, plus nature's resources, plus the cost for the use of capital in the shape of machines, buildings, etc. Or, to state the same thing in a different way: that the greatest prosperity can exist only as the result of the greatest possible productivity of the men and machines of the establishment—that is, when each man and each machine are turning out the largest

possible output; because unless your men and your machines are daily turning out more work than others around you, it is clear that competition will prevent your paying higher wages to your workmen than are paid to those of your competitor. And what is true as to the possibility of paying high wages in the case of two companies competing close beside one another is also true as to whole districts of the country and even as to nations which are in competition. In a word, that maximum prosperity can exist only as the result of maximum productivity. Later in this paper illustrations will be given of several companies which are earning large dividends and at the same time paying from 30 per cent. to 100 per cent. higher wages to their men than are paid to similar men immediately around them, and with whose employers they are in competition. These illustrations will cover different types of work, from the most elementary to the most complicated.

If the above reasoning is correct, it follows that the most important object of both the workmen and the management should be the training and development of each individual in the establishment, so that he can do (at his fastest pace and with the maximum of efficiency) the highest class of work for which his natural abilities fit him.

These principles appear to be so self-evident that many men may think it almost childish to state them. Let us, however, turn to the facts, as they actually exist in this country and in England. The English and American peoples are the greatest sportsmen in the world. Whenever an American workman plays baseball, or an English workman plays cricket, it is safe to say that he strains every nerve to secure victory for his side. He does his very best to make the largest possible number of runs. The universal sentiment is so strong that any man who fails to give out all there is in him in sport is branded as a "quitter," and treated with contempt by those who are around him.

When the same workman returns to work on the following day, instead of using every effort to turn out the largest possible amount of work, in a majority of the cases this man deliberately plans to do as little as he safely can—to turn out far less work than he is well able to do—in many instances to do not more than one-third to one-half of a proper day's work. And in fact if he were to do his best to turn out his largest possible day's work, he would be abused by his fellow-workers for so doing, even more than if he had proved himself a "quitter" in sport. Underworking, that is, deliberately working slowly so as to avoid doing a full day's work, "soldiering," as it is called in this country, "hanging it out," as it is called in England, "ca canae," as it is called in Scotland, is almost universal in industrial establishments, and prevails also to a large extent in the building trades; and the writer asserts without fear of contradiction that this constitutes the greatest evil with which the working-people of both England and America are now afflicted.

It will be shown later in this paper that doing away with slow working and "soldiering" in all its forms and so arranging the relations between employer and employé that each workman will work to his very best advantage and at his best speed, accompanied by the intimate cooperation with the management and the help (which the workman should receive) from the management, would result on the average in nearly doubling the output of each man and each machine. What other reforms, among those which are being discussed by these two nations, could do as much toward promoting prosperity, toward the diminution of poverty, and the alleviation of suffering? America and England have been recently agitated over such subjects as the tariff, the control of the large corporations on the one hand, and of hereditary power on the other hand, and over various more or less socialistic proposals for taxation, etc. On these subjects both peoples have been profoundly stirred, and yet hardly a voice has been raised to call attention to this vastly greater and more important subject of "soldiering," which directly and powerfully affects the wages, the prosperity, and the life of almost every working-man, and also quite as much the prosperity of every industrial establishment in the nation.

The elimination of "soldiering" and of the several causes of slow working would so lower the cost of production that both our home and foreign markets would be greatly enlarged, and we could compete on more than even terms with our rivals. It would remove one of the fundamental causes for dull times, for lack of employment, and for poverty, and therefore would have a more permanent and far-reaching effect upon these misfortunes than any of the curative remedies that are now being used to soften their consequences. It would insure higher wages and make shorter working hours and better working and home conditions possible.

Why is it, then, in the face of the self-evident fact that maximum prosperity can exist only as the result of the determined effort of each workman to turn out each day his largest possible day's work, that the great majority of our men are deliberately doing just the opposite, and that even when the men have the best of intentions their work is in most cases far from efficient?

There are three causes for this condition, which may be briefly summarized as:

First. The fallacy, which has from time immemorial been almost universal among workmen, that a material increase in the output of each man or each machine in the trade would result in the end in throwing a large number of men out of work.

Second. The defective systems of management which are in common use, and which make it necessary for each workman to soldier, or work slowly, in order that he may protect his own best interests.

Third. The inefficient rule-of-thumb methods, which are still almost universal in all trades, and in practising which our workmen waste a large part of their effort.

This paper will attempt to show the enormous gains which would result from the substitution by our workmen of scientific for rule-of-thumb methods.

To explain a little more fully these three causes:

First. The great majority of workmen still believe that if they were to work at their best speed they would be doing a great injustice to the whole trade by throwing a lot of men out of work, and yet the history of the development of each trade shows that each improvement, whether it be the invention of a new machine or the introduction of a better method, which results in increasing the productive capacity of the men in the trade and cheapening the costs, instead of throwing men out of work make in the end work for more men.

The cheapening of any article in common use almost immediately results in a largely increased demand for that article. Take the case of shoes, for instance. The introduction of machinery for doing every element of the work which was formerly done by hand has resulted in making shoes at a fraction of their former labor cost, and in selling them so cheap that now almost every man, woman, and child in the working-classes buys one or two pairs of shoes per year, and wears shoes all the time, whereas formerly each workman bought perhaps one pair of shoes every five years, and went barefoot most of the time, wearing shoes only as a luxury or as a matter of the sternest necessity. In spite of the enormously increased output of shoes per workman, which has come with shoe machinery, the demand for shoes has so increased that there are relatively more men working in the shoe industry now than ever before.

The workmen in almost every trade have before them an object lesson of this kind, and yet, because they are ignorant of the history of their own trade even, they still firmly believe, as their fathers did before them, that it is against their best interests for each man to turn out each day as much work as possible.

Under this fallacious idea a large proportion of the workmen of both countries each day deliberately work slowly so as to curtail the output. Almost every labor union has made, or is contemplating making, rules which have for their object curtailing the output of their members, and those men who have the greatest influence with the working-people, the labor leaders as well as many people with philanthropic feelings who are helping them, are daily spreading this fallacy and at the same time telling them that they are overworked.

A great deal has been and is being constantly said about "sweat-shop" work and conditions. The writer has great sympathy with those who are overworked, but on the whole a greater sympathy for those who are *under paid.* For every individual, however, who is overworked, there are a hundred who intentionally underwork—greatly underwork—every day of their lives, and who for this reason deliberately aid in establishing those conditions which in the end inevitably result in low wages. And yet hardly a single voice is being raised in an endeavor to correct this evil.

As engineers and managers, we are more intimately acquainted with these facts than any other class in the community, and are therefore best fitted to lead in a movement to combat this fallacious idea by educating not only the workmen but the whole of the country as to the true facts. And yet we are practically doing nothing in this direction, and are leaving this field entirely in the hands of the labor agitators (many of whom are misinformed and misguided), and of sentimentalists who are ignorant as to actual working conditions.

Second. As to the second cause for soldiering—the relations which exist between employers and employés under almost all of the systems of management which are in common use—it is impossible in a few words to make it clear to one not familiar with this problem why it is that the *ignorance of employers* as to the proper time in which work of various kinds should be done makes it for the interest of the workman to "soldier."

The writer therefore quotes herewith from a paper read before The American Society of Mechanical Engineers, in June, 1903, entitled "Shop Management," which it is hoped will explain fully this cause for soldiering:

"This loafing or soldiering proceeds from two causes. First, from the natural instinct and tendency of men to take it easy, which may be called natural soldiering. Second, from more intricate second thought and reasoning caused by their relations with other men, which may be called systematic soldiering.

"There is no question that the tendency of the average man (in all walks of life) is toward working at a slow, easy gait, and that it is only after a good deal of thought and observation on his part or as a result of example, conscience, or external pressure that he takes a more rapid pace.

"There are, of course, men of unusual energy, vitality, and ambition who naturally choose the fastest gait, who set up their own standards, and who work hard, even though it may be against their best interests. But these few uncommon men only serve by forming a contrast to emphasize the tendency of the average.

"This common tendency to 'take it easy' is greatly increased by bringing a number of men together on similar work and at a uniform standard rate of pay by the day.

"Under this plan the better men gradually but surely slow down their gait to that of the poorest and least efficient. When a naturally energetic man works for a few days beside a lazy one, the logic of the situation is unanswerable. 'Why should I work hard when that lazy fellow gets the same pay that I do and does only half as much work?'

"A careful time study of men working under these conditions will disclose facts which are ludicrous as well as pitiable.

"To illustrate: The writer has timed a naturally energetic workman who, while going and coming from work, would walk at a speed of from three to four miles per hour, and not infrequently trot home after a day's work. On arriving at his work he would immediately slow down to a speed of about one mile an hour. When, for example, wheeling a loaded wheelbarrow, he would go at a good fast pace even up hill in order to be as short a time as possible under load, and immediately on the return walk slow down to a mile an hour, improving every opportunity for delay short of actually sitting down. In order to be sure not to do more than his lazy neighbor, he would actually tire himself in his effort to go slow.

"These men were working under a foreman of good reputation and highly thought of by his employer, who, when his attention was called to this state of things, answered: 'Well, I can keep them from sitting down, but the devil can't make them get a move on while they are at work.'

"The natural laziness of men is serious, but by far the greatest evil from which both workmen and employers are suffering is the *systematic soldiering* which is almost universal under all of the ordinary schemes of management and which results from a careful study on the part of the workmen of what will promote their best interests.

"The writer was much interested recently in hearing one small but experienced golf caddy boy of twelve explaining to a green caddy, who had shown special energy and interest, the necessity of going slow and lagging behind his man when he came up to the ball, showing him that since they were paid by the hour, the faster they went the less money they got, and finally telling him that if he went too fast the other boys would give him a licking.

"This represents a type of *systematic soldiering* which is not, however, very serious, since it is done with the knowledge of the employer, who can quite easily break it up if he wishes.

"The greater part of the *systematic soldiering,* however, is done by the men with the deliberate object of keeping their employers ignorant of how fast work can be done.

"So universal is soldiering for this purpose that hardly a competent workman can be found in a large establishment, whether he works by the day or on piece work, contract work, or under any of the ordinary systems, who does not devote a considerable part of his time to studying just how slow he can work and still convince his employer that he is going at a good pace.

"The causes for this are, briefly, that practically all employers determine upon a maximum sum which they feel it is right for each of their classes of employees to earn per day, whether their men work by the day or piece.

"Each workman soon finds out about what this figure is for his particular case, and he also realizes that when his employer is convinced that a man is capable of doing more work than he has done, he will find sooner or later some way of compelling him to do it with little or no increase of pay.

"Employers derive their knowledge of how much of a given class of work can be done in a day from either their own experience, which has frequently grown hazy with age, from casual and unsystematic observation of their men, or at best from records which are kept, showing the quickest time in which each job has been done. In many cases the employer will feel almost certain that a given job can be done faster than it has been, but he rarely cares to take the drastic measures necessary to force men to do it in the quickest time, unless he has an actual record proving conclusively how fast the work can be done.

"It evidently becomes for each man's interest, then, to see that no job is done faster than it has been in the past. The younger and less experienced men are taught this by their elders, and all possible persuasion and social pressure is brought to bear upon the greedy and selfish men to keep them from making new records which result in temporarily increasing their wages, while all those who come after them are made to work harder for the same old pay.

"Under the best day work of the ordinary type, when accurate records are kept of the amount of work done by each man and of his efficiency, and when each man's wages are raised as he improves, and those who fail to rise to a certain standard are discharged and a fresh supply of carefully selected men are given work in their places, both the natural loafing and systematic soldiering can be largely broken up. This can only be done, however, when the men are thoroughly convinced that there is no intention of establishing piece work even in the remote future, and it is next to impossible to make men believe this when the work is of such a nature that they believe piece work to be practicable. In most cases their fear of making a record which will be used as a basis for piece work will cause them to soldier as much as they dare.

"It is, however, under piece work that the art of systematic soldiering is thoroughly developed; after a workman has had the price per piece of the work he is doing lowered two or three times as a result of his having worked harder and increased his output, he is likely entirely to lose sight of his employer's side of the case and become imbued with a grim determination to have no more cuts if soldiering can prevent it. Unfortunately for the character of the workman, soldiering involves a deliberate attempt to mislead and deceive his employer, and thus upright and straightforward workmen are compelled to become more or less hypocritical. The employer is soon looked upon as an antagonist, if not an enemy, and the mutual confidence which should exist between a leader and his men, the enthusiasm, the feeling that they are all working for the same end and will share in the results is entirely lacking.

"The feeling of antagonism under the ordinary piece-work system becomes in many cases so marked on the part of the men that any proposition made by their employers, however reasonable, is looked upon with suspicion, and soldiering becomes such a fixed habit that men will frequently take pains to restrict the product of machines which they are running when even a large increase in output would involve no more work on their part."

Third. As to the third cause for slow work, considerable space will later in this paper be devoted to illustrating the great gain, both to employers and employés, which results from the substitution of scientific for rule-of-thumb methods in even the smallest details of the work of every trade. The enormous saving of time and therefore increase in the output which it is possible to effect through eliminating unnecessary motions and substituting fast for slow and inefficient motions for the men working in any of our trades can be fully realized only after one has personally seen the improvement which results from a thorough motion and time study, made by a competent man.

To explain briefly: owing to the fact that the workmen in all of our trades have been taught the details of their work by observation of those immediately around them, there are many different ways in common use for doing the same thing, perhaps forty, fifty, or a hundred ways of doing each act in each trade, and for the same reason there is a great variety in the implements used for each class of work. Now, among the various methods and implements used in each element of each trade there is always one method and one implement which is quicker and better than any of the rest. And this one best method and best implement can only be discovered or developed through a scientific study and analysis of all of the methods and implements in use, together with accurate, minute, motion and time study. This involves the gradual substitution of science for rule of thumb throughout the mechanic arts.

This paper will show that the underlying philosophy of all of the old systems of management in common use makes it imperative that each workman shall be left with the final responsibility for doing his job practically as he thinks best, with comparatively little help and advice from the management. And it will also show that because of this isolation of workmen, it is in most cases impossible for the men working under these systems to do their work in accordance with the rules and laws of a science or art, even where one exists.

The writer asserts as a general principle (and he proposes to give illustrations tending to prove the fact later in this paper) that in almost all of the mechanic arts the science which underlies each act of each workman is so great and amounts to so much that the workman who is best suited to actually doing the work is incapable of fully understanding this science, without the guidance and help of those who are working with him or over him, either through lack of education or through insufficient mental capacity. In order that the work may be done in accordance with scientific laws, it is necessary that there shall be a far more equal division of the responsibility between the management and the workmen than exists under any of the ordinary types of management. Those in the management whose duty it is to develop this science should also guide and help the workman in working under it, and should assume a much larger share of the responsibility for results than under usual conditions is assumed by the management.

The body of this paper will make it clear that, to work according to scientific laws, the management must take over and perform much of the work which is now left to the men; almost every act of the workman should be preceded by one or more preparatory acts of the management which enable him to do his work better and quicker than he otherwise could. And each man should daily be taught by and receive the most friendly help from those who are over him, instead of being, at the one extreme, driven or coerced by his bosses, and at the other left to his own unaided devices.

This close, intimate, personal cooperation between the management and the men is of the essence of modern scientific or task management.

It will be shown by a series of practical illustrations that, through this friendly cooperation, namely, through sharing equally in every day's burden, all of the great obstacles (above described) to obtaining the maximum output for each man and each machine in the establishment are swept away. The 30 per cent. to 100 per cent. increase in wages which the workmen are able to earn beyond what they receive under the old type of management, coupled with the daily intimate shoulder to shoulder contact with the management, entirely removes all cause for soldiering. And in a few years, under this system, the workmen have before them the object lesson of seeing that a great increase in the output per man results in giving employment to more men, instead of throwing men out of work, thus completely eradicating the fallacy that a larger output for each man will throw other men out of work.

It is the writer's judgment, then, that while much can be done and should be done by writing and talking toward educating not only workmen, but all classes in the community, as to the importance of obtaining the maximum output of each man and each machine, it is only through the adoption of modern scientific management that this great problem can be finally solved. Probably most of the readers of this paper will say that all of this is mere theory. On the contrary, the theory, or philosophy, of scientific management is just beginning to be understood, whereas the management itself has been a gradual evolution, extending over a period of nearly thirty years. And during this time the employés of one company after another, including a large range and diversity of industries, have gradually changed from the ordinary to the scientific type of management. At least 50,000 workmen in the United States are now employed under this system; and they are receiving from 30 per cent. to 100 per cent. higher wages daily than are paid to men of similar caliber with whom they are surrounded, while the companies employing them are more prosperous than ever before. In these companies the output, per man and per machine, has on an average been doubled. During all these years there has never been a single strike among the men working under this system. In place of the suspicious watchfulness and the more or less open warfare which characterizes the ordinary types of management, there is universally friendly cooperation between the management and the men.

Several papers have been written, describing the expedients which have been adopted and the details which have been developed under scientific management and the steps to be taken in changing from the ordinary to the scientific type. But unfortunately most of the readers of these papers have mistaken the mechanism for the true essence. Scientific management fundamentally consists of certain broad general principles, a certain philosophy, which can be applied in many ways, and a description of what any one man or men may believe to be the best mechanism for applying these general principles should in no way be confused with the principles themselves.

It is not here claimed that any single panacea exists for all of the troubles of the working-people or of employers. As long as some people are born lazy or inefficient, and others are born greedy and brutal, as long as vice and crime are with us, just so long will a certain amount of poverty, misery, and unhappiness be with us also. No system of management, no single expedient within the control of any man or any set of men can insure continuous prosperity to either workmen or employers. Prosperity depends upon so many factors entirely beyond the control of any one set of men, any state, or even any one country, that certain periods

will inevitably come when both sides must suffer, more or less. It is claimed, however, that under scientific management the intermediate periods will be far more prosperous, far happier, and more free from discord and dissension. And also, that the periods will be fewer, shorter and the suffering less. And this will be particularly true in any one town, any one section of the country, or any one state which first substitutes the principles of scientific management for the rule of thumb.

That these principles are certain to come into general use practically throughout the civilized world, sooner or later, the writer is profoundly convinced, and the sooner they come the better for all the people.

8

The Hawthorne Experiment
Western Electric Company

Elton Mayo

Elton Mayo, an early industrial sociologist, conducted a series of observational studies at Western Electric in Chicago from 1926 to the early 1940s. This research included the famous Hawthorne experiments, whose results are described in this reading. The reading is excerpted from Mayo's 1933 book, *The Human Problems of an Industrial Civilization.*

. . . Acting in collaboration with the National Research Council, the Western Electric Company had for three years been engaged upon an attempt to assess the effect of illumination upon the worker and his work. No offi-

cial report of these experiments has yet been published, and it is consequently impossible to quote chapter and verse as to the methods employed and the results obtained. I can, however, state with confidence that the inquiry involved in one phase the segregation of two groups of workers, engaged upon the same task, in two rooms equally illuminated. The experimental diminution of the

---

Excerpts from *The Human Problems of an Industrial Civilization,* by Elton Mayo. Reprinted by permission of Baker Library, Harvard Business School.

lighting, in ordered quantities, in one room only, gave no sufficiently significant difference, expressed in terms of measured output, as compared with the other still fully illuminated room. Somehow or other that complex of mutually dependent factors, the human organism, shifted its equilibrium and unintentionally defeated the purpose of the experiment. . . .

In the institution of a second inquiry full heed was paid to the lesson of the first experiment. A group of workers was segregated for observation of the effect of various changes in the conditions of work. No attempt was made to "test for the effect of single variables." Where human beings are concerned one cannot change one condition without inadvertently changing others—so much the illumination experiment had shown. The group was kept small—six operatives—because the Company officers had become alert to the possible significance for the inquiry of changes of mental attitude; it was believed that such changes were more likely to be noticed by the official observers if the group were small. Arrangements were made to measure accurately all changes in output; this also meant that the group must be small. An accurate record of output was desired for two reasons: first, changes in production differ from many other human changes in that they lend themselves to exact and continuous determination; second, variations in output do effectively show "the combined effect" of all the conditions affecting a group. The work of Vernon and Wyatt supports the view that an output curve does indicate the relative equilibrium or disequilibrium of the individual and the group.

The operation selected was that of assembling telephone relays. . . . The operation ranks as repetitive; it is performed by women. A standard assembly bench with places for five workers and the appropriate equipment were put into one of the experi-

mental rooms. This room was separated from the main assembly department by a ten-foot wooden partition. The bench was well illuminated; arrangements were made for observation of temperature and humidity changes. An attempt was made to provide for the observation of other changes and especially of unanticipated changes as well as those experimentally introduced. This again reflected the experience gained in the illumination experiments. Thus constituted, presumably for a relatively short period of observation, the experimental room actually ran on from April, 1927, to the middle of 1932, a period of over five years. And the increasing interest of the experiment justified its continuance until the economic depression made further development impossible.

Six female operatives were chosen, five to work at the bench, one to procure and distribute parts for those engaged in assembly. I shall not discuss the method of choosing these operatives, except to say that all were experienced workers. This was arranged by those in charge because they wished to avoid the complications which learning would introduce. Within the first year the two operatives first chosen—numbers one and two at the outset—dropped out, and their places were taken by two other workers of equal or superior skill who remained as numbers one and two until the end. The original number five left the Hawthorne Works for a time in the middle period but subsequently returned to her place in the group. In effect, then, there exist continuous records of the output of five workers for approximately five years. These records were obtained by means of a specially devised apparatus which, as each relay was completed, punched a hole in a moving tape. The tape moved at a constant speed, approximately one-quarter of an inch per minute; it punched five rows of holes, one row for each worker. At the right of each worker's place at the bench was a chute within which was an electric gate. When the worker finished a relay she placed it in the chute; as it passed through, it operated the electric gate and the punching apparatus duly recorded the relay. By measuring the distance on the tape between one hole and the next it is possible to calculate the time elapsing between the completion of one relay and another. The Company thus has a record of every relay assembled by every operative in the experimental room for five years and in almost every instance has also a record of the time taken to assemble it. . . .

The transfer of the five workers into the experimental room was carefully arranged. It was clear that changes in output, as measured by the recording device, would constitute the most important series of observations. The continuity and accuracy of this record would obviously make it the chief point of reference for other observations. Consequently, for two weeks before the five operatives were moved into the special room, a record was kept of the production of each one without her knowledge. This is stated as the base output from which she starts. After this, the girls were moved into the experimental room and again for five weeks their output was recorded without the introduction of any change of working conditions or procedures. This, it was assumed, would sufficiently account for any changes incidental to the transfer. In the third period, which lasted for eight weeks, the experimental change introduced was a variation in the method of payment. In the department the girls had been paid a group piece rate as members of a group of approximately one hundred workers. The change in the third period was to constitute the five a unitary group for piece-rate payment. . . . It . . . meant that each girl was given a strong, though indirect, interest in the achievement of the group. After watching the effect of this change of grouping for

eight weeks, the Company officers felt that the more significant experimentation might begin.

In the fourth experimental period the group was given two rest-pauses of five minutes each, beginning at 10:00 in the mid-morning and at 2:00 in the afternoon respectively. The question had been discussed beforehand with the operatives—as all subsequent changes were—and the decision had been in favor of a five minute rather than a ten or fifteen minute pause partly because there was some feeling that, if the break were longer, the lost time would perhaps not be made up. This was continued for five weeks, at which time it was clear that just as total output had increased perceptibly after the constitution of the workers as a group for payment, so also had it definitely risen again in response to the rests. The alternative of the original proposals, two ten-minute rest-pauses, was therefore adopted as the experimental change in period five. This change was retained for four weeks, in which time both the daily and weekly output of the group showed a greater rise than for any former change. In the sixth period the group was given six five-minute rests for four weeks. The girl operatives expressed some dislike of the constant interruption and the output curve showed a small recession.

The seventh experimental period was destined to become standard for the remaining years of the experiment. The subsequent changes are, for the most part, some variation of it. It may be regarded as concluding the first phase of the inquiry which was devoted, first, to the transfer of the operative and the establishment of routines of observation and, second, to experiment with rest-pauses of varying incidence and length. Period seven was originally intended to discover the effect of giving some refreshment—coffee or soup and a sandwich—to the workers in the mid-morning period. The observers in charge had, in process of talking with the girls, found out that they frequently came to work in the morning after little or no breakfast. They became hungry long before lunch and it was thought that there was an indication of this in a downward trend of the output record before the midday break. It was therefore decided that the Company should supply each member of the group with adequate refection in the middle of the working morning and perhaps some slighter refreshment in the mid-afternoon. This, however, meant an abandonment of the six five-minute rests and a return to the two ten-minute rest-pauses. Such a return was in any event justified both by the expressed preference of the workers and by the fact that the output records seemed to indicate it as the better arrangement. The refreshment provided, however, made necessary some extension of the morning break. Period seven accordingly is characterized by a mid-morning break of fifteen minutes (9:30 A.M.) with lunch and a mid-afternoon break of ten minutes (2:30 P.M.). This arrangement persisted in uncomplicated form for eleven weeks and in that time production returned to its former high level and remained there.

In the second phase of experimentation, periods eight to eleven inclusive, the conditions of period seven are held constant and other changes are introduced. In period eight the group stopped work half an hour earlier every day—at 4:30 P.M. This was attended with a remarkable rise in both daily and weekly output. This continued for seven weeks until the tenth of March, 1928. Early in this period the original numbers one and two dropped out and their places were taken by those who rank as one and two for the greater part of the inquiry. In the ninth period the working day was shortened still further and the group stopped at 4:00 P.M. daily. This lasted for four weeks and in that time there was a slight fall both

in daily and weekly output—although the average hourly output rose. In the tenth period the group returned to the conditions of work of period seven—fifteen-minute morning rest-pause with refreshment, ten-minute rest-pause in the mid-afternoon and a full working day to five o'clock. This period lasted for twelve weeks and in that time the group in respect of its recorded daily and weekly output achieved and held a production very much higher than at any previous time. It was, perhaps, this "high" of production which brought to expression certain grave doubts which had been growing in the minds of the Company officers responsible for the experiment. Many changes other than those in production had been observed to be occurring; up to this time it had been possible to assume for practical purposes that such changes were of the nature of adaptation to special circumstance and not necessarily otherwise significant. Equally it had been possible to assume that the changes recorded in output were, at least for the most part, related to the experimental changes in working conditions—rest-pauses or whatnot—singly and successively imposed. At this stage these assumptions had become untenable—especially in the light of the previously expressed determination "not to test for single variables" but to study the situation.

Period eleven was a concession to the workers, at least in part. I do not mean that the Company had not intended to extend their second experimental phase—observation of the effect of shorter working time—to include a record of the effect of a five-day week. I am convinced that this was intended; but the introduction of a shorter working week—no work on Saturday—at this time refers itself to two facts, first, that the twelve weeks of this period run between the second of July and the first of September in the summer of 1928 and, second, it refers itself also by anticipation to the next experimental change. For it had already been agreed between the workers and the officers in charge that the next experiment, twelve, should be the restoration of the original conditions of work—no rest-pauses, no lunch, no shortened day or week. In period eleven—the shortened week in summer—the daily output continued to increase; it did not, however, increase sufficiently to compensate for the loss of Saturday morning's work, consequently the weekly output shows a small recession. It is important to note that although the weekly output shows this recession, it nevertheless remains above the weekly output of all other periods except periods eight and ten.

September, 1928, was an important month in the development of the inquiry. In September, the twelfth experimental change began and, by arrangement with the workers, continued for twelve weeks. In this period, as I have said, the group returned to the conditions of work which obtained in period three at the beginning of the inquiry; rest-periods, special refreshments, and other concessions were all abolished for approximately three months. In September, 1928, also began that extension of the inquiry known as "The Interview Programme." . . . Both of these events must be regarded as having strongly influenced the course of the inquiry.

The history of the twelve-week return to the so-called original conditions of work is soon told. The daily and weekly output rose to a point higher than at any other time and in the whole period "there was no downward trend." At the end of twelve weeks, in period thirteen, the group returned, as had been arranged, to the conditions of period seven with the sole difference that whereas the Company continued to supply coffee or other beverage for the mid-morning lunch, the girls now provided their own food. This arrangement lasted for thirty-one weeks—much longer than any previous change.

Whereas in period twelve the group's output had exceeded that of all the other performances, in period thirteen, with rest-pauses and refreshment restored, their output rose once again to even greater heights. It had become clear that the itemized changes experimentally imposed, although they could perhaps be used to account for minor differences between one period and another, yet could not be used to explain the major change—the continually increasing production. This steady increase as represented by all the contemporary records seemed to ignore the experimental changes in its upward development.

The fourteenth experimental period was a repetition of period eleven; it permitted the group to give up work on Saturday between the first of July and the thirty-first of August, 1929. The fifteenth period returned again to the conditions of the thirteenth, and at this point we may regard the conditions of period seven as the established standard for the group.

It had been the habit of the officers in charge to issue reports of the progress of the experiment from time to time. These reports were published privately to the Western Electric Company and certain of its officers. From these documents one can gain some idea of the contemporary attitude to the inquiry of those who were directing it. The third of these reports was issued on August 15, 1928, and consequently did not carry its comment or description beyond period ten. The fourth was issued on May 11, 1929, and in it one finds interesting discussion of the events I have just described. . . .

. . . From the "conclusions" I select the following passages:

"(b) There has been a continual upward trend in output which has been independent of the changes in rest-pauses. This upward trend has continued too long to be ascribed to an initial stimulus from the novelty of starting a special study."

"(c) The reduction of muscular fatigue has not been the primary factor in increasing output. Cumulative fatigue is not present."

"(f) There has been an important increase in contentment among the girls working under test-room conditions."

"(g) There has been a decrease in absences of about 80 per cent among the girls since entering the test-room group. Test-room operators have had approximately one-third as many sick absences as the regular department during the last six months" (p. 126).

"(v) Output is more directly related to the type of working day than to the number of (working) days in the week . . ." (p. 127).

"(y) Observations of operators in the relay assembly test room indicate that their health is being maintained or improved and that they are working within their capacity. . ." (p. 129).

The following conclusions in former reports are reaffirmed:

"(n) The changed working conditions have resulted in creating an eagerness on the part of operators to come to work in the morning" (p. 130).

"(s) Important factors in the production of a better mental attitude and greater enjoyment of work have been the greater freedom, less strict supervision and the opportunity to vary from a fixed pace without reprimand from a gang boss."

"The operators have no clear idea as to why they are able to produce more in the test room; but as shown in the replies to questionnaires . . . there is the feeling that better output is in some way related to the distinctly pleasanter, freer, and happier working conditions" (p. 131).

The report proceeds to remark that "much can be gained industrially by carrying greater personal consideration to the lowest levels of employment."

Mr. G. A. Pennock in a paper read before a conference of the Personnel Research Federation on September 15, 1929, in New York says: ". . . this unexpected and continual upward trend in productivity throughout the periods, even in period twelve when the girls were put on a full forty-eight hour week with no rest period or lunch, led us to seek some explanation or analysis." He goes on to mention three possibilities: first, fatigue which he finds it easy to exclude on the medical evidence, on the basis of certain physiological findings and on the obvious ground that the "gradually rising production over a period of two years" precludes such a possibility. He considers that the payment incentive of the higher group earnings may play some small part, but proceeds to state his conviction that the results are mainly due to changes in mental attitude. . . .

. . . Undoubtedly, there had been a remarkable change of mental attitude in the group. This showed in their recurrent conferences with high executive authorities. At first shy and uneasy, silent and perhaps somewhat suspicious of the Company's intention, later their attitude is marked by confidence and candor. Before every change of programme, the group is consulted. Their comments are listened to and discussed; sometimes their objections are allowed to negative a suggestion. The group unquestionably develops a sense of participation in the critical determinations and becomes something of a social unit. This developing social unity is illustrated by the entertainment of each other in their respective homes, especially operatives one, two, three, and four. . . .

The most significant change that the Western Electric Company introduced into its "test room" bore only a casual relation to the experimental changes. What the Company actually did for the group was to reconstruct entirely its whole industrial situation. Miss May Smith has wisely observed that the repetition work is "a thread of the total pattern," but "is not the total pattern." The Company, in the interest of developing a new form of scientific control—namely, measurement and accurate observation—incidentally altered the total pattern, in Miss Smith's analogy, and then experimented with that thread which, in this instance, was the work of assembling relays. The conse-quence was that there was a period during which the individual workers and the group had to re-adapt themselves to a new industrial milieu, a milieu in which their own self-determination and their social well-being ranked first and the work was incidental.

9

The Division of Labor

Harry Braverman

The late Harry Braverman is the author of the 1974 classic, *Labor and Monopoly Capital: The Degradation of Work in the Twentieth Century.* This book, excerpted in this reading, was extremely influential among sociologists of work in the 1980s and has continued to inspire research and debate.

The earliest innovative principle of the capitalist mode of production was the manufacturing division of labor, and in one form or another the division of labor has remained the fundamental principle of industrial organization. The division of labor in capitalist industry is not at all identical with the phenomenon of the distribution of tasks, crafts, or specialties of production throughout society, for while all known societies have divided their work into productive specialties, no society before capitalism systematically subdivided the work of each productive specialty into limited operations. This form of the division of labor becomes generalized only with capitalism. . . .

Our concern at this point, therefore, is not with the division of labor in society at large, but within the enterprise; not with the distribution of labor among various industries and occupations, but with the breakdown of occupations and industrial processes; not with the division of labor in "production in general," but within the capitalist mode of production in particular. It is not "pure technique" that concerns us, but rather the marriage of technique with the special needs of capital.

The division of labor in production begins with the *analysis of the labor process*—that is to say, the separation of the work of production into its constituent elements. But this, in itself, is not what brings into being the detail worker. Such an analysis or separation, in fact, is characteristic in every labor process organized by workers to suit their own needs.

For example, a tinsmith makes a funnel: he draws the elevation view on sheetmetal, and from this develops the outline of an unrolled funnel and its bottom spout. He then cuts out each piece with snips and shears, rolls it to its proper shape, and crimps or rivets the seams. He then rolls the top edge, solders the seams, solders on a hanging ring, washes away the acid used in soldering, and rounds the funnel to its final shape. But when he applies the same process to a quantity of identical funnels, his mode of operation changes. Instead of laying out the work directly on the material, he makes a pattern and uses it to mark off the total quantity of funnels needed; then he cuts them all out, one after the other, rolls them, etc. In this case, instead of making a single funnel in the course of an hour or two, he spends hours or even days on each step of the process, creating in each case fixtures, clamps, devices, etc. which would not be worth making for a single funnel but which, where a sufficiently large quantity of funnels is to be made, speed each step sufficiently so that the saving justifies the extra outlay of time. Quantities, he has discovered, will be produced with less trouble and greater economy of time in this way than by finishing each funnel individually before starting the next.

In the same way a bookkeeper whose job it is to make out bills and maintain office records against their future collection will, if he or she works for a lawyer who has only a few clients at a time, prepare a bill and post it at once to the proper accounts and the customer statement. But if there are hundreds of bills each month, the bookkeeper will accumulate them and spend a full day or two, from time to time, posting them to the proper accounts. Some of these postings will now be made by daily, weekly, or monthly totals instead of bill by bill, a practice which saves a great deal of labor when large quantities are involved; at the same time, the bookkeeper will now make use of other shortcuts or aids, which become practicable when operations are analyzed or broken up in this

way, such as specially prepared ledger cards, or carbon forms which combine into a single operation the posting to the customer's account and the preparation of a monthly statement.

Such methods of analysis of the labor process and its division into constituent elements have always been and are to this day common in all trades and crafts, and represent the first form of the subdivision of labor in detail. It is clear that they satisfy, essentially if not fully, the three advantages of the division of labor given by Adam Smith in his famous discussion in the first chapter of *The Wealth of Nations:*

> This great increase in the quantity of work, which, in consequence of the division of labour, the same number of people are capable of performing, is owing to three different circumstances; first, to the increase of dexterity in every particular workman; secondly, to the saving of the time which is commonly lost in passing from one species of work to another; and lastly, to the invention of a great number of machines which facilitate and abridge labour, and enable one man to do the work of many.[1]

The example which Smith gives is the making of pins, and his description is as follows:

> One man draws out the wire, another straightens it, a third cuts it, a fourth points it, a fifth grinds it at the top for receiving the head; to make the head requires two or three distinct operations; to put it on, is a peculiar business, to whiten the pins is another; it is even a trade by itself to put them into the paper; and the important business of making a pin is, in this manner, divided into about eighteen distinct operations, which, in some manufacto-

ries, are all performed by distinct hands, though in others the same man will sometimes perform two or three of them.[2]

In this example, the division of labor is carried one step further than in the examples of the tinsmith and the bookkeeper. Not only are the operations separated from each other, but *they are assigned to different workers.* Here we have not just the analysis of the labor process but the creation of the detail worker. Both steps depend upon the scale of production: without sufficient quantities they are impracticable. Each step represents a saving in labor time. The greatest saving is embodied in the analysis of the process, and a further saving, the extent varying with the nature of the process, is to be found in the separation of operations among different workers.

The worker may break the process down, but he never voluntarily converts himself into a lifelong detail worker. This is the contribution of the capitalist, who sees no reason why, if so much is to be gained from the first step—analysis—and something more gained from the second—breakdown among workers—he should not take the second step as well as the first. That the first step breaks up only the process, while the second dismembers the worker as well, means nothing to the capitalist, and all the less since, in destroying the craft as a process under the control of the worker, he reconstitutes it as a process under his own control. He can now count his gains in a double sense, not only in productivity but in management control, since that which mortally injures the worker is in this case advantageous to him.

The effect of these advantages is heightened by still another which, while it is given surprisingly little mention in economic literature, is certainly the most compelling reason of all for the immense popularity of the division of tasks among workers in the capitalist mode of production, and for its rapid spread. It was not formulated clearly nor emphasized strongly until a half-century after Smith, by Charles Babbage.

In "On the Division of Labour," Chapter XIX of his *On the Economy of Machinery and Manufactures,* the first edition of which was published in 1832, Babbage noted that "the most important and influential cause [of savings from the division of labor] has been altogether unnoticed." He recapitulates the classic arguments of William Petty, Adam Smith, and the other political economists, quotes from Smith the passage reproduced above about the "three different circumstances" of the division of labor which add to the productivity of labor, and continues:

> Now, although all these are important causes, and each has its influence on the result; yet it appears to me, that any explanation of the cheapness of manufactured articles, as consequent upon the division of labour, would be incomplete if the following principle were omitted to be stated.

> *That the master manufacturer, by dividing the work to be executed into different processes, each requiring different degrees of skill or of force, can purchase exactly that precise quantity of both which is necessary for each process; whereas, if the whole work were executed by one workman, that person must possess sufficient skill to perform the most difficult, and sufficient strength to execute the most laborious, of the operations into which the art is divided.*[3]

To put this all-important principle another way, in a society based upon the purchase and sale of labor power, dividing the craft cheapens its individual parts. To clarify this point, Babbage gives us an example drawn, like Smith's, from pin manufacture. He presents a table for the labor employed, by type (that is, by age and sex) and by pay, in the English manufacture of those pins known in his day as "Elevens."[4]

Drawing wire	Man	3s. 3d. per day
Straightening wire	Woman	1s. 0d.
	Girl	0s. 6d.
Pointing	Man	5s. 3d.
Twisting and	Boy	0s. 4½ d.
cutting heads	Man	5s. 4½ d.
Heading	Woman	1s. 3d.
Tinning or	Man	6s. 0d.
whitening	Woman	3s. 0d.
Papering	Woman	1s. 6d.

It is clear from this tabulation, as Babbage points out, that if the minimum pay for a craftsman capable of performing all operations is no more than the highest pay in the above listing, and if such craftsmen are employed exclusively, then the labor costs of manufacture would be more than doubled, *even if the very same division of labor were employed and even if the craftsmen produced pins at the very same speed as the detail workers.*

Let us add another and later example, taken from the first assembly line in American industry, the meatpacking conveyor (actually a *disassembly* line). J. R. Commons has realistically included in this description, along with the usual details, the rates of pay of the workers:

> It would be difficult to find another industry where division of labor has been so ingeniously and microscopically worked out. The animal has been surveyed and laid off like a map; and the men have been classified in over thirty specialties and twenty rates of pay, from 16 cents to 50 cents an hour. The 50-cent man is restricted to using the knife on the most delicate parts of

the hide (floorman) or to using the ax in splitting the backbone (splitter); and wherever a less-skilled man can be slipped in at 18 cents, 18½ cents, 20 cents, 21 cents, 22½ cents, 24 cents, 25 cents, and so on, a place is made for him, and an occupation mapped out. In working on the hide alone there are nine positions, at eight different rates of pay. A 20-cent man pulls off the tail, a 22½-cent man pounds off another part where good leather is not found, and the knife of the 40-cent man cuts a different texture and has a different "feel" from that of the 50-cent man.[5]

Babbage's principle is fundamental to the evolution of the division of labor in capitalist society. It gives expression not to a technical aspect of the division of labor, but to its social aspect. Insofar as the labor process may be dissociated, it may be separated into elements some of which are simpler than others and each of which is simpler than the whole. Translated into market terms, this means that the labor power capable of performing the process may be purchased more cheaply as dissociated elements than as a capacity integrated in a single worker. Applied first to the handicrafts and then to the mechanical crafts, Babbage's principle eventually becomes the underlying force governing all forms of work in capitalist society, no matter in what setting or at what hierarchical level.

In the mythology of capitalism, the Babbage principle is presented as an effort to "preserve scarce skills" by putting qualified workers to tasks which "only they can perform," and not wasting "social resources." It is presented as a response to "shortages" of skilled workers or technically trained people, whose time is best used "efficiently" for the advantage of "society." But however much this principle may manifest itself at times in the form of a response to the scarcity of skilled labor—for example, during wars or other periods of rapid expansion of production—this apology is on the whole false. The capitalist mode of production systematically destroys all-around skills where they exist, and brings into being skills and occupations that correspond to its needs. Technical capacities are henceforth distributed on a strict "need to know" basis. The generalized distribution of knowledge of the productive process among all its participants becomes, from this point on, not merely "unnecessary," but a positive barrier to the functioning of the capitalist mode of production.

Labor power has become a commodity. Its uses are no longer organized according to the needs and desires of those who sell it, but rather according to the needs of its purchasers, who are, primarily, employers seeking to expand the value of their capital. And it is the special and permanent interest of these purchasers to cheapen this commodity. The most common mode of cheapening labor power is exemplified by the Babbage principle: break it up into its simplest elements. And, as the capitalist mode of production creates a working population suitable to its needs, the Babbage principle is, by the very shape of this "labor market," enforced upon the capitalists themselves.

Every step in the labor process is divorced, so far as possible, from special knowledge and training and reduced to simple labor. Meanwhile, the relatively few persons for whom special knowledge and training are reserved are freed so far as possible from the obligations of simple labor. In this way, a structure is given to all labor processes that at its extremes polarizes those whose time is infinitely valuable and those whose time is worth almost nothing. This might even be called the general law of the capitalist division of labor. It is not the sole force acting upon the organization of work, but it is certainly the most powerful and general. Its results, more or less advanced in every industry and occupation, give massive testimony to its validity. It shapes not only work, but populations as well, because over the long run it creates that mass of simple labor which is the primary feature of populations in developed capitalist countries.

NOTES

1. Adam Smith, *The Wealth of Nations* (New York, 1937), p. 7.
2. Ibid., pp. 4–5.
3. Charles Babbage, *On the Economy of Machinery and Manufactures* (London, 1832; reprint ed., New York, 1963), pp. 175–76.
4. Ibid., p. 184.
5. J. R. Commons, *Quarterly Journal of Economics*, vol. XIX, p. 3; quoted in F. W. Taussig, *Principles of Economics* (New York, 1921), p. 42.

10

Contested Terrain
The Transformation of the Workplace in the Twentieth Century

Richard C. Edwards

Richard Edwards is dean of the college of liberal arts and sciences at the University of Kentucky, Lexington. An economist, Edwards has published widely on work and labor markets. This reading is drawn from his 1979 book, *Contested Terrain: The Transformation of the Workplace in the Twentieth Century.*

Roughly one hundred million Americans must work for a living. About ninety-five million of them, when they can find jobs, work for someone else. Three of those workers, who reflect both the unity and the diversity of the American working class, are Maureen Agnati, Fred Doyal, and Stanley Miller. These three share a condition common to all workers, past and present: they must sell their labor time to support themselves. Yet they also lead very different work lives, and the differences contain in kernel form the evolving history of work in twentieth-century America. Indeed, the study of how their jobs came to be so different goes far toward explaining the present weakness and future potential of the American working class.

Maureen Agnati assembles coils at Digitex, Incorporated, a small Boston-area manufacturer of electronics components.[1] Digitex's founder established the firm in the 1930s and continues to manage it today. The company employs about 450 people, four-fifths of whom are production workers. The labor force is mainly female and Portuguese,

with a sprinkling of other ethnic workers—Italian, Haitian, Greek, Polish, and Asian.

Maureen is a white, twenty-six-year-old mother of two girls. Her husband Tom works in a warehouse at a nearby sheet-metal company. Maureen has worked for Digitex off and on for a number of years; she started after her junior year in high school, quit at nineteen when her first child was born, returned for one month to get Christmas money, quit again, and then returned again to work the spring months until the end of her older daughter's school term. Frequent job changes do not seem to be any problem at Digitex, and indeed, in some ways the company appears to encourage high turnover.

Maureen's work involves winding coil forms with copper wire. To do this, Maureen operates a machine that counts and controls the number of wraps put on each collar. She does the same task all day.

Nearly half of Digitex's workers are on the piece-rate system, which means that their wages partly depend on how fast they work. The company pays both a guaranteed base wage and a piece-rate bonus on top of the base. But the guaranteed wage is always low—roughly equal to the legal minimum wage—so the worker's attention turns to making the bonus. To be eligible for extra pay, a worker must exceed the particular job's "rate"; that is, the assigned minimum level of output needed to trigger the incentive system. The worker then earns a bonus depending on how many units she produces above the rate. The problem is that the rates are high and are often changed. For example, when Maureen returned to work this last time, she found that the rates were so "tight" that she frequently did not make any incentive pay at all. It seems to be common that when workers begin to make large premiums, the time-study man appears to "restudy" the job, and the rates cause a great deal of resentment.

The pay system causes resentment among the hourly workers too. The company keeps most of the information about wages secret; a worker cannot learn, for example, what her job's top pay is, how the job is classified, or even what the wage schedule is. Often two workers will discover that, while they are doing nearly the same work, their pay differs greatly.

As for the conditions of work, employees are watched constantly, like children in a classroom. The design of the machinery pretty much dictates what tasks have to be done at each work station, but in other ways the foreman actively directs the work. One way he does this is by assigning workers to particular stations. For example, Maureen was not hired specifically for "winding" and when she returned to work her foreman simply put her at the station. But he can change job assignments whenever he wishes, and he often moves people around. Since some jobs have easy rates and others have tight ones, the job he assigns Maureen to will determine both how much she makes and how hard she has to work.

The foreman and supervisors at Digitex have other ways of directing the work, too. They watch closely over the hours and pace of work, and they ring a bell to signal the be-

ginning and end of work breaks. Workers must get permission to make phone calls or leave the work area. And despite the piece-rate system (which might seem to leave it up to the individual worker to determine how fast to work and hence how much pay she would receive), the bosses take a direct hand in speeding up production; workers who talk to nearby workers, who fail to make the rates, or who return late from breaks or lunch are likely to be targets for reprimands and threats. The various bosses (foremen, general foreman, and other officials) spend their days walking among the workers, noting and correcting any laggard performance.

The supervisors' immediate role in directing production gives them considerable power, of course, yet their full power springs from other sources as well. No real grievance process exists at Digitex, and supervisors can dismiss workers on the spot. Less drastically, foremen maintain a certain degree of control because they must approve any "benefits" the workers receive. They must approve in advance any requests for time off to attend a funeral, see a doctor, and so on. For hourly workers, the supervisors determine any pay raises; since the wage schedules are secret, supervisors can choose when and whom to reward, and in what amount. For piece-rate workers, who are not eligible for raises, the supervisors' decisions on rejects—what to count as faulty output and whether to penalize the workers for it—weigh heavily in bonus calculations. Foremen also choose favored workers for the opportunity to earn overtime pay. And when business falls off and the company needs to reduce its workforce, no seniority or other considerations intervene; the foremen decide which workers to lay off. Through these powers, supervisors effectively rule over all aspects of factory life. Getting on the foreman's good side means much; being on his bad side tends to make life miserable.

Maureen, like other production workers at Digitex, has few prospects for advancing beyond her current position. All people working under the piece-rate system, regardless of seniority, earn the same base pay. There are a few supervisory slots, but these jobs are necessarily limited in number and are currently filled. There simply is no place for them to grow. This fact perhaps accounts for the high turnover at Digitex: over half the employees have worked for the company for less than three years, and Maureen's pattern of frequently quitting her job does not seem to be unusual.

There has recently been a bitter struggle to build a union at Digitex. Maureen's attitude—"We could sure use one around here, I'll tell you that"—was perhaps typical, but the real issue was whether the company's powers of intimidation would prove stronger than the workers' desire for better conditions. Initially, the union won a federally monitored election to be the workers' bargaining agent. The company's hostility toward the union persisted, however; after signing an initial contract with the union it launched a vicious campaign to decertify the union. The second time around, the union lost. No union exists at Digitex today.

Fred Doyal works as process control inspector at General Electric's Ashland (Massachusetts) assembly plant. The plant used to be run by Telechron Clock Company, a small independent firm, but GE bought it out. Today, the plant's thousand or so workers manufacture small electrical motors, the kind used in clocks, kitchen timers, and other very small appliances. The plant is highly automated, and slightly over half of its workers are women.

Fred operates sound-testing machinery to check the motors' noise levels. He monitors two hundred or so motors a day. The procedure is routine—he picks up the motors from the assembly area, returns to the "silent room," mounts them on the decibel counter, and records the result—and he performs virtually the same sequence every day. GE pays Fred about $13,000 a year.

There is little need for the supervisor to direct the work pace; the machinery does that, and when "you come on the job, you learn that routine; unless there is some change in that routine, the foreman would not be coming to you and telling you what to do; he just expects you (and you do) to know your daily routine, when you do repetitious work." In fact, the foreman generally appears only when a special situation arises, such as defective materials or machine breakdown. Other than that, workers mainly have contact with their bosses on disciplinary problems.

Evaluation and discipline do bring in the supervisors, but the union's presence tends to restrict their power. In a sense, the company evaluates Fred's work daily: "Everything I do, I record, and I turn in daily reports." The reports provide information not only about the decibel level of the motors but also coincidentally about Fred's output. Yet he is very confident that if he does a reasonable amount of work, his job will be secure. If the company tried to fire him, it would have to demonstrate to an outside arbitrator that its action is justified. In fact, any time the company takes disciplinary action, the union contract says that arbitration is automatic. In arbitration, Fred notes, the union has found that "discharge on a long-service employee, unless there's a horrendous record on this person, or if it was for something like striking a supervisor or stealing, discharge would be considered too severe by an arbitrator. Usually, you know? Don't bet on it, but that's the usual case."

There are, of course, lesser penalties. The disciplinary procedure begins with the written warning, and when the worker gets three written warnings, he or she can be suspended. Fred himself has been suspended for two days for "refusing to do a certain type of work." Suspension means the loss of pay, and it is probably the most common discipline at Ashland. Fred has known people who were suspended for up to a week because of absenteeism, and for lesser periods because of tardiness and insubordination.

Fred is in his mid-fifties, and he has worked for GE for thirty years. He started as a stock handler in the Worcester (Massachusetts) plant, moved up to be a group leader in the packing department, then transferred to shipping. At one point he had several employees under him, but he was "knocked off that job in a cutback." When they consolidated the plants he moved to Ashland to work in quality control. Presently he does not supervise anyone.

While Fred was moving up, the company had no formal procedure for filling vacancies. Switching from one job to another depended on "merit and so forth . . . some of it was ass-kissing." Now, however, in a change that Fred traces directly to the coming of the union, a new system prevails. If any job opens up, it must be posted, and everyone can apply for it. Qualifications and seniority are supposed to be taken into account in determining who gets the job. The company usually wants to decide unilaterally who is qualified, but "the union fights the company on this all the way." In fact, in Fred's experience the union is usually successful: "The company, rather than get in a hassle, and if they have no particular bitch against this individual who has the most seniority, the company will give that person the job."

Men do a lot better at Ashland than women. The plant jobs seem quite rigidly stereotyped. Women fill most of the lower-paying positions on the clock-assembly conveyors, while the men tend to get the more skilled jobs elsewhere in the plant. Men's jobs are also more secure. In the event of a partial layoff, any worker in a higher-classified job can bump any other worker of equal or lesser seniority in a lower-classified job; but of course one cannot bump upwards. Women, since they tend to be in the lower classifications, have few others (mainly women) whom they can bump. Men have most of the women to bump.

Fred believes that General Electric has not overlooked the benefits of this system.

> Where that company has made all its money is on the conveyors; that's where they really build the clocks, see—a long assembly conveyor, thirty-five, forty women working on it. Those women are working every minute of the day; those women *really* make money for the company! The company didn't get rich on me, and the older I get, the less rich it's gonna get on me. But they got rich on those women. Those women are there every second, every second of their time is taken up. Now, they have on each of these conveyors what they call a group leader, and it's a woman, right? . . . Theses women are *highly* qualified, *highly* skilled, these group leaders. Way underpaid. There's a man that stock-handles the conveyor—man or a boy, whichever you want—he's just a "hunky," picks up boxes and puts them on the conveyor for the girls or moves heavy stuff. That man makes ten to fifteen dollars a week more than a woman who's a group leader.

In the supervisory staff, the sexual stereotyping is even more apparent. There are quite a few bosses, counting all the foremen, general foremen, and higher managers. Yet there are only two women. "There have always been two; not always the same two, but two."

Recently, the rigid sexual division seems to have lessened somewhat, and women have applied for jobs that formerly were off limits. According to Fred, the company is wary of turning them down, because it is worried about a government anti-discrimination suit. (GE subsequently settled the suit, agreeing to pay damages.) The union has made some attempt to change the ratio of women's to men's wages, but Fred acknowledges that it has been "unsuccessful."

At the plant, men and women alike are very concerned about the possibilities of a general layoff. As Fred puts it,

> I'll give it to the company; they're great with the public relations bit. GE puts out two, three bulletins a week, and they're always telling those people [the plant's workers] about the foreign competition. What they're trying to do, and they're successful, is getting the idea across that if they don't work harder, if they don't stop taking off days off, and quit taking so much time on their coffee break, and so forth, that they're gonna have to take the plant and move it to Singapore, which, by the way, they have a plant in Singapore that makes clocks. . . . They've been very successful at this productivity thing, you know. They've scared people with it. This company, like a lot of companies, runs the thing by fear.

Fred is a strong supporter of the union (the United Electrical Workers), and he has from time to time held various official positions in the local. He is completely disillusioned about the AFL-CIO ("They sold out a long time ago"). For him, just following the Democratic Party is not enough: "Any union movement that doesn't have a political philosophy in this country is doomed."

Stanley Harris works as a research chemist at the Polaroid Corporation. "Research chemist" may sound like a high-powered position, and indeed the pay is quite good: Stanley makes about $18,000. But in terms of the actual work involved, the position is more mundane. Stanley's bachelor degree equips him to do only relatively routine laboratory procedures. He cannot choose his own research, and he does not have a special area of expertise. He supervises no one, and instead his own work is done under supervision. Stanley is, in effect, a technical worker.

On first meeting Stanley, one is not surprised to learn of his middle-level occupation. He is white, roughly fifty years old, and seems well educated. Despite the fact that it is the middle of the workday, his proffered hand is clean (and soft). He wears no special work clothes, spurning both the heavy fabrics necessary in production jobs and the suit and tie affected by the managers. In the lab, of course, he wears a white protective smock, but beneath is an unstylish, small-collar Dacron sports shirt and chino pants.

Here and there, traces of a blue-collar background appear. Stanley has a few teeth missing. His speech retains a slight working-class accent, and occasionally his grammar betrays him. He mentions that he lives in Lynn (Massachusetts), an old working-class city outside of Boston.

Stanley's career tells much about the employment system at Polaroid. He joined the company nineteen years ago as a production worker, when he "ran out of money going through college." Having already completed the science curriculum, he went to night school to fulfill his liberal arts requirements while continuing to work at Polaroid. After obtaining his BS degree, he began applying for the research openings advertised on the company's bulletin boards, and since Polaroid's hiring policies give preference to those who are already employees, the company eventually promoted Stanley into one of the lab jobs. These jobs encompass many ranks, from assistant scientist all the way up to senior scientist. Stanley started at the bottom, and his current position, research scientist, appears in the middle of the hierarchy.

In most of the research jobs, the specific work to be done combines a particular product assignment with the general skills and work behavior expected of a research chemist. Stanley's supervisor assigns him a project within the "general sweep of problems, anything having to do with a company product." Stanley then methodically applies standard tests ("the state of the art"), one after the other, until he finds the answer or his supervisor redirects his efforts. Rather than having his workday closely supervised by his boss or directed by a machine, Stanley follows professional work patterns, habits that are, in fact, common to the eight hundred or so other research workers at Polaroid's Tech Square facility.

Stanley's supervisor formally evaluates his work performance in the annual review. Although the evaluation format seems to change frequently—"Right now it is very curt, either 'good,' 'bad,' or 'indifferent'; but in previous years it was something like four pages"—the purpose and importance of the review have not changed. Stanley believes that the evaluation is crucial to his chances for promotion. "It goes to someone who has to okay it, and if he doesn't know you and he sees on a piece of paper 'poor worker,' it hurts you."

The formal evaluations are especially important because, while Stanley's boss assigns him projects and evaluates his work, he has little say in Stanley's promotions or pay raises or discipline. Those decisions are made higher up, by applying the company's rules to the individual's case. As Stanley explains it, the company contributes the formula while the individual provides the numbers, and then somebody "upstairs" just has to do the calculation. The rules for advancement seem pretty clear.

An important illustration of Stanley's point is the company's layoff policy. When demand for Polaroid's cameras fell off during the 1974–1975 recession, the company laid off sixteen hundred workers, about 15 percent of its entire workforce. Such a deep cut could be expected to create lasting insecurity among Polaroid's workers, and it undoubtedly did among the younger workers. But not for Stanley; the company's seniority-based bumping system protects him. If Polaroid eliminates Stanley's current job, he can displace any worker with less seniority in any of the jobs that he has previously held. "I'm not worried because of the fact that I started at the bottom, and so in theory I could bump my way all the way back to the bottom." In Stanley's view, such an enormous economic disaster would be required before layoffs reached him that, "I figure we'll all be out of work."

Stanley summed up his attitude toward unions in one word: "antagonistic." But the reason for his hostility is, perhaps, surprising. "Like all the movements that are idealistic at the beginning, they [unions] have degenerated to where they benefit a select group.... I'm not saying the idea is bad, but they have been corrupted." Stanley sees no use for a union in his own job, since, "if I put out, I'll get the rewards; at least, that's what I've found."

Maureen Agnati, Fred Doyal, Stanley Miller. Three different workers, three different ways of organizing work. Today we observe their situations as simply different arrangements in production, but they are in fact endpoints in a long process of capitalist development that has transformed (and continues to transform) the American workplace. The change does not reflect inevitable consequences of modern technology or of industrial society, but rather . . . the transformation occurred because continuing capital accumulation has propelled workers and their employers into virtually perpetual conflict. And while both technology and the requirements of modern social production play a part in the story to come, the roots of this conflict lie in the basic arrangements of capitalist production. . . .

The Dimensions of Control

How much work gets done every hour or every day emerges as a result of the struggle between workers and capitalists. . . . Each side seeks to tip the balance and influence or determine the outcome with the weapons at its disposal. On one side, the workers use hidden or open resistance to protect themselves against the constant pressure for speed-up; on the other side, capitalists employ a variety of sophisticated or brutal devices for tipping the balance their way. But this is not exactly an equal fight, for employers retain their power to hire and fire, and on this foundation they have developed various methods of control by which to organize, shape, and affect the workers' exertions.

Control in this sense differs from coordination, a term that appears more frequently in popular literature describing what managers do, and it may be useful at the outset to distinguish the two. Coordination is required, of course, in all social production, since the product of such production is by definition the result of labor by many persons. Hence, whether a pair of shoes is produced in a Moroccan cobbler's shop, a Chinese commune, or an American factory, it is an inherent technical characteristic of the production process that the persons cutting and tanning the leather must mesh their efforts with those who sew the leather, those who attach the heels, and others. Without such coordinations, production would be haphazard, wasteful, and—where products more complex than shoes are involved—probably impossible as well. Hence, coordination of social production is essential.

Coordination may be achieved in a variety of ways, however, and the differences are crucial. Coordination may be achieved by tradition—through long-established ways of doing the work and the passing on of these trade secrets from master to apprentices. Or it may be achieved directly by the producers themselves, as occurs when the members of a cooperative or commune discuss their parts in the production process to ensure that their tasks are harmonized. As the scale of production increases, workers may designate one member (or even choose someone from the outside) to act as a full-time coordinator of their interests, thus establishing a manager. As long as the managerial staff, no matter how large, remains accountable to the producers themselves, we may properly speak of their efforts as "coordination" or "administration."

A different type of coordination characterizes capitalist workplaces, however; in capitalist production, labor power is purchased, and with that purchase—as with the purchase of every commodity in a capitalist economy—goes the right to designate the use (consumption) of the object bought. Hence there is a presumption, indeed a contractual right backed by legal force, for the capitalist, as owner of the purchased labor power, to direct its use. A corollary presumption (again backed by legal force) follows: that the workers whose labor power has been purchased have no right to participate in the conception and planning of production. Coordination occurs in capitalist production as it must inevitably occur in all social production, but it necessarily takes the specific form of top-down coordination, for the exercise of which the top (capitalists) must be able to control the bottom (workers). In analyzing capitalist production, then, it is more appropriate to speak of control than of coordination, although of course, control is a means of coordination.

"Control" is here defined as the ability of capitalists and/or managers to obtain desired work behavior from workers. Such ability exists in greater or lesser degrees, depending upon the relative strength of workers and their bosses. As long as capitalist production continues, control exists to some degree, and the crucial questions are: to what degree? how is control obtained? and how does control lead to or inhibit resistance on a wider scale? At one extreme, capitalists try to avoid strikes, sit-downs, and other militant actions that stop production; but equally important to their success, they attempt to extract, day by day, greater amounts of labor for a given amount of labor power.

In what follows, the *system of control* (in other words, the social relations of production within the firm) are thought of as a way in which three elements are coordinated:

1. Direction, or a mechanism or method by which the employer directs work tasks, specifying what needs to be done, in what order, with what degree of precision or accuracy, and in what period of time.
2. Evaluation, or a procedure whereby the employer supervises and evaluates to correct mistakes or other failures in production, to assess each worker's performance, and to identify individual workers or group of workers who are not performing work tasks adequately.
3. Discipline, or an apparatus that the employer uses to discipline and reward workers, in order to elicit cooperation and enforce compliance with the capitalist's direction of the labor process.

The Types of Control

Systems of control in the firm have undergone dramatic changes in response to changes in the firm's size, operations, and environment and in the workers' success in imposing their own goals at the workplace. The new forms did not emerge as sharp, discrete discontinuities in historical evolution, but neither were they simply points in a smooth and inevitable evolution. Rather, each transformation occurred as a resolution of intensifying conflict and contradiction in the firm's operations. Pressures built up, making the old forms of control untenable. The period of increasing tension was followed by a relatively rapid process of discovery, experimentation, and implementation, in which new systems of control were substituted for the older, more primitive ones. Once instituted, these new relations tend to persist until they no longer effectively contain worker resistance or until further changes occur in the firm's operations.

In the nineteenth century, most businesses were small and were subject to the relatively tight discipline of substantial competition in product markets. The typical firm had few resources and little energy to invest in creating more sophisticated management structures. A single entrepreneur, usually flanked by a small coterie of foremen and managers, ruled the firm. These bosses exercised power personally, intervening in the labor process often to exhort workers, bully and threaten them, reward good performance, hire and fire on the spot, favor loyal workers, and generally act as despots, benevolent or otherwise. They had a direct stake in translating labor power into labor, and they combined both incentives and sanctions in an idiosyncratic and unsystematic mix. There was little structure to the way power was exercised, and workers were often treated arbitrarily. Since workforces were small and the boss was both close and powerful, workers had limited success when they tried to oppose his rule. This system of "simple" control survives today in the small-business sector of the American economy, where it has necessarily been amended by the passage of time and by the borrowings of management practices from the more advanced corporate sector, but it retains its essential principles and mode of operation. It is the system of simple control that governs Maureen Agnati's job at Digitex.

Near the end of the nineteenth century, the tendencies toward concentration of economic resources undermined simple control; while firms' needs for control increased, the efficacy of simple control declined. The need for coordination appeared to increase not only with the complexity of the product but also with the scale of production. By bringing under one corporate roof what were formerly small independent groups linked through the market, the corporation more than proportionately raised the degree of coordination needed. Production assumed an increasingly social character, requiring greater "social" planning and implying an increased need for control. But as firms began to employ thousands of workers, the distance between capitalists and workers expanded, and the intervening space was filled by growing numbers of foremen, general foremen, supervisors, superintendents, and other minor officials. Whereas petty tyranny had been more or less successful when conducted by entrepreneurs (or foremen close to them), the system did not work well when staffed by hired bosses. The foremen came into increasingly severe conflict with both their bosses and their workers.

The workers themselves resisted speed-up and arbitrary rule more successfully, since they were now concentrated by the very growth of the enterprise. From the Homestead and Pullman strikes to the great 1919–1920 steel strike, workers fought with their bosses over control of the actual process of production. The maturing labor movement and an emergent Socialist Party organized the first serious challenge to capitalist rule. Intensifying conflict in society at large and the specific contradictions of simple control in the workplace combined to produce an acute crisis of control on the shop floor.

The large corporations fashioned the most far-reaching response to this crisis. During the conflict, big employers joined small ones in supporting direct repression of their adversaries. But the large corporations also began to move in systematic ways to reorganize work. They confronted the most serious problems of control, but they also commanded the greatest resources with which to attack the problems. Their size and their substantial market power released them from the tight grip of the short-run market discipline and made possible for the first time planning in the service of long-term profits. The initial steps taken by large companies—welfare capitalism, scientific management, and company unions—constituted experiments, trials with serious inherent errors, but useful learning experiences nonetheless. In retrospect, these efforts appear as beginnings in the corporations' larger project of establishing more secure control over the labor process.

Large firms developed methods of organization that are more formalized and more consciously contrived than simple control; they are "structural" forms of control. Two possibilities existed: more formal, consciously contrived controls could be embedded in either the physical structure of the labor process (producing "technical" control) or in its social structure (producing "bureaucratic" control). In time, employers used both, for they found that the new systems made control more institutional and hence less visible to workers, and they also provided a means for capitalists to control the "intermediate layers," those extended lines of supervision and power.

Technical control emerged from employers' experiences in attempting to control the production (or blue-collar) operations of the firm. The assembly line came to be the classic image, but the actual application of technical control was much broader. Machinery itself directed the labor process and set the pace. For a time, employers had the best of two worlds. Inside the firm, technical control turned the tide of conflict in their favor, reducing workers to attendants of prepaced machinery; externally, the system strengthened the employer's hands by expanding the number of potential substitute workers. But as factory workers in the late 1930s struck back with sit-downs, their action exposed the deep dangers to employers in thus linking all workers' labor together in one technical apparatus. The conflict at the workplace propelled labor into its "giant step," the CIO.

These forces have produced today a second type of work organization. Whereas simple control persists in the small firms of the industrial periphery, in large firms, especially those in the mass-production industries, work is subject to technical control. The system is mutually administered by management and (as a junior partner) unions. Jobs in the GE plant where Fred Doyal works fit this pattern.

There exists a third method for organizing work, and it too appeared in the large firms. This system, bureaucratic control, rests on the principle of embedding control in the social structure or the social relations of the workplace. The defining feature of bureaucratic control is the institutionalization of hierarchical power. "Rule of law"—the firm's law—replaces "rule by supervisor command" in the direction of work, the procedures for evaluating workers' performance, and the exercise of the firm's sanctions and rewards; supervisors and workers alike become subject to the dictates of "company policy." Work becomes highly stratified; each job is given its distinct title and description; and impersonal rules govern promotion. "Stick with the corporation," the worker is told, "and you can ascend up the ladder." The company promises the workers a *career*.

Bureaucratic control originated in employers' attempts to subject nonproduction workers to more strict control, but its success impelled firms to apply the system more broadly than just to the white-collar staff. Especially in the last three decades, bureaucratic control has appeared as the organizing principle in both production and nonproduction jobs in many large firms, and not the least of its attractions is that the system has proven especially effective in forestalling unionism. Stanley Miller's job at Polaroid is subject to bureaucratic control.

Continuing conflict in the workplace and employers' attempts to contain it have thus brought the modern American working class under the sway of three quite different systems for organizing and controlling their work: simple control, technical control (with union participation), and bureaucratic control. Of course, the specific labor processes vary greatly: Maureen Agnati's coil wrapper might have been a typewriter or a cash register, Fred Doyal's job might have been in a tire plant or a tractor factory, and Stanley Miller's work might have involved being a supervisor or skilled craftsman. Yet within this variety of concrete labors, the three patterns for organizing work prevail.

The typology of control embodies both the pattern of historical evolution and the array of contemporary methods of organizing work. On the one hand, each form of control corresponds to a definite stage in the development of the representative or most important firms; in this sense structural control succeeded simple control and bureaucratic control succeeded technical control, and the systems of control correspond to or characterize stages of capitalism. On the other hand, capitalist production has developed unevenly, with some sectors pushing far in advance of other sectors, and so each type of control represents an alternate method of organizing work; so long as uneven development produces disparate circumstances, alternate methods will coexist.

NOTE

1. This account is taken from Ann Bookman (1977); Bookman's work presents an exceptionally insightful description of supervision, control, and conflict at Digitex. Both the name of this firm and the names and personal details of all the workers have been changed to protect them.

REFERENCE

Bookman, Ann. *The Process of Political Socialization Among Women and Immigrant Workers: A Case Study of Unionization in the Electronics Industry.* Unpublished Ph.D. thesis, Harvard University, 1977.

TECHNOLOGICAL CHANGE AND THE WORKPLACE

11

In the Age of the Smart Machine

Shoshana Zuboff

Shoshana Zuboff is Benjamin and Lilian Hertzberg Professor of business administration at Harvard University, graduate school of business administration. In addition to her 1988 book, *In the Age of the Smart Machine*, Professor Zuboff has published widely on the subject of information technology in the workplace, and on the history and future of work.

Without a doubt, the part of mankind which has advanced intellectually is quite under the spell of technology. Its charms are twofold. On the one hand, there is the enticement of increasingly comfortable living standards; on the other, there is a reduction in the amount of work which is necessary to do. . . . The irresistible pull toward technological development . . . is caused, we should remember, by the unconscious and deep-rooted desire to free ourselves from the material oppression of the material world.

—FOLKERT WILKEN,
THE LIBERATION OF CAPITAL

The Body's Virtuosity at Work

In the older pulp and paper mills of Piney Wood and Tiger Creek, where a highly experienced work force was making the transition to a new computer-based technology, operators had many ways of using their bodies to achieve precise knowledge. One man judged the condition of paper coming off a dry roller by the sensitivity of his hair to electricity in the atmosphere around the machine. Another could judge the moisture content of a roll of pulp by a quick slap of his hand. Immediacy was the mode in which things were known; it provided a feeling of certainty, of knowing "what's going on." One worker in Piney Wood described how it felt to be removed from the physical presence of the process equipment and asked to perform his tasks from a computerized control room:

> It is very different now. . . . It is hard to get used to not being out there with the process. I miss it a lot. I miss being able to see it. You can see when the pulp runs over a vat. You know what's happening.

The worker's capacity "to know" has been lodged in sentience and displayed in action. The physical presence of the process equipment has been the setting that corresponded to this knowledge, which could, in turn, be displayed only in that context. As long as the action context remained intact, it was possible for knowledge to remain implicit. In this sense, the worker knew a great deal, but very little of that knowledge was ever articulated, written down, or made explicit in any fashion. Instead, operators went about their business, displaying their know-how and rarely attempting to translate that knowledge into terms that were publicly accessible. This is what managers mean when they speak of the "art" involved in operating these plants. As one manager at Piney Wood described it:

> There are a lot of operators working here who cannot verbally give a description of some piece of the process. I can ask them what is going on at the far end of the plant, and they can't tell me, but they can draw it for me. By taking away this physical contact that he un-

derstands, it's like we have taken away his blueprint. He can't verbalize his way around the process.

In this regard, the pulp and paper mills embody a historical sweep that is unavailable in many other forms of work. Unlike other continuous-process industries, such as oil refining or chemical production, the pulp-and-paper-making process has not yet yielded a full scientific explication. This has retarded the spread of automation and also has worked to preserve the integrity of a certain amount of craft know-how among those operators with lengthy experience in the industry. Like other continuous-process operations, the technological environment in these mills has created work that was more mediated by equipment and dependent upon indirect data than, say, work on an assembly line. However, discrete instrumentation typically was located on or close to the actual operating equipment, allowing the operator to combine data from an instrument reading with data from his or her own senses. Most workers believed that they "knew" what was going on at any particular moment because of what they saw and felt, and they used past experience to relate these perceptions to a set of likely consequences. The required sequences and routines necessary to control certain parts of the process and to make proper adjustments for achieving the best results represented a form of knowledge that the worker displayed in action as a continual reflection of this sentient involvement. Acquired experience made it possible to relate current conditions to past events; thus, an operator's competence increased as the passing of time enabled him or her to experience the action possibilities of a wide variety of operating conditions.

In Piney Wood and Tiger Creek, the technology change did not mean simply trading one form of instrumentation for another. Because the traditional basis of competence, like skilled work in most industries, was still heavily dependent upon sentient involvement, information technology was experienced as a radical departure from the taken-for-granted approach to daily work. In this sense, workers' experiences in these mills bridge two manufacturing domains. They not only illustrate the next phase of technological change within the continuous-process industries but also foreshadow the dilemmas that will emerge in other industrial organizations (for example, batch and assembly-line production) with the transition from machine to computer mediation.

When a process engineer attempts to construct a set of algorithms that will be the basis for automating some portion of the production process, he or she first interviews those individuals who currently perform the tasks that will be automated. The process engineer must learn the detail of their actions in order to translate their practice into the terms of a mathematical model. The algorithms in such a model explicate, rationalize, and institutionalize know-how. In the course of these interviews, the process engineer is likely to run up against the limits of implicit knowledge. A worker may perform competently yet be unable to communicate the structure of his or her actions. As one engineer discovered:

> There are operators who can run the paper machine with tremendous efficiency, but they cannot describe to you how they do it. They have built-in actions and senses that they are not aware of. One operation required pulling two levers simultaneously, and they were not conscious of the fact that they were pulling two levers. They said they were pulling one. The operators run the mill, but they don't understand how. There are operators who know exactly what to do, but they cannot tell you how they do it.

Though every operator with similar responsibilities performs the same functions, each will perform them in a unique way, fashioned according to a personal interpretation of what works best. A process engineer contrasted the personal rendering of skill with the impersonal but consistently optimal performance of the computer:

> There is no question that the computer takes the human factor out of running the machine. Each new person who comes on shift will make their own distinct changes, according to their sense of what is the best setting. In contrast, the computer runs exactly the same way all the time. Each operator thinks he does a better job, each one thinks he has a better intimate understanding of the equipment than another operator. But none of them can compete with the computer.

These comments describe a particular quality of skill that I refer to as *action-centered*. Four components of action-centered skill are highlighted in the experiences of these workers:

1. *Sentience.* Action-centered skill is based upon sentient information derived from physical cues.
2. *Action-dependence.* Action-centered skill is developed in physical performance. Although in principle it may be made explicit in language, it typically remains unexplicated—implicit in action.
3. *Context-dependence.* Action-centered skill only has meaning within the context in which its associated physical activities can occur.
4. *Personalism.* It is the individual body that takes in the situation and an individual's actions that display the required competence. There is a felt linkage between the knower and the known. The implicit quality of knowledge provides it with a sense of interiority, much like physical experience.

The Dissociation of Sentience and Knowledge

Computerization brings about an essential change in the way the worker can know the world and, with it, a crisis of confidence in the possibility of certain knowledge. For the workers of Piney Wood and Tiger Creek, achieving a sense of knowing the world was rarely problematical in their conventional environments. Certain knowledge was conveyed through the immediacy of their sensory experience. Instead of Descartes's "I think, therefore I am," these workers might say, "I see, I touch, I smell, I hear; therefore, I know." Their capacity to trust their knowledge was reflected in the assumption of its validity. In the precomputerized environment, belief was a seamless extension of sensory experience.

As the medium of knowing was transformed by computerization, the placid unity of experience and knowledge was disturbed. Accomplishing work depended upon the ability to manipulate symbolic, electronically presented data. Instead of using their bodies as instruments of *acting-on* equipment and materials, the task relationship became mediated by the information system. Operators had to work through the medium of what I will call the "data interface," represented most visibly by the computer terminals they monitored from central control rooms. The workers in this transition were at first overwhelmed with the feeling that they could no longer see or touch their work, as if it has been made both invisible and intangible by computer mediation.

> It's just different getting this information in the control room. The man in here can't see. Out there you can look around until you find something.

> The chlorine has overflowed, and it's all over the third floor. You see, this is what I mean . . . it's all over the floor, but you

can't see it. You have to remember how to get into the system to do something about it. Before you could see it and you knew what was happening—you just knew.

> The hardest thing for us operators is not to have the physical part. I can chew pulp and tell you its physical properties. We knew things from experience. Now we have to try and figure out what is happening. The hardest part is to give up that physical control.

In a world in which skills were honed over long years of physical experience, work was associated with concrete objects and the cues they provided. A worker's sense of occupational identity was deeply marked by his or her understanding of and attachment to discrete tangible entities, such as a piece of operating equipment. Years of service meant continued opportunities to master new objects. It was the immediate knowledge one could gain of these tangible objects that engendered feelings of competence and control. For workers, the new computer-mediated relationship to work often felt like being yanked away from a world that could be known because it could be sensed.

> Our operators did their job by feeling a pipe—"Is it hot?" We can't just tell them it's 150 degrees. They have to believe it.

> With computerization I am further away from my job than I have ever been before. I used to listen to the sounds the boiler makes and know just how it was running. I could look at the fire in the furnace and tell by its color how it was burning. I knew what kinds of adjustments were needed by the shades of color I saw. A lot of the men also said that there were smells that told you different things about how it was running. I feel uncomfortable being away from these sights and smells. Now I only

have numbers to go by. I am scared of that boiler, and I feel that I should be closer to it in order to control it.

It is as if one's job had vanished into a two-dimensional space of abstractions, where digital symbols replace a concrete reality. Workers reiterated a spontaneous emotional response countless times—defined by feelings of loss of control, of vulnerability, and of frustration. It was sharpened with a sense of crisis and a need for steeling oneself with courage and not a little adrenaline in order to meet the challenge. It was shot through with the bewilderment of a man suddenly blind, groping with his hands outstretched in a vast, unfamiliar space. "We are in uncharted water now," they said. "We have to control our operations blind." This oft-repeated metaphor spoke of being robbed of one's senses and plunged into darkness. The tangible world had always been thick with landmarks; it was difficult to cast off from these familiar moorings with only abstractions as guides.

One operator described learning to work with the new computer system in Tiger Creek's pulping area. "The difficulty," he said, "is not being able to touch things." As he spoke, his hands shot out before him and he wiggled all his fingers, as if to emphasize the sense of incompleteness and loss. He continued:

When I go out and touch something, I know what will happen. There is a fear of not being out on the floor watching things. It is like turning your back in a dark alley. You don't know what is behind you; you don't know what might be happening. It all becomes remote from you, and it makes you feel vulnerable. It was like being a new operator all over again. Today I push buttons instead of opening valves on the digester. If I push the wrong button, will I screw up? Will anything happen?

Many other descriptions conveyed a similar feeling:

With the change to the computer it's like driving down the highway with your lights out and someone else pushing the accelerator.

It's like flying an airplane and taking all the instruments out so you can't see. It's like if you had an airplane and you put pieces over each instrument to hide it. Then, if something went wrong, you have to uncover the right one in a split second.

Doing my job through the computer, it feels different. It is like you are riding a big, powerful horse, but someone is sitting behind you on the saddle holding the reins, and you just have to be on that ride and hold on. You see what is coming, but you can't do anything to control it. You can't steer yourself left and right; you can't control that horse that you are on. You have got to do whatever the guy behind you holding the reins wants you to do. Well, I would rather be holding the reins than have someone behind me holding the reins.

The feeling of being in control and the willingness to be held accountable require a reservoir of critical judgment with which to initiate informed action. In the past, operators like those at Piney Wood derived their critical judgment from their "gut feel" of the production process. Becoming a "good" operator—the kind that workers and managers alike refer to as an "artist" and invest with the authority of expertise—required the years of experience to develop a finely nuanced, felt sense of the equipment, the product, and the overall process. With computerization, many managers acknowledged that operators had lost their ability "to feel the machine." Without considering the new skill implications of this loss, many managers feared it would eliminate the kind of critical judgment that would have allowed operators to take action based upon an understanding that reached beyond the computer system.

Piney Wood's plant manager, as he presided over the massive technology conversion, asked himself what the loss of such art might mean:

> In the digester area, we used to have guys doing it who had an art. After we put the computer in, when they went down we could go to manual backup. People remembered how to run the digesters. Now if we try to go back, they can't remember what to do. They have lost the feel for it. We are really stuck now without the computer; we can't successfully operate that unit without it. If you are watching a screen, do you see the same things you would if you were there, face-to-face with the process and the equipment? I am concerned we are losing the art and skills that are not replenishable.

There were many operators who agreed. In one area of Piney Wood, the crew leader explained it this way:

> The new people are not going to understand, see, or feel as well as the old guys. Something is wrong with this fan, for example. You may not know what; you just feel it in your feet. The sound, the tone, the volume, the vibrations . . . the computer will control it, but you will have lost something, too. It's a trade-off. The computer can't feel what is going on out there. The new operators will need to have more written down, because they will not know it in their guts. I can't understand how new people coming in are ever going to learn how to run a pulp mill. They are not going to know what is going on. They

will only learn what these computers tell them.

Sam Gimbel was a young production coordinator in Piney Wood. Though trained as a chemical engineer, he had been particularly close to the operators whom he managed. He had shepherded them through the technology conversion and construction of the new control room, and worked closely with them as they grappled with new ways of operating:

> We are losing the context where hands-on experience makes sense. If you don't have actual experience, you have to believe everything the computer says, and you can't beat it at its own game. You can't stand up to it. And yet who will have the experience to make these kinds of judgments? It will surely be a different world. You lose the checkpoints in reality to know if you are doing it right; therefore, how will anyone be able to confront the computer information?

Piney Wood's management had approached the technology conversion with the following message: "We are simply providing you with new tools to do your job. Your job is to operate the equipment, and this is a new tool to operate the equipment with." Managers repeatedly made statements such as, "We told them this was a tool just like a hammer or a wrench." One manager even went so far as to say, "We hoped they wouldn't figure out that the terminal we were giving them was really a computer."

As experience with the new operating conditions began to accumulate, many managers began to see that treating the computer system like a physical object, "just another tool," could lead to chronic suboptimization of the technology's potential. A powerhouse worker with over twenty-five years of experience had developed a special way of kicking the boiler in order to make it function smoothly. He used the same approach with the terminal; if he hit a certain button on the keyboard, a particular reading would change in the desired direction, but he did not know why or how. Piney Wood's powerhouse manager put it this way:

> The guy who kicks the boiler is the same guy who mashes the button a certain way just to make the line go down. This person will never optimize the process. He will use too much chemical and too high pressure. He will never make you money because he doesn't understand the problem.

Just as the digester operators had lost their ability to cook manually, other workers throughout the mill felt equally powerless:

> In the old way, you had control over the job. The computer now tells you what to do. There is more responsibility but less control. We lost a boiler that was on computer control. We just had to sit there and stare. We were all shook up.

> Sometimes I am amazed when I realize that we stare at the screen even when it has gone down. You get in the habit and you just keep staring even if there is nothing there.

Ironically, as managers and operators across the mill watched the level of artistry decline, the senior technical designers continued to assume that manual skills would provide the necessary backup to their systems.

The problem was even more acute in Cedar Bluff, where most of the work force lacked the experience base from which felt sense and critical judgment are developed. Managers at Cedar Bluff engaged in a quiet debate as to how much of a problem this lack of experience would ultimately be. On one side of the argument were the "old-timers"—managers with years of experience in the industry:

> I like to smell and feel the pulp sometimes. It can be slick, it can be slimy, it can be all different consistencies. These are the artistic aspects of making pulp that the computer doesn't know about. Some of the operators have been picking up these aspects, but there are so many numbers so readily accessible, we have to shortcut it at times and solve more problems from the office. The information is so good and rapid we have to use it. . . . You have got to be able to recognize when you can run things from the office and when you have to go and look. Yet, I recognize that I am not as good a pulp maker as the people who trained me, and the new operators are not as good as I am. They are better managers and planners. I am very happy with the new managers, but not with the new pulp makers.

The younger engineers, schooled in computer-based analytic techniques, had little patience with anxious laments over the loss of the art of pulp making. They were relentlessly confident that a good computer model could reproduce anything that operators knew from experience—only better. Here is how the process engineers articulated the argument:

> Computer analysis lets us see the effects of many variables and their interactions. This is a picture of truth that we could not have achieved before. It is superior to the experience-based knowledge of an operator. You might say that truth replaces knowledge.

> People who have this analytic power do not need to have been around to know what is going on. All you need is to be able to formulate a model and perform the necessary confirmation checks. With

the right model you can manage the system just fine.

Most Cedar Bluff managers agreed that the computer system made it possible to do a better job running the plant with an inexperienced work force than otherwise would have been possible, though some wondered whether the levels of expertise would ever be as high as among workers with hands-on exposure to the pulping process. Yet even as managers argued over the essentiality of action-centered skill, technology was irreversibly altering the context in which the operators performed. The opportunities to develop such skills were becoming increasingly rare as the action context was paved over by the data highway.

Many of Cedar Bluff's managers believed that the traditional knowledge of the pulp mill worker would actually inhibit the development of creativity and flexibility. Under the new technological conditions, the young operators would develop their capacity to "know better" than the systems with which they worked as they struggled with the complexities of the new technology and the data it provided. The data interface would replace the physical equipment as the primary arena for learning.

Yet as months passed, other managers observed a disturbing pattern of interactions between the operators and the computer system. Some believed that the highly computerized task environment resulted in a greater than usual bifurcation of skills. One group of operators would use the information systems to learn an extraordinary amount about the process, while another group would make itself an appendage to the system, mechanically carrying out the computer's directives. These managers complained that the computer system was becoming a crutch that prevented many operators from developing a superior knowl-

edge of the process. One "old-timer" provided an example:

When there is a shift change and new operators come on, the good operator will take the process from the computer, put it on manual, make certain changes that the operator thinks are necessary, and then gives it back to the computer. The average operator will come in, see this thing on automatic control, and leave it with the computer. Sometimes that operator won't even realize that things are getting bad or getting worse. They should have known better, but they didn't.

Most Cedar Bluff operators spoke enthusiastically about the convenience of the computer interface, and some freely admitted what they perceived to be a dependence on the computer system:

The computer provides your hands. I don't think I could work in a conventional mill. This is so much more convenient. You have so much control without having to go out to the equipment and adjust things.

We can't run this mill manually. There are too many controls, and it is too complex. The average person can only run four or five variables at once in a manual mode, and the automatic system runs it all. If the computer goes down, we have to sit back and wait. We sit and we stare at the screens and we hope something pipes in.

Many managers observed with growing alarm the things that occurred when operators neither enjoyed the traditional sources of critical judgment nor had developed enough new knowledge for informed action.

In a conventional mill, you have to go and look at the equipment because you cannot get enough data in the control room. Here, you get all the data you need. The computer becomes a substitute tool. It replaces all the sensual data instead of being an addition. We had another experience with the feedwater pumps, which supply water to the boiler to make steam. There was a power outage. Something in the computer canceled the alarm. The operator had a lot of trouble and did not look at the readout of the water level and never got an alarm. The tank ran empty, the pumps tripped. The pump finally tore up because there was no water feeding it.

We have so much data from the computer, I find that hard drives out soft. Operators are tempted not to tour the plant. They just sit at the computer and watch for alarms. One weekend I found a tank overflowing in digesting. I went to the operator and told him, and he said, "It can't be; the computer says my level is fine." I am afraid of what happens if we trust the computer too much.

At least since the introduction of the moving assembly line in Ford's Highland Park plant, it has been second nature for managers to use technology to delimit worker discretion and, in this process, to concentrate knowledge within the managerial domain. The special dilemmas raised by information technology require managers to reconsider these assumptions. When information and control technology is used to turn the worker into "just another mechanical variable," one immediate result is the withdrawal of the worker's commitment to and accountability for the work. This lack of care requires additional managerial vigilance and leads to a need for increased automatic control. As this dynamic unfolds, it no longer seems shocking to contemplate an image of work laced with stupefaction and

passivity, in which the human being is a hapless bystander at the margins of productive activity. One young operator in Cedar Bluff discussed his prior job as a bank clerk. I asked him if his two employment experiences had anything in common. "Yes," he said, "in both cases you punch the buttons and watch it happen."

As automation intensifies, information technology becomes the receptacle for larger and larger portions of the organization's operating intelligence. Algorithms become the functional equivalent of a once diffuse know-how, and the action context in which know-how can be developed and sustained vanishes. Because many managers assume that more technology means a diminished need for human operating skill, they may recognize the waning of worker know-how without becoming concerned enough to chart a different course. Left unchallenged, these systems become more potent, as they are invested with an escalating degree of authority. Technical experts temporarily serve as resources, but once their knowledge has been depleted, and converted into systematic rules for decision making, their usefulness is attenuated. The analysts and engineers, who construct programs and models, have the capacity to manipulate data and, presumably, to make discoveries. Ultimately, they will become the most important human presence to offer any counterpoint to the growing density and opacity of the automated systems.

There is an alternative, one that involves understanding this technological change as an occasion for developing a new set of skills—skills that are able to exploit the information capacity of the technology and to become a new source of critical judgment. In order to assess the likelihood of this alternative—the forces that will drive organizations in this direction and those that will impede them—we first have to understand the nature of these new skills. What can the experiences of workers in these three mills teach us about the emerging requirements for competence at the data interface?

From Action-Centered to Intellective Skill

The pulp and paper mills reveal the shift in the grounds of knowledge associated with a technology that informates. Men and women accustomed to an intimate physical association with the production process found themselves removed from the action. Now they had to know and to do based upon their ability to understand and manipulate electronic data. In Piney Wood, a $200 million investment in technology was radically altering every phase of mill life. Managers believed they were merely "upgrading" in order to modernize production and to improve productivity. Tiger Creek was undergoing a similar modernization process. In both cases, informating dynamics tended to unfold as an unintended and undermanaged consequence of these efforts. Cedar Bluff had been designed with a technological infrastructure based on integrated information and control systems. In that organization, managers were somewhat more self-conscious about using the informating capacity of the technology as the basis for developing new operating skills.

The experiences of the skilled workers in these mills provide a frame of reference for a general appraisal of the forms of knowledge that are required in an informated environment. My contention is that the skill demands that can be deciphered from their experiences have relevance for a wider range of organizational settings in both manufacturing and service sectors. Later chapters will compare the experiences of clerks and managers to those of the mill operators. This joint appraisal will help to unravel the intrinsic and the contingent aspects of change and to gauge the generaliza-

tions that follow from the dilemmas of transformation described here.

A fundamental quality of this technological transformation, as it is experienced by workers and observed by their managers, involves a reorientation of the means by which one can have a palpable effect upon the world. Immediate physical responses must be replaced by an abstract thought process in which options are considered, and choices are made and then translated into the terms of the information system. For many, physical action is restricted to the play of fingers on the terminal keyboard. As one operator put it, "Your past physical mobility must be translated into a mental thought process." A Cedar Bluff manager with prior experience in pulping contemplates the distinct capacities that had become necessary in a highly computerized environment:

> In 1953 we put operation and control as close together as possible. We did a lot of localizing so that when you made a change you could watch the change, actually see the motor start up. With the evolution of computer technology, you centralize controls and move away from the actual physical process. If you don't have an understanding of what is happening and how all the pieces interact, it is more difficult. You need a new learning capability, because when you operate with the computer, you can't see what is happening. There is a difference in the mental and conceptual capabilities you need—you have to do things in your mind.

When operators in Piney Wood and Tiger Creek discuss their traditional skills, they speak of knowing things by habit and association. They talk about "cause-and-effect" knowledge and being able to see the things to which they must respond. They refer to "folk medicine" and knowledge that you don't even know you have until it is suddenly displayed in the ability to take a decisive action and make something work.

In plants like Piney Wood and Tiger Creek, where operators have relied upon action-centered skill, management must convince the operator to leave behind a world in which things were immediately known, comprehensively sensed, and able to be acted upon directly, in order to embrace a world that is dominated by objective data, is removed from the action context, and requires a qualitatively different kind of response. In this new world, personal interpretations of how to make things happen count for little. The worker who has relied upon an intimate knowledge of a piece of equipment—the operators talk about having "pet knobs" or knowing just where to kick a machine to make it hum—feels adrift. To be effective, he or she must now trade immediate knowledge for a more explicit understanding of the science that undergirds the operation. One Piney Wood manager described it this way:

> The workers have an intuitive feel of what the process needs to be. Someone in the process will listen to things, and that is their information. All of their senses are supplying data. But once they are in the control room, all they have to do is look at the screen. Things are concentrated right in front of you. You don't have sensory feedback. You have to draw inferences by watching the data, so you must understand the theory behind it. In the long run, you would like people who can take data and draw broad conclusions from it. They must be more scientific.

Many managers are not optimistic about the ability of experienced workers to trade their embodied knowledge for a more explicit, "scientific" inference.

The operators today know if I do "x," then "y" will happen. But they don't understand the real logic of the system. Their cause-and-effect reasoning comes from their experience. Once we put things under automatic control and ask them to relate to the process using the computer, their personal judgments about how to relate to equipment go by the wayside. We are saying your intuition is no longer valuable. Now you must understand the whole process and the theory behind it.

Now a new kind of learning must begin. It is slow and scary, and many workers are timid, not wanting to appear foolish and incompetent. Hammers and wrenches have been replaced by numbers and buttons. An operator with thirty years of service in the Piney Wood Mill described his experience in the computer-mediated environment:

> Anytime you mash a button you should have in mind exactly what is going to happen. You need to have in your mind where it is at, what it is doing, and why it is doing it. Out there in the plant, you can know things just by habit. You can know them without knowing that you know them. In here you have to watch the numbers, whereas out there you have to watch the actual process.

"You need to have in your mind where it is at"—it is a simple phrase, but deceptive. What it takes to have things "in your mind" is far different from the knowledge associated with action-centered skill.

This does not imply that action-centered skills exist independent of cognitive activity. Rather, it means that the process of learning, remembering, and displaying action-centered skills do not necessarily require that the knowledge they contain be made explicit. Physical cues do not require inference; learning in an action-centered context is more likely to be analogical than analytical. In contrast, the abstract cues available through the data interface do require explicit inferential reasoning, particularly in the early phases of the learning process. It is necessary to reason out the meaning of those cues—what is their relation to each other and to the world "out there"?

It is also necessary to understand the procedures according to which these abstract cues can be manipulated to result in the desired effects. Procedural reasoning means having an understanding of the internal structure of the information system and its functional capacities. This makes it possible both to operate skillfully through the system and to use the system as a source of learning and feedback. For example, one operation might require sixteen control actions spread across four groups of variables. The operator must first think about what has to be done. Second, he or she must know how data elements (abstract cues) correspond to actual processes and their systemic relations. Third, the operator must have a conception of the information system itself, in order to know how actions taken at the information interface can result in appropriate outcomes. Fourth, having decided what to do and executed that command, he or she must scan new data and check for results. Each of these processes folds back upon a kind of thinking that can stand independent from the physical context. An operator summed it up this way:

> Before computers, we didn't have to think as much, just react. You just knew what to do because it was physically there. Now, the most important thing to learn is to think before you do something, to think about what you are planning to do. You have to know which variables are the most critical and therefore what to be the most cautious about, what to spend time thinking about before you take action.

The vital element here is that these workers feel a stark difference in the forms of knowledge they must now use. Their experience of competence has been radically altered. "We never got paid to have ideas," said one Tiger Creek worker. "We got paid to work." Work was the exertion that could be known by its material results. The fact that a material world must be created required physical exertion. Most of the operators believed that some people in society are paid to "think," but they were not among them. They knew themselves to be the ones who gave their bodies in effort and skill, and through their bodies, they made things. Accustomed to gauging their integrity in intimate measures of strain and sweat, these workers find that information technology has challenged their assumptions and thrown them into turmoil. There was a gradual dawning that the rules of the game had changed. For some, this created panic; they did not believe in their ability to think in this new way and were afraid of being revealed as incompetent.

Such feelings are no mere accident of personality, but the sedimentation of long years of conditioned learning about who does the "thinking"—a boundary that is not meant to be crossed. As a Tiger Creek manager observed:

> Currently, managers make all the decisions. . . . Operators don't want to hear about alternatives. They have been trained to *do*, not to *think*. There is a fear of being punished if you think. This translates into a fear of the new technology.

In each control room, a tale is told about one or two old-timers who, though they knew more about the process than anyone else, "just up and quit" when they heard the new technology was coming. From one plant to another, reports of these cases were remarkably similar:

He felt that because he had never graduated high school, he would never be able to keep up with this new stuff. We tried to tell him different, but he just wouldn't listen.

Despite the anxiety of change, those who left were not the majority. Most men and women need their jobs and will do whatever it takes to keep them. Beyond this, there were many who were honestly intrigued with the opportunity this change offered. They seemed to get pulled in gradually, observing their own experiences and savoring with secret surprise each new bit of evidence of their unexpected abilities. They discussed the newness and strangeness of having to act upon the world by exerting a more strictly intellectual effort. Under the gentle stimulus of a researcher's questions, they thought about this new kind of thinking. What does it feel like? Here are the observations of an operator who spent twenty years in one of the most manually intensive parts of the Tiger Creek Mill, which has recently been computerized:

> If something is happening, if something is going wrong, you don't go down and fix it. Instead, you stay up here and think about the sequence, and you think about how you want to affect the sequence. You get it done through your thinking. But dealing with information instead of things is very . . . well, very intriguing. I am very aware of the need for my mental involvement now. I am always wondering: Where am I at? What is happening? It all occurs in your mind now.

Another operator discussed the same experience but added an additional dimen-

sion. After describing the demand for thinking and mental involvement, he observed:

> Things occur to me now that never would have occurred to me before. With all of this information in front of me, I begin to think about how to do the job better. And, being freed from all that manual activity, you really have time to look at things, to think about them, and to anticipate.

As information technology restructures the work situation, it abstracts thought from action. Absorption, immediacy, and organic responsiveness are superseded by distance, coolness, and remoteness. Such distance brings an opportunity for reflection. There was little doubt in these workers' minds that the logic of their jobs had been fundamentally altered. As another worker from Tiger Creek summed it up, "Sitting in this room and just thinking has become part of my job. It's the technology that lets me do these things."

The thinking this operator refers to is of a different quality from the thinking that attended the display of action-centered skills. It combines abstraction, explicit inference, and procedural reasoning. Taken together, these elements make possible a new set of competencies that I call *intellective skills*. As long as the new technology signals only deskilling—the diminished importance of action-centered skills—there will be little probability of developing critical judgment at the data interface. To rekindle such judgment, though on a new, more abstract footing, a reskilling process is required. Mastery in a computer-mediated environment depends upon developing intellective skills. . . .

12

Capital, Labor, and New Technology

Steven Peter Vallas

Steven Vallas is associate professor of sociology in the school of history, technology, and society at the Georgia Institute of Technology. Professor Vallas writes, "While in graduate school, I was involved in a union organizing campaign that was run with the assistance of the Communications Workers of America. That campaign put me in touch with some progressive union leaders in New Jersey and New York, who later encouraged me to study the workplace changes that communications workers faced. In keeping with the usual social scientific prejudices, I designed a tedious survey questionnaire and distributed it to telephone workers throughout the New York metropolitan area. That survey did prove useful, but not nearly so revealing as some very spirited interviews with ordinary workers and shop stewards. These exchanges forced me to explore the existing historical record on the industry, and to reconstruct the changes in authority relations—that is, in 'production politics'—that have unfolded in this industry. Without my serendipitous encounters with union members and organizers, this study would probably not have been done."

The Structure of the Bell System after World War II

Tradition amidst Bureaucracy

The Bell system at mid-century was a mammoth, vertically integrated monopoly that controlled its own manufacturing complex (Western Electric), research and development facilities (Bell Laboratories), long distance division (the Long Lines division) as well as twenty-two local operating companies spread throughout the United States. Although each operating company was nominally independent, its internal structure and functioning were subject to highly centralized controls emanating from AT&T's headquarters at 195 Broadway in New York.

Reprinted from *Power in the Workplace: The Politics of Production at AT&T,* by Steven Peter Vallas, by permission of the State University of New York Press.

. . . [T]he rules and practices employed in the provision of telephone service were largely standardized across the Bell system. This standardization of the company's operations eased management's problem of coordination and planning and enabled the company to deploy resources from its disparate parts without fear of incompatibility. Thus, virtually all operating companies manifested the same pattern of internal differentiation, dividing their operations into Traffic, Plant, Commercial, Accounting, Engineering, and other such departments.

The hierarchy that arose to control the Bell system's operations was labyrinthine in its complexity and rivaled only by the military. Crews of craftworkers or operators routinely reported to first-level supervisors, whose evaluations depended on the performance of their subordinates. First-liners reported to second-level managers, who in turn reported to District Managers. These District Managers oversaw part of their department's operations throughout a given geographic area. Above the District Managers stood a fourth link in the chain—the Divisions Managers—who controlled an entire department's operations within each geographic region (for example, managing the Traffic department's operations in downstate New York). Only at the fifth line of supervision—the General Manager's position—did control over the operations of several departments converge. A sixth level of authority—Assistants to the Vice President—approved major decisions made by the General Managers and set policy guidelines for them to enact. Ultimately, authority reached upward to the Vice Presidents, and finally the President, of each operating company. Beyond this corporate demiurge stood the parent firm, whose officers oversaw decisions made within each Bell firm.

AT&T's internal structure, then, reached as high as any of the company's skyscrapers and was as vertically differentiated as any major bureaucracy in the nation. Yet, owing to a combination of circumstances affecting Bell firms (such as their insulation from market competition, the legacy of paternalistic authority relations as well as the recruitment of managers from within the firm itself), there remained considerable room for customary or traditional forms of behavior between the various levels of managers and the work force they sought to control. In the Traffic department, the work remained highly routinized. But even there, managers sometimes sought to demonstrate some personal concern for their workers—for example, by bringing in snacks made at home or making sure fans were available on hot summer days. One senior operator I interviewed recalled having her manager bring lemonade around to the girls. "They made you feel like a person to some extent," she recalled. "It wasn't all rules and numbers then." The maintenance of informal social relations and customary procedures was

greatest in the Plant department, however, where craftworkers enjoyed substantial degrees of control over their work.

Retrospective interviews with older workers and retirees who entered the Bell system in the 1950s were virtually unanimous in depicting a set of work relations that remained highly traditional in character. Virtually all of the older Plant managers I interviewed recalled that during the 1960s craftworkers retained their customary ability to influence the pace and method of their work. Often, supervisors lacked detailed knowledge of their subordinates' work methods and were unable to directly supervise their work. This was especially true in older central offices, where repeated rewiring left frame equipment impenetrable to all but the local craft force. Thus, one second-line manager suspected that his craft personnel intentionally caused troubles in their switching equipment, "to make sure there was enough work to go around." Given his limited grasp of the equipment and work methods, he could not say for sure.

Respondents in office occupations commonly recalled working in locations where people of different rank shared holiday dinners together and where children's hand-me-downs were exchanged between supervisors and their workers. Symbolic of this set of social relations was the social fabric established at the district headquarters of New York Telephone's Nassau County operations. This office, a large complex in Hempstead, New York, was a bustling community whose members went fishing together, attended the weddings of their coworkers, and came to know one another's children as well. Despite the overarching formal structure within which telephone work was performed, then, the bureaucratic structure of many Bell firms was overlaid with substantial residues of personal or communal social ties.

That such recollections are more than a romanticized image of the past is partly attested to by data bearing on changes in AT&T's degree of bureaucratization. Presumably, any trend toward increasing bureaucratization during the postwar years would be evident in the relative growth of the system's administrative overhead—the ranks of its managerial, supervisory, and technical personnel. Detailed occupational data on this question are limited to the years 1945–1960, a period of dramatic economic growth for the firm and the wider economy. Yet we find little evidence of any trend toward increasing bureaucracy within the Bell system during these years. . . . [E]ven as the Bell system expanded by more than 200,000 employees, the proportion of its work force made up of executive, technical, and supervisory personnel remained constant, fluctuating between 15 and 17 percent of the firm's employees. One change which the data do reveal is the steady expansion of technical specialists—mainly, electrical engineers and professionals in kindred fields—who accounted for an increasing proportion of Bell's administrative personnel (rising from 24 percent in 1945 to 41.4 percent in 1960). This growth of technical professionals apparently stemmed from the system's growing use of mechanized switching systems . . . and the consequent need for specialists to oversee the modernization of each operating company's equipment. Such engineering personnel were rarely involved in the day-to-day operations of plant or traffic work, however, and remained peripheral to the line of authority. . . .

Information Technology and Work Processes

For roughly four decades after the 1920s, the tools and methods of Plant work had scarcely changed. Beginning in the mid-1960s, however, Bell Labs had begun to announce a series of new technologies that promised sweeping changes in the nature of communications work and which were quickly adopted across the Bell system. The most prominent of these were electronic or "stored program" switching systems (which revolutionized switching operations), Mechanized Loop Testing equipment (which automated the testing of lines), and various computerized systems for the management of Plant information that recast the nature of clerical functions. Initially, these changes were limited to isolated departments. By the end of the 1970s, however, more and more work locations were caught up in a movement toward electronic integration, as the labor process began to evolve into a complex web whose elements are electronically interwoven by mainframe computers located far from any given worksite.

To show how these changes have reshaped skill requirements and managerial control during the past two decades, I shall first present data gathered from field work and interviews conducted at New York Telephone's Plant department. I will then use quantitative data to model the precise interrelation among new technologies, skill requirements, and alienation from work.

The Automation of Craft Labor

Management's campaign to rationalize its operations began, logically enough, at the most pivotal unit within the C.O.—the Repair Service Bureaus. Beginning at the end of the 1960s, the company introduced two decisive changes directly bearing on the RSBs. The first involved the organization of the RSBs: management began to separate the functions of craft and clerical workers, distributing them into two distinct organizational units. This change enabled the company to consolidate the labor of the Repair

Service Attendants into larger and more concentrated bureaus that served much wider geographical areas, in this way reducing the number of offices the company needed to maintain. As will soon be discussed more fully, this reorganization enabled the company to establish what it called "a traffic environment" in the consolidated trouble-reporting bureaus.

A second change centered on the technologies used to test and interpret troubles. Hard upon the reorganization of the RSBs, the company installed microelectronic equipment called Mechanized Loop Testing (MLT) systems, which translated the Deskman's testing and interpretive skills into computer programs. No longer dependent on the Deskman as the supplier of testing skills, the company promoted lower-paid clerical personnel who lacked any technical knowledge of electrical circuits to take the Deskmen's place. Typically, the clerical personnel assigned to run the MLTs were recruited from the ranks of the RSAs (Repair Service Attendants), the very clerical workers whom the Deskmen had previously overseen.

In the old RSBs, trouble reports were literally handed to testing personnel by the RSAs standing adjacent to them. Now testing personnel receive trouble reports electronically, from consolidated 611 bureaus that are often hundreds of miles away. As RSAs forward trouble reports into a testing office (now called Installation and Maintenance Centers, or IMCs), clerical workers type the suspect telephone numbers into programmed interfaces ("masks") on their screens. Once the clerk presses the enter key, the system *automatically* tests the relevant cable and pair, outputting the test results in roughly forty seconds. A screenful of data comes up, showing the circuit's ohm and volt readings, AC and DC signatures, the status of the dial tone, as well as other data. Yet the only unit of information that concerns the clerical worker is the VER code,

which indicates the apparent source of the trouble. A VER code of 3, for example, indicates a probable trouble in switches; in this case, the clerk forwards it to a switching control center, where the system assigns it to a craftworker's log. When the VER code indicates a cable problem, the clerk sends the trouble to a repair garage where a splicer is assigned to locate the trouble and close it out. Virtually all elements of judgment and interpretation have in fact been encoded into the algorithms of the MLT system's software; clerical workers have little or no substantive knowledge of what the tests actually mean.

From management's perspective, this arrangement reduces the variable or contingent nature of the labor process. In the words of a top technical manager at New York Telephone, MLT technologies ensure that

> a VER code of 3 will *always* go to the switching location. A certain handle number will *always* get the right cable and pair. There are no decisions to be made along the way. *That's the way we want the work to be.*

Repercussions from the new technologies echoed throughout the Plant department, beginning a process that affected both the outside workers and switching crafts alike. One immediate impact of the MLTs was to introduce sharp conflict and tension between clerical workers (mainly women) in the automated IMCs and the craft personnel (men) who actually completed the relevant repairs. Such conflict typically occurred under two circumstances. One was when the MLT reports were erroneous or vague, and craftworkers had to call in to the IMC for further information. Because the company's aim was to reduce its labor costs, it kept its IMC staff to a minimum, often forcing craftworkers out in the field to wait long periods of time before getting through. Indeed, the splicers in one garage heard from their counterparts in the city that they had better brush up on their reading skills, for the new technologies would mean long delays. "Boy, were they ever right," he noted.

A second source of conflict occurred when craftworkers *did* get through, as workers in the skilled crafts now had to deal with workers who had been denied all but the most rudimentary knowledge of telephone circuitry. One splicer expressed a widespread feeling with particular force:

> These M.A.s [MLT operators] have *no idea* what it's like to hang up on a pole when it's ten degrees out, with your knees hurting and legs turning to jelly, with some bimbo fiddle-fucking around!

As splicers observed, the MLT operators passively read the results on their screens without adjusting for weather conditions or the age and type of the equipment. As a result, what they saw on their VDTs often had only the most tenuous bearing on the actual state of Plant equipment. With few other means of defense, MLT operators often clung to the organization's rules, insisting on the validity of the system's results and forcing craftworkers to "clear" troubles that sometimes didn't exist. As one splicer reported:

> An M.A. says the pair's no good, but I can see with my own eyes that it tests fine. I can get tone on it. The trouble was in the C.O., not in the pair! She [the MLT operator] is just not experienced enough to know what to do.

To some extent these conflicts reflected the organizational tensions that often accompany the restructuring of work methods. For one thing, the task of automating the Deskmen's job was extraordinarily complex; many of the tacit skills Deskmen had accumulated were not (could not be) incorporated into the MLT systems. This posed enormous threats to the validity of diagnostic work. Recalled one Deskman who works with the MLTs in a different department of the firm:

> See, when you test you're also *listening* to the circuit, and you can detect certain things that the [computer] system can't, because it can't hear the line. Also, when a machine tests a circuit, it doesn't have a memory, at least not in the same way we do. Like when we say, "Oh, I remember there was something like this before . . ." It can *try* to duplicate that. But it simply doesn't have the human capacity of relating a lot of different things together into one.

The results were sometimes highly wasteful. In one case, as many as a dozen workers were dispatched to the same location when the system failed to "see" the common source underlying several kindred troubles.

These technological sources of uncertainty were exacerbated by the company's effort to minimize its training and staffing costs. The automation of testing work had been undertaken to speed up the flow of work thought the Plant department and to reduce the cost of shooting troubles in Plant equipment. When the new system yielded an *increased* need for communication between the clerical workers and outside workers, however, the restructured system was more poorly equipped to handle such needs than ever before. The resulting tensions were directed at the MLT operators, who bore the brunt of the workers' resentment.

Even more important than these factors, however, has been the role of gender ideology and politics, which intensified the conflict between male outside workers and female MLT operators. Much as in printing, metal trades, and many other crafts, outside craftworkers had infused their tasks with the trappings of masculinity, defining their skills in terms of what Paul Willis has called the "manly confrontation with the task."[1] Peering out through this gendered lens, many of the men viewed the women in the testing offices as inherently incompetent in the analysis and interpretation of troubles. By pointing to the women's manifest lack of knowledge of Plant operations, moreover, the men could reaffirm the importance of their own skills. For these reasons, many outside craftworkers viewed the women as interlopers, in effect blaming them for organizational developments that were in fact well beyond the women's control. Only recently has such conflict begun to abate, as the company has taken steps to correct the problems it had itself created. . . .

The Automation of the Switching Crafts

The deskmen had played a central role in the detection and analysis of switching troubles, but the actual repairs were performed by switching craftworkers assigned to each frame location. The clearing of troubles within each C.O. required little outside intervention, as C.O.s were largely self-sufficient units. This arrangement began to shift in 1965, when Bell Laboratories announced the development of Electronic Switching Systems (ESS), more generally known as "stored program" equipment. In contrast to mechanical installations, ESS equipment uses digital technologies to store switching codes in memory, in effect assigning each telephone number an electronic address. In this way the computer views each telephone as a logical device attached to a wide area network. When a subscriber inputs a telephone number to be reached, the computer processes the call as an input/output operation, calculates the optimal path for the call, and establishes the connection electronically.[2]

The technical advantages of stored program switching systems are unmistakable. With such systems installed, Plant managers can achieve far greater flexibility in the use of their equipment, changing the as-

signment of particular cables and pairs without any manual intervention. Digital systems usually detect faults before customers ever become aware of them. Failing components can be automatically taken off line, achieving a level of fault tolerance not possible before. Finally, because digital systems make little or no use of mechanical devices, they require far less maintenance than their mechanical predecessors. From the perspective of the workers, however, stored program switching has had several less beneficial effects.

The *first* has been a virtual depopulation of most C.O. frame and switching installations. Before, in a large switching hub as existed in the Hempstead district office, switching craftworkers maintained their own miniature society, with playful rivalries between workers skilled in different systems. Each frame often required as many as twenty-five workers, who rotated on and off different shifts in order to keep service up and running. Now a typical frame location requires no more than a half-dozen of switching workers. Many workers have been transferred to other locations (e.g., to the computerized control centers) or else are retained on a roving basis (making repairs wherever they need to be dispatched). Still, when New York Telephone's switching services in Nassau County were cut over to digital equipment, the area's force requirements in switch fell by 40 percent between 1982 and 1991 (from 992 to 605).

The introduction of digital switching equipment has promoted a *second* and even more pronounced change in the work process—management's centralization of its switching operations—which has placed control over each territory's switching equipment in a new type of office, Automated Switching Control Centers. Much as in automated process industries, the Switching Control Centers constantly monitor the operations of the area's switching and frame installations, alerting workers to changes in the state of the system's functioning and even adjusting the network's behavior as the situation demands.

Before the shift toward Control Centers, New York Telephone maintained twenty-four distinct frame installations in Nassau County, each of which was a relatively autonomous organizational unit. By 1982, stored program switching systems enabled the company to establish ten Control Centers to oversee all of its switching installations. Three years later, the number of Control Centers had shrunk to four, and by 1990 to only one. While there remain twenty-four frame and switch installations in this county, a single highly automated complex located in the company's district office now "manages" their functioning from afar.

This shift toward more centralized controls has split the switching crafts in two. Some craftworkers continue to work in remote C.O.s, as system needs require. Other switching workers have been assigned to the Control Centers, working in entirely new situations. This had led to a *third* effect of the new technologies: switching craftworkers in the Control Centers have exchanged their older, physically based knowledge for a set of abstract, "intellective" skills (Zuboff 1987).

To be sure, there were important analytical skills required of inside craftworkers even before the introduction of ESS equipment. To find a trouble, switching craftworkers often had to run a battery of tests at their local installations, using schematic diagrams and manuals to interpret the results. Yet these tests were always conducted alongside the switching machines themselves, and workers had previously been part of a mechanical, hands-on working environment. The practical test of their diagnosis was physically present before their very eyes. For switching personnel who have been assigned to the Control

Centers, however, the material trappings of their craft have all but fallen away. Increasingly, switching craftworkers conduct their tasks at computer screens far removed from any concrete referent.

Workers employed at different sections of a Control Center perform varying sorts of functions. In one section, for example, workers oversee the operations of specific types of equipment—for example, maintaining Northern Telecom DMS switches, AT&T ESS-5 machines, or the few remaining Cross-Bar switches in the district. In a nearby area of the same office, workers run tests on troubles that have been reported to the 611 bureau and which have been traced to malfunctions in a switch. In yet another area, workers are assigned "control and surveillance" functions, analyzing computer-detected faults in the district's switching operations. What unites these workers is their constant use of computer systems in the conduct of their tasks.

One system that is commonly used in New York Telephone's Switching Control Centers is an installation called CIMAP (Circuit Installation and Maintenance Assistance Package). Pronounced SEE-MAP, the acronym reflects the system's goal of helping workers peer into the operations of the switching equipment distributed throughout the local terrain. In the words of one supervisor, CIMAP "is our universe."

Workers in the Control Center receive their tasks in different ways. A routine source of work stems from CIMAP's nightly testing of circuits in the district's switching systems. As the system locates components whose ohm readings violate acceptable thresholds, it routes calls around faulty circuits, flags them as troubles that need repair, and electronically sends each task to a given worker's log. Craftworkers then access their work logs and bring up each task, using an array of diagnostic programs to see what produced each trouble report. This type of assignment is called "programmable load work." A less routine source of work happens when CIMAP detects the sudden occurrence of a fault which is a potential threat to some portion of local service. In such situations, CIMAP sounds a bell and outputs the trouble report to a line printer, where it receives immediate attention. Whether they are performing programmable load work or responding to alarms, workers now receive their work assignments from CIMAP itself. *The computer system itself informs workers which of the system's parts to repair.*

When a switching craftworker accesses his work log, he opens a trouble report to see what type of fault he or she has been assigned. The worker then calls up a circuit history of the equipment involved, uses CIMAP and other, supplementary diagnostic systems to run a set of testing routines, and locates the trouble on the basis of the results. Sometimes, the trouble stems from a software error. In such cases, the trouble can be cleared electronically, simply by issuing a set of commands from within CIMAP. More often, the worker finds an open circuit, meaning that a specific electronic component has failed within a remote C.O., indicating the need for manual repair. In the latter case the craftworker forwards the test report (usually including a short narrative describing the trouble) to a repair worker out in the field.

Although a yawning distance now separates workers from the objects of their labor, few craftworkers have experienced the feeling that Zuboff called "epistemological distress," in which older ways of knowing are rapidly overturned, resulting in confusion and uncertainty about the actual condition of the production process. Even so, most switching workers feel a sense of discomfort with the increasingly abstract character of their jobs. Said one young Hispanic woman working in a Manhattan Control Center:

Part of the problem with working with the computer is that you have little view of what you are actually testing, and you need that. You see, when you're testing on the tube [using the terminal], the computer tells you what *it* sees, not what *you* would see with your own eyes. You don't have that same pulse on the circuit as you had before, when you'd hear certain irregularities on the line and kind of sense things that way.

This inability to "see" and "hear" the switching systems themselves persists despite the most sophisticated programming efforts to overcome it. This was clear in a Control Center that has experimented with a visually-oriented alternative to CIMAP. This new system, called Vision, graphically displays the functioning of the entire area's C.O.s on large computer monitors, with a rectangle representing each remote C.O. Blinking rectangles signal the existence of a troubled C.O., while a steady-state condition indicates normal functioning. Using a mouse, a switching worker can click on each rectangle, windowing into data on the operation of each C.O., even showing several trouble conditions on the screen simultaneously. Such systems do make it easier to *figuratively* "see" the conditions that prevail in remote C.O.s, but most workers still prefer work in the C.O.s, where they can *literally* see their tools in front of them and feel a sense of material connection with the objects of their work. One worker explained:

At the SCC you're responsible for *everything,* the whole system, so you don't get a proprietary sense about anything at all. You can feel really removed from what's going on out there. But at the C.O., there's a feeling of *owning your own switches* that you can't get at the Control Center.

One might easily conclude that this preference for the older, mechanical style of working is an expression of traditionalism that is destined to fade away. Yet the evidence suggests otherwise, indicating that workers' preference for the C.O.s is more than an irrational attachment to tradition. Rather, it reflects their aversion to the *fourth* and final effect of computerization—its establishment of an increasingly structured, more tightly constrained set of work relations within the Control Centers. Put simply, workers chafe at the tightened discipline the company has achieved in the Control Centers and prefer to work in the C.O.s, where they feel a greater sense of independence from managerial control.

No one could reasonably suggest that management has sought to introduce a "traffic environment" in its Control Centers. The work is still too varied and complex to allow for such complete standardization. For example, although the introduction of computers has automated the routine testing of circuits, workers must still set the program's ohm thresholds themselves, and to do this they need considerable knowledge of different types of equipment. (If the thresholds are set improperly, the system will report an excess of troubles, generating much more information than workers can possibly use). Given the differing types of equipment in use (mostly from Northern Telecom and AT&T), months of active use can go by before workers begin to understand the rudiments of each particular system. Despite the continuing complexity of workers' skills, however, systems such as CIMAP have quite clearly enabled management to establish a stricter set of production standards than had ever existed before.

When CIMAP allocates tasks to each technician's work log, it also establishes a "price" for each job that depends on its type, in this way maintaining an ongoing record of each worker's efficiency rating. If a worker's total number of production units falls below the value expected for the week, the worker's efficiency rating begins to suffer. Workers assigned to programmable load work, for example, are expected to achieve "96–99 percent completeness" as a matter of course. Ironically, the very system that detects "faults" in the switching network performs the same function with respect to the *human* network that keeps the system on line.

The importance of technology in maintaining an expected level of work discipline emerged clearly in the remarks of middle- and lower-level managers. Said one first-line supervisor:

> I don't need the machine to know who's not pulling their weight. I knew who wasn't pulling their weight even without it. *But it helps.* It makes a real difference. It means there are fewer confrontations. I have something *real* now I can show people to back up my point. *They can't argue with the hard copy.*

Almost every manager was quick to justify the use of performance measurement, portraying it as a tool that helps them develop their subordinates' skills. One supervisor told me:

> When one of my people is having a problem, I can see it more quickly now. I can sit down with him and determine what's wrong. Maybe there's something he hasn't tried yet that would help, some method that will bring his performance up a few notches.

This view of performance measurement as an aid in training and development contains an important element of truth. Yet it conveniently ignores another, less friendly function of the new technologies: with the new systems in place, the task of maintaining given levels of production became that much less dependent on personal forms of supervision. When asked how stored program technologies had affected his control over the work locations under his authority, a third-level manager of switching services alluded to precisely this point. He shook his head and identified an anomaly: "It's funny. Each office is much less supervised now, *but it's much more controlled.*"

This development is at times made graphically clear, as in one major Control Center that oversees the switches in a suburban New York county. The supervisors in this Control Center have installed a video projection system that magnifies a computer screen's display and projects it onto the front wall of the office. The image, involving data from CIMAP's tracking system, shows each outstanding fault in the Control Center, the name of the worker assigned to it and the time the worker has spent on each outstanding task. The effect is to "publicize" each worker's ongoing work performance, which is now apparent for all to see. A supervisor explained why he liked this arrangement:

> Now I don't have to constantly ask people how their work is coming. And I don't have to log into the system to check. I can see for myself *just by looking up at the wall.*

Even this office could not reasonably be called an electronic sweatshop. Workers have too much discretion for that term to fit and can still engage in casual conversation if their trouble schedules allow. As suggested, their work remains highly complex. Yet methods such as this serve to put switching workers on notice that the clock is ticking, and that the same computer system that assigns them their tasks is measuring their efficiency in handling each one. . . .

. . . [A] typical centralized repair bureau houses roughly one hundred workers, although only half that many are on the job at any given time. . . . [T]he overlapping and often rotating shifts that workers are assigned rule out the establishment of personal work areas. When an RSA arrives at

work, she selects one of the fifty-odd cubicles to use that day, plugs in her headset, and logs in her ID code. From that point on, the work is almost indistinguishable from that performed in Traffic bureaus. Calls automatically flow to the first available RSA. Just as in Traffic bureaus, work performance is measured using the AWT system.

The starting pay for an RSA is low (only $249 per week), but doubles within five years' time. Still, turnover is high, and many RSAs leave before this period elapses. The reasons are clear. The job involves friction with aggrieved subscribers, who often vent their frustrations at the company's workers. It offers little autonomy or discretion, for workers' tasks are highly standardized: they use a few structured questions to elicit data which they enter into computer fields on their screens. As in traffic, workers' performance is timed; expected AWTs hover at about 110 seconds per call. Finally, force requirements lead to strict enforcement of the rules governing absences and sick leave. As the second-line manager of a 611 bureau put it: "If I need 6.5 bodies, they've got to be there. If not, my service is impacted. So you better believe we're strict!"

Events in this manager's office are especially revealing. Despite the company's strict absence-control policy (or perhaps because of it), absenteeism has remained quite high. This fact, coupled with levels of turnover and poor performance, began to indicate to management that their rationalization efforts might have gone too far. Beginning in the late 1980s, third line management began to advise their second liners (including the manager of this office) to ease up on production standards and to emphasize quality more. The second-liner recalled,

> We used to beat them over the head with AWTs. Literally. But now I've been told to relax things, to raise the AWT and to look at my Telsam ratings [ser-

vice evaluations commissioned by the state] and not just the AWTs.

Nonetheless, this man is quick to point out that his office's AWT has loosened only slightly, moving from 110 to 120 seconds per call; he is proud that other offices have let their AWTs slide even more. Apparently, the calculus of productivity still informed his behavior.

Management has applied elementary Human Relations techniques to this office, to improve work attitudes among the RSAs. On Employee Recognition Day, the company presents awards to those RSAs who have performed especially well. At the last such event, workers were allowed to rotate off their positions for an hour or so on company time and to share hero sandwiches and cake, while middle- and top-level managers heaped praise on them, dubbing them the company's "unsung heroes." At the end of the festivities, commemorative mugs were distributed to the attendees. A party atmosphere prevailed for much of the day, with workers straggling in as their shifts allowed.

A further effort to counter employee alienation in this office has been the establishment of the Sunshine Club, a small group of supervisors and workers who try to enliven social relations at work by throwing parties on holidays and employee birthdays. On such days, members of the club affix crepe paper streamers to the ceilings and lay out a spread of cookies and soda. The evidence suggests, however, that none of these efforts—minimal relaxation of the AWT or the various Human Relations efforts—has had any appreciable effect on workers' attitudes. Workers eat the company's cookies and take home its mugs, yet feel little change in their orientation toward their jobs.

A small number of RSAs employed at the office described above was included in the 1985 regional survey of two Bell operating companies. Because the number of such workers was small, caution is clearly warranted in drawing inferences about this particular clerical group. Nonetheless, a relatively clear and consistent pattern emerges in the work attitudes and perceptions of these RSAs.

It is useful to view the workers in this industry on a continuum that ranges from the most highly alienated group (the telephone operators) at one end, to the least alienated group (craftworkers such as the splicers) at the other. When we locate the RSAs on this continuum, we find that their attitudes are now almost indistinguishable from those of their counterparts in the Traffic department. In light of their work attitudes, it is hard to believe that they are employed in the same industry as the splicers (see Table 1)

Only 6 percent of the splicers usually feel controlled by their machines, yet more than four-fifths (82.3 percent) of the RSAs "often" or "always" feel this way. Like the majority of the operators, most RSAs (76.5 percent) have come to feel "just like another part of the machinery" when they are at work, a sentiment accompanied by a clear sense of aversion toward the work itself. The same proportion of RSAs report a clearly instrumental view of their jobs, where only the pay serves as a motivating force; the comparable proportion among the splicers (32 percent) is less than half as large. Clearly, the work situation of the operators has reappeared in a newer context—the centralized Repair Service Bureaus.

There are at least some indications that clerical workers in other organizational units may escape the fullest development of this process, as countervailing trends have to some extent offset the de-skilling effects RSAs have felt. The automation of the Loop Assignment Centers, for example, has abolished the most routinized and repetitive functions (those of the data entry clerks), chiefly because the electronic integration of the labor process has reduced the need to re-enter the same data at different points in the

Table 1   Responses to Selected Indicators of Alienation from Work by Occupational Group

	Occupational Group		
Percent Who "Often" or "Always" Report Feeling the Following:	Directory Assistance Operators % (N)	Repair Service Attendants % (N)	Cable Splicers % (N)
On my job I feel as if the machines and equipment control me.*	68.0 (103)	82.3 (17)	6.0 (50)
When I'm working I feel like just another part of the machinery.*	71.0 (107)	76.5 (17)	22.0 (50)
I really have to force myself to go into work.*	51.9 (106)	70.5 (17)	18.0 (50)
The only thing I look forward to on my job is getting paid.	67.9 (103)	76.4 (17)	32.0 (50)

*P < .0005 using chi square.

productive circuit. In highly automated LACs (called Loop Data Maintenance Centers, or LDMCs), the great bulk of the information processing work that clerical workers had performed is now conducted automatically, as computers search their databases and assign cables and pairs to new equipment with little need for human intervention. Although such processes have tended to eliminate the least skilled clerical tasks, the bulk of the work in automated LACs remains highly routine. Workers perform auxiliary tasks, picking up whatever residual jobs the computers find too awkward to conduct. The programs that manage the flow of work through automated LDMCs contain routines for the measurement of each worker's performance, though they are not yet widely used.

While still preliminary, these observations begin to suggest that the de-skilling trend has been imposed with greater force on clerical than craft occupations, as workers in lower-level office jobs have felt the full effect of the rationalization trend. Clerks have at times been used as a wedge in management's battle against craftworkers. . . . More generally, clerical workers have tended

to experience what the company calls a "Traffic environment," involving the use of machine-pacing and electronic surveillance to maintain desired production standards.

Estimating the Linkages among Technology, Work, and Alienation

. . . Ideally, we should like to use longitudinal data to assess the impact of the new technologies.[3] The static, cross-sectional nature of the survey data falls short of this ideal. They do, however, permit us to approximate the nature of the changes at issue by creating a "synthetic cohort" of jobs situated at varying points in the automation process. The strategy adopted here has been to compare the content of similar jobs at low, medium, and high levels of automation, deciphering technologically related variations in job complexity and autonomy. To understand the attitudinal effects of these changes, we can explore data on alienation from work as well. In the following analysis, then, I shall fit the survey data with a structural model that reveals the nature of the links among new technologies, work content, and alienation from work for both craft and clerical occupations.

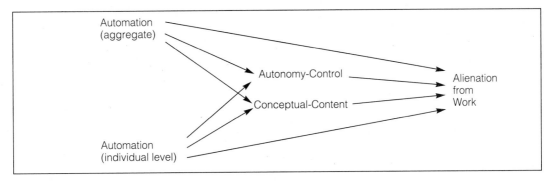

FIGURE 1 A Model of the Links between the Degree of Automation, Work Content, and Alienation from Work

Figure 1 displays the model used to guide the analysis. Similar heuristic devices have been commonly used by studies in the upgrading genre (e.g., Blauner, 1964; Faunce 1965; Shepard 1971; Hull, Friedman, and Rogers, 1982). In using the model, I make no assumptions that technology is an autonomous force, standing above or beyond social influences (as upgrading theorists have often assumed). I assume only that the introduction of new technologies has enabled management to reconfigure the work process in ways that the model can unearth. The dependent variables which the model employs include both structural and attitudinal variables (that is, both work content and levels of alienation). The measures I have used in the analysis can briefly be described as follows.

Alienation. . . . I have defined alienation from work in terms of a relation between the worker and the job that generates two subjective conditions: (1) the worker's feeling of separation or disengagement from his or her work, which comes to acquire a merely instrumental meaning, and (2) the worker's perception that he or she has become an *object* of the production process, falling under the control of his or her own tools. While multiple dimensions would ideally be developed to measure this construct, a more par-

simonious, one-dimensional scale has been developed on the basis of five survey items.[4]

Autonomy and Conceptual Content. My approach to studying work content follows Spenner's lead (1983), recognizing two distinct dimensions—autonomy-control and complexity (or conceptual content). By autonomy I mean the extent to which workers are free to direct the method and the pace of their work. By the conceptual content of their tasks I mean the degree to which their work requires "independent thought or judgment" (Spenner 1983:828), rather than what Braverman called the labor of execution alone. The analysis that follows uses multiple items to measure each dimension of work content, with indices that achieve reliability coefficients that were deemed at least acceptable.[5]

Automation. The degree of automation, finally, is defined in terms of the extent to which digital or other advanced technologies have replaced older, mechanical tools and machines. To measure this variable I have used a set of occupation-specific items that asked how often workers routinely use specific types of equipment. These items enable us to distinguish between workers using relatively primitive or manual equipment (coded as 1), those using equipment at intermediate or mechanical levels (coded as

2) and those using relatively advanced, digital technologies (coded as 3).[6]

One further point remains before presenting the results. The research design was planned in a manner that used distinct *workplaces* (rather than the individual *worker*) as the primary sampling units. (Once a workplace was selected for inclusion, questionnaires were administered to all the workers in it). This approach makes possible the use of a fuller, more structurally oriented measure of automation than could be done merely using individual automation scores. By aggregating the degree of automation that prevails in each workplace, we can form a measure of automation at two distinct levels of analysis—the structural or systemic level of the office as a whole, as well as the individual level of each worker's specific job. Presumably variations in work content and worker attitudes will be shaped by automation at both levels of analysis.

To form the contextual measure of office automation, worker's individual responses have been aggregated by work location (Kendall and Lazarsfeld 1955; Coleman 1969), yielding the mean level of automation that exists within each office. To separate out the individual effects of automation, I have constructed a term that represents each worker's deviation from the office mean (see Tannenbaum and Bachman 1964; Alwin 1976; and Lincoln and Zeitz 1980). The following analysis thus includes both contextual *and* individual measures of technology, enabling us to unravel the effects of automation at the two levels of analysis.

To form the "synthetic cohort" of jobs at different stages in the automation process, we must be able to compare occupations that are similar in all relevant respects save for their degree of automation. For this reason, I have broken down the regression equations into occupational subgroups, showing the links among automation, work content, and alienation within each specific job category. As we see in Tables 2 through 4, the results lend support to the qualitative analysis outlined above.

TABLE 2 Work Autonomy Regressed on the Degree of Automation and Controls, by Occupation Group. Unstandardized Coefficients (Beta in Parentheses)

Predictor	(1) Inside Crafts	(2) Outside Crafts	(3) Clerical Employees
Size	.70***	−.50	−.05
	(.34)	(−.12)	(−.02)
Seniority	−.02	.02	−.02
	(−.05)	(.05)	(−.03)
Gender	1.52	2.25	.26
	(.12)	(−.11)	(.15)
Automation (individual)	−1.56*	−.19	−1.54***
	(−.18)	(−.03)	(−.28)
Automation (contextual)	−2.27	2.87**	−2.57***
	(−.08)	(.30)	(−.26)
Constant	15.10	9.45	9.77
R^2	.21	.08	.18
N	(133)	(103)	(249)

***P < .001
**P < .01
*P < .05

TABLE 3 Conceptual Content Regressed on Degree of Automation and Controls. Unstandardized Coefficients (Beta in Parentheses)

	(1) Inside Crafts	(2) Outside Crafts	(3) Clerical Employees
Size	.09	.11	.02
	(.06)	(.04)	(.01)
Seniority	.03	−.01	.06**
	(.10)	(−.04)	(−.15)
Gender	1.24	−.54	1.49**
	(.12)	(−.04)	(.15)
Automation (individual)	−1.09	.29	−1.00***
	(−.17)	(.07)	(−.21)
Automation (contextual)	1.65	1.61*	−1.04
	(.08)	(.24)	(−.12)
Constant	6.34	8.74	9.21
R^2	.07	.10	.10
N	(133)	(103)	(249)

*P < .05
**P < .01
***P < .001

TABLE 4 Alienation from Work Regressed on Degree of Automation and Controls. Unstandardized Coefficients (Beta in Parentheses)

	(1) Inside Crafts	(2) Outside Crafts	(3) Clerical Employees
Size	−.03	.62*	.01
	(−.02)	(.19)	(.00)
Seniority	.00	.03	.00
	(.00)	(.09)	(.00)
Gender	1.64	1.33	.23
	(.15)	(.08)	(.02)
Automation (individual)	−1.64**	.36	.93**
	(−.23)	(.08)	(.18)
Automation (contextual)	2.51	.32	.00
	(.11)	(.04)	(.00)
Autonomy	.37***	−.41***	−.28***
	(−.43)	(−.52)	(−.31)
Conceptual Content	−.20*	−.10	−.25***
	(−.18)	(−.09)	(−.23)
Constant	10.22	7.80	12.20
R^2	.251	.34	.27
N	(133)	(103)	(249)

*P < .05
**P < .01
***P < .001

Consider first the effects of automation on the autonomy of the two craft groups. Table 2 begins to show that the effects of automation are not homogeneous across the craft categories. The autonomy of the inside craftworkers does indeed decline when workers are employed at automated switching systems, much as the qualitative data suggest. Among the outside craft group, however, automation has the opposite, upgrading effect: outside craftworkers who install and maintain the most sophisticated equipment tend to report significantly *greater* autonomy than their counterparts employed in less advanced contexts.

When we consider apparent shifts in the conceptual content of craft work, we find no evidence that automation brings about any simplification or loss of conceptual functions with respect to the switching crafts (Table 3). In fact, Equation 1 (which predicts conceptual content for the inside crafts) fails to attain statistical significance. Among the outside crafts, however, automation again acts to enhance work content: outside craftworkers who work in the most technically advanced contexts again report significantly *greater* conceptual complexity in their work than their counterparts in less advanced contexts.[7] Thus, while the work situation of the inside craft groups does seem to suffer (at least with respect to work autonomy), the functions of other groups are apparently enhanced. Hence we find no evidence of any wholesale erosion or destruction of skilled manual occupations. What seems to occur is the *transformation* or reproduction of craft work.

Again supporting the qualitative analysis, the data suggest that automation has strong and consistently adverse effects on the content of clerical workers' jobs. The autonomy of the clerks declines apace with automation at both the contextual *and* the individual levels of analysis (see Table 2). Likewise, the conceptual content of clerical

work quite clearly falls as computerization proceeds (Table 3). What these data suggest is that the experience of the RSAs, whose labor has been fully rationalized, does indeed hold wider relevance for the clerical work force as a whole, for the de-skilling process seems to bring its full weight to bear on this occupational group.[8]

The differential effects of automation on craft and clerical work grow even more apparent when we extend the analysis to include the subjective experience of work—that is, levels of alienation from work (see Table 4). By combining the results in the three tables we can estimate the total effects of new technology on alienation, including both its direct and indirect effects (i.e., those which operate independently of work content, and those which are mediated by shifts in job design). When we do this, a number of important conclusions emerge.

As we have already seen, the introduction of advanced technologies increases the autonomy and conceptual content of the outside crafts, in turn reducing their level of alienation. The total effect of such changes on workers' attitudes is, however, quite modest: on average, a standard deviation increment in the degree of automation is expected to reduce worker alienation by a total of .18 standard deviations.

Somewhat more surprising are the overall effects of automation on the inside crafts. As noted, the use of programmable automation reduces the autonomy of the switching crafts, indirectly increasing worker alienation. However, as Table 4 reveals, the direct effect of automation on alienation serves to *offset* this indirect, alienating effect: After adjusting for variations in work content, we find that automated switching technology tends to *reduce* workers' levels of alienation.[9] Because the direct and indirect effects of alienation move in opposite directions, the result cancels out any trend toward alienation that switching craftworkers might otherwise feel. Overall, we therefore find no pronounced changes in alienation among the two skilled craft groups.

As we have seen, automation exerts a pronounced de-skilling effect on the content of clerical labor, which in turn heightens these workers' alienation from their jobs. In addition to this indirect effect, automation also exerts a direct effect on clerical workers' attitudes, which in this case only *exacerbates* the trend toward increased alienation. Given the consistency and strength of these effects, we find that automation has an especially strong and adverse effect on work attitudes among the clerical group. Thus the model estimates that each standard deviation increase in the degree of office automation elevates clerical workers' alienation by an average of .40 standard deviations—an appreciable effect.

Hence the data largely conform to the qualitative observations just sketched and shed further light on the limitations of the de-skilling thesis when applied to skilled manual work as a whole. We again find evidence of a deterioration in the work situations of certain crafts (those in switching and frame locations) where programmable automation has reduced workers' autonomy. Yet we find no evidence of any overall trend toward the simplification or dilution of conceptual skill requirements. In fact, the only significant trends involving conceptual content are among the outside crafts, whose jobs demand *in*creasing levels of conceptual skill as automation rises. Again, the automation process seems not so much to *abolish* as to *recast* the nature of craft work. Where the position of one craft seems to weaken, that of another craft group is enhanced, redistributing skills among the various crafts (Penn, 1985). At the same time, automation seems to foster a clear de-skilling trend among clerical employees. The net effect is to reflect or reproduce the pattern of inequality that exists between craft and clerical workers. In fact, this pattern of inequality seems if anything to have grown more pronounced, as clerks have experienced the brunt of the rationalization process.

NOTES

1. See especially Willis (1977, 1979) and Cockburn (1983). The role of gender in the culture of telephone work is explored in Cynthia Epstein's research (e.g., 1988).

2. For technical discussions, see Almquist and Fessler (1979), Amin, et al. (1981). For a more sociological discussion from a de-skilling perspective, see Newman (1982).

3. The standard work here remains that of Spenner (1979, 1983, 1990).

4. Using a 4-point frequency coding, the items asked workers how often they experienced each of the feelings articulated in Table 1. (An additional statement not shown in the table was "the time really drags for me while I'm at work.") The resulting index has an alpha of .84. The index ranges from 5 through 20, with high scores indicating greater alienation from work.

5. To measure work autonomy, I designed six items that asked respondents how often each of the following characteristics described their jobs: "My job requires that I do things just the way I am told. If I leave my work area for a moment, my supervisor starts wondering where I am. The amount of work I do is carefully measured by the people above me. My job requires that I complete a certain amount of work per minute or hour. My job requires that I keep working every minute of the day. My job requires that I work very fast." Cronbach's alpha for the index is .85. The index ranges from 0 to 18, with high scores denoting greater autonomy.

To measure the conceptual content of workers' jobs, I adapted four items crudely based on the *Dictionary of Occupational Titles* index of occupational complexity (for discussion, see Spenner 1979, 1990; Kohn 1969; and Kohn and Schooler 1983). Each of these items presented respondents with roughly opposed ends of a continuum, and asked them to indicate where their job tasks typically fall. Items were designed to bear on the use of data, people and things, with one item bearing on overall levels of routinization. Although the Cronbach's alpha for the resulting index is low (.59), the index is a significant predictor of wages ($r = .50$). The index also correlates with the DOT scores from 1977 (Spearman's rho = .60). The index ranges from 0 through 16, with high scores denoting greater conceptual content.

6. Clerical workers' scores were based on the frequency with which they used VDTs in their work. Those using VDTs very little or not at all were assigned scores of 1; occasional VDT users (between 25% and 75% of the day) were given scores of 2; while constant VDT users (those who use terminals more than 75% of the day) were assigned values of 3.

   Automation scores for switching craftworkers were based on the generation of switching technology they mainly use. Those who work with electromechanical equipment (mainly Cross-Bar switches) were coded as 2, while users of electronic or other programmable systems were assigned the highest score (3).

   Scores of outside craftworkers, finally, were based on the number of advanced technologies (among them, SLC-96 equipment, Dimension systems, and fiber optic cables) the worker commonly uses in his or her job. Those using none of the technologies were given manual scores of 1; those using one type were scored at the intermediate level, while those using two or more of the new technologies were assigned the highest automation score(3) . . .

7. Note that these data were collected immediately before the CATs were introduced. If anything, they underestimate the upgrading trend apparent among the outside crafts.

8. The meaning of these findings can be explained in more concrete terms. If the degree of automation at an office increases by one standard deviation (as would occur when an office is cut over to a new system), workers who become constant users of VDTs can expect to find their autonomy reduced by more than half a standard deviation (.54 units).

9. This finding may reflect the preponderance of central office switching workers in the sample. As was suggested, these workers enjoy more of a sense of "owning your own switch" than do workers in the Control Centers, and apparently do not experience automation in the same way as do workers in the latter worksites.

REFERENCES

Almquist, Milton L., and George E. Fessler. 1979. "Switching Control Centers: Switching System Maintenance—and More." Bell Laboratories Report (June).

Alwin, Duane F. 1976. "Assessing School Effects: Some Identities." *Sociology of Education* 49 (October):249–303.

Amin, Ashok T., Walter Haun, and Donald Mulder. 1981. "Sleuthing for Troubles in ESS Networks." Bell Laboratories Report (October).

Blauner, Robert. 1964. *Alienation and Freedom: The Factory Worker and His Industry.* Chicago: University of Chicago Press.

Cockburn, Cynthia. 1983. *Brothers: Male Dominance and Technological Change.* London: Pluto.

Coleman, James R. 1969. "Relations Analysis: The Study of Social Organizations with Survey Methods." In A. Etzioni, ed., *A Sociological Reader on Complex Organizations.* New York: Holt, Rinehart and Winston.

Faunce, William. 1965. "Automation and the Division of Labor." *Social Problems* 13 (Fall).

Hull, Frank, N. S. Freidman, and T. Rogers. 1982. "The Effect of Technology on Alienation from Work: Testing Blauner's Inverted U-Curve Hypothesis." *Work and Occupations* 9,1 (February).

Kendall, Patricia, and Paul Lazarsfeld. 1955. "The Relation Between Individual and Group Characteristics in The American Soldier." In *The Language of Social Research,* edited by Lazarsfeld and Morris Rosenberg. Glencoe, Ill.: Free Press.

Kohn, Melvin. 1969. *Class and Conformity: A Study of Values.* Homewood, Ill.: Dorsey Press.

———. Carmi Schooler, et al., 1983. *Work and Personality: An Inquiry into the Impact of Social Stratification.* Norwood, New Jersey: Ablex.

Lincoln, James, and Gerald Zeitz. 1980. "Organizational Properties from Aggregate Data: Separating Individual from Structural Effects." *American Sociological Review* 45 (June): 391–408.

Newman, David. 1982. "New Technology and the Changing Labor Process in the Telephone Industry: The Union's Response," Unpublished manuscript. New Brunswick, N.J.: Rutgers University, Department of Labor Studies.

Penn, Roger. 1985. "Skill, Class and Labor: A Compensatory Model." *British Journal of Sociology.*

Shepard, Jon. 1971. *Automation and Alienation: A Study of Office and Factory Workers.* Cambridge, Mass.: MIT Press.

Spenner, Kenneth I. 1979. "Temporal Changes in Work Content." *American Sociological Review* 44:968–975.

Tannenbaum, Arnold, and Gerald Bachman. 1964. "Structural versus Individual Effects." *American Journal of Sociology* 69 (May): 585–595.

Vallas, Steven P. 1988. "New Technology, Job Content and Worker Alienation: A Test of Two

Rival Perspectives." *Work and Occupations: An International Journal* (May).

Vallas, Steven P., and Cynthia Fuchs Epstein. 1988. "The Workers' Response to the Labor Process: The Limits of Job Centered Analysis." Paper presented at the American Sociological Association meetings, Atlanta.

Willis, Paul. 1977. *Learning to Labour: How Working Class Kids Get Working Class Jobs.* New York: Columbia University Press.

———. 1979. "Shop Floor Culture, Masculinity and the Wage Form." In John Clarke, ed., *Working Class Culture.* London: Hutchinson.

13

Labor and Management in Uncertain Times
Renegotiating the Social Contract

Ruth Milkman

Ruth Milkman is professor of sociology at UCLA. Professor Milkman writes, "My interest in auto workers dates back many years. In the late 1970s, I was intrigued by the history of women auto workers during the Second World War, which my first book, *Gender At Work* (1987) dealt with in some detail. Then, in the 1980s, the auto industry as it had existed for most of this century was dramatically transformed once again—this time not by a war but instead by international economic competition. When I got the chance to research the impact of these changes on workers at GM, I jumped at it. The article—and my 1997 book, *Farewell to the Factory*—is the result."

The U.A.W. . . . is the largest labor union on earth. Its membership of 1,300,000 embraces most of the production workers in three major American industries. . . . The U.A.W. itself is diverse and discordant, both in its leaders and its members, among whom are represented every race and shape of political opinion. . . . The union's sharp insistence on democratic expression permits bloc to battle bloc and both to rebel at higher-ups' orders. They often do. But U.A.W. is a smart, aggressive, ambitious outfit with young, skillful leaders. . . . It has improved the working conditions in the sometimes frantically paced production lines. And it has firmly established the union shop in an industry which was once firmly open shop. . . . It is not a rich union. Its dues are one dollar a month, which is low. . . . U.A.W. makes its money go a long way. It sets up social, medical, and educational benefits. . . . In its high ranks are men like Reuther, who believes labor must more and more be given a voice in long-range economic planning of the country.[1]

Curious as it may seem to late-twentieth-century sensibility, this homage to the United Auto Workers is not from a union publication or some obscure left-wing tract. It appeared in *Life* magazine in 1945, a month after V-J Day and not long before the century's largest wave of industrial strikes, led by the auto workers, rocked the nation. The cover photo featured a 1940s Everyman: an unnamed auto worker in his work clothes, with factory smokestacks in the background. Blue-collar men in heavy industry, with powerful democratic unions and, at least implicitly, a strong class consciousness—only forty-five years ago this was standard iconography in the mass media and in the popular thinking that it both reflected and helped shape. Organized labor, then embracing over a third of the nation's nonfarm workers and 67 percent of those in manufacturing, was a central force in the Democratic party and a vital influence in public debate on a wide range of social questions. The industrial unions founded in the New Deal era were leaders in opposing race discrimination (and to some extent even sex discrimination) in this period, and their political agenda went far beyond the narrow, sectional interests of their members. Indeed, as historian Nelson Lichtenstein has written, in the 1940s "the union movement defined the left wing of what was possible in the political affairs of the day."[2]

Today, the history is all but forgotten. Blue-collar workers and labor unions are conspicuous by their absence from the mainstream of public discourse. Across the political spectrum, the conventional wisdom is that both industrial work and the forms of unionism it generated are fading relics of a bygone age, obsolete and irrelevant in today's postindustrial society. As everybody knows, while the unionized male factory worker was prototypical in 1945, today the labor force includes nearly as many women as men, and workers of both genders are more likely to sit behind a desk or perform a service than to toil on an assembly line. Union density has fallen dramatically, and organized labor is so isolated from the larger society that the right-wing characterization of it as a "special interest" prevails unchallenged. Public approval ratings of unions are

at a postwar low, and such new social movements as environmentalism and feminism are as likely to define themselves in opposition to as in alliance with organized labor (if they take any notice of it at all).

What has happened in the postwar decades to produce this change? Part of the story involves structural economic shifts. Most obviously, the manufacturing sector has decreased drastically in importance, accounting for only 20 percent of civilian wage and salary employment in the United States in 1987, compared to 34 percent in 1948.[3] And for complex political as well as economic reasons, unionization has declined even more sharply, especially in manufacturing, its historical stronghold. Although numbers fail to capture the qualitative aspects of this decline, they do indicate its massive scale: in 1989, only 16 percent of all U.S. workers, and 22 percent of those in manufacturing, were union members—half and one-third, respectively, of the 1945 density levels.[4] Alongside these massive processes of deindustrialization and deunionization, the widespread introduction of new technologies and the growing diffusion of the "new" industrial relations, with its emphasis on worker participation, have in recent years dramatically transformed both work and unionism in the manufacturing sector itself.

Few workplaces have been affected by these changes as dramatically as those in the automobile industry, the historical prototype of mass production manufacturing and the core of the U.S. economy for most of this century. Since the mid-1970s, hundreds of thousands of auto workers have been thrown out of work as some factories have closed and others have been modernized. And although the U.A.W. still represents the vast bulk of workers employed by the "Big Three" auto firms (General Motors, Ford, and Chrysler), in recent years the non-union sector of the industry has grown dramatically. Union coverage in the auto parts industry has fallen sharply since the mid-1970s, and the establishment of new Japanese-owned "transplants" in the 1980s has created a non-union beachhead in the otherwise solidly organized assembly sector. Profoundly weakened by these developments, the U.A.W. has gingerly entered a new era of "cooperation" with management, jettisoning many of its time-honored traditions in hopes of securing a place for itself in the future configuration of the industry. Meanwhile, the Big Three have invested vast sums of money in such new technologies as robotics and programmable automation. They have also experimented extensively with worker participation schemes and other organizational changes.

The current situation of auto workers graphically illustrates both the historical legacy of the glory days of American industrial unionism and the consequences of the recent unravelling of the social contract between labor and management that crystallized in the aftermath of World War II. This chapter explores current changes in the nature of work and unionism in the auto industry, drawing on historical evidence and on fieldwork in a recently modernized General Motors (GM) assembly plant in Linden, New Jersey. The analysis focuses particularly on the effects of new technology and the new, participatory forms of management. While it is always hazardous to generalize from any one industry to "the" workplace, the recent history of labor relations in the auto industry is nonetheless suggestive of broader patterns. The auto industry case is also of special interest because it figures so prominently in current theoretical debates about workplace change. . . .

Because so much of the recent behavior of automobile manufacturing managers and of the U.A.W. and its members is rooted in the past, the first step in understanding the current situation is to look back to the early days of the auto industry, when the system of mass production and the accompanying pattern of labor-management relations that is now unravelling first took shape.

Fordism and the History of Labor Relations in the U.S. Auto Industry

The earliest car manufacturers depended heavily on skilled craftsmen to make small production runs of luxury vehicles for the rich. But the industry's transformation into a model of mass production efficiency, led by the Ford Motor Company in the 1910s, was predicated on the systematic removal of skill from the industry's labor process through scientific management, or Taylorism (named for its premier theorist, Frederick Winslow Taylor). Ford perfected a system involving not only deskilling but also product standardization, the use of interchangeable parts, mechanization, a moving assembly line, and high wages. These were the elements of what has since come to be known as "Fordism," and they defined not only the organization of the automobile industry but that of modern mass production generally.

As rationalization and deskilling proceeded through the auto industry in the 1910s and 1920s, the proportion of highly skilled jobs fell dramatically. The introduction of Ford's famous Five Dollar Day in 1914 (then twice the going rate for factory workers) both secured labor's consent to the horrendous working conditions these innovations produced and helped promote the mass consumption that mass production required for its success. Managerial paternalism, symbolized by Ford's "Sociological Department," supplemented high wages in this regime of labor control. Early Ford management also developed job classification systems, ranking jobs by skill levels and so establishing an internal labor market within which workers could hope to advance.

Deskilling was never complete, and some skill differentials persisted among production workers. Even in the 1980s, auto body painters and welders had more skill than workers who simply assembled parts, for example. But these were insignificant gradations compared to the gap between production workers and the privileged stratum of craft workers known in the auto industry as the "skilled trades"—tool and die makers, machinists, electricians, and various other maintenance workers. Nevertheless, the mass of the industry's semiskilled operatives united with the skilled trades elite in the great industrial union drives of the 1930s, and in the U.A.W. both groups were integrated into the same local unions.

The triumph of unionism left the industry's internal division of jobs and skills intact, but the U.A.W. did succeed in narrowing wage differentials among production workers and in institutionalizing seniority (a principle originally introduced by management but enforced erratically in the pre-union era) as the basic criterion for layoffs and job transfers for production workers. For the first decade of the union era, much labor-management conflict focused on the definition of seniority groups. Workers wanted plantwide or departmentwide seniority to maximize employment security, while management sought the narrowest possible seniority classifications to minimize the disruptions associated with workers' movement from job to job. But once the U.A.W. won plantwide seniority for layoffs, it welcomed management's efforts to increase the number of job classifications for transfers, since this maximized opportunities for workers with high seniority to choose the jobs they preferred. By the 1950s, this system of narrowly defined jobs, supported by union and management alike, was firmly entrenched.

Management and labor reached an accommodation on many other issues as well in the immediate aftermath of World War II. But at the same time, the U.A.W. began to retreat from the broad, progressive agenda it had championed in the 1930s and during the war. The failure of the 1945–46 "open the books" strike, in which the union demanded that GM raise workers' wages without increasing car prices, and the national resurgence of conservatism in the late 1940s and 1950s led the U.A.W. into its famous postwar "accord" with management. Under its terms, the union increasingly restricted its goals to improving wages and working conditions for its members, while ceding to management all the prerogatives involved in the production process and in economic planning. The shop steward system in the plants was weakened in the post-war period as well, and in the decades that followed, the U.A.W. was gradually transformed from the highly democratic social movement that *Life* magazine had profiled in 1945 into a more staid, bureaucratic institution that concentrated its energies on the increasingly complex technical issues involved in enforcing its contracts and improving wages, fringe benefits, and job security for its members.

The grueling nature of production work in the auto industry changed relatively little over the postwar decades, even as the U.A.W. continued to extract improvements in the economic terms under which workers agreed to perform it. High wages and excellent benefits made auto workers into the blue-collar aristocrats of the age. It was an overwhelmingly male aristocracy, since women had been largely excluded from auto assembly jobs after World War II; blacks, on the other hand, made up a more substantial part of the auto production work force than of the nation's population. In 1987, at the Linden GM assembly plant where I did my fieldwork, for example, women were 12 percent of the production work force and less than 1 percent of the skilled trades. Linden production workers were a racially diverse group: 61 percent were white, 28 percent were black, and 12 percent were Hispanic; the skilled trades work force, however, was 90 percent white.

While the union did little to ameliorate the actual experience of work in the postwar period, with the job classification system solidified, those committed to a long-term career in the industry could build up enough seniority to bid on the better jobs within their plants. Although the early, management-imposed job classification systems had been based on skill and wage differentials, the union eliminated most of the variation along these dimensions. Indeed, the payment system the U.A.W. won, which persists to this day, is extremely egalitarian. Regardless of seniority or individual merit, assembly workers are paid a fixed hourly rate negotiated for their job classification, and the rate spread across classifications is very narrow. Formal education, which is in any case relatively low (both production workers and skilled trades at Linden GM averaged twelve years of schooling), is virtually irrelevant to earnings. At Linden GM, production workers rates in 1987 ranged from a low of $13.51 per hour for sweepers and janitors to a high of $14.69 for metal repair work in the body shop. Skilled trades workers' hourly rates were only slightly higher, ranging from $15.90 to $16.80 (with a twenty-cent-an-hour "merit spread"), although their annual earnings are much higher than those of production workers because of their extensive overtime.[5]

Since wage differentials are so small, the informal *de facto* hierarchy among production jobs is based instead on what workers themselves perceive as desirable job characteristics. While individual preferences always vary somewhat, the consensus is reflected in the seniority required to secure any given position. One testament to the intensely alienating nature of work on the assembly line is that among the jobs auto workers prefer most are those of sweeper and janitor, even though these jobs have the *lowest* hourly wage rates. Subassembly, inspection, and other jobs where workers could pace themselves rather than be governed by the assembly line are also much sought after. At Linden in 1987, the median seniority of unskilled workers in the material and maintenance departments, which include all the sweepers and janitors and where all jobs are "off the line," was 24 years—twice the median seniority of workers in the assembly departments! By contrast, jobs in particularly hot or dirty parts of the plant, or those in areas where supervision is especially hostile, are shunned by workers whose seniority gives them any choice. Such concerns are far more important to production workers than what have become marginal skill or wage differentials, although there is a group that longs to cross the almost insurmountable barrier between production work and the skilled trades.[6]

Such was the system that emerged from the post–World War II accord between the U.A.W. and management. It functioned reasonably well for the first three postwar decades. The auto companies generated huge profits in these years, and for auto workers, too, the period was one of unprecedented prosperity. Even recessions in this cyclically sensitive industry were cushioned by the supplementary unemployment benefits the union won in 1955. However, in the 1970s, fundamental shifts in the international economy began to undermine the domestic auto makers. As skyrocketing oil prices sent shock waves through the U.S. economy, more and more cars were imported from the economically resurgent nations of Western Europe and, most significantly, Japan. For the first time in their history, the domestic producers faced a serious challenge in their home market.

After initially ignoring these developments, in the 1980s the Big Three began to confront their international competition seriously. They invested heavily in computerization and robotization, building a few new high-tech plants and modernizing most of their existing facilities. GM alone spent more than $40 billion during the 1980s on renovating old plants and building new ones.[7] At the same time, inspired by their Japanese competitors, the auto firms sought to change the terms of their postwar accord with labor, seeking wage concessions from the union, reducing the number of job classifications and related work rules in many plants, and experimenting with new forms of "employee involvement" and worker participation, from quality circles to flexible work teams.

The U.A.W., faced with unprecedented job losses and the threat of more to come, accepted most of these changes in the name of labor-management cooperation. To the union's national leadership, this appeared to be the only viable alternative. They justified it to an often skeptical rank and file membership by arguing that resistance to change would only serve to prevent the domestic industry from becoming internationally competitive, which in turn would mean further job losses. Once it won job security provisions protecting those members affected by technological change, the union welcomed management's investments in technological modernization, which both parties saw as a means of meeting the challenge of foreign competition. Classification mergers and worker participation schemes were more controversial within the union, but the leadership accepted these, too, in the name of enhancing the domestic industry's competitiveness.

Most popular and academic commentators view the innovations in technology and industrial relations that the auto industry (among others) undertook in the 1980s in very positive terms. Some go so far as to suggest that they constitute a fundamental

break with the old Fordist system. New production technologies in particular, it is widely argued, hold forth the promise of eliminating the most boring and dangerous jobs while upgrading the skill levels of those that remain. In this view, new technology potentially offers workers something the U.A.W. was never able to provide, namely, an end to the deadening monotony of repetitive, deskilled work. Similarly, many commentators applaud the introduction of Japanese-style quality circles and other forms of participative management, which they see as a form of work humanization complementing the new technology. By building on workers' own knowledge of the production process, it is argued, participation enhances both efficiency and the quality of work experience. The realities of work in the auto industry, however, have changed far less than this optimistic scenario suggests.

New Technology and the Skill Question

Computer-based technologies are fundamentally different from earlier waves of industrial innovation. Whereas in the past automation involved the use of special-purpose, or "dedicated," machinery to perform specific functions previously done manually, the new information-based technologies are flexible, allowing a single machine to be adapted to a variety of specific tasks. As Shoshana Zuboff points out, these new technologies often require workers to use "intellective" skills. Workers no longer simply manipulate tools and other tangible objects, but also must respond to abstract, electronically presented information. For this reason, Zuboff suggests, computer technology offers the possibility of a radical break with the Taylorist tradition of work organization that industries like auto manufacturing long ago perfected, moving instead toward more skilled and rewarding jobs, and toward workplaces where learning is encouraged and rewarded. "Learning is the new form of labor," she declares.[8] Larry Hirschhorn, another influential commentator on computer technology, makes a similar agreement. As he puts it, in the computerized factory the "deskilling process is reversed. Machines extend workers' skill rather than replace it."[9]

As computer technology has transformed more and more workplaces, claims like these have won widespread public acceptance. They are, in fact, the basis for labor market projections that suggest a declining need for unskilled labor and the need for educational upgrading to produce future generations of workers capable of working in the factory and office of the computer age. Yet it is far from certain that workplaces are actually changing in the ways that Zuboff and Hirschhorn suggest.

The Linden GM plant is a useful case for examining this issue, since it recently underwent dramatic technological change. In 1985–86, GM spent $300 million modernizing the plant, which emerged from this process as one of the nation's most technologically advanced auto assembly facilities and as the most efficient GM plant in the United States. There are now 219 robots in the plant, and 113 automated guided vehicles (AGVs), which carry the car bodies from station to station as they are assembled. Other new technology includes 186 programmable logic controllers (PLCs), used to program the robots. (Before the plant modernization there was only one robot, no AGVs, and eight PLCs.)[10]

Despite this radical technological overhaul, the long-standing division of labor between skilled trades and production workers has been preserved intact. Today, as they did when the plant used traditional technology, Linden's skilled trades workers maintain the plant's machinery and equipment, while production workers perform the un-

skilled and semi-skilled manual work involved in assembling the cars. However, the number of production workers has been drastically reduced (by over 1,100 people, or 26 percent), while the much smaller population of skilled trades workers has risen sharply (by 190 people, or 81 percent). Thus the overall proportion of skilled workers increased—from 5 percent to 11.5 percent—with the introduction of robotics and other computer-based production technologies. In this sense, the plant's modernization did lead to an overall upgrading in skill levels.

However, a closer look at the impact of the technological change on GM-Linden reveals that pre-existing skill differentials among workers have been magnified, leading to skill *polarization* within the plant rather than across-the-board upgrading. After the plant modernization, the skilled trades workers enjoyed massive skill upgrading and gained higher levels of responsibility, just as Zuboff and Hirschhorn would predict. In contrast, however, the much larger group of production workers, whose jobs were already extremely routinized, typically experienced still further deskilling and found themselves subordinated to and controlled by the new technology to an even greater extent than before.

The skilled trades workers had to learn how to maintain and repair the robots, AGVs, and other new equipment, and since the new technology is far more complex than what it replaced, they acquired many new skills. Most skilled trades workers received extensive retraining, especially in robotics and in the use of computers. Linden's skilled trades workers reported an average (median) of forty-eight full days of technical training in connection with the plant modernization, and some received much more. Most of them were enthusiastic about the situation. "They were anxiously awaiting the new technology," one electrician recalled. "It was like a kid with a new toy.

Everyone wanted to know what was going to happen." After the "changeover" (the term Linden workers used for the plant modernization), the skilled trades workers described their work as challenging and intellectually demanding:

> We're responsible for programming the robots, troubleshooting the robots, wiping their noses, cleaning them, whatever. . . . Its interesting work. We're doing something that very few people in the world are doing, troubleshooting and repairing robots. It's terrific! I don't think this can be boring because there are so many things involved. There are things happening right now that we haven't ever seen before. Every day there's something different. We're always learning about the program, always changing things to make them better—every single day. [an electrician]
>
> With high technology, skilled trades people are being forced to learn other people's trades in order to do their trade better. Like with me, I have to understand that controller and how it works in order to make sure the robot will work the way it's supposed to. You have to know the whole system. You can't just say, "I work on that one little gear box, I don't give a damn about what the rest of the machine does." You have to have a knowledge of everything you work with and everything that is related to it, whether you want to or not. You got to know pneumatics, hydraulics—all the trades. Everything is so interrelated and connected. You can't be narrow-minded anymore. [a machine repairman]

However, the situation was quite different for production workers. Their jobs, as had always been the case in the auto industry, continued to involve extremely repetitive, machine-paced, unskilled or semi-

skilled work. Far from being required to learn new skills, many found their jobs were simplified or further deskilled by the new technology:

> It does make it easier to an extent, but also at the same time they figure, "Well, I'm giving you a computer and it's going to make your job faster, so instead of you doing this, this, and this, I'm going to have you do this and eight other things, because the time I'm saving you on the first three you're going to make it up on the last." Right now I'm doing more work in less time, the company's benefiting, and I am bored to death—more bored than before! [a trim department worker with nineteen years seniority]
>
> I'm working in assembly. I'm feeding the line, the right side panel, the whole right side of the car. Myself and a fellow worker, in the same spot. Now all we do, actually, is put pieces in, push the buttons, and what they call a shuttle picks up whatever we put on and takes it down the line to be welded. Before the changeover my job was completely different. I was a torch solderer. And I had to solder the roof, you know, the joint of the roof with the side panel. I could use my head more. I like it more. Because, you know, when you have your mind in it also, it's more interesting. And not too many fellow workers could do the job. You had to be precise, because you had to put only so much material, lead, on the job. [a body shop worker with sixteen years seniority]

Not only were some of the more demanding and relatively skilled traditional production jobs—like soldering, welding, and painting car bodies—automated out of existence, but also many of the relatively desirable off-the-line jobs were eliminated. "Before there were more people working subassembly, assembling parts," one worker recalled. "You have some of the old-timers working on the line right now. Before, if you had more seniority, you were, let's say, off the line, in subassembly."

Even when they operate computers—a rarity for production workers—they typically do so in a highly routinized way. "There is nothing that really takes any skill to operate a computer," one production worker in the final inspection area said. "You just punch in the numbers, the screen will tell you what to do, it will tell you when to race the engine and when to turn the air conditioner off, when to do everything. Everything comes right up on the screen. It's very simple."

The pattern of skill polarization between the skilled trades and production workers that these comments suggest is verified by the findings of an in-plant survey. Skilled trades workers at Linden, asked about the importance of twelve specific on-the-job skills (including "problem solving," "accuracy/precision," "memory," and "reading/spelling") to their jobs before and after the plant was modernized, reported that all but one ("physical strength") increased in importance. In contrast, a survey of the plant's production workers asking about the importance of a similar list of skills found that all twelve declined in importance after the introduction of the new technology. The survey also suggested that boredom levels had increased for production workers; 45 percent stated that their work after the changeover was boring and monotonous "often" or "all the time," compared to 35 percent who had found it boring and monotonous before the changeover. Similarly, 96 percent of production workers said that they now do the same task over and over again "often" or "all the time," up from 79 percent who did so before the changeover.

In the Linden case, the plant modernization had opposite effects on skilled trades and production workers, primarily because no significant job redesign was attempted. The boundary between the two groups and the kinds of work each had traditionally done was maintained, despite the radical technological change. While management might have chosen (and the union might have agreed) to try to transfer some tasks from the skilled trades to production workers, such as minor machine maintenance, or to redesign jobs more extensively in keeping with the potential of the new technology, this was not seriously attempted. Engineers limited their efforts to conventional "line balancing," which simply involves packaging tasks among individual production jobs so as to minimize the idle time of any given worker. In this respect they treated the new technology very much like older forms of machinery. The fundamental division of labor between production workers and the skilled trades persisted despite the massive infusion of new technology, and this organizational continuity led to the intensification of the already existing skill polarization within the plant.

GM-Linden appears to be typical of U.S. auto assembly plants in that new technology has been introduced without jobs having been fundamentally redesigned or the basic division of labor altered between production workers and the skilled trades. Even where significant changes in the division of labor—such as flexible teams—have been introduced, as in the new Japanese transplants, they typically involve rotating workers over a series of conventionally deskilled production jobs, rather than changing the basic nature of the work. While being able to perform eight or ten unskilled jobs rather than only one might be considered skill upgrading in some narrow technical sense, it hardly fits the glowing accounts of commentators who claim that with new technology "the deskilling process is reversed." . . .

Perhaps work in the auto industry *could* be reorganized along the lines Zuboff and Hirschhorn suggest, now that new technology has been introduced so widely. However, a major obstacle to this is bureaucratic inertia on the management side, for which GM in particular is legendary. As many auto industry analysts have pointed out, the firm's investments in new technology were typically seen by management as a "quick fix," throwing vast sums of money at the accelerating crisis of international competitiveness without seriously revamping the firm's organizational structure or its management strategies to make the most efficient possible use of the new equipment. As MaryAnn Keller put it, for GM "the goal of all the technology push has been to get rid of hourly workers. GM thought in terms of automation rather than replacing the current system with a better system."[11] The technology was meant to replace workers, not to transform work.

Reinforcing management's inertia, ironically, was the weakness of the U.A.W. The union has an old, deeply ingrained habit of ceding to management all prerogatives on such matters as job design. And in the 1980s, faced with unprecedented job losses, union concerns about employment security were in the forefront. The U.A.W. concentrated its efforts on minimizing the pain of "downsizing," generally accepting the notion that new technology and other strategies adopted by management were the best way to meet the challenge of increased competition in the industry. After all, if the domestic firms failed to become competitive, U.A.W. members would have no jobs at all. This kind of reasoning, most prominently associated with the U.A.W.'s GM Department director Donald Ephlin, until his retirement in 1989, also smoothed the path for management's efforts to transform the industrial relations system in the direction of in-

creased "employee involvement" and teamwork, to which we now turn.

Worker Participation and the "New Industrial Relations"

Inspired by both the non-union manufacturing sector in the U.S. and by the Japanese system of work organization, the Big Three began to experiment with various worker participation schemes in the 1970s. By the end of the 1980s, virtually every auto assembly plant in the United States had institutionalized some form of participation. Like the new technologies that were introduced in the same period, these organizational innovations—the "new industrial relations"—were a response to the pressure of international competition. And even more than the new technologies, they signaled a historic break with previous industrial practices. For both the Taylorist organization of work in the auto industry and the system of labor relations that developed around it had presumed that the interests of management and those of workers were fundamentally in conflict. In embracing worker participation, however, management abandoned this worldview and redefined its interests as best served by cooperation with labor, its old adversary.

For management, the goal of worker participation is to increase productivity and quality by drawing on workers' own knowledge of the labor process and by increasing their motivation and thus their commitment to the firm. Participation takes many different forms, ranging from suggestion programs, quality circles, and quality-of-work-life (QWL) programs, which actively solicit workers' ideas about how to improve production processes, to "team concept" systems, which organize workers into small groups that rotate jobs and work together to improve productivity and quality on an ongoing basis. All these initiatives promote communication and trust between management and labor, in the name of efficiency and enhanced international competitiveness. Like the new technologies with which they are often associated, the various forms of worker participation have been widely applauded by many commentators who see them as potentially opening up a new era of work humanization and industrial democracy.

In the early 1970s, some U.A.W. officials (most notably Irving Bluestone, then head of the union's GM department) actively supported experimental QWL programs, which they saw as a means for improving the actual experience of work in the auto industry, a long-neglected part of the union's original agenda. But many unionists were more skeptical about participation in the 1980s, when QWL programs and the team concept became increasingly associated with union "give-backs," or concessions. In a dramatic reversal of the logic of the postwar labor-management accord, under which economic benefits were exchanged for unilateral management control over the production process, now economic concessions went hand-in-hand with the promise of worker participation in decision making. However, QWL and the team concept were introduced largely on management's terms in the 1980s, for in sharp contrast to the period immediately after World War II, now the U.A.W. was in a position of unprecedented weakness. In many Big Three plants, participation schemes were forced on workers (often in the face of organized opposition) through what auto industry analysts call "whipsawing," a process whereby management pits local unions against one another by threatening to close the least "cooperative" plants. Partly for this reason, QWL and the team concept have precipitated serious divisions within the union, with Ephlin and other national union leaders who endorse participation facing op-

position from a new generation of union dissidents who view it as a betrayal of the union's membership.

The New United Motor Manufacturing, Inc., plant (NUMMI) in Fremont, California, a joint venture of Toyota and GM, is the focus of much of the recent controversy over worker participation. The plant is run by Toyota, using the team concept and various Japanese management techniques. (GM's responsibility is limited to the marketing side of the operation.) But unlike Toyota's Kentucky plant and the other wholly Japanese-owned transplants, at NUMMI the workers are U.A.W. members. Most of them worked for GM in the same plant before it was closed in 1982. Under GM, the Fremont plant had a reputation for low productivity and frequent wildcat strikes, but when it reopened as NUMMI two years later, with the same work force and even the same local union officers, it became an overnight success story. NUMMI's productivity and quality ratings are comparable to those of Toyota plants in Japan, and higher than any other U.S. auto plant. Efforts to emulate its success further accelerated the push to establish teams in auto plants around the nation.

Many commentators have praised the NUMMI system of work organization as a model of worker participation; yet others have severely criticized it. The system's detractors argue that despite the rhetoric of worker control, the team concept and other participatory schemes are basically strategies to enhance *management* control. Thus Mike Parker and Jane Slaughter suggest that, far from offering a humane alternative to Taylorism, at NUMMI, and at plants that imitate it, workers mainly "participate" in the intensification of their own exploitation, mobilizing their detailed firsthand knowledge of the labor process to help management speed up production and eliminate wasteful work practices. More generally, "whether through team meetings, quality circles, or suggestion plans," Parker and Slaughter argue, "the little influence workers do have over their jobs is that in effect they are organized to time-study themselves in a kind of super-Taylorism."[12] They see the team concept as extremely treacherous, undermining unionism in the name of a dubious form of participation in management decisions.

Workers themselves, however, seem to find intrinsically appealing the idea of participating in what historically have been exclusively managerial decision-making processes, especially in comparison to traditional American managerial methods. This is the case even though participation typically is limited to an extremely restricted arena, such as helping to streamline the production process or otherwise raise productivity. Even Parker and Slaughter acknowledge that at NUMMI, "nobody says they want to return to the days when GM ran the plant."[13] Unless one wants to believe that auto workers are simply dupes of managerial manipulation, NUMMI's enormous popularity with the work force suggests that the new industrial relations have some positive features and cannot simply be dismissed as the latest form of labor control.

Evidence from the GM-Linden case confirms the appeal of participation to workers, although reforms in labor relations there were much more limited than at NUMMI. Linden still has over eighty populated job classifications, and although 72 percent of the production workers are concentrated in only eight of them, this is quite different from NUMMI, where there is only one job classification for production workers and seniority plays a very limited role. Nor has Linden adopted the team system. However, when the plant reopened after its 1985–86 modernization, among its official goals was to improve communications between labor and management, and both parties embraced "jointness" as a principle of decision

making. At the same time, "employee involvement groups" (EIGs) were established. Production workers were welcomed back to the plant after the changeover with a jointly (union-management) developed two-week (eighty-hour) training program, in the course of which they were promised that the "new Linden" would be totally different from the plant they had known before. In particular, workers were led to expect an improved relationship with management, and a larger role in decision making and problem solving on the shop floor.[14]

Most workers were extremely enthusiastic about these ideas—at least initially. The problem was that after the eighty-hour training program was over, when everyone was back at work, the daily reality of plant life failed to live up to the promises about the "new Linden." "It's sort of like going to college," one worker commented about the training program. "You learn one thing, and then you go into the real world. . . . " Another agreed:

> It sounded good at the time, but it turned out to be a big joke. Management's attitude is still the same. It hasn't changed at all. Foremen who treated you like a fellow human being are still the same—no problems with them. The ones who were arrogant bastards are still the same, with the exception of a few who are a little bit scared, a little bit afraid that it might go to the top man, and, you know, make some trouble. Everyone has pretty much the same attitude.

Indeed, the biggest problem was at the level of first-line supervision. While upper management may have been convinced that workers should have more input into decision making, middle and lower management (who also went through a training program) did not always share this view. Indeed, after the training raised workers' expectations, foremen in the plant, faced with the usual pressures to get production out, seemed to quickly fall back into their old habits. The much-touted "new Linden" thus turned out to be all too familiar. As the workers pointed out:

> You still have the management that has the mentality of the top-down, like they're right, they don't listen to the exchange from the workers, like the old school. So that's why when you ask about the "new Linden," people say it's a farce, because you still . . . do not feel mutual respect, you feel the big thing is to get the jobs out. This is a manufacturing plant; they do have to produce. But you can't just tell this worker, you know, take me upstairs [where the training classes were held], give me this big hype, and then bring me downstairs and then have the same kind of attitude.
>
> With management, they don't have the security that we have. Because if a foreman doesn't do his job, he can be replaced tomorrow, and he's got nobody to back him up. So everybody's a little afraid of their jobs. So if you have a problem, you complain to your foreman, he tries to take care of it without bringing it to his general foreman; or the general foreman, he don't want to bring it to his superintendent, because neither of them can control it. So they all try to keep it down, low level, and under the rug, and "Don't bother me about it—just fix it and let it slide." And that is not the teachings that we went through in that eighty-hour [training] course!

Many Linden workers expressed similar cynicism about the EIGs. "A lot of people feel very little comes out of the meetings. It's just to pacify you so you don't write up grievances," one paint department worker said, articulating a widespread sentiment. "It's a half-hour's pay for sitting there and eating your lunch," he added.

Research on other U.S. auto assembly plants suggests that Linden, where the rhetoric of participation was introduced without much substantive change in the quality of the labor-management relationship, is a more representative case than NUMMI, where participation (whatever its limits) is by all accounts more genuine. Reports from Big Three plants around the nation suggest that typical complaints concern not the *concept* of participation—which workers generally endorse—but management's failure to live up to its own stated principles. Gerald Horton, a worker at GM's Wentzville, Missouri, plant "thinks the team concept is a good idea if only management would abide by it." Similarly, Dan Maurin of GM's Shreveport, Louisiana, plant observes, "it makes people resentful when they preach participative management and then come in and say, 'this is how we do it.' "[15] Betty Foote, who works at a Ford truck plant outside Detroit, expressed the sentiments of many auto workers about Employee Involvement (EI): "The supposed concern for workers' happiness now with the EI program is a real joke. It looks good on paper, but it is not effective. . . . Relations between workers and management haven't changed."[16]

At NUMMI, workers view participation far more positively. Critics of the team concept suggest that this is because workers there experienced a "significant emotional event" and suffered economically after GM closed the plant, so that when they were recalled to NUMMI a few years later they gratefully accepted the new system without complaint. But, given the uncertainty of employment and the history of chronic layoffs throughout the auto industry, that this would sharply distinguish NUMMI's workers from those in other plants seems unlikely. Such an explanation for the positive reception of the team concept by NUMMI workers is also dubious in light of the fact that even the opposition caucus in the local union, which criticizes the local U.A.W. officials for being insufficiently militant in representing the rank and file, explicitly supports the team concept.

Instead, the key difference between NUMMI and the Big Three assembly plants may be that workers have *more* job security at NUMMI, where the Japanese management has evidently succeeded in building a high-trust relationship with workers. When the plant reopened, NUMMI workers were guaranteed no layoffs unless management first took a pay cut; this promise and many others have (so far) been kept, despite slow sales. In contrast, the Big Three (and especially GM) routinely enrage workers by announcing layoffs and then announcing executive pay raises a few days later; while at the plant level, as we have seen, management frequently fails to live up to its rhetorical commitments to participation. On the one hand, this explains why NUMMI workers are so much more enthusiastic about participation than their counterparts in other plants. On the other hand, where teamwork and other participatory schemes have been forced on workers through "whipsawing," the result has been a dismal failure on its own terms. Indeed, one study found a negative correlation between the existence of participation programs and productivity.

Insofar as the U.A.W. has associated itself with such arrangements, it loses legitimacy with the rank and file when management's promises are not fulfilled. Successful participation systems, however, can help strengthen unionism. It is striking that at NUMMI, with its sterling productivity and quality record, high management credibility, and relatively strong job security provisions, the U.A.W. is stronger than in most Big Three plants. For that matter, the local union at NUMMI has more influence than do enterprise unions in Japanese auto plants, where teamwork systems are long-standing. But here, as in so many other ways, NUMMI

is the exceptional case. In most U.S. auto plants, the weakness of the U.A.W.—in the face of industry overcapacity and capital's enhanced ability to shift production around the globe—has combined with management's inability to transform its own ranks to undermine the promise of participation.

NOTES

1. "U.A.W.: World's Largest Union Is Facing Troubled Times," *Life,* 19 (September 10, 1945): 103–11.

2. . . . [T]he quote is from Nelson Lichtenstein, "From Corporatism to Collective Bargaining: Organized Labor and the Eclipse of Social Democracy in the Postwar Era," in *The Rise and Fall of the New Deal Order, 1930–1980,* ed. Steve Fraser and Gary Gerstle (Princeton, N.J.: Princeton University Press, 1989), 126.

3. These figures are for private sector manufacturing wage and salary workers as a proportion of all employed civilian wage and salary workers, and are computed from U.S. Bureau of Labor Statistics, *Labor Force Statistics Derived from the Current Population Survey, 1948–87,* Bulletin No. 2307 (Washington, D.C.: Government Printing Office, 1988), 383, 386.

4. Figures for 1989 are from U.S. Bureau of Labor Statistics, *Employment and Earnings* 37 (January 1990): 231–32. Enumeration methods are different from those used in 1945 (see note 2 for sources for 1945 data), so that the figures are not strictly comparable; yet there can be no doubt as to the magnitude and direction of the change.

5. *1987 Agreement between Chevrolet—Pontiac—GM of Canada, Linden Plant, General Motors Corporation and Local No. 595, United Auto Workers, Region 9* (privately published), 37–42.

6. Author's field interviews with GM workers in Linden, New Jersey.

7. Maryann Keller, *Rude Awakening: The Rise, Fall and Struggle for Recovery of General Motors* (New York: William Morrow, 1989), 204.

8. Shoshana Zuboff, *In the Age of the Smart Machine: The Future of Work and Power* (New York: Basic Books, 1988), 395.

9. Larry Hirschhorn, *Beyond Mechanization: Work and Technology in a Postindustrial Age* (Cambridge, Mass.: MIT Press, 1984), 97.

10. Data supplied by local management. The finding that Linden is the most efficient GM plant in the United States is from *The Harbour Report*, 139.

11. Keller quoted in Amal Nag, "Tricky Technology: Auto Makers Discover 'Factory of the Future' Is Headache Just Now," *Wall Street Journal* (May 13, 1986), 1.

12. Parker and Slaughter, *Choosing Sides*, 19.

13. Parker and Slaughter, *Choosing Sides*, 111.

14. The data on job classification are computed from rosters supplied by local management.

Other information is from the author's fieldwork. The quotes in the paragraphs that follow are from interviews with Linden workers.

15. Horton quoted in Peter Downs, "Wentzville: Strangest Job Training Ever," in Parker and Slaughter, Choosing Sides, 190; Maurin quoted in Choosing Sides, 130.

16. Foote quoted in Richard Feldman and Michael Betzold, *End of the Line: Autoworkers and the American Dream* (New York: Weidenfeld & Nicolson, 1988), 178–79.

14

The Electronic Sweatshop
How Computers Are Transforming the Office of the Future into the Factory of the Past

Barbara Garson

Barbara Garson is a playwright and author of books, stories, and essays. This reading is from her 1988 book, *The Electronic Sweatshop*.

People will adapt nicely to office systems if their arms are broken. We're in the twisting stage now.

WILLIAM F. LAUGHLIN
VICE PRESIDENT, IBM, 1975[1]

If you think a secretary without a boss is sad, you should see a boss without a secretary.

MARY L. _____
TYPIST, PROCTER & GAMBLE, 1985[2]

Front-Office Automation

During the most dynamic phases of the industrial revolution, vast enterprises were managed by their owners with the help of one or two clerks. In Victorian fiction "clerk," "bookkeeper" or "chief clerk" was the position to which a poor but diligent factory lad might rise—and then, of course, marry the boss's daughter.

In the small, family-style offices of that period, prudent supervision might simply mean watching over the clerk's shoulder from time to time. Standardization could be achieved by saying, "Here, do it my way." While factory workers were rigidly controlled, office workers were still basically independent or autonomous within their own spheres of responsibility.

But by the late nineteenth century, operations like payroll and billing had come to employ a significant amount of labor in manufacturing companies. Furthermore, there were now large institutions like banks and insurance companies whose entire function was keeping track of money and whose entire staff was clerical.

Eventually separate departments were created to handle the routine, repetitive tasks connected with payroll, billing, shipping, inventory control and so on. Staffed mostly by women whose status became more like that of clerks in the modern sense, these units were large enough to attract efficiency experts in earnest. Turn-of-the-century time-and-motion studies calculated by the tenth of a second how long it took to open envelopes, how long it took to close file drawers and even how long it took ink to dry. Office typewriters came equipped with mechanical meters that counted keystrokes. (Smart typists soon learned to raise their keystroke count by indenting paragraphs with five strokes of the space bar rather than one stroke of the tab key.)

Usually, these bookkeeping or operations departments were located in the back of the office, away from visitors and windows. Eventually, they became separate back offices with supervisors and managers of their own.

But the real managers, the real bosses, stayed in what became known as the front office—later called the corporate, executive or administrative office. The front office is the place where company policy is made and disseminated to all the other departments. It's the place where receptionists and secretaries interact with executives. It's the generic office my mother envisaged when she told me that a young lady should work in an office, not a factory.

By the time computers were introduced, the back office was thoroughly industrialized (and, in my opinion, one of the worst places to work).[3] Computers may have added physical discomforts—at first the noise of keypunch machines, later the glare of screens—but they didn't suddenly transform an office into a factory. In the back office, computers merely mechanized work that was already organized on the factory model.

Computers came to the front office, however, at the very moment that executives were (and are) beginning to be industrialized. Frankly, I'm surprised it took this long to begin industrializing the front office. Administrative offices had become enormous before corporations got serious about standardizing the work of managers and executives. But some time in the seventies it began to happen. As Harry Braverman noted in 1974 in his book *Labor and Monopoly Capital,* "There is ample evidence . . . that management is now nerving itself for major surgery upon its own lower limbs."[4]

Because this is happening at the same time that computers are being introduced, front-office automation is bound to look confusing. It's even more confusing because its most important goals are deliberately obscured.

When computers are set down in the front office, their valuable word- and number-juggling features are used to camouflage their monitoring functions. Nonspecific communication needs are used to justify reorganizations that undermine old social relationships and impose new controls. The artifice or caution used to introduce these changes suggests that top managers still feel a bit squeamish about operating "on their own lower limbs."

Nevertheless, the operation has begun. If word processing were merely about processing words, its introduction wouldn't be much more complicated than the introduction of electric typewriters. What we're about to see goes far beyond the installation of a new machine. . . .

In 1981 I wrote an article that was published in *Mother Jones* magazine about office automation and got the following response from Lucille Schmidt in Cincinnati.

Lucille Schmidt

Your article ["The Electronic Sweatshop"] was very powerful and, unfortunately, very true.

I have been employed with The Proctor & Gamble Company for 13 years now. Four years ago I was promoted from secretary to manager. About that time, our Division brought in Word Processing equipment. All the secretaries and quite a few of us managers were very interested in the new technology and eager to utilize it to streamline the work. But then something very strange happened.

There was a reorganization. . . all secretaries and clerks now became part of an organization called Administrative Services. . . .

One of the first visible signs that Administrative Services had arrived was the removal of the Executive Secretaries from the offices they had shared with their male bosses. No longer would there be 1:1 relationships as this did not "meet the needs of the business." All secretaries regardless of status, experience or rank were now "equal" and shared an office or "work center" with two or three others. They were given new job descriptions. Women whose typing was considered excellent became Information Processors and typed eight hours a day. Others were Support Secretaries. They were told they must learn to work as a team. . . . If there were conflicts involving workload or personality, they were given "feedback" in their

Performance Evaluation that they didn't understand the team concept. . . .

Secretaries were transferred from one job to another, from one location to another, with little warning and no prior discussion. This was called career planning. Questions were not tolerated: those who questioned any aspect of the system were "resistant to change."

A monthly newsletter extolled the virtues of the new system. "Production reports" displayed the weekly output—pages typed. There were team meetings, not to discuss the work or how to effectively get it done, but to learn the "team concept.". . . Administrative Services was the office of the future . . . improving productivity for managers and providing a challenging and rewarding work life for the secretaries and clerks.

Absenteeism and tardiness skyrocketed . . . There were disabilities, "stress related," as indicated on the medical reports. Many resigned. There were some early retirements. Requests for transfers to another Division were refused. They were told to "make the system work."

. . . Cost reduction reports "proved" the many thousands of dollars being saved.

[Lucille Schmidt was asked repeatedly to become a manager in Administrative Services, the new bureaucracy that provided clerical support for almost 3,000 engineers. But Lucille was already a manager. She didn't think of supervising secretaries as a step up.]

After all, my position as Personnel Manager provided regular interaction with the Paper hierarchy. [At Procter & Gamble there's a soup hierarchy, a soap hierarchy, a cosmetics hierarchy and so on.] I represented our division at various meetings at Corporate headquarters, I was respected for my technical and interpersonal skills and had well-established credibility. . . . For two years I was able to resist a transfer to Administrative Services. Then I was told it's this or the front door—there was no option.

I am now an Administrative Supervisor.

I am to take attendance (I forego the "bedcheck"), report any absence or overtime and arrange for LOs [Temps are called Low Overheads at Procter & Gamble] to cover any planned or unplanned absences. I am to provide a "joining up" plan for personnel new to my area. I am to give written performance evaluations and provide action steps for further "growth." I am to hand out the 3 × 5 cards notifying of a salary increase. I am to call meetings to share (read) organizational announcements . . .

Of course I know why I was transferred here. . . . Few positions in Personnel carry much responsibility and much authority. I held such a position but I am female, a former secretary, and my father's collar is blue. Now I am a leader of secretaries, all female, in an organization of female secretaries. Now I am "back" in my proper "place" and I can grow and progress all the hell I want. . . .

[Despite excellent benefits and seniority at Procter & Gamble, Lucille was thinking about leaving the company.]

I will probably have to relocate to another part of the U.S., but I'm angry and scared and starting to get bitter here and that's not healthy. . . .

Your article showed only the tip of an ever-growing iceberg. . . .

Four years later I phoned Lucille in Cincinnati. By then she'd left Procter & Gamble, taking a $10,000 pay cut—"Though I'm almost up to my old salary again"—to run the office of a small investment company.

Over the phone I didn't sense that knot of anguish in the throat that I could practically hear in her letter. "For a while there," she acknowledged, "I was getting to be the kind of person I don't like to be around. But now I work with three intelligent men, they respect me, they let me learn everything I can about the business. In fact, I'm going out later to shop for a word processing system to put on my own desk.

"At Procter, they give you a new machine and this somehow makes you 'a different kind of resource.'. . . Oh, Barbara, it's such a waste—such a waste of people. The way they put in word processing there, you had a lot of smart women getting dumb very fast."

At Procter & Gamble the Division Heads had been free to make certain choices about office automation. The system Lucille described was established in the Engineering Division in 1978 after the Director of Engineering read about word processing on an airplane and decided right then, "60,000 feet in the air" so the story goes, to try it out at once. Engineering, located on the outskirts of town a good distance from the new corporate headquarters, was known as a technically experimental and bureaucratically informal part of the company.

An automation team was formed. The team visited an IBM center and selected the IBM OS6 to be used in small work centers. (Later the IBMs were gradually replaced with Wangs. But the system remained the same.)

Lucille encouraged me to visit Cincinnati and see what the six-year experiment with word processing had wrought.

"Matter of fact, I've got a luncheon date this week with a couple of secretaries I used to supervise. I bet they'd love to talk to you. And I'll get you the extensions of some managers—some ADs and Ds (Associate Directors and Directors)—and a section head in Soup."

"In the soup department?" I tried to get it straight.

"No," Lucille corrected me, "not the Soup Division, Soup Engineering. Anyway, he's now in the Management Systems Division. I know it's confusing. I'll print up a road map of the company hierarchy. You'll need it to get around. . . ."

Procter & Gamble is among the top 50 of the "*Fortune* 500" and the largest advertiser in the world. The company was formed in 1837 when two brothers-in-law, James Gamble, a soap maker, and William Procter, a candlemaker, merged their businesses. By the Civil War they were the largest firm in Cincinnati. They supplied soap and candles to the Union army.

Though the presidency went out of the family in 1930, Procter & Gamble still has a family or paternal atmosphere. The company has a reputation as a decent employer. Among reporters, the company has a reputation for being secretive. It's difficult to interview anyone at P&G. The company prefers to get its messages across through paid advertising and well prepared public relations releases.

But Lucille knew many employees, and I arrived in Cincinnati with a few contacts of my own. Procter & Gamble employs over 20,000 people in Cincinnati, over 60,000 worldwide. So almost everyone who has ever lived in the city of seven hills has a cousin or a high school sweetheart who still works for P&G.

Lucille found that quite a few of the secretaries she knew had quit or been given outplacement in the two years since she herself left. I wasn't surprised, since one goal of the IBM system is to reduce the ratio of support staff to principals. But I soon found that a surprising number of principals in the Engineering Division were gone too. Many of the men I called from both my own list and from Lucille's were "no longer employed."

Those I managed to reach were either too busy to be interviewed or not sure they should be. But everyone had time for a caustic laugh when I mentioned that my subject was Administrative Services. Some of the men referred me to former associates who, they suspected, "might have more time to talk" now that they weren't with the company. One of those was Tom Oppdahl.

Tom Oppdahl

Tom Oppdahl had supervised a unit of over 100 engineers before his "early retirement." His fellow managers liked him and were gratified to tell me that he now had a good job—maybe even a better one—in Dayton.

I arranged to meet Oppdahl in Dayton, at the end of his work day. I could interview him in his car on the way home. (His new job entailed a long commute.) I felt embarrassed about questioning a fifty-five-year-old displaced engineer, a man who had commanded a group of 100 professionals at P&G and now worked in a small job shop over a clothing store.

But in Dayton I found Oppdahl well ensconced as Vice President for Engineering of a small but long-established job shop that even did a little design work for Procter & Gamble. "That didn't come through me," Tom made clear. "They had the contract already."

Tom's chief concern was modernizing the shop, which meant finding and training employees to use computer-aided design (CAD) systems. He was glad to answer my questions about CAD and good at explaining it.

It was harder for him to talk about his early retirement from Procter & Gamble. It's not that he was ashamed of being displaced. It's more that he was uncomfortable expressing anything that sounded like a personal feeling or a complaint. It's as if he wasn't entitled. But eventually I got the story from Tom, his wife, and his daughter.

Oppdahl had been overseeing an engineering project in California when rumors drifted West about accelerated attrition in the home office. Then, after more than twenty two years, Tom got his first less-than-superior rating. He was surprised and hurt, but he accepted it as a normal evaluation. It took his wife to point out that Procter might be preparing the ground for firing him. A poor rating could help protect the firm from an age discrimination suit. Tom confronted the company directly (he was proud of that) and learned that they were only waiting for his fifty-fifth birthday. For the sake of the early retirement benefits (there were still two more boys to put through college), he stuck it out for a year and a half while looking for a new job.

"That must have been a difficult year and a half," I said.

"A couple of my friends died in the process. Fortunately I had already had my heart attack."

Tom had been the head of a section that published P&G's internal engineering manuals, built industrial models of their manufacturing plants and designed the thermal systems—boilers, air conditioning, and sprinklers—for all P&G plants worldwide.

"I had three key subordinates, each of them had about thirty, thirty-five engineers. But I was stretched too darn far. I had more going on than I could keep track of.

"Then, before Administrative Services, I got a young secretary, right out of high school. She was a darn smart and aggressive person. She and I sat down and made an outline of the things that had to be done and I said, 'Erin, I want you to take all the administrative tasks that you can and let me focus on the engineering.'

"It was fabulous. . . . She handled reports, sending them out wherever they needed to go; personnel, if a person needed

to move from this building to that she'd handle the paperwork, get all the corporate approvals; travel arrangements, you just tell her where you wanted to go, what meetings you needed to attend, she'd work out the flights, the hotels. It didn't take long before I could describe the intent of a nontechnical letter and she could compose and sign it herself or prepare it for my signature.

"The bottom line is that our team approach increased my productivity at least 50 percent, possibly doubled it. She was so good that I lost her. She got promoted to another organization in P&G. I think she's still classified as a secretary over there but with a level of pay I couldn't command.

"After Erin left, I was loaned out by P&G to another corporation to supervise an engineering project. So I didn't experience the first six months of Administrative Services. I was 'off campus,' so to speak, the day it was announced. I missed the day when your personal secretary couldn't talk to you anymore.

"Actually, there was never a time when a secretary couldn't talk to her former boss. But there were secretaries who chose not to talk to their former bosses, the kind of bosses who had abused them. There were also some secretaries who I did not then, nor do I now, respect, who used Administrative Services as an excuse to say 'I can't do that,' or 'I don't take dictation; use the telephone,' or 'You have to fill out the form before I can get your airplane tickets.' There were two causes for that type of behavior, either she was lazy or she resented the bastard."

"But no," I rushed to defend the women, "they were not supposed to serve as personal secretaries anymore. One typist told me about lectures from the head of Admin. Services, like sermons she said, 'The one-to-one relationship is the office of the past: in the office of the future we will move forward into. . . .' "

"True," Tom stopped me, "but some of them took it to the extreme."

"Did you feel personally demoted," I asked, "when a typist said, 'You'll have to fill out a form,' or 'I'm sorry but I don't take dictation'?"

"Demoted?" He played thoughtfully with the concept. "No, I did not feel demoted. I felt that I had lost a quality of service and I resented that.

"Well . . . ," he thought some more, "in one respect I was demoted. I was demoted in that I had to do more things for myself.

"A letter had to be transcribed by a voice telephone and done by a pool of people you didn't see. Everything was in order of the queue. If it was an emergency you handed it in Monday, it went into the queue and you would get it back Wednesday. And if you needed a correction it would go back in the queue. To make changes or small corrections was extremely time consuming."

And the whole beauty of the word processor is the quick way you can make little changes, I thought. How profoundly perverse—it hadn't hit me this clearly before—to take the miraculous typewriter that could make changes in an instant and set it up so an executive has to fill out a form and wait hours (or even days) for the new version to come back from the pool. Just filling out the form takes longer than making most corrections.

The second great advantage of a word processor is that it specifically eliminates routine retyping. This should leave people freer to do more varied work. Yet the work center system creates a huge caste of people who do nothing but type.

So a rigid, regulating schema had negated the two main advantages of this wonderful, flexible machine.

"Travel arrangements," Tom continued. "You'd have to fill out a form saying when you wanted to leave. They even had on it, 'What flight do you want to take and what hotel?' So you had to go to the travel guide and look that up yourself. If you didn't fill in those details, you couldn't predict the arrangements you'd get back. Like you could have a plane that left at an inconvenient time. Or you could get a plane that left Florida just when you asked, but it terminated in Atlanta and you'd catch the next leg the next day. Your hotel could be an hour from where you had to work. Common sense and judgment seemed to disappear."

"What did you do if you had to get a report out fast?" I asked.

"Sometimes it didn't get out. Really your performance depended on the friendships you could make and how much you could get done unofficially. You'd try to use the system and not abuse friendships. But where you had a critical situation, friendship was the only thing that made it happen."

"If it depended on friendship," I suggested "there must have been some men who could never get anything done."

"Yup," he laughed, "and they deserved it. There is some justice.

"But if you were on good terms with a secretary you could walk over and hand something to her and say, 'Could you make those changes? I need it today.' And you'd have it promptly. But if it was one of the malingerers she'd cover up with all the bureaucratic answers why it couldn't be done and how you couldn't get it till 2 o'clock and if you don't like it, go talk to my boss."

"Weren't the supervisors supposed to keep the manager away from the typist?" I asked. "I'm surprised they let you go directly to her desk."

"Early on, some supervisors tried to say, 'You can't come in here and talk to her.' But then what happened was *they* became the mailman. The support secretary had twenty or more people to support. So they'd let you deliver your own.

"The real way they kept the principal away from the typist was to put your typist down four floors and in a corner. You'd ask someone for a change and she'd say, 'Gee I don't have that document on my Wang. It's on a different system.'

"Eventually I got proficient on the word processor myself. That's how I finally got the best out of the system. What I'd do was make a rough draft of my letters on the terminal as quickly as I could have dictated them. Then I'd use the Administrative Services secretary to call up the document, format it, correct the spelling and tell me when she was finished. After that I'd call it up on my terminal, do the editing and instruct her when it was to be printed. Writing directly on the computer like that was the best system, better than dictating on tape or telephone, better than hand-written copy. I was the only manager I know that had a terminal in my office."

"How'd you get it?" I asked.

"A little bit of pulling strings, a little bit of authority."

"And how did you get the typist to call up your document quickly? Didn't she still say it had to go in the queue?"

"I was sharing her workload by typing the first draft, so she was more cooperative. And even though it was via machine, she would know who she was doing it for. It was personal. I could thank her.

"You see," Tom explained, "in theory you can be more efficient if you just handle the mail, or you just make reservations, or you just type. But they made the typists do just one thing and then took away the accountability. They weren't working for anyone."

"They were accountable to Administrative Services," I said.

"Their bosses in Administrative Services had them accountable by how many pages they did but not what pages or how well. I'd rather have a letter on time with a couple of typos that can be corrected with Wite-Out than a perfect letter two days late.

They were judged by errors per page or typeovers per line, not on responsiveness to the needs of the business.

"Under Administrative Services," Oppdahl summed up, "I went from 150 percent efficiency down to less than 100 percent because I was doing secretarial functions just to get things done. It's inefficient. You had $30,000–$40,000 engineers doing what a $15,000 secretary could do better if she had the motivation or the permission to do it. It was just inefficient."

"But Ivan [the head of Administrative Services] told me," I said, becoming devil's advocate, "that Administrative Services cut the ratio of support staff to principals by 30 to 40 percent where there was no resistance."

"IBM and Wang and idiots like Ivan are selling the computer, so they redesign the office to match the machine instead of vice versa."

"They say their system offers a countable and a predictable output," I continued.

"What's countable may not be what counts. The bean counters can count the keystrokes but the intangibles get lost. I take that back; it's not only intangibles they miss. They measure the easily measurable things, but they can't even differentiate between a typo and a mistake that makes the letter nonsense.

"The department was bloated, so yes," Tom declared, "there was a need for efficiency. But they answered the need with a corrupt system. They needed transportation, so they went out and bought a camel."

Sophia Crandall

The majority of Procter & Gamble secretaries felt demoted or exiled when they were moved into work centers. But to Sophia Crandall, the separation of the secretary and the boss promised a kind of liberation.

Mrs. Crandall had been a certified executive secretary when word processing was first considered in the Engineering Department. She was part of the original team that visited the IBM center and selected the IBM OS6.

With the start-up of Administrative Services she became a group leader. In the P&G hierarchy that was only one rank below Tom Oppdahl. She outranked most of the men that her group of clericals supported.

Even the engineers who most resented Administrative Services respected Sophia Crandall's skill and honesty. "She'd probably be willing to talk to you," I was advised by an executive who declined to be interviewed himself, "because she doesn't owe her position to any clique at Procter."

Sophia was a tall woman of sixty with tight gray ringlets. She had a large jaw and thick-rimmed glasses. But bubbles of wit rising to the surface kept threatening to subvert her severe demeanor. She looked like Lily Tomlin playing my second-grade teacher.

At her home after work she gave me a formal history of Administrative Services.

"In the beginning," she acknowledged, "there was a lot of trauma for the managers. We started out with a survey trying to get them to write down what they did over a month's time. We asked them what support work they needed. We didn't realize that a lot of managers don't know what a secretary does. They have no idea what reports flow through their office.

"Some of them could understand the benefits to them of the increased productivity in word processing. But there were other needs. I call them the ego needs. The people who think of their secretary as a fixture or a perk to do personal-type things. Those were the people who tried to undermine the system. Those were the ones who would fuss or complain about any minor thing. And who

tried to get the support staff to do personal-type things without the other managers knowing about it."

"What kind of personal things?"

"To run and get stamps if they brought their bills in to be mailed. To run from one building to another for a personal stamp. Or to make tennis appointments. One manager had this large tennis club and used secretarial support to line up the tennis games and to type up the league's schedule. A lot of personal letters, too.

"One man," Sophia remembered, "his secretary had always baked a birthday cake for him. He bragged about her baking skills to the other managers. But his secretary had been transferred into a work center. As a part of our survey of support needs we never took down his birthday or arranged a cake. When it came to the birthday he kept coming out of the office looking, but there was no cake. (He wasn't the kind of man you'd bake a cake for unless he was your boss.) That was the kind of issue."

"But weren't there real trade-offs under the old system?" I asked. "I mean, you typed his personal letters and he let you make personal phone calls; you typed his kid's term paper, he let you leave early on a school holiday."

"But the trade-off was never money."

I'd never heard it stated that simply.

"He could brag that his secretary was the best baker, but the number of times you took things back to the store, or the number of personal letters you typed or the number of cups of coffee won't get you a raise in a large company. A secretary may be quite appreciated by her boss, but when it comes to advancement . . ."

"What about praise?" I asked. "That's not money, but I talked to one Information Processor who complained about typing all day and then, she said, 'You do a big project with complicated charts, lots of tabs, you type all day then the support secretary carries it back and gets the credit. You don't hear anyone say, 'That's a good job.' "

"That is accurate," Sophia said. "And that is one of the things that made us evolve the system back to combined roles [the sharing of administrative support and word processing]. The information processor didn't get to hear the praise.

"But for a lot of people," Sophia said disapprovingly, "the problem of praise is still the separation from the man. If I tell them, as a woman, they've done a good job, it's not received as much. Really, it depends on the level of their own confidence. The best secretaries, they knew themselves when they'd done a good job. They knew how to recognize it. A few still had to go back and hear it from a man." She brooded over these weak sisters.

"Wasn't that another problem?" I asked. "Didn't the secretaries keep running back to their old bosses, and the bosses to their old secretaries?"

"More the managers," she said, "the older managers. A lot of secretaries wanted change.

"There was a problem at first because we had not done much assertiveness training to help them deal better with the managers hanging around their desks expecting them to do this or find that."

"Assertiveness training?"

"Oh yes. We had a number of formal assertiveness training sessions to help them explain to the men that their work load did not allow them to go get stamps. We practiced with role playing."

I pressed for examples.

"If he stands over you, 'Just make this change please,' you say, 'You make me nervous standing there. I'll be glad to make your change and return it to you.' The women had to practice to be able to say 'The work will get done in order. You won't get it any faster by standing there.' "

"One man claimed," I said to Sophia, "that some women were just waiting for the chance to say no to the men, especially the ones who had had abusive bosses before."

"For some," she acknowledged, "as they did the role playing they got a new . . . uh . . . perspective and they would be anxious to go back and put it into practice. It really all hinged on the male-female dynamics.

"One manager came into my office storming because a woman had told him she couldn't do something. He said, 'I have never been told no by any woman!' I thought, 'At your age it's about time some woman told you no. '

"We had one male information processor and he never had near the same problem with managers trying their games on him. He did not need assertiveness training. . . .

"A lot of the complaints about Administrative Services," Sophia drew herself up to make a controversial point, "a lot of the complaints were because a female organization held a bit of power for once.

"One of the things certain managers did to test us at the beginning was to put everything in as rush to see what the system could handle. That was one of their underhanded ways of doing it."

Sophia had to recapitulate the history of Administrative Services' monitoring attempts in order to explain the method that evolved to counter these artificial rushes.

"At start-up we had the operators fill out daily production reports. Most of the information they could take right off the machine. The computer would tell them how many pages they typed. There was a systems manager at the beginning," she remembered, "who was pushing for us to count everything. He wanted us to measure the lines of type with a special ruler. Some areas did it but I said 'No, I won't do that.' I refused. But in regard to the rushes, we did ask the women to keep sheets on. . . ."

"Why did you refuse to measure lines?" I interrupted her train of thought.

"I always felt strongly, it's one of P&G's beliefs, that the human resource is a valuable asset of the company. Our staff were very honest. I was not going to measure what they did with a ruler.

"But they were asked to keep a sheet on the rushed pages and the author of those rush documents. If you found a manager who had 75 percent rush work, then you asked some questions about it. 'Does this say you're not so organized as you need to be? We could help you with that.' "

Sophia Crandall had refused to make the typists measure their own lines but she insisted on keeping track of the managers' production, at least in regard to rushed pages.

"Could anything else on these clerical productivity reports be used to evaluate the managers?" I asked. "Did *their* superiors ever ask to see them?"

"If someone is going to write a document and he has to keep revising it ten, eleven times before you can send it out, then yes, someone at the higher level could ask for that kind of information. Our daily productivity report included the number of rushes, the number of draft pages, the number of revisions and whether the revisions were due to managers' changes or our errors. Yes, some of the higher executives did feel we could give them some information on their staff, that we could have an input on the communications skills of the managers and how they interfaced with the organization."

"Were there any typists," I asked, "who always looked for their old boss's tapes or continued to give them special service?"

"A few secretaries that would take care of their old boss's work ahead of other people would be moved further away. If the team concept is to work, if we are to move forward to the idea of supporting the larger group in total, it is essential to break the one-to-one relationship between the secretary and the principal. Most of the women had no trouble with that."

"You are really some feminist," I said.

"My husband used to kid that I was a woman's libber before my time. Since 1960, I have never carried a cup of coffee as a secretary. Even when I worked for a senior vice president."

"Did six years of Administrative Services change the staffing patterns?" I asked.

"The ratio of secretaries to managers was just about double when we started," Sophia answered. "Of course we began with a lot of cuts. Probably too drastic at the beginning.

"As I look back on it, I believe we tried to make too many changes at once. Everybody had to change, the secretaries, the bosses, the whole system. People had to adjust to a technical change and a social change. They had to learn the machine and they had to learn the team concept. As I think about it, I believe the first thing should have been the split of the boss/secretary relationship."

"Why?" I asked. "Why not just give the secretary a word processor, especially now that we have small computers. I never met a secretary who didn't like her own word processor."

Sophia agreed with the last observation. "I don't know anyone who would want to go back to a Selectric."

"Then why not put the word processor on the secretary's desk first?"

"Because the first would be the last," she answered. "If you brought your word processor in first, the secretaries would be more productive but the individual manager still wouldn't allow his secretary to move into a team concept and support others. She might finish two hours earlier but he would not admit that he didn't have the work for her. He would rather have his secretary do nothing 40 percent of the time, just so long as she was totally available outside his door.

"Besides, if you brought the word processors in first, you'd have to give them to everybody. You could not afford to do that and keep all those people on.

"No," Sophia insisted with unflinching logic, "if you're going to move to the team concept you have to change the social relationship first. You have to move to the work center first and bring the technology in after. Of course you wouldn't be able to cut your staff until after you had the word processors. But you cannot begin to move forward," she concluded with conviction, "till you split the one-to-one relationship."

My jaw dropped with admiration. All by herself Sophia Crandall had reformulated one of the toughest tenets of industrial revolution. *First* you rationalize the job, change the physical layout, break the old social relationships, *then* you bring in the new machinery. . . .

By the mid-1980s executives had adapted to the IBM word processing system in many different ways. Traditional managers like the men I met at Procter & Gamble felt slighted, helpless or even lonely when their secretaries were moved away to word processing centers. They missed the personal services they had received through the one-to-one relationships. Often they adapted by trying to cajole the old kind of personal attention from the new communal support staff.

But younger managers tended to make a different adjustment. Instead of trying to wheedle their way around the work center, they learned how to get a letter out by themselves. In just about a decade the predominant managerial support system shifted from private secretary to communal secretary to no secretary at all.

For all but the top executives, the office relationship of the future will be neither monogamy nor polygamy, but celibacy. With a few electronic aids, the rising MBA can do it himself. Many young executives prefer it that way. . . .

Les Cummings

"Among our thousand employees," Les Cummings told me, "we have exactly two secretaries. Actually one and a half. I don't keep my secretary occupied, so I release her for other work."

Mr. Cummings is the Executive Vice President of a medium-size firm on the American Stock Exchange. He's about forty, plays tennis and loves computers.

"With the economic modeling programs I've developed," he told me, "I can see from the top to the bottom of the company—past, present, and future—just by pushing a few buttons on a keyboard."

Les was glad to give me some of his time because he's interested in literature. He means to write a book himself someday.

"With my PC and soon my laser printer, I can, myself, produce a document with higher quality in terms of content, formatting and appearance, in less time than I could with a secretary.

"A secretary is superfluous and, even worse, gets in the way.

"I can put my entire Rolodex on my computer; Rolodex makes a program. Let's say I'm in the middle of typing a memo, I realize I want to speak to Barbara. Since I have 'Sidekick,' I can exit from word processing and flip to my Rolodex. I simply press 'Barbara,' and your phone rings at home. I don't have to bother with my secretary, who might be on a coffee break.

"Right now, today, her only function for me is screening my calls. I'll never want to answer my own phone. By 1990, where you now have ten secretaries, you'll have two receptionists.

"For the manager who isn't afraid of it, the computer means greater and greater control over his or her life. It means the security of less and less dependency on other people.

"For those other people, it means unemployment of course." This thought, apparently new, slowed Mr. Cummings down. But he recovered his positive spirit and raced ahead with another idea.

"Why don't you write a book about the Death of the Secretary?"

"The traditional secretary will soon be displayed in a glass case in the natural history museum, with her steno pad. By 1990 most managers won't want to use secretaries. In ten years the traditional secretary will be obsolete. . . . You want to take down the reasons?

"First, managers want to be independent.

"Two, education. There are fewer people coming out of school literate enough to be good secretaries. The better-trained woman can get a management job in her own right. So a truly good secretary is harder and harder to find anyway.

"Three, feminism has taken away the fun of having a secretary.

"Hey, this could be a big seller!" he interrupted himself enthusiastically. "How many millions of secretaries are out there? They're literate; they buy books. They see the computer coming into the office but what will it mean to their jobs? *The Death of the Secretary,* that's the book you should write."

NOTES

1. *Business Week,* 6/30/75.

2. Conversation between "Mary L_____" and the author, 1985.

3. I described some back-office jobs I held just before and during the introduction of computers in *All the Livelong Day: The Meaning and Demeaning of Routine Work* (New York: Penguin, 1977).

4. Harry Braverman, *Labor and Monopoly Capital: The Degradation of Work in the Twentieth Century* (New York: Monthly Review Press, 1975).

PART III

Work and Inequality

There are rewards and costs attached to all forms of work. The fact that some jobs pay more and some pay less is an obvious way in which rewards diverge. Jobs also can be rewarding for other reasons—such as allowing creativity or autonomy—and access to these rewards also varies from job to job. The costs of work, such as exposure to stress, harassment, or dangerous chemicals, are also variable. Because jobs vary in their rewards and costs, inequality is an inevitable aspect of work in American society. What factors determine the rewards or costs of a particular job? To what extent is access to rewarding jobs a function of a worker's race and gender? These questions are among those addressed in Part III.

Work, Wages, and Inequality

During the 1980s, the gap between rich and poor widened in the United States (Gordon 1996; Phillips 1990). Although the reasons for this pattern are complex, no explanation of it can ignore the workplace. The economic fates of most people in the United States are tied to paid work. Children's livelihoods depend on their parents' or caretakers' access to jobs and wages. The vast majority of adults either work for pay or are supported by someone who does. When jobs are unavailable, the consequences for individuals, their families, and their communities are devastating (Wilson 1996). Moreover, as debates about poverty and welfare policy make clear, nonemployed adults in American society who are perceived as being able to work (and who are not supported by another paid worker) are viewed negatively by many

(Katz 1989). Thus, not only is access to paid work important for economic survival, but it has come to define one's worth as a person. Under these circumstances, it becomes important to understand how wages are assigned to jobs, the factors that determine how wages are distributed to individuals, and the broader trends in wages and wage inequality.

Obviously, some earn more than others; sociologists (and economists) have devoted much attention to understanding why wages vary. In general, these analyses suggest that one's wages depend on three sets of factors: individual characteristics, such as education and experience; the characteristics of one's job, such as skill requirements and level of authority; and the characteristics of the organization where one is employed, such as the size of the company or its profitability. These models thus assume that wage differences between individuals or groups derive from differences in one or more of these factors. This logic has been applied to the study of gender- and race-based wage inequality (Tomaskovic-Devey 1993). Researchers want to know not only whether women earn lower wages than men, or whether African-Americans (or Latinos, Native Americans, or Asians) earn less than whites, but also what factors account for these patterns. Determining these factors is essential to understand the sources of wage discrimination in the labor market.

Donald Tomaskovic-Devey's reading describes an analysis designed to examine these questions. Women in Tomaskovic-Devey's North Carolina sample earned approximately 71 percent of male workers' earnings, while African-Americans earned approximately 78 percent of whites' earnings. Using a quantitative approach, Tomaskovic-Devey identifies the factors that explain these wage gaps. Though his analyses are fairly sophisticated, Tomaskovic-Devey's findings are clear and suggest that somewhat different factors explain the gender gap in pay than those that explain the pay gap between African-Americans and whites. In particular, his analysis shows that, although gender and racial segregation play important roles in creating wage inequality, the gender composition of jobs has a much more powerful impact on the gender gap in earnings than the racial composition of jobs has on the earnings gaps between African-Americans and whites.

Whereas Tomaskovic-Devey's reading examines the nature of wage inequality among those who are employed, the next reading addresses another form of labor market disadvantage: the lack of a job (and, hence, a wage). As William Julius Wilson argues, "the disappearance of work" has disproportionately affected lower-skilled men in inner cities, many of whom are African-American. Wilson shows how patterns of industrial restructuring on a national level have contributed to increased joblessness in inner-city areas. When employment prospects are dim, increasing poverty and declining neighborhoods are two inevitable results.

Increasing wage inequality has become a concern of politicians, policy-makers, and researchers. The next two selections examine this issue from an economic viewpoint. David Gordon's reading, "The Wage Squeeze," is drawn from his book, *Fat and Mean: The Corporate Squeeze of Working Americans and the Myth of Managerial "Downsizing"* (1996). Gordon shows that the wages of most working Americans have been "squeezed" downward in recent years, and, consistent with some of the themes developed by Wilson and Tomaskovic-Devey, he notes that not all

groups of workers have suffered equally. Whereas Gordon devotes some attention to understanding the forces behind the wage squeeze, these forces are explored in more depth by the final reading in this section.

Richard Freeman and Lawrence Katz conclude that the wage squeeze is a peculiarly American phenomenon. These Harvard economists compare wage inequality in the United States with the trends in other advanced capitalist societies and find that "less educated and lower-paid American workers suffered the largest erosion of economic well-being among workers in advanced capitalist countries" (Freeman and Katz 1994, p. 39). In explaining why the United States is different, Freeman and Katz identify factors discussed throughout this anthology, including technological change, unions, demographic shifts, and the globalization of the economy.

The Dynamics of Race and Gender on the Job

The increasing demographic heterogeneity of the U.S. workforce is a well-documented trend (Johnston and Packer 1987). The implications of this trend are clear: "More and more individuals are likely to work with people who are demographically different from them in terms of age, gender, race, and ethnicity" (Tsui, Egan, and O'Reilly 1992, p. 549). This transformation has inspired many studies of the experiences of workers belonging to numerically underrepresented and numerically overrepresented groups. The selections in this section offer a sampling of these studies.

The first reading in the section is drawn from Rosabeth Moss Kanter's classic study, *Men and Women of the Corporation* (1977). Kanter (1977, p. 207) offers a simple proposition: "As proportions begin to shift, so do social experiences." This statement implies that people's experience of work, their interactions with others, and how they are perceived by co-workers depend in part on how many of their "type" are present in the workplace. A man working in a disproportionately female job, such as nursing, thus should experience work differently from a man employed in a predominately male job, such as engineering; an African-American manager should have different experiences than a white manager in the same firm. Kanter's proposition thus provides a clear rationale as to why the demographics of a job, work group, or firm may be sociologically meaningful.

The next reading, by Barbara Reskin, also focuses on the demographics of the workplace, but from a more macrohistorical perspective. Tracing historical changes in the sex composition of the book editing profession, Reskin identifies some of the factors contributing to the feminization of this occupation. She shows that changes in the publishing industry, such as the shift to outside ownership, made publishing a less attractive field for men, while other societal changes increased the supply of women available for these jobs. Although women's movement into publishing desegregated this once predominantly male domain, this change, Reskin suggests, has not necessarily produced equality between women and men in that industry. Reskin's argument is important, as it implies that women's entrance into predominantly male occupations may coincide with declining rewards and diminishing opportunities for advancement in those fields.

Gender and race are highly salient social categories in American society and operate in every sphere of social life. Because members of different social categories occupy different places in the world both inside and outside the workplace, their perceptions and experiences of work are likely to vary. These dynamics and their consequences for how workers identify sexual harassment are the focus of Reading 20, by Patti Giuffre and Christine Williams. These authors' finding

that the "gender, race, status, and sexual orientation of the assailant" enter into workers' decisions whether to label a behavior sexual harassment underscores the ways in which work life is structured by the dynamics of difference.

Race and gender also shape employers' perceptions, expectations, and behavior. These influences may have serious consequences, because it is employers' actions that largely determine the hiring, placement, and promotion of workers. In addition, as Joleen Kirschenman and Kathryn Neckerman (1991, p. 123) note, "employers' expectations may become self-fulfilling prophecies." Although racial discrimination is illegal (as is discrimination on the basis of gender, color, ethnicity, national origin, and religion), Kirschenman and Neckerman describe how race nevertheless is an important factor in the hiring practices of inner-city employers. Their discussion of the ways that a job applicant's race becomes a proxy for other characteristics, such as work ethic and productivity, illustrates the ways that stereotypes and statistical discrimination operate to disadvantage poor black workers from the inner city.

REFERENCES

Freeman, Richard B. and Lawrence F. Katz. 1994. *Working Under Different Rules.* New York: Russell Sage Foundation.

Gordon, David M. 1996. *Fat and Mean: The Corporate Squeeze of Working Americans and the Myth of Managerial "Downsizing."* New York: The Free Press.

Johnston, William B. and Arnold E. Packer. 1987. *Workforce 2000: Work and Workers for the 21st Century.* Indianapolis, IN: The Hudson Institute, Inc.

Kanter, Rosabeth Moss. 1977. *Men and Women of the Corporation.* New York: Basic Books.

Katz, Michael B. 1989. *The Undeserving Poor: From the War on Poverty to the War on Welfare.* New York: Pantheon Books.

Kirschenman, Joleen and Kathryn M. Neckerman. 1991. "'We'd Love to Hire Them, But. . .':" The Meaning of Race for Employers." Pp. 203–232 in *The Urban Underclass,* edited by C. Jencks and P. E. Peterson. Washington, D.C.: The Brookings Institution.

Phillips, Kevin. 1990. *The Politics of Rich and Poor.* New York: Random House.

Tomaskovic-Devey, Donald. 1993. *Gender and Racial Inequality at Work.* Ithaca, NY: ILR Press.

Tsui, Anne S., Terry D. Egan, and Charles O'Reilly III. 1992. "Being Different: Relational Demography and Organizational Attachment." *Administrative Science Quarterly* 37: 549–579.

Wilson, William Julius. 1996. *When Work Disappears: The World of the New Urban Poor.* New York: Knopf.

WORK, WAGES, AND INEQUALITY

15

Sex and Racial Segregation and Pay Gaps
Donald Tomaskovic-Devey

Donald Tomaskovic-Devey is professor of sociology at North Carolina State University. Professor Tomaskovic-Devey writes, "I study inequality because I think it is important for social science to be politically and socially relevant. I endeavor to make my teaching, research, and public policy advocacy politically engaged. This reading is part of an ongoing research project on inequality in workplaces. The quality of jobs and who gets them—the basic issues of class, race, and gender inequities—are my focus. The social violence created by class, gender, and race inequality spill over into all aspects of social life. I believe that these inequalities must be understood and fought if we are to enjoy a just society."

Sex segregation in employment has come to represent the dominant (but certainly not the exclusive) explanation in the sociological literature for the male-female earnings gap (see Marini 1989 for a fairly complete review of competing explanations). It is well established that the earnings of both males and females fall as the percentage of females in an occupation rises (e.g., Baron and Newman 1990; Bridges and Nelson 1989; England et al. 1988; Jacobs and Steinberg, 1990; Parcel 1989; Sorenson 1989a, 1989b).[1] Less is known about racial segregation in employment, but researchers have found that as the percentage of minorities in an occupation rises, earnings tend to decline for minorities and dominants alike (Baron and Newman 1990; Parcel 1989; Semyonov and Lewin-Epstein 1989 [for Israel]; Sorenson 1989a, 1989b).

From *Gender & Racial Inequality at Work*, by Donald Tomaskovic-Devey. Used by permission of the publisher, Cornell University Press.

Although the research is fairly conclusive on the link between sex composition and earnings, interpretations of this conclusion are still being debated. Most sociologists argue that the link reflects . . . status closure and status composition processes. . . . Women are allocated into low-quality jobs, and high concentrations of women further depress the value assigned to jobs. In particular, the sociological perspective suggests that sex composition becomes a part of the organizational value of a position. This interpretation is disputed by neoclassically inclined economists such as Randall K. Filer (1989, 1990), who expect that market mechanisms will allocate rewards to individuals. Filer's expectation is that there are compensating differentials that make women's work more desirable and that women are compensated with these nonmonetary but still valued rewards. . . . [T]he empirical support for this contention is weak (see England et al. 1988; Glass 1990; Jacobs and Steinberg 1990; chap. 5). Filer (1990) points out, however, that the strongest tests of the sex composition–earnings relationship and the refutation of the compensating differentials argument have focused on state civil service positions (see Baron and Newman 1990; Bridges and Nelson 1989; and especially Jacobs and Steinberg 1990). Filer argues that market mechanisms are unlikely to have strong effects in the state sector in that organizational practices are administered rather than market controlled. This study has a clear advantage in meeting this criticism in that it includes the whole labor market, not a single organization, and it includes the private sector. . . .

Developing an Earnings Model

Two similar approaches to estimating earnings inequality were explored for this chapter. The first approach follows the typical strategy of comparable worth or pay equity models and focuses on the effects of the sex and racial compositions of jobs on earnings, controlling for relevant job characteristics. The second approach is more closely related to the typical human capital or sociological wage determination models in that wage-setting processes are estimated separately for men and women and blacks and whites. The substantive results are similar with both approaches. The discussion will focus on the simpler comparable worth approach.

Comparable worth models are generally developed to ascertain the degree to which organizations create discriminatory job structures. Discrimination here refers to the worth attributed to black-dominated or female-dominated jobs, that is, independent of the real differences in skills required to perform the work. A comparable worth model conceptualizes earnings as a function of the productivity or skill-related characteristics attached to jobs and the percentage of blacks or females in the job. The effect of the percentage of females or blacks in the job is

interpreted as a status composition effect on the compensation polices of the firm. It is anticipated that the effect on wages will be negative if firms are creating gendered and racial job structures.

To extend this generic model to a general population of jobs with identifiable incumbents, we need to modify the model to take into account the potential impact of individual-level variations in skills, productivity, and organizational value and extend the model to include interfirm as well as intrafirm wage variations. This expanded model implies that wage variations across jobs are a function of job-related characteristics, firm characteristics, individual skill-related characteristics, the racial and sex compositions of the job, and the race and sex of the individuals in the job. This model is substantively similar to comparable worth models in that it assumes that a single process sets wages for all jobs. It diverges from these models in that it controls for the variation in wages attributable to individual characteristics and differences in a firm's resources. . . .

I examine the degree to which racial and gender inequalities in wages reflect individual human capital, organizational resources, job-skill characteristics, and the status composition of jobs. . . . I refer . . . to these as human capital, organizational closure, job-skill closure, and status composition processes. In this chapter, the wage gaps will be decomposed into those portions attributable to these four basic processes of inequality.

It is also useful to distinguish between the interpretation of job characteristics in this study and that of the typical comparable worth model. In pay equity and comparable worth models (and their academic counterparts), measures of job characteristics are treated as unambiguously representative of real job differences in skill requirements (e.g., Sorenson 1989a, 1989b; Gerhart and Milkovich 1989; Filer 1989). Many sociologists see jobs as defined not only by their production skills but also as power struggles over control of the organization (e.g., Kalleberg, Wallace, and Althauser 1981; Acker 1987). The job characteristics measured in this chapter (complexity, autonomy, training time, required credentials, required experience, supervisory power) are known to be both the outcome and the playing field for struggles between management and labor and between groups of employees for control of organizational activity. . . . Complexity, autonomy, internal labor market opportunity, and supervisory power are certainly all influenced by job-status composition. That these characteristics are typically evaluated as embodying varying levels of skill is undeniable. The actual organization of jobs, however, is not the unambiguous product of efficiency considerations but represents the outcome of organizational gender, racial, and class politics in the workplace.

The general pay equity model assumes that the earnings process is the same for racial and gender groups. Many scholars have noted that the earnings process can be quite different across these groups. This implies that it is appropriate to examine the general model separately for males and females and blacks and whites. The earnings process will be examined first for the whole sample and then separately for men and women and whites and blacks.[2]

The model estimated for the whole sample probably represents the best policy model in that there is a normative assumption that the earnings process should be the same for blacks and whites and men and women. Some economists have assumed that earnings models estimated for white males only represent nondiscriminatory labor market operations (e.g., Daymont and Andrisani 1984). This is a naive perspective. To the extent that blacks or women are discriminated against in labor markets, some group must benefit, and that group often includes white male employees. In some situations, it may be that employers pocket all of the profits from discrimination, but overall both the historical accounts and the status closure perspective employed in this study lead to the conclusion that superordinates benefit. If only employers benefited, there would be no material incentive for white male employees to support race and gender status hierarchies. Since white males clearly fare better in the quality of their jobs, they certainly benefit, at least given the current distribution of opportunity.[3]

Models that control for human capital, organizational resources, and job-skill variables and that include both racial and sex composition and dummy variables for gender and race can be interpreted fairly unambiguously. The estimated effects of the racial and sex compositions of jobs on earnings represent the institutionalization of an earnings disadvantage over and beyond any individual or job-related productivity or other valued organizational characteristics. Estimates of the sex and race of individuals represent direct estimates of the amount of discrimination not tied to the job. . . . Years of education, experience, experience squared, and years of tenure with current employer are the indicators of individual human capital. . . . Job characteristics include whether the job is directly supervised, the degree of supervisory authority, job complexity, closeness of supervision, union membership, job-required credentials, prior experience requirements, and the weeks necessary to learn to do the job well. This is an unusually broad range of job characteristics that can be expected to influence earnings somewhat independently of the racial and sex compositions of the job.

Characteristics of the firms are used to model possible interfirm variations in wages that might reflect differences in their resources (Kalleberg, Wallace, and Althauser 1981; Hodson 1983; Tomaskovic-Devey 1989). The measures used to model such variations include twelve industrial sectors,

TABLE 1 Male-Female and White-Black Hourly Wage Inequalities among North Carolina Employees, 1989

Panel A	Male	Female	Pay Gap	Female as % Male
Average hourly wage	11.83	8.37	3.46	70.75
(standard deviation)	(10.93)	(4.11)		

Panel B	White	Black	Pay Gap	Black as % White
Average hourly wage	10.33	8.03	2.30	77.73
(standard deviation)	(8.69)	(4.00)		

establishment size, and whether or not the establishment is a for-profit firm.

Findings

Table 1 reports the average hourly wages and pay gaps of male and female and white and black employees in North Carolina in 1989. Female employees earned, on average, $3.46 less per hour than male employees, or 71 percent of the males' wages. Black employees earned $2.30 less per hour than white employees, or 78 percent. The pay gaps are, of course, larger when the self-employed are included in the sample and when monthly earnings rather than hourly wages are compared. Females make only 53 percent of males' monthly earnings, reflecting their lower probability of being self-employed and the fact that, on average, they work substantially fewer hours than males. This gap is very similar to current national male-female hourly wage gaps (Marini 1989). Blacks earn in a month only 64 percent of whites' monthly earnings.

Figure 1 is the starting point for our investigation into the degree to which these observed pay gaps can be attributed to the sex and racial compositions of jobs. Figure 1 reports the simple regression of earnings on the percent black and percent female in the job for the entire sample. As the percent black in the job rises, earnings fall dramatically. The picture is even more dramatic for percent female.

Table 2 reports earnings consequences for five samples and four different models of a rise in percent female and percent black. The numbers in the table represent the earnings loss associated with a 1 percent rise in

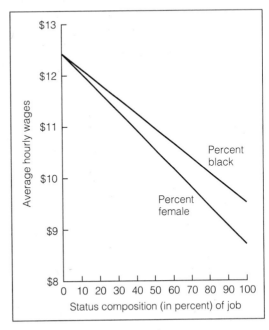

FIGURE 1 Percent Female and Percent Black and Hourly Wages of North Carolina Jobs, 1989

TABLE 2   Effects of Racial and Sex Compositions on Hourly Wages of Employed North Carolinians for Various Models, 1989

	All (N = 654)	Males (N = 294)	Females (N = 360)	Whites (N = 539)	Blacks (N = 115)
Gross effect					
Percent female	**−.027**	.008	**−.020**	**−.040**	**−.023**
Percent black	**−.029**	**−.041**	**−.020**	**−.026**	.006
Effect net of human capital					
Percent female	**−.036**	**−.020**	**−.016**	**−.038**	**−.024**
Percent black	**−.018**	−.021	**−.013**	−.016	−.001
Effect net of human capital, job characteristics, and firm characteristics					
Percent female	**−.024**	**−.063**	**−.013**	**−.027**	**−.016**
Percent black	**−.012**	**−.028**	**−.009**	−.018	.003
Effect net of human capital, job characteristics, firm characteristics, and individual gender and/or race					
Percent female	**−.023**	**−.063**	**−.012**	**−.036**	.006
Percent black	−.009	−.027	−.002	−.018	.003
Minority	−.459	−.126	**−1.24**	—	—
Female	−.120	—	—	.968	**−2.48**

Note: Metric regression coefficients reported. **Bold** indicates statistically significant at or below the .10 probability level, although almost all **bold** coefficients are significant below the .05 probability level. All tests of statistical significance are one-tailed tests. . . .

percent female or percent black. The samples represent the whole population of jobs and those subsamples of jobs filled only by males, females, whites, and blacks respectively. The first set of models reports the gross effects of percent black and percent female on earnings controlling for no other variables. The next model controls for individual human capital characteristics. The third model adds to the human capital control variables statistical controls for job and firm characteristics. The final model adds individual variables that reflect sex and race. Sex and racial differences in earnings that are not explained by these models are reported in the final two rows.

For the whole population as well as the sex and race subsamples, we see that as the proportion minority and proportion female in the job rises, hourly earnings fall. There are two exceptions at the level of gross effects. Among the black subsample, the relationship between percent black in the job and earnings is consistently nonsignificant. This may reflect the small size of the sample and limited variation for this variable among blacks. Percent female is not significantly related to earnings among males at the level of gross effects. It is significant, however, once job characteristics are controlled, reflecting that sex-integrated jobs are somewhat more common when the educational requirements are higher.

Once we control for individual human capital characteristics, the effect of percent black is reduced substantially for all models, suggesting that variations in human capital between whites and blacks as well as between white-dominated and black-dominated jobs account for some of the observed association between racial composition and earnings. Controlling for human capital differences does not substantially influence the relationship between percent female and earnings. . . . Controlling for job and firm characteristics reduces the size of the effect of both percent female and percent black in the model that contains the whole population. The percent black relationship with earnings is quite weak at this point. The percent female coefficient is now strongly statistically significant for the male subsample. Overall, percent female is associated significantly with lower wages for all subsamples, even when human capital, firm resources, and an extensive set of job skill and power characteristics are statistically controlled. The effect of percent black is weaker, and although it is significant for the whole population and for the male and female subsamples, it is not significant within the race subsamples when control variables are included.

The final set of models adds (where appropriate) individual race and gender variables. For the whole-population model, percent female remains significantly negatively associated with the earnings net of human capital, firm resources, job characteristics, and even the individuals' sex. Sex is not significantly associated with earnings in this model. Neither the individuals' race nor the racial composition of the job is significantly associated with the earnings net of human capital, job, and firm characteristics. The results from this model are consistent with previous findings that the percent female influences the earnings net of job and human capital controls but that percent black does not. When race dummies are not included in the model, however, the relationship between percent black and earnings is significant for the whole population as well as for the male and female subsamples.

The results across the subsamples are consistent for percent female. Males and females experience declining real wages as percent female rises. In fact, the earnings penalty for males associated with a rise in percent female is much higher than the penalty for females. For every 10 percent increase in percent female in their jobs, males' wages decline by $.63; for the same increase, females' wages decline by only $.13. Percent female becomes nonsignificant in the model for the black subsample once the female dummy variable is entered. Black females, however, do have significantly lower wages ($2.48) than black males even after controlling for human capital, job, and firm characteristics.

Racial composition is consistently nonsignificant in the final models, although black women seem to face a direct earnings disadvantage not tied to any job characteristic. . . .

Table 3 decomposes the pay gap into its constituent parts for the pay equity model. . . . The $3.46 male-female pay gap is almost totally explained (all but $.02) by this model. Fifty-six percent of this gap is associated with the sex composition of jobs even after extensive controls for human capital, job characteristics, and firm characteristics. Job characteristics explain an additional 28 percent. Firm-level segmentation is associated with 13 percent of the gap, and human capital characteristics with 3 percent. Thus, status composition effects explain 56 percent, status closure effects (job + firm characteristics) 41 percent, and human capital only 3 percent of the male-female pay gap.

The pattern for the black-white pay gap is quite different. Black-white differences in their mean levels of job characteristics explain 38 percent of the pay gap, and human capital differences explain an additional 31 percent. Only 21 percent is attributable to the racial composition of jobs. Finally, firm characteristics play a trivial role in creating the black-white pay gap. Thus, status

TABLE 3   Proportion of Pay Gap among Employed North Carolinians Attributable to Racial and Sex Compositions, Human Capital, and Job and Firm Characteristics, Based on Pooled Pay Equity-Type Model, 1989

	Male-Female Dollar Pay Gap	Proportion of Gap	White-Black Dollar Pay Gap	Proportion of Gap
Total	3.46	100%	2.30	100%
Percent female	1.92	56	−.13	−6
Percent black	.01	0	.48	21
Human capital	.12	3	.70	31
Job characteristics	.95	28	.88	38
Firm characteristics	.44	13	.04	2
Unexplained	.02	1	.33	14

composition effects explain 21 percent, status closure 40 percent, and human capital 31 percent of the black-white pay gap.

Conclusions

At the very least, 56 percent of the $3.46 hourly earnings gap between men and women employees in North Carolina can be attributed to the sex composition of jobs. . . . Although the effects of racial composition on earnings were weaker than the effects of sex composition, this study did find signifi-

cant racial composition effects in models that control for human capital, job characteristics, and firms' resources. The models suggest that at the very least 21 percent of the black-white gap in earnings among North Carolina employees in 1989 may have been attributable to racial segregation at the job level (see Figures 2 and 3). . . .

There are also substantively different processes by which the black-white and male-female wage gaps are generated. The male-female wage gap is not the result of sex differences in human capital, whereas black-white differences in human capital are

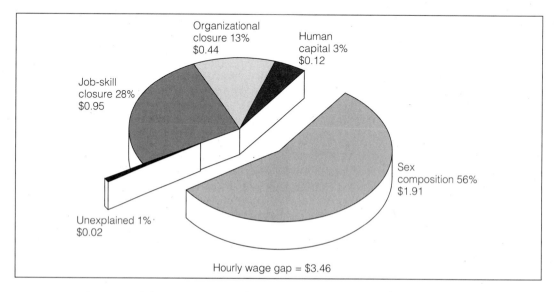

FIGURE 2   Sources of the Male-Female Pay Gap among North Carolina Employees, 1989

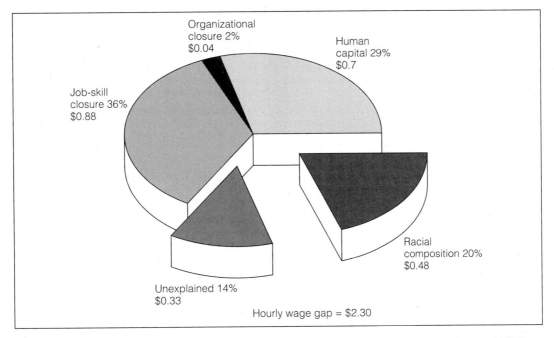

FIGURE 3   Sources of the White-Black Pay Gap among North Carolina Employees, 1989

extremely important sources of black-white differences in earnings. Exclusionary status closure processes are important sources of both race-based and sex-based wage inequalities. Both earnings gaps are substantially linked to segregation in the skills and power invested in jobs. It is quite likely that some of this skill and power segregation reflects status processes whereby the sex and racial compositions of jobs influence the social organization of the work. Most of this skill and power segregation, however, probably reflects discrimination in hiring. The characteristics of firms seem to explain more of the male-female gap than the black-white gap in earnings. Finally, although both the sex and racial compositions of jobs influence their respective earnings gaps, the effect of gender is much more powerful.

NOTES

1. For the single study that does not provide evidence of a sex composition wage effect after controlling for multiple job characteristics, see Filer 1989.

2. Although it would be preferable to estimate separate equations for each group by both sex and race (e.g., black females), the sample is too small for this level of detail.

3. It may be that the elimination of patriarchal and racist tendencies in the labor market will increase the overall bargaining power of the working class and over the long term raise the wages of all employees. Over the short term, however, white men and women benefit from their race and white men and black men benefit from their sex. Black women are doubly disadvantaged.

REFERENCES

Acker, Joan. 1987. "Sex Bias in Job Evaluation: A Comparable Worth Issue." In *Ingredients for Women's Employment Policy*, ed. Christine E. Bose and Glenna D. Spitze, 183–96. Albany: State University of New York Press.

Baron, James N., and Andrew E. Newman. 1990. "For What It's Worth: Organizations, Occupations and the Value of Work Done by Women and Nonwhites." *American Sociological Review* 55:155–75.

Bridges, William P., and Robert L. Nelson. 1989. "Markets in Hierarchies: Organizational and Market Influences on Gender Inequality in a State Pay System." *American Journal of Sociology* 95:616–59.

Daymont, Thomas, and Paul Andrisani. 1984. "Job Preferences, College Major, and the Gender Gap in Earnings." *Journal of Human Resources* 18:408–28.

England, Paula, et al. 1988. "Explaining Occupational Sex Segregation and Wages: Findings from a Model with Fixed Effects." *American Sociological Review* 53:544–58.

Filer, Randall K. 1989. "Occupational Segregation, Compensating Differentials, and Comparable Worth." In *Pay Equity: Empirical Inquiries,* ed. Robert T. Michael, Heidi I. Hartmann, and Brigid O'Farrell, 153–70. Washington, D.C.: National Academy Press.

———. 1990. "Compensating Differentials and the Male-Female Wage Gap: A Comment." *Social Forces* 69:469–73.

Gerhart, Barry A., and George T. Milkovich. 1989. "Salaries, Salary Growth, and Promotions of Men and Women in a Large, Private Firm." In *Pay Equity: Empirical Inquiries,* ed. Robert T. Michael, Heidi I. Hartmann, and Brigid O'Farrell, 23–41. Washington, D.C.: National Academy Press.

Glass, Jennifer. 1990. "The Impact of Occupational Segregation on Working Conditions." *Social Forces* 68:779–96.

Hodson, Randy. 1983. *Workers' Earnings and Corporate Economic Structure.* New York: Academic Press.

Jacobs, Jerry A., and Ronnie Steinberg. 1990. "Compensating Differentials and the Male-Female Wage Gap: Evidence from the New York State Comparable Worth Study." *Social Forces* 69:439–68.

Kalleberg, Arne, Michael Wallace, and Robert Althauser. 1981. "Economic Segregation, Worker Power, and Income Inequality." *American Journal of Sociology* 87:651–83.

Marini, Margaret Mooney. 1989. "Sex Differences in Earnings in the United States." *Annual Review of Sociology* 15:348–80.

Parcel, Toby. 1989. "Comparable Worth, Occupational Labor Markets and Occupational Earnings: Results from the 1980 Census." In *Pay Equity: Empirical Inquiries,* ed. Robert T. Michael, Heidi I. Hartmann, and Brigid O'Farrell, 134–52. Washington, D.C.: National Academy Press.

Semyonov, Moshe, and Noah Lewin-Epstein. 1989. "Segregation and Competition in Occupational Labor Markets." *Social Forces* 68:379–96.

Sorenson, Elaine. 1989a. "The Crowding Hypothesis and Comparable Worth." *Journal of Human Resources* 25:55–89.

———. 1989b. "Measuring the Effect of Occupational Sex and Race Composition on Earnings." In *Pay Equity: Empirical Inquiries,* ed. Robert T. Michael, Heidi I. Hartmann, and Brigid O'Farrell, 49–70. Washington, D.C.: National Academy Press.

Tomaskovic-Devey, Donald. 1989. "Organizational Stratification and the Size of the Pie: Environmental Constraints on Organizational Income Streams." Paper presented at the annual meeting of the American Sociological Association, San Francisco, August.

16

When Work Disappears
The World of the New Urban Poor

William Julius Wilson

William Julius Wilson is the Malcolm Wiener Professor of Social Policy at the John F. Kennedy School of Government at Harvard University. Professor Wilson writes, "For the last several years my research has been devoted to problems of urban poverty and joblessness as reflected in two of my latest books—*The Truly Disadvantaged: The Inner City, the Underclass, and Public Policy* and *When Work Disappears: The World of the New Urban Poor.* My interest in the problems of the disadvantaged is in part derived from my own experiences of living in poverty as a child after my father, who worked in the Pittsburgh steel mills, died."

The disappearance of work in many inner-city neighborhoods is partly related to the nationwide decline in the fortunes of low-skilled workers. Although the growing wage inequality has hurt both low-skilled men and women, the problem of declining employment has been concentrated among low-skilled men. In 1987–89, a low-skilled male worker was jobless eight and a half weeks longer than he would have been in 1967–69. Moreover, the proportion of men who "permanently" dropped out of the labor force was more than twice as high in the late 1980s than it had been in the late 1960s. A precipitous drop in real wages—that is, wages adjusted for inflation—has accompanied the increases in joblessness among low-income workers. If you arrange all wages into five groups according to wage percentile (from highest to lowest), you see that men in the bottom fifth of this income distribution experienced more than a 30 per-

cent drop in real wages between 1970 and 1989.

Even the low-skilled workers who are consistently employed face problems of economic advancement. Job ladders—opportunities for promotion within firms—have eroded, and many less-skilled workers stagnate in dead-end, low-paying positions. This suggests that the chances of improving one's earnings by changing jobs have declined: if jobs inside a firm have become less available to the experienced workers in that firm, they are probably even more difficult for outsiders to obtain.

But there is a paradox here. Despite the increasing economic marginality of low-wage workers, unemployment dipped below 6 percent in 1994 and early 1995, many workers are holding more than one job, and overtime work has reached a record high. Yet while tens of millions of new jobs have been created in the past two decades, men who are well below retirement age are working less than they did two decades ago—and a growing percentage are neither working nor looking for work. The proportion of male workers in the prime of their life (between the ages of

22 and 58) who worked in a given decade full-time, year-round, in at least eight out of ten years declined from 79 percent during the 1970s to 71 percent in the 1980s. While the American economy saw a rapid expansion in high technology and services, especially advanced services, growth in blue-collar factory, transportation, and construction jobs, traditionally held by men, has not kept pace with the rise in the working-age population. These men are working less as a result.

The growth of a nonworking class of prime-age males along with a larger number of those who are often unemployed, who work part-time, or who work in temporary jobs is concentrated among the poorly educated, the school dropouts, and minorities. In the 1970s, two-thirds of prime-age male workers with less than a high school education worked full-time, year-round, in eight out of ten years. During the 1980s, only half did so. Prime-age black men experienced a similar sharp decline. Seven out of ten of all black men worked full-time, year-round, in eight out of ten years in the 1970s, but only half did so in the 1980s. The figures for those who reside in the inner city are obviously even lower. . . .

Joblessness and declining wages are . . . related to the recent growth in ghetto poverty. The most dramatic increases in ghetto poverty occurred between 1970 and 1980, and they were mostly confined to the large industrial metropolises of the Northeast and Midwest, regions that experienced massive industrial restructuring and loss of blue-collar jobs during that decade. But the rise in ghetto poverty was not the only problem. Industrial restructuring had devastating effects on the social organization of many inner-city neighborhoods in these regions. The fate of the West Side black community of North Lawndale vividly exemplifies the cumulative process of economic and social dislocation that has swept through Chicago's inner city.

After more than a quarter century of continuous deterioration, North Lawndale resembles a war zone. Since 1960, nearly half of its housing stock has disappeared; the remaining units are mostly run-down or dilapidated. Two large factories anchored the economy of this West Side neighborhood in its good days—the Hawthorne plant of Western Electric, which employed over 43,000 workers; and an International Harvester plant with 14,000 workers. The world headquarters for Sears, Roebuck and Company was located there, providing another 10,000 jobs. The neighborhood also had a Copenhagen snuff plant, a Sunbeam factory, and a Zenith factory, a Dell Farm food market, an Alden's catalog store, and a U.S. Post Office bulk station. But conditions rapidly changed. Harvester closed its doors in the late 1960s. Sears moved most of its offices to the Loop in downtown Chicago in 1973; a catalog distribution center with a workforce of 3,000 initially remained in the neighborhood but was relocated outside of the state of Illinois in 1987. The Hawthorne plant gradually phased out its operations and finally shut down in 1984.

The departure of the big plants triggered the demise or exodus of the smaller stores, the banks, and other businesses that relied on the wages paid by the large employers. "To make matters worse, scores of stores were forced out of business or pushed out of the neighborhoods by insurance companies in the wake of the 1968 riots that swept through Chicago's West Side after the assassination of Dr. Martin Luther King, Jr. Others were simply burned or abandoned. It has been estimated that the community lost 75 percent of its business establishments from 1960 to 1970 alone." In 1986, North Lawndale, with a population of over 66,000, had only one bank and one supermarket; but it was also home to forty-eight state lottery agents, fifty currency exchanges, and ninety-nine licensed liquor stores and bars.

The impact of industrial restructuring on inner-city employment is clearly apparent to urban blacks. The UPFLS [Chicago Urban

Poverty and Family Life Survey] survey posed the following question: "Over the past five or ten years, how many friends of yours have lost their jobs because the place where they worked shut down—would you say none, a few, some, or most?" Only 26 percent of the black residents in our sample reported that none of their friends had lost jobs because their workplace shut down. Indeed, both black men and black women were more likely to report that their friends had lost jobs because of plant closings than were the Mexicans and the other ethnic groups in our study. Moreover, nearly half of the employed black fathers and mothers in the UPFLS survey stated that they considered themselves to be at high risk of losing their jobs because of plant shutdowns. Significantly fewer Hispanic and white parents felt this way.

Some of the inner-city neighborhoods have experienced more visible job losses than others. But residents of the inner city are keenly aware of the rapid depletion of job opportunities. A 33-year-old unmarried black male of North Lawndale who is employed as a clerical worker stated: "Because of the way the economy is structured, we're losing more jobs. Chicago is losing jobs by the thousands. There just aren't any starting companies here and it's harder to find a job compared to what it was years ago."

A similar view was expressed by a 41-year-old black female, also from North Lawndale, who works as a nurse's aide:

Chicago is really full of peoples. Everybody can't get a good job. They don't have enough good jobs to provide for everybody. I don't think they have enough jobs period. . . . And all the factories and the places, they closed up and moved out of the city and stuff like that, you know. I guess it's one of the reasons they haven't got too many jobs now, 'cause a lot of the jobs now, factories and business, they're done moved out. So that way it's less jobs for lot of peoples.

Respondents from other neighborhoods also reported on the impact of industrial restructuring. According to a 33-year-old South Side janitor:

The machines are putting a lot of people out of jobs. I worked for Time magazine for seven years on a videograph printer and they come along with the Abedic printer, it cost them half a million dollars: they did what we did in half the time, eliminated two shifts.

"Jobs were plentiful in the past," stated a 29-year-old unemployed black male who lives in one of the poorest neighborhoods on the South Side.

You could walk out of the house and get a job. Maybe not what you want but you could get a job. Now, you can't find anything. A lot of people in this neighborhood, they want to work but they can't get work. A few, but a very few, they just don't want to work. The majority they want to work but they can't find work.

Finally, a 41-year-old hospital worker from another impoverished South Side neighborhood associated declining employment opportunities with decreasing skill levels:

Well, most of the jobs have moved out of Chicago. Factory jobs have moved out. There are no jobs here. Not like it was 20, 30 years ago. And people aren't skilled enough for the jobs that are here. You don't have enough skilled and educated people to fill them.

The increasing suburbanization of employment has accompanied industrial restructuring and has further exacerbated the problems of inner-city joblessness and restricted access to jobs. "Metropolitan areas captured nearly 90 percent of the nation's employment growth; much of this growth occurred in booming 'edge cities' at the metropolitan periphery. By 1990, many of these 'edge cities' had more office space and retail sales than the metropolitan downtowns." Over the last two decades, 60 percent of the new jobs created in the Chicago metropolitan area have been located in the northwest suburbs of Cook and Du Page counties. African-Americans constitute less than 2 percent of the population in these areas.

In *The Truly Disadvantaged,* I maintained that one result of these changes for many urban blacks has been a growing mismatch between the suburban location of employment and minorities' residence in the inner city. Although studies based on data collected before 1970 showed no consistent or convincing effects on black employment as a consequence of this spatial mismatch, the employment of inner-city blacks relative to suburban blacks has clearly deteriorated since then. Recent research, conducted mainly by urban and labor economists, strongly shows that the decentralization of employment is continuing and that employment in manufacturing, most of which is already suburbanized, has decreased in central cities, particularly in the Northeast and Midwest. As Farrell Bloch, an economic and statistical consultant, points out, "Not only has the number of manufacturing jobs been decreasing, but new plants now tend to locate in the suburbs to take advantage of cheap land, access to highways, and low crime rates; in addition, businesses shun urban locations to avoid buying land from several different owners, paying high demolition costs for old buildings, and arranging parking for employees and customers."

Blacks living in central cities have less access to employment, as measured by the ratio of jobs to people and the average travel time to and from work, than do central-city whites. Moreover, unlike most other groups of workers across the urban/suburban divide, less educated central-city blacks receive lower wages than suburban blacks who have similar levels of education. And the decline in earnings of central-city blacks is related to the decentralization of employment—that is,

the movement of jobs from the cities to the suburbs—in metropolitan areas.

But are the differences in employment between city and suburban blacks mainly the result of changes in the location of jobs? It is possible that in recent years the migration of blacks to the suburbs has become much more selective than in earlier years, so much so that the changes attributed to job location are actually caused by this selective migration. The pattern of black migration to the suburbs in the 1970s was similar to that of whites during the 1950s and 1960s in the sense that it was concentrated among the better-educated and younger city residents. However, in the 1970s this was even more true for blacks, creating a situation in which the education and income gaps between city and suburban blacks seemed to expand at the same time that the differences between city and suburban whites seemed to contract. Accordingly, if one were to take into account differences in education, family background, and so on, how much of the employment gap between city and suburbs would remain?

This question was addressed in a study of the Gautreaux program in Chicago. The Gautreaux program was created under a 1976 court order resulting from a judicial finding of widespread discrimination in the public housing projects of Chicago. The program has relocated more than 4,000 residents from public housing into subsidized housing in neighborhoods throughout the Greater Chicago area. The design of the program permitted the researchers, James E. Rosenbaum and Susan J. Popkin, to contrast systematically the employment experiences of a group of low-income blacks who had been assigned private apartments in the suburbs with the experiences of a control group with similar characteristics and histories who had been assigned private apartments in the city. Their findings support the spatial mismatch hypothesis. After taking into account the personal characteristics of the respondents (including family background, family circumstances, levels of human capital, motivation, length of time since the respondent first enrolled in the Gautreaux program), Rosenbaum and Popkin found that those who moved to apartments in the suburbs were significantly more likely to have a job after the move than those placed in the city. When asked what makes it easier to obtain employment in the suburbs, nearly all the suburban respondents mentioned the high availability of jobs.

The African-Americans surveyed in the UPFLS clearly recognized a spatial mismatch of jobs. Both black men and black women saw greater job prospects outside the city. For example, only one-third of black fathers from areas with poverty rates of at least 30 percent reported that their best opportunities for employment were to be found in the city. Nearly two-thirds of whites and Puerto Ricans and over half of Mexicans living in similar neighborhoods felt this way. Getting to suburban jobs is especially problematic for the jobless individuals in the UPFLS because only 28 percent have access to an automobile. This rate falls even further to 18 percent for those living in the ghetto areas.

Among two-car middle-class and affluent families, commuting is accepted as a fact of life; but it occurs in a context of safe school environments for children, more available and accessible day care, and higher incomes to support mobile, away-from-home lifestyles. In a multitiered job market that requires substantial resources for participation, most inner-city minorities must rely on public transportation systems that rarely provide easy and quick access to suburban locations. A 32-year-old unemployed South Side welfare mother described the problem this way:

> There's not enough jobs. I thinks Chicago's the only city that does not have a lot of opportunities opening in it. There's not enough factories, there's not enough work. Most all the good jobs are in the suburbs. Sometimes it's hard for the people in the city to get to the sub-

urbs, because everybody don't own a car. Everybody don't drive.

After commenting on the lack of jobs in his area, a 29-year-old unemployed South Side black male continued:

> You gotta go out in the suburbs, but I can't get out there. The bus go out there but you don't want to catch the bus out there, going two hours each ways. If you have to be at work at eight that mean you have to leave for work at six, that mean you have to get up at five to be at work at eight. Then when wintertime come you be in trouble.

Another unemployed South Side black male had this to say: "Most of the time . . . the places be too far and you need transportation and I don't have none right now. If I had some I'd probably be able to get one [a job]. If I had a car and went way into the suburbs, 'cause there ain't none in the city." This perception was echoed by an 18-year-old unemployed West Side black male:

> They are most likely hiring in the suburbs. Recently, I think about two years ago, I had a job but they say that I need some transportation and they say that the bus out in the suburbs run at a certain time. So I had to pass that job up because I did not have no transport.

An unemployed unmarried welfare mother of two from the West Side likewise stated:

> Well, I'm goin' to tell you: most jobs, more jobs are in the suburbs. It's where the good jobs and stuff is but you gotta have transportation to get there and it's hard to be gettin' out there in the suburbs. Some people don't know where the suburbs is, some people get lost out there. It is really hard, but some make a way.

One employed factory worker from the West Side who works a night shift described the situation this way:

From what I, I see, you know, it's hard to find a good job in the inner city 'cause so many people moving, you know, west to the suburbs and out of state. . . . Some people turn jobs down because they don't have no way of getting out there. . . . I just see some people just going to work—and they seem like they the type who just used to—they coming all the way from the city and go on all the way to the suburbs and, you know, you can see 'em all bundled and—catching one bus and the next bus. They just used to doing that.

But the problem is not simply one of transportation and the length of commuting time. There is also the problem of the travel expense and of whether the long trek to the suburbs is actually worth it in terms of the income earned—after all, owning a car creates expenses far beyond the purchase price, including insurance, which is much more costly for city dwellers than it is for suburban motorists. "If you work in the suburbs you gotta have a car," stated an unmarried welfare mother of three children who lives on Chicago's West Side, "then you gotta buy gas. You spending more getting to the suburbs to work, than you is getting paid, so you still ain't getting nowhere."

Indeed, one unemployed 36-year-old black man from the West Side of Chicago actually quit his suburban job because of the transportation problem. "It was more expensive going to work in Naperville, transportation and all, and it wasn't worth it. . . . I was spending more money getting to work than I earned working."

If transportation poses a problem for those who have to commute to work from the inner city to the suburbs, it can also hinder poor ghetto residents' ability to travel to the suburbs just to seek employment. For example, one unemployed man who lives on the South Side had just gone to O'Hare Airport looking for work with no luck. His

complaint: "The money I spent yesterday, I coulda kept that in my pocket—I coulda kept that. 'Cause you know I musta spent about $7 or somethin'. I coulda kept that."

Finally, in addition to enduring the search-and-travel costs, inner-city black workers often confront racial harassment when they enter suburban communities. A 38-year-old South Side divorced mother of two children who works as a hotel cashier described the problems experienced by her son and his coworker in one of Chicago's suburbs:

> My son, who works in Carol Stream, an all-white community, they've been stopped by a policeman two or three times asking them why they're in the community. And they're trying to go to work. They want everyone to stay in their own place. That's what society wants. And they followed them all the way to work to make sure. 'Cause it's an all-white neighborhood. But there're no jobs in the black neighborhoods. They got to go way out there to get a job.

These informal observations on the difficulties and cost of travel to suburban employment are consistent with the results of a recent study by the labor economists Harry J. Holzer, Keith R. Ihlandfeldt, and David L. Sjoquist (1994). In addition to finding that the lack of automobile ownership among inner-city blacks contributed significantly to their lower wages and lower rate of employment, these authors also reported that African-Americans "spend more time traveling to work than whites," that "the time cost per mile traveled is . . . significantly higher for blacks," and that the resulting gains are relatively small. Overall, their results suggest that the amount of time and money spent in commuting, when compared with the actual income that accrues to inner-city blacks in low-skill jobs in the suburbs, acts to discourage poor people from seeking employment far from their own neighborhoods. Holzer and his colleagues concluded that it was quite rational for blacks to reject these search-and-travel choices when assessing their position in the job market.

Changes in the industrial and occupational mix, including the removal of jobs from urban centers to suburban corridors, represent external factors that have helped to elevate joblessness among inner-city blacks. But important social and demographic changes within the inner city are also associated with the escalating rates of neighborhood joblessness, and we shall consider these next.

The increase in the proportion of jobless adults in the inner city is also related to changes in the class, racial, and age composition of such neighborhoods—changes that have led to greater concentrations of poverty. Concentrated poverty is positively associated with joblessness. That is, when the former appears, the latter is found as well. As stated previously, poor people today are far more likely to be unemployed or out of the labor force than in previous years. In *The Truly Disadvantaged* (1987), I argue that in addition to the effects of joblessness, inner-city neighborhoods have experienced a growing concentration of poverty for several other reasons, including (1) the out-migration of nonpoor black families; (2) the exodus of nonpoor white and other nonblack families; and (3) the rise in the number of residents who have become poor while living in these areas. Additional research on the growth of concentrated poverty suggests another factor: the movement of poor people into a neighborhood (inmigration). And one more factor should be added to this mix: changes in the age structure of the community.

I believe that the extent to which any one factor is significant in explaining the decrease in the proportion of nonpoor individuals and families depends on the poverty level and racial or ethnic makeup of the neighborhood at a given time. . . .

One of the important demographic shifts that had an impact on the upturn in the jobless rate has been the change in the age structure of inner-city ghetto neighborhoods. Let us . . . examine the three Bronzeville neighborhoods of Douglas, Grand Boulevard, and Washington Park. . . . [T]he proportion of those in the age categories (20–64) that roughly approximate the prime-age workforce has declined in all three neighborhoods since 1950, whereas the proportion in the age category 65 and over has increased. Of the adults age 20 and over, the proportion in the prime-age categories declined by 17 percent in Grand Boulevard, 16 percent in Douglas, and 12 percent in Washington Park between 1950 and 1990. The smaller the percentage of prime-age adults in a population, the lower the proportion of residents who are likely to be employed. The proportion of residents in the age category 5–19 increased sharply in each neighborhood from 1950 to 1990, suggesting that the growth in the proportion of teenagers also contributed to the rise in the jobless rate. However, if we consider the fact that male employment in these neighborhoods declined by a phenomenal 46 percent between 1950 and 1960, these demographic changes obviously can account for only a fraction, albeit a significant fraction, of the high proportion of the area's jobless adults.

The rise in the proportion of jobless adults in the Bronzeville neighborhoods has been accompanied by an incredible depopulation—a decline of 66 percent in the three neighborhoods combined—that magnifies the problems of the new poverty neighborhoods. As the population drops and the proportion of nonworking adults rises, basic neighborhood institutions are more difficult to maintain: stores, banks, credit institutions, restaurants, dry cleaners, gas stations, medical doctors, and so on lose regular and potential patrons. Churches experience dwindling numbers of parishioners and shrinking resources; recreational facilities, block clubs, community groups, and other informal organizations also suffer. As these organizations decline, the means of formal and informal social control in the neighborhood become weaker. Levels of crime and street violence increase as a result, leading to further deterioration of the neighborhood.

The more rapid the neighborhood deterioration, the greater the institutional disinvestment. In the 1960s and 1970s, neighborhoods plagued by heavy abandonment were frequently "redlined" (identified as areas that should not receive or be recommended for mortgage loans or insurance); this paralyzed the housing market, lowered property values, and further encouraged landlord abandonment. The enactment of federal and state community reinvestment legislation in the 1970s curbed the practice of open redlining. Nonetheless, "prudent lenders will exercise increased caution in advancing mortgages, particularly in neighborhoods marked by strong indication of owner disinvestment and early abandonment."

As the neighborhood disintegrates, those who are able to leave depart in increasing numbers; among these are many working- and middle-class families. The lower population density in turn creates additional problems. Abandoned buildings increase and often serve as havens for crack use and other illegal enterprises that give criminals footholds in the community. Precipitous declines in density also make it even more difficult to sustain or develop a sense of community. The feeling of safety in numbers is completely lacking in such neighborhoods.

Although changes in the economy (industrial restructuring and reorganization) and changes in the class, racial, and demographic composition of inner-city ghetto neighborhoods are important factors in the shift from institutional to jobless ghettos since 1970, we ought not to lose sight of the fact that this process actually began immediately following World War II.

The federal government contributed to the early decay of inner-city neighborhoods by withholding mortgage capital and by making it difficult for urban areas to retain or attract families able to purchase their own homes. Spurred on by massive mortgage foreclosures during the Great Depression, the federal government in the 1940s began underwriting mortgages in an effort to enable citizens to become homeowners. But the mortgage program was selectively administered by the Federal Housing Administration (FHA), and urban neighborhoods considered poor risks were redlined—an action that excluded virtually all the black neighborhoods and many neighborhoods with a considerable number of European immigrants. It was not until the 1960s that the FHA discontinued its racial restrictions on mortgages.

By manipulating market incentives, the federal government drew middle-class whites to the suburbs and, in effect, trapped blacks in the inner cities. Beginning in the 1950s, the suburbanization of the middle class was also facilitated by a federal transportation and highway policy, including the building of freeway networks through the hearts of many cities, mortgages for veterans, mortgage-interest tax exemptions, and the quick, cheap production of massive amounts of tract housing.

In the nineteenth and early twentieth centuries, with the offer of municipal services as an inducement, cities tended to annex their suburbs. But the relations between cities and suburbs in the United States began to change following a century-long influx of poor migrants who required expensive services and paid relatively little in taxes. Annexation largely ended in the mid-twentieth century as suburbs began to resist incorporation successfully. Suburban communities also drew tighter boundaries through the manipulation of zoning laws and discriminatory land-use controls and site-selection practices, making it difficult for inner-city racial minorities to penetrate.

As separate political jurisdictions, suburbs exercised a great deal of autonomy in their use of zoning, land-use policies, covenants, and deed restrictions. In the face of mounting pressures calling for integration in the 1960s, "suburbs chose to diversify by race rather than class. They retained zoning and other restrictions that allowed only affluent blacks (and in some instances Jews) to enter, thereby intensifying the concentration and isolation of the urban poor."

Other government policies also contributed to the growth of jobless ghettos, both directly and indirectly. Many black communities were uprooted by urban renewal and forced migration. The construction of freeway and highway networks through the hearts of many cities in the 1950s produced the most dramatic changes, as many viable low-income communities were destroyed. These networks not only encouraged relocation from the cities to the suburbs, "they also created barriers between the sections of the cities, walling off poor and minority neighborhoods from central business districts. Like urban renewal, highway and expressway construction also displaced many poor people from their homes."

Federal housing policy also contributed to the gradual shift to jobless ghettos. Indeed, the lack of federal action to fight extensive segregation against African-Americans in urban housing markets and acquiescence to the opposition of organized neighborhood groups to the construction of public housing in their communities have resulted in massive segregated housing projects. The federal public housing program evolved in two policy stages that represented two distinct styles. The Wagner Housing Act of 1937 initiated the first stage. Concerned that the construction of public housing might depress

private rent levels, groups such as the U.S. Building and Loan League and the National Association of Real Estate Boards successfully lobbied Congress to require, by law, that for each new unit of public housing one "unsafe or unsanitary" unit of public housing be destroyed. As Mark Condon (1991) points out, "This policy increased employment in the urban construction market while insulating private rent levels by barring the expansion of the housing stock available to low-income families."

The early years of the public housing program produced positive results. Initially, the program mainly served intact families temporarily displaced by the Depression or in need of housing after the end of World War II. For many of these families, public housing was the first step on the road toward economic recovery. Their stay in the projects was relatively brief. The economic mobility of these families "contributed to the sociological stability of the first public housing communities, and explains the program's initial success."

The passage of the Housing Act of 1949 marked the beginning of the second policy stage. It instituted and funded the urban renewal program designed to eradicate urban slums. "Public housing was now meant to collect the ghetto residents left homeless by the urban renewal bulldozers." A new, lower-income ceiling for public housing residency was established by the federal Public Housing Authority, and families with incomes above that ceiling were evicted, thereby restricting access to public housing to the most economically disadvantaged segments of the population.

This change in federal housing policy coincided with the mass migration of African-Americans from the rural South to the cities of the Northeast and Midwest. Since smaller suburban communities refused to permit the construction of public housing, the units were overwhelmingly concentrated in the overcrowded and deteriorating inner city ghettos—the poorest and least socially organized sections of the city and the metropolitan area. "This growing population of politically weak urban poor was unable to counteract the desires of vocal middle- and working-class whites for segregated housing," housing that would keep blacks out of white neighborhoods. In short, public housing represents a federally funded institution that has isolated families by race and class for decades, and has therefore contributed to the growing concentration of jobless families in the inner-city ghettos in recent years.

Also, since 1980, a fundamental shift in the federal government's support for basic urban programs has aggravated the problems of joblessness and social organization in the new poverty neighborhoods. The Reagan and Bush administrations—proponents of the New Federalism—sharply cut spending on direct aid to cities, including general revenue sharing, urban mass transit, public service jobs and job training, compensatory education, social service block grants, local public works, economic development assistance, and urban development action grants. In 1980, the federal contribution to city budgets was 18 percent; by 1990 it had dropped to 6.4 percent. In addition, the economic recession which began in the Northeast in 1989 and lasted until the early 1990s sharply reduced those revenues that the cities themselves generated, thereby creating budget deficits that resulted in further cutbacks in basic services and programs along with increases in local taxes.

For many cities, especially the older cities of the East and Midwest, the combination of the New Federalism and the recession led to the worst fiscal and service crisis since the Depression. Cities have become increasingly underserviced, and many have been on the brink of bankruptcy. They have therefore not been in a position to combat effec-

tively three unhealthy social conditions that have emerged or become prominent since 1980: (1) the prevalence of crack-cocaine addiction and the violent crime associated with it; (2) the AIDS epidemic and its escalating public health costs; and (3) the sharp rise in the homeless population not only for individuals but for whole families as well.

Although drug addiction and its attendant violence, AIDS and its toll on public health resources, and homelessness are found in many American communities, their impact on the ghetto is profound. These communities, whose residents have been pushed to the margins of society, have few resources with which to combat these social ills that arose in the 1980s. Fiscally strapped cities have watched helplessly as these problems—exacerbated by the new poverty, the decline of social organization in the jobless neighborhoods, and the reduction of social services—have made the city at large seem a dangerous and threatening place in which to live. Accordingly, working- and middle-class urban residents continue to relocate in the suburbs. Thus, while joblessness and related social problems are on the rise in inner-city neighborhoods, especially in those that represent the new poverty areas, the larger city has fewer and fewer resources with which to combat them.

Finally, policymakers indirectly contributed to the emergence of jobless ghettos by making decisions that have decreased the attractiveness of low-paying jobs and accelerated the relative decline in wages for low-income workers. In particular, in the absence of an effective labor-market policy, they have tolerated industry practices that undermine worker security, such as the reduction in benefits and the rise of involuntary part-time employment, and they have "allowed the minimum wage to erode to its second-lowest level in purchasing power in 40 years." After adjusting for inflation, "the minimum wage is 26 percent below its av-erage level in the 1970s." Moreover, they virtually eliminated AFDC benefits for fam-ilies in which a mother is employed at least half-time. In the early 1970s, a working mother with two children whose wages equaled 75 percent of the amount desig-nated as the poverty line could receive AFDC benefits as a wage supplement in forty-nine states; in 1995 only those in three states could. . . . [E]ven with the expansion of the earned income tax credit (a wage sub-sidy for the working poor) such policies make it difficult for poor workers to sup-port their families and protect their chil-dren. The erosion of wages and benefits

forces many low-income workers in the in-ner city to move or remain on welfare.

REFERENCES

Condon, Mark. 1991."Public Housing, Crime, and the Urban Labor Market: A Study of Black Youths in Chicago." Working paper series, Malcom Wiener Center for Social Policy, John F. Kennedy School of Government, Harvard University, March, no. H-91-3.

Holzer, Harry J., Keith R. Ihlanfeldt, and David L. Sjoquist. 1994. "Work, Search and Travel Among White and Black Youth." *Journal of Urban Economics* 35:320–45.

Wilson, William Julius. 1987. *The Truly Disadvantaged: The Inner City, The Underclass, and Public Policy.* Chicago: University of Chicago Press.

17

THE WAGE SQUEEZE
David M. Gordon

David M. Gordon is Dorothy H. Hirshon Professor of Economics and Director of the Center for Economic Policy Analysis at the New School of Research. His chapter is drawn from his 1996 book, *Fat and Mean: The Corporate Squeeze of Working Americans and the Myth of Managerial "Downsizing."*

For years Craig Miller had been a sheet-metal worker at a major airline. After he lost his job in 1992, he and his wife—parents of four kids—had to scramble. Craig took on two lower-paying jobs and started a small sideline business. His wife worked

nights as a stock clerk. They were patching together, counting his business, four part-time jobs and they were still earning less than half Craig's previous paycheck.

"Sure we've got four jobs," Craig told a reporter. "So what? So you can work like a dog for $5 an hour?"[1]

The Miller family saga is hardly unique. Since the mid-1970s, more and more U.S. workers and their families have been suf-fering the *wage squeeze*, enduring steady downward pressure on their hourly take-home pay. The wage squeeze has afflicted not merely the unskilled and disadvantaged but the vast majority of U.S. households, not merely the poor and working class but the middle class as well. Most people in the United States used to be able to look forward to a future of steadily rising earnings. Now they have to race merely to stay in place.

The wage squeeze has even broader consequences. It not only pinches workers and their immediate families. It sends tremors through entire communities, eroding their stability, ripping their social fabric. The frustration and anger it provokes begins to attach the body politic like a plague, spreading virulent strains of cynicism and discontent, of disaffection from government and hatred toward "others" like immigrants who are often blamed for the scourge. Many observers in the United States are inclined to turn their heads, viewing falling wages as somebody else's problem. But the effects are too far-reaching, too extensive. It won't work to play the ostrich, sticking one's head in the sand. The sand is eroding all around us.

Back to the 1960s

The public receives mixed signals about the wage squeeze. On the one hand, more and more observers have taken note of the vise closing around workers' earnings—citing the pressure to work longer hours, the "disappearing middle class," the increasingly elusive American Dream, the mounting gap between the rich and the poor. Personal stories of declining fortunes abound. Statistical studies of stagnant earnings and soaring inequality have become a growth industry. In my research . . ., finding journalistic accounts and scholarly analyses of the wage squeeze was as easy as following the trail of Newt Gingrich's newfound notoriety.

By late 1995, . . . the issue was becoming inescapable. *Business Week,* often a leader in tracking changes in the economic climate, devoted a cover story to "The Wage Squeeze" in July 1995. Surveying the atmospheric conditions they reported:[2]

> Four years into a recovery, profits are at a 45-year high, unemployment remains relatively low, and the weak dollar has put foreign rivals on the defensive. Yet U.S. companies continue to drive down costs as if the economy still were in a tailspin. Many are tearing up pay systems and job structures, replacing them with new ones that slice wage rates, slash raises, and subcontract work to lower-paying suppliers.

"Although the problem [of slumping wages] has been plaguing Americans for years," wrote *New York Times* economics reporter Louis Uchitelle that same summer, "it is just now rising to the level of a major campaign issue."[3] "Nearly everyone by now knows the situation," economic columnist William Greider wrote in November 1995, "either from the headlines or from their own daily lives: the continuing erosion of wage incomes for most American families."[4] Commenting on yet another twelve months of stagnant wage growth, Robert D. Hershey Jr. wrote in late 1995: "The frustration and insecurity that have resulted are expected to play a major role in shaping next year's Presidential race as politicians of both parties try to portray themselves as the best choice to provide economic growth that will benefit the middle class."[5]

On the other hand, many pundits, economists and business leaders seem not to lament the wage squeeze but rather to praise it. Instead of wringing their hands about working households' living standards, many express relief about the moderation of wage pressure on prices and profits—a trend they hope will dampen inflationary pressure, keep U.S. firms competitive in global markets, and protect small enterprises against business failure. When journalists report monthly data on workers' hourly earnings, they are much more likely to celebrate wage moderation or decline than to worry about its consequences for the millions who depend on that labor income.

Take the *New York Times'* report in April 1994 on real wage trends in the first quarter of the year. Noting that nominal wages and prices had grown at roughly the same rates, leaving real wages flat, the story appeared to welcome this "relatively benign reading on wages and benefits . . . ": "American workers are obtaining less in pay and benefit increases from employers these days . . . ," with the result that ". . . price pressures remained subdued." The reporter observed hopefully that "bond prices rallied at the news." Nowhere in the story did he wonder how workers themselves might regard these "relatively benign" developments.[6]

So there are, indeed, two sides to the news about wages. "The good news is labor costs are under control," economic forecaster Michael Evans put it in 1992. "The bad news is that employees are broke."[7]

More often than not, however, the good news for business seems to blot out the bad for nearly everyone else. I was recently struck by the prevalence of these priorities at a conference about macroeconomic policy in Washington, D.C. in the spring of 1994. At lunch we heard from a Presidential economic adviser. A distinguished scholar, the speaker had been an economic liberal, more to the left than to the right of the mainstream of economic discourse. In a recent policy book, he had expressed concern about a polarized society in which the economic extremes of the 1980s had made the rich richer and set the rest adrift.

The economist lauded the progress of the economy in the spring of 1994 and the continuing signs, in the Administration's view, of a decent economic recovery. He noted with approval the evidence of (modest) growth in consumer spending, investment, and exports. He applauded the Federal Reserve's and the markets' continuing restraint in interest rates and pointed proudly to the tepid pace of inflation. He projected 1994 real wage growth at zero percent.

What is notable about this presentation is what was *not* said. A projection of zero real wage growth, but no reflections on the hardships experienced by ordinary working people. No lament about the twenty-year decline in real earnings. And this from a key economic adviser to the president who had promised, in his initial economic message to Congress, that "our economic plan will redress the inequities of the 1980s."[8]

This widespread inattention to workers' living standards even shows up in the preferences of government data collectors. For decades, since the end of the Depression and the spread of the union movement, the U.S. Bureau of Labor Statistics had kept track of the living standards of the average American worker with published data on *spendable earnings.* The series measured the real after-tax value of workers' weekly take-home pay. But in 1981 the Reagan Administration discontinued the index, citing conceptual and measurement problems. They proposed no replacement, leaving us without any official series intended specifically to monitor the effective purchasing power of workers' earnings.

Had the government data apparatchiki actually cared about illuminating the trends in workers' income, the statistical problems they cited would not have been especially difficult to overcome—hardly so vexing that they warranted dropping this kind of series altogether. But their priorities lay elsewhere.

At more or less the same time as the discontinuation of the weekly spendable earnings series, the Bureau of Labor Statistics, reflecting the Reaganites' ever-extending solicitude for the needs of business, was expanding the range and variety of its *employment cost indices,* tracking the hourly costs to corporations of their wage-and-salary employees. As a result, in recent years, corporations need merely dial the phone to get up-to-date data about changes in labor costs faced by them and their competitors.

More than a decade ago, in response to this change in priorities, my collaborators Samuel Bowles, Thomas E. Weisskopf, and I proposed an alternative version of the spendable earnings index, with modifications designed to address each of the specific problems raised about the traditional indicator. Where the traditional series on *weekly* earnings had conflated movements in hourly earnings and changes in hours worked per week, we proposed relying on a much simpler index of *hourly* earnings. Where the traditional series had relied on a somewhat implausible adjustment for the taxes paid by the "average" worker, we suggested a much more immediate and direct calculation. We called our proposed alternative an index of *real spendable hourly earnings.*

Our proposal was graciously published in the Bureau of Labor Statistics official journal, but, hardly to our surprise, the Reagan Administration ignored our advice, persisting in providing no official record of trends in workers' take-home pay. So we have continued ourselves to maintain and update what we consider to be the most salient indicator of workers' earnings.

Our index of *real spendable hourly earnings* provides a straightforward measure of the real value of the average production or nonsupervisory worker's take-home pay. "Production and nonsupervisory" workers, as they're defined in the official BLS surveys of business establishments, comprised 82 per-

cent of total employment in 1994.[9] They represent that group in the labor force that is most clearly dependent on wage and salary income. They include both blue-collar and white-collar workers, both unskilled and skilled. They cover not only laborers and machinists but also secretaries, programmers and teachers.

I focus primarily on these "production and nonsupervisory" employees at least partly to avoid distortions in the data from the huge increases during the 1980s in the salaries of top management—a group covered by the earnings data for the other fifth of employees excluded from our measure, a category called "nonproduction or supervisory" employees. In further discussion in this chapter . . ., in order to avoid the cumbersome terminology used by the BLS, I shall refer to the "production and nonsupervisory" category in the establishment data as *production* workers and to the other grouping as *supervisory* employees, respectively.

Spendable hourly earnings measure the average production worker's hourly wage-and-salary income minus personal income taxes and Social Security taxes. These earnings are then expressed in constant dollars in order to adjust for the effects of inflation on the cost of living. They measure how much per hour, controlling for taxes and inflation, the average production worker is able to take home from his or her job.

Figure 1 charts the level of average real hourly spendable earnings for private nonfarm production employees in the United States from 1948 to 1994.

The data show a clear pattern. The average worker's real after-tax pay grew rapidly through the mid-1960s. Its growth then slowed, with some fluctuation, until the early 1970s. After a postwar peak in 1972, this measure of earnings declined with growing severity, with cyclical fluctuation around this accelerating drop, through the rest of the 1970s and 1980s. The average an-

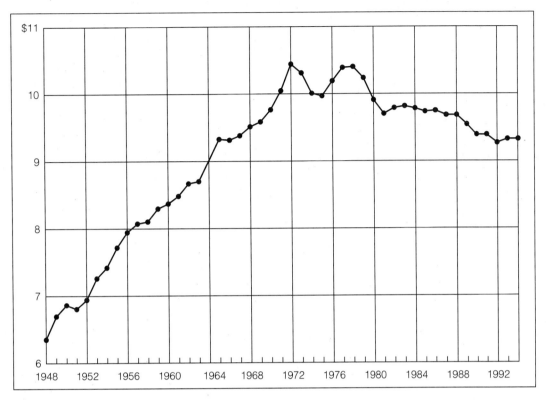

FIGURE 1　The Wage Squeeze—Real Spendable Hourly Earnings ($1994), Production/Nonsupervisory Employees, Private Nonfarm Sector, 1948–94
Source: See text and notes; series maintained by author.

nual growth of real spendable hourly earnings reached 2.1 percent a year from 1948 to 1966, slowed to 1.4 percent between 1966 and 1973, and then dropped with gathering speed at a shade less than *minus* one percent per year from 1973 to 1989.

Despite the recovery from the recession of 1990–91, real spendable hourly earnings were lower in 1994 than they had been in the business-cycle trough of 1990. Even though the economy had been growing steadily for three years from the bottom of the recession, they continued to decline at an average annual rate of −0.6 percent from the peak in 1989 through 1994.

By 1994, indeed, real hourly take-home pay had dropped by 10.4 percent since its postwar peak in 1972. More dramatically still, *real spendable hourly earnings had fallen back to below the level they had last reached in 1967.* Growing massively over those nearly three decades, the economy's real gross output per capita in 1994 was 53 percent larger than it had been in 1967, but real hourly take-home pay was four cents lower.[10] Referring to these trends since the early 1970s as "the wage squeeze" is polite understatement. Calling it the "wage collapse" might be more apt.

These harsh winds have continued to blow through the recent recovery. Most economic meteorologists have described them in similarly cloudy terms. But a few have recently tried to present a sunnier weather report.

In one highly visible piece in late 1994, for example, the *New York Times* published a long news story beginning on its front page. Sylvia Nasar, the *Times* reporter, broadcast a considerably more sanguine view about wage trends: "it is practically gospel that the growing American economy cannot deliver the higher pay that American workers want," she wrote. But she claimed that wage changes during the early 1990s appeared to suggest a turnaround, with the majority of new jobs paying above-average wages. "As a result," she concluded, "average hourly pay for all employees, adjusted for inflation, is slowly rising."[11]

The source of Nasar's discrepant conclusions was not hard to find. Unlike all the data reviewed thus far in this chapter, which cover production employees—accounting for roughly four-fifths of the wage-and-salary workforce—Nasar was looking at wage trends for *all* workers. These data cover those at the top of the earnings distribution, including top-level executives whose total compensation has continued to soar straight through the mid-1990s. Those who have long pointed to the wage squeeze have never denied that the top 10 to 20 percent of the earnings distribution has fared much better than everyone else. If you mix together those in the middle and bottom with those at the top, you're bound to get a different and ultimately misleading story. Nasar's story was effectively demonstrating a penetrating glimpse into the obvious—that supervisory employees have continued to enjoy rising real hourly compensation.

In his recent book *Values Matter Most*, commentator Ben J. Wattenberg makes the same mistake. Hoping to create the space for his argument that we should concentrate on social values, not the economy, he seeks to cast doubt on the economic pressures cited by many. He notes that many highlighting the wage squeeze focus on real earnings series for production and nonsupervisory workers. He argues that this series gives an "inaccurate" picture because it "concerns cash only, ignoring benefits."[12] Then, almost quicker than the eye can blink, he shifts our attention to the same series Nasar reported, the index for total employee compensation per hour. "That line," he observes hopefully, "is clearly trending *upward* . . . ," lending support to his ultimate conclusion that "our economic situation is somewhat less than grievous."[13] But while the eye was blinking, Wattenberg switched to a series that differed from the first in *two* respects, not just one: including benefits, it traced total compensation; *and*, tracking all workers, it included those at the top who have been feeding at the trough. . . [Just] including benefits in our series, while continuing to focus on production and nonsupervisory workers, tells almost exactly the same story as earnings without benefits. Whether we look at earnings or full compensation, the wage squeeze for production workers remains severe.

For the vast majority of workers, then, these have been hard times indeed. In 1994, the average production employee working thirty-five hours a week and fifty-two weeks a year was able to take home about $16,833 after taxes, barely above the official poverty standard for a family of four.[14] An earlier generation had expected that their earnings would rise over their working lifetimes and that their children could anticipate higher living standards than their own. For the past two decades, however, more and more workers have had to adjust their expectations, reconciling themselves to toil at what are sometimes derisively called "McJobs."[15]

One Michigan woman, talking in a pollster's focus group in the early 1990s about deflated expectations, lamented:[16]

I think about when I was married, a week of groceries cost me $13 and my husband thought that was entirely too much money to spend for a week's groceries. Now I spend $150. I feel like I'm always running—and this big snowball is behind me getting bigger and bigger—and just trying to keep it from running over me.

Another focus group participant talked about shifting expectations across generations. "[Our kids]'ll have to be good to us if they want to have a home to live in, because the only way they'll get one is if we will them ours. They're never going to be able to buy a house."[17]

You don't have to organize your own focus groups to get a strong whiff of these kinds of economic concerns. Recent national polls repeatedly reveal such fears about economic pressure and the cloudy future for this and future generations. In a 1992 Gallup poll, for example, more than three-fifths said they were dissatisfied with "the opportunity for the next generation of Americans to live better than their parents"; 58 percent were dissatisfied with the "opportunity for a poor person in this country to get ahead by working hard."[18] In a June 1993 *LA Times*/CNN poll, 39 percent of participants described their personal finances as "shaky," while more than half—51 percent—said they "expect the next generation of Americans will have a worse standard of living than the one we have now."[19] Even though the economy was well into its recovery, in a November 1993 *LA Times*/CNN poll two-thirds reported that job security was "worse for Americans now, compared to two years ago" and 53 percent that they felt this "greater job insecurity will occur over the long term, for many years."[20] Even further into the recovery, a March 1994 *New York Times* poll found that two-fifths of respondents expressed "worry" that during the next two years they might be laid off, required to work reduced hours, or forced to take pay cuts. Nearly two-fifths also reported that in order "to try to stay even financially" during the last two years they had had to work overtime or take on extra jobs.[21] In a March 1995 *Business Week*/Harris poll, people were asked whether "the American Dream . . . has become easier or harder to achieve in the *past* 10 years." Two-thirds answered that it has become "harder." Participants were also asked if it would be "easier or harder to achieve in the *next* 10 years." Three-quarters chose "harder."[22]

A Crowded Boat

Andrew Flenoy, a twenty-one-year-old living in Kansas City, did better in 1994 than many, holding down a steady job paying a cut above the minimum wage. In fact, he had even enjoyed some recent promotions, rising at a food catering firm from dishwasher to catering manager. Through that sequence of promotions, however, his earnings had increased from $5.50 an hour to only $6.50 an hour—the equivalent of only about $12,000 a year working full-time year-round. Whatever satisfaction he had enjoyed from his promotions had quickly paled. "Now he is tired of the burgundy and black uniform he must wear," a reporter concluded, "and of the sense that he works every day from 6 A.M. to 2 P.M. just to earn enough money so that he can come back and work some more the next day." "My resolution for 1994," Flenoy remarked, "is that if nothing comes along, I'll relocate and start from scratch somewhere else."[23]

Flenoy attended only a semester of community college after high school and suffered the additional employment disadvantage of being African American. Many are inclined to assume, indeed, that the wage squeeze has mostly afflicted the young, the unskilled, and the disadvantaged.

Although some have suffered more than others, however, a much wider band of the working population has been caught in the vise. For most Americans, the wage squeeze has been a profoundly democratizing trend.

Indeed, the data on the breadth of the wage squeeze seem finally to have persuaded skeptics not normally known for their empathy with workers. Recently confronted with some of these data, for example, Marvin Kosters, a well-known conservative economist at the American Enterprise Institute who had earlier challenged reports about trends toward growing inequality, admitted surprise at the variety of subgroups affected by wage erosion. "It's really quite amazing," he acknowledged.[24] The data would scarcely seem "amazing," of course, to those who've been directly feeling the pinch.

In order to assess the breadth of the wage squeeze, we need to turn to data from household surveys, which unlike the establishment surveys afford considerable detail on workers' personal characteristics. We can look at trends in real hourly earnings between 1979 and 1993 for a variety of different groups in the private nonfarm workforce, since it is trends in the private sector with which I am most concerned. . . .[25]

Looking at this universe, we find that real hourly earnings for *all* private nonfarm employees, including those at the top, remained essentially flat from 1979 to 1993—barely rising from $11.62 to $11.80 (in 1993 prices). (Government workers did somewhat better.)

But we know that those at the top did fairly well. The more telling comparison looks at real wage trajectories for the bottom four-fifths of the real wage distribution and for the top fifth. As anticipated from the data for production workers reviewed in the previous section, it was the bottom 80 percent that experienced actual real wage decline, with the 1993 level dropping by 3.4 percent below the 1979 figure. For the top 20 percent times were not so harsh; they en-

joyed a healthy rate of increase, with their real hourly earnings rising by 1993 to almost three times those for the bottom four-fifths.

We can also compare workers by race and ethnic origin. Looking at workers in the bottom 80 percent of the overall wage distribution, it is true, not surprisingly, that African Americans and Hispanics fared less well than whites. But even among whites in the bottom 80 percent, real hourly earnings dropped by nearly 3 percent. (Of course, a much larger percentage of African Americans and Hispanics were situated in the bottom four-fifths of the wage distribution than of whites.) Not just the disadvantaged but the advantaged racial group joined the wake.

TABLE 1   The Wage Squeeze Across the Work Force—Real Hourly Earnings, Nonfarm Private Sector ($1993)

	1979	1993	% Change
All workers	$11.62	11.80	1.5%
Bottom 80 percent	8.93	8.59	−3.4
Top 20 percent	22.41	24.66	10.04
White workers, bottom 80 percent	9.03	8.77	−2.9
Black workers, bottom 80 percent	8.28	7.98	−3.6
Hispanic workers, bottom 80 percent	8.53	7.86	−7.9
Male workers, bottom 80 percent	9.94	9.05	−9.0
Female workers, bottom 80 percent	7.94	8.16	2.8
High school dropout	10.31	8.19	−20.6
High school graduate	11.11	10.05	−9.5
Some college education	13.12	11.03	−15.9
College graduate	16.01	16.57	3.5
Postgraduate	19.84	21.59	8.8

Sources and Notes: Based on author's own tabulations from data samples extracted from Current Population Survey.

Hourly earnings for all nonfarm private workers and all subgroupings defined as usual weekly earnings divided by usual weekly hours worked. Hourly earnings deflated by CPI-U-X1 price deflator.

Looking at wage trends by gender, we find a major difference in the impact of the wage squeeze. While male workers in the bottom 80 percent of the distribution experienced devastating declines in their real hourly earnings—facing a decline of close to 10 percent—women workers in the bottom 80 percent enjoyed modest real wage growth, with a total increase over the full period of 2.8 percent. Despite these gains, however, women's wages still lagged substantially behind men's. In 1993, the median female hourly wage had reached barely more than three-quarters of the median male wage, at 78 percent. Women were gaining on men, to be sure, but their gains occurred primarily because real male wages were plummeting, not because real female earnings were themselves growing rapidly. Indeed, almost three-quarters of the decline in the wage gap between men and women from 1979 and 1993 can be attributed to the decline in male earnings—a trend which undoubtedly contributed to the widespread frustration which many males have apparently been feeling and venting.[26]

A final comparison looks at the experience of workers with different levels of education. It was the bulk of workers on the bottom, those with less than a college degree, who experienced actual wage decline. Only those with a college degree or better were able to gain some measure of protection against the unfriendly winds. And the most recent trends have been harsh even for a large number in that group. From 1989 to 1993, for example, even male workers with just a college degree, but no postgraduate education, were hit with declining real earnings.

Table 1 pulls together these separate tabulations for different groups of workers. The wage squeeze has caught a huge proportion of U.S. workers in its grip.

In better times, of course, workers in a pinch often pulled up stakes and migrated in search of greener pastures—in Andrew Flenoy's words, "to relocate and start from scratch somewhere else." But the greener pastures have mostly turned brown. *New York Times* reporter Louis Uchitelle tells the story about workers in Peoria, Illinois, where layoffs and givebacks at Caterpillar had cast long shadows over the local economy:[27]

Today the adventurous search for opportunity is no longer rewarding. For generations, Americans migrated—going West, so to speak—when jobs in their communities became scarce or failed to pay well. But income stagnation is a nationwide phenomenon. Migration has become futile. Peorians, for example, uprooted themselves by the thousands in the early 1980's, when recession and then massive layoffs at Caterpillar and the numerous local companies that supply Caterpillar pushed the unemployment rate here above 16 percent. By the late 1980's, they were trickling home again.

"When they got to Oklahoma and Texas, they found that the promise of good wages was a lot of talk; they worked hard and had little to show for it," said David Koehler, executive director of the Peoria Area Labor Management Council. "Now, many have come home to jobs that pay less than they once earned, but they have returned because this is where their families are to help them."

. . . Those caught in the vise have no illusions about the consequences. A union activist in the continuing labor struggles at Caterpillar in Illinois looked down the road toward the turn of the millennium and saw hardship: "If we don't put an end to this drift of the country to drive wages down," he said, "there's no future for my three boys. There will be an upper class and a lower class, and I know where [my boys] will be."[28] A middle-class Michigan resident echoed this view: "Everybody is going to be either very rich or very poor. There's going to be the rich in their little towers, and there's going to be everybody else floundering around trying to survive."[29] A 48-year-old Milwaukee woman, laid off in June 1995 after seventeen years on the job, wondered when the wage pressure from corporations will end. "How far can this go," she asked, "before they ruin everything?"[30]

NOTES

1. Dirk Johnson, "Family Struggles to Make Do After Fall From Middle Class," New York Times, March 11, 1994, p. A1.

2. Aaron Bernstein, "The Wage Squeeze," Business Week, July 17, 1995, p. 55.

3. Louis Uchitelle, "Flat Wages Seen as Issue in '96 Vote," New York Times, August 13, 1995, p. 26.

4. William Greider, "Middle-Class Funk," Rolling Stone, November 2, 1995, p. 35.

5. Robert D. Hershey Jr., "U.S. Wages Up 2.7% in Year, A Record Low," New York Times, November 1, 1995, p. A1.

6. Robert D. Hershey Jr., "Wage Increases Are Small, But Confidence Jumps," New York Times, April 27, 1994, p. D1.

7. Quoted in "A 4.3% Gain for Workers," New York Times, January 29, 1992, p. D8.

8. Executive Office of the President, "A Vision of Change for America," February 17, 1993, p. 8.

9. See Employment and Earnings, January 1995, Tables 48–49.

10. GDP per capita from Economic Report of the President, 1995, Tables B-2, B-32.

11. Sylvia Nasar, "Statistics Reveal Bulk of New Jobs Pay Over Average," New York Times, October 17, 1994, p. A1.

12. Ben J. Wattenberg, Values Matter Most: How Republicans or Democrats or a Third Party Can Win and Renew the American Way of Life (New York: The Free Press, 1995), p. 78.

13. Ibid., pp. 79, 81 [emphasis in original].

14. In 1993 the official government poverty line for a family of four was $14,763. U.S. Bureau of the Census, "Income, Poverty, and Valuation of Noncash Benefits: 1993," Current Population Reports, Series P-60, No. 188, February 1995, Table A-1.

15. I first came across this designation in Tamar Lewin, "Low Pay and Closed Doors Confront Young Job Seekers," New York Times, March 10, 1994, p. B12. The author defines McJobs as "jobs that pay $6 an hour or less, and offer little in the way of a career path."

16. Quoted in Stanley B. Greenberg, Middle Class Dreams: The Politics and Power of the New American Majority (New York: Times Books, 1995), p. 168.

17. Quoted in Greenberg, Middle Class Dreams, p. 169.

18. Gallup Poll News Service, "Recession Shakes Faith in American Dream," News Release, February 2, 1992.

19. Los Angeles Times, "Los Angeles Times Poll: Study #317, National Politics," July 15, 1993, p. 1.

20. Los Angeles Times, "Los Angeles Times Poll: Employment," November 15, 1993, p. 7.

21. Michael R. Kagay, "From Coast to Coast, From Affluent to Poor, Poll Shows Anxiety Over Jobs," New York Times, March 11, 1994, p. A14.

22. "Portrait of an Anxious Public," Business Week, March 13, 1995, p. 80 [emphases added].

23. Lewin, "Low Pay and Closed Doors Confront Young Job Seekers," p. B12.

24. Quoted in New York Times, March 31, 1994, p. A18.

25. All data in the following discussion are based on the author's tabulations from the outgoing rotation samples of the Current Population Survey for March 1979 and March 1993. The 1979 earnings figures were converted to 1993 dollars by the CPI-U-X1 price index.

26. Lawrence Mishel and Jared Bernstein, The State of Working America, 1994–95 (Armonk, NY: M. E. Sharpe, 1994), Table 3.9.

27. Louis Uchitelle, "Trapped in the Impoverished Middle Class," New York Times, November 17, 1991, Sec. 3, p. 1.

28. David Moberg, "Prairie Fires," In These Times, July 25, 1994, p. 21.

29. Quoted in Greenberg, Middle Class Dreams, p. 165.

30. Quoted in Bernstein, "The Wage Squeeze," p. 55.

18

Rising Wage Inequality
The United States vs. Other Advanced Countries

Richard B. Freeman • *Lawrence F. Katz*

Richard B. Freeman holds the Herbert Ascherman Chair in Economics at Harvard University. He is also director of the Labor Studies Program at the National Bureau of Economic Research, and executive programme director of the Comparative Labour Market Institutions Programme at the London School of Economics' Centre for Economic Performance. He is currently a member of the Secretary of Labor and Commerce's Commission on The Future of Worker-Management Relations. His research interests include youth labor market problems, trade unionism, high-skilled labor markets, crime, economic discrimination, philanthropic behavior, income distribution and equity in the marketplace, and labor in developing countries.

Lawrence F. Katz is Chief Economist of the U.S. Department of Labor. He is currently on leave from his positions as a professor of economics at Harvard University and a research associate of the National Bureau of Economic Research. His research interests include family income inequality, labor mobility and unemployment, changes in the structure of wages, theories of wage determination, the problems of disadvantaged youth, and regional economic growth. He is currently an editor of the *Quarterly Journal of Economics*.

One of the "big stories" in American economic life in the 1980s was the large increase in income inequality. Inequality grew as the economic expansion of the latter half of the 1980s failed to benefit the majority of American families enough to offset the losses they had incurred during the recession of the early 1980s. In the early 1980s it was possible to make a plausible case for trickle-down economics, but by the end of the decade it was clear that policies to increase the income of the wealthy had not generated prosperity for the majority of the population. Many American families saw a decline in their living standards in the 1980s. A large number were no better off at the outset of the 1990s than they had been ten years earlier; in 1989 the real money incomes for the bottom 40 percent of American families were similar to the incomes of the bottom 40 percent of families in 1979. In contrast, the incomes of the upper 20 percent of families in 1989 were almost 20 percent higher than those of analogous families in 1979 (U.S. Bureau of the Census, 1992, pp. B-11 and B-13).

Since most Americans make their living from work, the story behind this rising inequality and the deteriorating income of lower-paid workers is a story about changes in the labor market. Underlying the rising disparity in the fortunes of American families was a rise in labor market inequality that shifted wage and employment opportunities in favor of the more educated and more skilled. Less educated men, particularly the young, suffered substantial losses in real earnings and were at greater risk of unemployment than in years past. For many of them, the American dream of economic progress was seriously threatened, as it had not been since the Great Depression.

Was the twist in the job market against less educated workers unique to the United States, or was it part of a general pattern of decline in the well-being of the less skilled in advanced countries? Does it mark a new era in modern economic development—a reversal of the broad trend of income inequality falling with economic growth? Have other advanced countries avoided or ameliorated the rise in wage inequality that has characterized the United States?

To examine these questions we begin with a summary of the changes in the American wage structure during the 1980s, and then look at the extent to which similar changes occurred in other industrial nations. Our analysis of the overseas experience relies largely on studies by researchers at the National Bureau of Economic Research (NBER) that use computerized records of the earnings and employment of tens of thousands of workers in advanced Western countries—the United States and its major trading partners and competitors in the world economy. Given the facts, we assess why inequality rose so rapidly in the United States, and draw lessons for the United States from the experience overseas.

Our analysis highlights four aspects of wage inequality across countries:

1. During the 1980s, the countries with the most decentralized labor markets and wage-setting systems—the United States and the United Kingdom—had exceptional increases in earnings inequality and in wage differentials by skill. Only in the United States, however, did low-wage workers (even those in full-time employment) have large declines in real earnings (earnings adjusted for inflation). Most other developed countries had only moderate or slight increases in wage inequality, and in Britain real wages rose even for low-paid workers.

2. The major cause of increasing inequality was a shift in relative labor demand that favored more educated workers and workers with problem-solving skills combined with a reduced rate of growth in the supply of highly educated workers relative to less educated workers. The shift in demand was driven by skill-biased technological change associated with the "computer revolution" and, to a lesser extent, by changes in international trade. However, because shifts in demand were similar across countries, demand forces do not explain many of the differences among countries in the rise of inequality.

3. Slower growth in the supply of highly educated workers relative to less educated workers in the United States contributed to the especially great increase in wage differentials by education. The slackened growth was due largely to a slower expansion of the college-educated work force in the 1980s than in the 1970s, but was also affected by the influx of immigrants who had less than a high school education. Wage differentials by education increased much less in countries where the relative supply of more educated workers continued to grow rapidly in the 1980s.

4. Differences in wage setting institutions and training and education systems also contributed to international differences in the growth of inequality. Countries where unions, employer federations, and government agencies play a greater role in wage setting and where better training or

education for non-college-educated workers is provided had smaller increases in inequality than in the United States. In addition, the decline of unionization in the United States and the United Kingdom contributed to the rapid rise in wage inequality in those countries, while the weakening of centralized wage-setting institutions in countries such as Sweden allowed for modest increases in historically compressed wage differentials.

Changes in the United States

As a starting point for examining what happened in other countries, we summarize the facts about changes in the U.S. wage and employment structure in the 1980s. In this case, unlike in many areas of economic analysis, there is strong evidence and a broad consensus that lets us use the word *facts* rather than *claims* or *assertions*. Researchers using several data sources, including household survey data from the Current Population Survey (CPS), other household surveys, and establishment surveys, have documented that wage inequality and skill differentials in earnings and employment increased sharply in the United States (Bound and Johnson, 1992; Blackburn, Bloom, and Freeman, 1992; Davis and Haltiwanger, 1991; Katz and Murphy, 1992; Levy and Murnane, 1992; Murphy and Welch, 1992). The finding that inequality increased is not sensitive to the choice of data set, sample, or wage measure. The following is a summary of the changes in the American wage and employment structure that give us benchmarks for assessing the labor market performance of other countries.

Fact One In the 1980s overall wage dispersion increased in the United States to levels greater than at any time since 1940. The hourly earnings of a full-time worker

in the ninetieth percentile of the U.S. earnings distribution (someone whose earnings exceeded those of 90 percent of all workers) relative to a worker in the tenth percentile (someone whose earnings exceeded those of just 10 percent of all workers) grew by 20 percent for men and 25 percent for women from 1979 to 1989. This pattern was not offset by improved fringe benefits for less skilled workers nor by increases in their chances of holding a job relative to more educated workers. It marks a worsening in the economic well-being of lower-paid workers.

Fact Two Pay differentials by education and age increased. The college/high school wage premium doubled for young workers, as the weekly wages of young male college graduates increased by some 30 percent relative to those of young males with twelve or fewer years of schooling. In addition, among workers without college degrees the wages of older workers rose relative to those of younger workers. The only earnings differential that decreased was that between men and women, which dropped by 10 percent or so in all education and age groups in the 1980s.

Fact Three Wage dispersion increased within demographic and skill groups. The wages of individuals of the same age, education, and sex, working in the same industry and occupation, were more unequal at the end of the 1980s than they had been ten or twenty years earlier. Much of this increase took the form of greater wage differentials for "similar" workers across establishments in the same industry. A worker's formal educational qualifications and employer mattered more for his or her earnings in 1990 than in the past.

Fact Four The real earnings of less educated and lower paid workers fell compared with the real earnings of analogous individuals a decade earlier. Most striking, the real hourly wages of young men with twelve or fewer years of schooling dropped by some 20 percent from 1979 to 1989.

This list of facts summarizes the evidence in terms of statistical measures of earnings distributions. But the same data can be organized in another way that some find more appealing: as changes in the share of jobs that provide "middle-class" earnings. For instance, rather than reporting the ratio of the wages of ninetieth percentile to tenth percentile workers, we could report the proportion of workers whose incomes fall within a fixed middle-class income band. Organized this way, the data show that the fraction of workers in the middle of the income distribution declined substantially. Published CPS Consumer Income Reports reveal, for instance, that in 1990, 35 percent of twenty-five- to thirty-four-year-old men had incomes that were in a 30 percent band around the mean for that age group, down 6 percentage points from 41 percent in 1980.[1] The middle of the income distribution was "squashed" relative to the top and bottom.

The "jobs" measure of changes in labor market inequality tells the same story as the income distribution measures, since both reflect the same changes in the pattern of individual earnings. Under reasonable circumstances, an increase in earnings inequality implies a decline in the proportion of jobs around the middle of the earnings distribution; conversely, a decline in the proportion of workers with middle-class earnings implies a rise in inequality. . . .

Will the increase in inequality continue into the twenty-first century? The increase in overall wage inequality was initially driven by rising within-group inequality but was counteracted, in part, by declines in the college wage premium in the 1970s. When within-group inequality and educational wage differentials expanded in the 1980s, inequality rose along all dimensions except gender. While there is no economic law preventing further increases in inequality, the rise in educational differentials has induced some offsetting forces—notably, increased enrollments in college in response to the increased payoff of college degrees—that have arrested the upward trend in educational premiums in the early 1990s, and that will weigh against any sustained further rise in inequality.

Changes in Other Advanced Countries

Did labor market differentials by skill and overall wage inequality rise in other advanced industrial nations as they did in the United States, or is rising inequality unique to the United States?

To answer this question, we used studies that gathered comparable earnings data and examined wage structures for many countries in the 1980s, including the United States, United Kingdom, Canada, Australia, Japan, Sweden, France, Italy, Germany, South Korea, and the Netherlands (Freeman and Katz, 1994). The data come from diverse sources, ranging from CPS-style household surveys to establishment surveys to surveys comparable to the United States' Survey of Consumer Finances. Virtually all of the data sets measure earnings as before-tax earnings.

There are, of course, noncomparabilities between data sets for various countries. Definitions of educational and occupational groups differ depending on national education and training systems and data gathering procedures. Sample survey coverage and measures of earnings differ. The meaning of earnings also differs across countries. In the United States living standards depend largely on personal earnings, whereas in countries with extensive welfare states the government provides elements of compensation to all citizens or workers, such as health insurance, that many Americans must buy with their take-home pay and gives child allowances and diverse forms of social insurance that make living standards less dependent on earnings than in the United States. . . . If Europeans, for example, have benefits that Americans must buy with their pay, measures of inequality based on wages will overstate inequality in Europe relative to the United States, since all European workers will obtain similar benefits that are not counted in their wages. Differences in the progressivity of tax-transfer systems across countries also affect how before-tax earnings translate into economic well-being. Earnings differentials based on before-tax earnings overstate inequality when the tax system is progressive. On the other hand, high marginal tax rates induce firms to give in-kind payments to workers (such as company cars, subsidies on transportation, lunch, and so on), so that wage differentials may even understate true inequality.

Differences in data sets by country and in modes of pay make cross-country comparisons difficult, but they do not make such comparisons impossible or meaningless. In many cases, we know how reporting practices or definitions vary and can adjust results for these differences or, if that is impossible, specify whether the differences lead to an overstatement or understatement of inequality compared with the United States. More important in terms of the theme of this chapter, differences in definitions and reporting procedures that are constant over time are unlikely to distort trends in inequality.

Table 1 categorizes countries by the way their wage patterns changed in the 1970s and 1980s. From the late 1960s to the late 1970s all of the countries shared a common pattern of

TABLE 1   Changes in Educational/Occupational Skill Differentials in Advanced Countries

Countries That Experienced:	1970s	1980s
Large Fall in Differentials	Australia Canada France Germany Italy Japan Netherlands Sweden United Kingdom United States	Korea[a]

Modest Changes in Differentials
  Modest fall in differentials
  No noticeable change in differentials
		Netherlands
		France
		Germany
		Italy

Modest rise in differentials		Australia Canada Japan Sweden
A large rise in differentials		United Kingdom United States

Sources: For the 1970s, Richard B. Freeman "The Changing Economic Value of Higher Education in Developed Economies: A Report to the OECD," NBER Working Paper no. 820, December 1981; for the 1980s, Freeman and Katz, 1994.
[a]Developing country moving into advanced state.

TABLE 2   Wage Inequality for Full-Time Workers, Selected OECD Countries, 1970 to 1990[a]

Log of Ratio of Wage of 90th Percentile Earner to 10th Percentile Earner

Country	1979	1984	1987	1990	Change from 1979 to Latest Year
Men					
United Kingdom	0.88	1.04	1.10	1.16	0.28
United States	1.23	1.36	1.38	1.40	0.17
Japan	0.95	1.02	1.01	1.04	0.09
France	1.19	1.18	1.22	—	0.03
Italy[b]	0.74	0.69	0.73	—	−0.01
Netherlands	0.82	0.77	—	0.80	−0.02
Germany I[c]	0.78	0.80	—	—	}−0.03[d]
Germany II	—	0.96	0.91	—	
Canada[e]	1.23	—	1.44	—	0.21
Women					
United States	0.96	1.16	1.23	1.27	0.31
United Kingdom	0.84	0.98	1.02	1.11	0.27
Japan	0.78	0.79	0.84	0.83	0.05
France	0.96	0.93	1.00	—	0.04
Italy	0.87	0.69	0.69	—	−0.18
Men and Women					
Sweden, all	—	0.66	—	0.73	0.06
Sweden, blue-collar	0.30	0.30	0.31	0.35	0.05

Sources: The data for the United States, United Kingdom, France, and Japan are from Blanchflower, Katz, and Loveman, 1994; the data for Canada are from Davis, 1992; the data for Germany are from Abraham and Houseman, 1994; the data for Sweden are from Edin and Holmlund, 1994; the data for Italy are from Erickson and Ichino, 1994; and the data for the Netherlands are from Teulings, 1992.

[a]The samples consist of full-time workers, with the exception of Japan, which covers regular workers. Wages are measured by hourly earnings for the United States, United Kingdom, France, and Sweden; weekly earnings for workers covered by the social security system for Germany I; and gross average monthly earnings plus holiday allowances from the German socioeconomic panel for Germany II.

[b]The data in the second and third columns are for 1985 and 1989.

[c]The Germany I data are for years 1979 and 1983.

[d]This change is the sum of Germany I from 1979–84 and Germany II from 1984-87.

[e]Canada data are for years 1981 and 1985.

narrowing educational and occupational wage differentials. With the exception of the United States, all had a decline in overall wage dispersion for males in the 1970s—and all saw the trend toward lower educational wage differentials and a more compressed wage structure end by the early to mid-1980s.

In the 1980s, however, wage inequality changed differently in different countries.[2] Overall inequality and differentials by education grew in several countries, but much more modestly than in the United States. Canada, Australia, Japan, and Sweden had small increases in wage inequality and occupational differentials beginning in the early 1980s, and the Canadian rise seemingly began to reverse itself in the late 1980s (Bar-Or et al., 1992; MacPhail, 1993). Wage differentials narrowed in Italy and France through the mid-1980s with some hint of expanding differentials in the late 1980s. There is no evidence of rising wage inequality or educa-

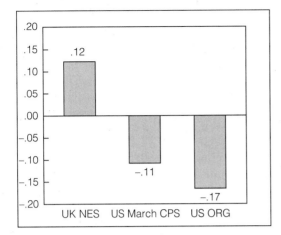

FIGURE 1 Change in Log of Hourly Real Earnings at the Tenth Percentile, Male Workers, 1979 to 1989

Source: Blanchflower, Katz, and Loveman, 1994.
Notes: UK NES–United Kingdom New Earnings Survey;
US March CPS—U.S. March Current Population Survey;
US ORG—U.S. Current Population Survey Outgoing Rotation Groups.
U.S. nominal wages are turned into constant dollars by using the implicit price deflator for personal consumption expenditures from the National Income and Products Account. British nominal wages are deflated by the Consumer Price Index.

tional differentials during the 1980s in the Netherlands nor in West Germany, and no evidence of rising educational differentials in Australia. The only country where wage differentials widened by an amount similar to the United States was Great Britain.

Table 2 measures changes in inequality in terms of the log of the ratio of the earnings of the top decile to the bottom decile of earnings from 1979 to 1990 (or the latest year available). The data show that only the United States and United Kingdom had double-digit increases in inequality. But there is a difference between the change in wages in the United Kingdom and in the United States (see Figure 1). In the United Kingdom, real earnings for all workers rose

rapidly, so that despite greater inequality, the real pay of those at the bottom of the distribution grew (Katz, Loveman, and Blanchflower, 1994; Schmitt, 1994). By contrast, in the United States real earnings at the bottom of the earnings distribution fell sharply. From 1979 to 1989 the real earnings of lower-decile Americans dropped by 11 to 17 percent (depending on the survey used) compared to an *increase* in the real earnings of lower-decile British workers of 12 percent.

That low wage workers need not suffer losses in economic well-being even when inequality rises is also shown in the pattern of change in Japan. Inequality rose somewhat in Japan in the 1980s, but economic growth was so rapid that the living standards of the low-paid workers improved immensely. From 1979 to 1989, the real earnings of the tenth percentile Japanese male employee increased by more than 40 percent—an increase that exceeded that of the ninetieth percentile American male worker.

We conclude that less educated and lower-paid American workers suffered the largest erosion of economic well-being among workers in advanced countries.

Did the relative earnings of women improve in other countries as they did in the United States? Figure 2 shows that the gap in earnings between men and women declined in most countries during the period under investigation. Given the widening of the overall earnings distribution and the historical concentration of women in the bottom part of the distribution, the reduction in the male-female wage gap in the United States in particular was a remarkable achievement. After all, when lower-paid workers are falling further behind higher-paid workers, one would expect a group that has traditionally been lower-paid, such as women, to lose ground relative to men who traditionally receive higher pay. That women gained ground against the tide of rising inequality implies that distinct forces

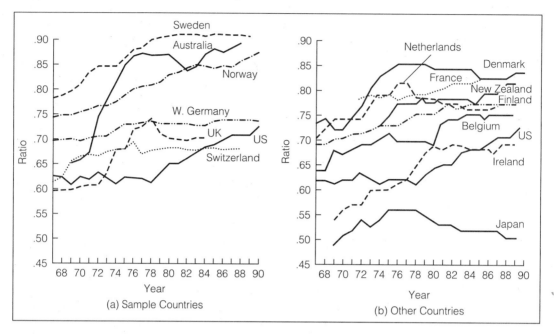

FIGURE 2   Female-to-Male Hourly Earnings Ratios, Nonagricultural Workers, 1967 to 1990
Source: Blau and Kahn, 1994.

were operating in favor of women in the job market (Blau and Kahn, 1994).

When looking at changes among countries in the ratio of employment to population or in unemployment rates by level of skill, two things stand out. In terms of levels, the ratio of employment to population in all countries was higher for the more educated workers. Similarly, the less educated were invariably more likely to be unemployed than the more-educated. In terms of changes, the trend was against the less educated. Their employment-population ratio fell relative to that of more educated workers in many countries during the 1980s (OECD, 1989, chap. 2); and the difference in unemployment associated with education tended to rise. While in the early 1990s white-collar unemployment became a larger problem in the United States, the fact that the more skilled and more highly paid workers can often do the work of the less skilled, while the latter

lack the education needed for professional, technical, or many managerial jobs, implies that rates of unemployment are likely to remain higher among the less educated.

Explaining the Changes

Why did wage inequality and educational wage differentials rise more in the United States than in other advanced countries? We attribute the exceptional experience of the United States to the way shifts in the supply of and demand for skills work themselves out in the decentralized U.S. labor market, compared with how they operate in other labor markets. Our explanation has three parts.

The first is that changes in the supply of and demand for labor skills substantially alter wages and employment of different groups of workers in the manner predicted by economists' supply-and-demand market-clearing model. This statement is more than the squawking of an economic parrot that knows nothing beyond supply and demand. For the supply-demand model to be relevant to the observed changes, wages must respond to market forces in situations with very different wage-setting institutions—collective bargaining, minimum wages, individual bargaining—and in situations where markets may not fully clear. Different demographic, education, and skill groups must be imperfect substitutes in production. We further expect supply and demand to have their largest effect on young or less experienced workers on the active job market as opposed to experienced workers with substantial job tenure (Freeman, 1976).

Supply and demand factors, however, cannot by themselves explain all of the differing changes in inequality among advanced countries. Why? Because supply and demand moved in roughly similar ways in these countries. Developed economies, after all, operate in the same world markets, using similar technology, and they have similar industry and occupation mixes. Changes in demand will not differ significantly among these countries. Supply changes will diverge more, because the countries expanded their higher education systems at different times, but even so a trend toward a greater proportion of workers obtaining college degrees is found everywhere. To fully understand the differences in labor market outcomes across countries, something beyond supply and demand is needed.

The second part of our explanation identifies that "something" as differences in wage setting and other labor market institutions across countries. . . . In a world in which the labor market is not a bourse (a stock exchange where prices continuously fluctuate), identical shifts in supply and demand will have different wage and employment consequences, depending on the wage-setting institutions or pay-setting norms in a country and on its education and training institutions. The stronger the role of institutions in wage determination, the smaller will be the effect of shifts in supply and demand on relative wages and, as a consequence, the greater will be their effect on relative employment. In addition, education and training institutions also mediate the effect of market forces on wages and employment. . . . They determine the level of workplace skills for the less educated workers and the degree to which more and less skilled workers can be substituted for each other in production. A more egalitarian distribution of skills should dampen the effects of market shifts on wages and employment. Social insurance and income maintenance institutions also affect labor outcomes. For instance, generous income maintenance or unemployment benefits that allow workers to remain unemployed for a long period can reduce their willingness to take low wages to obtain work and thus reduce supply-side pressure for pay cuts.

For the third part of our explanation we turn to institutional changes, such as product market deregulation and changes in unionization that alter the wage-setting calculus. In part, forces outside the labor market, such as political developments, will change labor institutions, but these institutions also respond to shifts in supply and demand. The important institutional changes in the 1980s were the decline in trade union power, which was exceptional in the United States, and the decentralization of collective bargaining that characterized diverse European countries. Both of these developments are likely to produce greater earnings differentials. . . .

Conclusion: Leaning against the Wind

Market forces are working to ameliorate the huge increase in inequality in the United

States. The massive college-education-wage premium of the 1980s increased college enrollments despite sharply rising tuition costs (Blackburn, Bloom, and Freeman, 1992). In 1990, 60 percent of new American high school graduates enrolled in two- or four-year colleges in the October following their graduation, compared with 49 percent of the high school graduating class of 1980 (U.S. Department of Education, 1992)—a huge change that will accelerate the growth of the college-graduate work force in the 1990s. An increased supply of graduates will, in turn, offset demand increases favoring the more educated and act to lower education differentials. Having proportionately fewer workers with less than a college degree will decrease downward pressure on the pay of the less educated, and may possibly lead to real wage gains for them.

Will this be enough to restore an economic future to less educated workers? Given continued trade and technological changes favoring those who are more educated, we doubt that increasing the supply of college graduates and reducing that of less educated workers will by itself undo the rise in inequality seen in the 1980s. The experiences of other advanced nations suggest additional ways to lean against the forces toward greater inequality. Indeed, developments in Europe and Japan in the 1980s showed that international competition and the implementation of new technologies do *not* necessarily imply sharp increases in wage inequality and declines in the real earnings of less educated workers.

Two broad national strategies were associated with little increase in skill differentials and in overall wage inequality in the 1980s. The first was the European model of greater institutional influence in the wage-setting process through increases in minimum wages and extensions of the terms of collective bargaining agreements to firms not directly involved in such agreements. Strategies of this type succeeded in preventing the wage structures from widening in Italy and France in the early 1980s. But these policies do not deal directly with a changing demand for skills, and they can run into economic difficulties over the long run. Policies that limit market wage adjustments without directly addressing changed market conditions can prevent wage inequality from increasing, but they risk stagnant employment growth, persistent unemployment for young workers (as in France), and a shift of resources to an underground economy to avoid wage regulations (as in Italy).

The second type of national strategy combines some institutional wage interventions with education and training systems that invest heavily in non-college-educated workers. Of this approach, Germany and Japan are exemplars in training. . . . German and Japanese firms treat college-educated and non-college-educated workers as much closer substitutes in production than do U.S. or British firms, reducing the effect of technological change on relative skill demand and lowering pressure for wage structure changes in those countries as compared with the United States. German institutions affect wage setting, but they also offer apprenticeships to ensure that the nation's skill structure is consistent with its wage policies. Buffering the earnings of the less educated with institutional wage setting seems to work best when institutions augment workers' skills as well.

From this perspective, an economic strategy that involves policies to augment the skills of the less educated, that develops institutions to protect workers' interests in the labor market, and that encourages market responses in the form of greater investments in higher education could produce a more desirable long-term solution to the rise of inequality in the United States than could any of these approaches taken separately.

NOTES

1. Specifically we computed the proportion of all men who had income between 1.3 times the mean and 0.7 times the mean income in the relevant tables reporting total money income by age, in CPS Consumer Income Reports Series P-60, *Money Income of Households, Families, and Persons in the United States.*

2. This generalization is based on the following studies: Blanchflower, Katz, and Loveman, 1994; Edin and Holmlund, 1994; Freeman and Needels, 1993; Abraham and Houseman, 1994; Erickson and Ichino, 1994; Gregory and Vella, 1994; and Hartog, Oosterbeek, and Teulings, 1992.

REFERENCES

Abraham, Katherine G., and Susan Houseman. 1994. "Earnings Inequality in Germany." In R. Freeman and L. Katz, eds., *Differences and Changes in Wage Structures.* Chicago: University of Chicago Press for NBER.

Bar-Or, Yuval, John Burbridge, Lonnie Magee, and A. Leslie Robb. 1992. "Canadian Experience-Earnings Profiles and the Return to Education in Canada: 1971–90." McMaster University, Department of Economics, Working Paper no. 93-4, December.

Blackburn, McKinley L., David E. Bloom, and Richard B. Freeman. 1992. "Changes in Earnings Differentials in the 1980s: Concordance, Convergence, Causes and Consequences." NBER Working Paper no. 3901, November.

Blanchflower, David G., Lawrence F. Katz, and Gary W. Loveman. 1994. "A Comparison of Changes in the Structure of Wages in Four OECD Countries." In R. Freeman and L. Katz, eds., *Differences and Changes in Wage Structures.* Chicago: University of Chicago Press for NBER.

Blau, Francine, and Lawrence Kahn. 1994. "The Gender Earnings Gap: Some International Evidence." In R. Freeman and L. Katz, eds., *Differ-*

ences and Changes in Wage Structures. Chicago: University of Chicago Press for NBER.

Bloom, David E., and Richard B. Freeman. 1992. "The Fall in Private Pension Coverage in the United States." *American Economic Review* 82, no. 2 (May): 539–548.

Bound, John, and George Johnson. 1992. "Changes in the Structure of Wages in the 1980s: An Evaluation of Alternative Explanations." *American Economic Review* 82 (June): 371–392.

Davis, Steven J., and John Haltiwanger. 1991. "Wage Dispersion within and between Manufacturing Plants." *Brookings Papers on Economic Activity: Microeconomics.* Washington, D.C.: Brookings Institution, Pp. 115–180.

Edin, Per-Anders, and Bertil Holmlund. 1994. "The Swedish Wage Structure: The Rise and Fall of Solidarity Wage Policy." In R. Freeman and L. Katz, eds., *Differences and Changes in Wage Structures.* Chicago: University of Chicago Press for NBER.

Erickson, Christopher, and Andrea Ichino. 1994. "Wage Differentials in Italy: Market Forces, Institutions, and Inflation." In R. Freeman and L. Katz, eds., *Differences and Changes in Wage Structures.* Chicago: University of Chicago Press for NBER.

Freeman, Richard B., and Lawrence F. Katz. 1994. *Differences and Changes in Wage Structures.* Chicago: University of Chicago Press for NBER.

Freeman, Richard B., and Karen Needels. 1993. "Skill Differentials in Canada in an Era of Rising Labor Market Inequality." In D. Card and R. Freeman, eds., *Small Differences That Matter.* Chicago: University of Chicago Press for NBER.

Gregory, Robert, and Frank Vella. 1994. "Aspects of Real Wage and Employment Changes in the Australian Male Labour Market." In R. Freeman and L. Katz, eds., *Differences and Changes in Wage Structures.* Chicago: University of Chicago Press for NBER.

Hartog, Joop, Hessel Oosterbeek, and Coen Teulings. 1992. "Age, Wage and Education in the Netherlands." Unpublished paper, University of Amsterdam.

Katz, Lawrence F., Gary Loveman, and David Blanchflower. 1994. "A Comparison of Changes in the Structure of Wages in Four OECD Countries." In R. Freeman and L. Katz, eds., *Differences and Changes in Wage Structures.* Chicago: University of Chicago Press for NBER.

Katz, Lawrence F., and Kevin M. Murphy. 1992. "Changes in Relative Wages, 1963–1987: Supply and Demand Factors." *Quarterly Journal of Economics* 107 (February): 35–78.

Levy, Frank, and Richard Murnane. 1992. "U.S. Earnings Levels and Earnings Inequality: A Review of Recent Trends and Proposed Explanations." *Journal of Economic Literature,* September.

MacPhail, Fiona. 1993. "Has the 'Great U-Turn' Gone Full Circle? Recent Trends in Earnings Inequality in Canada 1981–1989." Dalhouse University, Halifax, Department of Economics, Working Paper no. 93-01, January.

Murphy, Kevin M., and Finis Welch. 1992. "The Structure of Wages." *Quarterly Journal of Economics* 107 (February): 285–326.

Organization for Economic Cooperation and Development (OECD). 1991. *Employment Outlook.* Paris: OECD.

Schmitt, John. 1994. "The Changing Structure of Male Earnings in Britain, 1974–88." In R. Freeman and L. Katz, eds., *Differences and Changes in Wage Structures.* Chicago: University of Chicago Press for NBER.

U.S. Bureau of the Census. 1992. *Money Income of Households, Families, and Persons in the United States: 1991.* Current Population Reports, Series P-60, No. 180. Washington D.C.: U.S. Department of Commerce, August.

U.S. Department of Education. 1992. National Center for Education Statistics, *The Condition of Education 1992.* Washington D.C.: U.S. Government Printing Office, June.

RACE AND GENDER ON THE JOB

19

Numbers
Minorities and Majorities

Rosabeth Moss Kanter

Rosabeth Moss Kanter holds the Class of 1960 chair as professor of business administration at the Harvard Business School and is former editor of the Harvard Business Review. Kanter is the author of eleven books, including her 1977 classic (excerpted here), *Men and Women of the Corporation.*

The token woman stands in the square of the Immaculate Exception blessing pigeons from a blue pedestal. . . . The token woman is placed like a scarecrow in the long haired corn: her muscles are wooden. Why does she ride into battle on a clothes horse?

—MARGE PIERCY, LIVING IN THE OPEN

Excerpts from *Men and Women of the Corporation,* by Rosabeth Moss Kanter. Copyright © 1977 by Rosabeth Moss Kanter. Reprinted by permission of BasicBooks, a division of HarperCollins Publishers, Inc.

. . . The situations of Industrial Supply Corporation men and women . . . point to the significance of numerical distributions for behavior in organizations: how many of one social type are found with how many of another. As proportions begin to shift, so do social experiences.

The Many and the Few: The Significance of Proportions for Social Life

. . . To understand the dramas of the many and the few in the organization requires a theory and a vocabulary. Four group types can be identified on the basis of different proportional representations of kinds of people, as Figure 1 shows. *Uniform* groups have only one kind of person, one significant social type. The group may develop its own differentiations, of course, but groups called uniform can be considered homogeneous with respect to salient external master statuses such as sex, race, or ethnicity. Uniform

groups have a typological ratio of 100:0. *Skewed* groups are those in which there is a large preponderance of one type over another, up to a ratio of perhaps 85:15. The numerically dominant types also control the group and its culture in enough ways to be labeled "dominants." The few of another type in a skewed group can appropriately be called "tokens," for, like the Indsco exempt women, they are often treated as representatives of their category, as symbols rather than individuals. If the absolute size of the skewed group is small, tokens can also be solos, the only one of their kind present; but even if there are two tokens in a skewed group, it is difficult for them to generate an alliance that can become powerful in the group, as we shall see later. Next, *tilted* groups begin to move toward less extreme distributions and

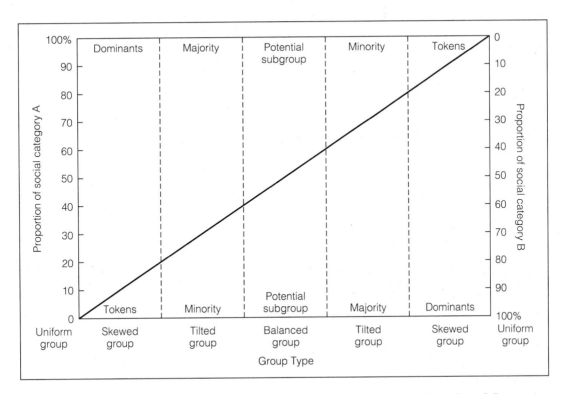

FIGURE 1   Group Types as Defined by Proportional Representation of Two Social Categories in the Membership

less exaggerated effects. In this situation, with ratios of perhaps 65:35, dominants are just a "majority" and tokens become a "minority." Minority members have potential allies among each other, can form coalitions, and can affect the culture of the group. They begin to become individuals differentiated from each other as well as a type differentiated from the majority. Finally, at about 60:40 and down to 50:50, the group becomes *balanced.* Culture and interaction reflect this balance. Majority and minority turn into potential subgroups that may or may not generate actual type-based identifications. Outcomes for individuals in such a balanced peer group, regardless of type, will depend more on other structural and personal factors, including formation of subgroups or differentiated roles and abilities. . . .

Viewing the Few: Why Tokens Face Special Situations

The proportional rarity of tokens is associated with three perceptual tendencies: visibility, contrast, and assimilation. These are all derived simply from the ways any set of objects are perceived. If one sees nine X's and one 0:

$$X \ X \ x \ x \ X \ X \ 0 \ X \ x \ X$$

the 0 will stand out. The 0 may also be overlooked, but if it is seen at all, it will get more notice than any X. Further, the X's may seem more alike than different because of their contrast with the 0. And it will be easier to assimilate the 0 to generalizations about all 0's than to do the same with the X's, which offer more examples and thus, perhaps, more variety and individuation. The same perceptual factors operate in social situations, and they generate special pressures for token women.

First, tokens get attention. One by one, they have higher visibility than dominants looked at alone; they capture a larger aware-

ness share. . . . Contrast—or polarization and exaggeration of differences—is the second perceptual tendency. In uniform groups, members and observers may never become self-conscious about the common culture and type, which remain taken for granted and implicit. But the presence of a person or two bearing a different set of social characteristics increases the self-consciousness of the numerically dominant population and the consciousness of observers about what makes the dominants a class. . . . Assimilation, the third perceptual tendency, involves the use of stereotypes, or familiar generalizations about a person's social type. The characteristics of a token tend to be distorted to fit the generalization. Tokens are more easily stereotyped than people found in greater proportion. . . .

Visibility, contrast, and assimilation are each associated with particular forces and dynamics that, in turn, generate typical token responses. These dynamics are, again, similar regardless of the category from which the tokens come, although the specific kinds of people and their history of relationships with dominants provide cultural content for specific communications. Visibility tends to create *performance pressures* on the token. Contrast leads to heightening of *dominant culture boundaries,* including isolation of the token. And assimilation results in the token's *role encapsulation.*

The experiences of exempt women at Industrial Supply Corporation took their shape from these processes.

Performance Pressures: Life in the Limelight

Indsco's upper-level women, especially those in sales, were highly visible, much more so than their male peers. Even those who reported they felt ignored and overlooked were known in their immediate divisions and spotted when they did something unusual. But the ones who felt ignored also seemed to be those in jobs not enmeshed in the interpersonal structure of the company: for example, a woman in public relations who had only a clerical assistant reporting to her and whose job did not occupy a space in the competitive race to the top.

In the sales force, where peer culture and informal relations were most strongly entrenched, everyone knew about the women. They were the subject of conversation, questioning, gossip, and careful scrutiny. Their placements were known and observed through the division, whereas those of most men typically were not. Their names came up at meetings, and they would easily be used as examples. Travelers to locations with women in it would bring back news of the latest about the women, along with other gossip. In other functions, too, the women developed well-known names, and their characteristics would often be broadcast through the system in anticipation of their arrival in another office to do a piece of work. A woman swore in an elevator in an Atlanta hotel while going to have drinks with colleagues, and it was known all over Chicago a few days later that she was a "radical." And some women were even told by their managers that they were watched more closely than the men. Sometimes the manager was intending to be helpful, to let the woman know that he would be right there behind her. But the net effect was the same as all of the visibility phenomena. Tokens typically performed their jobs under public and symbolic conditions different from those of dominants. . . .

Symbolic Consequences

The women were visible as category members, because of their social type. This loaded all of their acts with extra symbolic consequences and gave them the burden of representing their category, not just themselves. Some women were told outright that their performances could affect the prospects of other women in the company. In the men's informal conversations, women were often measured by two yardsticks: how *as women* they carried out the sales or management role; and how *as managers* they lived up to images of womanhood. In short, every act tended to be evaluated beyond its meaning for the organization and taken as a sign of "how women perform." This meant that there was a tendency for problematic situations to be blamed on the woman—on her category membership—rather than on the situation, a phenomenon noted in other reports of few women among many men in high-ranking corporate jobs. In one case of victim-blaming, a woman in sales went to her manager to discuss the handling of a customer who was behaving seductively. The manager jumped to the assumption that the woman had led him on. The result was an angry confrontation between woman and manager in which she thought he was incapable of seeing her apart from his stereotypes, and he said later he felt misunderstood.

Women were treated as symbols or representatives on those occasions when, regardless of their expertise or interest, they would be asked to provide the meeting with "the woman's point of view" or to explain to a manager why he was having certain problems with his women. They were often expected to be speaking for women, not just for themselves, and felt, even in my interviews, that they must preface personal statements with a disclaimer that they were speaking for themselves rather than for women generally. Such individuality was difficult to find when among dominants. But this was not always generated by dominants. Some women seized this chance to be a symbol as an opportunity to get included in particular gatherings or task forces, where they could come to represent all women at Indsco. "Even if you don't want *me* personally," they seemed to be saying to dominants, "you can want me as a symbol." Yet, if they did this, they would always be left with uncertainty about the grounds for their inclusion; they were failing to distinguish themselves as individuals.

Women also added symbolic consequences to each other's affairs. Upper-level women were scrutinized by those on a lower level, who discussed the merits of things done by the higher-ranking women and considered them to have implications for their own careers. One woman manager who was passed over for a promotion in her department was the subject of considerable discussion by other women, who felt she should have pushed to get the opening and complained when she did not.

The extension of consequences for those in token statuses may increase their self-consciousness about their self-presentation and about their decisions, and can change the nature of the decisions that get made. Decisions about what to wear and who to sit with at lunch are not casual. One executive woman knew that her clothing and leisure choices would have impact. She deliberately wore pants one day as she walked through an office—not her own—of female clerks supervised by a man who wanted them to wear dresses, and she noted that a few women cautiously began to wear pants occasionally. She decided to let it be known that she was leaving at four p.m. for ballet lessons once a week, arguing that the men at her level did the same thing to play golf, but also knowing that ballet was going to have a very different meaning from golf. Her act was a gesture performed with an audience in mind as much as an expression of preference. The meaning of "natural" in such situations is problematic, for in doing what they might find natural as private beings, tokens as public personae are also sending messages to the organization.

Business as well as personal decisions were handled by tokens with an awareness of their extended symbolic consequences. One woman manager was faced with the

dilemma of deciding what to do about a woman assistant who wanted to go back to the secretarial ranks from which she had recently been promoted. The manager felt she jeopardized her own claims for mobility and the need to open the system to more women if she let her assistant return and had to admit that a woman who was given opportunity had failed. She spent much more time on the issue than a mere change of assistants would have warranted, going privately to a few men she trusted at the officer level to discuss the situation. She also kept the assistant on much longer than she felt was wise, but she thought herself trapped.

Sometimes the thought of the symbolic as well as personal consequences of acts led token women to outright distortions. One was an active feminist in a training staff job who, according to her own reports, "separated what I say for the cause from what I want for myself." Her secret ambition was to leave the corporation within a year or two to increase her own professional skills and become an external consultant. But when discussing her aspirations with her own manager in career reviews or with peers on informal occasions, she always smiled and said, "Chairman of the board of Industrial Supply Corporation." Every time a job at the grade level above her became vacant, she would inquire about it and appear to be very interested, making sure that there was some reason at the last minute she could not take it. "They are watching me," she explained, "to see if women are really motivated or if they will be content to stay in low-level jobs. They are expecting me to prove something one way or the other." . . .

Boundary Heightening and Membership Costs: Tokens in Dominants' Groups

Contrast, or exaggeration of the token's differences from dominants, sets a second set of dynamics in motion. The presence of a token or two makes dominants more aware of what they have in common at the same time that it threatens that commonality. Indeed, it is often at those moments when a collectivity is threatened with change that its culture and bonds become exposed to itself; only when an obvious "outsider" appears do group members suddenly realize aspects of their common bond as insiders. The "threat" a token poses is twofold. First, the token represents the danger of challenge to the dominants' premises, either through explicit confrontation by the token or by a disaffected dominant who, through increased awareness, sees the culture for what it is and sees the possibility of alternatives. Second, the self-consciousness created by the token's presence is uncomfortable for people who prefer to operate in casual, superficial, and easygoing ways, without much psychological self-awareness and without the strain of reviewing habitual modes of action—a characteristic stance in the corporate environment.

Furthermore, as Everett Hughes pointed out, part of the hostility peer groups show to new kinds of people stems from uncertainty about their behavior when non-structured, non-routine events occur. Tokens cannot be assumed to share the same unspoken understandings that the rest of the members share, because of their common membership in a social category, one basis for closing ranks against those who are different. . . . For smooth interaction, groups require both discretion (the ability to put statements in their proper perspective) and a shared vocabulary of attitudes (the ability to take feeling and sentiments for granted) so that they can avoid the time-consuming process of translation. At best, then, members of the dominant category are likely to be uncomfortable and uncertain in the presence of a member of a different category. Other analysts have also shown that people with "incongruent statuses," like women in male jobs, strain group

interaction by generating ambiguity and lack of social certitude.[1] It is not only the first of a kind that arouses discomfort. People who are usually not found in that setting and come from a category with a history of special forms of interaction with the numerical dominants, as rare women among men, are also potentially disruptive of peer interaction.

The token's contrast effect, then, can lead dominants to exaggerate both their commonality and the token's "difference." They move to heighten boundaries of which, previously, they might even have been aware. They erect new boundaries that at some times exclude the token or at others let her in only if she proves her loyalty.

Exaggeration of Dominants' Culture

Indsco men asserted group solidarity and reaffirmed shared in-group understandings in the presence of token women, first, by emphasizing and exaggerating those cultural elements they shared in contrast to the token. The token became both occasion and audience for the highlighting and dramatizing of those themes that differentiated her as the outsider. Ironically, tokens, unlike people of their type represented in greater proportion, are thus instruments for under*lining* rather than under*mining* majority culture. At Indsco, this phenomenon was most clearly in operation on occasions that brought together people from many parts of the organization who did not necessarily know each other well, as in training programs and at dinners and cocktail parties during meetings. Here the camaraderie of men, as in other work and social settings, was based in part on tales of sexual adventures, ability with respect to "hunting" and capturing women, and off-color jokes. Other themes involved work prowess and sports, especially golf and fishing. The capacity for and enjoyment of drinking provided the context for displays of these themes. They were dramatized and acted out more fervently in the presence of token women than when only men were present.[2] When the men were alone, they introduced these themes in much milder form and were just as likely to share company gossip or talk of domestic matters such as a house being built. This was also in contrast to more equally mixed male-female groups in which there were a sufficient number of women to influence and change group culture and introduce a new hybrid of conversational themes based on shared male-female concerns.

Around token women, then, men sometimes exaggerated displays of aggression and potency: instances of sexual innuendos, aggressive sexual teasing, and prowess-oriented "war stories." When a woman or two were present, the men's behavior involved "showing off," telling stories in which "masculine prowess" accounted for personal, sexual, or business success. They highlighted what they could do, as men, in contrast to the women. In a set of training situations for relatively junior salespeople, these themes were even acted out overtly in role plays in which participants were asked to prepare and perform demonstrations of sales situations. In every case involving a woman, the men played the primary, effective roles, and the women were objects of sexual attention. Sexual innuendos were heightened and more obvious and exaggerated than in all-male role plays. . . . After these role plays, the group atmosphere seemed quite tense, and the women especially appeared highly uncomfortable.

The women themselves reported other examples of "testing" to see how they would respond to the "male" culture. They said that many sexual innuendos or displays of locker-room humor were put on for their benefit, especially by the younger men. (The older men tended to parade their business successes.) One woman was a team leader at a work-

shop (and the only woman), when her team decided to use as its slogan, "The [obscenity] of the week," looking at her for a reaction. By raising the issue and forcing the woman to choose not to participate, the men in the group created an occasion for uniting against the outsider and asserting dominant group solidarity. Such events, it must be pointed out, were relatively rare and occurred only at those informal occasions outside of the business routine in which people were unwinding, letting themselves go, or, as in the training role plays, deliberately creating unreal situations. Most behavior at Indsco was more businesslike in tone. But the fact that such interaction ever occurred, even infrequently, around women served to isolate them and make them uncomfortable at those very moments when, ironically, people were supposed to be relaxing and having fun.

A sales meeting at Indsco provided an interesting example of how the dominant culture could simultaneously acknowledge the presence of tokens and retain its own themes and flavor. It was traditional for sales men to tell traveling salesman/farmer's daughter jokes at informal gatherings. On this occasion, four years after women first entered the sales force, a raunchy traveling sales*woman*/farmer's *son* joke was told, a story currently going around the company. The form was the same, but the content reflected the presence of women.

Tokens' functions as audience for dominant cultural expressions also played a part in the next set of processes.

Interruptions as Reminders of "Difference"

On more formal occasions, as in meetings, members of the numerically dominant category underscored and reinforced differences between tokens and dominants, ensuring that tokens recognized their outsider status, by making the token the occasion for "interruptions" in the flow of group events. Dominants prefaced acts with apologies or questions about appropriateness directed at the token; they then invariably went ahead with the act, having placed the token in the position of interrupter or interloper, of someone who took up the group's time. This happened often in the presence of the saleswomen. Men's questions or apologies represented a way of asking whether the old or expected cultural rules were still operative—the words and expressions permitted, the pleasures and forms of release indulged in. (Can we still swear? Toss a football? Use technical jargon? Go drinking? Tell "in" jokes?) Sometimes the questions seemed motivated by a sincere desire to put the women at ease and treat them appropriately, but the net effect was the same regardless of dominants' intentions. By posing these questions overtly, dominants made the culture clear to tokens, stated the terms under which tokens enter the relationship, and reminded them that they were special people. It is a dilemma of all cross-cultural interaction that the very act of attempting to learn what to do in the presence of the different kind of person so as to integrate him can reinforce differentiation. . . .

Via difference-reminding interruptions, then, dominants both affirm their own shared understandings and draw the cultural boundary between themselves and tokens. The tokens learned that they caused interruptions in "normal" communication, and that their appropriate position was more like that of audience than that of full participant. But the women also found the audience position frustrating or wearying, as these statements indicated: "I felt like one of the guys for a while. Then I got tired of it. They had crude mouths and were very immature. I began to dread the next week because I was tired of their company. Finally, when we were all out drinking, I admitted to myself, this is not me; I don't want to play their game."

And: "I was at a dinner where the men were telling dirty jokes. It was fun for a while; then it got to me. I moved and tried to have a real conversation with a guy at the other end of the table. The dinner started out as a comrade thing, but it loses its flavor, especially if you're the only woman. I didn't want them to stop on my account, but I wish I had had an alternative conversation."

Overt Inhibition: Informal Isolation

In some cases, dominants did not wish to have tokens around all the time; they had secrets to preserve or simply did not know how far they could trust the women, especially those who didn't seem to play by all the rules. They thus moved the locus of some activities and expressions from public settings to which tokens had access to more private settings from which they could be excluded. When information potentially embarrassing or damaging to dominants is being exchanged, an outsider-audience is not desirable, because dominants do not know how far they can trust the tokens. As Hughes . . . pointed out, colleagues who rely on unspoken understandings may feel uncomfortable in the presence of "odd kinds of fellows" who cannot be trusted to interpret information in just the same way or to engage in the same relationships of trust and reciprocity.[3] There was a sense that it was not possible to level with a woman or be real with her, as one could with other men.

The result was sometimes "quarantine"—keeping tokens away from some occasions. Informal pre-meeting meetings were sometimes held. Some topics of discussion seemed rarely raised by men in the presence of many of their women peers, even though they discussed them among themselves: admissions of low commitment to the company or concerns about job performance, ways of getting around formal rules, political plotting for mutual advantage, strategies for impressing certain corporate executives. Many of the women did not tend to be included in the networks by which informal socialization occurred and politics behind the formal system were exposed, as researchers have found in other settings. . . . Toward the upper levels of the corporation, any tendency for peer groups to quarantine women was reinforced by men-only social establishments; a senior personnel administrator committed to placing more women in top executive jobs was concerned about whether they could overcome the limitation on their business effectiveness placed by exclusion from informal exchanges at male clubs.

In a few cases, overt inhibition worked directly against women in their jobs. They missed out on important informal training by peers. There were instances in which women trainees did not get direct criticism in time to improve their performance and did not know they were the subjects of criticism in the company until told to find jobs in other divisions. They were not part of the buddy network that uncovered such information quickly, and their managers were reluctant to criticize a woman out of uncertainty about how she would receive the information. (One man put quite simply how he felt about giving negative feedback to a woman: "I'm chicken.") Here feelings that it was impossible to level with a different kind of person stood in the way.

Loyalty Tests

At the same time that tokens may be kept on the periphery of colleague interaction, they may also be expected to demonstrate loyalty to their dominant peers. Failure to do so could result in further isolation; signs of loyalty, on the other hand, permitted the token to come closer to being included in more of the dominants' activities. Through loyalty tests, the group sought reassurance that the tokens would not turn against the dominants or use any of the information gained through their viewing of the dominants' world to do harm to the group. In the normal course of peer interactions, people learn all sorts of things about each other that could be turned against the other. Indeed, many colleague relationships are often solidified by the reciprocal knowledge of potentially damaging bits of information and the understanding that they both have an interest in preserving confidentiality. Tokens, however, pose a different problem and raise uncertainties, for their membership in a different social category could produce loyalties outside the peer cadre.

This was a quite rational concern on occasion. With government pressures and public interest mounting, Indsco women were often asked to speak to classes or women's groups or to testify before investigating committees. One woman was called in by her manager before her testimony at hearings on discrimination against women in business; he wanted to hear her testimony in advance and have censorship rights. She refused, but then made only very general and bland statements at the hearing anyway.

Peers seek reassurance about embarrassing as well as damaging disclosures. There is always the possibility that tokens will find some of what the dominants naturally do silly or ridiculous and will insult them where they feel vulnerable. Dominants also want to know that tokens will not use their inside information to make the dominants look bad or turn them into figures of fun to members of the token's category outside with whom they must interact. The joking remarks men made when seeing women colleagues occasionally eating with the secretaries (e.g., "What do you 'girls' find so interesting to talk about?") revealed some of their concerns.

Assurance could be gained by asking tokens to join with or identify with the dominants against those who represented competing loyalties; in short, dominants pressured tokens to turn against members of their own category . . . If tokens colluded, they made themselves psychological hostages to the majority group. For token women, the price of being "one of the boys" was a willingness to occasionally turn against "the girls." . . .

Role Encapsulation

Tokens can never really be seen as they are, and they are always fighting stereotypes, because of a third tendency. The characteristics of tokens as individuals are often distorted to fit preexisting generalizations about their category as a group—what I call "assimilation." Such stereotypical assumptions about what tokens "must" be like, such mistaken attributions and biased judgments, tend to force tokens into playing limited and caricatured roles. This constrains the tokens but is useful for dominant group members. Whatever ambiguity there might be around a strange person is reduced by providing a stereotyped and thus familiar place for tokens in the group, allowing dominants to make use of already-learned expectations and modes of action, like the traditional ways men expect to treat women. Familiar roles and assumptions, further, can serve to keep tokens in a bounded place and out of the mainstream of interaction where the uncertainties they arouse might be more difficult to handle. In short, tokens become encapsulated in limited roles that give them the security of a "place" but constrain their areas of permissible or rewarded action.

Status Leveling

Tokens were often initially misperceived as a result of their numerical rarity. That is, an unusual woman would be treated as though she resembled women on the average—a function of what has been called "statistical discrimination" rather than outright prejudice.[4] Since people make judgments about the role being played by others on the basis of probabilistic reasoning about what a particular kind of person will be doing in a particular situation, such misperceptions are the result of statistical mistakes. Thus, women exempts at Indsco, like other tokens, encountered many instances of "mistaken identity"—first impressions that they were occupying a *usual female* position rather than their *unusual* (for a woman) job. In the office, they were often taken for secretaries; on sales trips on the road, especially when they traveled with a male colleague, they were often taken for wives or mistresses; with customers, they were first assumed to be temporarily substituting for a man who was the "real" salesperson; with a male peer at meetings, they were seen as the assistant; when entertaining customers, they were assumed to be the wife or date. (One woman sales trainee accompanied a senior salesman to call on a customer, whose initial reaction was laughter: "What won't you guys think up next? A woman!" She had the last laugh, however, for that company's chief engineer happened to be a woman with whom she had instant rapport.)

Mistaken first impressions can be corrected, although they give tokens an extra burden of spending more time untangling awkward exchanges and establishing accurate and appropriate role relations. But meanwhile, status leveling occurs. Status leveling involves making adjustments in perception of a token's professional role to fit with the expected position of the token's category—that is, bringing situational status in line with what has been called "master status," the token's social type. Even when others knew that the women were not secretaries, for example, there was still a tendency to treat them like secretaries or to make secretary-like demands on them. In one blatant case, one woman was a sales trainee along with three men, all four of whom were to be given positions as summer replacements. The men were all assigned to replace salesmen; the woman was asked to replace a secretary—and only after a long and heated discussion with the manager was she given a more professional assignment. Similarly, when having professional contacts with customers and managers, the women felt themselves to be treated in more wife-like or date-like ways than a man would treat another man, even though the occasion was clearly professional. A professional woman at Indsco asked for a promotion and talked about looking for a better job; her manager's first assumption was that she did not feel "loved" and it was his fault for failing to give love to a woman. . . . In all these instances, it was easier for others to fit the token woman to their preexisting generalizations about women than to change the category; numerical rarity provided too few examples to contradict the generalization. . . . ([I]n the case of tokens whose master status is higher than their situational status, leveling can work to their advantage, as when male nurses are called "Dr.")

The Woman's Slot

There was also a tendency to encapsulate women and to maintain generalizations by defining special roles for women, even on the managerial and professional levels, that put them slightly apart as colleagues. Again, it was easy to do this with a small number and would have been much harder with many more women spilling over the bounds of such slots. A woman could ensure her membership by accepting a special place but then find herself confined by it. Once women began to occupy certain jobs, those jobs sometimes gradually came to be defined as "women's slots." One personnel

woman at Indsco pointed this out. In her last career review, she had asked to be moved, feeling that, in another six months, she would have done and learned all she could in her present position and was ready to be upgraded. "They [the managers] told me to be patient; if I waited a year or two longer, they had just the right job for me, three grades up. I knew what they had in mind. Linda Martin [a senior woman] would be retiring by then from a benefits administration job, and they wanted to give it to me because it was considered a place to put a woman. But it had no *real* responsibilities despite its status; it was all routine work."

Affirmative action and equal employment opportunity jobs were also seen as "women's jobs." Many women, who would otherwise be interested in the growth and challenge they offered, said that they would not touch such a position: "The label makes it a dead end. It's a way of putting us out to pasture." There was no way to test the reality of such fears, given the short time the jobs had been in existence, but it could be observed that women who worked on women's personnel or training issues were finding it hard to move out into other areas. These women also found it hard to interest some other, secretly sympathetic managerial women in active advocacy of upward mobility for women because of the latter's own fears of getting too identified with a single issue. (Others, though, seized on it as a way to express their values or to get visibility.)

Committees, task forces, and other ad hoc events had a tendency, too, to develop a woman's slot for those women selected to participate. Sometimes it would take the form of giving the women areas of responsibility that were stereotypically "female" concerns, or, as mentioned earlier, giving them the role in the group of "expert on women." This posed major dilemmas for the women seriously interested in being women's advocates but who were also aware of how the role encapsulation process could undercut their effectiveness and limit their organizational mobility. They had to carefully balance the time spent as woman-symbols with other activities and with attention to the technical/professional aspects of their jobs.

Stereotyped Informal Roles

Dominants can incorporate tokens and still preserve their generalizations by inducting tokens into stereotypical roles that preserve familiar forms of interaction between the kinds of people represented by the token and the dominants. In the case of token women in colleague groups at Indsco, four informal role traps were observed, all of which encapsulated the tokens in a category the men could respond to and understand. Each was formed around one behavioral tendency of the token, building this into an image of the token's place in the group and forcing her to continue to live up to the image; each defined for dominants a single response to the token's sexuality. Two of the roles are classics in Freudian theory: the "mother" and the "seductress." Freud wrote of the need for men to handle women's sexuality by envisioning them either as "madonnas" or "whores"— as either asexual mothers or overly sexual, debased seductresses, perhaps as a function of Victorian family patterns, which encouraged separation of idealistic adoration toward the mother and animalistic eroticism.[5] The others, termed the "pet" and the "iron maiden," also have family counterparts in the kid sister and the virgin aunt.

Mother A token woman sometimes found that she became a "mother" to men in the group. One by one, they brought her their private troubles, and she was expected to comfort them. The assumption that women are sympathetic, good listeners and easy to talk to about one's problems was common,

even though, ironically, men also said it was hard to level with women over task-related issues. One saleswoman was constantly approached by her all-male peers to listen to their problems with their families. In a variety of residential training groups, token women were observed acting out other parts of the traditional nurturant-maternal role: doing laundry, sewing on buttons for men.

The mother role was comparatively safe. A mother is not necessarily vulnerable to sexual pursuit (for Freud it was the very idealization of the madonna that was in part responsible for men's ambivalence toward women), nor do men need to compete for her favors, since they are available to everyone. However, the typecasting of women as nurturers can have three negative consequences for the woman's task performance: (1) The mother is rewarded primarily for service and not for independent action. (2) The dominant, powerful aspects of the maternal image may be feared, and thus the mother is expected to keep her place as a non-critical, accepting, "good mother" or lose her rewards. Since the ability to differentiate and be critical is often an indicator of competence in work groups, the mother is prohibited from exhibiting this skill. (3) The mother becomes an emotional specialist. This provides her with a place in the life of the group and its members. Yet, at the same time one of the stereotypically "feminine" characteristics men in positions of authority in industry most often criticize in women is excess "emotionality." . . . Although the mother herself might not ever cry or engage in emotional outbursts in the group, she remains identified with emotional matters. As long as she is in the scarce position of token, however, it is unlikely that nurturance, support, and expressivity will be valued or that a mother can demonstrate and be rewarded for critical, independent, task-oriented behaviors.

Seductress   The role of seductress or sexual object is fraught with more tension than the maternal role, for it introduces an element of sexual competition and jealousy. The mother can have many sons; it is more difficult for the sexually attractive to have many swains. Should the woman cast as sex object (that is, seen as sexually desirable and potentially available—seductress is a perception, and the woman herself may not be consciously behaving seductively) share her attention widely, she risks the debasement of the whore. Yet, should she form a close alliance with any man in particular, she arouses resentment, particularly so because she represents a scarce resource; there are just not enough women to go around.

In several situations I observed, a high status male allied himself with the seductress and acted as her "protector," partly because of his promise of rescue from sex-charged overtures of the rest of the men as well as because of his high status *per se*. The powerful male (staff member, manager, sponsor, etc.) could easily become the "protector" of the still "virgin" seductress, gaining through masking his own sexual interest what the other men could not gain by declaring theirs. However, this removal of the seductress from the sexual marketplace contained its own problems. The other men could resent the high-status male for winning the prize and resent the woman for her ability to get an "in" with the high-status male that they could not obtain as men. Although the seductress was rewarded for her femaleness and insured attention from the group, then, she was also the source of considerable tension; and needless to say, her perceived sexuality blotted out all other characteristics.

Men could adopt the role of protector toward an attractive woman, regardless of her collusion, and by implication cast her as sex object, reminding her and the rest of the group of her sexual status. In the guise of "helping" her, self-designated protectors may actually put up further barriers to the solitary woman's full acceptance by inserting themselves, figuratively speaking, between the woman and the rest of the group. A male management trainer typically offered token women in management assessment groups extra help and sympathetic attention to the problems their male peers might cause, taking them out alone for drinks at the end of daily sessions. But this kind of "help" also preserved the sex object role.

Pet   The "pet" was adopted by the male group as a cute, amusing little thing and symbolically taken along on group events as mascot—a cheerleader for shows of prowess. Humor was often a characteristic of the pet. She was expected to admire the male displays but not to enter into them; she cheered from the sidelines. Shows of competence on her part were treated as special and complimented just because they were unexpected (and the compliments themselves can be seen as reminders of the expected rarity of such behavior). One woman reported that when she was alone in a group of men and spoke at length on an issue, comments to her by men after the meeting often referred to her speech-making ability rather than the content of what she said (e.g., "You talk so fluently"), whereas comments the men made to one another were almost invariably content- or issue-oriented. Competent acts that are taken for granted when performed by males were often unduly "fussed over" when performed by exempt women, considered precocious or precious—a kind of look-what-she-did-and-she's-only-a-woman attitude. Such attitudes on the part of men encouraged self-effacing, girlish responses on the part of solitary women (who, after all, may be genuinely relieved to be included and petted) and prevented them from realizing or demonstrating their own power and competence.

Iron Maiden   The "iron maiden" is a contemporary variation of the stereotypical roles into which strong women are placed. Women who failed to fall into any of the first three roles and, in fact, resisted overtures that would trap them in a role (such as flirtation) might consequently be responded to as "tough" or dangerous. (One woman manager developed such a reputation in company branches throughout the country.) If a token insisted on full rights in the group, if she displayed competence in a forthright manner, or if she cut off sexual innuendos, she could be asked, "You're not one of those women's libbers, are you?" Regardless of the answer, she was henceforth regarded with suspicion, undue and exaggerated shows of politeness (by inserting references to women into conversations, by elaborate rituals of *not* opening doors), and with distance, for she was demanding treatment as an equal in a setting in which no person of her kind had previously been an equal. Women inducted into the "iron maiden" role were stereotyped as tougher than they are (hence the name) and trapped in a more militant stance than they might otherwise take. Whereas seductresses and pets, especially, incurred protective responses, iron maidens faced abandonment. They were left to flounder on their own and often could not find peers sympathetic to them when they had problems. . . .

Effects on Tokens as Individuals: Stresses and Costs in the Token Situation

The point is not that all of these things happen to token women, or that they happen only to people who are tokens. Some young men at Indsco complained that as new-hires they, too, felt performance pressures, uncertainties about their acceptance, and either over-protected or abandoned. But these issues were part of a transitional status out of which new-hires soon passed, and, in any event, men did not so routinely or dramatically encounter them. Similarly, age and experience helped women make a satisfactory accommodation, and over time, many

women settled into comfortable and less token-like patterns. Some said that there was no problem they could not handle with time and that the manifestations of discrimination in their jobs were trivial. But still, the issues stemming from rarity and scarcity arose for women in every new situation, with new peers, and at career transitions. Even successful women who reported little or no discrimination said that they felt they had to "work twice as hard" and expend more energy than the average man to succeed. It is also clear that not all women in the token situation behave alike or engender the same responses in others. There was variety in the individual choices, and there were alternative strategies for managing the situation. But a system characteristic—the numerical proportion in which women and men were found—set limits on the behavioral possibilities and defined the context for peer interaction. . . .

NOTES

1. The Hughes citation is to Everett Hughes, *Men and Their Work* (Glencoe, Illinois: Free Press, 1958), p. 109. See also Hughes, "Dilemmas and Contradictions of Status," *American Journal of Sociology*, 50 (March 1944): pp. 353–59. Judith Lorber came to some similar conclusions in "Trust, Loyalty, and the Place of Women in the Informal Organization of Work," presented at the 1975 Meetings of the American Sociological Association. On "status incongruence" as an explanatory variable in group member behavior, used in many of the same ways I use "tokenism" but without the explicit numerical connotations, see A. Zaleznik, C. R. Christensen, and F. J. Roethlisberger, *The Motivation, Productivity, and Satisfaction of Workers: A Prediction Study* (Boston: Harvard Business School Division of Research, 1958), especially pp. 56–68.

2. Clearly I was limited in first-hand observations of how the men acted when alone, since, by definition, if I, as a female researcher, were present, they would not have been alone. For my data here I relied on tape recordings of several meetings in which the tape was kept running even during breaks, and on informants' reports immediately after informal social events and about meetings.

3. Hughes, "Men and Their Work" and "Dilemmas and Contradictions of Status"; Lorber, "Trust, Loyalty, and the Place of Women."

4. *Annual Report of the Council of Economic Advisers* (Washington, D.C.: U.S. Government Printing Office, 1973), p. 106.

5. Philip Rieff, ed., *Freud: Sexuality and the Psychology of Love* (New York: Collier Books, 1963); Byran Strong, "Toward a History of the Experiential Family: Sex and Incest in the Nineteenth Century Family," *Journal of Marriage and the Family,* 35 (August 1973): pp. 457–66.

20

Culture, Commerce, and Gender
The Feminization of Book Editing

Barbara F. Reskin

Barbara Reskin is professor of sociology at Ohio State University. Professor Reskin writes, "This reading is from a study of why women made unprecedented headway in some primarily male occupations (e.g., bartending, baking, insurance sales, pharmacy). I found that women got in after the occupations had deteriorated in ways that made them less attractive to men. The occupational studies and my theoretical explanation appear in *Job Queues, Gender Queues: Explaining Women's Inroads into Male Occupations* (with Patricia Roos). My other research examines how and why workers' sex, race, and ethnicity affect their jobs and career advancement. My book *Women and Men on the Job* (with Irene Padavic) summarizes these and many other studies."

For centuries book editing was a "gentlemen's profession" (Tebbel, 1972: 207), yet in the 1970s women made such large gains in the occupation that some have speculated that editing is becoming a women's ghetto (Geracimos, 1974:25). How can we explain women's gains? This chapter examines the changes in the publishing industry and the editorial role that have led to women's increasing representation among editors. . . .

Women in Publishing

Until the 1960s, publishing was "predominantly a business of middle-aged and older men" (Tebbel, 1975:101), but between 1963 and 1968, women accounted for 62 percent of employment growth in publishing (compared with 52 percent for the printing and publishing industry overall and 35 percent for all manufacturing), and during this period the numbers of men and women employed in the industry rose by 19 percent and 41 percent, respectively (U.S. Bureau of Labor Statistics, cited in *Publishers Weekly,* 1971:69). By 1980, publishing's sex composition had changed (Tebbel, 1981:728), and observers were calling it a "women's business" (Caplette, 1982a:148). By the late 1970s and early 1980s, estimates put women's employment share at about two-thirds of the industry's workforce (Association of American Publishers, 1977:27; Cornelius, 1983:34; U.S. Bureau of the Census, 1984b: Table 4).

Sex Segregation in Publishing

Even when men dominated the industry, publishing employed women for some jobs. While college publishing was predominantly male, scholarly publishing was so to a lesser degree (university presses could take advantage of the captive labor market that faculty wives represented). Women were concentrated in children's publishing, in mass-market paperbacks (Coser et al., 1982)—which enjoyed little status and lacked a "cultural" image because these houses reissued hard-cover editions and published lightly edited genre books, such as mysteries and historical romances—and in certain jobs in trade publishing.

Men dominated marketing and management, the highest-paying jobs in the industry, and except in paperback publishing the majority of editors—particularly acquisitions editors—were men (Strainchamps, 1974:133; Caplette, 1982a:157). Women were typically relegated to lower-level editorial jobs (copyeditor, editorial assistant), normally behind-the-scenes positions (Caplette, 1982a:154). Most began their careers as manuscript readers, secretaries, or editorial assistants, jobs whose low pay and clerical duties could attract few men (Tebbel, 1981:728).

Other female ghettos were the noneditorial "service" jobs of publicity and subsidiary rights (Geracimos, 1974:27; Caplette, 1982a:158). Selling subsidiary rights is complex, detailed work but—until recently—not especially profitable (Tebbel, 1975:140). A former subsidiary-rights director described it as "a pro forma job: . . . sending out notes, keep-

ing track of things, and then the [male] editor-in-chief would step in to do the razzle-dazzle deal" (*Publishers Weekly*, 1979). Publicity, according to a former publicity director, "was naturally a female job" because it involved "lots of handholding, nurturing, socializing," and like subsidiary rights it was not considered a moneymaking function until the 1970s.

Until 1970, publishers rarely hired women as sales representatives, the traditional entry-level job for college editors; before that, "it was almost inconceivable that a woman should go on the road alone" (Strainchamps, 1974:159–60). Publishers feared, informants explained, that women would find the books too heavy, would not be able to find the colleges, or would get raped—or that professors would feel insulted if a woman called on them (Strainchamps, 1974:155). One editor recounted that a university press denied her a sales job in 1964, although she had six years editorial experience, because they "couldn't allow a pretty young lady to travel alone" even two or three days a month. Another interviewee recalled that when her employer transferred a woman to college sales in the mid-1960s, the male representatives "tormented her" until she quit. She added, "It was an object lesson to us all."

The Sex Composition of Editors

Although women were underrepresented in editorial jobs until the late 1960s and early 1970s, they have held some editorial positions since early in the century. About the time of World War I a survey of 82 publishing firms revealed that 14 percent of the 1,400 female employees were working in editorial jobs (Tebbel, 1975:177). Yet a world war later, publisher Henry Holt still described editors as male (Bechtold, 1946:14). Industry histories (Cerf, 1977; Tebbel, 1978) rarely mentioned women editors. Bechtold (1946:14) noted that women editors earned less than men and had to wait longer and work harder to succeed. Women with editorial titles usually copyedited or styled manuscripts for publication. Only in children's books was editing fully open to women (Laskey, 1969:13); indeed, men rarely held these jobs through the early 1960s (Tebbel, 1978).

Many female secretaries and editorial assistants did editorial work without the title, including screening the thousands of unsolicited manuscripts that swamped publishers (see, e.g., Caplette, 1982a:152–54). The secretarial and editorial assistant jobs were in a secondary labor market with a nonexistent or weakly defined career ladder to full editorial positions (Caplette, 1979), though finding a promising book in the "slushpile" of unsolicited manuscripts sometimes meant a step up the editorial ladder. Moreover, the ratio of aspirants to openings was—and remains—enormous. It took women extraordinary effort to get out of the secretarial–assistant ghetto, and few female editorial assistants became editors (Caplette, 1982a:161; Tebbel, 1987). In contrast, the few men who began as assistants moved up rapidly (Caplette, 1982a:154). Thus, the considerable sex segregation across editorial jobs revealed in a survey made by Chicago Women in Publishing (1973:2) probably reflected the industry as a whole.

The educational sector of the industry did not resemble trade publishing with respect to women's access to editorial jobs. College publishers required sales experience of editors because of the importance of marketing in college sales; sales representatives acted as "field editors" who scouted out potential authors (Coser et al., 1982:20, 102). As a result, men's monopoly over sales jobs ensured that editing was also their preserve (Caplette, 1979:5). No large college firms employed women as acquisitions editors in major disciplines until early in the 1970s, and late in the decade three-quarters of college editors were still men (Coser et al., 1982). In school publishing the sex ratio was more balanced because firms hired former teachers as editors. Scholarly—particularly university—presses employed relatively more women than did other sectors (Powell, 1985:30).

Women's Increased Representation among Editors

By 1970 just under half the editors employed in book and periodical publishing were women (U.S. Bureau of the Census, 1972: Table 8), but only 5,025 of these 26,745 workers edited books (Association of American Publishers, 1977:24). Unfortunately, no data enumerate book editors by sex, but by all accounts women were underrepresented, and female editors were concentrated in school and paperback publishing or in low-level editorial positions in trade, college, and scholarly houses. During the 1970s women made considerable strides in editing in most sectors of the industry; by mid-decade their number had increased so much that a *Publishers Weekly* article (Geracimos, 1974:25) called 1974 "the year of the woman" in trade publishing (see also Tebbel, 1975:101), and in 1978 a survey of 117 publishing employees showed women outnumbering men two to one in editorial acquisitions and manuscript editing (Caplette, 1982a:155). However, the wage gap in one large publishing house, in which women editors averaged 54 cents for each dollar men received, indicates that although two-thirds of its 195 editors were female, they either held lower-level positions or were paid less than male editors in the same jobs (Osterman, 1979). Nonetheless, by 1980 women made up more than 57 percent of the 36,161 editors employed in book and periodical publishing (U.S. Bureau of the Census, 1984b: Table 4), although again we do not know their proportion among the approximately 10,000 *book* editors (Wright, 1984:589). Caplette (1982b:158) observed that "the gradual increase of women editors in the last decade has, within the last few years, become an upsurge—nearly half of trade and mass-market paperback editors are now women." Confirming her impressions are those of more than forty industry informants who agreed that the 1970s brought dramatic progress for women in editing and other publishing jobs.

Explaining Women's Progress in Editing

Although women advanced in many occupations in the 1970s, their gains in editing outstripped those in most other occupations. To account for their progress, I used a variety of documentary data and published sources, including memoirs of editors and publishers, scholarly analyses of the publishing industry, articles from *Publishers Weekly* between 1968 and 1987, and forty-one interviews, including eleven that Michele Caplette (1981) conducted in 1978.[1] I found that changes in the publishing industry and the editorial role set the stage for women's gains by altering both the supply of male would-be editors and the demand for women.

Industrial Growth and Change

First in the chain of events that transformed publishing was its pronounced growth over fifteen to twenty years, beginning about 1960 (Lofquist, 1970:6, 9; Powell, 1985:5). Rising personal income and educational levels, unprecedented federal investments in public education, and the information explosion (Powell, 1982:33) stimulated record book sales. Profits led existing firms to expand their lists and attracted new firms to the industry (Altbach, 1975:11; Dessauer,

1982:34). At least three hundred new firms set up shop between 1967 and 1978 (Noble, 1978:35); between 1972 and 1977 the number of firms increased by almost half (Gilroy, 1980:8,11), and between 1954 and 1977 the number more than doubled (Powell, 1985:213). Both title output and sales volume showed increases of 50 to 100 percent between 1959 and 1980 (Powell, 1985:4).[2]

These two decades of expansion set the stage for dramatic changes in the culture of publishing. Rapid growth and solid profits led to a spate of mergers in the late 1960s and again in the late 1970s and middle 1980s (Gilroy, 1980:12) and inevitably drew the interest of nonpublishing firms and conglomerates looking for profitable acquisitions (Tebbel, 1981:733). Conglomerization, which hit publishing in the early 1970s, transformed the industry (Navasky, 1973b); it "became less of a gentleman's industry and more of a business" that emphasized "the bottom line" (Galassi, 1980:28).

Although concern with profits was not new, according to industry analyst John Dessauer (1982:36), "it has become more virulent [as] opportunities for making a quick buck have increased with a growing market, and the big-money ownership that has entered the field is more easily tempted by the quick buck than were the other-worldly types that used to constitute the industry's core." As Powell (1985:6) noted, "Outside ownership brought modern management practices that fundamentally altered the craftlike nature of book publishing." Commercialization eroded publishing's reputation as an industry outside the fray, and in so doing, transformed editorial work. As a result, it also transformed the publishing workforce.

Changes in Editorial Work

To understand the changes in the role of editor that figure importantly in women's gains in the occupation, I begin by examining the traditional editorial role. The predecessors of modern editors were readers—often established writers or academicians (Lane, 1975:38)—whom publishers paid to evaluate manuscripts and help writers improve their work (Sifton, 1985:43). Twentieth-century editors perform similar functions: acquisitions editors select manuscripts and work with authors in completing them, and manuscript editors concentrate on the production side (Lane, 1975:35). Of the two functions, producing books enjoys less status and lower wages than the more exciting job of acquiring them (Carter, 1984:24). However, acquisitions can be demanding work in many sectors of the industry. Editors typically handle upward of forty books a year, a few of which are culled from thousands of unsolicited manuscripts (Rawson and Dolin, 1985:28). A book's existence and ultimate success depend on its editor's efforts to sell the manuscript to the editorial board and the marketing people (Rawson and Dolin, 1985:25). As the publishers' representatives, editors work closely with authors to negotiate contracts, monitor progress, suggest revisions (Sifton, 1985:43–45), and offer encouragement. The last function may extend to serving as friend, cheerleader, confessor, and psychotherapist (Giroux, 1982:55; Dong, 1984:22); some (Canfield, 1969:27; Rawson and Dolin, 1985:23) have characterized editors as surrogate parents. "You hear from authors on weekends, . . . they may even end up living in your house" (Dong, 1984:26). Editorial responsibilities include looking out for an author's interests within the firm: translating royalty statements, arranging advances, touting the book. Some editors also emphasize the importance of subordinating their egos to "literature" and to authors: "An editor . . . must be willing to play second fiddle" (Lehman, 1987:89; also see Evans, 1979:31).

Editors have written extensively about the qualifications their work demands. Common themes depict the ideal editor as charming, sophisticated, and willing to take risks; as a person with taste, intuition, and empathy who can be persuasive yet tactful in dealing with "difficult" authors and who is willing to make her- or himself an "agreeable nuisance" (Association of American Publishers, 1977:22; Galassi, 1980:29; Giroux, 1982:55; Carter, 1984:24–25). Besides all this, in most sectors of the industry, editors must be willing to work long hours for sometimes notoriously low salaries.

The shift to outside ownership strained the traditionally amiable relations between publishers and editors and profoundly altered editorial work. The pursuit of the blockbuster in large trade houses sharply circumscribed editorial autonomy in acquisition decisions (Wendroff, 1980): "Editors could no longer simply sign a book and then tell their house to sell it" (Powell, 1982:47). By 1973, "fewer and fewer editors [had] the right to commission books without first securing the approval of a Publishing Committee, and most often it [was] the editor-in-chief who [made] the presentation to the committee rather than the editor" (Navasky, 1973a). The new emphasis on packaging and sales gave publicity, marketing, and subsidiary-rights people much more sway in editorial decisions (Phalon, 1981:253; Powell, 1982:47), thereby eroding editorial autonomy. Bringing the views of the corporate boardroom into the editorial side also discouraged creative risk taking (Tebbel, 1981:733), an important source of satisfaction in editorial work. Instead, editors were under pressure to sign up best sellers or, in the smaller and still-independent houses, to acquire more books (Powell, 1982). An editor who noted that publication committees' choices are based largely on budget considerations wondered "whether editors have as much power as they once did, whether their power is more circumscribed, and . . . who controls what editors do" (Geracimos, 1974:25).

A second consequence of outside ownership was the deterioration of the traditional close relationship between editors and their authors. With more money at stake, authors changed houses frequently in pursuit of better deals and hired agents or lawyers to represent them in negotiating with editors (Powell, 1982). The growing role of literary agents in getting books published (Bannon, 1972:102; Doebler, 1978:27) further circumscribed editor–author contacts. Agents are more influential than editors in acquiring books and have assumed other traditional editorial functions in the publication process (Gabriel, 1989). Besides having less close contact with authors, editors interact less with other editors, thus fragmenting "the old sense of a community of bookmen" (Powell 1982:49).

The absorption of book publishing by other media also altered editors' duties. Arranging the fat subsidiary-rights agreements or movie tie-ins essential for big trade profits meant that editors "had to change their habits and spend more time working on deals." In his insightful analysis of the impact of outside ownership on book publishing, Powell (1982:48–49) quoted an editor whose small firm had been acquired by a large diversified publishing corporation: "After-[ward] I never had time to see authors. I spent all my time in meetings with various corporate executives and 'selling' our imprint within the parent company." After being promoted to head the trade department in a large house, another editor Powell interviewed, who had formerly helped his authors develop their work, said that he was "in danger of becoming simply a well-paid retailer of ideas and entertainment."

New ownership patterns also threatened editors' job security, the only economic compensation for publishing's low wages. The frequent mergers of the 1960s and 1970s often precipitated corporate shake-ups that cost editors their jobs (Evans, 1978:45; Carter, 1983:8). The corporate focus on performance further eroded job security (Tebbel, 1981:733) and forced editors to compete with corporate executive staff from outside the publishing industry for the only top-level positions to which senior editors could aspire—publisher and director.

Changes in the Supply of Would-Be Editors

For most of this century, publishing's glamour and its image as a "gentlemen's profession" were sufficient to attract more than enough qualified recruits. Then, although industrial expansion heightened the demand for editorial workers, the concomitants of that growth reduced the industry's attractiveness to its traditional workforce: talented young men from high socioeconomic backgrounds.

Dwindling Attraction for Men Publishing's primary draw for such men had been entree into the world of culture without the taint of commerce. But commerce is exactly what outside ownership meant. At the same time, as we have seen, editorial work lost many of the features that had compensated nonwealthy workers for low wages. To make matters worse, commerce was supplanting culture without conferring the usual economic incentives of commercial careers. Although editorial wages had always been low, there were other compensations. One editor said, "I consider the right to publish books which don't make money a part of my salary" (Navasky, 1973a). Just as some editors lost that right, wages may have actually declined (Tebbel, 1981:728; Rosenthal et al., 1986). In 1982, entry-level pay for editorial assistants was as low as $9,000 a year (Powell, 1985:225), and several people I interviewed noted that it is increasingly difficult, perhaps impossible, to survive—much less support a family—in Manhattan on editorial wages. An industry expert said, only partly in jest: "Only college graduates with rich parents willing to subsidize them can afford to work in editorial jobs any more" (Tebbel, 1981:728). In the face of society's growing emphasis on a fashionable life-style and the increasing tendency to use income as "the measure of a man," publishing's low wages further deterred men from pursuing editorial jobs (Tebbel, 1987). Better-paying media jobs (technical writing for high-tech companies, corporate public relations, film) and graduate school lured away talented men interested in communications.

With declining opportunities for mobility (Coser et al., 1982:112) and challenges to the traditional promotion practices that had given men a fast track to the top (Strainchamps, 1974), little remained to draw men to editorial work. A woman editor whom Caplette interviewed in 1978 remarked, "The average man thinks that he has a God-given right to start in as an editor." To the extent that this was true, entry-level jobs as editorial assistants (often a euphemism for secretary when these were women's jobs) attracted few men, and the industry increasingly relied on women as editorial assistants.

Increasing Supply of Women   The gentility that had rendered publishing jobs appropriate for upper-status men did so too for "respectable" women whom traditional values encouraged to pursue cultural and aesthetic pursuits (Veblen, 1899). As a long-time assistant at Harper & Brothers said, "Young women getting out of college were so anxious to get a job in something they could be proud of that they would go into publishing and work for practically nothing" (Caplette, 1982a:151). Gender-role socialization further enhanced women's qualifications for publishing by schooling them in verbal and communications skills that equipped them with the facility and

inclination to work with words and predisposed them toward the interpersonal work that editing often involved. One female holder of a master's degree said of her secretarial job in the mid-1950s, "I thought it was an honor to read books and write . . . flap copy" (Caplette, 1982a:169). Working in an intellectual and cultural industry situated in one of the metropolitan publishing "capitals" offered an added incentive to women graduating from prestigious eastern colleges, particularly before the 1970s, when few alternatives presented themselves to career-minded women.

The massive influx of women into the labor force during the 1970s expanded the pool of women available for editorial jobs, and the women's liberation movement encouraged women to consider occupations customarily reserved for men. Publishing attracted women also because it reputedly presented fewer obstacles than many other industries. Moreover, male occupations in predominantly female industries—particularly growing industries—tend to be more hospitable and hence more attractive to women (O'Farrell and Harlan, 1984). Thus, although women knew they faced discrimination in publishing, they probably realized that other commercial fields were worse (Dessauer, 1974:42). Publishing's low wages were less likely to deter women than men because their socialization had not encouraged them to maximize income. Because women lacked access to many better-paying jobs, they did not have to forgo more lucrative opportunities for jobs as assistants or editors, and their limited alternatives presumably also explained their willingness to accept the changes that were making editorial work less desirable to men. As a result, the supply of female applicants remained unabated or grew, while that of males declined. Moreover, several interviewees contended that because publishing could no longer attract the most qualified men, female applicants often had better credentials than the males who did apply. If publishers chose the best applicant (as the new emphasis on profits dictated), it would probably be a woman.

The operation of the publishing labor market enhanced women's gains in editing. Several prestigious colleges close to the industry's centers in New York and Boston generated a supply of qualified women eager to work in publishing. The proliferation of publishing training programs (the first was established at Radcliffe) augmented that supply—by 1980 the director of the popular Denver Publishing Institute estimated that three-quarters of its students were women (Caplette, 1982a:169)—and helped women make contacts with employers. Most women began in entry-level positions on the editorial ladder. For years, sex discrimination and the high ratio of assistants to editors kept most secretaries and assistants from advancing. When the barriers to women began to crumble, however, most houses had a large number of talented, experienced women ready and able to edit books (Geracimos, 1974:25).

Even in college publishing, in the 1970s women successfully challenged both their exclusion from sales and the job ladder that made sales the only route to acquisitions (Association of American Publishers, 1977:16). Some companies began hiring women sales representatives, and others promoted to acquisitions one or two women who lacked sales experience. An early female sales representative speculated half-jokingly that her activity in a women's caucus at her firm may have won her a sought-after transfer to sales. The success of these first saleswomen who, as she said, "tore up the territory" eased the way for others, as well as putting women on the editorial ladder. Once college sales and acquisitions were recast as jobs to which women could aspire and the career ladder was re-

structured, a supply of women became available to work as acquisitions editors.

The Growing Demand for Women Editors

Two decades of growth in the publishing industry created a demand for additional personnel; nonproduction (white-collar) employment increased by approximately 50 percent during the 1970s.[3] High turnover generated further demand for new editorial assistants and editors (Dong, 1980; Dessauer, 1982:34). Previously, publishing had never had trouble finding "eager bodies" to fill openings (Association of American Publishers, 1977:19), but as editing became less attractive to men, the demand for women grew. Publishing had long relied on women for many jobs, for reasons that are easy to understand. For one thing, gender-role socialization and a liberal-arts education qualified women for editorial jobs by encouraging literacy, deftness in interpersonal relations, and attention to detail—skills valued in an industry whose stock in trade is communicating ideas. As editor Elizabeth Sifton put it, "We all knew how to type, we were good work horses, and we were willing to learn the ropes" (quoted in Lehman, 1987:43). Moreover, their low profit margin restricted publishers to workers who would settle for low wages because either they had another source of income, placed low priority on earnings, or lacked better-paying alternatives. In fact, industry analyst John Dessauer (1974:64) contended that women won managerial-level jobs partly because publishers knew they could pay them less than men.

In addition to across-the-board growth, several traditionally female sectors grew disproportionately. The growth of subsidiary rights particularly benefited women. Long confined in a female ghetto, women who had developed expertise in rights rose to positions of power when rights directors began making million-dollar movie and paperback deals in the 1970s (*Publishers Weekly*, 1979). Editors consulted them in acquisition decisions, opening a path from subsidiary rights to editorial positions (Coser et al., 1982:104) and later to top management jobs. The detailed, technical nature of the work probably prevented inexperienced men from invading this "empty field" (Tuchman and Fortin, 1984), although Powell (1988) has pointed out that men with legal degrees are now entering subsidiary rights.

When the paperback industry exploded in the late 1960s and the 1970s (Benjamin, 1981:42; Tebbel, 1981:738) and paperback publishers began to acquire and publish original manuscripts, they needed more editors. Massive federal spending on education led to the expansion of school publishing, a sector in which the sexes were already integrated at the editorial level. Public interest in social issues spurred growth in the social sciences, a disproportionately female specialty in both college and mass-market houses. The women's movement gave birth to women's studies, creating jobs for editors knowledgeable about the women's movement and sympathetic to it. Finally, in order to cut costs, the industry increasingly contracted work out, fueling the demand for freelance editors—a predominantly female specialty.

A highly sex-differentiated society creates a demand for workers (such as coaches, counselors, and prison guards) who are the same sex as their occupational role partners (Bielby and Baron, 1984). Once women made up the majority of the fiction-reading and -buying public (*Publishers Weekly*, 1974:25), publishers sought female editors for insight into women's taste (Geracimos, 1974:23). Women also compose a growing percentage of authors and the majority of the literary agents who are playing an increasingly im-

portant role in getting books published (Lane, 1975:41-42; Doebler, 1978:27), so the likelihood that the editor's role partners will be female has increased. To the extent that authors or literary agents prefer same-sex editors, the demand for female editors may have grown accordingly.

In other words, women became attractive to publishers because of their literary and interpersonal skills, their presumed ability to read for a largely female readership, and their expertise in growing segments of the industry—and because they would work cheap. These factors, combined with their availability as a surplus labor pool that could be readily drawn into the workforce, made women an acceptable solution to publishing's economic fluctuations (Caplette, 1982a:151).

Declining Sex Discrimination

Early in this century the feminist movement prompted publishing "to open its doors to [women], however reluctantly" (Tebbel, 1975:176). This process was repeated on a larger scale in the 1970s. Inspired by the women's liberation movement to reject the low-level jobs to which most women had been relegated, some women mobilized against sex discrimination and pressed for better opportunities in publishing (Dessauer, 1974:42; Strainchamps, 1974). Their efforts included both pressure from within and litigation.

By 1970 a group of women had formed Women in Publishing, an organization that carried out actions against some publishing houses, partly in conjunction with labor-organizing issues (*Publishers Weekly*, 1970), and women's groups soon emerged at publishing houses (Strainchamps, 1974:154; Caplette, 1987). When these groups confronted their employers with evidence of wage and job discrimination, some houses began to rectify disparities. For example, after a year-long campaign for job posting by Boston Women in Publishing, five houses posted openings (Reuter, 1976:18). In 1974 the president of Harper & Row, in a letter to *Publishers Weekly* (Knowlton, 1974:12), described that firm's efforts to provide equal opportunities for women, including salary reviews and broader job posting. The industry reclassified secretaries as "editorial assistants"—although their duties did not change (Coser et al., 1982:108); and many firms eliminated separate career ladders for men and women, giving women greater access to senior-level editorial jobs and tempering their preference for men in certain jobs.

Other firms were less receptive. In 1974 New York state's attorney general challenged several companies privately and brought suit against Macmillan (Geracimos, 1974:27; Maryles, 1974; *Publishers Weekly*, 1975a), which subsequently established an affirmative-action plan (*Publishers Weekly*, 1976b). In 1975 a sex-discrimination suit by women editors in Houghton Mifflin's school division led to a cash settlement and to Houghton Mifflin's expansion of its job-representation goals (Smith, 1981:19). In the same year the publishing committee of the Boston chapter of the women's rights organization called 9to5 charged Addison-Wesley and Allyn & Bacon with race and sex discrimination (*Publishers Weekly*, 1975b; 1976a). As a result of these suits, "wages [rose] and management practices . . . changed," according to Massachusetts Attorney General Francis X. Bellotti (Mello, 1980; Reuter, 1980).

The spate of actions against other media giants, including *Newsday*, Time-Life, and NBC, heightened the impact of the suits against book publishing firms. A former editor at Holt, Rinehart & Winston claimed that a three-million-dollar suit against NBC prompted CBS (Holt's parent company) to implement a broad program to recruit and promote women and minorities: "You can-

not imagine the amount of [management activity] there was around here [right after the NBC suit] in getting women up to speed."

A minority publisher claimed that no enforcement agency "is really after book publishers" and added, "If somebody zeroed in, there'd be a difference" (Weyr, 1980:31). However, most observers claimed that pressure from women's groups, litigation, and the risk of government intervention had companies running scared and that the pressure from women's groups had led publishers to curtail sex discrimination (Geracimos, 1974:25). For example, according to an editor in college publishing, "The threat of litigation made a difference. One major responsibility of the personnel director at [a large firm] that especially feared being sued was to keep the company out of trouble by encouraging the hiring of blacks and women."

Another observer commented, "They were worried primarily about the legal cost—not the loss of creative input, because they had gotten along without that." Educational publishers were especially vulnerable to government action in the early 1970s because they held large government contracts. A Harper & Row vice-president for personnel confirmed that affirmative action occurred because publishers—especially large trade and educational houses—had to implement affirmative-action regulations in order to get or keep government contracts (*Publishers Weekly*, 1980).

The women's liberation movement in conjunction with changing social values helped to alert gatekeepers who "consider[ed] themselves *avant garde*" to the contradiction between their behavior and their liberal values. One school publishing editor recalled that after the National Organization for Women (NOW) protested sex stereotyping in some materials she had developed, she and her male boss found stereotyped material in many of their other books. She said, "To have [NOW] protest has a consciousness-raising effect—whether you're a man or a woman." She believed that such experiences had helped men to recognize sex inequality in publishing employment.

The opening of management positions to women further enhanced women's access to editorial jobs. When men dominate management, hiring decisions for desirable jobs tend to favor men (Kanter, 1977). My interviews with women in top-level positions suggest that women's attaining organizational power fostered opportunities for women in lower ranks without necessitating preferential treatment of women. The presence of a few women who had finally attained top-level positions encouraged decision makers to ignore sex in filling lower-level editorial positions (see also Caplette, 1979:17). It also conveyed to women below that they could hope to advance. For example, Sherry Arden (quoted in Geracimos, 1974:23) recalled how moved the secretaries were when she was made a vice-president: "They felt . . . they had a chance at this point." Thus, "the notion that women [couldn't] be acquisitions editors gave way before the insistence of women" (Strainchamps, 1974:159–60; also see Tebbel, 1981:728), and the knowledge that opportunities existed generated a supply of applicants for them (Reskin and Hartmann, 1986).

Conclusions

In sum, the factors that facilitated women's increased representation in editing and the decline in sex segregation across editorial roles began with outside ownership and conglomerization, which tarnished the industry's image and reshaped the editor's role— especially that of the trade editor—robbing it of autonomy and the chance for creative risk taking. Job security declined, and wages failed to rise and may have declined. As a re-

sult of these changes, publishing could no longer attract the caliber of men it desired because they had better alternatives.

The decline in the number of qualified men seeking editorial careers paired with industrial growth to increase the ever present demand for editors, and the growth of several female-dominated specialties led the industry to turn to the large number of women who continued to seek work as editors. Women's availability at lower wages than men commanded no doubt contributed to their attractiveness to publishers. By the time these changes were under way, publishing was already a predominantly female industry, with women monopolizing the lower rungs on the editorial ladder. Pressure by women's groups and fear of government action encouraged publishers to modify their personnel practices to eliminate sex discrimination, creating opportunities for women in editorial jobs. Although sometimes women simply got titles to match the jobs they had been doing all along, many were promoted into senior editorships in trade and college houses. Publishing historian John Tebbel (1987) concluded, "Corporations were virtually forced to give women more opportunities, and women took advantage of [them]." Indeed, women now hold some of the top jobs in the industry (McDowell, 1987)—although they still report to the men who run the corporations that have come to control publishing.

In 1981 Michael and Susan Carter subtitled an article on women in the professions "Women get a ticket to ride after the gravy train has left the station." Although book editing has never been a gravy train, for most of this century its nonmonetary rewards compensated practitioners for low wages. Now, as many of those rewards have diminished, so too has the pool of male would-be editors on whom the industry formerly drew. The result has been both a higher proportion of female editors and a breakdown of sex segregation among editors. Most editors with whom I spoke indicated that male and female assistant editors now do the same jobs. A few expressed concern that editing is becoming resegregated as a female job (e.g., Geracimos, 1974:25). . . . But as Powell (1982) and others have pointed out, trends in publishing are fickle: mergers were common at the turn of the century, then ceased, only to reappear in the 1960s and 1970s; some conglomerates have sold their publishing houses, and others may look for greener pastures; firms may effectively resist takeovers (see, e.g., Glabberson, 1987). In short, the changes in the editorial role need not be irreversible. The data are not all in, and the final chapter remains to be written. What seems likely is that women will edit it.

NOTES

Acknowledgments: I completed this chapter while I was a fellow at the Center for Advanced Study in the Behavioral Sciences, where I was supported in part by a grant from the John D. and Catherine T. MacArthur Foundation. I am happy to acknowledge the assistance of many individuals—particularly Michele Caplette, who generously lent me her dissertation data; John Tebbel, who explained changes in the publishing industry; Miriam E. Phelps, research librarian at R. R. Bowker, who provided articles and indexes for back volumes of *Publishers Weekly;* Barbara Kritt of the University of Michigan, who did the spade work for this chapter; and Pauline Pang, who as an undergraduate at the University of Illinois provided valuable research assistance. This chapter benefited from the comments of Lowell Hargens, Walter Powell, Patricia Roos, and Kathleen Much, who also provided editorial assistance. My greatest debt is to the thirty overworked members of the publishing industry who generously shared their experiences and impressions.

1. I identify by name only editors whom I quote from published sources and industry experts whom I interviewed.
2. I computed sales rates from statistics of the Association of American Publishers, which appear annually in *Publishers Weekly*.
3. There were 40,900 nonproduction employees in 1970 (Lofquist, 1970:6, 9), 46,200 in 1977 (U.S. Department of Commerce, 1977b: Table 1a) and an estimated 66,000 in 1980 (Wright, 1984:589).

REFERENCES

Altbach, Philip G. 1975. "Publishing and the Intellectual System." *Annals of the American Academy of Political and Social Science* 421 (September): 1–13.

Association of American Publishers, Education for Publishing Committee. 1977. *The Accidental Profession: Education, Training, and the People of Publishing.* New York: Association of American Publishers.

Bannon, Barbara A. 1972. "Writers and Editors, the Publishing Lifeline." *Publishers Weekly* 201 (April 10): 100-106.

Bechtold, Grace. 1946. *Book Publishing.* Vocational and Professional Monographs. Boston: Bellman.

Benjamin, Curtis G. 1981. "The Weaving of a Tangled Economic Web." *Publishers Weekly* 219 (April 24): 41–45.

Bielby, Denise D., and William T. Bielby. 1987. "Writing for the Screen: Gender, Jobs, and Stereotypes in the Entertainment Industry." Paper presented at the meeting of the American Sociological Association, Chicago, August.

Bielby, William T., and James N. Baron. 1984. "A Woman's Place Is with Other Women: Sex Segregation within Organizations." In Barbara F. Reskin, ed., *Sex Segregation in the Workplace: Trends, Explanations, Remedies,* 27–55. Washington, D.C.: National Academy Press.

Bingley, Clive. 1972. *The Business of Book Publishing.* Oxford: Pergamon Press.

Canfield, Cass. 1969. "The Real and the Ideal Editor." *Publishers Weekly* 195 (March 31): 24–27.

Caplette, Michele. 1979. "Editorial Career Paths in College Textbook Publishing." Paper presented to the annual meeting of the American Sociological Association, Boston.

————. 1981. "Women in Publishing: A Study of Careers in Organizations." Ph.D. diss., State University of New York at Stony Brook.

————. 1982a. "Women in Book Publishing: A Qualified Success Story." In Lewis Coser, Charles Kadushin, and Walter Powell, eds., *Books: The Culture and Commerce of Publishing,* 148–74. Chicago: University of Chicago Press.

————. 1982b. "Women in Book Publishing: Common Denominators in the Careers of Twelve Successful Women." Presented to the Women's National Book Association.

Carter, Robert A. 1984. "Acquiring Books for Fun and Profit." *Publishers Weekly* 225 (March 23): 24–26.

Cerf, Bennett. 1977. *At Random.* New York: Random House.

Chaney, Bev, ed. 1984. *The First Hundred Years: Association of Book Travelers, 1884–1984.* New York: Association of Book Travelers.

Charnizon, Marlene. 1987. "Women at the Top." *Publishers Weekly* 231 (January 23): 27–31.

Chicago Women in Publishing. 1973. "Survey II: Comparative Status of Women and Men in Chicago Area Book Publishing." Unpublished report, Fall.

Cornelius, James. 1983. "Staying Alive—Young People in Publishing." *Publishers Weekly* 25 (November): 32–35.

Coser, Lewis, Charles Kadushin, and Walter Powell. 1982. *Books: The Culture and Commerce of Publishing.* Chicago: University of Chicago Press.

Dong, Stella. 1980. "Publishing's Revolving Door." *Publisher's Weekly* 218 (December 18): 20–23.

————. 1984. "What Authors Look For in Editors." *Publisher's Weekly* 226 (December 14): 22–27.

Gabriel, Trip. 1989. "Call My Agent!" *New York Times Magazine,* February 19, pp. 45–80.

Galassi, Jonathan W. 1980. "Double Agent: The Literary Editor in the Commercial House." *Publishers Weekly* 217 (March 7):28–30.

Geracimos, Ann. 1974. "Women in Publishing: Where Do They Feel They're Going?" *Publishers Weekly* 206 (November 11):22–27.

Gilroy, Angele A. 1980. "An Economic Analysis of the U.S. Domestic Book Publishing Industry." *Printing and Publishing* 21(4): 8–11.

Giroux, Robert. 1982. "The Education of an Editor." *Publishers Weekly* 221 (January 8): 54–60.

Glabberson, William. 1987. "Will Takeovers Be Bad for Books?" *New York Times.* April 5, p. 3.

Grannis, Chandler B. 1985. "The Structure and Function of the Book Business." In Elizabeth Geiser et al., eds., *The Business of Book Publishing,* 12–20. Boulder, Colo.: Westview Press.

James, Caryn. 1987. "New York's Spinning Literary Circles." *The World of New York, New York Times Magazine* supplement, April 26, pp. 40, 50–53.

Kanter, Rosabeth Moss. 1977. *Men and Women of the Corporation.* New York: Basic Books.

Laskey, Burton. 1969. "Who'll Do the Work?" *Publisher's Weekly* 196 (December 15): 13–14.

McDowell, Edwin. 1987. "Women Move to Top in Publishing." *New York Times,* October 25, p. E24.

Maryles, Daisy. 1974. "Macmillan Charged with Sex Bias in Hiring." *Publishers Weekly* 206 (September 30): 19.

Mello, John P., Jr. 1980. "Allyn and Bacon Settles in Sex Discrimination Suit." *Publishers Weekly* 217 (May 23): 23.

Much, Kathleen. 1988. Personal communication.

Navasky, Victor S. 1973a. "In Cold Print: What Is an Editor Worth?" *New York Times Book Review,* April 15, p. 2.

————. 1973b. "In Cold Print: Selling Out and Buying In." *New York Times Book Review,* May 20, p. 2.

Noble, Kendrick. 1978. "Assessing the Merger Trend." *Publishers Weekly* 214 (July 31): 35–42.

O'Farrell, Brigid, and Sharon Harlan. 1984. "Job Integration Strategies: Today's Programs and Tomorrow's Needs." In Barbara F. Reskin, ed., *Sex Segregation in the Workplace: Trends, Explanations, Remedies,* 267–91. Washington, D.C.: National Academy Press.

Osterman, Paul. 1979. "Sex Discrimination in Professional Employment: A Case Study." *Industrial and Labor Relations Review* 32(4): 451–64.

Phalon, Richard. 1981. "Publishing." *Forbes* 5 (January): 253–54.

Powell, Walter. 1982. "From Craft to Corporation: The Impact of Outside Ownership on Book Publishing." In J. S. Ettema and D. C. Whitney, eds., *Individuals in Mass Media Organizations,* 33–52. Beverly Hills, Calif.: Sage.

————. 1985. *Getting into Print.* Chicago: University of Chicago Press.

————. 1988. Personal communication.

Publishers Weekly. 1969. "Who's Who among the Travelers?" Vol. 195 (March 10): 3.

————. 1970. "McGraw-Hill Picketed by Women in Publishing." Vol. 198 (July 6): 35.

————. 1971. "The Rise of Women in Publishing," Vol. 199 (February 15): 66, 69.

————. 1974. "Some Harsh Words on How Women Fare in Publishing." Vol. 205 (March 25): 25.

————. 1975a. "Women Editors File Suit against HM for Sex Bias." Vol. 208 (November 24): 18.

————. 1975b. "News Brief." Vol. 208 (December 8): 13.

————. 1976a. "Mass. Attorney General Joins Sex Bias Suit against HM." Vol. 209 (March 8): 27.

————. 1976b. "Sex Bias Complaint Settled at Macmillan." Vol. 200 (April 19): 28.

————. 1979. "Why Are Women So Successful in Sub Rights?" Vol. 215 (June 18): 58–62.

————. 1980. "Affirmative Action and Inaction." Vol. 218 (August 8): 25–26.

Rawson, Hugh, and Arnold Dolin. 1985. "The Editorial Process: An Overview." In Elizabeth Geiser et al., eds., *The Business of Book Publishing,* 21–42. Boulder, Colo.: Westview Press.

Reskin, Barbara F., and Heidi I. Hartmann. 1986. *Women's Work, Men's Work: Sex Segregation on the Job.* Washington, D.C.: National Academy Press.

Reuter, Madalynne. 1976. "Boston Women in Publishing Hails Job Posting Efforts." *Publishers Weekly* 210 (October 11): 18.

————. 1980. "Addison-Wesley Agrees to $360,000 Sex-Bias Accord." *Publishers Weekly* 217 (April 11): 10.

Roos, Patricia A., and Barbara F. Reskin. 1984. "Institutional Factors Contributing to Sex Segregation in the Workplace." In Barbara F. Reskin, ed., *Sex Segregation in the Workplace: Trends, Explanations, Remedies,* 235–60. Washington, D.C.: National Academy Press.

Rosenthal, Ellen, Carter Smith, Hope Steele, Clifford Crouch, et al. 1986. "My Say." *Publishers Weekly* 230 (August 29): 392.

Sifton, Elisabeth. 1985. "The Editor's Job in Trade Publishing." In Elizabeth Geiser et al., eds., *The Business of Book Publishing,* 43–61. Boulder, Colo.: Westview Press.

Smith, Wendy. 1981. "Houghton Reaches Accord in Sex Bias Suit." *Publishers Weekly* 219 (January 16): 19.

Strainchamps, Ethel. 1974. *Rooms with No View: A Woman's Guide to the Man's World of Publishing.* New York: Harper & Row.

Tebbel, John. 1972. *A History of Book Publishing in the United States.* Vol. 1, *The Creation of an Industry.* New York: Bowker.

————. 1975. *A History of Book Publishing in the United States.* Vol. 2, *The Expansion of an Industry.* New York: Bowker.

————. 1978. *A History of Book Publishing in the United States.* Vol. 3, *The Golden Age between Two Wars, 1920–1940.* New York: Bowker.

————. 1981. *A History of Book Publishing in the United States.* Vol. 4, *The Great Change, 1940–1980.* New York, Bowker.

————. 1987. Personal communication.

Tuchman, Gay, and Nina Fortin. 1984. "Women Writers and Literary Tradition." *American Journal of Sociology* 90 (July): 72–96.

U.S. Bureau of the Census. 1972. *1970 Census of Population: Occupation by Industry.* Subject Reports, PC(2)-7C. Washington, D.C.: Government Printing Office.

————. 1984b. *1980 Census of Population: Subject Reports.* Vol. 2, *Occupation by Industry.* PC80-2-7C. Washington, D.C.: Government Printing Office.

U.S. Bureau of Labor Statistics. 1972. *Occupational Outlook Handbook.* 1972–73 ed. Bulletin 1700. Washington, D.C.: Government Printing Office.

————. 1984b. *Occupational Outlook Handbook.* 1984–85 ed. Bulletin 2205. Washington, D.C.: Government Printing Office.

U.S. Department of Commerce. 1977b. *Census of Manufacturing.* Subject Statistics, vol. 2, pt. SIC Major Groups 37–34. Washington, D.C.: Government Printing Office.

Weber, Max. 1978. *Economy and Society.* Vol. 2. Berkeley: University of California Press.

Wendroff, Michael. 1980. "Should We Do the Book?" *Publishers Weekly* 218 (August 15): 24–30.

Weyr, Thomas. 1980. "Minorities in Publishing." *Publishers Weekly* 218 (October 17): 31–35.

Wright, John W. 1984. *The American Almanac of Jobs and Salaries.* New York: Avon Books.

21

Boundary Lines
Labeling Sexual Harassment in Restaurants

Patti A. Giuffre • Christine L. Williams

Patti Giuffre is assistant professor of sociology at Grand Valley State University. Her co-author, Christine L. Williams, is associate professor of sociology at the University of Texas, Austin. Giuffre's current interests include exploring the institutionalized nature of sexual harassment, and the management of sexuality in medicine and nursing. Professor Giuffre observes, "I was a waitperson for over eight years, and was working as a waitress when I began my data collection for this project (my masters thesis, which was supervised by Christine Williams). I noticed that sexual banter and innuendo were common among restaurant employees, and wanted to examine how people draw the line between sexual harassment and more acceptable sexual behaviors in the restaurant. This 'insider status' gave me a more contextualized view of this workplace setting."

Sexual harassment occurs when submission to or rejection of sexual advances is a term of employment, is used as a basis for making employment decisions, or if the advances create a hostile or offensive work environment (Konrad and Gutek 1986). Sexual harassment can cover a range of behaviors, from leering to rape (Ellis, Barak, and Pinto 1991; Pryor 1987; Reilly et al. 1992; Schneider 1982). Researchers estimate that as many as 70 percent of employed women have experienced behaviors that may legally constitute sexual harassment (MacKinnon 1979; Powell 1986); however, a far lower percentage of women claim to have experienced sexual harassment. Paludi and Barickman write that "the great majority of women

Abridgment from "Boundary Lines: Labeling Sexual Harassment in Restaurants," by Patti A. Giuffre and Christine L. Williams, *Gender & Society*, Vol. 8, No. 3, September 1994. Copyright © 1994 Sociologists for Women in Society. Reprinted by permission of Sage Publications Inc.

who are abused by behavior that fits legal definitions of sexual harassment—and who are traumatized by the experience—do not label what has happened to them 'sexual harassment'" (1991, 68).

Why do most women fail to label their experiences as sexual harassment? Part of the problem is that many still do not recognize that sexual harassment is an actionable offense. Sexual harassment was first described in 1976 (MacKinnon 1979), but it was not until 1986 that the U.S. Supreme Court included sexual harassment in the category of gender discrimination, thereby making it illegal (Paludi and Barickman 1991); consequently, women may not yet identify their experiences as sexual harassment because a substantial degree of awareness about its illegality has yet to be developed.

Many victims of sexual harassment may also be reluctant to come forward with complaints, fearing that they will not be believed, or that their charges will not be taken seriously (Jensen and Gutek 1982). As the Anita Hill-Clarence Thomas hearings demonstrated, women who are victims of sexual harassment often become the accused when they bring charges against their assailant.

There is another issue at stake in explaining the gap between experiencing and labeling behaviors "sexual harassment": many men and women experience some sexual behaviors in the workplace as pleasurable. Research on sexual harassment suggests that men are more likely than women to enjoy sexual interactions at work (Gutek 1985; Konrad and Gutek 1986; Reilly et al. 1992), but even some women experience sexual overtures at work as pleasurable (Pringle 1988). This attitude may be especially strong in organizations that use and exploit the bodies and sexuality of the workers (Cockburn 1991). Workers in many jobs are hired on the basis of their attractiveness and solicitousness—including not only sex industry workers, but also service sector workers such as receptionists, airline attendants, and servers in trendy restaurants. According to Cockburn (1991), the sexual exploitation is not completely forced: many people find this dimension of their jobs appealing and reinforcing to their own sense of identity and pleasure; consequently, some men and women resist efforts to expunge all sexuality from their places of work.

This is not to claim that all sexual behavior in the workplace is acceptable, even to some people. The point is that it is difficult to label behavior as sexual harassment because it forces people to draw a line between illicit and "legitimate" forms of sexuality at work—a process fraught with ambiguity. Whether a particular interaction is identified as harassment will depend on the intention of the harasser and the interpretation of the interchange by the victim, and both of these perspectives will be highly influenced by workplace culture and the social context of the specific event. . . .

Methods

The occupation of waiting tables was selected to study the social definition of sexual harassment because many restaurants have a blatantly sexualized workplace culture (Cobble 1991; Paules 1991). According to a report published in a magazine that caters to restaurant owners, "Restaurants . . . are about as informal a workplace as there is, so much so as to actually encourage—or at the very least tolerate—sexual banter" (Anders 1993, 48). Unremitting sexual banter and innuendo, as well as physical jostling, create an environment of "compulsory jocularity" in many restaurants (Pringle 1988, 93). Sexual attractiveness and flirtation are often institutionalized parts of a waitperson's job description; consequently, individual employees are often forced to draw the line for themselves to distinguish legitimate and illegitimate expressions of sexuality, making this occupation an excellent context for examining how people determine what constitutes sexual harassment. In contrast, many more sexual behaviors may be labeled sexual harassment in less highly sexualized work environments.

Eighteen in-depth interviews were conducted with male and female wait staff who work in restaurants in Austin, Texas. Respondents were selected from restaurants that employ equal proportions of men and women on their wait staffs. Overall, restaurant work is highly sex segregated: women make up about 82 percent of all waitpeople (U.S. Department of Labor 1989), and it is common for restaurants to be staffed only by either waitresses or waiters, with men predominating in the higher-priced restaurants (Cobble 1991; Hall 1993; Paules 1991). We decided to focus only on waitpeople who work in mixed-sex groups for two reasons. First, focusing on waitpeople working on integrated staffs enables us to examine sexual

harassment between co-workers who occupy the same position in an organizational hierarchy. Co-worker sexual harassment is perhaps the most common form of
sexual harassment (Pryor 1987; Schneider
1982); yet most case studies of sexual harassment have examined either unequal
hierarchical relationships (e.g., boss-secre-
tary harassment) or harassment in highly
skewed gender groupings (e.g., women
who work in nontraditional occupations)
(Benson and Thomson 1982; Carothers and
Crull 1984; Gruber and Bjorn 1982). This
study is designed to investigate sexual harassment in unequal hierarchical relationships, as well as harassment between organizationally equal co-workers.

Second, equal proportions of men and
women in an occupation implies a high degree of male-female interaction (Gutek
1985). Waitpeople are in constant contact
with each other, help each other when the
restaurant is busy, and informally socialize
during slack periods. In constant, men and
women have much more limited interactions in highly sex-segregated restaurants
and indeed, in most work environments.
The high degree of interaction among the
wait staff provides ample opportunity for
sexual harassment between men and
women to occur and, concomitantly, less opportunity for same-sex sexual harassment to
occur.

The sample was generated using
"snowball" techniques and by going to area
restaurants and asking waitpeople to volunteer for the study. The sample includes eight
men and ten women. Four respondents are
Latina/o, two African American, and twelve
white. Four respondents are gay or lesbian;
one is bisexual; thirteen are heterosexual.
(The gay men and lesbians in the sample are
all "out" at their respective restaurants.)
Fourteen respondents are single; three are
married; one is divorced. Respondents' ages
range from 22 to 37. . . .

Findings

Respondents agreed that sexual banter is
very common in the restaurant: staff members talk and joke about sex constantly. With
only one exception, respondents described
their restaurants as highly sexualized. This
means that 17 of the 18 respondents said
that sexual joking, touching, and fondling
were common, everyday occurrences in
their restaurants. For example, when asked
if he and other waitpeople ever joke about
sex, one waiter replied, "about 90 percent of
[the jokes] are about sex." According to a
waitress, "at work . . . [we're] used to pat-
ting and touching and hugging." Another
waiter said, "I do not go through a shift
without someone . . . pinching my nipples or
poking me in the butt or grabbing my
crotch. . . . It's just what we do at work."

These informal behaviors are tantamount to "doing heterosexuality," a process
analogous to "doing gender" (West and
Zimmerman 1987).[1] By engaging in these
public flirtations and open discussions of
sex, men and women reproduce the dominant cultural norms of heterosexuality and
lend an air of legitimacy—if not inevitability—to heterosexual relationships. In other
words, heterosexuality is normalized and
naturalized through its ritualistic public display. Indeed, although most respondents
described their workplaces as highly sexualized, several dismissed the constant sexual
innuendo and behaviors as "just joking,"
and nothing to get upset about. Several respondents claimed that this is simply "the
way it is in the restaurant business," or "just
the way men are."

With only one exception, the men and
women interviewed maintained that they
enjoyed this aspect of their work.
Heterosexuality may be normative, and in
these contexts, even compulsory, yet many
men and women find pleasure in its expression. Many women—as well as men—

actively reproduce hegemonic sexuality and apparently enjoy its ritual expression; however, in a few instances, sexual conduct was labeled as sexual harassment. Seven women and three men said they had experienced sexual harassment in restaurant work. Of these, two women and one man described two different experiences of sexual harassment, and two women described three experiences. . . .

We analyzed these 17 accounts of sexual harassment to find out what, if anything, these experiences shared in common. With the exception of two episodes (discussed later), the experiences that were labeled "sexual harassment" were not distinguished by any specific words or behaviors, nor were they distinguished by their degree of severity. Identical behaviors were considered acceptable if they were perpetrated by some people, but considered offensive if perpetrated by others. In other words, sexual behavior in the workplace was interpreted differently depending on the context of the interaction. In general, respondents labeled their experiences sexual harassment only if the offending behavior occurred in one of three social contexts: (1) if perpetrated by someone in a more powerful position, such as a manager; (2) if perpetrated by someone of a different race/ethnicity; or (3) if perpetrated by someone of a different sexual orientation.

Our findings do not imply that sexual harassment did not occur outside of these three contexts. Instead, they simply indicate that our respondents *labeled* behavior as "sexual harassment" when it occurred in these particular social contexts. We will discuss each of these contexts and speculate on the reasons why they were singled out by our respondents.

Powerful Position

In the restaurant, managers and owners are the highest in the hierarchy of workers. Generally, they are the only ones who can hire or fire waitpeople. Three of the women and one of the men interviewed said they had been sexually harassed by their restaurants' managers or owners. In addition, several others who did not personally experience harassment said they had witnessed managers or owners sexually harassing other waitpeople. This finding is consistent with other research indicating people are more likely to think that sexual harassment has occurred when the perpetrator is in a more powerful position (e.g., Ellis et al. 1991).

Carla describes being sexually harassed by her manager:

> One evening, [my manager] grabbed my body, not in a private place, just grabbed my body, period. He gave me like a bear hug from behind a total of four times in one night. By the end of the night I was livid. I was trying to avoid him. Then when he'd do it, I'd just ignore the conversation or the joke or whatever and walk away.

She claimed that her co-workers often give each other massages and joke about sex, but she did not label any of their behaviors sexual harassment. In fact, all four individuals who experienced sexual harassment from their managers described very similar types of behavior from their co-workers, which they did not define as sexual harassment. For example, Cathy said that she and the other waitpeople talk and joke about sex constantly: "Everybody stands around and talks about sex a lot. . . . Isn't that weird? You know, it's something about working in restaurants and, yeah, so we'll all sit around and talk about sex." She said that talking with her co-workers about sex does not constitute sexual harassment because it is "only joking." She does, however, view her male manager as a sexual harasser:

My employer is very sexist. I would call that sexual harassment. Very much of a male chauvinist pig. He kind of started [saying] stuff like, "You can't really wear those shorts because they're not flattering to your figure. . . . But I like the way you wear those jeans. They look real good. They're tight." It's like, you know [I want to say to him], "You're the owner, you're in power. That's evident. You know, you need to find a better way to tell me these things." We've gotten to a point now where we'll joke around now, but it's never ever sexual, ever. I won't allow that with him.

Cathy acknowledges that her manager may legitimately dictate her appearance at work, but only if he does so in professional—and not personal—terms. She wants him "to find a better way to tell me these things," implying that he is not completely out-of-line in suggesting that she wear tight pants. He "crosses the line" when he personalizes his directive, by saying to Cathy "*I like* the way you wear those jeans." This is offensive to Cathy because it is framed as the manager's personal prerogative, not the institutional requirements of the job.

Ann described a similar experience of sexual harassment from a restaurant owner:

Yeah, there's been a couple of times when a manager has made me feel real uncomfortable and I just removed myself from the situation. . . . Like if there's something I really want him to hear or something I think is really important there's no touching. Like, "Don't touch me while I'm talking to you." You know, because I take that as very patronizing. I actually blew up at one of the owners once because I was having a rough day and he came up behind me and he was rubbing my back, like up and down my back and saying, you know, "Oh, is Ann having a

bad day?" or something like that and I shook him off of me and I said, "You do not need to touch me to talk to me."

Ann distinguishes between legitimate and illegitimate touching: if the issue being discussed is "really important"—that is, involving her job status—she insists there be no touching. In these specific situations, a back rub is interpreted as patronizing and offensive because the manager is using his powerful position for his *personal* sexual enjoyment.

One of the men in the sample, Frank, also experienced sexual harassment from a manager:

I was in the bathroom and [the manager] came up next to me and my tennis shoes were spray-painted silver so he knew it was me in there and he said something about, "Oh, what do you have in your hand there?" I was on the other side of a wall and he said, "Mind if I hold it for a while?" or something like that, you know. I just pretended like I didn't hear it.

Frank also described various sexual behaviors among the waitstaff, including fondling, "joking about bodily functions," and "making bikinis out of tortillas." He said, "I mean, it's like, what we do at work. . . . There's no holds barred. I don't find it offensive. I'm used to it by now. I'm guilty of it myself." Evidently, he defines sexual behaviors as "sexual harassment" only when perpetrated by someone in a position of power over him.

Two of the women in the sample also described sexual harassment from customers. We place these experiences in the category of "powerful position" because customers do have limited economic power over the waitperson insofar as they control the tip (Crull 1987). Cathy said that male customers often ask her to "sit on my lap" and provide them with other sexual favors. Brenda, a lesbian, described a similar experience of sexual harassment from women customers:

> One time I had this table of lesbians and they were being real vulgar towards me. Real sexual. This woman kind of tripped me as I was walking by and said, "Hurry back." I mean, gay people can tell when other people are gay. I felt harassed.

In these examples of harassment by customers, the line is drawn using a similar logic as in the examples of harassment by managers. There customers acted as though the waitresses were providing table service to satisfy the customers' private desires, instead of working to fulfill their job descriptions. In other words, the customers' demands were couched in personal—and not professional—terms, making the waitresses feel sexually harassed.

It is not difficult to understand why waitpeople singled out sexual behaviors from managers, owners, and customers as sexual harassment. Subjection to sexual advances by someone with economic power comes closest to the quid pro quo form of sexual harassment, wherein employees are given the option to either "put out or get out." Studies have found that this type of sexual harassment is viewed as the most threatening and unambiguous sort (Ellis et al. 1991; Fitzgerald 1990; Gruber and Bjorn 1982).

But even in this context, lines are drawn between legitimate and illegitimate sexual behavior in the workplace. As Cathy's comments make clear, some people accept the employers' prerogative to exploit the workers' sexuality, by dictating appropriate "sexy" dress, for example. Like airline attendants, waitresses are expected to be friendly, helpful, and sexually available to the male customers (Cobble 1991). Because this expectation is embedded in restaurant culture, it becomes difficult for workers to separate sexual harassment from the more or less accepted forms of sexual exploitation that are routine features of their jobs. Consequently, some women are reluctant to label blatantly offensive behaviors as sexual harassment. For example, Maxine, who claims that she has never experienced sexual harassment, said that customers often "talk dirty" to her:

> I remember one day, about four or five years ago when I was working as a cocktail waitress, this guy asked me for a "Slow Comfortable Screw" [the name of a drink]. I didn't know what it was. I didn't know if he was making a move or something. I just looked at him. He said, "You know what it is, right?" I said, "I bet the bartender knows!" (laughs). . . . There's another one, "Sex on the Beach." And there's another one called a "Screaming Orgasm." Do you believe that?

Maxine is subject to a sexualized work environment that she finds offensive; hence her experience could fit the legal definition of sexual harassment. But because sexy drink names are an institutionalized part of restaurant culture, Maxine neither complains about it nor labels it sexual harassment: Once it becomes clear that a "Slow Comfortable Screw" is a legitimate and recognized restaurant demand, she accepts it (although reluctantly) as part of her job description. In other words, the fact that the offensive behavior is institutionalized seems to make it beyond reproach in her eyes. This finding is consistent with others' findings that those who work in highly sexualized environments may be less likely to label offensive behavior "sexual harassment" (Gutek 1985; Konrad and Gutek 1986).

Only in specific contexts do workers appear to define offensive words and acts of a sexual nature as sexual harassment—even when initiated by someone in a more powerful position. The interviews suggest that workers use this label to describe their experiences only when their bosses or their customers couch their requests for sexual attentions in explicitly personal terms. This way of defining sexual harassment may obscure and legitimize more institutionalized—and hence more insidious—forms of sexual exploitation at work.

Race/Ethnicity

The restaurants in our sample, like most restaurants in the United States, have racially segregated staffs (Howe 1977). In the restaurants where our respondents are employed, men of color are concentrated in two positions: the kitchen cooks and bus personnel (formerly called busboys). Five of the white women in the sample reported experiencing sexual harassment from Latino men who worked in these positions. For example, when asked if she had ever experienced sexual harassment, Beth said:

> Yes, but it was not with the people . . . it was not, you know, the people that I work with in the front of the house. It was with the kitchen. There are boundaries or lines that I draw with the people I work with. In the kitchen, the lines are quite different. Plus, it's a Mexican staff. It's a very different attitude. They tend to want to touch you more and, at times, I can put up with a little bit of it but . . . because I will give them a hard time too but I won't touch them. I won't touch their butt or anything like that.
>
> [Interviewer: So sometimes they cross the line?]
>
> It's only happened to me a couple of times. One guy, like, patted me on the butt and I went off. I lost my shit. I went off on him. I said, "No. Bad. Wrong. I can't speak Spanish to you but, you

know, this is it." I told the kitchen manager who is a guy and he's not . . . the head kitchen manager is not Hispanic. . . . I've had to do that over the years only a couple of times with those guys.

Beth reported that the waitpeople joke about sex and touch each other constantly, but she does not consider their behavior sexual harassment. Like many of the other men and women in the sample, Beth said she feels comfortable engaging in this sexual banter and play with other waitpeople (who were predominantly white), but not with the Mexican men in the kitchen.

Part of the reason for singling out the behaviors of the cooks as sexual harassment may involve status differences between waitpeople and cooks. Studies have suggested that people may label behaviors as sexual harassment when they are perpetrated by people in lower status organizational positions (Grauerholz 1989; McKinney 1990); however, it is difficult to generalize about the relative status of cooks and waitpeople because of the varied and often complex organizational hierarchies of restaurants (Paules 1991, 107-10). If the cook is a chef, as in higher-priced restaurants, he or she may actually have more status than waitpeople, and indeed may have the formal power to hire and fire the waitstaff. In the restaurants where our respondents worked, the kitchen cooks did not wield this sort of formal control, but they could exert some informal power over the waitstaff by slowing down food orders or making the orders look and/or taste bad. Because bad food can decrease the waitperson's tip, the cooks can thereby control the waitperson's income; hence servers are forced to negotiate and to some extent placate the wishes and desires of cooks to perform their jobs. The willingness of several respondents to label the cooks' behavior as sexual harassment may reflect their perception that the cooks' informal demands had become unreasonable. In such cases, subjection to the offensive behaviors is a term of employment, which is quid pro quo sexual harassment. As mentioned previously, this type of sexual harassment is the most likely to be so labeled and identified.

Because each recounted case of sexual harassment occurring between individuals of different occupational statuses involved a minority man sexually harassing a white woman, the racial context seems equally important. For example, Ann also said she and the other waiters and waitresses joke about sex and touch each other "on the butt" all the time, and when asked if she had ever experienced sexual harassment, she said,

> I had some problems at [a previous restaurant] but it was a communication problem. A lot of the guys in the kitchen did not speak English. They would see the waiters hugging on us, kissing us and pinching our rears and stuff. They would try to do it and I couldn't tell them, "No. You don't understand this. It's like we do it because we have a mutual understanding but I'm not comfortable with you doing it." So that was really hard and a lot of times what I'd have to do is just sucker punch them in the chest and just use a lot of cuss words and they knew that I was serious. And there again, I felt real weird about that because they're just doing what they see go on everyday.

Kate, Carla, and Brenda described very similar racial double standards. Kate complained about a Mexican busser who constantly touched her:

> This is not somebody that I talk to on a friendly basis. We don't sit there and laugh and joke and stuff. So, when he touches me, all I know is he is just touching me and there is no context about it. With other people, if they said something or they touched me, it would

be funny or . . . we have a relationship. This person and I and all the other people do not. So that is sexual harassment.

And according to Brenda:

> The kitchen can be kind of sexist. They really make me angry. They're not as bad as they used to be because they got warned. They're mostly Mexican, not even Mexican-American. Most of them, they're just starting to learn English.
>
> [Interviewer: What do they do to you?]
>
> Well, I speak Spanish, so I know. They're not as sexual to me because I think they know I don't like it. Some of the other girls will come through and they will touch them like here [points to the lower part of her waist]. . . . I've had some pretty bad arguments with the kitchen.
>
> [Interviewer: Would you call that sexual harassment?]
>
> Yes. I think some of the girls just don't know better to say something. I think it happens a lot with the kitchen guys. Like sometimes, they will take a relleno in their hands like it's a penis. Sick!

Each of these women identified the sexual advances of the minority men in their restaurants as sexual harassment, but not the identical behaviors of their white male co-workers; moreover, they all recognize that they draw boundary lines differently for Anglo men and Mexican men: each of them willingly participates in "doing heterosexuality" only in racially homogamous contexts. These women called the behavior of the Mexican cooks "sexual harassment" in part because they did not "have a relationship" with these men, nor was it conceivable to them that they *could* have a relationship with them, given cultural and language barriers—and, probably, racist attitudes as well. The white men, on the other hand, can "hug, kiss, and pinch rears" of the white women because they have a "mutual understanding"—implying reciprocity and the possibility of intimacy.

The importance of this perception of relationship potential in the assessment of sexual harassment is especially clear in the cases of the two married women in the sample, Diana and Maxine. Both of these women said that they had never experienced sexual harassment. Diana, who works in a family-owned and -operated restaurant, claimed that her restaurant is not a sexualized work environment. Although people occasionally make double entendre jokes relating to sex, according to Diana, "there's no contact whatsoever like someone pinching your butt or something." She said that she has never experienced sexual harassment:

> Everybody here knows I'm married so they're not going to get fresh with me because they know that it's not going to go anywhere, you know so . . . and vice versa. You know, we know the guys' wives. They come in here to eat. It's respect all the way. I don't think they could handle it if they saw us going around hugging them. You know what I mean? It's not right.

Similarly, Maxine, who is Colombian, said she avoids the problem of sexual harassment in her workplace because she is married:

> The cooks don't offend me because they know I speak Spanish and they know how to talk with me because I set my boundaries and they know that. . . . I just don't joke with them more than I should. They all know that I'm married, first of all, so that's a no-no for all of them. My brother used to be a manager in that restaurant so he probably took care of everything. I never had any problems anyway in any other jobs

because, like I said, I set my boundaries. I don't let them get too close to me.

[Interviewer: You mean physically?]

Not physically only. Just talking. If they want to talk about, "Do you go dancing? Where do you go dancing?" Like I just change the subject because it's none of their business and I don't really care to talk about that with them . . . not because I consider them to be on the lower levels than me or something but just because if you start talking with them that way then you are just giving them hope or something. I think that's true for most of the guys here, not just talking about the cooks. . . . I do get offended and they know that so sometimes they apologize.

Both Maxine and Diana said that they are protected from sexual harassment because they are married. In effect, they use their marital status to negotiate their interactions with their co-workers and to ward off unwanted sexual advances. Furthermore, because they do not view their co-workers as potential relationship "interests," they conscientiously refuse to participate in any sexual banter in the restaurant.

The fact that both women speak Spanish fluently may mean that they can communicate their boundaries unambiguously to those who only speak Spanish (unlike the female respondents in the sample who only speak English). For these two women, sexual harassment from co-workers is not an issue. Diana, who is Latina, talks about "respect all around" in her restaurant; Maxine claims the cooks (who are Mexican) aren't the ones who offend her. Their comments seem to reflect more mutual respect and humanity toward their Latino co-workers than the comments of the white waitresses. On the other hand, at least from Maxine's vantage point, racial harassment is a bigger problem in her workplace than is sexual harassment. When asked if she ever felt excluded from any groups at work, she said:

> Yeah, sometimes. How can I explain this? Sometimes, I mean, I don't know if they do it on purpose or they don't but they joke around you about being Spanish. . . . Sometimes it hurts. Like they say, "What are you doing here? Why don't you go back home?"

Racial harassment—like sexual harassment— is a means used by a dominant group to maintain its dominance over a subordinated group. Maxine feels that, because she is married, she is protected from sexual harassment (although, as we have seen, she is subject to a sexualized workplace that is offensive to her); however, she does experience racial harassment where she works, and she feels vulnerable to this because she is one of very few nonwhites working at her restaurant.

One of the waiters in the sample claimed that he had experienced sexual harassment from female co-workers, and race may have also been a factor in this situation. When Rick (who is African American) was asked if he had ever been sexually harassed, he recounted his experiences with some white waitresses:

> Yes. There are a couple of girls there, waitpeople, who will pinch my rear.
>
> [Interviewer: Do you find it offensive?]
>
> No (laughs) because I'm male. . . . But it is a form of sexual harassment.
>
> [Interviewer: Do you ever tell them to stop?]
>
> If I'm really busy, if I'm in the weeds, and they want to touch me, I'll get mad. I'll tell them to stop. There's a certain time and place for everything.

Rick is reluctant about labeling this interaction "sexual harassment" because "it doesn't bother me unless I'm, like, busy or something like that." In those cases where he is

busy, he feels that his female co-workers are subverting his work by pinching him. Because of the race difference, he may experience their behaviors as an expression of racial dominance, which probably influences his willingness to label the behavior as sexual harassment.

In sum, the interviews suggest that the perception and labeling of interactions as "sexual harassment" may be influenced by the racial context of the interaction. If the victim perceives the harasser as expressing a potentially reciprocal relationship interest, they may be less likely to label their experience sexual harassment. In cases where the harasser and victim have a different race/ethnicity and class background, the possibility of a relationship may be precluded because of racism, making these cases more likely to be labeled "sexual harassment."

This finding suggests that the practices associated with "doing heterosexuality" are profoundly racist. The white women in the sample showed a great reluctance to label unwanted sexual behavior sexual harassment when it was perpetrated by a potential (or real) relationship interest—that is, a white male co-worker. In contrast, minority men are socially constructed as potential harassers of white women: any expression of sexual interest may be more readily perceived as nonreciprocal and unwanted. The assumption of racial homogamy in heterosexual relationships thus may protect white men from charges of sexual harassment of white women. This would help to explain why so many white women in the sample labeled behaviors perpetrated by Mexican men as sexual harassment, but not the identical behaviors perpetrated by white men.

Sexual Orientation

There has been very little research on sexual harassment that addresses the sexual orientation of the harasser and victim (exceptions include Reilly et al. 1992; Schneider 1982, 1984). Surveys of sexual harassment typically include questions about marital status but not about sexual orientation (e.g., Fain and Anderton 1987; Gruber and Bjorn 1982; Powell 1986). In this study, sexual orientation was an important part of heterosexual men's perceptions of sexual harassment. Of the four episodes of sexual harassment reported by the men in the study, three involved openly gay men sexually harassing straight men. One case involved a male manager harassing a male waiter (Frank's experience, described earlier). The other two cases involved co-workers. Jake said that he had been sexually harassed by a waiter:

> Someone has come on to me that I didn't want to come on to me. . . . He was another waiter [male]. It was laughs and jokes the whole way until things got a little too much and it was like, "Hey, this is how it is. Back off. Keep your hands off my ass." . . . Once it reached the point where I felt kind of threatened and bothered by it.

Rick described being sexually harassed by a gay baker in his restaurant:

> There was a baker that we had who was really, really gay. . . . He was very straightforward and blunt. He would tell you, in detail, his sexual experiences and tell you that he wanted to do them with you. . . . I knew he was kidding but he was serious. I mean, if he had a chance he would do these things.

In each of these cases, the men expressed some confusion about the intentions of their harassers—"I knew he was kidding but he was serious." Their inability to read the intentions of the gay men provoked them to label these episodes sexual harassment. Each man did not perceive the sexual interchange as reciprocal, nor did he view the harasser as a potential relationship interest.

Interestingly, however, all three of the men who described harassment from gay men claimed that sexual banter and play with other *straight* men did not trouble them. Jake, for example, said that "when men get together, they talk sex," regardless of whether there are women around. He acceded, "people find me offensive, as a matter of fact," because he gets "pretty raunchy" talking and joking about sex. Only when this talk was initiated by a gay man did Jake label it as sexual harassment.

Johnson (1988) argues that talking and joking about sex is a common means of establishing intimacy among heterosexual men and maintaining a masculine identity. Homosexuality is perceived as a direct challenge and threat to the achievement of masculinity and consequently, "the male homosexual is derided by other males because he is not a real man, and in male logic if one is not a real man, one is a woman" (p. 124). In Johnson's view, this dynamic not only sustains masculine identity, it also shores up male dominance over women; thus, for some straight men, talking about sex with other straight men is a form of reasserting masculinity and male dominance, whereas talking about sex with gay men threatens the very basis for their masculine privilege. For this reason they may interpret the sex talk and conduct of gay men as a form of sexual harassment.

In certain restaurants, gay men may in fact intentionally hassle straight men as an explicit strategy to undermine their privileged position in society. For example, Trent (who is openly gay) realizes that heterosexual men are uncomfortable with his sexuality, and he intentionally draws attention to his sexuality in order to bother them:

> [Interviewer: Homosexuality gets on whose nerves?]
>
> The straight people's nerves. . . . I know also that we consciously push it just

because, we know, "Okay. We know this is hard for you to get used to but tough luck. I've had my whole life trying to live in this straight world and if you don't like this, tough shit." I don't mean like we're shitty to them on purpose but it's like, "I've had to worry about being accepted by straight people all my life. The shoe's on the other foot now. If you don't like it, sorry."

[Interviewer: Do you get along well with most of the waitpeople?]

I think I get along with straight women. I get along with gay men. I get along with gay women usually. If there's ever going to be a problem between me and somebody it will be between me and a straight man.

Trent's efforts to "push" his sexuality could easily be experienced as sexual harassment by straight men who have limited experience negotiating unwanted sexual advances. The three men who reported being sexually harassed by gay men seemed genuinely confused about the intentions of their harassers, and threatened by the possibility that they would actually be subjected to and harmed by unwanted sexual advances. But it is important to point out that Trent works in a restaurant owned by lesbians, which empowers him to confront his straight male co-workers. Not all restaurants provide the sort of atmosphere that makes this type of engagement possible; indeed, some restaurants have policies explicitly banning the hiring of gays and lesbians. Clearly, not all gay men would be able to push their sexuality without suffering severe retaliation (e.g., loss of job, physical attacks).

In contrast to the reports of the straight men in this study, none of the women interviewed reported sexual harassment from their gay or lesbian co-workers. Although Maxine was worried when she found out that one of her co-workers was lesbian, she claims that this fact no longer troubles her:

> Six months ago I found out that there was a lesbian girl working there. It kind of freaked me out for a while. I was kind of aware of everything that she did towards me. I was conscious if she walked by me and accidentally brushed up against me. She's cool. She doesn't bother me. She never touches my butt or anything like that. The gay guys do that to the [straight] guys but they know they're just kidding around. The [straight] guys do that to the [straight] girls, but they don't care. They know that they're not supposed to do that with me. If they do it, I stop and look at them and they apologize and they don't do it anymore. So they stay out of my way because I'm a meanie (laughs).

Some heterosexual women claimed they feel *more* comfortable working with gay men and lesbians. For example, Kate prefers working with gay men rather than heterosexual men or women. She claims that she often jokes about sex with her gay co-workers, yet she does not view them as potential harassers. Instead, she feels that her working conditions are more comfortable and more fun because she works with gay men. Similarly, Cathy prefers working with gay men over straight men because "gay men are a lot like women in that they're very sensitive to other people's space." Cathy also works with lesbians, and she claims that she has never felt sexually harassed by them.

The gays and lesbians in the study did not report any sexual harassment from their gay and lesbian co-workers. Laura, who is bisexual, said she preferred to work with gays and lesbians instead of heterosexuals because they are "more relaxed" about sex. Brenda said she feels comfortable working around all of her male and female colleagues—regardless of their sexual orientation:

> The guys I work with [don't threaten me]. We always run by each other and pat each other on the butt. It's no big deal. Like with my girlfriend [who works at the same restaurant], all the cocktailers and hostesses love us. They don't care that we're gay. We're not a threat. We all kind of flirt but it's not sexual. A lesbian is not going to sexually harass another woman unless they're pretty gross anyway. It has nothing to do with their sexuality; it has to do with the person. You can't generalize and say that gays and lesbians are the best to work with or anything because it depends on the person.

Brenda enjoys flirtatious interactions with both men and women at her restaurant, but distinguishes these behaviors from sexual harassment. Likewise, Lynn, who is a lesbian, enjoys the relaxed sexual atmosphere at her workplace. When asked if she ever joked about sex in her workplace, she said:

> Yes! (laughs) All the time! All the time—everybody has something that they want to talk about on sex and it's got to be funny. We have gays. We have lesbians. We have straights. We have people who are real Christian-oriented. But we all jump in there and we all talk about it. It gets real funny at times. . . . I've patted a few butts. . . . and I've been patted back by men, and by the women, too! (laughs).

Don and Trent, who are both gay, also said that they had never been sexually harassed in their restaurants, even though both described their restaurants as highly sexualized.

In sum, our interviews suggest that sexual orientation is an important factor in understanding each individual's experience of sexual harassment and his or her willingness to label interactions as sexual harassment. In particular, straight men may perceive gay men as potential harassers. Three of our straight male respondents claimed to enjoy the sexual banter that commonly occurs among straight men, and between heterosexual men and women, but singled out the sexual advances of gay men as sexual harassment. Their contacts with gay men may be the only context where they feel vulnerable to unwanted sexual encounters. Their sense of not being in control of the situation may make them more willing to label these episodes sexual harassment.

Our findings about sexual orientation are less suggestive regarding women. None of the women (straight, lesbian, or bisexual) reported sexual harassment from other female co-workers or from gay men. In fact, all but one of the women's reported cases of sexual harassment involved a heterosexual man. One of the two lesbians in the sample (Brenda) did experience sexual harassment from a group of lesbian customers (described earlier), but she claimed that sexual orientation is *not* key to her defining the situation as harassment. Other studies have shown that lesbian and bisexual women are routinely subjected to sexual harassment in the workplace (Schneider 1982, 1984); however, more research is needed to elaborate the social contexts and the specific definitions of harassment among lesbians.

The Exceptions

Two cases of sexual harassment were related by respondents that do not fit in the categories we have thus far described. These were the only incidents of sexual harassment reported between co-workers of the same race: in both cases, the sexual harasser is a white man, and the victim, a white woman. Laura—who is bisexual—was sexually harassed at a previous restaurant by a cook:

> This guy was just constantly badgering me about going out with him. He like grabbed me and took me in the walk-in one time. It was a real big deal. He got fired over it too. . . . I was in the back doing something and he said, "I need to talk to you," and I said, "We have nothing to talk about." He like took me and threw me against the wall in the back. . . . I ran out and told the manager, "Oh my God. He just hit me," and he saw the expression on my face. The manager went back there . . . and then he got fired.

This episode of sexual harassment involved violence, unlike the other reported cases. The threat of violence was also present in the other exception, a case described by Carla. When asked if she had ever been sexually harassed, she said,

> I experienced two men, in wait jobs, that were vulgar or offensive and one was a cook and I think he was a rapist. He had the kind of attitude where he would rape a woman. I mean, that's the kind of attitude he had. He would say totally, totally inappropriate [sexual] things.

These were the only two recounted episodes of sexual harassment between "equal" co-workers that involved white men and women, and both involved violence or the threat of violence. . . .

Discussion and Conclusion

We have argued that sexual harassment is hard to identify, and thus difficult to eradicate from the workplace, in part because our hegemonic definition of sexuality defines certain contexts of sexual interaction as legitimate. The interviews with waitpeople in Austin, Texas, indicate that how people currently identify sexual harassment singles out only a narrow range of interactions, thus disguising and ignoring a good deal of sexual domination and exploitation that take place at work.

Most of the respondents in this study work in highly sexualized atmospheres where sexual banter and touching frequently occur. There are institutionalized policies and practices in the workplace that encourage—or at the very least tolerate—a continual display and performance of heterosexuality. Many people apparently accept this ritual display as being a normal or natural feature of their work; some even enjoy this behavior. In the in-depth interviews, respondents labeled such experiences as sexual harassment in only three contexts: when perpetrated by someone who took advantage of their powerful position for personal sexual gain; when the perpetrator was of a different race/ethnicity than the victim—typically a minority man harassing a white woman; and when the perpetrator was of a different sexual orientation than the victim—typically a gay man harassing a straight man. In only two cases did respondents label experiences involving co-workers of the same race and sexual orientation as sexual harassment—and both episodes involved violence or the threat of violence.

These findings are based on a very small sample in a unique working environment, and hence it is not clear whether they are generalizable to other work settings. In less sexualized working environments, individuals may be more likely to label all offensive sexual advances as sexual harassment, whereas in more highly sexualized environments (such as topless clubs or striptease bars), fewer sexual advances may be labeled sexual harassment. Our findings do suggest that researchers should pay closer attention to the interaction context of sexual harassment, taking into account not only gender but also the race, occupational status, and sexual orientation of the assailant and the victim. . . .

NOTE

1. We thank Margaret Andersen for drawing our attention to this fruitful analogy.

REFERENCES

Anders, K. T. 1993. Bad sex: Who's harassing whom in restaurants? *Restaurant Business,* 20 January, pp. 46–54.

Benson, Donna J., and Gregg E. Thomson. 1982. Sexual harassment on a university campus: The confluence of authority relations, sexual interest and gender stratification. *Social Problems* 29:236–51.

Britton, Dana M., and Christine L. Williams. Forthcoming. Don't ask, don't tell, don't pursue: Military policy and the construction of heterosexual masculinity. *Journal of Homosexuality.*

Carothers, Suzanne C., and Peggy Crull. 1984. Contrasting sexual harassment in female- and male-dominated occupations. In *My troubles are going to have trouble with me: Everyday trials and triumphs of women workers,* edited by K. B. Sacks and D. Remy. New Brunswick, NJ: Rutgers University Press.

Cobble, Dorothy Sue. 1991. *Dishing it out: Waitresses and their unions in the twentieth century.* Urbana: University of Illinois Press.

Cockburn, Cynthia. 1991. *In the way of women.* Ithaca, NY: I.L.R. Press.

Crull, Peggy. 1987. Searching for the causes of sexual harassment: An examination of two prototypes. In *Hidden aspects of women's work,* edited by Christine Bose, Roslyn Feldberg, and Natalie Sokoloff. New York: Praeger.

Ellis, Shmuel, Azy Barak, and Adaya Pinto. 1991. Moderating effects of personal cognitions on experienced and perceived sexual harassment of women at the workplace. *Journal of Applied Social Psychology* 21:1320–37.

Fain, Terri C., and Douglas L. Anderton. 1987. Sexual harassment: Organizational context and diffuse status. *Sex Roles* 17:291–311.

Fitzgerald, Louise F. 1990. Sexual harassment: The definition and measurement of a construct. In *Ivory power: Sexual harassment on campus,* edited by Michele M. Paludi. Albany: State University of New York Press.

Grauerholz, Elizabeth. 1989. Sexual harassment of women professors by students: Exploring the dynamics of power, authority, and gender in a university setting. *Sex Roles* 21:789–801.

Gruber, James E., and Lars Bjorn. 1982. Blue-collar blues: The sexual harassment of women auto workers. *Work and Occupations* 9:271–98.

Gutek, Barbara A. 1985. *Sex and the workplace.* San Francisco: Jossey-Bass.

Hall, Elaine J. 1993. Waitering/waitressing: Engendering the work of table servers. *Gender & Society* 7:329–46.

Howe, Louise Kapp. 1977. *Pink collar workers: Inside the world of women's work.* New York: Avon.

Jensen, Inger W., and Barbara A. Gutek. 1982. Attributions and assignment of responsibility in sexual harassment. *Journal of Social Issues* 38:122–36.

Johnson, Miriam. 1988. *Strong mothers, weak wives.* Berkeley: University of California Press.

Konrad, Alison M., and Barbara A. Gutek. 1986. Impact of work experiences on attitudes toward sexual harassment. *Administrative Science Quarterly* 31:422–38.

MacKinnon, Catherine A. 1979. *Sexual harassment of working women: A case of sex discrimination.* New Haven, CT: Yale University Press.

McKinney, Kathleen. 1990. Sexual harassment of university faculty by colleagues and students. *Sex Roles* 23:421–38.

Paludi, Michele, and Richard B. Barickman. 1991. *Academic and workplace sexual harassment.* Albany: State University of New York Press.

Paules, Greta Foff. 1991. *Dishing it out: Power and resistance among waitresses in a New Jersey restaurant.* Philadelphia: Temple University Press.

Powell, Gary N. 1986. Effects of sex role identity and sex on definitions of sexual harassment. *Sex Roles* 14:9–19.

Pryor, John B. 1987. Sexual harassment proclivities in men. *Sex Roles* 17:269–90.

Reilly, Mary Ellen, Bernice Lott, Donna Caldwell, and Luisa DeLuca. 1992. Tolerance for sexual harassment related to self-reported sexual victimization. *Gender & Society* 6:122–38.

Schneider, Beth E. 1982. Consciousness about sexual harassment among heterosexual and lesbian women workers. *Journal of Social Issues* 38:75–98.

———. 1984. The office affair: Myth and reality for heterosexual and lesbian women workers. *Sociological Perspectives* 27:443–64.

U.S. Department of Labor, Bureau of Labor Statistics. 1989, January. *Employment and earnings.* Washington, DC: Government Printing Office.

West, Candace, and Don H. Zimmerman. 1987. Doing gender. *Gender & Society* 1:125–51.

22

"We'd Love to Hire Them, But . . ."
The Meaning of Race for Employers

Joleen Kirschenman
Kathryn M. Neckerman

Joleen Kirschenman is an affiliate of the Center for the Study of Urban Inequality at the University of Chicago. Kathryn M. Neckerman is assistant professor of sociology at Columbia University. She writes, "My research interests include education and race and ethnic relations, and I am writing a book about minority education in Chicago, 1900–1960. My latest project was inspired by the employer survey described here, in which white-collar employers wanted their employees to speak standard English, often considered a white middle-class style. For the new research, I interviewed African-American, Latino, and West Indian students who were enrolled in business college to prepare for white-collar jobs, to see how these students reconciled ethnic identity with pressure to 'talk white.'"

. . . In this paper we explore the meaning of race and ethnicity to employers, the ways race and ethnicity are qualified by—and at times reinforce—other characteristics in the eyes of employers, and the conditions under which race seems to matter most. Our interviews at Chicago-area businesses show that employers view inner-city workers, especially black men, as unstable, uncooperative, dishonest, and uneducated. Race is an important factor in hiring decisions. But it is not race alone: rather it is race in a complex interaction with employers' perceptions of class and space, or inner-city residence. Our findings suggest that racial discrimination deserves an important place in analyses of the underclass.

Excerpt from "'We'd Love to Hire Them, But . . .': The Meaning of Race for Employers," by Joleen Kirschenman and Kathryn M. Neckerman, in C. Jencks and P. F. Peterson, eds., *The Unseen Underclass*, 1991. Reprinted by permission of The Brookings Institution.

Race and Employment

In research on the disadvantages blacks experience in the labor market, social scientists tend to rely on indirect measures of racial discrimination. They interpret as evidence of this discrimination the differences in wages or employment among races and ethnic groups that remain after education and experience are controlled. With a few exceptions they have neglected the processes at the level of the firm that underlie these observed differences.[1] . . .

The theoretical literature conventionally distinguishes two types of discrimination, "pure" and "statistical." In pure discrimination, employers, employees, or consumers have a "taste" for discrimination, that is, they will pay a premium to avoid members of another group.[2] Statistical discrimination is a more recent conception that builds on the discussions of "signaling."[3] In statistical discrimination, employers use group membership as a proxy for aspects of productivity that are relatively expensive or impossible to measure. Those who use the concept disagree about whether employers' perceptions of group differences in productivity must reflect reality. In this discussion, we are concerned with statistical discrimination as a cognitive process, regardless of whether the employer is correct or mistaken in his or her views of the labor force. . . .

The distinction between pure and statistical discrimination is a useful one. However, it is also useful to recognize the relationship between the two. There are several ways in which a taste for discrimination in employment practices may lead to perceived and actual productivity differences between groups, making statistical discrimination more likely. Social psychological evidence suggests that expectations about group differences in productivity may bias evaluation of job performance. These expectations may also influence job placement. In particular, workers of lower expected productivity may be given less on-the-job training. Finally, and most important for our study, productivity is not an individual characteristic; rather, it is shaped by the social relations of the workplace. If these relations are strained because of tastes for discrimination on the part of the employer, supervisor, coworkers, or consumers, lower productivity may result. Thus what begins as irrational practice based on prejudice or mistaken beliefs may end up being rational, profit-maximizing behavior.

Data

This research is based on face-to-face interviews with employers in Chicago and surrounding Cook County between July 1988 and March 1989. Inner-city firms were oversampled; all results here are weighted to adjust for this oversampling. Our overall response rate was 46 percent, and the completed sample of 185 employers is representative of the distribution of Cook County's employment by industry and firm size.[4]

Interviews included both closed- and open-ended questions about employers' hiring and recruitment practices and about their perceptions of Chicago's labor force and business climate. Our initial contacts, and most of the interviews themselves, were conducted with the highest ranking official at the establishment. Because of the many open-ended questions, we taped the interviews.

Most of the structured portion of the interview focused on a sample job, defined by the interview schedule as "the most typical entry-level position" in the firm's modal occupational category—sales, clerical, skilled, semiskilled, unskilled, or service, but excluding managerial, professional, and technical. The distribution of our sample jobs approximates the occupational distribution in the 1980 census for Cook County, again excluding professional, managerial, and technical categories. In effect, what we have is a sample of the opportunities facing the Chicago jobseeker with minimal skills. . . .

Although we do not present our findings as necessarily representative of the attitudes of all Chicago employers, as the rules of positivist social science would require, they are representative of those Chicago employers who spoke to a particular issue. A standard rule of discourse is that some things are acceptable to say and others are better left unsaid. Silence has the capacity to speak volumes. Thus we were overwhelmed by the degree to which Chicago employers felt comfortable talking with us—in a situation where the temptation would be to conceal rather than reveal—in a negative manner about blacks. In this paper we make an effort to understand the discursive evidence by relating it to the practice of discrimination, using quantitative data to reinforce the qualitative findings.

We'd Love to Hire Them, But . . .

. . . Explanations for the high rates of unemployment and poverty among blacks have relied heavily on the categories of class and space.[5] We found that employers also relied on those categories, but they used them to refine the category of race, which for them is primary. Indeed, it was through the interaction of race with class and space that these categories were imbued with new meaning. It was race that made class and space important to employers.

Although some employers regarded Chicago's workers as highly skilled and having a good work ethic, far more thought that the labor force has deteriorated. When asked why they thought business had been leaving Chicago, 35 percent referred to the inferior quality of the work force. . . . Several firms in our sample were relocating or seriously considering a move to the South in a search for cheap skilled labor. Employers of less skilled labor can find an ample supply of applicants, but many complained that it was becoming more difficult to find workers with basic skills and a good work ethic.

These employers coped with what they considered a less qualified work force through various strategies. Some restructured production to require either fewer workers or fewer skills. These strategies included increasing automation and deemphasizing literacy requirements—using color-coded filing systems, for example. But far more widespread were the use of recruiting and screening techniques to help select "good" workers. For instance, employers relied more heavily on referrals from employees, which tend to reproduce the traits and characteristics of the current work force: the Chicago Association

of Commerce and Industry has reported a dramatic increase in the use of referral bonuses in the past few years. Or employers targeted newspaper ads to particular neighborhoods or ethnic groups. The rationale underlying these strategies was, in part, related to the productivity employers accorded different categories of workers.

For instance, whether or not the urban underclass is an objective social category, its subjective importance in the discourse of Chicago employers cannot be denied. Their characterizations of inner-city workers mirrored many descriptions of the underclass by social scientists. Common among the traits listed were that workers were unskilled, uneducated, illiterate, dishonest, lacking initiative, unmotivated, involved with drugs and gangs, did not understand work, had no personal charm, were unstable, lacked a work ethic, and had no family life or role models.

Social scientists discover pathologies; employers try to avoid them. After explaining that he hired "the best applicant," the owner of a transportation firm added, "Probably what I'm trying to say is we're not social minded. We're not worried about solving the problems of sociology. We can't afford to." But despite not being worried about the "problems of sociology," employers have become lay social theorists, creating numerous distinctions among the labor force that then serve as bases for statistical discrimination. From their own experiences and biases, those of other employers, and accounts in the mass media, employers have attributed meaning to the categories of race and ethnicity, class, and space. These have then become markers of more or less desirable workers.

These categories were often confounded with each other, as when one respondent contrasted the white youth (with opportunities) from the North Shore with the black one (without opportunities) from the South

Side. Although the primary distinction that more than 70 percent of our informants made was based on race and ethnicity, it was frequently confounded with class: black and Hispanic equaled lower class; white equaled middle class. And these distinctions also overlapped with space: "inner-city" and at times "Chicago" equaled minority, especially black; "suburb" equaled white. In fact, race was important in part because it signaled class and inner-city residence, which are less easy to observe directly. But employers also needed class and space to draw distinctions within racial and ethnic groups; race was the distinguishing characteristic most often referred to, followed respectively by class and space. . . .

Race and Ethnicity

When they talked about the work ethic, tensions in the workplace, or attitudes toward work, employers emphasized the color of a person's skin. Many believed that white workers were superior to minorities in their work ethic. A woman who hires for a suburban service firm said, "The Polish immigrants that I know and know of are more highly motivated than the Hispanics. The Hispanics share in some of the problems that the blacks do." These problems included "exposure to poverty and drugs" as well as "a lack of motivation" related to "their environment and background." A man from a Chicago construction company, expressing a view shared by many of our informants, said, "For all groups, the pride [in their work] of days gone by is not there, but what is left, I think probably the whites take more pride than some of the other minorities." (Interviewer: "And between blacks and Hispanics?") "Probably the same."

In the discourse of "work ethic," which looms large among the concerns of employers, whites usually came out on top. But although white workers generally

looked good to employers, East European whites were repeatedly praised for really knowing how to work and caring about their work. Several informants cited positive experiences with their Polish domestic help. In the skilled occupations, East European men were sought. One company advertised for its skilled workers in Polish- and German-language newspapers, but hired all its unskilled workers, 97 percent of whom were Hispanic, through an employee network.

When asked directly whether they thought there were any differences in the work ethics of whites, blacks, and Hispanics, 37.7 percent of the employers ranked blacks last, 1.4 percent ranked Hispanics last, and no one ranked whites there. Another 7.6 percent placed blacks and Hispanics together on the lowest level; 51.4 percent either saw no difference or refused to categorize in a straightforward way. Many of the latter group qualified their response by saying they saw no differences once one controlled for education, background, or environment, and that any differences were more the result of class or space.

Although blacks were consistently evaluated less favorably than whites, employers' perceptions of Hispanics were more mixed. Some ranked them with blacks; others positioned them between whites and blacks. . . .

They also believed that a homogenous work force serves to maintain good relations among workers. . . . A personnel manager from a large, once all-white Chicago manufacturing concern lamented the tensions that race and ethnic diversity had created among workers: "I wish we could all be the same, but, unfortunately, we're not." An employer of an all-white work force said that "if I had one [black worker] back there it might be okay, but if I have two or more I would have trouble." But although some employers found a diverse work force more difficult to manage, few actually maintained a homogeneous labor force, at least in terms of race and ethnicity.

Employers worried about tensions not only between white and minority workers but also between Mexicans and blacks, Mexicans and Puerto Ricans, and even African and American blacks. A restaurateur with an all-white staff of waiters and a Hispanic kitchen said, "The Mexican kids that work in the kitchen, they're not, they're not kids anymore, but they don't like to work with black guys. But they don't like to work with Puerto Rican guys either." . . .

Blacks are by and large thought to possess very few of the characteristics of a "good" worker. Over and over employers said, "They don't want to work." "They don't want to stay." "They've got an attitude problem." One compared blacks with Mexicans: "Most of them are not as educated as you might think. I've never seen any of these guys read anything outside of a comic book. These Mexicans are sitting here reading novels constantly, even though they are in Spanish. These guys will sit and watch cartoons while the other guys are busy reading. To me that shows basic laziness. No desire to upgrade yourself." When asked about discrimination against black workers, a Chicago manufacturer related a common view: "Oh, I would in all honesty probably say there is some among most employers. I think one of the reasons, in all honesty, is because we've had bad experience in that sector, and believe me, I've tried. And as I say, if I find—whether he's black or white, if he's good and, you know, we'll hire him. We are not shutting out any black specifically. But I will say that our experience factor has been bad. We've had more bad black employees over the years than we had good." This negative opinion of blacks sometimes cuts across class lines. For instance, a personnel officer of a professional service company in the suburbs com-

mented that "with the professional staff, black males that we've had, some of the skill levels—they're not as orientated to details. They lack some of the leadership skills."

One must also consider the "relevant nots": what were some employers not talking about? They were not talking about how clever black workers were, they were not talking about the cultural richness of the black community, nor were they talking about rising divorce rates among whites. Furthermore, although each employer reserved the right to deny making distinctions along racial lines, fewer than 10 percent consistently refused to distinguish or generalize according to race.

These ways of talking about black workers—they have a bad work ethic, they create tensions in the workplace, they are lazy and unreliable, they have a bad attitude—reveal the meaning race has for many employers. If race were a proxy for expected productivity and the sole basis for statistical discrimination, black applicants would indeed find few job opportunities.

Class

Although some respondents spoke only in terms of race and ethnicity, or conflated class with race, others were sensitive to class distinctions. Class constituted a second, less easily detected signal for employers. Depending somewhat on the demands of the jobs, they used class markers to select among black applicants. The contrasts between their discourse about blacks and Hispanics were striking. Employers sometimes placed Hispanics with blacks in the lower class: an inner-city retailer confounded race, ethnicity, and class when he said, "I think there's a self-defeating prophecy that's maybe inherent in a lot of lower-income ethnic groups or races. Blacks, Hispanics." But although they rarely drew class distinctions among Hispanics, such distinctions were widely made for black workers. As one manufacturer said, "The black work ethic. There's no work ethic. At least at the unskilled. I'm sure with the skilled, as you go up, it's a lot different." Employers generally considered it likely that lower-class blacks would have more negative traits than blacks of other classes.

In many ways black business owners and black personnel managers were the most expressive about class divisions among blacks. A few believed poor blacks were most likely to be dishonest because of the economic pressures they face. A black jeweler said the most important quality he looked for in his help was "a person who doesn't need a job."

> (Interviewer: That's what you're looking for?)
>
> That's what we usually try to hire. People that don't need the job.
>
> (Interviewer: Why?)
>
> Because they will tend to be a little more honest. Most of the people that live in the neighborhoods and areas where my stores are at need the job. They are low-income, and so, consequently, they're under more pressure and there's more of a tendency to be dishonest, because of the pressure. . . .

Other employers mentioned problems that occur in the workplace when there are class divisions among the workers. These are reminiscent of the tensions created by the racial and ethnic diversity described earlier. One black businesswoman told of a program wherein disadvantaged youths were sent to private schools by wealthy sponsors. She herself was a sponsor and held the program in high regard, but she hired some of these youths and they did not get along with her other young employees: "Those kids were too smart 'cause they were from a middle-class background." (Interviewer:

"So these were primarily middle-class kids?") "No, they're not middle class, but they have middle-class values because they're exposed to them all the time." They made excellent employees, she said, "if you kept your store filled with just them. They're more outgoing and less afraid of the customers. But they're very intimidating to the supervisors because they know everything by the time they get to be a sophomore in high school." . . .

Thus, although many employers assumed that black meant "inner-city poor," others—both black and white—were quick to see divisions within the black population. Of course, class itself is not directly observable, but markers that convey middle- or working-class status will help a black job applicant get through race-based exclusionary barriers. Class is primarily signaled to employers through speech, dress, education levels, skill levels, and place of residence. Although many respondents drew class distinctions among blacks, very few made those same distinctions among Hispanics or whites; in refining these categories, respondents referred to ethnicity and age rather than class.

Space

Although some employers spoke implicitly or explicitly in terms of class, for others "inner-city" was the more important category. For most the term immediately connoted black, poor, uneducated, unskilled, lacking in values, crime, gangs, drugs, and unstable families. "Suburb" connoted white, middle-class, educated, skilled, and stable families. Conversely, race was salient in part because it signaled space; black connoted inner city and white the suburbs. . . . When asked what it would take for their firm to relocate to the inner city, respondents generally thought it an implausible notion. They were sure their skilled workers would not consider working in those neighborhoods because they feared for their safety, and the employers saw no alternative labor supply there.

The skepticism that greets the inner-city worker often arises when employers associate their race and residence with enrollment in Chicago's troubled public education system. Being educated in Chicago public schools has become a way of signaling "I'm black, I'm poor, and I'm from the inner city" to employers. Some mentioned that they passed over applicants from Chicago public schools for those with parochial or suburban educations. If employers were looking at an applicant's credentials when screening, blacks in the inner city did not do well. As one employer said, "The educational skills they come to the job with are minimal because of the schools in the areas where they generally live."

A vice president of a television station complained of the inner-city work force:

> They are frequently unable to write. They go through the Chicago public schools or they dropped out when they were in the eighth grade. They can't read. They can't write. They can hardly talk. I have another opinion which is strictly my own and that is that people who insist on beating themselves to the point where they are out of the mainstream of the world suffer the consequences. And I'm talking about the languages that are spoken in the ghetto. They are not English.

Employers were clearly disappointed, not just in the academic content and level of training students receive, but in the failure of the school system to prepare them for the work force. Because the inner city is heavily associated with a lack of family values, employers wished the schools would compensate and provide students the self-discipline needed for workers' socialization. Additionally, they complained that black work-

ers had no "ability to understand work." . . . It is not only educational content per se that employers were looking for; some were concerned with the educational "experience." One talked about how it just showed "they could finish something." Thus inner city is equated with public school attendance, which in turn signifies insufficient work skills and work ethic.

. . . Another employer used space to refine the category of race: "We have some black women here but they're not inner city. They're from suburbs and . . . I think they're a little bit more willing to give it a shot, you know, I mean they're a little bit more willing [than black men] to give a day's work for a day's pay."

Employers readily distinguished among blacks on the basis of space. They talked about Cabrini Green or the Robert Taylor Homes or referred to the South Side and West Side as a shorthand for black. But they were not likely to make these distinctions among whites and Hispanics. They made no reference to Pilsen (a largely immigrant Mexican neighborhood), Humboldt Park (largely Puerto Rican), or Uptown (a community of poor whites and new immigrants).

For black applicants, having the wrong combination of class and space markers suggested low productivity and undesirability to an employer. The important finding of this research, then, is not only that employers make hiring decisions based on the color of a person's skin, but the extent to which that act has become nuanced. Race, class, and space interact with each other. Moreover, the precise nature of that interaction is largely determined by the demands of the job. . . .

Conclusion

Chicago's employers did not hesitate to generalize about race or ethnic differences in the quality of the labor force. Most associated negative images with inner-city workers, and particularly with black men. "Black" and "inner-city" were inextricably linked, and both were linked with "lower-class."

Regardless of the generalizations employers made, they did consider the black population particularly heterogeneous, which made it more important that they be able to distinguish "good" from "bad" workers. Whether through skills tests, credentials, personal references, folk theories, or their intuition, they used some means of screening out the inner-city applicant. The ubiquitous anecdote about the good black worker, the exception to the rule, testified to their own perceived success at doing this. So did frequent references to "our" black workers as opposed to "those guys on the street corner."

And black job applicants, unlike their white counterparts, must indicate to employers that the stereotypes do not apply to them. Inner-city and lower-class workers were seen as undesirable, and black applicants had to try to signal to employers that they did not fall into those categories, either by demonstrating their skills or by adopting a middle-class style of dress, manner, and speech or perhaps (as we were told some did) by lying about their address or work history.

By stressing employers' preconceptions about inner-city workers, we do not mean to imply that there are no problems of labor quality in the inner city: the low reading and mathematics test scores of Chicago public school students testify to these problems. But if the quality of the inner-city labor force has indeed deteriorated, then it is incumbent on employers to avoid hiring inner-city workers. This is precisely the result one would expect from William Julius Wilson's account of increased social dislocations in the inner city since the early 1970s. Because race and inner-city residence are so highly correlated, it would not be surprising if race were to become a key marker of worker productivity.

However, productivity is not an individual characteristic. Rather it is embedded in social relations. The qualities most likely to be proxied by race are not job skills but behavioral and attitudinal attributes—dependability, strong work ethic, cooperativeness—that are closely tied to interactions among workers and between workers and employers. Our evidence suggests that more attention should be paid to social relations in the workplace. Antagonisms among workers and between workers and their employers are likely to diminish productivity. Thus employers' expectations may become self-fulfilling prophecies.

NOTES

1. One of the exceptions is Braddock and McPartland (1987).
2. Becker (1957).
3. Phelps (1972); Arrow (1973); and Spence (1973).
4. The sample and survey methods are described in more detail in the "Employer Survey Final Report," available from the authors.
5. Wilson (1980, 1987); and Kasarda (1985). We use the term "space" in the tradition of urban geography. We do this to draw attention to the way people categorize and attach meaning to geographic locations.

REFERENCES

Arrow, Kenneth. 1973. "The Theory of Discrimination." In *Discrimination in Labor Markets*, edited by Orley Aschenfelter and Albert Rees. Princeton University Press.

Braddock, Jomills Henry II, and James M. McPartland. 1987. "How Minorities Continue to Be Excluded from Equal Employment Opportunities: Research on Labor Market and Institutional Barriers." *Journal of Social Issues* 43, pp. 5–39.

Kasarda, John D. 1985. "Urban Change and Minority Opportunities." In *The New Urban Reality*, edited by Paul E. Peterson. Brookings.

Phelps, Edmund S. 1972. "The Statistical Theory of Racism and Sexism." *American Economic Review* 62 (September), pp. 659–61.

Spence, Michael. 1973. "Job Market Signalling." *Quarterly Journal of Economics* 87 (August), pp. 355–74.

Wilson, William Julius. 1980. *The Declining Significance of Race: Blacks and Changing American Institutions.* 2d ed. University of Chicago Press.

———. 1987. *The Truly Disadvantaged: The Inner City, the Underclass, and Public Policy.* University of Chicago Press.

TYPES OF WORK

How do medical students learn to be doctors? How do workers in routine production jobs avoid boredom and make the workday interesting? How do restaurant workers, whose jobs require them to interact with the public, cope with angry customers? Whereas some forces shaping the workplace are relevant for virtually all types of workers (e.g., technological change and race and gender dynamics), answering these questions requires us to narrow our focus and examine the forces affecting particular occupational groups. The three sections in Part IV are designed to address some of these occupation-specific topics.

Industrial Work

For the purposes of this anthology, *industrial work* refers to "blue-collar" occupations—craft worker, operator, and laborer positions. These occupations may have received more attention from sociologists than any other type of work. In fact, what is now called the sociology of work used to be known more narrowly as industrial sociology (or, in Thompson's words, "plant sociology," 1989, p. 14). The historical importance of industrial work for sociologists stemmed from several factors. First, a relatively large segment of the labor force worked in these occupations. In the immediate post–World War II era, for example, approximately 40 percent of the labor force held blue-collar jobs (Tausky 1996, p. 48). More important than their numbers, however, was the fact that industrial workers formed a major force in labor unions. The ability and willingness of industrial work-

ers to collectively challenge their employers was apparent even in the early stages of industrialization. As modern industry developed, industrial conflict increased, inspiring the efforts of people like Frederick Taylor and the attention of sociologists. Industrial sociology tended to focus heavily on workers' behavior inside the workplace, and this concern continues to be expressed in participant observation–based studies of blue-collar jobs.

In the first reading of this section, Michael Burawoy examines the "art of making out" among operators in a machine shop. In contrast to those who view industrial workers as tightly controlled by management and technology, Burawoy argues that operators retain a degree of autonomy that they use to pursue their own objectives. In particular, by manipulating the rules of the organization of work, machine-shop operators increased their production levels to earn higher pay.

The ability of workers to "self-organize" and thus to expand their control over production is also a theme of Tom Juravich's reading, "Women on the Line." Like Burawoy's, Juravich's analysis of assembly line labor is based on participant observation. Juravich challenges accepted accounts of industrial work, especially of that traditionally performed by women. He argues that this work is often portrayed as deskilled, menial, and routine. Instead, however, Juravich reveals women workers' hidden "craft knowledge" and shows how this knowledge can be used to subvert management directives.

The Japanese model of industrial work has received much attention in recent years. The economic success of Japanese firms and their movement into the United States heightened sociological and popular interest in Japanese methods for organizing industrial work. Laurie Graham's study of a "non-union Japanese automobile transplant" (1995, p. 13)—Subaru-Isuzu Automotive—offers an in-depth analysis of a U.S.-based Japanese firm. Graham provides a detailed description of life on the assembly line at Subaru-Isuzu. This discussion is particularly important for its portrayal of the ways that "shop floor reality" diverges from both company philosophy and popular accounts of Japanese work organization. In particular, Graham shows how workers' health suffered as a result of their employment in highly routinized, factory jobs.

Personal Service Work

By all accounts, the United States has become a service society. The vast majority of new jobs being created are service occupations, whereas goods-producing occupations are in decline (Kutscher 1987). What is a service job? Definitions vary, but at the most general level, service jobs are those in which "face-to-face or voice-to-voice interaction is a fundamental element of the work" (Macdonald and Sirianni 1996, p. 3). Because they involve interaction, these jobs also typically require workers to perform "emotional labor." This latter term refers to the work involved in managing feelings and emotional expression so as to produce a particular state of mind in another (Hochschild 1983).

As we will see, emotional labor is also a component of many professional jobs, such as litigator (see Reading 30). In fact, there are many different types of service jobs that vary widely in their earnings and organization. The three service jobs described in this section represent a type of service employment known as "personal services." These are services that are produced primarily for individuals and families and hence involve the worker directly in service delivery. Two additional factors differentiate the occupations discussed in this section from professionals and other higher-level service workers. The first is the degree of control workers exercise over their interactions and, hence, emotions. Unlike professionals, who monitor their own behavior, the workers described in these readings tend to be closely supervised by others. The second is the fact that the *clients* of professionals have less power in the interaction than do the *customers* of service workers. The authority relations in the two types of occupations thus are different, with professionals having much greater authority over their clients than service workers have over customers. As a result, workers in personal service occupations constitute what Macdonald and Sirianni (1996, p. 3) call "the emotional proletariat."

The fast food industry has become a symbol of a service economy, and McDonald's is undoubtedly one of the most well known American corporations. McDonald's success can be partly attributed to its ability to produce a highly standardized product: "Not only is the food supposed to taste the same every day everywhere in the world, but McDonald's promises that every meal will be served quickly, courteously, and with a smile" (Leidner 1993, p. 45). As this quote reveals, standardization of the product also implies a certain standardization of workers' behavior. This theme is developed in more detail by Robin Leidner, whose reading is drawn from her study, *Fast Food, Fast Talk: Service Work and the Routinization of Everyday Life* (1993). As a participant-observer working in a Chicago-area McDonald's, Leidner gained a firsthand account of McDonald's efforts to routinize service interactions.

Whereas McDonald's workers have relatively little opportunity to improvise or tailor their interactions with customers, restaurant wait staff are not quite so restricted. At the same time, because workers in this occupation depend heavily on tips, they face pressures to interact with customers in ways that will maximize their earnings and preserve their dignity. The tipping relationship underscores the service worker's subordinate position vis-à-vis customers. As Greta Foff Paules describes in Reading 27, while tipping places the balance of power in the customers' hands, female servers pursue strategies to challenge this power imbalance and resist the negative symbolism of service work.

Racial and gender stratification are parts of service work just as they are in other occupations. Racial and gender distinctions have played a particularly important role in certain sectors of service work—namely, those associated with "social reproduction." This term refers to the labor involved in "the creation and recreation of people as cultural and social, as well as physical beings" (Glenn 1996, p. 117). Domestic service is a form of reproductive labor that has historically been performed by subordinate racial and ethnic groups. Indeed, African-American and Hispanic women continue to be overrepresented in this occupational category. In the final reading in this section, "Between Women: Domestics and Their Employers," Judith Rollins examines the work experiences of domestic laborers, paying particular attention to African-American women workers' relations with their white female employers. Like employers in other sectors of the economy, employers of domestics exercise primary control over the conditions of their employees' work. Rollins provides a rich description of domestic workers' views of their jobs and employers, underscoring the fact that, although domestic service is "between women," the employer-employee relationship in this arena is structured by some of the same forces operating in other economic sectors.

Professional and Managerial Work

By most accounts, professional and managerial workers constitute the most privileged sector of the labor force. Higher average earnings, lower average rates of unemployment, and greater access to job autonomy than other workers have are a few examples of these privileges. In addition, as the core of the "new middle class," professional and managerial workers occupy an important role in the larger society (Ehrenreich 1989; Gouldner 1979; Brint 1985).

What are the professions? Though the term *profession* is often used synonymously with *occupation*, sociologists prefer to reserve the former label for occupations with a distinct set of characteristics. As Ehrenreich observes, "Professions, as opposed to *jobs*, are understood to offer some measure of intrinsic satisfaction, some linkage of science and service, intellect and conscience, autonomy and responsibility. No one has such expectations of a mere *job*; and it is this, as much as anything, which defines the middle-class advantage over the working-class majority" (1989, pp. 260–261).

Understanding how and why some occupations achieved professional status while others did not were early concerns in the sociological study of professions. Another concern was the experience of professional work, especially professionals' relations with their clients. More recently, the sociological study of professions has taken a somewhat more macro turn. The political, social, and economic power of professions have become important sociological issues (Bok 1993).

The first reading on professionals in this section is drawn from Eliot Friedson's classic study, *Professional Powers: A Study of the*

Institutionalization of Formal Knowledge.
Friedson's book aims "to clarify the relations
between knowledge and power by grounding them in the institutions of professionalism in the United States" (1986, p. xi).
Friedson suggests that formal knowledge
has become an increasingly important element of modern life, playing an expanded
role in organizing human affairs. As the
"agents of formal knowledge," professionals
thus exercise considerable power in contemporary society.

Lawyering represents one of the oldest
professions. In Reading 30, we turn our attention to this arena. Like other professions, the legal profession involves the
mastery of highly abstract, specialized
knowledge. Prospective lawyers thus must
undergo a lengthy training period. During
this time, students are expected not only to
acquire technical knowledge, but also to
take on the persona of their profession.
Becoming a professional thus involves the
acquisition of a distinct occupational identity, culture, and behavioral style. For example, as Jennifer Pierce shows, being an
effective litigator requires learning more
than the law. As one of her respondents
stated, "To be a really good litigator, you
have to be a jerk" (Pierce 1995, p. 50).

Pierce's discussion of the emotional dimension of lawyering uncovers the emotional demands and expectations associated with being a litigator. These legal
professionals must display a particular demeanor in order to elicit cooperation from
others in the courtroom and to achieve
their broader objectives. Pierce suggests
that the gamesmanship that is at the center
of the litigator's presentation of self is a
highly gendered style. As a historically
male-dominated profession, definitions of
good lawyering and expectations for professional behavior have come to be expressed in masculine terms. Pierce thus
shows how gender can become embedded

in occupational expectations for behavior,
which can create different dilemmas for
male and female professionals.

Professional identity and self-presentation are also subjects of the reading by
James Woods and Jay Lucas on gay professionals. Expressions of sexuality have generally been considered taboo in the professional workplace—and, indeed, in most
workplaces. As these authors explain: "We
imagine that work is a rational activity and
that workplaces depend on order. Sexuality,
in contrast, is perceived as a threat to all
that is rational and ordered, the antithesis
of organization" (Woods and Lucas 1993,
p. 33). These assumptions may be especially pervasive in professional jobs, where
the appearance of objectivity and the
avoidance of excessive emotion help professionals maintain authority over clients.
These pressures for professionals to be
asexual require them to constantly manage
and monitor their sexuality. Furthermore,
Woods and Lucas suggest, gay men and lesbians are especially sensitive to these pressures and may be ambivalent about the
need to deny their sexuality on the job.

The last two readings in this section focus on managerial occupations. This occupational group covers a variety of jobs—from
supervisors to chief executives—and thus is
difficult to characterize. Robert Jackall's focus in "The Social Structure of Managerial
Work" is the ranks of "middle managers,"
whose authority puts them above first-line
supervisors and below the chief executive.
Managers at this level must learn to operate
within a complex, hierarchical system in
which relationships among authority figures
must be constantly negotiated. For example,
as Jackall shows, details are "pushed down"
the hierarchy and credit is "pushed up."
More generally, Jackall reveals the uncertainty and ambiguity that permeate managerial work and the ways managers cope
with these features.

Managerial hierarchies are also discussed in Sharon Collins's reading, "The Marginalization of Black Executives." Collins shows that, despite increased numbers of blacks in managerial positions, racial segregation within managerial ranks persists. In particular, Collins suggests, black managers often find themselves in racialized positions that are highly vulnerable to changing economic and social policies. At a more general level, Collins's reading is important for two related reasons. First, she underscores the earlier claim that management occupations differ widely in their authority, pay, and security. Hence, we must resist the temptation to generalize about managerial work. Second, Collins shows that the rising number of African-American managers does not necessarily imply a move toward greater racial equality in managerial ranks. As has been true with respect to the gender integration of some fields (see, e.g., Reading 20), the racial integration of management may be accompanied by the concentration of African-American (and other nonwhite) managers in lower-paying, less prestigious, and less secure management positions.

REFERENCES

Bok, Derek. 1993. *The Cost of Talent.* New York: The Free Press.

Brint, Steven G. 1985. "The Political Attitudes of Professionals." *Annual Review of Sociology* 11: 389–414.

Ehrenreich, Barbara. 1989. *Fear of Falling: The Inner Life of the Middle Class.* New York: Pantheon.

Friedson, Eliot. 1986. *Professional Powers: A Study of the Institutionalization of Formal Knowledge.* Chicago: University of Chicago Press.

Glenn, Evelyn Nakano. 1996. "From Servitude to Service Work: Historical Continuities in the Racial Division of Paid Reproductive Labor." Pp. 115–156 in *Working in the Service Society,* edited by Cameron Lynne Macdonald and Carmen Sirianni. Philadelphia: Temple University Press.

Gouldner, Alvin J. 1979. *The Future of the Intellectuals and the Rise of the New Class.* London: Macmillan Press.

Hochschild, Arlie. 1983. *The Managed Heart.* Berkeley: University of California Press.

Kutscher, Ronald E. 1987. "Projections 2000: Overview and Implications of the Projections to 2000." *Monthly Labor Review* (September): 3–9.

Leidner, Robin. 1993. *Service Work and the Routinization of Everyday Life.* Berkeley: University of California Press.

Macdonald, Cameron Lynne and Carmen Sirianni. 1996. "The Service Society and the Changing Experience of Work." Pp. 1–26 in *Working in the Service Society,* edited by Cameron Lynne Macdonald and Carmen Sirianni. Philadelphia: Temple University Press.

Paules, Greta Foff. 1991. *Dishing It Out: Power and Resistance among Waitresses in a New Jersey Restaurant.* Philadelphia: Temple University Press.

Pierce, Jennifer L. 1995. *Gender Trials: Emotional Lives in Contemporary Law Firms.* Berkeley: University of California Press.

Tausky, Curt. 1996. *Work and Society.* Itasca, IL: F.E. Peacock Publishers, Inc.

Thompson, Paul. 1989. *The Nature of Work.* London: Macmillan.

Woods, James D. with Jay H. Lucas. 1993. *The Corporate Closet: The Professional Lives of Gay Men in America.* New York: The Free Press.

INDUSTRIAL WORK

23

Thirty Years of Making Out

Michael Burawoy

Michael Burawoy is professor of sociology at the University of California, Berkeley. Professor Burawoy writes, "Academic sociologists too easily forget what life is like for those chained to machines eight hours at a time. I tried to explore such lives by joining workers in their space and time. In addition to the machine operators I worked with in South Chicago, I have studied copper miners in Zambia, steel workers in Hungary, and furniture makers in Russia. By participating at the same time as observing I came to appreciate the commitment and skills, often invisible from the outside, of blue collar workers. I began to glimpse how they constructed their social and political worlds differently in different places. My findings would remain inaccessible to research conducted at a distance, from behind the walls of the university."

Making Out—A Game Workers Play

. . . In this section I propose to treat the activities on the shop floor as a series of games in which operators attempt to achieve levels of production that earn incentive pay, in other words, anything over 100 percent. The precise target that each operator aims at is established on an individual basis, varying with job, machine, experience, and so on. Some are satisfied with 125 percent, while others are in a foul mood unless they achieve 140 percent—the ceiling imposed and recognized by all participants. This game of making out provides a framework for evaluating the productive activities and the social relations that arise out of the organization of work. We can look upon

From *Manufacturing Consent,* by Michael Burawoy. Reprinted by permission of the University of Chicago Press and the author.

making out, therefore, as comprising a sequence of stages—of encounters between machine operators and the social or nonsocial objects that regulate the conditions of work. The rules of the game are experienced as a set of externally imposed relationships. The art of making out is to manipulate those relationships with the purpose of advancing as quickly as possible from one stage to the next.

At the beginning of the shift, operators assemble outside the time office on the shop floor to collect their production cards and punch in on the "setup" of their first task. If it has already been set up on the previous shift, the operator simply punches in on production. Usually operators know from talking to their counterpart, before the beginning of the shift, which task they are likely to receive. Knowing what is available on the floor for their machine, an operator is sometimes in a position to bargain with the scheduling man, who is responsible for distributing the tasks.

. . . the scheduling man's duties [did not] end with the distribution of work, but . . . he also assumed some responsibility for ensuring that the department turned out the requisite parts on time. Therefore, he is often found stalking the floor, checking up on progress and urging workers to get a move on. Because he has no formal authority over the operators, the scheduling man's only recourse is to his bargaining strength, based on the discretion he can exert in distributing jobs and fixing up an operator's time. Operators who hold strategic jobs, requiring a particular skill, for example, or who are frequently called upon to do "hot jobs" are in a strong bargaining position vis-à-vis the scheduling man. He knows this and is careful not to upset them. . . .

After receiving their first task, operators have to find the blueprint and tooling for the operation. These are usually in the crib, although they may be already out on the floor. The crib attendant is therefore a strategic person whose cooperation an operator must secure. If the crib attendant chooses to be uncooperative in dispensing towels, blueprints, fixtures, etc., and, particularly, in the grinding of tools, operators can be held up for considerable lengths of time. Occasionally, operators who have managed to gain the confidence of the crib attendant will enter the crib themselves and expedite the process. Since, unlike the scheduling man, the crib attendant has no real interest in whether the operator makes out, his cooperation has to be elicited by other means. For the first five months of my employment my relations with the crib attendant on second shift were very poor, but at Christmas things changed dramatically. Every year the local union distributes a Christmas ham to all its members. I told Harry that I couldn't be bothered picking mine up from the union hall and that he could have it for himself. He was delighted,

and after that I received good service in the crib. . . .

While I was able to secure the cooperation of the crib attendant, I was not so fortunate with the truck drivers. When I was being broken in on the miscellaneous job, I was told repeatedly that the first thing I must do was to befriend the truck driver. He or she was responsible for bringing the stock from the aisles, where it was kept in tubs, to the machine. Particularly at the beginning of the shift, when everyone is seeking their assistance, truck drivers can hold you up for a considerable period. While some treated everyone alike, others discriminated among operators, frustrating those without power, assisting those who were powerful. Working on the miscellaneous job meant that I was continually requiring the truck driver's services, and, when Morris was in the seat, he used to delight in frustrating me by making me wait. There was nothing I could do about it unless I was on a hot job; then the foreman or scheduling man might intervene. To complain to the foreman on any other occasion would only have brought me more travail, since Morris could easily retaliate later on. It was better just to sit tight and wait. Like the crib attendants, truckers have no stake in the operator's making out, and they are, at the same time, acutely conscious of their power in the shop. All they want is for you to get off their backs so that they can rest, light up, chat with their friends, or have a cup of coffee—in other words, enjoy the marginal freedoms of the machine operator. As one of the graffiti in the men's toilet put it, "Fuck the company, fuck the union, but most of all fuck the truckers because they fuck us all." Operators who become impatient may, if they know how, hop into an idle truck and move their own stock. But this may have unfortunate consequences, for other operators may ask them to get their stock too. . . .

As they wait for the stock to arrive, each operator sets up his machine, if it is not already set up. This can take anything from a few minutes to two shifts, but normally it takes less than an hour. Since every setup has a standard time for completion, operators try to make out here, too. When a setup is unusually rapid, an operator may even be able to make time so that, when he punches in on production, he has already turned out a few pieces. A setup man is available for assistance. Particularly for the inexperienced, his help is crucial, but, as with the other auxiliary personnel, his cooperation must be sought and possibly bargained for. He, too, has no obvious stake in your making out, though the quicker he is through with you, the freer he is. Once the machine is set up and the stock has arrived, the operator can begin the first piece, and the setup man is no longer required unless the setup turns out to be unsatisfactory.

The quality and concern of setup men vary enormously. For example, on day shift the setup man was not known for his cooperative spirit. When I asked Bill, my day man, who the setup man was on day shift, he replied, "Oh, he died some years ago." This was a reference to the fact that the present one was useless as far as he was concerned. On second shift, by contrast, the setup man went about his job with enthusiasm and friendliness. When he was in a position to help, he most certainly did his best, and everyone liked and respected him. Yet even he did not know all the jobs in the shop. Indeed, he knew hardly any of my machines and so was of little use to me. . . .

The assigned task may be to drill a set of holes in a plate, pipe, casting, or whatever; to mill the surface of some elbow; to turn an internal diameter on a lathe; to shave the teeth on a gear; and so on. The first piece completed has to be checked by the inspector against the blueprint. Between inspector and operator there is an irrevocable conflict of interest because the former is concerned with quality while the operator is concerned with quantity. Time spent when an operation just won't come right—when piece after piece fails, according to the inspector, to meet the specifications of the blueprint—represents lost time to the operator. Yet the inspector wants to OK the piece as quickly as possible and doesn't want to be bothered with checking further pieces until the required tolerances are met.

When a piece is on the margin, some inspectors will let it go, but others will enforce the specifications of the blueprint to the nth degree. In any event, inspectors are in practice, if not in theory, held partly responsible if an operator runs scrap. Though formally accountable only for the first piece that is tagged as OK, an inspector will be bawled out if subsequent pieces fall outside the tolerance limits. Thus, inspectors are to some extent at the mercy of the operators, who, after successfully getting the first piece OK'd, may turn up the speed of their machine and turn out scrap. An operator who does this can always blame the inspector by shifting the tag from the first piece to one that is scrap. Of course, an inspector has ample opportunity to take revenge on an operator who tries to shaft him. Moreover, operators also bear the responsibility for quality. During my term of employment, charts were distributed and hung up on each machine, defining the frequency with which operators were expected to check their pieces for any given machine at any particular tolerance level. Moreover, in the period immediately prior to the investigation of the plant's quality-assurance organization by an outside certifying body, operators were expected to indicate on the back of the inspection card the number of times they checked their pieces. . . .

When an inspector holds up an operator who is working on an important job but is unable to satisfy the specifications on the blueprint, a foreman may intervene to persuade the inspector to OK the piece. When this conflict cannot be resolved at the lowest level, it is taken to the next rung in the management hierarchy, and the superintendent fights it out with the chief inspector. . . . [P]roduction management generally defeated quality control in such bargaining . . . which reflects an organizational structure in which quality control is directly subordinated to production. Not surprisingly, the function of quality control has become a sensitive issue and the focus of much conflict among the higher levels of Allied's engine division. Quality control is continually trying to fight itself clear of subordination to production management so as to monitor quality on the shop floor. This, of course, would have deleterious effects on levels of production, and so it is opposed by the production management. Particularly sensitive in this regard is control of the engine test department, which in 1975 resided with production management. The production manager naturally claimed that he was capable of assessing quality impartially. Furthermore, he justified this arrangement by shifting the locus of quality problems from the shop floor to the design of the engine, which brought the engineers into the fray. Engineering management, not surprisingly, opposes the trend toward increasing their responsibility for quality. Therefore, the manager of engineering supported greater autonomy for quality control as a reflection of his interest in returning responsibility for quality to the shop floor. . . .

After the first piece has been OK'd, the operator engages in a battle with the clock and the machine. Unless the task is a familiar one—in which case the answer is known, within limits—the question is: Can I make out? It may be necessary to figure some angles, some short cuts, to speed up the machine, make a special tool, etc. In these un-

dertakings there is always an element of risk—for example, the possibility of turning out scrap or of breaking tools. If it becomes apparent that making out is impossible or quite unlikely, operators slacken off and take it easy. Since they are guaranteed their base earnings, there is little point in wearing themselves out unless they can make more than the base earnings—that is, more than 100 percent. That is what Roy refers to as goldbricking. The other form of "output restriction" to which he refers—quota restriction—entails putting a ceiling on how much an operator may turn in—that is, on how much he may record on the production card. In 1945 the ceiling was $10.00 a day or $1.25 an hour, though this did vary somewhat between machines. In 1975 the ceiling was defined as 140 percent for all operations on all machines. It was presumed that turning in more than 140 percent led to "price cuts" (rate increases), and this was indeed the case.

In 1975 quota restriction was not necessarily a form of restriction of *output,* because operators *regularly* turned *out* more than 140 percent, but turned *in* only 140 percent, keeping the remainder as a "kitty" for those operations on which they could not make out. Indeed, operators would "bust their ass" for entire shifts, when they had a gravy job, so as to build up a kitty for the following day(s). Experienced operators on the more sophisticated machines could easily build up a kitty of a week's work. There was always some discrepancy, therefore, between what was registered in the books as completed and what was actually completed on the shop floor. Shop management was more concerned with the latter and let the books take care of themselves. Both the 140 percent ceiling and the practice of banking (keeping a kitty) were recognized and accepted by everyone on the shop floor, even if they didn't meet with the approval of higher management.

Management outside the shop also regarded the practice of "chiseling" as illicit, while management within the shop either assisted or connived in it. Chiseling (Roy's expression, which did not have currency on the shop floor in 1975) involves redistributing time from one operation to another so that operators can maximize the period turned in as over 100 percent. Either the time clerk cooperates by punching the cards in and out at the appropriate time or the operators are allowed to punch their own cards. In part, because of the diversity of jobs, some of them very short, I managed to avoid punching any of my cards. At the end of the shift I would sit down with an account of the pieces completed in each job and fiddle around with the eight hours available, so as to maximize my earnings. I would pencil in the calculated times of starting and finishing each operation. No one ever complained, but it is unlikely that such consistent juggling would have been allowed on first shift. . . .

The Organization of a Shop-Floor Culture

So far we have considered the stages through which any operation must go for its completion and the roles of different employees in advancing the operation from stage to stage. In practice the stages themselves are subject to considerable manipulation, and there were occasions when I would complete an operation without ever having been given it by the scheduling man, without having a blueprint, or without having it checked by the inspector. It is not necessary to discuss these manipulations further, since by now it must be apparent that relations emanating directly from the organization of work are understood and attain meaning primarily in terms of making out. Even social interaction not occasioned by the structure of work is dominated by and couched in the idiom of making out. When someone comes over to talk, his first question is, "Are you making out?" followed by "What's the rate?" If you are not making out, your conversation is likely to consist of explanations of why you are not: "The rate's impossible," "I had to wait an hour for the inspector to check the first piece," "These motherfucking drills keep on burning up." When you are sweating it out on the machine, "knocking the pieces out," a passerby may call out "Gravy!"—suggesting that the job is not as difficult as you are making it appear. Or, when you are "goofing off"—visiting other workers or gossiping at the coffee machine—as likely as not someone will yell out, "You've got it made, man!" When faced with an operation that is obviously impossible, some comedian may bawl out, "Best job in the house!" Calling out to a passerby, "You got nothing to do?" will frequently elicit a protest of the nature, "I'm making out. What more do you want?" At lunchtime, operators of similar machines tend to sit together, and each undertakes a postmortem of the first half of the shift. Why they failed to make out, who "screwed them up," what they expect to accomplish in the second half of the shift, can they make up lost time, advice for others who are having some difficulty, and so on—such topics tend to dominate lunchtime conversations. As regards the domination of shop-floor interaction by the culture of making out . . . the idiom, status, tempo, etc., of interaction at work continue to be governed by and to rise out of the relations in production that constitute the rules of making out.

In summary, we have seen how the shop-floor culture revolves around making out. Each worker sooner or later is sucked into this distinctive set of activities and language, which then proceed to take on a meaning of their own. Like Roy, when I first entered the shop I was somewhat contemptuous of this game of making out, which appeared to advance Allied's profit margins more than the operators' interests. But I experienced the same shift of opinion that Roy reported:

> . . . attitudes changed from mere indifference to the piecework incentive to a determination not to be forced to respond, when failure to get a price increase on one of the lowest paying operations of his job repertoire convinced him that the company was unfair. Light scorn for the incentive scheme turned to bitterness. Several months later, however, after fellow operator McCann had instructed him in the "angles on making out," the writer was finding values in the piecework system other than economic ones. He struggled to attain quota "for the hell of it," because it was a "little game" and "keeps me from being bored."[1]

Such a pattern of insertion and seduction is common. In my own case, it took me some time to understand the shop language, let alone the intricacies of making out. It was a matter of three or four months before I began to make out by using a number of angles and by transferring time from one operation to another. Once I knew I had a chance to make out, the rewards of participating in a game in which the outcomes were uncertain absorbed my attention, and I found myself spontaneously cooperating with management in the production of greater surplus value. Moreover, it was only in this way that I could establish relationships with others on the shop floor. Until I was able to strut around the floor like an experienced operator, as if I had all the time in the world and could still make out, few but the greenest would condescend to engage me in conversation. Thus, it was in terms of the culture of making out that individuals evaluated one another and themselves. It provided the basis of status hierarchies on the shop floor, and it was reinforced by the fact that the more sophisticated machines requiring greater skill also had the easier rates. Auxiliary personnel developed characters in accordance with their willingness to cooperate in making out: Morris was a lousy guy because he'd always delay in bringing stock; Harry was basically a decent crib attendant (after he took my ham), tried to help the guys, but was overworked; Charley was an OK scheduling man because he'd try to give me the gravy jobs; Bill, my day man, was "all right" because he'd show me the angles on making out, give me some kitty if I needed it, and sometimes cover up for me when I made a mess of things. . . .

What we have observed is the expansion of the area of the "self-organization" of workers as they pursue their daily activities. We have seen how operators, in order to make out at all, subvert rules promulgated from on high, create informal alliances with auxiliary workers, make their own tools, and so on. In order to produce surplus value, workers have had to organize their relations and activities in opposition to management, particularly middle and senior management. . . . For Cornelius Castoriadis, this represents the fundamental contradiction of capitalism:

> In short, it [the deep contradiction] lies in the fact that capitalism . . . is obliged to try and achieve the simultaneous exclusion and participation of people in relation to their activities, in the fact that people are forced to ensure the functioning of the system half of the time *against* the system's own rules and therefore in struggle against it. This fundamental contradiction appears constantly wherever the process of management meets the process of execution, which is precisely (and par excellence) the social moment of production.[2]

But if the self-organization of workers is necessary for the survival of capitalism, it also questions the foundations of capitalism.

When the shop-floor collective establishes norms that informally sanction both "slackers" and "speeders," when it constantly constitutes and reconstitutes itself in "informal" groups that respond to both the requirements of the work process and to personal affinities, it can only be viewed as actively opposing to capitalist principles new principles of productive and social organization and a new view of work.[3]

But is making out as radical as Castoriadis claims? Or is it, as Herbert Marcuse would argue, a mode of adaptation that reproduces "the voluntary servitude" of workers to capital? Are these freedoms and needs, generated and partially satisfied in the context of work and harnessed to the production of surplus value, a challenge to "capitalist principles"? Does making out present an anticipation of something new, the potential for human self-organization, or is it wholly contained within the reproduction of capitalist relations?[4] . . .

NOTES

1. Donald Roy, "Work Satisfaction and Social Reward in Quota Achievement," *American Journal of Sociology* 57 (1953): 509–10.

2. Paul Cardan (alias Cornelius Castoriadis), *Redefining Revolution* (London: Solidarity Pamphlet 44, n.d.), p. 11.

3. Cornelius Castoriadis, "On the History of the Workers' Movement," *Telos* no. 30 (Winter 1976–77): 35.

4. See, for example, Herbert Marcuse, *One Dimensional Man* (Boston: Beacon Press, 1964), chap. 1; *An Essay on Liberation* (Boston: Beacon Press, 1969); *Eros and Civilization* (Boston: Beacon Press, 1955), chap. 10.

24

Women on the Line

Tom Juravich

Tom Juravich is director of the Labor Relations and Research Center at the University of Massachusetts. Professor Juravich writes, "Growing up in a working class family and having done factory work before college, I knew that it would be inadequate to write a dissertation about work and labor from the comfort of a chair in the library or the computer lab. While the ten months in National Wire was the hardest, most boring, and in many ways the most difficult work I've ever done, it was fundamental in defining the work I have done since. My research and teaching for the past fifteen years has built on *Chaos on the Shop Floor,* describing and giving voice to workers' lives as well as advocating for workers and their unions, whether analyzing union organizing and bargaining strategies, critically assessing the impact of employee involvement programs, or writing and performing as a labor singer-songwriter."

Until recently, the role played by women in the industrial labor force has been severely underestimated. Although the postwar bias emphasized the extent to which women remained in the home, women have played fundamental roles in American industry; as Barbara Wertheimer has written, "We Were There" (Wertheimer, 1977). We tend to forget that it was women who first left the New England farms (leaving the men behind) to work in the new industrial centers of Lawrence, Massachusetts and Manchester, New Hampshire. In addition, entire industries, such as the garment industry, hired primarily female workers.

It is important, however, to characterize the nature of women's participation in the industrial labor force. Despite great shifts in American industry (textiles in New England have been replaced by high-tech, for example), "women's work" has remained essentially the same. For the most part women have occupied the lowest paid, most tedious "handwork" positions. In the textile industry women nimbly replaced spools of thread and tied swift weavers' knots as well as similar handwork. In today's high-tech industry they assemble electrical components and micro chips. As in the garment industry, women hold the majority of assembly positions (Grossman, 1980).

Thus the women at National are part of a continuing American tradition, one that our conventional view of the industrial workplace has generally downplayed. In what follows we will observe assembly work at National—and see that in addition to low pay and repetition, it is characterized by a considerable degree of chaos.

Women's Work

On the average there were twenty women working on the second floor at National.

The number fluctuated greatly while I was there. It plummeted to a low of eight during two different lay-offs, and rose to forty during peak production (for about two months when a four-hour second shift was added). The women were extremely young. A handful were in their forties and fifties, but most were in their early twenties. At least eight were under twenty.

There were ten to fifteen small machines on the floor that were used sporadically for a variety of jobs. Two or three might be running at any given time. But most of the women worked on the three-wire assembly, the major product of the floor. The production of these assemblies was broken down into six separate tasks.

The process began at the SELM, where terminals were placed on various lengths of wire. It was the operator's job to inspect these leads (wires) as they came off the machine. They were then stacked in cardboard boxes and put in a shelf near the SELM at the back of the floor.

The assembly itself began in the next phase. Between four and eight women took three different colors (and lengths) of wire and inserted them into a small plastic block an inch square and a quarter of an inch deep. This was by far the hardest and most tedious job. Each lead had a square terminal on the end which had to be pushed into a square channel in the plastic block until it locked. It was not an easy task. It took a certain amount of force and some finesse as well. If you held the lead too far back you bent the terminal. If you held the lead too close you banged your fingers.

You could always tell who was new on the job by their bandaged fingers. Without exception, new employees were assigned to "blocking," as this job was called, and without exception their hands bled. If they lasted beyond the first few weeks, which most did not, they developed the calluses necessary to do the job.

Besides being physically difficult, "blocking" demanded speed. The women were expected to block close to two hundred assemblies per hour, although we had no bonus system (where workers can earn extra money by being more productive). If after a training period that rate was not met, the women would be called into the office repeatedly and threatened with dismissal, although to my knowledge that never happened. Usually they quit long before that.

From the blockers the assemblies moved down the line to be sewed. Although I use the phrase "down the line," the assemblies were not moved down a belt or automatic assembly line. They were stacked in boxes which the women shifted from station to station. At any given time the floor was stacked with a variety of boxes containing assemblies at different stages of production. The sewers took assemblies that had been blocked and on specially designed machines sewed around the three wires. Sewing was the most favored job on the line, and it was usually assigned to women who had been at National the longest. The younger women competed hard for these positions.

The assemblies then passed to the singers (singe-ers) and trimmers. The actual stitching of the assemblies was fairly loose, and it was the singer's job to pass a heat gun (which looked like a large hair dryer) over the stitching to shrink the thread around the wires. After singeing, the loose end of the thread was cut off by the trimmers. In many ways the easiest job, trimming, was often held back as a reward or to be done when there was little else to do.

These five steps—making the leads on the SELM, blocking, sewing, singeing, and trimming—produced the assembly. The sixth and final stage was to inspect and pack the finished product. The inspectors checked the length of the wire, the sewing, the blocks (to see that they were not scratched in the blocking process), and a variety of other characteristics. Depending on the work load, one or two women worked as inspectors.

For a while my knowledge of the women's work was only that of an outsider. I had observed them repeating their tasks over and over, but my attention had been focused on the SELMs. Their work seemed straightforward, and although boring, appeared to present little confusion. Yet in the coming months, as I spent more time with the women, I began to understand that their work was quite different. Although these six tasks appeared so simple that one would expect the process to be automatic, it was actually the source of much confusion, conflict, and disagreement. A careful look at the production process reveals why women on the line were beset with their own kind of chaos.

The Craft Knowledge of Deskilled Workers

Much has been written about the deskilling of labor in the twentieth century. Perhaps the best example is Harry Braverman's *Labor and Monopoly Capital* (1974). Throughout the book, as well as in related volumes (see Zimbalist, 1979), we are given numerous examples of how technology has taken away the skill from a job, leaving only routine to the workers.

If there ever were an example of this degradation of labor, it was the kind of work performed by the women at National. There is no way that their work could be seen as exciting, satisfying, or rewarding. It was tolerable at best. Even Carroll recognized this. He once told me, "It takes a special kind of girl [sic] to do this kind of work. The guys could never do it, they don't have the patience. We like the neat ones, the ones who like this close work."

One comes away from Braverman convinced that little skill is necessary to perform most factory jobs. This conviction is very much shared as a conventional wisdom. Yet these "simple" tasks often look quite different from the shop floor.

One of my first jobs working closely with the women involved changing the belts on the sewing machines. The belts were made of leather and stretched or broke over time. Installing a new belt involved cutting a new piece of leather to the proper length and fastening it together with a metal staple. This took about half an hour (until much later when I discovered a special tool which was designed to punch the holes and fasten the staple). The women poked fun at my somewhat clumsy style (the task actually was quite difficult), especially Carol (not to be confused with Carroll), whose machine I started on. She was a large woman in her late thirties with a hot temper but also a good sense of humor.

After replacing the belt, I sat down at her machine and asked her to show me how to sew. I never heard such laughter. The other women thought that a man sewing was the funniest thing they ever saw. It took me five minutes to sew a single assembly, and it came out completely wrong. "You'll never make your rate that way, honey," said Carol. "You think your job is hard," said one of the other sewers. Carroll would also sew while repairing or testing a machine. He was a little better at it than me, but not much. The women used the opportunity to give him all the grief they could. "See if you can keep that up all day," one of the women used to say.

It was clear to me, and to anyone else watching, that a worker could not walk in off the street, sit down at the machine, and make her rate. Yet despite his own experience, this is how Carroll often threatened the women: "Why, I could get somebody right off the street who could do that job faster than you." Perhaps Carroll believed it. The usual explanation is that these jobs require a certain manual dexterity, though no real skill, and some people simply lack the physical coordination. Yet this explanation is not adequate. As I found out, many of our assembly positions required more than deftness.

At one point I was called over to adjust a small press. It applied a spade terminal (like the one on your television antenna) to an already cut and stripped length of wire. The repair amounted essentially to cleaning out the applicator with the air line and some lubricant, but in the process I discovered that Betty, the operator of the machine, had perfected an ingenious technique.

The wire was approximately sixteen inches long, and terminals had to be placed on each end parallel to each other. I had seen other women struggle with this job, placing a terminal on one end, turning the wire around, lining it up and applying the other terminal. Betty, however, had found another way to do it. As I was checking the machine, I saw her pick up a handful of wires and bounce them in her hand. When I asked what she was doing, she said she was finding the "bend" in the wire. This 'bend' she referred to was due to the fact that the wire had originally been coiled on a spool. Although the machine that stripped and cut the wire included a mechanical device called a straightener, it was impossible to remove the bend entirely, and when lined up in a tray, the wires bent one way or the other.

Once Betty had bounced the wires and they lined up the same way (with the ends bending down as she held them); still holding them as a bunch, she put a terminal on one end of all of them. She then turned the bundle around and put terminals on the other end. Because she let the memory of the wire keep the ends turned the same way, the terminals were easily applied in the proper parallel fashion.

I was impressed. This was hardly a deskilled worker performing routine procedures. When I asked her how she learned to do it, she responded casually that she had figured it out doing the job. As I began to see the women's work from the inside, I noticed a host of skills like Betty's that facilitated production. In fact, I was surprised how fundamental this "craft knowledge" was to the day-to-day operation of the mill. By "craft knowledge," most people think of skills possessed by someone like a violin maker. It is knowledge that cannot be rigidly systematized or reduced to procedural rules but is developed through years of experience. I would argue that the women on the line possessed skills very much akin to those of a craftsman.

Even so, I would hardly argue that working in National was anything like making violins. Indeed, as we have seen, the work itself was menial. Yet contrary to Braverman, a job that involves repetitive, boring tasks is not necessarily devoid of skill or craft. As Manwaring and Wood conclude, the recognition of "working knowledge does not in and of itself refute the deskilling thesis, but it does provide a different vantage point, one in which the central notion is that work is both degrading and constructive, both crippling and enriching" (Manwaring and Wood, 1984: 56).

It is not that craft knowledge at National merely facilitated speedier production. Rather, it was integral to getting the job done at all. Based on research in a paper cone factory, Ken Kusterer (1978) implies this point in his distinction between basic and supplemental (craft) knowledge.

Basic knowledge includes all the procedures necessary to routinely carry out their work tasks: how to start and stop the machine, clean it in a prescribed manner, "bridge the cones," label the case, etc. Supplemental knowledge includes all the know-how necessary to handle obstacles to this routine work performance that arise from time to time: how to keep the machinery running, overcome "bad paper," diagnose the cause of the defects (Kusterer, 1978: 45).

Thus, when Carroll told the women that he could replace them with "somebody off the street," what he really meant was, "Provided that all the materials are perfect, the machines are running well, and with constant supervision," then "somebody off the street" would do. But as we have seen, National hardly ever ran under those conditions. The machines were in constant disrepair, the materials were inconsistent, and most of the actual decisions on the floor were made by the women themselves, not by Carroll or June. If the managers had to make every decision themselves, production schedules would never be met.

The high labor turnover at National always threatened production. A new assembler would be trained for a day or two and then left on her own. This worked fine as long as things went smoothly. But a problem could spell disaster. For example, one new blocker was doing fine until she blocked 5,000 assemblies with wire that was too heavy. A more experienced blocker would have detected the overly heavy gauge simply by feeling the wire, and could have avoided the lost time and materials. (In a way Carroll was right about taking workers directly off the street. This blocker had made her rate all right, but her work had to be tossed in the scrap pile.)

Thus, the day-to-day operation of the mill required more than mere routine assembly. Yet the constant need for decision-making had mixed implications for the women on the line.

Chaos on the Line

As Kusterer demonstrates in *Know-How on the Job* (1978), all jobs from bank teller to longshoreman demand an insider's knowledge, without which the job cannot be done effectively. This craft knowledge is important to workers in a number of ways. First, it is an important source of pride and dignity. That jobs involve more than menial tasks contributes in fundamental ways to workers' self-esteem. Second, craft knowledge can be an important source of power for workers. Because for the most part it is hidden from management, it can become a tool for workers to assert power in the workplace.

Yet the degree to which this kind of decision-making was constantly needed on the line indicates how confused production really was. The women did not really mind making decisions—it was by far the most interesting part of their day—but making the right decision was not always clear, and the wrong decision often carried strong sanctions.

For example, the leads produced by the SELM were supposed to be measured on an ongoing basis by the operator and once an hour by an inspector. They checked the overall length of the wire, the length of the strip, and how the wire was placed in the terminal. The specifications for these leads were extremely rigid, with the tolerance on each measure plus or minus one-sixty-fourth of an inch. Given the condition of the machines, the quality of the materials, and the experience of the workers, this tolerance was nearly impossible to achieve. In fact, the manual for the machine specified that it would work only to a one-thirty-second of an inch tolerance. In actuality, the machines were running plus or minus one-sixteenth of an inch.

Everyone in the mill, from the operator Alice to the inspectors, was aware of this. They knew that by official specifications most of the leads were beyond tolerance. Yet they also knew that the leads were probably acceptable to the purchaser, and that if they rejected too many items Carroll would be on their backs. Thus everyone was in an ambiguous position that required a constant negotiation of the rules.

From my experience, this goes on in other mills, where official specifications only serve as general guidelines, and where actual specifications are actually much looser. Yet I never witnessed anywhere near the negotiation that occurred daily at National. If the women actually obeyed the specifications, they would do no work. Yet if they accepted (or produced) something beyond an acceptable tolerance, they ran the risk of being held responsible for producing "bad" items.

This uncertainty led to endless "crises" at National. Every two or three weeks, management shut down the production line and called everyone into the cafeteria. Carroll or June would show us some assemblies and ask us what was wrong with them. It was a test. It was amazing how much we could find wrong if we looked hard enough, although what we found was often not what they had in mind. One time the blocks were scratched, another time the tab on the end of the terminals was bent, and once the sewing pulled out. They would chew us out and send us back to the line, usually with some new procedure or inspection to eliminate the problem.

However, if we focused on one detail or aspect of production, the line would immediately slow down. As long as the women stuck close to specifications, the production rate dropped. Interestingly, most of these crises ended the same way. For a week or two the women were very careful, but before long they went back to their old ways. The new inspection or procedure was usually forgotten, and the uncertainty in the production line remained essentially the same. It was amazing to me that despite a series of these crises, the line ran basically the same when I left National as when I arrived.

Much More Than Just a Routine Job

From this in-depth look at the women on the line at National, we have discovered that what they do is much more than just routine work. Not denying that it was boring and repetitive, working at National required constant decision-making and precarious negotiation of what was expected. At first glance, it might be argued that the women at National were "lucky" to have this high level of decision-making, to the extent that it relieved them of the boredom they would otherwise experience. Yet upon further analysis, this constant decision-making cannot be seen as relieving boredom. Decision-making took place in such a confusing and contradictory context that in fundamental ways it added to the pressure.

Workers have a number of ways of dealing with monotony. For some it is dreams of summer vacations or a new car, for others it is the beer at lunch, while others try radios and singing on the job. If you observe a mill carefully, you will notice all kinds of routines that appear pointless at first glance. For example, one of the older women on the floor had a routine she followed religiously. Every day at morning coffeebreak she went to the corner store and bought a newspaper. She brought it to her table and then went to the bathroom for a paper towel that she spread on her table. She then proceeded to eat half of her sandwich, no more, no less, every working day. There were numerous other examples of women "setting up" their meager possessions—radio, cigarettes, and coffee cup—in similar fashion.

At first you wonder if these routines are the product of working too long in an alienating workplace. Yet over time you see the purpose behind these rituals. Most of what the workers at National did was out of their control. They knew they would produce thousands of assemblies each day, yet had no control over the conditions under which that production occurred. These rituals, then, in important and fundamental ways served to impose some, if only a small amount, of personal impact on the day. The woman who eats just half a sandwich at the same time each day in her own way is imposing some order on the day's events. Although these jobs are clearly "too small for people," it is through this imposition of order that they somehow become "enough."

Jobs become less boring to the extent that workers control their daily activities. For example, if workers' rates were computed by the day instead of by the hour, workers could work harder in the morning when they were fresh, and slower in the afternoon when tired. A break in the work routine, however, when not tied to an increase in control, does not necessarily make a job less boring. For instance, when management stopped production at National because of problems with tolerances, it did not alleviate boredom. Since constant decision-making made the workday more unpredictable, the women felt less in control than if their jobs were utterly routine.

Psychologists agree that random punishment is the worst kind because it threatens an individual's sense of control and order. A punishment that follows from a certain behavior or occurs at some fixed interval is much easier to deal with than one that occurs at random times. In a similar fashion, the ongoing decision-making and the confusion that resulted made the work at National difficult to bear.

Especially confusing times (during one of our "crises," for instance) had an obvious effect on the women who worked on the line. Tempers flared, arguments were more common, people took more days off, and some worked as slowly as they could. They complained as well. "I wish they'd make up their damn minds," said one of the blockers to me. "It's bad enough having such boring work, and then there's so much confusion all the time. One day it'll pass, the next day it won't." As another woman said to me, "All I want to do is to be able to do my job without anyone bothering me, and then go home."

REFERENCES

Braverman, Harry. 1974. *Labor and Monopoly Capital: The Degradation of Work in the Twentieth Century.* New York: Monthly Review Press.

Grossman, Rachael. 1980. "Women's Place in the Integrated Circuit." *Radical America* 14: 29–50.

Kusterer, Ken C. 1978. *Know-How on the Job: The Important Working Knowledge of "Unskilled" Workers.* Boulder, Colo.: Westview Press.

Wertheimer, Barbara Mayer. 1977. *We Were There: The Story of Working Women in America.* New York: Pantheon.

Zimbalist, Andrew, ed. 1979. *Case Studies on the Labor Process.* New York: Monthly Review Press.

25

On the Line at Subaru–Isuzu

Laurie Graham

Laurie Graham is associate professor of labor studies at Indiana University, Kokomo. Professor Graham writes, "In the early 1970s I managed to land my first factory job. This job was different for me not only because it was factory work, but also because it was a 'man's' job; therefore, the pay was good. The effect that job had on my life was very mixed. Although the increased money allowed me greater freedom and autonomy at home, I found myself under more control and pressure while at work. It seemed as though I had given up one form of freedom in exchange for another. Soon, however, my co-workers and I voted to form a union. This process of working together in support of each other changed my experience of work. As workers, we had gained a unique form of control over our lives. This experience awakened in me an unending questioning of why life is organized around work and how our experience of work affects every aspect of our lives. My twenty years of work experience—from delivery driver, waitress, cook, and service worker to factory worker and union organizer—were good preparation for becoming a sociologist."

Life on the assembly line, whether operated under the Japanese model or under traditional U.S. methods, continues to be a monotonous grind. However, there is one critical difference between the two systems: a key feature of the Japanese model is speedup and work intensification (Berggren 1992; Kamata 1982; Parker and Slaughter 1988). This chapter describes SIA's process of vehicle production with its flat management structure and rigid work process built on extensive Taylorist principles. An immediate and widespread effect of the Japanese model was physical injury, injuries which reached beyond the plant floor to touch the personal lives of the workers.

From *On the Line at Subaru–Isuzu,* by Laurie Graham. Used by permission of the publisher, Cornell University Press.

The Subaru–Isuzu plant spans more than fifty acres, and Trim and Final occupies about one-third of that area. Trim and Final has a "car side" where the Subaru Legacy is assembled and a "truck side" where Isuzu trucks are built. I worked in the Trim and Final department as a member of Team 1 in "trim one" on the car side. We were the first team to work on the bodies after they came out of Paint. About fourteen teams assembled the cars and a few more than fourteen worked on the truck side. The rest of the teams were in final inspection or in In Process Control (IPC), neither of which is directly connected to the main assembly lines.

The car side of Trim and Final consists of four areas: trim one, trim two, chassis, and final. . . . Trim one and two runs the full length of the department, about the distance of a couple of city blocks. It takes several minutes to walk from one end to the other. There are four teams in trim one and two teams in trim two. Trim installs virtually everything inside the passenger compartment except for the seats, carpeting, and steering wheel. It also assembles the doors and attaches a few items to the engine compartment.

Since both the truck and car lines run the length of Trim and Final and then back again, Team 1 is located between the final line on the truck side and the final line on the car side. We were the first team to work on the cars and, at the same time, we watched as they were driven off the line, as finished products.

. . . [A] relatively flat management structure exists at SIA with only a few levels of authority between the worker and the Operating Committee—the highest level decision-making body in the plant. . . . [T]he Operating Committee consists of the president and five vice presidents. Below them are six department managers—one for Trim and Final—and below managers are group leaders, team leaders, and production Associates.

In Trim and Final, salaried workers consist of nine group leaders, one car line manager, a truck line manager, and a single department manager. The team leaders are hourly employees. There were twenty-nine teams in all of Trim and Final, each with one team leader, and the average team size was seven. In 1989, the first year of production, Associates' pay started at $11.60 per hour and team leaders received $12.15 per hour. The following year production Associates' wages were raised to $12.49 and those of team leaders to $13.14. (As of February 1994, Associates with seniority dates equal to mine were making about $16.35 per hour.)

The department manager was not usually present on the floor, so the car and truck managers acted as "foremen." Group leaders worked as the managers' assistants and as troubleshooters for their teams. Team 1's group leader had four teams under his control: Team 1 and Team 2 on the main assembly line and two teams which assembled the doors on a separate, smaller line. Most group leaders had three or four teams under them. However, two of the nine group leaders in Trim and Final were engineers who directed no teams. In addition to those nine, there was a group leader from Human Resources who worked as a liaison between that department and Trim and Final. Since the Human Resources group leader and the engineers directed no teams, their designation was misleading. For them, it was more an indication of wage and organizational rank than a description of their jobs.

On the car side, the fourteen teams were broken down into sixty-nine stations on both sides of the line. Team members referred to the stations and the people working them as though they were same. In other words, when team members referred to the work I performed, it was the work done by "one left"; however, team members did not refer to each other by station when away from the line. Team 1 was divided into twelve stations, six to a side. Eventually, one person would be responsible for each station. When I left, we were still short one person. When fully staffed, there would be thirteen on the team, including the team leader. Team 1 was one of the largest teams.

During the six months I worked at SIA, we never had a "group" meeting involving all four teams. However, the four team leaders met with the group leader every morning and all the group leaders met with the car manager every afternoon. The only direct connection that Team 1 experienced with the other teams in our group was on the line. If one team was short several workers, the group leader would pull a worker from one of the other teams to assist that team.

Team 1 is located at one end of Trim; at the other end is an area called the U-turn. Here the cars literally make a U-turn. They are lifted up to about twenty feet and brought around to face in the opposite direction, ready to be lowered into the chassis area.

Some observations about the human component of the work setting at Trim and Final are in order before I describe the work itself. Concerning the sexual division of labor at SIA, men dominated the authority structure. Women accounted for only five out of the twenty-nine team leaders in Trim and Final, and none of the group leaders. Most of the women in production were located in Trim and Final, the lowest skilled and most labor-intensive area of the plant. Only three women held positions in the highest paying production jobs located in the Maintenance department. The three were all highly skilled millwrights from a local factory.

Selections from my field notes reflect the sexual division of labor, the ways in which that division was maintained, and the impact that it held for women at SIA:

> "On the way to work Joan told me about the problems she has had with her team leader. He came right out and told her that he did not want any women working under him. . . . She said that Mary (her teammate) has carpal tunnel and he makes fun of her for having it. Joan said that no matter how bad her hands ever hurt, she will not go to the doctor because of him. (October 24, 1989)

During down time, when the line was not moving, Team 1 performed tasks such as cleaning the area, fixing parts, and kaizening racks (designing and building racks to hold our parts). As the following excerpt indicates, despite the egalitarian ethic promoted by the company, a sexual division of labor emerges:

> Karen brought up today how our team leader assigns all the work according to sex. Karen and I always do the sweep-

ing and the guys always kaizen. Karen and I make signs and repair wiring harnesses unless we can rope some of the guys into helping us. (November 3, 1989)

A woman from the final line experienced sexual discrimination which, if allowed to go unchecked, would have prevented her from ever advancing within the company. The following conversation took place during down time while we were hiding in a room containing personal computers, trying to look busy and stay out of the way so that we did not get work assignments that we disliked, such as sweeping and mopping the floor:

> Teresa (from the final line) told Randa, Karen (both from Team 1), Mindy (Team 2), and me about her evaluation by her team leader. (Anyone who wants to be a team leader has to have one of these evaluations.) Teresa said that she was devastated afterwards. He ranked her unacceptable on ability to train, oral communication and one other thing. When she asked him for an explanation, he said that he had never seen her train anyone nor speak before a group. She told us that she also had to do a self-evaluation and she told him that she had ranked herself very high in those two categories because she was formerly a music teacher and spoke in front of groups and trained people all day long. Her team leader then said that she had never worked any of the other stations, so she was not qualified to be a team leader because you have to master your entire area. Teresa said that the reason she hasn't is because he will not let her rotate. (She is the only woman on the team.) He also told her at the evaluation that she simply did not have the physical ability to perform any of the

other stations. She will never qualify for team leader unless she can cross-train. (January 5, 1990).

With our encouragement, Teresa discussed this problem with her group leader. The group leader talked with her team leader and she was allowed to participate in team leader training. The following is another example of how the sexual division of labor was maintained:

> Teresa told us that when the company tried to move another woman down to their team right before Christmas, her team leader threw a fit. He was going to have to put the woman on the last station driving the cars off the line because the woman was in wrist splints and the group leader thought she could do that job. The team leader said that that was the station he used to reward the men during the rotation, and another woman would prevent the men from receiving this reward. The group leader put the other woman back on her original team. (January 5, 1990)

Concerning racial division of labor, there were no blacks in positions of authority above team leader. I was aware of only one black man attaining the position of team leader in Trim and Final. He was in charge of one of the door lines on our group. In general, it seemed that very few blacks worked at SIA. The month after I started work at SIA, I counted ten blacks at a meeting of all Trim and Final Associates, about 150 people. Later one of the black workers in Materials was stymied in his attempt to advance within the company because his team leader would not give permission for him to attend team leader training classes after work. Team 1 members felt that he was a victim of racial discrimination:

John told me today that Frank—the forklift driver who services my side of the line—asked him if we were satisfied with his work. John told him that of course we were and asked him why he wanted to know. Frank (who is black) said that his group leader refused to sign off for him so he could take the team leader training course (this was necessary in order to enter the pool of applicants for team leader). . . . I told the other members of the team about it. . . . Everyone is upset and says it's unfair. John said that Frank could file a grievance if there was a union. (November 16, 1989)

On July 22, 1993, the local newspaper reported that SIA was being sued for racial discrimination by a worker who claimed that he was fired because he is black and that the company maintains an atmosphere hostile to African Americans. The possibility of grounds for such conditions in transplants is evident in research on these operations. For example, there have been suggestions in the literature on the Japanese model that it uses site location to avoid hiring African Americans (Cole and Deskins 1988) and that "the screening procedures are discriminatory not only against unions, but also minorities, and perhaps older workers and women as well" (International Metalworkers Federation 1992:27).

A Typical Day

A typical day at SIA began at 6:25 A.M. (five minutes before the scheduled start of work) when music played over the loudspeaker, signaling morning exercises. Team members would line up and the team leader would lead us in our daily exercise routine. Team members had varied reactions to the exercises. Our team leader and one team member consistently seemed enthusiastic about the exercises; however, for the rest of us and for others in Trim and Final it was a different story. During my first day in the shop, there was a department meeting with the Trim and Final manager. At the end of the meeting questions were taken from the workers. The following field note entries illuminate how the workers felt about exercising:

A woman asked: "What about the exercise policy, do we get slapped on the wrist for being late for exercises, or are we early for work?"

The manager's response: "We encourage everyone to exercise."

The woman: "Our team leader said he wanted to see everybody there."

The manager: "They are not mandatory. That's why they are before the shift. But I'm not going to tell you not to do them."

At this point, one of my teammates whispered to the rest of us: "Now she's ready for her team leader, she's got the manager's word." (July 31, 1989)

Today was the first morning after the Trim and Final meeting. . . . This morning I noticed, and Terry mentioned it to me later, that there were fewer people exercising and several people entered the plant while we were performing ours (anyone entering the plant through the main door goes past our station). The team we face while doing ours was nonexistent. Dave (teammate) said that even though our group leader had never said that they had to be there, they did feel a general pressure even though it is on their own time. (August 4, 1989)

The inspection team that exercised on the other side of final line has totally stopped. (August 10, 1989)

The team leader left Terry in charge today so no one exercised this morning, except Reese; he did it because he said it makes him feel better. The rest of us sat at the picnic table drinking coffee watching him. (November 10, 1989)

The first time I exercised I remember feeling embarrassed. It seemed juvenile. However, as time went on I began to feel differently about stretching out. Once the line was moving continually, I knew how easily it was to pull a muscle; so unless we refused as a team, to protest something, I exercised. The Japanese trainer usually joined us when we exercised; however, he was often late because the head trainer held meetings prior to work. About thirty seconds or so after exercises, the buzzer sounded to signal the beginning of our shift. The team did not wait for the buzzer. Instead, we formed a circle and began the morning team meeting. (According to the follow-up interviews in 1994, no one exercised by then. The music still plays, but workers no longer exercise.)

When official production was under way, the morning team meeting lasted only five minutes and team members found that they had little to say. During August and even into September, we generally had more time for meetings. Team members would bring up problems and suggestions. They complained, however, that their suggestions were seldom acted upon. Several times team members brought up their desire to rotate and to vote. Requests were acknowledged but simply ignored. Team members resented this. Once the line was moving continuously, team members also expressed resentment at even the brief time (five minutes) scheduled for the meetings because it interfered with their ability to get their station set up for the day. The line began moving exactly at 6:35 A.M. whether our stations were ready or not.

At the end of those meetings the team performed a daily ritual. Team members would huddle in a manner similar to that of a sports team before a game. During the huddle, each person extended his or her left arm into the center of the circle, hands clenched into fists. The team leader then called on one member to deliver an inspirational message to the team. The usual message was, "Let's have a safe and productive day." A few team members sometimes told good-natured jokes, making light of the ritual. For the most part, it was embarrassing to be called upon and the jokes were a way for us to insert some control over the process. For example, during my last week in the plant the following occurred:

> This morning Tony gave the inspirational message for the group. He said: "This is Laurie's last week and working with her has been a pleasure. Let's build these cars for Laurie!" It was all a joke. Most of the messages are jokes. Terry will often give some Chinese proverb and then say some puffed up thing like—"I'm proud to be an American"—in a real deep voice. Everyone laughs. (January 8, 1990)

After the message, we all brought our right arms around into the circle with everyone's hands meeting in the center clenched into fists. While doing this, members shouted "Yosh!" and then broke up and went to work. Every team in the plant was instructed in performing this same ritual. It was our understanding that *yosh* was a cheer meaning something similar to "Let's go!"

At exactly 6:35 A.M. a buzzer sounded and the assembly line began to move. Unless someone pulled the cord and stopped the line, it ran until 8:30 A.M. when we took a ten-minute break. The line would screech to a halt and everyone in Trim and Final rested. Exactly ten minutes later the buzzer sounded and the line immediately began

to move. There was no warning for team members to put on their aprons and gloves and walk back to their stations. Team members working the stations farthest from the break table were seen running back to the line.

At 10:30 A.M., the line stopped for a thirty-minute, unpaid lunch. Two or three team members often ate in the cafeteria with workers from their Orientation and Training classes. At 11:00 A.M. the line started up, again with no warning. At 1:00 P.M. the line stopped for another ten-minute break and at 3:00 P.M. the work day was over. Bathroom breaks were strongly discouraged when the line was moving. If you had to leave the line, you first had to get the team leader to take over your station. If the team leader was busy, you were out of luck. When there were no line stoppages it was a long and grueling day.

At one end of Team 1's area was a set of small lockers for personal items and opposite the lockers was a desk for the team leader. . . . The lockers provided a kind of boundary between the line and a large picnic table where team members congregated during breaks. Every team had its own set of lockers and picnic table to provide a small break area. Nearly all of us spent breaks with our own team because ten minutes simply was not enough time to leave the immediate area. Team 1's break area was located right under the conveyer system bringing the cars to our team.

The noise in Trim and Final was constant and loud. Even during breaks, when the conveyers stopped, there was noise. Inevitably, during break time, contract employees would work on maintenance projects. Almost everyone on Team 1 wore ear plugs provided by the company.

The type of work each team member performed varied as to its physical demands, its potential for injury, the speed at which it could be performed, and whether or not the team member could readily speak to others. For the most part, however, working on the line required our undivided attention. During plant start-up, workers had time for conversations between cars and even while working the stations. During our first few months, before line speed picked up, Team 1 played a guessing game while working on the line. One of us would think of a famous person and the rest of the team tried to figure out who it was within ten questions. (We made certain to stop playing when management came around.) As line speed increased, time for interactions between workers and for periods of rest continually decreased. Not only were we more isolated as we were unable to interact; increased line speed was also accompanied by the emergence of injuries. At one point seven of the twelve members of Team 1 suffered from hand and wrist injuries. Once the speedup began, workers experienced constant pressure from the assembly line. Everyone was forced to work at a continuous, rapid pace. . . .

Shop Floor Reality vs. Company Philosophy

The *SIA Associate Handbook* had told us "We are a company that places great importance on respect for people, commitment to safety, and quality in everything we do. These three are essential to our success. *People, safety,* and *quality* are the watchwords that dominate our workday" (1989:7).

The issue of stopping the line and who had the authority to pull the red cord was one of several inconsistencies between the company's egalitarian philosophy and our experience on the shop floor. In Orientation and Training, we had been told that "everyone is an Associate at SIA, from the company president on down." Team members, however, felt that the term *Associate* was used to designate those of us who worked on the

line or in support areas like material handling, not for management. When addressing team members, management would often begin statements with the phrase, "We are all Associates here at SIA." Even though team members used terms like *team leader* or *group leader* to refer to people in those positions, they never referred to each other or other line workers as Associates. Workers referred to each other by name, team, or department. Managers and group leaders used Associate when referring to workers collectively, and often as individuals. Sometimes it was even used to refer to one of us in the third person, while we were present. For example, once while the car manager was talking to my group leader and me, he turned to the group leader and said: "Well, it looks like the Associate is doing her job," speaking as though I was not present.

The term *Associate* was one way of distinguishing workers directly employed by SIA from contract workers. Contract workers did everything from maintaining the conveyer systems, cleaning the locker rooms and office area, running the cafeteria, and working in security to keeping up the grounds. Some of them even held clerical positions. For the most part, there was no interaction between these contract workers and Associates. (Contract workers are not the same as the temporary workers SIA widely employs today. Temporaries work on the line with regular team workers. I discovered through interviews during February 1994 that up to half of some teams are temporary workers. Temporaries are hired through a local agency and it was reported by Associates that they receive about ten dollars per hour. SIA pays them no benefits.)

But the overriding discrepancy between shop floor reality and company philosophy involved injuries. Immediately after official start of production (SOP), there was an outbreak of hand and wrist injuries. Since Team 1 was located at one end of the plant, anyone using the bathrooms on that side of the building had to walk past us. Because of our location and the easily identified method of treatment for hand and wrist injuries, we could observe the dramatic increase. Within only a few weeks, dozens of workers were wearing splints on their wrists and forearms. People continued to work, but their wrists were immobilized in splints. According to several injured workers, the company physician had either diagnosed them with carpal tunnel syndrome or, more typically, told them they were showing symptoms of it and their diagnosis was "overwork syndrome." At first, no one was taken off the line. Unless the company physician gave a direct order to remove an injured person from a station, each continued on the same job that had caused the injury.

The type of work we engaged in at SIA made us especially vulnerable to various repetitive-motion injuries, as was and is the case throughout the auto industry. Nationally, repetitive-motion injuries such as carpal tunnel syndrome increased 58 percent in 1989 over 1987 and workers in the automobile industry had an injury rate of 28.5 for every 100 full-time workers, more than three times the rate of all workplaces (*Labor Notes*, January 1990:4). At Mazda, the Fucinis found an alarming increase in worker injuries when the plant began approaching full production. Recordable injuries increased by 50 percent between June and September of 1988—a rate of 42.6 days lost for every 100 workers from June 1988 to May 1989—and injuries were considerably higher than in the Big Three auto plants in Michigan (1990:175).

At SIA we were living proof that the speedup, repetition, and physical stress of assembly line work was detrimental to our health. Berggren, Bjorkman, and Hollander's (1991) field trip to the Japanese transplants reported growing health and safety complaints due to the intense pace, repetitive-

ness, and long working hours. These conditions led to cumulative trauma disorders or repetitive strain injuries. At Mazda they found an unusually high incidence of carpal tunnel syndrome with the total number of work-related injuries at three times the level of that in comparable American plants (Berggren et al. 1991:55). When Berggren's team visited Honda in Anna, Ohio, management would not even admit that this was a problem in any way related to conditions of production. Instead, the company blamed the workers, stating: "There are weak and strong people. And there are right and wrong attitudes" (Berggren et al. 1991:55).

My field notes make reference to some of our injuries:

> I went to the (company) doctor this morning because my thumbs have been bothering me since we stepped up production—about a month now. He said I have tendonitis. He gave me wrist splints to wear at work, prescribed exercises for my hands, and told me not to push any more plugs on the cars for a week when he'll see me again. (November 22, 1989)

> Randa went to the doctor today. She has early signs of carpal tunnel. She is restricted from doing the toeboard insulator. . . . Half of Tom's team (Team 2) is down. Candy cannot do any kind of pinching motion or her hand goes immediately numb, and Tammy is on light duty. Ike is home with strep. (December 7, 1989)

> I saw Joan from the truck side in the bathroom this morning and she said that everyone on her team is now in splints (4 of them). . . . I know a lot of people in splints—the four on Joan's team, a woman right across from us on the truck finish line, two people on Tom's team, Karen, Randa, Mike and me. Plus there are many people I see

with them on that I simply don't know, or don't know what team they are on. (December 11, 1989)

Three of the men on our team have been to the doctor with wrist and thumb complaints, just as many as the women. (December 11, 1989)

I talked to Debbie on the truck line from my training class. She has splints on both arms. . . . Debbie used to be a line supervisor at a factory. She said that she now understands what the women under her went through with their carpal tunnel. The doctor told her she has it in one hand and is symptomatic in the other. He is sending her to physical therapy. (December 14, 1989)

Our team leader is going to go to the doctor tonight after work. She has been waking up all through the night with carpal tunnel symptoms (numbness in her hands). . . . Terry told me he is also going to go back to the doctor because his wrists are still bothering him. There are now two men with splints on from the door line. They are both big men. . . . Our team leader has never taken Karen off her station (the station where she sustained her wrist injury). (December 18, 1989)

Karen and Randa went in for checkups today; they are still in splints and Mindy (another team member) went in for the first time. Now she is also in splints. Randa told me that her friend Carey on the truck finish line is probably going to get splints also; her hands have been waking her up at night. . . . A third person is now wearing them on the door line. . . . I asked Steve from Team 2 how many people he thought were having wrist problems. He said he would guess that easily 25% are having problems, even if they haven't been put in splints. (December 20, 1989)

Candy from Team 2 experienced some of the earliest and most severe symptoms associated with hand injuries. She was one of the first to suffer pain and numbness in her hands, which continued for several weeks before she finally saw the company doctor. During that time, she said that she often complained to her team leader about pain and numbness, hoping that he would change her job or send her for medical help. Unfortunately, she did not realize—as none of us did at that time—that we had to ask to be seen by the doctor. No team leader that Team 1 members were aware of ever directed an Associate with a wrist or hand complaint to see the doctor without a specific request from the injured individual.

Candy finally sought help after she noticed someone from Team 1 in splints. Karen from Team 1 described to Candy how her hands were "falling asleep" at night and causing her to wake up. Once awake, she would shake them to get some feeling back. Finally, Karen saw a leaflet the company had distributed to our team and posted on a bulletin board, describing the symptoms associated with carpal tunnel syndrome. That was when she sought help. Karen asked our team leader to refer her to the company doctor and Candy followed her lead.

Nearly everyone with early carpal tunnel symptoms was put into splints and given anti-inflammatory medication. In addition, Candy wore isotoner support gloves to help control the swelling. Her injuries progressed to the point that with almost any movement, her hands became numb. Finally they began to fall asleep just hanging at her sides. Eventually, she had cortisone injected into each wrist and a few weeks later she was sent home on Worker's Compensation. She was called back a few times (once to the Paint department to inspect cars), but only on a temporary basis. After a few days in each job she would be sent home. Candy was afraid of losing her job but she was even more afraid of having permanently damaged her hands. No one seemed to be able to tell us what the long-term effects are from such injuries.

Debbie and Candy represented only a fraction of the workers who experienced hand and wrist injuries in Trim and Final. In our group alone, seven of twelve people on Team 1, three of nine from Team 2, and three people on the door line had such injuries. The man who took over Candy's station ended up in the same situation as hers: off work with hand injuries. All of these injuries occurred within a matter of weeks after SOP.

Needless to say, wrist injuries became a constant topic of conversation. Workers discussed them before work in the bathroom and on breaks, anxiously comparing notes on symptoms, diagnoses, and progress reports from the doctor. We discussed the pros and cons of the different types of splints and the exercises given for therapy. In addition to the injuries, the splints themselves were a cause of embarrassment and interfered with the normal routine of life outside of work. Getting them clean was a major concern. After being worn twenty-four hours a day, they smelled terrible. One woman said her husband was embarrassed to be seen in public with her while she wore splints— afraid people would think that he beat her. Another woman complained that the splints made it difficult to bathe her children, cook supper, or do any normal household chores.

Besides interfering with home life, splints also were an interference on the job. Some people even resorted to removing the splints at work because they slowed one down so much; people were afraid of not being able to keep up with the line. Others could not perform their jobs at all because their hands would no longer fit into tight places. Workers were afraid that their injuries would become more than an inconvenience and eventually progress into disabling conditions like Candy's. For her, it was not simply difficult or awkward to do

household chores; she was physically unable to cook, sweep, or do even the most minor task. The greatest fear, however, was not knowing what the long-term effects might be. As one young team member said: "When I'm finally a grandmother I want to be able to pick up my grandkids and do things for them. No job is worth giving up that."

Although the company attempted to cut back on the injury rate, Team 1 members were not impressed with its approach. On the surface, it appeared that the company was doing everything possible, but team members believed that it was only treating the symptoms, not the cause. The doctor tried to stress prevention and worked with many of us on programs for strengthening our hands. The company began talking to new workers during their training classes, warning them of the possibilities of injury and encouraging them to exercise their wrists and hands. Eventually, an occupational therapist was brought in to work with the injured. We were not dissatisfied with the company's medical response to our injuries. It was prevention that was weak. Strengthening one's hands was obviously important but we knew that the underlying causes of injury were greater than what could be addressed by physical strength.

The company hired an ergonomist to observe our work. He observed many of the jobs which were repeatedly causing injuries to our team. However, Team 1 never experienced any tangible evidence that such observations actually led to substantial changes in the structure or timing of our jobs. For example, he observed us installing the bulkhead harness, making the wiring connections for the dash and fuse box, installing the toeboard insulator, and putting in the rear wiring harness. All of these jobs were known to cause injury but only one change was ever made to any of them while I was there and it was made by a Japanese trainer, not by the ergonomist.

The job that was changed was the installation of the toeboard insulator. The problem with the toeboard was that the vendor manufacturing the toeboard for SIA was at one extreme of the tolerance for placing the holes in the toeboard, while the body shop welding the stud bolts that the holes fit over was at the opposite extreme. This meant that the burden of fit fell on three right and three left, the workers doing the installation. When the fit was really bad, installing the toeboard required a tremendous amount of twisting and straining and it was necessary to bend one's wrists backward to a sharp, unnatural angle in order to do the job. While that team member worked, she said, she could feel her wrists tingle under the stress.

The change to the toeboard installation was made by our Japanese kaizen trainer. His solution was to hang a heat lamp over the toeboards, making them more pliable. The heat lamps helped but were not a sufficient remedy. As the pile of toeboards went down, the lamps were farther away and less effective. Those of us with experience on that job suggested that the company send back those toeboards and make the vendor concentrate on designing a toeboard that fit the car, instead of making a line worker force the part to fit. (That did not happen while I was there.) After Randa was injured on the toeboard, our group leader filled out the accident report with her. His immediate solution to the problem: "Put a stronger Associate on the job." Randa's response: "Pretty soon, that 'strong' Associate will be on 'his' knees."

A work change suggestion made by the ergonomist and the company doctor involved the door assembly on the truck line. As a preventive measure, they provided splints to everyone doing that job and told people to wear these while they worked. In theory they had the right approach but it was an impractical and impossible solution.

People could not fit their hands inside the doors with the splints on! Even though the company seemed to have good intentions, the management approach to preventing injuries never penetrated the underlying causes. It tried to change people to fit the job, instead of making the job fit for people. Team members believed that line speedup, as well as repetition and stress, were the keys to the injury rate. As soon as the line began its steady speedup, the injury rate skyrocketed.

At first, a majority of workers with hand and wrist injuries seemed to be women; however, men soon experienced the same injuries. Nevertheless, since women appeared to be afflicted sooner and more often than men, a form of sexual harassment emerged which threatened to interfere further with safety. For example, in Paint, one of the men who operated a hand sprayer wore splints. Some of his male fellow workers in Paint said that he had "Corporal Klinger's disease," implying that the man was faking a woman's disease in order to get out of work. (A character from the movie and television program *MASH*, Corporal Klinger is a man who wears women's clothes in an attempt to be released from duty in the army.) Besides being stigmatizing, it was untrue. No one that any of us was aware of, aside from Candy, had ever been taken off the line because of having hands in splints and even she was not removed immediately. Faking carpal tunnel was not the road to an easier job.

Team 1's concern was that once carpal tunnel became a stigma, many men and women would be too embarrassed to seek help when their wrists were bothering them. In fact, it did take a great amount of encouragement from the rest of us before some of the injured men on Team 1 sought medical help, even though they were aware that they were experiencing symptoms associated with carpal tunnel. A woman from the truck line told me that her team leader made fun of another woman on the team because she had carpal tunnel. Her response was: "No matter how bad my hands hurt me, I will never go in to the doctor because of him." A woman from another team on the truck side had carpal tunnel in one wrist. She reported that her team leader told her: "The women at SIA are a bunch of weaklings and we should send them off to lift barbells for a few weeks."

In reality, both men and women were afflicted with hand and wrist injuries and eventually workers began to perceive this as a plant-wide problem. I asked one worker from Team 2 how widespread he thought the problem was. He believed that it was very widespread, stating: "I would guess that easily twenty-five percent [of the workforce] are having problems [with their wrists and hands]."

According to the company nurse, Trim and Final had by far the most hand complaints but she said these were increasing in other departments. While waiting for the doctor, sometimes we met people from other departments. One man from Body mentioned that he had been a welder for the last fifteen years. Since he came to SIA he developed what the doctor referred to as a "trigger finger." His hand was in a clenched position around his welding gun all day long and when he tried to open up his fingers, they did not move. While sitting in the doctor's office, he closed his fingers across his palm and then tried to open them; they jerked open about an inch and then closed up again. He was visibly shaken. Welding was his trade and he said he was worried that he had jeopardized it by coming to SIA.

During one of my visits to the company doctor, I talked to a man who worked in Body on the assembly line. His job was to hang doors on the trucks. He said that when he first started, the doors did not fit properly

and he had to use all the strength he could muster to push doors up and against each body to get the hinges to fit. He had pulled many of the muscles around his chest, which left him feeling weak all over. His main concern, however, was that his hands went numb after he fell asleep at night and this woke him up. He was not getting any sleep.

When I talked to the doctor, he seemed convinced that, for the most part, the injuries occurred because we were lacking in strength. During one examination I asked him if men got carpal tunnel as well as women, or if it was a "woman's disease." He assured me that there were plenty of men out there who were "out of shape" and not used to working at a physically demanding job.

One can understand how a lack of strength could contribute to injury; however, in many cases the injuries could be attributed to more specific conditions associated with the work process rather than to a worker's physical capacity. Consistently working with poorly fitting parts or working with wrists bent at unnatural angles created problems for workers' health regardless of their strength. Another common problem on both the car and truck sides was having to use one's thumbs to push plugs and clips into the vehicle bodies. In addition, there was the constant repetition, which seemed especially damaging when it involved small hand movements such as fitting nuts onto bolts with one's fingers.

At one point our Japanese trainer brought to work some "Japanese medicine" for our hands. Terry and I decided to try it during morning break. The trainer unwrapped a box of what appeared to be small cone-shaped incense candles. He placed them at certain points on our wrist and lit them with a match. We were told to leave them on while they heated up. He told us that these were what workers used in Japan to relieve their pains. They did not work for us, but then neither did aspirin after a while.

No matter how concerned about safety the company claimed to be, Team 1 could see no substantial improvement forthcoming. Jobs were not restructured or retimed and safety was our responsibility instead of the company's. SIA was unable to provide us with a "safe" workplace. It was not unsafe as regards common hazards, things that cause accidents and can easily be fixed; it was unsafe because of the work process itself. The repetition and speed of assembly line work was inherently harmful to workers. Any solutions that would reduce the work intensity created by repetition and line speed would threaten production quotas—something team members believed the company would never consider. Instead, we were left to our own devices of cobbling together makeshift tools and turning to each other for help. SIA might claim to be different from other companies but in terms of safety, the same forces that cause other automobile manufacturers to push their workers to the limit are at work at SIA. Providing a truly safe workplace is beyond their control in a competitive environment where the priority is quotas first rather than safety first.

Capitalist principles still operate in Japanese companies. Flexibility for the company does not begin to translate into flexibility for the workers. When we were hired at SIA, team members were asked to make a commitment to the company. However, ours was an ill-informed commitment. Team members could not have imagined the kind of effort they would expend while "working with others in a fast-paced environment," as the Subaru-Isuzu *Facts and Information* booklet put it. Nor could they envision the negative health effects that routine, expected work tasks would inflict on their bodies.

REFERENCES

Berggren, Christian. 1992. *Alternatives to Lean Production: Work Organization in the Swedish Auto Industry.* Ithaca, N.Y.: ILR Press.

Berggren, Christian, Torsten Bjorkman, and Ernst Hollander. 1991. *Are They Unbeatable? Report from a Field Trip to Study Transplants, the Japanese Owned Auto Plants in North America.* Stockholm: Royal Institute of Technology.

Cole, Robert, and Donald Deskins, Jr. 1988. "Racial Factor in Site Location and Employment Patterns of Japanese Auto Firms in America." *California Management Review* Fall: 9–22.

International Metalworkers Federation. 1992. *Toyota Motors towards 2000: A Report for Workers and Their Unions.* Toyota City, Japan: Toyota World Auto Council, May 27–29.

Kamata, Satoshi. 1982. *Japan in the Passing Lane.* New York: Pantheon Books.

Parker, Mike, and Jane Slaughter. 1988. *Choosing Sides: Unions and the Team Concept.* Boston: South End.

Subaru-Isuzu Automotive Inc. 1989. *SIA Associate Handbook.* August (first edition).

26

Over the Counter
McDonald's

Robin Leidner

Robin Leidner is associate professor of sociology at the University of Pennsylvania. Professor Leidner writes, "Before becoming a sociologist, I held a variety of jobs—cashier, waitress, actor—that involved interacting with the public and projecting a particular presentation of self. Perhaps that's why I was struck by how poorly many existing sociological theories of work fit the realities of service jobs. Routinizing such work presents unusual problems of autonomy, authenticity, and personal identity because there is no clear distinction between the product being sold and the person doing the work, giving employers a stake in controlling workers' ideas, moods, and personalities. Recently, I've continued to look at the rationalization of people's identities and interactions with others by studying how parents respond to advice about childrearing."

McDonald's

No one ever walks into a McDonald's and asks, "So, what's good today?" except satirically. The heart of McDonald's success is its uniformity and predictability. Not only is the food supposed to taste the same every day everywhere in the world, but McDonald's promises that every meal will be served quickly, courteously, and with a smile. Delivering on that promise over 20 million times a day in 54 countries is the company's colossal challenge (*McDonald's Annual Report* for 1990: 2). Its strategy for meeting that chal-

lenge draws on scientific management's most basic tenets: find the One Best Way to do every task and see that the work is conducted accordingly.

To insure that all McDonald's restaurants serve products of uniform quality, the company uses centralized planning, centrally designed training programs, centrally approved and supervised suppliers, automated machinery and other specially designed equipment, meticulous specifications, and systematic inspections. To provide its customers with a uniformly pleasant "McDonald's experience," the company also tries to mass-produce friendliness, deference, diligence, and good cheer through a variety of socialization and social control techniques. Despite sneers from those who equate uniformity with mediocrity, the success of McDonald's has been spectacular.

McFacts

By far the world's largest fast-food company, McDonald's has over 11,800 stores worldwide (*McDonald's Annual Report* for 1990: 1), and its 1990 international sales surpassed those of its three largest competitors combined (Berg 1991: sec. 3, 6) In the United States, consumer familiarity with McDonald's is virtually universal: the company estimates that 95 percent of U.S. consumers eat at a McDonald's at least once a year (Koepp 1987a: 58). McDonald's 1990 profits were $802.3 million, the third highest profits of any retailing company in the world (*Fortune* 1991: 179). At a time when the ability of many U.S. businesses to compete on the world market is in question, McDonald's continues to expand around the globe—most recently to Morocco—everywhere remaking consumer demand in its own image.

As politicians, union leaders, and others concerned with the effects of the shift to a service economy are quick to point out, McDonald's is a major employer. McDonald's restaurants in the United States employ about half a million people (Bertagnoli 1989a: 33), including one out of fifteen first-time job seekers (Wildavsky 1989: 30). The company claims that 7 percent of all current U.S. workers have worked for McDonald's at some time (Koepp 1987a: 59). Not only has McDonald's directly influenced the lives of millions of workers, but its impact has also been extended by the efforts of many kinds of organizations, especially in the service sector, to imitate the organizational features they see as central to McDonald's success.

For a company committed to standardization, McDonald's inspires strikingly varied reactions, both as an employer and as a cultural icon. On one side, Barbara Garson (1988), for instance, presents work at McDonald's as so systematized, automated, and closely monitored that all opportunity for thought, initiative, and human contact, let alone self-development, has been removed. To other critics, the ubiquity and uniformity of McDonald's epitomize the homogenization of U.S. culture and its imperialist export. At McDonald's, they point out, local culture is invisible and irrelevant, personal interactions are flattened into standardized patterns, and individual preferences are subordinated to efficient production. processes. Nutritionists scorn McDonald's menu, environmentalists its packaging.

However, McDonald's has been as widely admired as reviled. To its supporters, McDonald's represents efficiency, order, familiarity, good cheer, and good value. Many business writers hold McDonald's up as an example of excellence in service management (see, e.g., Heskett, Sasser, and Hart 1990; Peters and Austin 1985; Zemke with Schaaf 1989). A pioneer in the standardization and mass-production of food and service, the company is often represented as emblematic of American capitalist knowhow. It is a company whose phenomenal growth has resulted from steadfast commitment to its basic promise to customers of fast service, hot food, and clean restaurants.

The relentless standardization and infinite replication that inspire both horror and admiration are the legacy of Ray Kroc, a salesman who got into the hamburger business in 1954, when he was fifty-two years old, and created a worldwide phenomenon.[1] His inspiration was a phenomenally successful hamburger stand owned by the McDonald brothers of San Bernardino, California. He believed that their success could be reproduced consistently through carefully controlled franchises, and his hamburger business succeeded on an unprecedented scale. The basic idea was to serve a very few items of strictly uniform quality at low prices. Over the years, the menu has expanded somewhat and prices have risen, but the emphasis on strict, detailed standardization has never varied.

Kroc set out to achieve the kind of tight control over work routines and product quality that centralized production in factories makes possible, although the fast-food business is necessarily highly decentralized. Not only are the stores geographically dispersed, but approximately 75 percent of McDonald's outlets are owned by individual franchisees rather than by the corporation (*McDonald's Annual Report* for 1989: i). In his autobiography, Kroc describes how he approached the problem of combining standardization with decentralization (Kroc with Anderson 1977: 86):

> Our aim, of course, was to insure repeat business based on the system's reputation rather than on the quality of a single store or operator. This would require a continuing program of educating and assisting operators and a constant review of their performance. It would also require a full-time program of research and development. I knew in my bones that the key to uniformity would be in our ability to provide techniques of preparation that operators would accept because they were superior to methods they could dream up for themselves.

McDonald's franchise owners retain control over some matters, including pay scales, but the company requires that every store's production methods and products meet McDonald's precise specifications. The company encourages and enforces compliance with its standards in a variety of ways. The franchise agreements detail the obligations of both the owners and the corporation; the corporation requires that all potential owners go through its rigorous store-management training program; the corporation provides training materials for crew people and managers that include step-by-step instructions for every task in the store; raters from the corporation regularly visit franchises to evaluate their quality, service, and cleanliness; and

owners must purchase their equipment and food products from suppliers approved by the corporation. For those aspects of store operation not specifically covered by the franchise agreement, the corporation must persuade franchisees that they will maximize their profits by following the recommendations of the corporation. Given McDonald's phenomenal success, this persuasive power is considerable, as Kroc intended.

Luxenberg (1985: 77) writes that "Kroc introduced an extreme regimentation that had never been attempted in a service business." This regimentation is not limited to food-preparation techniques. McDonald's has standardized procedures for bookkeeping, purchasing, dealing with workers and customers, and virtually every other aspect of the business. But it is the assembly-line techniques used to produce and serve identical products in every McDonald's that are most salient for workers and most relevant to customers. These are the procedures designed to ensure that the food served to customers will be up to McDonald's standards and that customers will not have to wait more than a few minutes for their meal. The most comprehensive guide to corporate specifications for producing and serving "McDonald's quality" food is the "Operations and Training Manual"—McDonald's managers call it "the Bible"—which describes company procedures and standards in painstaking detail. Its 600 pages include, for instance, full-color photographs illustrating the proper placement of ketchup, mustard, and pickle slices on each type of hamburger on the menu. McDonald's stresses that these specifications are not arrived at arbitrarily, but are the accumulated fruits of years of experience and research. Franchise owners are kept up-to-date on corporate specifications by means of regularly issued bulletins.

Enforcement of McDonald's standards has been made easier over the years by the introduction of highly specialized equipment. Every company-owned store in the United States now has an "in-store processor," a computer system that calculates yields and food costs, keeps track of inventory and cash, schedules labor, and breaks down sales by time of day, product, and worker (*McDonald's Annual Report* for 1989: 29). In today's McDonald's, lights and buzzers tell workers exactly when to turn burgers or take fries out of the fat, and technologically advanced cash registers, linked to the computer system, do much of the thinking for window workers. Specially designed ketchup dispensers squirt exactly the right amount of ketchup on each burger in the approved flower pattern. The french-fry scoops let workers fill a bag and set it down in one continuous motion and help them gauge the proper serving size.

The extreme standardization of McDonald's products, and its workers, is closely tied to its marketing. The company advertises on a massive scale—in 1989, McDonald's spent $1.1 billion system-wide on advertising and promotions (*McDonald's Annual Report* for 1989: 32). In fact, McDonald's is the single most advertised brand in the world (*Advertising Age* 1990: 6). The national advertising assures the public that it will find high standards of quality, service, and cleanliness at every McDonald's store. The intent of the strict quality-control standards applied to every aspect of running a McDonald's outlet, from proper cleaning of the bathrooms to making sure the hamburgers are served hot, is to help franchise owners keep the promises made in the company's advertising.

The image of McDonald's outlets promoted in the company's advertising is one of fun, wholesomeness, and family orientation. Kroc was particularly concerned that his stores not become teen-age hangouts, since that would discourage families' patronage. To minimize their attractiveness to teenage loiterers, McDonald's stores do not have jukeboxes, video games, or even telephones. Kroc

initially decided not to hire young women to work behind McDonald's counters for the same reason: "They attracted the wrong kind of boys" (Boas and Chain 1976: 19). . . .

One McDonald's Franchise

I was assigned to a McDonald's in the downtown area of a small city near Chicago. It was a new store, only about fifteen months old when I began my fieldwork, but an exemplary one; it had recently won a major McDonald's award. The store was far more elegant than the average McDonald's. Adjacent to an expensive hotel, the restaurant was designed to seem "high-class," not garish or tacky. The interior decor included marble walls, a mahogany dining counter, black Art Deco fixtures, and mauve draperies. Outside were window boxes filled with flowers or greenery, and a relatively small Golden Arches sign, since the city council would not permit a large one.

This McDonald's differed from most in that it had neither a parking lot nor a drive-thru [sic] service window. It depended on pedestrian traffic for business, and its clientele included business people, college students, senior citizens, and shoppers. Fewer families came in than is typical for a McDonald's, and more people ordered just coffee or ice cream rather than a full meal; the average check size was accordingly smaller than at most McDonald's stores. At the time of my research in 1986, the store served 1,700 customers on an average day. In the course of a year, those customers collectively spent about one and a half million dollars. (The average McDonald's store brought in $1.34 million in 1985, half of it in drive-thru sales [training center lecture].)

The franchisee who owned the store owned three other McDonald's stores in the Chicago suburbs. The business had made him wealthy, and he proudly showed off a "new toy" to me, a Corvette convertible, complete with telephone. He also had a yacht. He, his wife, and some of their grown children were closely involved in running the store, coming in several times a week, planning improvements, and overseeing the operation. Such involvement is encouraged by the corporation, which wants all of its franchisees to be "owner/operators," not just investors.

This McDonald's store had five salaried managers, all male, three white and two black. The owner's son, another white, also worked as a manager on occasion. In addition, there were as many as five hourly swing managers at a time (all female; three black, one white, one Native American). During my fieldwork, two crew people, a black woman and an Asian man, were promoted to that level of management.

The store's crew fluctuated in size between sixty-five and about one hundred people in the course of six months; the store manager believed that eighty-five was optimal. There were about equal numbers of window workers and grill workers.

Personnel policies at McDonald's franchises, including pay scales, are determined by the franchise owners, not by the corporation. Many press reports have described fast-food franchises raising wages and offering benefits to compete for the declining number of teenage workers, but the crew at this franchise, both grill and window workers, started work at the federal minimum wage, $3.35 in 1986, and they received no benefits such as health insurance, paid holidays, or paid sick days. Merit raises of five or ten cents per hour were granted quarterly, when job performance reviews were made, and crew people promoted to crew trainer or crew chief received raises of five to fifteen cents per hour as well. The pay remained quite low, however. One crew trainer who had worked at the franchise for about a year and a half was earning $3.75.

Most, though not all, male crew members worked on the grill and most female crew members worked on the window. This pattern was usually based on managers' decisions when hiring workers. Some crew people reported having been given a choice about where they would start out, but more than half said that they had been assigned to their first job. A couple of crew people reported that the first women to be crosstrained to work on the grill had to persuade managers that they should be allowed to do so. In my interview sample of window people, 75 percent of the workers were women; according to the store's manager, this proportion accurately approximated the actual gender composition of the job category.

Salaried managers were expected to work forty-six to fifty hours per week. Officially, all of McDonald's crew workers are part-time, but 25 percent of my interview sample of window crew said that they usually worked thirty-five hours or more per week. The number of hours worked by crew people varied greatly, since many of them were students who only wished to work a few hours per week. Those who did want longer hours were expected to compete for them, proving themselves deserving through conscientious job performance. In practice, a core group of about twenty steady workers was sure to get its preferred hours, but cutting back an employee's hours was a standard way the managers showed their displeasure over poor job performance or attitude. The usual strategy for getting rid of poor workers, the store manager told me, was to decrease the hours they were scheduled to work until they got the message.

Through its scheduling practices McDonald's attempted to minimize labor costs without sacrificing speedy service for customers. As in almost all restaurants, McDonald's business normally came in waves rather than in a steady stream, with big rushes at meal times. On the one hand, managers did not want to have to pay crew people for hours they were not needed, since crew labor productivity is one of the main criteria by which managers are judged (Garson 1988: 32). On the other hand, they wanted to be sure to have enough people to keep lines moving quickly when business was brisk. The computerized cash-register system analyzed sales by hour of the day and day of the week, and managers used these figures to schedule work crews.

Since, however, computer projections are never entirely accurate, the schedules at this McDonald's were designed so that workers bore much of the burden of uncertainty. On the work schedule, posted one week in advance, a line for each crew person showed the hours she or he was scheduled to work. A solid line indicated hours the employee could count on working, and a zigzag line marked an additional hour or so. If the store was busy when a worker's guaranteed hours were finished, she or he would be required to work that extra time; if it was not busy, she or he would be asked to leave. In addition, it was quite common at unexpectedly quiet times for managers to tell workers they could leave before their scheduled hours were completed or even to pressure them to leave when they would rather have kept on working. I heard one manager say, "Come on, can't I make a profit today?" when a crew person resisted being sent home fifteen minutes early. Conversely, when the store was busy, managers were reluctant to let workers go when their scheduled hours, including the optional time, were done. When lines of people were waiting to be served, workers—I was one of them—would often have to ask repeatedly to be "punched out" (off the time clock) at the end of their shift.

Workers' preferences for longer or shorter hours varied; some wanted to earn as much as possible, others preferred to have more time for other activities. Whatever their preferences, the scheduling practices made it difficult for workers to plan ahead. Arrangements for transportation, social activities, child care, and so on could be disrupted by unexpected changes in the schedule, and workers could not accurately predict how much money they would earn in a given week. Furthermore, one of the most common complaints among the workers was that they had been scheduled to work at times they had said they were not available. Once on the schedule, they were held responsible for finding a replacement (see Garson 1988: 32–33). Since the McDonald's schedule was made up of such small units of time, however, it was usually relatively easy for workers to arrange hours for their convenience, an advantage McDonald's emphasized in recruitment. For example, workers who played on a high school team could cut down their hours during the sports season, and workers who needed to take a particular day off could usually arrange it if they gave sufficient notice.

The Interview Sample

Thirty-five percent of my sample was of high school age. (It is possible that I undersampled high school students simply because, since they were less likely to work many hours, I had less opportunity to meet them.) Although the majority of my sample (65 percent) were eighteen years old or over, 60 percent of the crew people told me that this was their first job.

The great majority of the crew people in the store were black, although blacks are a minority, albeit a large one, of the city's population. In my interview sample, 80 percent were black (including three Caribbean immigrants), one person was Hispanic-American, one was an Asian immigrant, and the rest were American-born white. A sizable minority of the workers commuted long distances, from the South Side and the West Side of Chicago. A full 25 percent of my sample had one-way commutes that took at least an hour and required at least one change of train, and I knew of several other workers with commutes at least that long. Given that the crew people started work at McDonald's at minimum wage, this pattern strongly suggests that these workers had been unable to find work near their homes or better-paying jobs elsewhere.

About two-thirds of the store's crew people were trained to work at the window. My sample of twenty-six window workers was not completely representative of all of the employees who worked behind the counter during the months I was there. Since my sampling method depended on my meeting the worker in the crew room, I probably oversampled those who worked relatively long or relatively steady hours and missed both those who worked only a few hours per week and those who worked for only a short time before quitting. I oversampled crew trainers and crew chiefs—30 percent of my sample had been promoted to one of these jobs. However, according to the store's manager, my sample was fairly representative of the store's population of customer-service workers in its gender, race, and age distributions. . . .

The Routine

McDonald's had routinized the work of its crews so thoroughly that decision making had practically been eliminated from the jobs. As one window worker told me, "They've tried to break it down so that it's almost idiot-proof." Most of the workers agreed that there was little call for them to use their own judgment on the job, since there were rules about everything. If an unusual problem arose, the workers were supposed to turn it over to a manager.

Many of the noninteractive parts of the window workers' job had been made idiot-proof through automation. The soda machines, for example, automatically dispensed the proper amount of beverage for regular,

medium, and large cups. Computerized cash registers performed a variety of functions handled elsewhere by human waitresses, waiters, and cashiers, making some kinds of skill and knowledge unnecessary. As a customer gave an order, the window worker simply pressed the cash register button labeled with the name of the selected product. There was no need to write the orders down, because the buttons lit up to indicate which products had been selected. Nor was there any need to remember prices, because the prices were programmed into the machines. Like most new cash registers, these added the tax automatically and told workers how much change customers were owed, so the window crew did not need to know how to do those calculations. The cash registers also helped regulate some of the crew's interactive work by reminding them to try to increase the size of each sale. For example, when a customer ordered a Big Mac, large fries, and a regular Coke, the cash register buttons for cookies, hot apple pies, ice cream cones, and ice cream sundaes would light up, prompting the worker to suggest dessert. It took some skill to operate the relatively complicated cash register, as my difficulties during my first work shift made clear, but this organizationally specific skill could soon be acquired on the job.

In addition to doing much of the workers' thinking for them, the computerized cash registers made it possible for managers to monitor the crew members' work and the store's inventory very closely. For example, if the number of Quarter Pounder with Cheese boxes gone did not match the number of Quarter Pounders with Cheese sold or accounted for as waste, managers might suspect that workers were giving away or taking food. Managers could easily tell which workers had brought in the most money during a given interval and who was doing the best job of persuading customers to buy a particular item. The computerized system could also complicate what would otherwise have been simple customer requests, however. For example, when a man who had not realized the benefit of ordering his son's food as a Happy Meal came back to the counter to ask whether his little boy could have one of the plastic beach pails the Happy Meals were served in, I had to ask a manager what to do, since fulfilling the request would produce a discrepancy between the inventory and the receipts. Sometimes the extreme systematization can induce rather than prevent idiocy, as when a window worker says she cannot serve a cup of coffee that is half decaffeinated and half regular because she would not know how to ring up the sale.[2]

The interactive part of window work is routinized through the Six Steps of Window Service and also through rules aimed at standardizing attitudes and demeanors as well as words and actions. The window workers were taught that they represented McDonald's to the public and that their attitudes were therefore an important component of service quality. Crew people could be reprimanded for not smiling, and often were. The window workers were supposed to be cheerful and polite at all times, but they were also told to be themselves while on the job. McDonald's does not want its workers to seem like robots, so part of the emotion work asked of the window crew is that they act naturally. "Being yourself" in this situation meant behaving in a way that did not seem stilted. Although workers had some latitude to go beyond the script, the short, highly schematic routine obviously did not allow much room for genuine self-expression.

Workers were not the only ones constrained by McDonald's routines, of course. The cooperation of service-recipients was crucial to the smooth functioning of the operation. In many kinds of interactive service work . . . constructing the compliance of service-recipients is an important part of the service worker's job. The routines such workers use may be designed to maximize the control each worker has over customers. McDonald's window workers' routines were not intended to give them much leverage over customers' behavior, however. The window workers interacted only with people who had already decided to do business with McDonald's and who therefore did not need to be persuaded to take part in the service interaction. Furthermore, almost all customers were familiar enough with McDonald's routines to know how they were expected to behave. For instance, I never saw a customer who did not know that she or he was supposed to come up to the counter rather than sit down and wait to be served. This customer training was accomplished through advertising, spatial design, customer experience, and the example of other customers, making it unnecessary for the window crew to put much effort into getting customers to fit into their work routines.

McDonald's ubiquitous advertising trains consumers at the same time that it tries to attract them to McDonald's. Television commercials demonstrate how the service system is supposed to work and familiarize customers with new products. Additional cues about expected customer behavior are provided by the design of the restaurants. For example, the entrances usually lead to the service counter, not to the dining area, making it unlikely that customers will fail to realize that they should get in line, and the placement of waste cans makes clear that customers are expected to throw out their own trash. Most important, the majority of customers have had years of experience with McDonald's, as well as with other fast-food restaurants that have similar arrangements. The company estimates that the average customer visits a McDonald's twenty times a year (Koepp 1987a: 58), and it is not uncommon for a customer to come in several times per week. For many customers, then, ordering at McDonald's is as routine an interaction as it is for the window worker. Indeed, because employee turnover is so high, steady customers may be more familiar with the work routines than the workers serving them are. Customers who are new to McDonald's can take their cue from more experienced customers.

Not surprisingly, then, most customers at the McDonald's I studied knew what was expected of them and tried to play their part well. They sorted themselves into lines and gazed up at the menu boards while waiting to be served. They usually gave their orders in the conventional sequence: burgers or other entrees, french fries or other side orders, drinks, and desserts. Hurried customers with savvy might order an item "only if it's in the bin," that is, ready to be served. Many customers prepared carefully so that they could give their orders promptly when they got to the counter. This preparation sometimes became apparent when a worker interrupted to ask, "What kind of dressing?" or "Cream and sugar?", flustering customers who could not deliver their orders as planned.

McDonald's routines, like those of other interactive service businesses, depend on the predictability of customers, but these businesses must not grind to a halt if customers are not completely cooperative. Some types of deviations from standard customer behavior are so common that they become routine themselves, and these can be handled through subroutines (Stinchcombe 1990b: 39). McDonald's routines work most efficiently when all customers accept their products exactly as they are usually prepared; indeed, the whole business is based on this premise. Since, however, some people give special instructions for customized products, such as "no onions," the routine allows for these exceptions. At the franchise I studied, workers could key the special requests into their cash registers, which automatically printed out "grill slips" with the instructions for the grill workers to follow. Under this system, the customer making the special order had to wait for it to be prepared, but the smooth flow of service for other customers was not interrupted. Another type of routine difficulty was customer dissatisfaction with food quality. Whenever a customer had a complaint about the food—cold fries, dried-out burger—window workers were authorized to supply a new product immediately without consulting a supervisor.

These two kinds of difficulties—special orders and complaints about food—were the only irregularities window workers were authorized to handle. The subroutines increased the flexibility of the service system, but they did not increase the workers' discretion, since procedures were in place for dealing with both situations. All other kinds of demands fell outside the window crew's purview. If they were faced with a dispute about money, an extraordinary request, or a furious customer, workers were instructed to call a manager; the crew had no authority to handle such problems.

Given the almost complete regimentation of tasks and preemption of decision making, does McDonald's need the flexibility and thoughtfulness of human workers? As the declining supply of teenagers and legislated increases in the minimum wage drive up labor costs, it is not surprising that McDonald's is experimenting with electronic replacements. So far, the only robot in use handles behind-the-scenes work rather than customer interactions. ARCH (Automated Restaurant Crew Helper) works in a Minnesota McDonald's where it does all the frying and lets workers know when to prepare sandwich buns, when supplies are running low, and when fries are no longer fresh enough to sell. Other McDonald's stores (along with Arby's and Burger King units) are experimenting with a touch-screen computer system that lets customers order their meals themselves, further curtailing the role of the window worker. Although it requires increased customer socialization and cooperation, early reports are that the system cuts service time by thirty seconds and increases sales per window worker 10–20 percent (Chaudhry 1989: F61).

Getting Workers to Work

The extreme routinization does not mean that McDonald's work is undemanding. I found that the company asked a lot of its workers, and the stresses of the job could be considerable. Especially when the store was busy, window work was extraordinarily hectic. From the grill area came the sounds of buzzers buzzing and people shouting instructions. Workers dashed from side to side behind the counter to pick up the various products they needed. Just getting around was extremely difficult. There might be six window workers, a manager or two overseeing the flow of food from the grill and backing up window workers, and another worker in charge of french fries, all trying to maneuver in a very small area, all hurrying, often carrying drinks, ice cream cones, stacks of burgers. Workers with pails of soapy water would frequently come to mop up the greasy floor, leaving it slippery and treacherous even for workers in the regulation nonskid shoes. Traffic jams formed around the soda machines and the salad cases. In the course of a shift various supplies would run out, and there would be no lids for the large cups, no clean trays, no Italian dressing, no ice, until someone found a moment to replenish the stock. Food products were frequently not ready when needed, frustrating window workers' efforts to gather their orders speedily—the supply of Big Macs in the food bin could be wiped out at any moment by a worker with an order for four of them, forcing several other workers to explain to their customers that they would have to wait for their food. The customers, of course, could be a major source of stress themselves. All in all, McDonald's work may be regarded as unskilled, but it was by no means easy to do

well. Window workers had to be able to keep many things in mind at once, to keep calm under fire, and to exhibit considerable physical and emotional stamina.

Even when the store was not crowded, workers were expected to keep busy, in accordance with the McDonald's slogan "If there's time to lean, there's time to clean." I was struck by how hard-working most of the crew people were:

> Matthew moves very fast, sweeps up whenever he has a spare moment. In fact, all of the crew people work like beavers—backing each other up, cleaning, etc.

Considering workers' low wages and limited stake in the success of the enterprise, why did they work so hard? Their intensity of effort was produced by several kinds of pressures. First, it seemed to me that most workers did conceive of the work as a team effort and were loath to be seen by their peers as making extra work for other people by not doing their share. Even workers who had what managers would define as a "bad attitude"—resentment about low wages, disrespectful treatment, or any other issue—might work hard in order to keep the respect of their peers.

Naturally, managers played a major role in keeping crew people hard at work. At this store, managers were virtually always present behind the counter and in the grill area. During busy periods several managers would be there at once, working side by side with the crew as well as issuing instructions. Any slacking off by a worker was thus very likely to be noticed. Managers insisted on constant effort; they clearly did not want to pay workers for a moment of nonproductive time. For instance, I heard a manager reprimand a grill worker for looking at the work schedule: "Are you off work? No? You look at the schedule on your time, not on my time." A handwritten sign was posted recommending that window workers come in fifteen minutes early to count out the money in their cash-register drawers on their own time so that, if the amount was wrong, they would not later be held responsible for a shortage. Crew trainers and crew chiefs were encouraged to let managers know about any workers who were shirking or causing problems.

The presence of customers on the scene was another major factor in intensifying workers' efforts. When long lines of people were waiting to be served, few workers had to be told to work as swiftly as possible. The sea of expectant faces provided a great deal of pressure to keep moving. Window workers in particular were anxious to avoid antagonizing customers, who were likely to take out any dissatisfactions on them. The surest way to keep people happy was to keep the lines moving quickly. The arrangement of the workplace, which made window workers clearly visible to the waiting customers as they went about their duties, and customers clearly visible to workers, was important in keeping crew people hard at work. This pressure could have an effect even if customers did not complain. For example, on the day I was to be trained to work window during breakfast, I spent quite a while standing behind the counter, in uniform, waiting to be given instructions and put to work. I was acutely aware that customers were likely to wonder why I did not take their orders, and I tried to adopt an air of attentive expectancy rather than one of casual loitering, in the hope that the customers would assume there was a good reason for my idleness.

These sorts of pressures were not the only reasons crew people worked hard and enthusiastically, however. Managers also tried to motivate them to strenuous efforts through positive means. The managers' constant presence meant that good work would not go unnoticed. McDonald's Corporation stresses the importance of acknowledging workers' efforts, and several workers men-

tioned that they appreciated such recognition. Indeed, I was surprised at how much it cheered me when a manager complimented me on my "good eye contact" with customers. Various incentive systems were in place as well, to make workers feel that it was in their individual interest to work hard. Free McDonald's meals (instead of the usual half-priced ones) and free record albums were some of the rewards available to good workers. Contests for the highest sales totals or most special raspberry milk shakes sold in a given hour encouraged window workers to compete in speed and pushiness. The possibility of promotion to crew trainer, crew chief, or swing manager also motivated some workers to work as hard as possible.

Group incentives seemed to be especially effective in motivating the crew. As part of a national advertising effort stressing service, all of the stores in McDonald's Chicago region competed to improve their speed. The owner of the store where I worked promised that if one of his stores came out near the top in this competition, the entire crew would be treated to a day at a large amusement park and the crew trainers would be invited for a day's outing on his yacht. The crew trainers and many other workers were very excited about this possibility and were willing to try to achieve unprecedented standards of speed. (They did not win the prize, but the crew of one of the owner's other stores did.) Some workers, though, especially the more disaffected ones, had no desire for either promotions or the low-cost rewards available and spoke derisively of them.

Managers also tried to make workers identify with the interests of the store, even when it clearly resulted in harder work for the same pay. At a monthly meeting for crew trainers, a manager acknowledged that workers were always asking why the store would not pay someone for an extra fifteen minutes to sweep up or do other such tasks not directly related to production, instead of making workers squeeze these tasks in around their main duties. He explained the importance to management of keeping labor costs down:

> "Say we use four extra hours a day—we keep extra people to [wash] the brown trays" or some other tasks. He reels off some calculations—"that's 120 hours a month, times—let's pay them the minimum wage—times twelve months. So that's 1,440 hours times $3.35, equals $4,825." There are oohs and ahs from the trainers—this sounds like a lot of money to them. I don't think it sounds like that much out of $1.5 million (which he had just said the store brought in annually). The manager went on, "So how do we get extra labor? By watching how we schedule. A $200 hour [an hour with $200 in sales], for instance, will go smoother with four window people, but three good people could do it. We save money, and then we can use it on other things, like training, for instance."

The crew trainers were willing to agree that it was only reasonable for the store to extract as much labor from them as possible, though resentments about overwork certainly did not disappear. The manager was also successful enough in getting the crew trainers to identify with management that they were willing to give the names of crew people who were uncooperative. . . .

For the most part, it seemed that sticking to corporate directives on proper management produced good results, while, predictably, more authoritarian and arbitrary interactions with staff produced resentment. The apparently respectful, even-handed, psychologistic management style that McDonald's encourages helped make the repetitive, fast-paced, low-autonomy, low-paid jobs tolerable to workers. Workers learned to accept even rules that were quite disadvantageous to them when they per-

ceived those rules to be fairly administered by people who regarded them as human beings. The official McDonald's stance was likely to anger workers, however, when, faced with customers who did not treat the crew as human beings, managers felt it was more important to satisfy the paying public than to defend the workers' dignity. . . .

Overview

. . . Most McDonald's work is organized as low-paying, low-status, part-time jobs that give workers little autonomy. Almost every decision about how to do crew people's tasks has been made in advance by the corporation, and many of the decisions have been built into the stores' technology. Why use human workers at all, if not to take advantage of the human capacity to respond to circumstances flexibly? McDonald's does want to provide at least a simulacrum of the human attributes of warmth, friendliness, and recognition. For that reason, not only workers' movements but also their words, demeanor, and attitudes are subject to managerial control.

Although predictability is McDonald's hallmark, not all factors can be controlled by management. One of the most serious irregularities that store management must deal with is fluctuation in the flow of customers, both expected and unexpected. Since personnel costs are the most manipulable variable affecting a store's profitability, managers want to match labor power to consumer demand as exactly as possible. They do so by paying all crew people by the hour, giving them highly irregular hours based on expected sales—sometimes including split shifts—and sending workers home early or keeping them late as conditions require. In other words, the costs of uneven demand are shifted to workers whenever possible. Since most McDonald's crew people cannot count on working a particular number of hours at precisely scheduled times, it is hard for them to make plans based on how much money they will earn or exactly what times they will be free. Workers are pressured to be flexible in order to maximize the organization's own flexibility in staffing levels. In contrast, of course, flexibility in the work process itself is minimized.

Routinization has not made the crew people's work easy. Their jobs, although highly structured and repetitive, are often demanding and stressful. Under these working conditions, the organization's limited commitment to workers, as reflected in job security, wages, and benefits, makes the task of maintaining worker motivation and discipline even more challenging. A variety of factors, many orchestrated by the corporation, keeps McDonald's crew people hard at work despite the limited rewards. Socialization into McDonald's norms, extremely close supervision (both human and electronic), individual and group incentives, peer pressure, and pressure from customers all play their part in getting workers to do things the McDonald's way. . . .

NOTES

1. Information about McDonald's history comes primarily from Boas and Chain 1976; Kroc with Anderson 1977; Love 1986; Luxenberg 1985; and McDonald's training materials. Reiter's (1991) description of Burger King reveals numerous parallels in the operation of the two companies, although Burger King, unlike McDonald's, is a subsidiary of a multinational conglomerate.

2. Thanks to Charles Bosk for this story.

REFERENCES

Advertising Age. 1990. "Adman of the Decade: McDonald's Fred Turner: Making All the Right Moves." (January 1): 6.

Boas, Max, and Steve Chain. 1976. *Big Mac: The Unauthorized Story of McDonald's.* New York: New American Library.

Braverman, Harry. 1974. *Labor and Monopoly Capital: The Degradation of Work in the Twentieth Century.* New York: Monthly Review Press.

Chaudhry, Rajan. 1989. "Burger Giants Singed by Battle." *Nation's Restaurant News* (August 7): F36.

Fortune. 1991. "Fortune Global Service 500: The 50 Largest Retailing Companies." (August 26): 179.

Goldman, Marshall. 1990. Presentation at colloquium on Reforming the Soviet Economy. University of Pennsylvania, May 17.

Heskett, James L., W. Earl Sasser, Jr., and Christopher W. L. Hart. 1990. *Service Breakthroughs: Changing the Rules of the Game.* New York: Free Press.

Howard, Robert. 1985. *Brave New Workplace.* New York: Viking.

Koepp, Stephen. 1987a. "Big Mac Strikes Back." *Time* (April 13): 58–60.

Kroc, Ray, with Robert Anderson. 1977. *Grinding It Out: The Making of McDonald's.* Chicago: Contemporary Books.

Love, John F. 1986. *McDonald's: Behind the Arches.* New York: Bantam Books.

Luxenberg, Stan. 1985. *Roadside Empires: How the Chains Franchised America.* New York: Viking.

McDonald's Annual Report Various years Oak Brook, Ill.

Peters, Tom, and Nancy Austin. 1985. *A Passion for Excellence: The Leadership Difference.* New York: Random House.

Reiter, Ester. 1991. *Making Fast Food: From the Frying Pan into the Fryer.* Montreal: McGill-Queen's University Press.

Wildavsky, Ben. 1989. "McJobs: Inside America's Largest Youth Training Program." *Policy Review* 49: 30–37.

Zemke, Ron, with Dick Schaaf. 1989. *The Service Edge: 101 Companies That Profit from Customer Care.* New York: NAL Books.

27

"Getting" and "Making" a Tip

Greta Foff Paules

Greta Foff Paules is a cultural anthropologist who received her Ph.D. from
Princeton University. This reading is drawn from her 1991 book, *Dishing It Out:
Power and Resistance among Waitresses in a New Jersey Restaurant.*

*The waitress can't help feeling a sense of per-
sonal failure and public censure when she is
"stiffed."*

—WILLIAM F. WHYTE, "WHEN WORKERS AND
CUSTOMERS MEET"

*They're rude, they're ignorant, they're obnox-
ious, they're inconsiderate. . . . Half these people don't deserve to come out and eat, let alone
try and tip a waitress.*

—ROUTE WAITRESS

Making a Tip at Route

A common feature of past research is that
the worker's control over the tipping system
is evaluated in terms of her efforts to con,
coerce, compel, or otherwise manipulate a
customer into relinquishing a bigger tip.
Because these efforts have for the most part
proven futile, the worker has been seen as
having little defense against the financial vicissitudes of the tipping system. What these
studies have overlooked is that an employee
can increase her tip income by controlling
the number as well as the size of tips she receives. This oversight has arisen from the

tendency of researchers to concentrate narrowly on the relationship between server
and served, while failing to take into account the broader organizational context in
which this relationship takes place.

Like service workers observed in earlier
studies, waitresses at Route strive to boost
the amount of individual gratuities by rendering special services and being especially
friendly. As one waitress put it, "I'll sell you
the world if you're in my station." In general
though, waitresses at Route Restaurant seek
to boost their tip income, not by increasing
the amount of individual gratuities, but by
increasing the number of customers they
serve. They accomplish this (a) by securing
the largest or busiest stations and working
the most lucrative shifts; (b) by "turning"
their tables quickly; and (c) by controlling
the flow of customers within the restaurant.

Technically, stations at Route are assigned on a rotating basis so that all waitresses, including rookies, work fast and slow
stations equally. Station assignments are
listed on the work schedule that is posted in
the office window where it can be examined
by all workers on all shifts, precluding the
possibility of blatant favoritism or discrimination. Yet a number of methods exist
whereby experienced waitresses are able to
circumvent the formal rotation system and
secure the more lucrative stations for themselves. A waitress can trade assignments

with a rookie who is uncertain of her ability to handle a fast station; she can volunteer to take over a large station when a *call-out* necessitates reorganization of station assignments;[1] or she can establish herself as the only waitress capable of handling a particularly large or chaotic station. Changes in station assignments tend not to be formally recorded, so inconsistencies in the rotation system often do not show up on the schedule. Waitresses on the same shift may notice of course that a co-worker has managed to avoid an especially slow station for many days, or has somehow ended up in the busiest station two weekends in a row, but the waitresses' code of noninterference . . . inhibits them from openly objecting to such irregularities.

A waitress can also increase her tip income by working the more lucrative shifts. Because day is the busiest and therefore most profitable shift at Route, it attracts experienced, professional waitresses who are most concerned and best able to maximize their tip earnings. There are exceptions: some competent, senior-ranking waitresses are unable to work during the day due to time constraints of family or second jobs. Others choose not to work during the day despite the potential monetary rewards, because they are unwilling to endure the intensely competitive atmosphere for which day shift is infamous.

The acutely competitive environment that characterizes day shift arises from the aggregate striving of each waitress to maximize her tip income by serving the greatest possible number of customers. Two strategies are enlisted to this end. First, each waitress attempts to *turn* her tables as quickly as possible. Briefly stated, this means she takes the order, delivers the food, clears and resets a table, and begins serving the next party as rapidly as customer lingering and the speed of the kitchen allow. A seven-year veteran of Route describes the strategy and its rewards:

What I do is I prebus my tables. When the people get up and go all I got is glasses and cups, pull off, wipe, set, and I do the table turnover. But see that's from day shift. See the girls on graveyard . . . don't understand the more times you turn that table the more money you make. You could have three tables and still make a hundred dollars. If you turn them tables.

As the waitress indicates, a large part of turning tables involves getting the table cleared and set for the next customer. During a rush, swing and grave waitresses tend to leave dirty tables standing, partly because they are less experienced and therefore less efficient, partly to avoid being given parties, or *sat*, when they are already behind. In contrast, day waitresses assign high priority to keeping their tables cleared and ready for customers. The difference in method reflects increased skill and growing awareness of and concern with money-making strategies.

A waitress can further increase her customer count by controlling the flow of customers within the restaurant. Ideally the hostess or manager running the front house rotates customers among stations, just as stations are rotated among waitresses.[2] Each waitress is given, or *sat*, one party at a time in turn so that all waitresses have comparable customer counts at the close of a shift. When no hostess is on duty, or both she and the manager are detained and customers are waiting to be seated, waitresses will typically seat incoming parties.

Whether or not a formal hostess is on duty, day waitresses are notorious for bypassing the rotation system by racing to the door and directing incoming customers to their own tables. A sense of the urgency with which this strategy is pursued is conveyed in the comment of one five-year veteran, "They'll run you down to get that person at the door, to seat them in their station." The competition for customers is so intense during the day that some waitresses claim they cannot afford to leave the floor (even to use the restroom) lest they return to find a co-worker's station filled at their expense. "In the daytime, honey," remarks an eight-year Route waitress, "in the daytime it's like pulling teeth. You got to stay on the floor to survive. To survive." It is in part because they do not want to lose customers and tips to their co-workers that waitresses do not take formal breaks. Instead, they rest and eat between waiting tables or during lulls in business, returning to the floor intermittently to check on parties in progress and seat customers in their stations.

The fast pace and chaotic nature of restaurant work provide a cover for the waitress's aggressive pursuit of customers, since it is difficult for other servers to monitor closely the allocation of parties in the bustle and confusion of a rush. Still, it is not uncommon for waitresses to grumble to management and co-workers if they notice an obvious imbalance in customer distribution. Here again, the waitress refrains from directly criticizing her fellow servers, voicing her displeasure by commenting on the paucity of customers in her own station, rather than the overabundance of customers in the stations of certain co-waitresses. In response to these grumblings, other waitresses may moderate somewhat their efforts to appropriate new parties, and management may make a special effort to seat the disgruntled server favorably.

A waitress can also exert pressure on the manager or hostess to keep her station filled. She may, for instance, threaten to leave if she is not seated enough customers.

I said, "Innes [a manager], I'm in [station] one and two. If one and two is not filled at all times from now until three,

I'm getting my coat, my pocketbook, and I'm leaving." And one and two was filled, and I made ninety-five dollars.

Alternatively, she can make it more convenient for the manager or hostess to seat her rather than her co-workers, either by keeping her tables open (as described), or by taking extra tables. If customers are waiting to be seated, a waitress may offer to pick up parties in a station that is closed or, occasionally, to pick up parties in another waitress's station.[3] In attempting either strategy, but especially the latter, the waitress must be adept not only at waiting tables, but in interpersonal restaurant politics. Autonomy and possession are of central concern to waitresses, and a waitress who offers to pick up tables outside her station must select her words carefully if she is to avoid being accused of invading her co-workers' territory. Accordingly, she may choose to present her bid for extra parties as an offer to help—the manager, another waitress, the restaurant, customers—rather than as a request.

The waitress who seeks to increase her tip income by maximizing the number of customers she serves may endeavor to cut her losses by refusing to serve parties that have stiffed her in the past. If she is a low-ranking waitress, her refusal is likely to be overturned by the manager. If she is an experienced and valuable waitress, the manager may ask someone else to take the party, assure the waitress he will take care of her (that is, pad the bill and give her the difference), or even pick up the party himself. Though the practice is far from common, a waitress may go so far as to demand a tip from a customer who has been known to stiff in the past.

This party of two guys come in and they order thirty to forty dollars worth of food . . . and they stiff us. Every time. So Kaddie told them, "If you don't tip us, we're not going to wait on you." They said, "We'll tip you." So Kaddie waited on them, and they tipped her. The next night they came in, I waited on them and they didn't tip me. The third time they came in [the manager] put them in my station and I told [the manager] straight up, "I'm not waiting on them . . ." So he made Hailey pick them up. And they stiffed Hailey. So when they came in the next night . . . [they] said, "Are you going to give us a table?" I said, "You going to tip me? I'm not going to wait on you. You got all that money, you sell all that crack on the streets and you come here and you can't even leave me a couple bucks?" . . . So they left me a dollar. So when they come in Tuesday night, I'm telling them a dollar ain't enough.

The tactics employed by waitresses, and particularly day-shift waitresses, to increase their customer count and thereby boost their tip earnings have earned them a resounding notoriety among their less competitive co-workers. Day (and some swing) waitresses are described as "money hungry," "sneaky little bitches," "self-centered," "aggressive," "backstabbing bitches," and "cutthroats over tables." The following remarks of two Route waitresses, however, indicate that those who employ these tactics see them as defensive, not aggressive measures. A sense of the waitress's preoccupation with autonomy and with protecting what is hers also emerges from these comments.

You have to be like that. Because if you don't be like that, people step on you. You know, like as far as getting customers. I mean, you know, I'm sorry everybody says I'm greedy. I guess that's why I've survived this long at Route. Cause I am greedy. . . . *I want what's mine,* and if it comes down to me cleaning your table or my table, I'm going to clean my table. Because see I went through all that stage where I

would do your table. To be fair. And you would walk home with seventy dollars, and I'd have twenty-five, cause I was being fair all night. (emphasis added)

If the customer comes in the door and I'm there getting that door, don't expect me to cover your backside while you in the back smoking a cigarette and I'm here working for myself. You not out there working for me. . . . When I go to the door and get the customers, when I keep my tables clean and your tables are dirty, and you wonder why you only got one person . . . then that's just tough shit. . . . You're damn right my station is filled. *I'm not here for you.* (emphasis added)

Whether the waitress who keeps her station filled with customers is acting aggressively or defensively, her tactics are effective. It is commonly accepted that determined day waitresses make better money than less competitive co-workers even when working swing or grave. Moreover Nera, the waitress most infamous for her relentless use of "money-hungry tactics," is at the same time most famous for her consistently high daily takes. While other waitresses jingle change in their aprons, Nera is forced to store wads of bills in her shoes and in paper bags to prevent tips from overflowing her pockets. She claims to make a minimum of five hundred dollars a week in tip earnings; her record for one day's work exceeds two hundred dollars and is undoubtedly the record for the restaurant.

Inverting the Symbolism of Tipping

It may already be apparent that the waitress views the customer—not as a master to pamper and appease—but as substance to be processed as quickly and in as large a quantity as possible. The difference in perspective is expressed in the objectifying terminology of waitresses: a customer or party is referred to as a *table,* or by table number, as *table five* or simply *five;* serving successive parties at a table is referred to as *turning the table;* taking an order is also known as *picking up a table;* and to serve water, coffee, or other beverages is to *water, coffee,* or *beverage* a table, number, or customer. Even personal acquaintances assume the status of inanimate matter, or tip-bearing plants, in the language of the server:

> I got my fifth-grade teacher [as a customer] one time. . . . I kept her coffeed. I kept her boyfriend coked all night. Sodaed. . . . And I kept them filled up.

If the customer is perceived as material that is processed, the goal of this processing is the production or extraction of a finished product: the tip. This image too is conveyed in the language of the floor. A waitress may comment that she "got a good tip" or "gets good tips," but she is more likely to say that she "made" or "makes good tips." She may also say that she "got five bucks out of" a customer, or complain that some customers "don't want to give up on" their money. She may accuse a waitress who stays over into her shift of "tapping on" her money, or warn an aspiring waitress against family restaurants on the grounds that "there's no money in there." In all these comments (and all are actual), the waitress might as easily be talking about mining for coal or drilling for oil as serving customers.

Predictably, the waitress's view of the customer as substance to be processed influences her perception of the meaning of tips, and especially substandard tips. At Route, low tips and stiffs are not interpreted as a negative reflection on the waitress's personal qualities or social status. Rather, they are felt to reveal the refractory nature or poor quality of the raw material from which the tip is extracted, produced,

or fashioned. In less metaphorical terms, a low tip or stiff is thought to reflect the negative qualities and low status of the customer who is too cheap, too poor, too ignorant, or too coarse to leave an appropriate gratuity. In this context, it is interesting to note that *stiff,* the term used in restaurants to refer to incidents of nontipping or to someone who does not tip, has also been used to refer to a wastrel or penniless man (Partridge 1984), a hobo, tramp, vagabond, deadbeat, and a moocher (Wentworth and Flexner 1975).

Evidence that waitresses assign blame for poor tips to the tipper is found in their reaction to being undertipped or stiffed. Rather than breaking down in tears and lamenting her "personal failure," the Route waitress responds to a stiff by announcing the event to her co-workers and managers in a tone of angry disbelief. Co-workers and managers echo the waitress's indignation and typically ask her to identify the party (by table number and physical description), or if she has already done so, to be more specific. This identification is crucial for it allows sympathizers to join the waitress in analyzing the cause of the stiff, which is assumed a priori to arise from some shortcoming of the party, not the waitress. The waitress and her co-workers may conclude that the customers in question were rude, troublemakers, or bums, or they may explain their behavior by identifying them as members of a particular category of customers. It might be revealed for instance, that the offending party was a church group: church groups are invariably tightfisted. It might be resolved that the offenders were senior citizens, Southerners, or businesspeople: all well-known cheapskates. If the customers were European, the stiff will be attributed to ignorance of the American tipping system; if they were young, to immaturity; if they had children, to lack of funds.

These classifications and their attendant explanations are neither fixed nor trustworthy. New categories are invented to explain otherwise puzzling incidents, and all categories are subject to exception. Though undependable as predictive devices, customer typologies serve a crucial function: they divert blame for stiffs and low tips from the waitress to the characteristics of the customer. It is for this reason that it is "important" for workers to distinguish between different categories of customers, despite the fact that such distinctions are based on "unreliable verbal and appearance clues." In fact, it is precisely the unreliability, or more appropriately the flexibility, of customer typologies that makes them valuable to waitresses. When categories can be constructed and dissolved on demand, there is no danger that an incident will fall outside the existing system of classification and hence be inexplicable.

While waitresses view the customer as something to be processed and the tip as the product of this processing, they are aware that the public does not share their understanding of the waitress–diner–tip relationship. Waitresses at Route recognize that many customers perceive them as needy creatures willing to commit great feats of service and absorb high doses of abuse in their anxiety to secure a favorable gratuity or protect their jobs. They are also aware that some customers leave small tips with the intent to insult the server and that others undertip on the assumption that for a Route waitress even fifty cents will be appreciated. One waitress indicated that prior to being employed in a restaurant, she herself subscribed to the stereotype of the down-and-out waitress "because you see stuff on television, you see these wives or single ladies who waitress and they live in slummy apartments or slummy houses and they dress in rags." It is these images of neediness and desperation, which run so strongly

against the waitress's perception of herself and her position, that she attacks when strained relations erupt into open conflict.

> Five rowdy black guys walked in the door and they went to seat themselves at table seven. I said, "Excuse me. You all got to wait to be seated." "We ain't got to do *shit*. We here to eat. . . ." So they went and sat down. And I turned around and just looked at them. And they said, "Well, I hope you ain't our waitress, cause you blew your tip. Cause you ain't getting nothing from us." And I turned around and I said, "You need it more than I do, baby."

This waitress's desire to confront the customer's assumption of her destitution is widely shared among service workers whose status as tipped employees marks them as needy in the eyes of their customers. Davis (1959:162–63) reports that among cabdrivers "a forever repeated story is of the annoyed driver, who, after a grueling trip with a Lady Shopper, hands the coin back, telling her, 'Lady, keep your lousy dime. You need it more than I do.'" Mars and Nicod (1984:75) report a hotel waitress's claim that "if she had served a large family with children for one or two weeks, and then was given a 10p piece, she would give the money back, saying, 'It's all right, thank you, I've got enough change for my bus fare home.'" In an incident I observed (not at Route), a waitress followed two male customers out of a restaurant calling, "Excuse me! You forgot this!" and holding up the coins they had left as a tip. The customers appeared embarrassed, motioned for her to keep the money, and continued down the sidewalk. The waitress, now standing in the outdoor seating area of the restaurant and observed by curious diners, threw the money after the retreating men and returned to her work. Episodes such as these allow the worker to repudiate openly the evaluation of her financial status that is implied in an offensively small gratuity, and permit her to articulate her own understanding of what a small tip says and about whom. If customers can only afford to leave a dime, or feel a 10p piece is adequate compensation for two weeks' service, they must be very hard up or very ignorant indeed.

In the following incident the waitress interjects a denial of her neediness into an altercation that is not related to tipping, demonstrating that the customer's perception of her financial status is a prominent and persistent concern for her.

> She [a customer] wanted a California Burger with mayonnaise. And when I got the mayonnaise, the mayonnaise had a little brown on it. . . . So this girl said to me, she said, "What the fuck is this you giving me?" And I turned around, I thought, "Maybe she's talking to somebody else in the booth with her." And I turned around and I said, "Excuse me?" She said, "You hear what I said. I said, "What the fuck are you giving me?" And I turned around, I said, "I don't know if you're referring your information to *me*," I said, "but if you're referring your information to *me*," I said, "I don't *need* your bullshit." I said, "I'm not going to even take it. . . . Furthermore, I could care less if you eat or *don't* eat. . . . And you see this?" And I took her check and I ripped it apart. . . . And I took the California Burger and I says, "You don't have a problem anymore now, right?" She went up to the manager. And she says, "That black waitress"—I says, "Oh. By the way, what is my name? I don't have a name, [using the words] 'that black waitress'. . . . My name happens to be Nera. . . . That's N-E-R-A. . . . And I don't need your bullshit, sweetheart. . . . People like you I can walk on, because you don't know how to talk to human beings." And

I said, "I don't need you. I don't need your quarters. I don't need your nickels. I don't need your dimes. So if you want service, be my guest. Don't you *ever* sit in my station, cause I won't wait on you." The manager said, "Nera, please. Would you wait in the back?" I said, "No. I don't take back seats no more for nobody."

In each of these cases, the waitress challenges the customer's definition of the relationship in which tipping occurs. By speaking out, by confronting the customer, she demonstrates that she is not subservient or in fear of losing her job; that she is not compelled by financial need or a sense of social hierarchy to accept abuse from customers; that she does not, in Nera's words, "take back seats no more for nobody." At the same time, she reverses the symbolic force of the low tip, converting a statement on her social status or work skills into a statement on the tipper's cheapness or lack of savoir faire.

Symbolic Dimensions of Tipping

Of 1.5 million restaurant servers employed in the United States, 90 percent are women who receive at least two-thirds of their earnings in the form of gratuities (Butler and Skipper 1980:489). For some waitresses the fact that tips have traditionally gone un- or underreported and therefore un- or undertaxed contributes to their economic appeal, despite the adverse consequences of underreporting for social security and unemployment benefits (L. Howe 1977:123). For others, the immediacy of tipping income is its central redeeming factor. "Waiting and waitressing is a MAC card," a Route waiter commented. "You walk in, you punch in your five hours of work, you walk out, you got forty bucks in your hand." For those whose financial needs are often small but urgent, the fast cash factor of the tipping system may be more valuable than the security of a steady weekly wage. This was the case for a seventeen-year-old hostess at Route who justified her demand to be trained for the floor partly on the grounds that if she were a waitress, whenever her baby needed something (Pampers, for example), she could come in and make the money by the end of her shift.

But a tip is more than payment for service rendered; it is a potent symbol capable of evoking a profound sense of triumph or provoking an angry blitz of expletives. It is, moreover, a symbol that embodies in coarse, even vulgar material form the myriad whisperings of power and control that pervade the server–served relationship. . . .

In drawing attention to the waitress's ability to subvert this complex and potentially degrading symbolism and moderate the financial risks of tipping, my purpose has been to demonstrate the waitress's power of resistance, her spirit of defiance, and her ability to manipulate her work environment to protect her interests. It has not been my intention to question the exploitive nature of a system of compensation that compels women to compete against one another to secure a fair wage, and absolves employers from responsibility for the economic security of workers from whose labor they profit. Nor has it been the aim of this discussion to suggest that waitresses are immune to the financial and emotional dangers of the tipping system. However skillfully the waitress maximizes her customer count, she remains vulnerable to the vicissitudes of the food service industry. Route servers suffered periodic drops in their tip income because of seasonal fluctuations in customer volume and unexpected slumps in business, as when the restaurant stood nearly empty for three weeks while road construction obscured the entrance to the parking lot. Likewise, though waitresses blame their customers and not themselves

for low tips, being stiffed or undertipped remains an emotionally taxing experience. At Route as elsewhere, the failure of a customer to provide adequate compensation for service was the frequent cause of impassioned outbursts. Nonetheless, throughout the course of research and in five years' prior experience waiting tables, I never encountered a waitress who interpreted a bad tip as a "personal failure." What tears were shed were shed in anger, not in self-rebuke.

NOTES

1. *Call-out:* an employee calls the restaurant to say she will not be coming to work because of sickness, transportation problems, or a personal emergency. Employees often call out shortly before they are supposed to start work, or after their scheduled shift has begun, making it difficult for management to find replacements in time.

2. *Front house:* area of restaurant open to customers, including the floor, the register and waiting area, and the customer restrooms. The back house comprises all areas to which the public does not have access, including the kitchen, dish room, managers' office, stockroom, main waitresses' station, and employee break room and restrooms. To *run the front house* is primarily to perform the duties of hostess, though the expression carries supervisory connotations.

3. *Pick up:* to take the order from or wait on a party.

REFERENCES

Butler, Suellen, and James K. Skipper, Jr. 1980. "Waitressing, Vulnerability, and Job Autonomy: The Case of the Risky Tip." *Sociology of Work and Occupations* 7(4):487–502.

Davis, Fred. 1959. "The Cabdriver and His Fare: Facets of a Fleeting Relationship." *American Journal of Sociology* 65(2):158–65.

Mars, Gerald, and Michael Nicod. 1984. *The World of Waiters.* London: George Allen & Unwin.

Wentworth, Harold, and Stuart Berg Flexner, eds. and comps. 1975. *Dictionary of American Slang.* 2d supplemental ed., s.v. "stiff." New York: Thomas Y. Crowell Co.

28

Between Women
Domestics and Their Employers

Judith Rollins

Judith Rollins is currently professor of africana studies and sociology at Wellesley College. The following excerpt is from her 1985 book, *Between Women: Domestics and Their Employers,* which received the Jessie Bernard Award of the American Sociological Association for its contribution to women's studies. She writes, "Examining this topic allowed me to explore the social psychology of domestic service, an occupation that has been a significant one for American women since the nineteenth century, and a situation where factors of class, race, and gender intersect." Professor Rollins published articles on the ideological role of domestic service, the Civil Rights Movement, and the American Women's Movement. Recently, she has been involved in "biography as sociology" and has completed an oral history with an elderly Louisiana woman: *All Is Never Said: The Narrative of Odette Harper Hines,* which was published by Temple University Press in 1995.

The Labor

Northern employers have a week's work cut out for you for a day or half a day. They pay you good but nine times out of ten you've got to take that money and go to the doctor with it.

Cleaning is indeed hard on the body. The older domestics I interviewed[1] had various physical ailments associated with their work: lower back problems, varicose veins, and, most common, ankle and foot problems. Two had switched to childcare and cooking because they were less tiring. In the early part of this century, black women frequently became laundresses and, according to the three women in my study who had done such work, this was the most physi-

cally demanding task of all. Washing machines may have replaced laundresses and other technology may have shortened and lightened other household tasks, but scrubbing floors, ironing, vacuuming with often outdated and heavy machines, and cleaning out closets for four to eight hours at a time remain exhausting work. When riding the trolley and bus home from my domestic jobs, I saw other domestics—usually older women—with a profound and sad, hollow-eyed weariness on their faces, often fighting sleep, ankles swollen, having lost the energy and sociability of the morning's ride to work. My own exhaustion debilitated me for a period of time every evening I worked a full day. And although it may be justly claimed that my previous academic life had hardly prepared me for any kind of all-day physical labor, my reaction was not at all unique. Forty-four-year-old Julia Henry explained why she stopped working for a family in Brookline after three months:

It was too much work from the beginning. It was two days' work in one. I was washing clothes, ironing. Then I had to do two bathrooms, three bedrooms, vacuum. I'd be so tired. I'd come home. I couldn't go anywhere except to bed. It really wasn't worth it. I told her I couldn't do it all in one day. I finally left.

Esther Jones describes the woman she has worked for for eighteen years:

She's a driver. Seems like that's where she gets her therapy from—working you. She likes to *work you*. Seems like the harder she works you the better she feels. She just keeps giving you more and more work, telling you what to do and how to do it. That's the reason today I require a lot of rest.

When she interviewed me she told me I'd get a two-hour rest every afternoon. But once I started working, she tried to stop me from doing that by telling me to do things. She just likes to see you work!

Four years earlier, Ms. Jones had to have an operation on her ankle. When her doctor advised her against returning to domestic work, this employer suggested she go on welfare. Unwilling to do that, Ms. Jones returned to the same employer, now working full-time, live-out, rather than live-in as before the operation.

Other domestics and a few employers also said that employers liked to see domestics working. Employer Margaret Slater described her displeasure at her worker's inactivity this way: "She really was very good. The only thing that annoyed me was when I would come home and find her sitting down. She'd be just playing with the kids or something. All the cleaning would be finished but it still bothered me to see her sitting." Retired domestic Anne Ryder remembered a time in the 1940's in Cambridge when she was so exhausted she lay on the kitchen floor in the middle of the day. When her employer came in, Ms. Ryder said, "'I'm tired and if you say one word to me I'm going to get up and go home.' 'Oh,' [the employer] said, 'you rest yourself and come and get something to drink.' But, you know, as soon as I had that drink, she had something else for me to do." And May Lund, talking about one of her early day-work experiences in the 1960's, described a pattern I repeatedly encountered in my domestic work:

The ad stated, "light housekeeping." When I went there she said, "Oh, just take the damp mop and run over the kitchen floor and make the beds and dust and this, that and the other." When I got finished, I said, "Oh, wow, this is not bad. I like this!" And then I go back the next week: "When you dust the furniture, put a little polish on that too." Then you go back the next week and: "Oh, would you just throw the clothes in the washer and dryer?" And every week you go back, they're adding more and more and more. And then it was a struggle, I mean it was a *job,* a *race* to get everything done in that eight hours. Every time you go there, there's something else added.

Few of the employers I interviewed mentioned the physical demands of the work. Fifty-five-year-old Frances Stewart related this story about a young Jamaican woman she had imported to be a live-in servant in Chestnut Hill:

Oh, a funny thing. I thought she must be very homesick. She'd brought up rum and we noticed she was using a *lot* of rum. We wondered if she had a drinking problem. But it turned out she was rubbing her muscles with it [laughter] so they wouldn't tire so much.

And sixty-eight-year-old Marna Houston, who has always done most of her own housework herself, employing help only when her children were small and recently since she's been ill, expresses her understanding of the amount of work involved both in the salary she pays (ten dollars an hour to an Italian-American woman) and in these statements:

> Well, the good thing about it is the independence. One can change jobs easily; you're not tied down by benefits. But the bad part is the labor itself. It can be *hard* physical labor. And, sometimes, there's no gratitude and very poor pay. I think the low prestige of the job is because of the low pay and menial nature of the work. It's really too bad.

Of my ten employers, only one—a Greek-American woman from a working-class background—was what I considered reasonable and realistic in her expectations. The others, to varying degrees, always demanded more than any one person could accomplish in the given time. At first I actually tried to do everything and would feel frustration as well as exhaustion at my failure; in time I realized that their being overdemanding was the norm and paced myself more wisely. One employer fired me for not working fast enough; the others seemed to expect that I would not complete everything they had asked be done. But seeing me breathing hard, perspiring, and visibly weary never prompted any employer to suggest I take a break—not even when I worked an eight-hour day (with a half-hour for lunch). And this apparently is typical: none of the domestics I talked with took breaks in addition to their lunch. Those working only four or five hours in one house did not stop at all. After a while, I began taking ten-minute breaks in the morning and afternoon on my eight-hour days—incurring reactions ranging from approval to pointed glares. On one occasion, when I sat down to eat an apple after working particularly hard from 9:00 A.M. to 12:30 P.M., the husband of my employer made his disapproval clear. My field notes read as follows:

> It was 12:30 and I, weary and hungry, decided to take a short break and have lunch later. Since he [a fifty-five-year-old psychiatrist] was on the phone in the kitchen, I sat in the dining area, ate an apple I had brought and read a magazine. He could hear me but not see me. As soon as he got off the phone, he walked a roundabout route to go upstairs, apparently so he could see what I was doing. Walking by slowly, he literally glared at me. I smiled slightly; he did not return the smile, seeming to want to make it clear he was checking me out and disapproved of my not working. He glared, said nothing, continued upstairs. I resumed work after about ten minutes.

But the reader should be reminded that my taking breaks was entirely out of the ordinary for this occupation; the morning and afternoon breaks other blue-collar workers take for granted are practically unknown in household work.

Like former domestic Elizabeth Roy, whose quote opens this section on work, many of the women who had worked in both the North and South commented that Northern employers worked domestics harder. They attributed it to Northerners' being less caring and paying more. When most forms of private household work were included in minimum-wage legislation (1974), Northern employers reacted by raising the salaries to at least the legal minimum but cutting back hours. (The day-work salaries of the 1960's, according to the domestic interviewees, ranged from 60¢ to $1.65 an hour in the Boston area.) While decreasing hours, however, employers did not decrease the amount of work they wanted done. And the crunch was on. Elizabeth Roy explains it this way:

Any time you do "day work," you make more than a regular five days a week in one place—because some of the people will want you to do a whole week's work in one day! You make more money but it's not worth it. You really have to break your neck.

You'd be surprised at the mess some of these people leave. It's really bad. I went out to Newton one day and I tell you! She wanted the *whole house* cleaned in one day. And it was awful—dust you could sprout any kind of seeds in! She wanted the windows, the blinds, everything done. I told her I'd do what I could.

She didn't want me to come back after I put the price to her: $35 for the day. [That's the price she'd been told on the phone] but she probably thought I'd do it for less. They con some of our people with old clothes and stuff. And the people coming from the [West Indian] Islands, they're really being exploited!

Note that Ms. Roy, a former vulnerable and exploited migrant from the South who has since become a matron in a state-run women's shelter, is conscious of the fact that today it is foreign-born Third World women who are "really being exploited." And domestic May Lund describes the change to partial days similarly:

You see, what happened was, the people cut down the hours. They generally don't want you more than four or five hours a day. Only one lady I worked for eight hours a day. Just one lady. The people cannot afford to pay you. . . . Even though, back then, you worked eight hours and got ten dollars—they got the whole house cleaned.

Another element of domestic service that too often adds to the physical demands of the work is the poor quality of the equipment supplied by the employers. I found this

statement by May Lund to be true in over half of the houses in which I worked: "Some of the equipment you work with, you don't know if it will make it from one cleaning to the next." Dilapidated, outdated, or very cheap equipment forces the worker to compensate for its ineffectiveness with extra physical effort. In a split-level ranch house in Needham, I was asked to scour kitchen counter tops, stove, and sink using only bar soap and cotton rags. In a luxurious house in Wayland, filled with original Picassos, Braques, and Chagalls, I was given a cheap five-and-ten-cents-store mop and pail to clean a particularly dirty kitchen floor. And in a modest but comfortable three-story home in Newton, where I worked along with a domestic who had been there fifteen years, we had to vacuum with a twenty-five to thirty pound cleaner that had been there even longer. One wonders how long the employing women would retain such equipment if they themselves had to use it.

Hours

Intense and exhausting work is more characteristic of day work than of live-in or full-time live-out work. But the trade-off is in hours and pay. Ten- and twelve-hour work days are not, as one might assume, a thing of the distant past, particularly not for live-in domestics. In 1964, seventeen-year-old Edith Lincoln was brought to Milton by a couple who had met her during their vacation on the Cape. Though they had no children, Ms. Lincoln left after four months because she considered the work and hours excessive.

I worked from the time I got up 'till the time I went to bed. I said, "This is not for me!" It was a big house. I had my own apartment on the third floor. When you work for older people, they like everything done just so. You got your floors, you got the walls, the windows. . . . During the day, it's a lot.

Asha Bell lived in for three years in the early 1970's in Chestnut Hill:

I had to see after the baby, make the beds, keep the house clean, things like that. I was free after the kids went to bed, about 7:30 or 8:00 unless the [employers] went out. Then I had to listen out for the kids until they came home. I started about 7:30 in the morning, but in the afternoon after lunch, I had a rest period. It was when the baby took her nap that I had a rest for about an hour, hour and a half. And I had Sundays and Thursdays off.

For this fifty- to seventy-hour week, Ms. Bell was paid seventy dollars.

Marva Woods lived with a family with two children in Chestnut Hill for eleven years from the mid-1960's to the mid-1970's. The family had brought her up from South Carolina:

I just worked until I got the children to bed. Every Thursday and every other Sunday was off. I got up in the morning, fixed breakfast, got the children ready for school, and carried little John to nursery school. I'd get them all off then start doing my housework: the washing, cleaning up. John would come home about twelve. I'd go and get him and give him his lunch and put him to bed. I would iron or something while he was in bed. When he got up, I'd take him for a walk. Then I'd cook dinner and serve it. After I cleaned up the kitchen and got the children to bed, I was finished. . . . She started me off at thirty-seven dollars a week, then she gave me a raise and I was making fifty-five dollars.

It is not coincidental that at the time of these experiences, all of these women were recent arrivals to Boston or were recruited from their homes specifically for these jobs. Margo Townsend, who directed a local black women's club's program for domestics in the late 1960's and early 1970's, and who, as part of her job, regularly talked to employers, explains their preference for such women this way:

At one time, they would stipulate, "I want a Southern girl." They like the "Yes, Ma'am" and the "Yes, Sir." They *loved* that. But, later on, they'd say "I want a West Indian girl." Now the reason for that was when they got on that job, they'd do anything, they'd work any number of hours—because here's an opportunity to come to this country. And they would work for less money. So everybody wanted a West Indian. No one ever asked for a Northern girl. They felt they'd get more loyalties from people from other places.

And the director of a Newton employment agency that places domestics in both live-in and live-out positions confirmed this view:

Right now I'm getting a lot of calls from people who have heard about the boat people—the people from Vietnam, Cambodia, Haiti, Cuba, and anybody that's coming in—Chinese people. The living over there and the living here—they don't understand what's going on. They'll do anything. I just had one woman come in who requested a Cambodian or Vietnamese. Why? Because she can get them cheap!

The Pay

But what is the pay really like? From the point of view of domestics, it is "fair," "much better than years ago," "better for whites than for blacks," "slave wages," "OK now," et cetera. Domestics' attitudes toward it range as widely as the pay scale itself. I encountered situations of live-out workers making from $3.50 to $10.00 an hour (though the highest salary I found for a black worker was $8.00 an hour). I heard of employers paying the foreign-born below the minimum wage but never encountered this situation first hand. And recall that before 1974, domestics in Boston were making from 60¢ to $1.65 an hour. My impression, from my own job hunts and from my discussions with employers and domestics, is that since 1974 most Boston employers have paid live-out help above the minimum wage.

Employers' attitudes toward the pay also varied widely. A few, like Elsa Coleman, demonstrated compassion and sensitivity to the low rewards of this occupation: "I think they work awfully hard and don't get a tremendous salary for the amount of work they do. There's such insecurity that goes along with not making a lot of money. I have a sense of their barely making it; it's a hand-to-mouth existence." Many more were like Alice Lynch, expressing little interest in the topic. Having had cleaners and childcare workers for over thirty years, Ms. Lynch has never given paid vacation or deducted for Social Security. When asked if she thought wages had been fair, she responded indifferently: "They probably haven't been, but I just paid the prevailing wage."

Other employers rationalized the low wages they had paid (particularly before 1974) by suggesting the workers did not care about their lack of money. Jocelyn Minor, for example, has always paid at the lower end of the wage scale. Talking about a former employee, she justified her wages in this way: "Well, I drove her home a couple of times and she lived in this dreadful hotel-type place in Newton. But she liked it! So I think the pay was fair in view of that. I never thought about it really." Frances Stewart dis-

played similar thoughtlessness when talking about a black domestic she had brought from Alabama through an agency. The woman had come to Boston to work and support three children in Alabama whom she eventually was able to bring up. Yet speaking of the forty dollars a week she was paying (in the early 1960's), Ms. Stewart said, "She never cared much about not having money. It never bothered her." Ava Pearson justified the wages to her fifteen-year Irish domestic (wages she was unable to remember) in a similar fashion: "She has a very positive attitude. She's always been poor. Her husband was a hod carrier. I don't know that the lack of material things were that important in her life." And a few of the older employers were openly resentful about the federally mandated increase in pay. This Chestnut Hill school teacher was the most explicit:

I used to have a woman for a full day. But now they charge so much! We have to just make do. . . . Domestics make too much money now. You know, I'm a teacher and I don't make as much an hour as some domestics do. It's gotten all out of hand. . . . It's unskilled labor; you don't need any training for it. Maybe there was a time when domestics weren't paid enough but now it's gotten to the opposite extreme. Do you think that that's right? That an unskilled worker should make more than a teacher? . . . I remember when I was paying twenty-four dollars a week! And my mother had a full-time woman for six dollars a week!

Live-in pay is more difficult to measure because room and board are given free and because of the ill-defined hours of work. The director of a Newton employment agency exclusively for domestics, whom I interviewed as a researcher, told me live-in pay ranged from $175 to $300 a week. The director of another Newton agency, to whom I talked as a job applicant, said the range was from $125 to $200. And the head of the newly formed domestics section of a large downtown Boston employment agency told me (as a researcher) that live-in positions were paying from $100 to $175. Since none of the domestics or employers I interviewed were currently involved in live-in situations, my information on this is limited to these figures supplied by employment agency personnel. The rather large discrepancies between them may be accounted for by their serving different employing clienteles and/or their wish to inflate their figures to attract or impress me.

From the interviews with domestics and employers came the fact that a wage hierarchy within the occupation indeed exists. The domestics I interviewed confirmed my impression that the further out one works from central Boston, the higher the pay. May Lund said:

> When you don't have transportation, you have to get on the busline. You had to keep in mind what a convenient location was, as far as transportation. Blacks end up working in Brookline, Chestnut Hill, Newton because most of them don't have cars and those are the areas convenient to get to. But I drive and the further out you go, the more money you get. . . . They know they have to pay for the distance. They know no one's going out that far for nothing. The best you can get in Brookline is five-fifty. And I'm getting eight dollars in Wayland.

Comments by other domestics, however, indicated they felt the wage differences were based on race. For example, Nancy Clay, a domestic for over twenty-five years now making five dollars an hour, asked me what was the highest salary I had heard of a day worker making. At the time it was eight dollars an hour. Her response was: "Oh, yes,

but if they're willing to pay that much, they'll only give it to a white domestic."

It is a fact that the areas of Boston in which most black domestics live—Roxbury, Dorchester, and Mattapan—connect most conveniently on public transportation with those areas that appear to pay the lowest— Brookline, Chestnut Hill, and Newton. But do these areas pay the lowest because the people in them know they have access to a large labor pool or because there is a deliberate design to pay black women less? In any case, a wage hierarchy does exist in domestic service in the Boston area and, whether because of racism, geography, or poverty (not owning a car), black women are on the bottom of it.

Though domestics varied in their attitudes toward current wages, they were unanimous in their complaints about the lack of benefits in this occupation. Dorothy Aron's remarks were typical: "The worst thing about domestic work is that there are no benefits, no sense of security. You're not covered for any unforeseen emergency. You're not even covered for tomorrow: they'll go away in a minute and leave you stuck." No domestic worker I talked with nor any past or present employee of the employers I interviewed had any form of medical coverage through their jobs. None had sick leave; if they were unable to make it to work, they forfeited their pay. Nine of the eleven women still active in domestic work received paid vacations ranging from one to two weeks. As the above quote indicates, day workers are particularly vulnerable to employers' out-of-town trips; whether for two days or two months, no day worker was paid for the period employers were away. And although all of the situations in my study were covered by the Social Security law, only eight domestics had Social Security taken out and two of the employers interviewed were taking it out. None of my ten employers mentioned Social Security. Clearly, in domestic service, non-compliance with Social Security legislation is rampant.

The reasons for such widespread disregard for the Social Security laws are numerous. The employer would have to do additional paperwork and contribute 5.85 percent of the employee's wages as her share of the Social Security tax. Many domestics, too, prefer not to have Social Security withheld: the typical hand-to-mouth existence of low-wage workers makes immediate cash more important than protection for the future. Employer Karen Edwards would prefer to take out Social Security but "I have never found anyone who would let me take it out. I would always offer. My husband is a lawyer and likes to be honest; it makes him feel good. And I believe it's right; it's really best for people." A few employers expressed ignorance that the Social Security law covered their employees. Frances Stewart, for example, maintained: "No, I've never taken out Social Security or given her a paid vacation. You have no such responsibility to day workers, to my knowledge." But Holly Woodward's deliberate neglect is more typical: "No, I never took out Social Security. We rationalized it. Nobody did it; why should you be a dope and add to your burdens?"

The two women who did take out Social Security, Ava Pearson and Elsa Coleman, both stated that they did so at their husbands' insistence:

> I always took out Social Security. My husband is very firm on this. He's a financial officer in a corporation. He's conscious of the law and basically I think it's the best thing. This sometimes presents a problem. . . . Some help is not willing to do this. (Ms. Pearson)

> We have gotten into discussions with the last few people. My husband and I feel very strongly that we have to pay employee taxes on the money that we pay domestic help—because that is legal, what we're supposed to do. . . . We do it because it's illegal not to and because my husband wants the childcare deduction on his taxes. (Ms. Coleman)

The prevalence of disregard for the law and the comfort expressed with that disregard by both domestics and employers suggests that the women may see domestic work as exceptional, not quite as legitimate a job as others, not to be taken entirely seriously as an employer-employee relationship. Pamela Kane comes close to saying this: "No, I've never taken out for Social Security or made arrangements about sick pay or vacation. In this kind of job, there is no formalized arrangement. I can't imagine what the [vacation arrangement] would be, but certainly time without pay." The isolation of the relationship undoubtedly facilitates this attitude. But the historical basis of the occupation—in slavery and feudalism where the servant was owned or considered a part of the household—may also explain the personal, extra-legal approach most women take toward this labor arrangement.

A part of that slavery/feudalistic type of domestic service was the protective obligations of the master or mistress. While many possible forms of protection, like health insurance or retirement pensions, do not exist, one form, the giving of gifts, is a still flourishing carryover of that tradition. Employers reported having given all kinds of items—beds, tables, refrigerators, leftover food—but, most commonly, they gave old clothes. By far, most of the employers who had given such gifts (and this included all of the women over forty-five) were entirely comfortable with, even proud of, having done so. (Only two employers expressed reservations because they had detected resentment in their domestics.) Domestics reported having been given such items in the North and in the South, in the 1980's as much as in earlier decades. Domestics said they always accepted anything offered and acted grateful. This was what was expected of them; this was "part of the job.". . . [W]hat is important is that this form of "payment in kind" is an extremely common practice in this occupation and can be considered one of the material compensations of domestic service.

Other Aspects of the Work

Four other aspects of the work that came up in my interviews with employers and domestics are worthy of mention: the aloneness of the job, the monotony of the work, the immediate gratification of the payment system, and the sense of accomplishment physical labor yields. . . .

These issues were noteworthy but by no means universally expressed. Not every domestic mentioned the monotony of the work nor the sense of accomplishment from it. Not every employer said domestics work less overtime. Only former live-in workers were unanimous on the existence of loneliness, and, as stated, only Ms. Lund brought up the immediate gratification of

the payment system. But I consider each of these issues noteworthy to complete the picture (along with the description of the physical demands of the work, the wages and other compensations, hours, and time off) of the overall work conditions of domestic work.

NOTE

1. . . . "[P]rivate household work," as the occupation is termed by the U.S. Census Bureau, includes a number of categories of workers: launderers and ironers, cooks, housekeepers, child care workers, and cleaners and servants. However, because the last category ("cleaners and servants") contains the largest proportion of all female domestics and because all of my domestic interviewees had spent most of their professional housework careers as cleaners, this is the type of work on which this chapter focuses (U.S. Department of Commerce, Bureau of the Census, *Detailed Occupation and Years of School Completed by Age, for the Civilian Labor Force by Sex, Race, and Spanish Origin: 1980 Census of the Population,* Supplementary Report [Washington, D.C.: U.S. Government Printing Office, March 1983], p. 22; and Allyson Sherman Grossman, "Women in Domestic Work: Yesterday and Today," *Monthly Labor Review,* Aug. 1980, p. 20).

29

Formal Knowledge, Power, and the Professions

Eliot Freidson

Eliot Freidson recently retired from the department of sociology at New York University. Freidson has authored numerous books on professions, including his 1986 publication, *Professional Powers: A Study of the Institutionalization of Formal Knowledge,* a portion of which is excerpted here.

Knowledge is power, it is said. If we consider the overwhelming growth of knowledge—particularly scientific knowledge—over the past hundred years, we might be inclined to think that the power of knowledge has grown as well. And surely there is ground for that. The power to render whole continents, if not the entire planet, virtually uninhabitable has grown out of the physical sciences, while unprecedented power over the shape of life itself seems to be developing out of the biological sciences. These are the most widely known and widely feared bodies of knowledge, but there are also others that seek the sources of power over personal and social as well as physical and biological existence. Such knowledge is said by many to constitute a new form of domination over our lives, to create a new form of pervasive social control hiding its face behind a mask of benevolence but leaving us helpless and dependent on others for guidance in the conduct of even our intimate lives in our families (cf. Lasch 1979).

From *Professional Powers,* by Eliot Freidson. Reprinted by permission of the University of Chicago Press and the author.

The question is, What is the relationship between those who create, transmit, and apply that knowledge and the actual exercise of power? Can it be said that scientists are a "new priesthood" (Lapp 1965) or "new Brahmans" (Klaw 1969)? Can we speak of the "tyranny of the experts" (Lieberman 1970) without hyperbole? Do people actually come to rule by virtue of their knowledge? Or, what may come to be the same thing, do they influence so completely the way we think about the world and conceive of solutions to our problems that, while politicians may nominally rule, their decisions are predetermined by the authoritative knowledge of their expert advisers? In what way can it be said accurately that knowledge is power? That is the broad question around which this [reading] revolves. . . .

The Rise of Secular Formal Knowledge

Knowledge is intrinsic to human culture, embracing the facts believed to compose the world, the proper methods or techniques by which to cope with them in order to gain a particular end, the attitudes or orientations that are appropriate to adopt toward them, and the ideas or theories by which one makes sense of facts, methods, and attitudes, explaining and legitimizing them. All human beings everywhere may be said to have some sort of knowledge.

But not all people have the same body of knowledge. Obviously, the substance of the knowledge of people in one culture can be quite different from that of people in another. Furthermore, within any particular culture of any complexity and size one can locate both a body of knowledge common to all and specialized knowledge that is available only to some. The social division of labor, constituting the interlinked system of specialized activities in a society, represents diverse bodies of specialized knowledge manifested through those activities. Thus we commonly distinguish everyday or commonsense knowledge shared by all normal adults in the course of the activities they all perform from specialized knowledge shared by particular groups of people who perform activities on a regular basis that others do not.

In the ancient great civilizations, however, and in our own today, yet other distinctions arise—distinctions between sacred and profane knowledge, theoretical and practical knowledge, elite and popular or mass knowledge, and higher and lower knowledge. In the West, higher knowledge was formalized into theories and other abstractions, on efforts at systematic, reasoned explanation, and on justification of the facts and activities believed to constitute the world. Formalization so distinctly marks modern higher knowledge that it is appropriate to call it formal knowledge. Formal knowledge remains separated from both common, everyday knowledge and nonformal specialized knowledge. Originally rooted in arcane lore and in texts in ancient languages known only to a few, higher knowledge is now still expressed in terms unfamiliar to and impenetrable by the many

and discussed by techniques of discourse that are opaque to outsiders. Those who developed modern higher knowledge—the secular scholars of the Renaissance, for example—addressed each other and members of the ruling elite who shared some of their knowledge and belief in its virtues. They did not address the common people or the common, specialized trades. So it is in our time.

If there is a single concept by which the nature of formal knowledge can be characterized, the most appropriate is likely to be *rationalization,* a concept that is central to Max Weber's analysis of the development of Western civilization. Rationalization consists in the pervasive use of reason, sustained where possible by measurement, to gain the end of functional efficiency. Rational action is organized to address both the material and the human world, and it is manifested most obviously in technology but also in law, the management of institutions, the economy, indeed, in the entire institutional realm of modern society. It is intimately associated with the accounting and management methods that developed with capitalism and the administrative methods of developing predictable social order that rose along with the modern state in the form of "rational-legal bureaucracy." Above all it is intimately associated with the rise of modern science and the application of the scientific method to technical and social problems. Much of the formal knowledge developed in universities over the past century may not have the capacity to control its object of study that the natural sciences have gained—that is to say, may not be adequately scientific—but it nonetheless adopts the same technical or functional rationality, the same effort to develop rational theories on which to base practice and to codify "knowledge with abstract systems of symbols that, as in any axiomatic system, can be used to illuminate many different and varied areas of experience" (Bell 1976, 20). There can be no doubt that formal knowledge, so defined as the subjects of research and teaching in the modern university, has increased at an extraordinarily rapid rate over the past century, with a parallel increase in specializations or disciplines (ibid., 177–78).

Formal Knowledge and Democracy

There is a tendency for prestige and respect to be given to formal knowledge by those who lack it. At least since Francis Bacon's *New Atlantis* there has been a strong belief in the capacity of science to improve human life. Indeed, that belief has been expressed frequently and forcefully from the latter part of the eighteenth century down through our own day. But there is also a tendency to fear it, a tradition that goes back long before the rise of modern science and that, with perhaps better justification than before, continues into our day. Formal knowledge is arcane to everyday people, and some of it can be thought to be powerful and dangerous. It is true that not all formal knowledge is feared: dusty scholars studying obscure minutiae that have no perceptible connection with everyday life are more an object of ridicule than respect even though their knowledge is arcane. But science, like alchemy before it, is thought to be consequential knowledge and therefore potentially dangerous.

By definition, formal knowledge is not part of everyday knowledge. This means that it is elite knowledge. And insofar as it is used to direct human enterprises, decision making on its basis is not democratic, not open to the active participation of all. Thus formal knowledge can be seen as a threat to democracy. Since formal knowledge has grown enormously over the century, and since it is increasingly used in the advanced industrial societies in virtually every sphere of life, it can mean that democracy itself may be at risk. Some visionaries, such as Saint-Simon early in the nineteenth century, have actually argued in favor of a society that is ruled by "objective" knowledge in the face of which opinion is irrelevant and democracy meaningless. Most writers, however, seem concerned with maintaining democracy, and many of them have considered growth in the importance of formal knowledge to human affairs to be a threat to democracy.

Perhaps the most direct and unqualified statement of the importance of such knowledge to modern societies has been made by Jacques Ellul, who characterized the essential spirit of its application to human concerns as "technique"—the state of mind and method of procedure of the scientifically oriented. The "intervention of reason and consciousness . . . can be described as the quest for the one best means in every field. And this 'one best means' is, in fact, the technical means" (Ellul 1964, 21). Technique is seen to be an irresistibly developing force, similar to Weber's "rationalization" and by no means limited to the natural sciences and technology. It embraces the methods used by the police, the management of factories, of education, and of medical care, and in politics the management of the public by propaganda and other techniques. The outcome is order: "Technique has only one principle: efficient ordering. Everything, for technique, is centered on the concept of order" (ibid., 110). Insofar as technique is the one best means, then there is really no choice on the part of politicians but to accept the solutions offered by technique. So it is that Ellul can see a society in which police technique in suppressing crime has been advanced to the point of true efficiency as a concentration camp and can see technique as the boundary of democracy (ibid., 209; for a summary of Ellul's work, see Kuhns 1973, 82–111).

Other commentators have also considered knowledge to be a tool employed for the purpose of controlling or dominating everyday lives, shaping them to the purposes of the state. The technique or rationalization inherent in such formal knowledge so orders and structures the possibilities for choice and action on the part of ordinary people that true choice is prevented. People become a function of the system created by others to control them. The most sweeping and complex statement of this emerges from the work of Michel Foucault. His historical analysis tries to show how domination, or imposed order, was generated in the course of the development of a variety of institutions from the ideas growing out of a number of formal or scientific disciplines. The formal knowledge of the disciplines shapes the way human institutions are organized and the way the behavior of human beings is conceived, providing justification for particular methods of interpreting and disposing of a wide variety of human behaviors. They "define how one may have a hold over others' bodies, not only so that they may do what one wishes, but so that they may operate as one wishes, with the techniques, the speed and the efficiency that one determines. Thus, discipline produces subjected and practised bodies, 'docile' bodies" (Foucault 1979, 138).

Discipline has a double meaning; it is both a segment of formal knowledge and the consequence of its application to the affairs of others. Such disciplines establish the power of the norm, statistical or otherwise, which is used as a "principle of coercion" in a variety of standardized institutions—in education, in health care, and in industrial work, for example. "Normalization becomes one of the great instruments of power" (ibid., 184). Power becomes no longer simply physical coercion but something much more comprehensive, "working to incite, reinforce, control, monitor, optimize and organize the forces under it: a power bent on generating forces, making them grow, and ordering them, rather than one dedicated to impeding

them, making them submit, or destroying them" (Foucault 1980, 136). The disciplines are powerful enough to mold human beings to their will and to the will of the state.

Formal Knowledge and Power

The use of formal knowledge to order human affairs is of course an exercise of power, an act of domination over those who are the object. Ellul might regard such domination as an inevitable outcome of the dynamism of technique. Others, however, would distinguish formal knowledge and technique themselves from power and argue that those who hold the power of decision making are not necessarily the same as those who possess formal knowledge and technique. Politics and politicians hold the power, and it is they who decide what formal knowledge to apply and to what. Daniel Bell is quite firm in asserting that it is the politician who ultimately holds the power: "The control system of the society is lodged . . . in the political order, and the question of who manages the political order is an open one" (Bell 1976, 374; see also 360). Given the growing importance of formal knowledge, however, Eulau (1973) postulates a change in the nature of political decision making in which a complex consultative relationship develops between politicians and those with the relevant skills. Lane (1966) argues that some decisions will be entirely removed from politics and thus from the process of democracy by virtue of having become objectively technical instead of political in character.

Habermas, following Marcuse and others of the Frankfurt School, adopts a critical rather than a descriptive perspective on the matter. He agrees that the growth of formal knowledge during this century has been so great as to create a qualitatively new situation. To him the present represents a second, new stage of the process of rationalization analyzed by Weber, for "the exercise of power . . . [has] been structurally transformed by the objective exigencies of new technological strategies" (Habermas 1971, 62). He does not see formal knowledge as a threat to democracy because of an intrinsic tendency inevitably to preempt political decisions and democratic participation. He denies the inevitability of the influence of technique. The threat he sees is the inappropriate and fallacious use of technique as ideology to justify decisions that are actually not technical or scientific in character. He argues that reason expressed through technology is only one dimension of knowledge and action and cannot adequately legitimate "practical decision in concrete situations," which is a different dimension (ibid., 63). For this reason he asserts that, "as little as we can accept the optimistic [belief in] the convergence of technology and democracy, the pessimistic assertion that technology [inevitably] excludes democracy is just as untenable" (ibid., 61).

The danger is that, whatever may be the logical case for the difference between formal, rational knowledge and "practical decision in concrete situations," it is entirely possible, as Habermas observes, that the former can be used as a false but politically effective justification for the undemocratic exercise of power. Under such circumstances political decisions are not subject to popular debate because they are presented as "technical" decisions. People are not allowed to choose among a variety of alternatives because the issue is presented as a technical one that involves the necessary use of the "one best method." Thus, as formal knowledge grows in magnitude and complexity, and as it is developed into disciplines addressed to an increasing number of areas of human life, one can see an increasing tendency toward rule by technique rather than by public debate about and participation in political decision making. One

can see a tendency, in short, away from democracy and toward technocracy.

Technocracy

Apart from programmatic or wishful statements like the utopian *New Atlantis* of Bacon or the scientifically based society of Saint-Simon, the concept of technocracy is rather opaque and its thrust uncertain and ambivalent. (For summaries of the "technocratic" utopians like Saint-Simon, Comte, and Veblen and some historical material, particularly on engineering, see Armytage 1965.) Meynaud (1969), who provides a balanced review of various conceptions of technocracy, himself arrives at a somewhat equivocal conclusion addressed particularly to France, in which elected representatives who nominally wield political power become a kind of reflex of the decisions that are prepared in advance for them by technical experts. In this sense, what he sees and what, for that matter, writers such as Sarfatti-Larson (1972–73) see is not literal rule of the polity by those with formal knowledge but rather a position in the structure of rule that mediates, qualifies, and sometimes directs the actions taken by those who actually rule. The "technocrat" is a high-level adviser perhaps, or a high-level member of the staff of the politically powerful, or a high-level administrator with technical training (cf. ibid., 4). But the technocrat is not the one who makes the ultimate decisions of the polity.

Beyond programmatic writers who are not describing the world as it is, then, there is little inclination to postulate anything more than a "tendency" to technocracy. Formal knowledge is an instrument of power, a source for guiding and facilitating the exercise of power, but not power in itself. Insofar as those with access to formal knowledge are in power, they are politicians rather than literal technocrats, as Bell (1976, 79) indicates, and must operate like politicians. What we must do if we wish to understand better the relation between formal knowledge and power, therefore, is to avoid the trap of assuming that knowledge itself is a system of domination that controls the ultimate power of the polity, as Foucault seems to imply. Furthermore, we must avoid the trap of assuming that there is only one method appropriate for making all political decisions, as Ellul seems to imply. Both writers treat knowledge and method as forces that are independent of human action and choice.

The Agents of Formal Knowledge

The question we must ask is, How is it possible for formal knowledge to have an impact on anything? In and of itself knowledge is an abstraction. Insofar as it is tangible, its "growth" over the past century or so can be "measured" by counting the number of books and journals that were published (Price 1961), but in order to exist in books and journals knowledge must have human creators and consumers. How does knowledge establish a consequential relationship to the everyday world? To have any impact on either the natural or the social world knowledge must have human agents or carriers, and the impact it makes must be influenced in part by the characteristics of those agents. Thus we cannot understand the role of formal knowledge in our world without understanding the character of those who create it and apply it. This, then, raises another question, namely, What are the characteristics of those who are the carriers or agents of formal knowledge? Who are they? and What are the characteristics of the institutions that make their activities as agents of knowledge viable? In identifying the agents of knowledge the literature is somewhat confusing, for it

has employed a number of different terms to characterize them. Sometimes the word *expert* is used for them and sometimes *technician*, sometimes the word *technocrat* and sometimes *professional*, sometimes *intellectual* and sometimes *intelligentsia*. Let us examine those terms.

The term *intelligentsia*, apparently first used in Poland in 1844 (Gella 1976, 12), was widely used in Poland and Russia by the 1860s and is still used widely, though in a different manner, in the Soviet Union and its surrounding Central European countries. In its traditional use in those countries, Gella argues persuasively, it referred to a social stratum joined together by a common education that, while secondary, was "higher" and "academic" in character. It was not a stratum composed of all those with a *gymnasium* education, however. The stratum was distinct from others with the same education in the middle and upper classes because it shared a "specific combination of psychological characteristics, manners, style of life, social status and, above all, value system" (ibid., 13). That value system, with roots in the ideals of the landed nobility, emphasized the obligation to serve the nation and lead it to what was defined as its destiny through fundamental sociopolitical change (cf. Konrád and Szelényi 1979, 85–142).

Members of the intelligentsia were active in the Russian Revolution and in the government of the Polish Republic between 1918 and 1939 but were supplanted by the new *working intelligentsia* of eastern Europe, a much broader stratum. The term became an official government label for all people who performed white-collar rather than manual labor and who had more education than the general population. As Churchward (1973) shows, it is a very heterogeneous category. In eastern European state socialist regimes today, which are based on state-directed "rational redistribution" of resources to the population, Konrád and

Szelényi (1979) argue that an elite segment of the working intelligentsia has developed that in essence directs the process of redistribution and is developing into a technocratic class. Bailes (1978) paints a somewhat more complex and qualified picture of the technical intelligentsia of the Soviet Union, but he would certainly agree that they exercise important influence on policy.

If *intelligentsia* is the eastern European word for the carriers and disseminators of formal knowledge, *intellectual* is its western European and North American analogue. While it may be a function of the translation from Hungarian to English, it is nonetheless a happy coincidence that Konrád and Szelényi alternate during the course of their analysis between the use of *intelligentsia* and the use of *intellectuals.* Who are the intellectuals? and What are their characteristics?

The term *intellectual* as used to designate a special group of people is even more modern than *intelligentsia,* having first been used widely in France at the end of the nineteenth century (cf. Feuer 1976, 48–49; Nettl 1969, 95). Those writers who have attempted to identify or define intellectuals tend to employ two criteria. On the one hand some emphasize the kind of knowledge that intellectuals pursue and transmit and the orientation of that knowledge. To those writers, it is not all formal knowledge that concerns intellectuals but only that which in some sense transcends the practical affairs of daily life. As Coser (1970, viii) put it, "Intellectuals feel the need to go beyond the immediate concrete task and to penetrate a more general realm of meaning and value." Thus intellectuals do not characteristically address the pursuits of everyday life as a practical problem and cannot be considered to be synonymous with, let us say, technocrats. In a sense they are concerned with ideas rather than with systematic bodies of knowledge or intellectual disciplines.

Furthermore, a number of influential writers have portrayed intellectuals as being somehow detached from or marginal to their societies and intrinsically critical of them (cf. Nettl 1969, 88). In his superb essay on the sociology of intellectuals in capitalist societies, Schumpeter (1950, 145–55) characterized them as those "whose interest it is to work up and organize resentment, to nurse it, to voice it and to lead it" (ibid., 145). Dahrendorf put that detached, critical perspective of the intellectual more mildly and, through his reference to the earlier role of the court jester, in a more ironic context: "All intellectuals have the duty to doubt everything that is obvious, to make relative all authority, to ask all those questions that no one else dares to ask" (Dahrendorf 1969, 55). Shils, however, in his broad, comparative view, analyzes the intellectual's dissent from and distrust of authority as a secondary characteristic that is comparatively recent in history (Shils 1969, 46–51; Shils 1982, 224–72).

Lipset employs functional criteria to distinguish the "hard core" of creators and distributors of culture from a peripheral group "composed of those who apply culture as part of their jobs—professionals like physicians and lawyers" (Lipset 1963, 311). Similarly, Shils (1982, 224) distinguishes the creation, cultivation, and transmission of knowledge as the primary role of the intellectual, with the secondary role being "the performance of intellectual-practical (or intellectual-executive) actions in which intellectual works are intimately involved." This distinction between those who are "pure" and those who are "applied" is in fact an important one in the literature. Parsons (1969, 13) adopts it along with distinctions between those affiliated with the lower ranks of society and those with the upper ranks and between those employing humanistic knowledge and those employing scientific knowledge.

On the whole, those who see intellectuals as having a singular mission in the employment of their knowledge would agree with Coser in ruling out scientists as a group and ruling out as well the practicing professions "unless they talk or write about subjects outside their [strictly defined] professional competence" (Schumpeter 1950, 146). But that discrimination presupposes accepting as the critical mark of intellectuals a particular preoccupation with transcendent values and ideas, including the aims or goals of the society they speak for. In that view, the knowledge of intellectuals is not technical in character but deliberately "teleological" with "cross-contextual" significance (cf. Konrád and Szelényi 1979, 6–9, 29–35). To accept that criterion would of course shrink the population of intellectuals into a very small segment of all who can be appropriately considered agents of formal knowledge and markedly shrink the corpus of knowledge they represent.

However, the distinction between the technical and the teleological leads us to recognize other terms that have been used to designate the creators and carriers of formal knowledge. Jacques Ellul and Michel Foucault, at least in English translation, frequently declare the agents of "technique" and "discipline" to be *technicians* and *experts*. Those words are also fairly modern inventions: the *Oxford English Dictionary* records the first use of the word *expert* as a person who is expert in 1825 (1971, 1:930) and of *technician* in 1833. (1971, 2:3248) But the words are singularly uninformative in their generality, for both, taken literally, refer to all sorts of specialists, including those who are neither exposed to nor thought to use formal knowledge in their activities. My own suspicion is that those words are used by Ellul and Foucault primarily because the French language and the structure of French society does not bring to mind a convenient and appropriate term that most Anglo-American writers could use comfortably in English—namely, the term *profession*.

Daniel Bell, whose *The Coming of Post-Industrial Society* consists in elaborating the view that formal knowledge has become the axial principle of advanced societies, asserts that "the heart of the post-industrial society is a class that is primarily a professional class. . . . A profession is a learned (i.e., scholarly) activity, and thus involves formal training, but with a broad intellectual context" (Bell 1976, 374). One does not have to subscribe to Bell's thesis about the preeminence of professionals to accept the notion that they are carriers of formal knowledge. And indeed others, who write of intellectuals rather than of postindustrial society, also identify at least some professionals as intellectuals and at least some intellectuals as engaged in professional pursuits. Parsons (1969, 15–20) seems to make the two virtually synonymous, though as I have noted already some exclude professionals entirely insofar as they are merely practitioners who apply their knowledge to practical affairs without dissenting from the status quo or being consciously preoccupied with transcendent issues.

The Material Prerequisites for Agency

We have seen that a variety of terms is used to designate those people who create, disseminate, and employ formal knowledge—*intelligentsia, intellectuals, experts, technicians,* and *professionals*. Each term has its ambiguities, and there is disagreement in every case about the particular people each refers to as the agents of formal knowledge. I cannot pretend to be able to lay any of those controversies to rest, for any solution is arbitrary. One issue that can be raised here appropriately, however, is the question of how it is possible for someone as a concrete human being to be an agent or carrier of formal knowledge and to exercise power. That question cannot be answered by referring to the nature of the knowledge itself—that is, whether it is objectively transcendent or not, teleological or not, pure or not, humanistic or not. One can answer it only by reference to the circumstances that are necessary in order for the activity of producing, transmitting, or applying such knowledge to go on. As Coser notes, one condition for the "intellectual vocation" is economic support for the intellectual (Coser 1970, 3). Man may not live by bread alone, but bread is a prerequisite for living. No matter what one's definition of those who are agents of formal knowledge, part of it must include or at least imply the characteristic way they get a living, without which they cannot exist.

As a number of writers have pointed out, there has been great historical variation in the way the agents of formal knowledge have characteristically gotten economic support. Since I am concerned with the recent period, in which formal knowledge has assumed far greater qualitative and quantitative importance than it had previously, I shall not dwell on those variations but merely cite Coser (1970), Znaniecki (1968), and Nettl (1969, 90–107), among others, as sources. In those and other discussions, however, one must note important national variations in how economic support is obtained and in how that affected the creation and distribution of knowledge. England and, later, the United States show important differences from the continental nations of Europe, and western European nations show important differences from those of eastern Europe. The discussions of intellectuals in modern times by such writers as Parsons (1969), Shils (1969, 1982), and Coser (1970) clearly reflect the circumstances of the United States in particular and at the most Western capitalist societies in general. This limitation of reference becomes immediately apparent when one compares their discussions with Gella's sketch of Russia and Poland (1976, 9–34) and the more sustained analysis of Konrád and Szelényi (1979, 74–142). In spite of those differences, however, the modern intelligentsia of eastern Europe can be defined as professionals who are trained and gain their living as "lawyers, physicians, economists, teachers, scientists, engineers, journalists, artists and others" (Bailes 1978, 15), just as Parsons, Bell, and Lipset could describe as professionals the intellectuals of the United States and other capitalist countries. Economic support for the agents of formal knowledge is provided in modern times most often by professional pursuits.

A reasonable method of identifying the agents of formal knowledge in modern times in such a way as to be able to discern how they can gain the living that is necessary to allow them to serve as such agents is to identify them as members of professions. Explicitly connected with the idea of profession is training in higher education, the institutions of which are without doubt the major source of the transformation of the source and role of agents of formal knowledge in all advanced countries (cf. Parsons 1969, 15–18; Shils 1969, 38–39). But the university's importance does not lie solely in its role in training those who engage in knowledge-based pursuits in the world outside, many of whom compose the practicing professions. Perhaps more important for the substance and role of formal knowledge is the fact that the university itself provides a professional pursuit to most of the intelligentsia and the intellectuals who are concerned with the transcendent and the teleological. That profession is university teaching.

In contrast to schoolteachers in "lower" educational institutions, university professors are granted enough time free from teaching to make it possible for them to do scientific, scholarly, and intellectual research and writing that does not generally have sufficient market value to provide a living by itself. Some can work as extremely specialized scientists or humanistic scholars who report their obscure investigations in academic journals and monographs (cf. Coser 1970, 249–96).

By virtue of their sinecures they are free to address only each other rather than the general public, on whose support they would otherwise depend, as Bender (1984, 84–106) notes. Others, however, are made similarly free by their sinecures to spend much of their time serving as critical intellectuals in nonscholarly journals of opinion. They can address the general public on broader subjects as "intellectuals" if they so choose but without having to depend on the public's economic support because they gain their living from teaching. This subsidization of activities that have little monetary value in the marketplace is what makes it possible for academics to play such a strategic role in the creation rather than in mere transmission of formal knowledge. By virtue of being members of the profession of teaching they gain the opportunity to be preoccupied with the pure, the transcendent, and the teleological, none of which are ordinarily considered to be strictly professional issues.

Understanding that the professions include many people of a sort that some analysts would not be willing to admit into the ranks of the elect, I nonetheless argue that as a term or a category profession constitutes the most useful source for identifying the agents of formal knowledge in our day. Furthermore, it includes most, if not all, of the elect. Being members of professions provides intellectuals, the intelligentsia, experts, and others represented as agents of formal knowledge with a living and therefore makes it possible for them to function as agents of formal knowledge, whether pure or applied. . . .

REFERENCES

Armytage, W. H. G. 1965. *The rise of the technocrats.* London: Routledge & Kegan Paul.

Bailes, K. E. 1978. *Technology and society under Lenin and Stalin.* Princeton, N.J.: Princeton University Press.

Bell, D. 1976. *The coming of post-industrial society.* New York: Basic Books.

Bender, T. 1984. The erosion of public culture: Cities, discourses and professional disciplines. In *The authority of experts,* edited by T. L. Haskell, 84–106. Bloomington: Indiana University Press.

Bledstein, B. J. 1976. *The culture of professionalism.* New York: W. W. Norton & Co.

Churchward, L. G. 1973. *The Soviet intelligentsia: An essay on the social structure and roles of the Soviet intellectuals during the 1960s.* Boston: Routledge & Kegan Paul.

Coser, L. A. 1970. *Men of ideas: A sociologist's view.* New York: Free Press.

Dahrendorf, R. 1969. The intellectual and society: The social function of the "fool" in the twentieth century. In *On intellectuals,* edited by P. Rieff, 53–56. New York: Anchor Books.

Ellul, J. 1964. *The technological society.* New York: Vintage Books.

Eulau, H. 1973. Skill revolution and consultative commonwealth. *American Political Science Review* 62:169–91.

Feuer, L. S. 1976. What is an intellectual? In *The intelligentsia and the intellectuals,* edited by A. Gella, 47–58. Beverly Hills, Calif.: Sage Publications.

Foucault, M. 1979. *Discipline and punish: The birth of the prison.* New York: Vintage Books.

———. 1980. *The history of sexuality.* Vol. 1, *An introduction.* New York: Vintage Books.

Gella, A. 1976. An introduction to the sociology of the intelligentsia. In *The intelligentsia and the intellectuals,* edited by A. Gella, 9–34. Beverly Hills, Calif: Sage Publications.

Habermas, J. 1971. *Toward a rational society.* Boston: Beacon Press.

Klaw, S. 1969. *The new Brahmans: Scientific life in America.* New York: William Morrow & Co.

Konrád, G., and I. Szelényi. 1979: *The intellectuals on the road to class power.* New York: Harcourt Brace Jovanovich.

Kuhns, W. 1973. *The post-industrial prophets.* New York: Harper Colophon.

Lane, R. E. 1966. The decline of politics and ideology in a knowledgeable society. *American Sociological Review* 31:649–62.

Lapp, R. E. 1965. *The new priesthood: The scientific elite and the uses of power.* New York: Harper & Row.

Lasch, C. 1979. *Haven in a heartless world.* New York: Basic Books.

Lieberman, J. K. 1970. *The tyranny of the experts: How professionals are closing the open society.* New York: Walker & Co.

Lipset, S. M. 1963. American intellectuals: Their politics and status. In *Political man,* edited by S. M. Lipset, 332–71. New York: Anchor Books.

Meynaud, J. 1969. *Technocracy.* New York: Free Press.

Nettl, J. P. 1969. Ideas, intellectuals, and structures of dissent. In *On intellectuals,* edited by P. Rieff, 57–134. New York: Anchor Books.

Oxford English Dictionary. 1971. Vols. 1, 2, compact ed. New York: Oxford University Press.

Parsons, T. 1969. "The intellectual": A social role category. In *On intellectuals,* edited by P. Rieff, 3–26. New York: Anchor Books.

Price, D. 1961. *Science since Babylon.* New Haven, Conn.: Yale University Press.

Sarfatti-Larson, M. 1972–73. Notes on technocracy: Some problems of theory, ideology and power. *Berkeley Journal of Sociology* 17:1–34.

Schumpeter, J. A. 1950. *Capitalism, socialism and democracy.* 3d ed. New York: Harper Torchbooks.

Shils, E. 1969. The intellectuals and the powers. In *On intellectuals,* edited by P. Rieff, 27–51. New York: Anchor Books.

———. 1982. Intellectuals and the center of society in the United States. In *The constitution of society,* edited by E. Shils, 224–72. Chicago: University of Chicago Press.

Znaniecki, F. 1968. *The social role of the man of knowledge.* New York: Harper Torchbooks.

30

Rambo Litigators
Emotional Labor in a Male Dominated Job

Jennifer L. Pierce

Jennifer L. Pierce is assistant professor in the department of sociology and an affiliate with the Center for Advanced Feminist Studies at the University of Minnesota. Professor Pierce's interest in legal workers and sex segregation "grew out of my own experiences working as a paralegal in large law firms before I attended graduate school. Litigation or trial work is one of the most stressful areas in the legal profession. Hours are long. Schedules are highly unpredictable. And, the adversarial model itself is emotionally demanding. Trial lawyers are called upon to present themselves one moment as aggressive and intimidating and in another as friendly and polite. Burnout was a frequent complaint. Part of what spurred my research interests was my curiosity about why people continued to do work that was so stressful. What meanings did it have for them? How did they derive psychological satisfaction from it? This reading is an attempt to answer these questions."

Late in the afternoon, I was sitting with Ben and Stan. . . . They were complaining about being litigators, or as they put it, how "litiga-

---

tion turns people into bastards—you don't have any real choices." Stan said that if you don't fit in, you have to get out because you won't be successful. And Ben added, "To be a really good litigator, you have to be a jerk. Sure you can get by being a nice guy, but you'll never be really good or really successful."

FIELD NOTES

The comments made by these two young lawyers suggest that the legal profession often requires behavior that is offensive not only to other people, but to oneself: "To be a really good litigator, you have to be a jerk." In popular culture and everyday life, jokes and stories abound that characterize lawyers as aggressive, manipulative, unreliable, and unethical. This image is expressed in the joke about why the lawyer who falls overboard in shark-infested waters is not eaten alive—it's professional courtesy. Our popular wisdom is that lawyers are ruthless con artists who are more concerned with making money than they are with fairness (Post 1987; *National Law Journal* 1986). Few consider, as these two young men do, that the requirements of the profession itself support and reinforce this behavior. . . .

Gamesmanship and the Adversarial Model

Popular wisdom and lawyer folklore portray lawyering as a game, and the ability to play as gamesmanship (Fox 1978; Spence 1988). As one of the trial attorneys I interviewed said,

> The logic of gamesmanship is very interesting to me. I like how you make someone appear to be a liar. You know, you take them down the merry path and before they know it, they've said something pretty stupid. The challenge is getting them to say it without violating the letter of the law.

Lawyering is based on gamesmanship—legal strategy, skill, and expertise. But trial lawyers are much more than chess players; their strategies are not simply cerebral, rational, and calculating moves, but highly emotional, dramatic, flamboyant, shocking presentations that evoke sympathy, distrust, or outrage. In litigation practice, gamesmanship involves the utilization of legal strategy through a presentation of an emotional self that is designed specifically to influence the feelings and judgment of a particular legal audience—the judge, the jury, the witness, or opposing counsel. Furthermore, in my definition, the choices litigators make about selecting a particular strategy are not simply individual; they are institutionally constrained by the structure of the legal profession, by formal and informal professional norms, such as the American Bar Association's Model Code of Professional Responsibility (1982), and by training in trial advocacy, through programs such as those sponsored by the National Institute of Trial Advocacy.

The rules governing gamesmanship derive from the adversarial model that underlies the basic structure of our legal system. This is a method of adjudication in which two advocates (the attorneys) present their sides of the case to an impartial third party (the judge and the jury), who listens to evidence and argument and declares one party the winner (Luban 1988; Menkel-Meadow (1985)). As Menkel-Meadow (1985) observes, the basic assumptions that underlie this set of arrangements are "advocacy, persuasion, hierarchy, competition and binary results (win/lose)." She writes: "The conduct of litigation is relatively similar . . . to a sporting event—there are rules, a referee, an object to the game, and a winner is declared after play is over" (1985: 51).

Within this system, the attorney's main objective is to persuade the impartial third party that his client's interests should prevail (American Bar Association 1982: 34). However, clients do not always have airtight, defensible cases. How then does the "zealous advocate" protect his client's interests and achieve the desired result? When persuasion by appeal to reason breaks down, an appeal to emotions becomes paramount (Cheatham

1955: 282–83). As legal scholar John Buchan writes, "the root of the talent is simply the power to persuade" (1939: 211–13). And in "Basic Rules of Pleading," Jerome Michael writes:

> The decision of an issue of fact in a case of closely balanced probabilities therefore, must, in the nature of things, be an emotional rather than a rational act; and the rules regulating that stage of a trial which we call the stage of persuasion, the stage when lawyers sum up to the jury. . . . The point is beautifully made by an old Tennessee case in which the plaintiff's counsel, when summing up to the jury began to weep. . . . The lawyer for the defendant objected and asked the trial judge to stop him from weeping. Weeping is not a form of argument. . . . Well, the Supreme Court of Tennessee said: "It is not only counsel's privilege to weep for his client; it is his duty to weep for his client." (1950: 175)

By appealing to emotions, the lawyer becomes a con man. He acts as if he has a defensible case; he puffs himself up; he bolsters his case. Thus, the successful advocate must not only be smart, but, as the famous turn-of-the-century trial lawyer Francis Wellman observed, he must also be a good actor (1986 [1903]: 13). In *The Art of Cross-Examination,* first published in 1903 and reprinted to the present, Wellman describes how carefully the litigator must present himself to the judge and jury:

> The most cautious cross-examiner will often elicit a damaging answer. Now is the time for the greatest self-control. If you show by your face how the answer hurt, you may lose by that one point alone. How often one sees a cross-examiner fairly staggered by such an answer. He pauses, blushes, [but seldom regains] control of the witness. With the really experienced trial lawyer, such answers, instead of appearing to surprise or disconcert him, will seem to come as a matter of course, and will fall perfectly flat. He will proceed with the next question as if nothing happened, or else perhaps give the witness an incredulous smile, as if to say, "Who do you suppose would believe that for a minute." (1986 [1903]: 13–14)

More recently, teacher and lawyer David Berg (1987) advises lawyers to think of themselves as actors and the jury as an audience:

> Decorum can make a difference, too. . . . Stride to the podium and exude confidence, even if there is a chance that the high school dropout on the stand is going to make you look like an idiot. Take command of the courtroom. Once you begin, do not grope for questions, shuffle through papers, or take breaks to confer with cocounsel. Let the jury know that you are prepared, that you do not need anyone's advice, and that you care about the case . . . because if you don't care, the jurors won't care. (1987: 28)

Wellman and Berg make a similar point: in the courtroom drama, attorneys are the leading actors. Appearance and demeanor are of utmost importance. The lawyer's manner, his tone of voice, and his facial expressions are all means to persuade the jury that his client is right. Outrageous behavior, as long as it remains within the letter of the law, is acceptable. Not only are trial lawyers expected to act, but they are expected to act with a specific purpose in mind: to favorably influence feelings of the judge and jurors.

This emphasis on acting is also evident in the courses taught by the National Institute for Trial Advocacy, where neophyte litigators learn the basics of presenting a case for trial. NITA's emphasis is on "learning by doing" (Kilpatrick quoted in Rice 1989). Attorneys do not simply read about cases but practice presenting them in a simulated courtroom with a judge, a jury, and witnesses. In this case, doing means acting. As one of the teachers/lawyers said on the first day of class, "Being a good trial lawyer means being a good actor. . . . Trial attorneys love to perform." Acting, in sociological terms, constitutes emotional labor, that is, inducing or suppressing feelings in order to produce the outward countenance that influences the emotions of others. The instructors discuss style, delivery, presentation of self, attitude, and professionalism. Participants, in turn, compare notes about the best way to "handle" judges, jurors, witnesses, clients, and opposing counsel. The efforts of these two groups constitute the teaching and observance of "feeling rules," or professional norms that govern appropriate lawyerly conduct in the courtroom. . . .

Intimidation

Litigation is war. The lawyer is a gladiator and the object is to wipe out the other side.
CLEVELAND LAWYER QUOTED IN THE *NEW YORK TIMES*, AUGUST 5, 1988

The most common form of emotional labor associated with lawyers is intimidation. In popular culture, the tough, hard-hitting, and aggressive trial lawyer is portrayed in television shows such as *L.A. Law* and *Perry Mason* and in movies such as *The Firm, A Few Good Men,* and *Presumed Innocent.* The news media's focus on famous trial attorneys such as Arthur Liman, the prosecutor of Oliver North in the Iran-Contra trial, also reinforces this image. Law professor Wayne Brazil (1978) refers to this style of lawyering as the "professional

combatant." Others have termed it the "Rambo litigator" (a reference to the highly stylized, super-masculine role Sylvester Stallone plays in his action movies), "legal terrorists," and "barbarians of the bar" (Margolick 1988; Sayler 1988; Miner 1988). Trial attorneys themselves call litigators from large law firms "hired guns" (Spangler 1986). And books on trial preparation, such as McElhaney's *Trial Notebook* (1987), endorse the litigator-as-gladiator metaphor by portraying the attorney on the book's dust jacket as a knight in a suit of armor ready to do battle (McElhaney 1987).

The recurring figure in these images is not only intimidating but strongly masculine. In the old West, hired guns were sharpshooters; men who were hired to kill other men. The strong, silent movie character Rambo is emblematic of a highly stylized, supermasculinity. The knight in shining armor preparing to do battle on the front cover of McElhaney's *Trial Notebook* is male, not female. Finally, most of the actors who play tough, hard-hitting lawyers in the television shows and movies mentioned above are men. Thus, intimidation is not simply a form of emotional labor associated with trial lawyers, it is a masculinized form of labor.

Intimidation is tied to cultural conceptions of masculinity in yet another way. In a review of the literature on occupations, Connell (1987) observes that the cult of masculinity in working-class jobs centers on physical prowess and sexual contempt for men in managerial or office positions (1987: 180). Like the men on the shop floor in Michael Burawoy's (1979) study who brag about how much they can lift or produce, lawyers in this study boast about "destroying witnesses," "playing hard-ball," and "taking no prisoners" and about the size and amount of their "win." In a middle-class job such as the legal profession, however, intimidation depends not on physical ability but on mental quickness and a highly developed set of social skills. Thus, masculinizing practices such as aggression and humiliation take on an emotional and intellectual tone in this occupation. . . .

In the sections on cross-examination at NITA, teachers trained lawyers to "act mean." The demonstration by the teachers on cross-examination best exemplified this point. Two male instructors reenacted an aggressive cross-examination in a burglary case. The prosecutor relentlessly hammered away until the witness couldn't remember any specific details about the burglar's appearance. At the end of his demonstration, the audience clapped vigorously. Three male students who had been asked to comment responded unanimously and enthusiastically that the prosecutor's approach had been excellent. One student commentator said, "He kept complete control of the witness." Another remarked, "He blasted the witness's testimony." And the third added, "He destroyed the witness's credibility." The fact that a destructive cross-examination served as the demonstration for the entire class underscores the desirability of aggressive behavior as a model for appropriate lawyer-like conduct in this situation. Furthermore, the students' praise for the attorney's tactics collectively reinforce the norm for such behavior.

Teachers emphasized the importance of using aggression to motivate oneself as well. Before a presentation on cross-examination, Tom, one of the students, stood in the hallway with one of the instructors trying to "psyche himself up to get mad." He repeated over and over to himself, "I hate it when witnesses lie to me. It makes me so mad!" The teacher coached him to concentrate on that thought until Tom could actually evoke the feeling of anger. He said later in an interview, "I really felt mad at the witness when I walked into the courtroom." In the actual cross-examination, each time the witness made an inconsistent statement,

Tom became more and more angry: "First, you told us you could see the burglar, now you say your vision was obstructed! So, which is it, Mr. Jones?" The more irate he became, the more he intimidated and confused the witness, who at last completely backed down and said, "I don't know" in response to every question. The teacher characterized Tom's performance as "the best in the class" because it was "the most forceful" and "the most intimidating." Students remarked that he deserved to "win the case."

NITA's teachers also utilized mistakes to train students in the rigors of cross-examination. For example, when Laura cross-examined [a] witness . . . , a teacher commented on her performance:

> Too many words. You're asking the witness for information. Don't do that in cross-examination. You tell them what the information is. You want to be destructive in cross-examination. When the other side objects to an answer, you were too nice. Don't be so nice! Next time, ask to talk to the judge, tell him, "This is crucial to my case." You also asked for information when you didn't know the answer. Bad news. You lost control of the witness.

By being nice and losing control of the witness, Laura violated two norms underlying the classic confrontational cross-examination. A destructive cross-examination is meant to impeach the witness's credibility, thereby demonstrating to the jury the weakness in opposing counsel's case. In situations that call for such an aggressive cross-examination, being nice implies that the lawyer likes the witness and agrees with her testimony. By not being aggressive, Laura created the wrong impression for the jury. Second, Laura lost control of the witness. Rather than guiding the witness through the cross with leading questions that were damaging to opposing counsel's case, she allowed the witness to make his own points. As we will see in the next section of the chapter, being nice can also be used as a strategy for controlling a witness; however, such a strategy is not effective in a destructive cross-examination.

Laura's violation of these norms also serves to highlight the implicitly masculine practices utilized in cross-examination. The repeated phrase, "keeping complete control of the witness," clearly signals the importance of dominating other women and men. Further, the language used to describe obtaining submission—"blasting the witness," "destroying his credibility," pushing him to "back down"—is quite violent. In addition, the successful control of the witness often takes on the character of a sexual conquest. One brutal phrase used repeatedly in this way is "raping the witness." Within this discursive field, men who "control," "destroy," or "rape" the witness are seen as "manly," while those who lose control are feminized as "sissies" and "wimps," or in Laura's case as "too nice."

The combative aspect of emotional labor carries over from the courtroom to other lawyering tasks, such as depositions, negotiations, communications with opposing counsel, and discovery. Attorneys "shred" witnesses not only in the courtroom but in depositions as well. When I worked at the private firm, Daniel, one of the partners, employed what he called his "cat and mouse game" with one of the key witnesses, Jim, in a deposition I attended. During the deposition, Daniel aggressively cross-examined Jim. "When did you do this?" "You were lying, weren't you?" Jim lost his temper in response to Daniel's hostile form of interrogation—"You hassle me, man! You make me mad!" Daniel smiled and said, "I'm only trying to get to the truth of the situation." Then he became aggressive again and said, "You lied to the IRS about how much profit you made, didn't you, Jim!" Jim lost his temper

again and started calling Daniel a liar. A heated interchange between Daniel and opposing counsel followed, in which opposing counsel objected to Daniel's "badgering the witness." The attorneys decided to take a brief recess.

When the deposition resumed, Daniel began by pointing his index finger at John, the other attorney, and accusing him of withholding crucial documents. Opposing counsel stood up and started yelling in a high-pitched voice—"Don't you ever point your finger at me! Don't you ever do that to me! This deposition is over. . . . I'm leaving." With that he stood up and began to cram papers into his briefcase in preparation to leave. Daniel immediately backed down, apologized, and said, "Sit down John, I promise, I won't point my finger again." He went on to smooth the situation over and proceeded to tell John in a very calm and controlled voice what his objections were. John made some protesting noises, but he didn't leave. The deposition continued.

In this instance, the deposition, rather than the courtroom, became the "stage" and Daniel took the leading role. His cross-examination was confrontational, and his behavior with the witness and opposing counsel was meant to intimidate. After the deposition Daniel boasted to me and several associates about how mad he had made the witness and how he had "destroyed his credibility." He then proceeded to reenact the final confrontation by imitating John standing up and yelling at him in a falsetto voice. In the discussion that followed, Daniel and his associates gave the effects of his behavior on the "audience" utmost consideration. Hadn't Daniel done a good job forcing the witness to lose control? Hadn't he controlled the situation well? Didn't he make opposing counsel look like a "simpering fool?"

The reenactment and ensuing discussion reveal several underlying purposes of the deposition. First, they suggest that for the attorney the deposition was not only a fact-finding mission but a show designed to influence a particular audience—the witness. Daniel effectively flustered and intimidated the witness. Second, Daniel's imitation of John with a falsetto voice "as if" he were a woman serves as a sort of "degradation ceremony" (Garfinkel 1956). By reenacting the drama, he ridicules the man on the other side before an audience of peers, further denigrating him by inviting collective criticism and laughter from colleagues. Third, the discussion of the strategy builds up and elevates Daniel's status as an attorney for his aggressive, yet rational control of the witness and the situation. Thus, the discussion creates an opportunity for collectively reinforcing Daniel's intimidation strategy. . . .

Masculine images of violence and warfare—destroying, blasting, shredding, slaying, burying—are used repeatedly to characterize the attorney's relationship to legal audiences. They are also used to describe discovery tactics and filing briefs. Discovery tactics such as enormous document requests are referred to as "dropping bombs" or "sending missiles" to the other side. And at the private firm, when a lawyer filed fourteen pretrial motions the week before trial, over three hundred pages of written material, he referred to it as "dumping an avalanche" on the other side.

Strategic Friendliness

Mr. Choate's appeal to the jury began long before final argument. . . . His manner to the jury was that of a friend, a friend solicitous to help them through their tedious investigation; never an expert combatant, intent on victory, and looking upon them as only instruments for its attainment.

(WELLMAN 1986 [1903]: 16–17)

The lesson implicit in Wellman's anecdote about famous nineteenth century lawyer Rufus Choate's trial tactics is that friendliness is another important strategy the litigator must learn and use to be successful in the courtroom. Like aggression, the strategic use of friendliness is a feature of gamesmanship, and hence, a component of emotional labor. As Richard, one of the attorney/teachers at NITA, stated, "Lawyers have to be able to vary their styles; they have to be able to have multiple speeds, personalities, and style." In his view, intimidation did not always work, and he proposed an alternative strategy, what he called "the toe-in-the-sand, aw-shucks routine." Rather than adopting an intimidating stance toward the witness, he advocated "playing dumb and innocent": "Say to the witness, 'Gee, I don't know what you mean. Can you explain it again?' until you catch the witness in a mistake or an inconsistent statement." Other litigators such as Leonard Ring (1987) call this the "low-key approach." Ring describes how opposing counsel delicately handled the cross-examination of a child witness:

The lawyer for the defendant . . . stood to cross-examine. Did he attack the details of her story to show inconsistencies? Did he set her up for impeachment by attempting to reveal mistakes, uncertainties and confusion? I sat there praying that he would. But no, he did none of the things a competent defense lawyer is supposed to do. He was old enough to be the girl's grandfather [and] the image came through. He asked her very softly and politely: "Honey, could you tell us again what you saw?" She told it exactly as she had on my direct. I felt relieved. He still wasn't satisfied. "Honey, would you mind telling us again what you saw?" She did again exactly as she had before. He still wasn't satisfied. "Would you do it once more?" She did. She repeated, again, the same story—the same way, in the same words. By that time I got the message. The child had been rehearsed by her mother the same way she had been taught "Mary Had a Little Lamb." I won the case, but it was a very small verdict. (1987: 35–36).

Ring concludes that a low-key approach is necessary in some situations and advises against adhering rigidly to the prototypical combative style.

Similarly, Scott Turow (1987), the lawyer and novelist, advises trying a variety of approaches when cross-examining the star witness. He cautions against adopting a "guerrilla warfare mentality" in cross-examination and suggests that the attorney may want to create another impression with the jury:

> Behaving courteously can keep you from getting hurt and, in the process, smooth the path for a win. [In one case I worked on] the cross examination was conducted with a politesse appropriate to a drawing room. I smiled to show that I was not mean-spirited. The chief executive officer smiled to show that he was not beaten. The commissioners smiled to show their gratitude that everybody was being so nice. And my client won big (1987: 40–42).

Being nice, polite, welcoming, playing dumb, or behaving courteously are all ways that a trial lawyer can manipulate the witness in order to create a particular impression for the jury. I term this form of gamesmanship strategic friendliness. Rather than bully or scare the witness into submission, this tactic employs friendliness, politeness and tact. Yet it is simply another form of emotional manipulation of another person for a strategic end—winning one's case. For instance, the attorney in Ring's account is gentle and considerate of the child witness

for two strategic reasons. First, by making the child feel comfortable, he brings to light the fact that her testimony has been rehearsed. Second, by playing the polite, gentle grandfatherly role, he has made a favorable impression on the jury. In this way, he improves his chances for winning. As, in fact, he did. Although he didn't win the case, the verdict for the other side was "small."

Although strategic friendliness may appear to be a softer approach than intimidation, it carries with it a strongly manipulative element. Consider the reasoning behind this particular approach. Ring's attorney is nice to the child witness not because he's altruistically concerned for her welfare, but to achieve the desired result, as simply a means to an end. This end is best summed up by litigator Mark Dombroff: "So long as you don't violate the law, including the rules of procedure and evidence or do violence to the canons of ethics, winning is the only thing that matters" (1989: 13).

This emphasis on winning is tied to traditional conceptions of masculinity and competition. Sociologist Mike Messner (1989) argues that achievement in sporting competitions such as football, baseball, and basketball serve as a measure of men's self-worth and their masculinity. This can also be carried over into the workplace. For example, as I have suggested, by redefining production on the shop floor as a "game," Burawoy's factory workers maintain their sense of control over the labor process, and hence, their identity as men. In her research on men in sales, Leidner (1991) finds that defining the jobs as competition becomes a means for construing the work as masculine:

> The element of competition, the battle of wills implicit in their interactions with customers, seemed to be a major factor which allowed agents to interpret their work as manly. Virtually every step of

the interaction was understood as a challenge to be met—getting in the door, making the prospect relax and warm up, being allowed to start the presentation . . . making the sale, and perhaps even increasing the size of the sale. (1991: 168)

For litigators, keeping score of wins in the courtroom and the dollar amount of damages or settlement awards allows them to interpret their work as manly. At Bonhomie Corporation and at Lyman, Lyman and Portia, the first question lawyers often asked others after a trial or settlement conference was "Who won the case?" or "How big were the damages?" Note that both Ring and Turow also conclude their pieces with descriptions of their win—"I won the case, but the verdict was small" and "I won big." Trial attorneys who did not "win big" were described as "having no balls," or as being "geeks" or "wimps." The fact that losing is associated with being less than a man suggests that the constant focus on competition and winning is an arena for proving one's masculinity.

One important area that calls for strategic friendliness and focuses on winning is jury selection or voir dire. The main purpose of voir dire is to obtain personal information about prospective jurors in order to determine whether they will be "favorably disposed to you, your client, and your case, and will ultimately return a favorable verdict" (Mauet 1980: 31). Once an attorney has made that assessment, biased jurors can be eliminated through challenges for cause and peremptory challenges. In an article on jury selection, attorney Peter Perlman maintains that the best way to uncover the prejudices of the jury "is to conduct voir dire in an atmosphere which makes prospective jurors comfortable about disclosing their true feelings" (1988: 5). He provides a checklist of

strategies for lawyers to utilize which enable jurors to feel more comfortable. Some of these include:

> Given the initial intimidation which jurors feel, try to make them feel as comfortable as possible; approach them in a natural, unpretentious and clear manner.
>
> Since jurors don't relate to "litigants" or "litigation," humanize the client and the dispute.
>
> Demonstrate the sincere desire to learn of the jurors' feelings.
>
> The lawyer's presentation to the jury should be positive and radiate sincerity. (1988: 5–9).

Perlman's account reveals that the underlying goal of jury selection is to encourage the jury to open up so that the lawyer can eliminate the jurors he doesn't want and develop a positive rapport with the ones who appear favorable to his case.

This goal is supported not only by other writings on jury selection (Blinder 1978; Cartwright 1977; Mauet 1980; Ring 1983; Wagner 1981) but also through the training offered by NITA. As one teacher, a judge, said after the class demonstration on jury selection, "Sell your personality to the jury. Try to get liked by the jury. You're not working for a fair jury, but one favorable to your side." This fact is also recognized by a judge in Clifford Irving's best-selling novel *Trial*: "Assuming his case has some merit, if a lawyer gets a jury to like him and then trust him more than the son of a bitch who's arguing against him, he's home free" (1990: 64).

At NITA, teachers emphasized this point on the individual level. In their sessions on voir dire, students had to select a jury for a case which involved an employee who fell down the steps at work and severely injured herself. (Jurors for the case were classmates, including me.) Mike, one of the students, began his presentation by explaining that he was representing the woman's employer. He then went on to tell the jury a little bit about himself: "I grew up in a small town in Indiana." The he began to ask each of the jurors where they were from, whether they knew the witness or the experts, whether they played sports, had back problems, suffered any physical injuries, and had ever had physical therapy. The instructor gave him the following comments:

> The personal comments about yourself seem forced. Good folksy approach, but you went overboard with it. You threw stuff out and let the jury nibble and you got a lot of information. But the main problem is that you didn't find out how people feel about the case or about their relatives and friends.

Another set of comments:

> Nice folksy approach, but a bit overdone. Listen to what jurors say, don't draw conclusions. Don't get so close to them, it makes them feel uncomfortable. Use body language to give people a good feeling about you. Good personality, but don't cross certain lines. Never ask someone about their ancestry. It's too loaded a question to ask. Good sense of humor, but don't call one of your prospective jurors a "money man." And don't tell the jury jokes! You don't win them over that way.

The sporting element to voir dire becomes "winning over the jury." This theme also became evident in discussions student lawyers had before and after jury selection. They discussed at length how best "to handle the jurors," "how to get personal information out of them," "how to please them," "how to make them like you," and "how to seduce them to your side." The element of sexual seduction is apparent in the often used phrase "getting in bed with the jury." The direct reference to sexual seduction and

conquest suggests, as did the intimidation strategy used in cross-examination, that "winning over the jury" is also a way to prove one's masculinity. Moreover, the desired result in both strategic friendliness and intimidation is similar: obtaining the juror's submission, and winning.

Strategic friendliness is also utilized in the cross-examination of sympathetic witnesses. In one of NITA's hypothetical cases, a woman dies of an illness related to her employment. Her husband sues his deceased wife's employer for her medical bills, lost wages, and "lost companionship." One of the damaging facts in the case, which could hurt his claim for "lost companionship," was the fact that he had a girlfriend long before his wife died. In typical combative, adversarial style, some of the student lawyers tried to bring this fact out in cross-examination to discredit his claims about his relationship with his wife. The teacher told one lawyer who presented such an aggressive cross-examination:

> It's too risky to go after him. Don't be so confrontational. And don't ask the judge to reprimand him for not answering the question. This witness is too sensitive. Go easy on him.

The same teacher gave the following comments to another student who had "come on too strong":

> Too stern. Hasn't this guy been through enough already! Handle him with kid gloves. And, don't cut him off. It generates sympathy for him from the jury when you do that. It's difficult to control a sympathetic witness. It's best to use another witness's testimony to impeach him.

And to yet another student:

> Slow down! This is a dramatic witness. Don't lead so much. He's a sympathetic

witness—the widower—let him do the talking. Otherwise you look like an insensitive jerk to the jury.

. . . Strategic friendliness carries over from the courtroom to depositions. Before deposing a particularly sensitive or sympathetic witness, Joe, one of the attorneys in the private firm, asked me whether "there is anything personal to start the interview with—a sort of warm-up question to start things off on a personal note?" I had previously interviewed the woman over the phone, so I knew something about her background. I told him that she was a young mother who had recently had a very difficult delivery of her first child. I added that she was worried about the baby's health because he had been born prematurely. At the beginning of the deposition later that afternoon, Joe said in a concerned voice that he understood the witness had recently had a baby and was concerned about its health. She appeared slightly embarrassed by the question, but with a slow smile and lots of encouragement from him, she began to tell him all about the baby and its health problems. By the time Joe began the formal part of the deposition, the witness had warmed up and gave her complete cooperation. Later, the attorney bragged to me and one of the associates that he had the witness "eating out of his hand."

After recording these events in my field notes, I wrote the following impressions:

On the surface, it looks like social etiquette to ask the witness these questions because it puts her at ease. It lets her know he takes her seriously. But the "personal touch" is completely artificial. He doesn't care about the witness as a person. Or, I should say, only insofar as she's useful to him. Moreover, he doesn't even bother to ask the witness these questions himself the first time

around. He asks me to do it. I'm to find the "personal hook" that he can use to manipulate her to his own ends.

Thus an innocuous personal remark becomes another way to create the desired impression with a witness and thereby manipulate him or her. Perhaps what is most ironic about strategic friendliness is that it requires a peculiar combination of sensitivity to other people and, at the same time, ruthlessness. The lawyer wants to appear kind and understanding, but that is merely a cover for the ulterior motive—winning. Although the outward presentation of self for this form of emotional labor differs from intimidation, the underlying goal is the same: the emotional manipulation of the witness for a favorable result.

Attorneys also employed strategic friendliness when dealing with clients. As I mentioned in the previous section, intimidation is rarely used with clients, particularly at the private firm, who are typically treated with a politesse, courtesy, and reassurance. The sensitivity to the client's needs and interests does not reflect genuine concern, however, but rather serves as a means to an end—obtaining and maintaining the client's current and future business. The importance of clients to lawyers can be gauged by one of the criteria for determining partnership at private law firms: the ability to attract and maintain a client base (Nelson 1988; Smigel 1969). In this light, clients become another important legal audience for whom the lawyer performs and obtaining a client's business is construed as another form of "winning."

Articles in legal newspapers such as the *National Law Journal* address the importance of lawyers' efforts to attract new clients (O'Neil 1989; Foster and Raider 1988). These articles underscore the importance not only of obtaining business but of appealing to clients through "communication," "cultural sensitivity," and "creating good first impressions." Thus, "finding" new clients is not simply an instrumental role as Nelson (1988) suggests, it also carries with it an emotional dimension.

"Wooing clients" to the firm, or "making rain," as lawyers call it, is a common practice at the private firm. Partners were rewarded in annual bonuses for their ability to bring in new business. In informal conversations, partners often discussed the competition between firms for the clients' business. For example, when one of the partners procured a case from a large San Francisco bank that typically did business with another large firm in the city, he described it as a "coup." Attorneys boasted not only about bringing clients into the firm but about how much revenue "their client" brought into the firm's coffers. The constant focus on capturing clients, "making rain," and making big money betrays male lawyers' need to prove themselves through accomplishments and achievements. Further, those who lost big clients were considered "weak," "impotent," and no longer "in with the good old boys." In this way, winning clients' business is also associated with manly behavior. . . .

REFERENCES

American Bar Association. *Model Code of Professional Responsibility and Code of Judicial Conduct.* Chicago, Ill.: National Center for Professional Responsibility and the American Bar Association, 1982.

Berg, David. "Cross-Examination." *Litigation: Journal of the Section of Litigation, American Bar Association* 14, no. 1 (Fall 1987): 25–30.

Blinder, Martin. "Picking Juries." *Trial Diplomacy* 1, no. 1 (Spring 1978): 8–13.

Blumberg, Abraham. "The Practice of Law as Confidence Game: Organizational Co-optation of a Profession," *Law and Society Review* 1, no. 2 (June 1967): 15–39.

Brazil, Wayne. "The Attorney as Victim: Toward More Candor about the Psychological Price Tag of Litigation Practice," *The Journal of the Legal Profession* 3 (1978): 107–17.

Buchan, John. "The Judicial Temperament." In his *Homilies and Recreations.* Third edition. London: Hodder and Stoughton, 1939.

Burawoy, Michael. *Manufacturing Consent: Changes in the Labor Process Under Monopoly Capitalism.* Chicago: University of Chicago Press, 1979.

Cartwright, John. 1977. "Jury Selection," *Trial* 28 (December 1977): 13.

Cheatham, Elliott. *Cases and Materials on the Legal Profession.* Second edition. Brooklyn: Foundation Press, 1955.

Connell, Robert. *Gender and Power: Society, the Person and Sexual Politics.* Stanford: Stanford University Press, 1987.

Dombroff, Mark. "Winning Is Everything!" *National Law Journal,* 25 September 1989: 13.

Foster, Dean, and Ellen Raider. "Bringing Cultural Sensitivity to the Bargaining Table." *San Francisco Banner,* 17 October 1988: 14.

Fox, Priscilla. "Good-bye to Game Playing." *Juris Doctor,* January 1978: 37–42.

Garfinkel, Harold. "Conditions of Successful Degradation Ceremonies." *American Journal of Sociology* 61, no. 11 (March 1956): 420–24.

Irving, Clifford. *Trial.* New York: Dell, 1990.

Luban, David. *Lawyers and Justice: An Ethical Study.* Princeton, N.J.: Princeton University Press, 1988.

Mauet, Thomas. *Fundamentals of Trial Techniques.* Boston, Mass.: Little Brown, 1980.

McElhaney, James. *McElhaney's Trial Notebook.* Second edition. Chicago: Section of Litigation, American Bar Association, 1987.

Menkel-Meadow, Carrie. "Portia in a Different Voice: Speculations on a Women's Lawyering Process." *Berkeley Women's Law Review* 1, no. 1 (Fall 1985): 39–63.

Messner, Michael. "Masculinities and Athletic Careers." *Gender & Society* 3, no. 1 (March 1989): 71–88.

Michael, Jerome. "The Basic Rules of Pleading." *The Record: New York City Bar Association* 5 (1950): 175–99.

O'Neil, Suzanne. "Associates Can Attract Clients, Too." *National Law Journal,* 16 January 1989: 17.

Perlman, Peter. "Jury Selection." *The Docket: Newsletter of the National Institute for Trial Advocacy,* Spring 1988: 1.

Post, Robert. "On the Popular Image of the Lawyer: Reflections in a Dark Glass." *California Law Review* 75, no. 1 (January 1987): 379–89.

Rice, Susan. "Two Organizations Provide Training, In-House or Out." *San Francisco Banner,* 24 May 1989: 6.

Ring, Leonard. "Cross-examining the Sympathetic Witness." *Litigation: Journal of the Section of Litigation, American Bar Association* 14, no. 1 (Fall 1987): 35–39.

Sayler, R. "Rambo Litigation: Why Hardball Tactics Don't Work." *American Bar Association Journal,* 1 March 1988: 79.

Smigel, Erwin. *The Wall Street Lawyer: Professional or Organizational Man?* Second edition. New York: Free Press, 1969.

Spence, Gary. *With Justice For None.* New York: Times Books, 1989.

Turow, Scott. "Crossing the Star." *Litigation: Journal of the Section of Litigation, American Bar Association* 14, no. 1 (Fall 1987): 40–42.

Wagner, Ward. *The Art of Advocacy: Jury Selection.* New York, N.Y.: Matthew Bender, 1981.

Wellman, Francis. *The Art of Cross-Examination: with the Cross-Examinations of Important Witnesses in Some Celebrated Cases.* Fourth Edition. New York: Collier, 1986 [1903].

31

The Corporate Closet
The Professional Lives of Gay Men in America

James D. Woods with Jay H. Lucas

James D. Woods received his Ph.D. from the Annenberg School of Communications at the University of Pennsylvania and was later appointed assistant professor of communications at the City University of New York, College of Staten Island. With Jay H. Lucas, Woods authored the 1993 book, *The Corporate Closet: The Professional Lives of Gay Men in America.* Woods died in 1996 at the age of 32.

In 1980 it was revealed that Mary Cunningham, then vice president of strategic planning at Joseph E. Seagram & Sons, was having an affair with the chairman of its parent company, William Agee. The result was an unprecedented flurry of speculation and criticism in the national press. Although she was an honors graduate of the Harvard Business School, Cunningham was portrayed as a sexual opportunist. She had won a string of promotions and raises since joining the company in 1979, and these were now subject to intense scrutiny. Why had she been promoted so quickly? Had she been rewarded for professional performance or for her extraprofessional dealings with her boss? Agee, meanwhile, was accused of behavior unbefitting a chief executive officer. The relationship with Cunningham wasn't the issue, according to his critics; the problem was the lapse in judgment it reflected. Dogged by these accusations, her credibility in question, Cunningham resigned.

The Agee-Cunningham affair, like countless others that attract less attention, highlights one of our most cherished beliefs about the workplace: that it is, or at least should be, asexual. Whether it's a company, law office, hospital, or charity, an organization is usually described as a structure, as a hierarchy of abstract "slots" to be filled by generic, asexual "workers." Activity within is organized around getting something done—managing an activity, manufacturing a commodity, providing a service—and behavior not relating to that central endeavor is kept at the fringes. Sexuality, when acknowledged at all, is assigned one of several labels: It's a friendly social diversion, an imprudent distraction, or an unwanted (and in the case of harassment, illegal) intrusion. Whatever it is, it's not official business.

Indeed, the legitimacy of bureaucratic authority is grounded in its apparent asexuality. Bureaucratic principles emphasize formal chains of command and official channels through which power and influence are presumed to flow. Few circumstances invite more resentment or are more discrediting to a manager than the appearance that he or she acquired a position of power "unfairly"—that is, by establishing romantic or sexual ties to those above. "Even when decision-makers actually remain uninfluenced by personal loyalties, the appearance of impartiality that a bureaucracy must maintain to preserve its legitimacy can be threatened if intimate relationships are publicized."[1]

Because they appear to short-circuit formal lines of authority, relationships like the one that developed between Agee and Cunningham are seen as threats to the organization. Eleven years after the liaison was made public, Standley H. Hoch's resignation as president of the General Public Utilities Corporation suggests that the rules have changed very little. In the summer of 1991, word traveled through the company that Hoch was having an affair with Susan Schepman, the company's vice president of communications. The only difference this time was who paid the penalty: It was the senior officer, Hoch, who was forced to resign. As the *New York Times* noted in its headline to the story, "The Boss Who Plays Now Pays."[2]

The Asexual Imperative

Our most powerful metaphor for the workplace is the machine, a comparison that en-

courages us to judge organizations according to their efficiency, productivity, and the smoothness of their output. We imagine that work is a rational activity and that workplaces depend on order. Sexuality, in contrast, is perceived as a threat to all that is rational and ordered, the antithesis of organization. It is part of an animal nature—biologically or psychodynamically driven, irrational, innate—that exists prior to (and is at war with) civilization, society, and the forces that would repress or tame it.

With their emphasis on the rational, goods-producing side of work, organizational theorists have traditionally ignored sexuality in the workplace. As a topic of study, sex is largely neglected in textbooks and journals concerned with organizational theory. Except when it can be commodified and made part of the output (as it is, for example, by models, entertainers, and others for whom physical appeal is explicitly part of the job), sexuality has no place in traditional organizational theory. In most cases this means that sexuality is viewed as an external threat to an organization, something that interferes with its primary purpose—something that must be regulated, prohibited, or otherwise held at the company gates. Our dominant ideologies and images of organization make sexuality an outsider.

Indeed, one can identify an array of policies and informal rules designed to eliminate "personal" considerations like sexuality from business. Most organizations have official or unofficial rules against nepotism, and some forbid fraternizing with clients. Managers are usually expected to absent themselves from decisions involving coworkers who are also friends, just as judges routinely disqualify themselves from trials involving people to whom they have personal ties. Employment statutes distinguish private and professional roles by prohibiting an interviewer from asking questions about an applicant's ancestry, national origin, marital status, parental status, birthplace, spouse, children, or other relatives. Implicit in these restrictions is the assumption that such matters have no impact on a candidate's ability to do the job; an employer presumably cares only about the "worker" who lies beneath the various "personal" characteristics on the surface. Even when violated, these rules establish an ideal type, an expectation about the proper way of doing business.

When sex does appear, the informal policy in most organizations is to look the other way. A 1987 survey of thirty-seven Fortune 500 companies found, for example, that only two had formal policies on romantic relationships at work (though sixteen had policies on nepotism).[3] When personnel managers were asked how they handled relationships in the office, most replied that they either "tried to overlook them" (36 percent) or "felt the problem [would] resolve itself" (18 percent). Only two (6 percent) gave new employees any kind of orientation or instruction on the matter of romantic involvements at work. Asked at what point they would have "a sense of responsibility" for their subordinates' sexual behavior, the managers replied that they would step in only when it "blatantly interfere[d] with their credibility with other employees," "[became] a source of gossip so that others might avoid the person," or "became offensive to others or disrupted the normal flow of business."[4] Likewise, when asked by *Business Week* to describe his company's policy on in-house romance, a senior manager at Leo Burnett Co., an advertising agency, explained that his company didn't have one: "As long as the relationship doesn't affect our ability to get out ads, it is none of our damn business."[5]

As a result sexual liaisons in the office are more often governed by informal custom and taboo than by company policy. Explaining the absence of a formal etiquette on sex between coworkers, for example, Letitia Baldrige advises in her *Complete Guide to Executive*

Manners: "There is no book of sexual manners in the office, because sex simply doesn't belong in the office. It exists, in lesser and greater degrees, but the greater the degree becomes, the closer the situation approaches disaster."[6] Indeed, when sexuality is acknowledged in employee manuals and hiring policies, it is usually to guard the organization against it. Policies that prohibit nepotism, fraternizing with clients, and immodest clothing all take the form of organizational prophylaxis; office romances can be stopped before they start (an implicit purpose of most dress codes) or firmly escorted outside company doors. When coworkers marry, for example, one of them is usually asked to leave.

Most often, however, sexuality goes unacknowledged until someone files a charge of sexual harassment, a matter on which most companies now have an explicit policy. The prescribed solution is usually the same: The sexual offender is simply expelled from the organization. Consequently, while some researchers have explored the definition of what constitutes harassment, most have attempted only to gauge the frequency and effect of particular harassing behaviors: "There is little systematic description of non-harassing sexual behavior at work and few attempts to understand sexuality at work aside from determining whether some particular class of behavior is or is not harassment."[7] While useful for policymakers and law enforcement officials, this approach scarcely suggests the protean role sexuality plays at work.

Sexuality is thus seen as the transgression of asexual actors into sexual territory, not as an inherent component of organizational behavior. The official, top-down view of a company classifies sexuality as an extra-organizational phenomenon. Formal and informal policies acknowledge it only when it seems to trespass on company grounds. When organizations do acknowledge sexuality, they define it narrowly, as a category of discrete "acts" (innuendos, affairs, flirtations), not as a broad subtext to all organizational behavior (sexual identities and sex-appropriate behaviors and assumptions). Indeed, if sexuality were rightly seen as an inherent component of all human interaction—something constitutive of, rather than threatening to, a professional relationship—formal policies on the matter might serve very different ends. Rather than simplistic prohibitions on sexuality, we might have an etiquette that sought to shape and police it.

The resulting sex-work dichotomy means that when professionals step into their offices, they cross an important cultural boundary. They leave the private world and assume their public roles as bankers and doctors, lawyers and teachers; sexuality stays behind in the realm of pleasure and emotion. They imagine that sex and work utilize different skills and satisfy different appetites. Each is given its characteristic time slots (the workday versus evenings and weekends) and its intended spaces (offices versus bedrooms). Geographically, temporally, and ideologically, we keep them apart. Social space is partitioned accordingly, permitting us to distinguish professional and social friends, work and leisure clothing, official and unofficial business. However it is expressed, the dichotomy implies that there is a public, work-producing, professional "self," one that can be shorn of its sexuality during office hours.

And that's how it *should* be, according to most professionals, both gay and straight. When asked to describe the role their sexuality plays at work, gay men often volunteer the conclusion that it is entirely fair and proper that the two be kept apart. In addition to formal policies that ignore or attempt to expel sexuality, they cite informal rules and normative beliefs that define sexuality as marginal, inappropriate organizational behavior. In office hallways one hears the familiar remarks: Sexuality is a private matter and doesn't belong in the office; it isn't relevant to the task at hand; people shouldn't be that intimate at work; it's impolite, a breach of office etiquette. Office decor is expected to be in "good taste," and off-color jokes are usually off limits. The cumulative message is loud and clear.

Taken together these entwined beliefs about privacy, professionalism, and office etiquette comprise an "asexual imperative," a multilayered argument that sexuality doesn't belong in the workplace at all. Gay men did not invent the imperative; on the contrary, their defense of conventional notions about privacy and professionalism merely echoes the values of the larger culture, which have a long and tangled history. But if they did not invent the imperative, they make special and insistent use of it. Like their straight peers, they often believe that sexuality has no place at work; unlike them, however, they use the imperative to protect themselves, to rationalize their own visibility. Recognizing the penalties they might pay for being openly gay at work—fearing they cannot be candid about their sexuality—they embrace the idea that they should not be, that it would be unprofessional, rude, disruptive, or tacky. The asexual imperative, although voiced by gay and straight professionals alike, is therefore most meaningful to those whose sexuality has been a source of stigma.

"My Sex Life Is Private"

Without thinking, we often use the terms *sex* and *private life* interchangeably. When asked if they've come out at work, for example, gay men often answer in euphemisms: "My boss doesn't know about my private life," or, "I haven't told her about my personal situation." Steve, an accountant with a Houston firm, remembers his dismay when a coworker moved into the same apartment complex. "He used the stairwell that runs right up to my front door," Steve recalls. "So I had to be careful. I kept my personal life—my personal life didn't come to my apartment. I went out for my personal life." Because romantic encounters were now arranged off site, Steve felt that his "personal life" no longer took place at home.

Offices, by contrast, are defined as public places, and the result is a familiar syllogism: Sexuality is private; offices are public; therefore sexuality doesn't belong in the office. When asked why he was reluctant to tell coworkers about his lover, Martin invoked the same binary logic: "Sex belongs in the bedroom, not the boardroom." Brent, a Houston manager in his late twenties, attributes the same thinking to his employer: "I think management would probably look at my coming out as a conflict of interests, in other words, that I'm bringing my personal life to work and I shouldn't be." Brent expects to be promoted within the next few years, provided "my life isn't becoming a problem with the job I'm doing."

Sexual secrecy can thus be justified as a matter of boundary maintenance, as gay men try to keep private behavior in its proper domain. In a 1992 survey by *Out/Look*, 36 percent of lesbians and gay men cited the "desire for privacy" as a reason they have remained secretive with one or more coworkers.[8] "There are lines you don't cross," says Carter, a sales representative with Hilton Hotels. "Personal matters, private matters, just don't belong in the office. You have to be aware of those boundaries." Glen, the general counsel at a large Houston company, agrees. "I need to have balance," he says. "I don't need to be socializing more with the people I work with. Likewise, I don't particularly need for my parents to know more of the details of my private life than they already know. It's *mine*. Privacy has a function, it seems to me. I've got an equilibrium that I'm comfortable with." Glen's "private life" is thus posed as something distinct from (and opposed to) his work, something that can be balanced

against the counterweight of work. As he explains it, one must seek "equilibrium."

Sometimes it may be an influential boss or coworker who draws the boundaries. Jeff is one of three analysts in a small Philadelphia investment firm. Though he considers his coworkers liberal and open minded, he is reluctant to talk about sexuality at work. "I don't think they'd have any problem with it," he says. "I think about telling my boss sometimes. I'm just not sure what the reason would be. I know his attitude is that he really keeps his private life private. He doesn't talk much about his wife and kids. I'd be bringing my private life into the office, to a degree." In keeping his sexuality a secret, Jeff feels he's merely taking his cue from his boss. "We all keep our social lives pretty separate," Jeff says.

With this conceptual framework in place, even the most elaborate efforts to mislead coworkers can be justified in the interest of privacy. Louis, a lawyer in his mid-forties, recalls his first few years at one of Boston's most prestigious firms. With a growing client base and considerable expertise in tax law, Louis was considered one of the firm's rising stars. Other associates found him easy to work with, and in a few years he was considered a likely candidate for partner. The word in the hallways was that Louis was going places.

There were others, however, who considered him something of an enigma. He rarely attended office social events, and although invitations were often extended, no one at the firm had met his wife and family. She never called him at work. One Christmas Louis had invited several of the partners to a holiday party for which a lavish meal had been prepared, but even then his wife had been unexpectedly called away and was unable to meet the guests. An otherwise friendly, sociable man, Louis avoided conversations about his home life and would sometimes protest that he "wanted to keep private matters private" or that it was "unprofessional" to bring family concerns to work. When a secretary asked where Louis and his wife would be spending a summer vacation, he replied, half jokingly, that it was a secret.

His notion of privacy seems somewhat strict until one learns—as the partners ultimately did, after Louis made partner—that the wife in question was actually a man, a lover of many years who had been carefully kept out of sight, disguised in countless conversations, and excluded from office gatherings and parties. Louis's wedding ring was a family heirloom, and the photographs on his desk were of a college girlfriend long since married to someone else. At the mysterious dinner party, Louis's lover had dutifully prepared the meal and hidden in the garage until the guests were gone. While the other attorneys were surprised by the news, Louis says that they understood his reasons for doing what he did. The scheme had been an attempt, Louis explains, "to set up some boundaries and mark off a little space for my private life."

"I Don't Want to Be That Intimate with Coworkers"

Most of us learn early on to associate sexuality with intimacy. Sex, we are taught, is to be shared by those who are emotionally or conjugally attached; sex between strangers, even when morally condoned, is considered an indulgence, a substitute for the real thing. The same can be said about conversations on the subject. We are usually reluctant to discuss our sexual lives with strangers and are encouraged to reserve the topic for chats with lovers, close friends, or therapists of one sort or another.

As a result explicit sexual conversations often serve as milestones in the development of an intimate friendship. By withholding information about our sexuality, we place limits on the growth of a relationship. Terry, a

Houston attorney, feels that being secretive about his sexuality has made him "a bit colder than I might otherwise be at work." Tony, who works for a Philadelphia financial services firm, is also somewhat distant at work. "Coming out might make us closer," he says. "It might open up the opportunity for us to become close friends. In fact, I might be blocking it." The converse is also true. By coming out at work, men invite coworkers to treat them as intimates, sometimes without intending to. Sean, who works for a large public relations firm in New York, remembers coming out to his secretary. "Suddenly she assumed she knew me really well, that we were really close friends, just because she knew that I was gay."

Professional asexuality is often justified on precisely these grounds. Gay men imagine that relationships with coworkers are categorically different from friendships. A "strictly professional" relationship encompasses only the work at hand, which means that when confidences are exchanged, they should be of a business nature. "It's not as if I have a personal friendship with most of these people," says Randy. "I've socialized once with three or four of them, but we're not close friends." Work relationships that grow more intimate, as many do, are said to have "crossed over" from one category to another. As Charles, a travel agent in Virginia, explains: "After a while, somebody's not your coworker, they're your friend—someone who's stepped over the boundary from coworker to friend. They have a new definition in your life."

To keep their distance, some men avoid all mention of sexuality at work. "I just don't think it's proper behavior in the office," says Roland, an art director for a small Manhattan advertising agency. "I don't come here to socialize with everybody. I work with these people, and if I like them, fine. And if we get along, great. But I'm not going to do it on a regular basis." Many fear that if the lines are blurred, if professional relationships become too intimate, they won't be able to do their jobs. "I have too many other things on my mind during the course of the day," says Arthur, who insists: "It isn't appropriate to get that involved in other people's personal lives." Dan warns: "There's the potential for it to get too loose, too comfortable, too friendly," when coworkers are open with one another. "It's real nice to have that comfortable feeling," he says, "but you can't cross the line. People start personalizing and not being objective."

Often they fear that their judgment will be compromised by intimate knowledge of a coworker's life. Glen refers to office friendships as a form of "modified nepotism." Brent avoids even casual lunches with coworkers. "I just think you have a better workplace if people keep their private lives to themselves," he says. "If they bring too much of it to the office, if I know too much about a person's social life, it's going to influence my decisions on merit increases or disciplinary actions, that sort of thing. Specifically, if I know that someone has gone through a divorce, and it's an unpleasant divorce and there are children involved, I'm going to be more sympathetic in my treatment of that person. And that really shouldn't impact what goes on in the office. You leave that outside the door at 8 A.M." Les, the business manager of a technical high school in Pennsylvania, lives by the same rule. "There's an old adage," he says. "You never dip your pen in the company inkwell. There must have been half a dozen times in my life when I wanted to. But I'm always glad that I didn't, because eventually I'd have to fire someone, or there'd be some static or something."

"Professionalism" is the term often invoked in defense of these boundaries. In the survey of *Out/Look* readers, 15 percent of lesbian and gay respondents said they would consider it "unprofessional" to come out at work.[9] Dan insists that the gay men on his staff be discreet about their sexuality in the presence of clients, and last year threatened to fire a male therapist who came to work wearing an earring, attire that Dan considered "unprofessional." When asked if female therapists were allowed to wear earrings in the clinic, Dan confessed that there was a double standard. The problem wasn't the earring per se but the message it might send to patients. "On a man an earring will arouse suspicion that he's gay, and that poses a problem from a professional point of view," according to Dan. "A mental health professional has to be a blank screen, so that a client can project whatever they have on you. If you disclose something inappropriate about yourself, that makes the process less clean and effective than it could be. I try to maintain the professional atmosphere you need in this society." Patrick's boss has a similar rule. Herself a lesbian, she heads a small staff of personnel trainers, including Patrick, at a large teaching hospital in Washington. "She thinks that trainers should be anonymous," Patrick says. "It would be inappropriate to come out at work, because that draws attention to yourself." Brent agrees. "It could become dangerously unprofessional around here if people found out that I'm gay," he says.

Chip, who manages the information system in a Houston company, received a harsh lesson in professionalism. Several years ago, he confronted a former coworker when she made a negative remark about gay people and AIDS. In the ensuing argument, Chip revealed that he is gay. Although he thought the disagreement had ended amicably, he received notice several days later that he had been fired. The official explanation: "unprofessional behavior."

"My Sexuality Isn't Relevant to Work"

Like arguments about privacy and intimacy, the relevance argument is grounded in the notion that "work" and "sexuality" are distinct classes of activity. It assumes that the separation of spheres is natural and normal, that the boundary between them should be breached only when there is a compelling reason. "I don't think that personal knowledge about one's sexuality is necessary for working relationships," says George, a senior airline executive, and "if there's no reason to bring it up, then why go to all the trouble?" Roland offers a similar explanation. "I'm not one of those people to go around advertising my sexuality because I don't think it's necessary. What's necessary is what I do for a living, and the job is not who I sleep with or who I date."

Typical of this view is an emphasis on the job itself and the insistence that all other matters, including sexuality, are of secondary importance. When asked if coworkers know that he is gay, Les assured me that it makes no difference. "I do my job. I'm competent. I treat them fairly. My sexuality is irrelevant." Matt, an executive at Ford, says that his boss "doesn't care if people come to work in their fucking pajamas, as long as they do the job." Jerry, a securities trader, is even more adamant. "On Wall Street, a place of work, it really isn't a place to discuss sexuality. With your friends, on nonwork time, it's perfectly fine to discuss sexuality. And if your friends happen to be coworkers, when you're not on work time, if you want to discuss sexuality, that's fine. But in a business setting there really isn't any reason to gossip." "You want to be judged on your accomplishments," says Grey, the public relations director for a Houston mall, "not on your relationships."

In saying that sex has nothing to do with work, these men imagine that asexuality is a man's natural, initial state of being. Asexuality is his status by default, the role he assumes passively. Until he indicates otherwise, he simply *remains* asexual. Jason, a senior executive at Johnson & Johnson, remembers speaking to a friend at a meeting of the gay physicians' group in Philadelphia.

The woman asked if Jason thought she should tell a potential employer, a local hospital, that she is a lesbian. "I told her that if somebody came into my office with that information, applying for a job in our organization, I would wonder, 'Why are you telling me this?' I would question their judgment. People don't come in and tell me they're heterosexual or bisexual or homosexual. That's not a part of the employment interview." Implicit in Jason's advice is the notion that workers are asexual—not heterosexual, bisexual, or homosexual—until they affirm otherwise. In a working environment, he says, such affirmations are a sign of poor judgment.

If sexuality is indeed irrelevant to work, then "coming out" can be made to appear trivial, even laughable. Milton says that "if someone ever said to me 'Are you gay?' my immediate response would be, 'Well, why on earth are you asking me?'" Jim imagined this scenario: "I've thought about it a couple of times—actually coming out at work—but I don't see how it's relevant. I don't need to go round saying, 'I'm gay, I'm gay,' and write a memo to everyone saying, 'Oh, by the way, I'm gay.' It doesn't seem like it's really important." Others described equally unlikely situations. "Unless you're a prostitute or a porn actor," asks Martin, "what does your sexuality have to do with work?"

Joel, who runs his own consulting firm in Washington, says that the same applies to most of his friendships. "Sometimes people need to know everything about you to be your friend, but I don't feel that that's the basis for friendship. My friends are not Republicans, or Lutherans, or rich people, or gay people. They're *all* people. I have lots of minorities, straights, non-Lutherans as friends. So it won't enhance our relationship for them to know that I'm gay." Only under unusual circumstances, Joel says, does he reveal his sexuality to any but close friends. As an example he describes an encounter that took place several years ago. A member of a local church organization, Joel frequently hosts dinners for students from Georgetown, American, and other universities in the Washington area. "They come in and have dinner here and socialize," he explains. After one of these dinners, one student in particular seemed eager to talk. "He said to me, as he discussed his life, that he was gay. He wanted to talk to me. He was a graduate student, and he taught Bible studies. And as I listened to him, my sense was that he needed a gay friend. He was really reaching out for help."

For Joel this at last was ample "reason" to reveal himself. "So I told him that I was also gay and invited him to go with me to get a broader range of experience in gay life in Washington." Joel admits that he rarely finds himself in situations like this, but says that "when there's a need, I'm happy to address my sexuality. But if there's no need, I'm not prepared to take the risk."

"It's Rude to Talk about Sex"

It can also be objected that sexual disclosures constitute a breach in office etiquette, that they are rude or tacky. Talking about sex, gay or otherwise, is potentially offensive, intrusive, or rude. Coworkers may find the subject distasteful, and their sensitivities must be taken into account.

Gay men are aware that sexual topics are often unwelcome, that coworkers may be upset by even the intimation of sex. "I put a joke on the messaging system once," says Chip. "The question was, 'What has a thousand teeth and eats weenies?' The answer is 'a zipper.' One of the guys called me and said he didn't think that was appropriate, because women were on the system." Arthur feels that "lawyerly etiquette" prohibits such jokes at his firm. "I think lawyers have it easier than any other profession," he says. "It's just not an inquisitive profession. We're paid

to ask questions, and when it comes to our intramural relations, we just don't. It would be unseemly for me to ask another single associate—I might ask what he did over the weekend, and he'd say, 'I saw *Postcards from the Edge.'* But it would be unseemly to say, 'Well, did you go with a girl with big tits, and did you, you know, *do it?'* "

Conversations about homosexuality, in particular, are off limits. "I always find them—because of my southern background—to be a bit crass," explains Chris, an arts management consultant in New York. "You know, as southerners we don't talk about things like that. We just do them." Dave, likewise, is certain that his secretary knows his secret. "But she would *never* bring it up. She knows that it would make me uncomfortable, so she wouldn't do it. She would consider it inappropriate."

The list of examples could go on. The asexual imperative is a central, pervasive feature of professional culture, and some version of it was reported by all of the men to whom we spoke. It was defended in different ways, sometimes as a matter of privacy, productivity, or professionalism, sometimes as plain "good manners."

However it is articulated, asexuality becomes the model against which professionals judge their own behavior, a norm they observe even in the breach. The particular arguments made on its behalf differ in certain respects but are joined at the base in the shared assumption that "work" (and its corollaries "organization," "professional," and so forth) and "sexuality" (or "personal life") are inherently distinct.

Marginalizing Sex

But what happens when sexuality *does* find its way through the office door? How do professionals respond to behavior, at work, that they *do* interpret as being sexual?

One need not look far to find countless work situations that involve sexuality in one way or another. As we've already seen, sexuality suffuses the workplace. At the personal, social, and symbolic levels of organizational life, one invariably finds sexual attractions and impulses, roles and appearances, flirtations and jokes, expectations and assumptions. They range from sexual feelings, fantasies, and innuendos right through to sexual relationships, sexual acts, violations, and harassment.

On a day-to-day basis, few of these activities are categorized as sex. When they are, however, the asexual imperative supplies the conceptual framework with which we label, evaluate, and make sense of them. The imperative ensures, in particular, that while we may sometimes acknowledge sexuality in work settings, we never see it as an inherent component of work. We recognize that sexual and professional activities may at times overlap—temporarily, accidentally, illegally—but believe that we can nonetheless tell them apart, disentangling them when necessary. Indeed, even in work environments that are overtly and explicitly sexual, the imperative encourages us to see sex as the perpetual visitor, external to the true life and purpose of the organization. As workers, we signal one another that sex is (or should be) marginal to work.

One tactic is to trivialize sexual displays. We devalue work environments in which physical attractiveness is emphasized and are reluctant to assign "professional" status to those whose jobs require them to be physically attractive. Recent efforts to "professionalize" some jobs, for example by turning "stewardesses" into "flight attendants" or "secretaries" into "office managers," are often little more than campaigns to desexualize them. Professional women, especially, find it insulting to be told that their appearance is part of the job. Because we imagine a distinction between "real work" and sex appeal, such compliments are seen as a trivialization of their professional skills. Workers who do acknowledge their use of sexuality are usually deemed nonprofessional or are criticized for being unprofessional.

We frame sexual discussions as jokes or distractions and use special labels to distinguish sexuality from the flow of "real" work. When sex is the subject of conversation, we are trading "gossip" or "just kidding around." "We joke about it, you know," according to Ralph, an executive with an oil and gas exploration company in Houston. "We'll say, 'So, did you get any sex this weekend?' Or, 'I'm gonna go out and get some sex this weekend.' I'll ask Perry, this guy at work, when's the last time he and his girlfriend Jackie had sex. You know, we joke about that a lot."

Sometimes the discussion is accompanied by a disclaimer, a protestation of surprise that denotes its forbidden status. "It's *amazing* what people will tell you if you ask them," says Peter, a Philadelphia realtor who claims to know "a lot" about the private lives of his coworkers. Matt adds, "I'm always *astounded* that people will engage in that sort of locker-room talk" about their sexual conquests. Others confess a sort of guilty pleasure in talking about sex while at work. "It's terrible," Peter says, "but we shock each other by saying outrageous things, just to pass the time when the market is slow." Scott, who works for Blue Cross in Philadelphia, agrees. "You'd be amazed—or maybe you wouldn't—at what people will ask after they've had a couple of beers or a couple of drinks. And how forward people will get!"

When work environments are especially matter-of-fact about sexuality, they are usually described as being "unusual" in this respect. George feels that his company is unique because most of its senior executives are Scandinavian. "People talk about sex in Scandinavia like they talk about going to the store. They just don't have the hangups we have in America. It took some getting used to." Others say they don't appreciate the sexual candor. Burt, a paralegal for a large Philadelphia firm, has no patience for the "constant heterosexual jokes" he hears at work. "As I'm taking notes, my boss will say things like, 'Did you see the piece of ass on that chick?' To me that's just gross. There's no place for that kind of talk in the office." Whether they are deemed amusing or offensive, trivial or inappropriate, sexual conversations are thus seen as a sort of lived exception to the asexual imperative. They are considered surprising or shocking, an indulgence or a distraction. By labeling sex in these ways, professionals signify its tenuous status in the organization.

Professionals also tend to limit their discussion of sex to those below or beside them in the hierarchy. Like other discrediting or "unprofessional" behavior, sex talk travels downward along the chain of command. Of the men we interviewed, only one felt that he could discuss sexual matters openly with his superior. "With people below you in the hierarchy, no problem," Burt adds, to clarify his earlier comment. "You can joke and have a good time, you can do whatever you want. But there are lines of demarcation about what you say to people above you." The result is a tendency to save one's sexual puns or confidences for those who are less powerful, those who share one's status, or those who are discredited. Steve shares a series of "secret nicknames" with the other junior accountants in his Houston firm (like "The FF Look," for the "fresh-fucked look"). Grey regularly "cruises" the aisles of the mall during his lunch hour, usually with the women in his secretarial pool.

Some men even suggest that sexual conversations are typical of a category of person, usually those of lower status within the organization. "My boss is a professional, and my colleagues are somewhat professional," according to Brent. "Everyone else

is clerical, so it's a different kind of person. They tend to be busybodies, discussing people's personal—you know, gossiping and that sort of thing, not as serious about their work." Like most men, Brent says that sex talk isn't something a rising executive should indulge in.

The formal hierarchy is further supplemented in most organizations by a gender hierarchy, which makes it easier for gay men to confide in women than in other men. Gay professionals sometimes accumulate a coterie of female subordinates (nurses, secretaries, and so forth) with whom they share their secrets. Tip has this sort of relationship with the support staff at his hospital. Though he avoids sexual topics with his various supervisors, Tip is close to several of the female nurses. "Because of the intensity of the emergency room and operating room, you bond with everyone," he explains. "The nurses that I run into know that I'm gay—I seek them out. I go down there when I have nothing to do and visit. We chat and discuss relationships."

In short, sexual banter is considered a trivial activity and is generally reserved for trivial people. Professionals feel they are being casual or frivolous when talking about sex, and are reluctant to take this tone with those who are more senior. "A lot of flirting goes on at our office," says Darren, whose clinic employs a number of young, female dental hygienists. "As you can imagine, there are so many young women in our office, and I'm the only unmarried man there. So you have a lot of women between twenty and thirty, and flirting with me is a big part of their lives."

The asexual imperative further compels professionals to marginalize sexuality, to grant it the sort of limited access one accords any visitor: only to certain physical areas and at certain times, usually when "normal" office activities have been temporarily suspended (during lunches, breaks, travel, or special events). Overtly sexual behaviors are thus confined to the temporal and spatial margins of "work," permitted only in personal spaces or during specks of personal time.

In the most obvious sense, personal time commences when the workday ends, during the transition from business hours to social or leisure time. The restraint that coworkers show during the day dissolves over drinks or dinner, and after-work outings often raise sexual or romantic possibilities (for many gay men, a compelling reason to avoid them). "If you want to talk about sex, you should talk about it after work or some other time," says Roland. "If a coworker said to me, 'Can we go out after work and talk about X, Y or Z?', I'd say 'Sure'," Jerry makes the same distinction. "With your friends, on nonwork time, it's perfectly fine to discuss sexuality. It's also fine if your friends happen to be coworkers, when you're not on work time."

Blocks of personal time or space can also be snatched at other times during the day, provided official duties have been temporarily suspended. Sometimes, a verbal cue signals the transition. Martin remembers feeling a "pang of fear" when his boss at Ogilvy & Mather suggested that they "have a friendly chat." "I knew that meant he wanted to talk about personal stuff, which made me uncomfortable." Other men chuckle at the tendency of their coworkers to whisper when talking about personal matters, as if they were sharing a dirty secret. "They don't say, 'She works in respiratory therapy and she happens to be gay,'" according to Patrick. "It's more like [he whispers and points], 'She's gay.'" Verbal ("Let's get back to work") or nonverbal cues (withdrawing eye contact, shuffling papers) can signal the end of a personal moment.

At other times the transition is spatial. Coworkers may seek the refuge of a private office or call one another "aside" in the hallways before trafficking in sexual information. Men's restrooms become "personal space,"

in which the usual restrictions on sex talk are suspended. Business travel occupies a hazy gray area, bringing coworkers together in settings (hotels, airports) that mingle the personal and the professional. Company picnics, dinners, and outings are in fact designed for this purpose, to encourage social relationships between those who might otherwise know each other only on a limited, professional basis. As any corporate caterer knows, nothing kills a company party more quickly than the decision to hold it on company grounds. Perhaps because the spatial location (work space) is at odds with its temporal location (after work) and purpose (nonwork), the frequent result is ambiguity about appropriate social behavior and a lousy time for all. The move from company space signals a transition to personal time.

When coworkers encounter one another unexpectedly in such settings, the boundaries can become fuzzy. Martin ran into his secretary at a gay disco, and was distressed the following Monday when she complimented him on "the shirt I was wearing on Saturday night." Though no one else overhead their exchange, he felt she had "intruded" on his social life. Arthur remembers running into Robert, one of the firm's paralegals, at a concert. "I've known for a long time that Robert is gay," says Arthur. "You know, I see him sitting on the Long Island Railroad, getting off at the right stops, that kind of stuff. He's seen me with all-male groups; I've seen him with all-male groups, having dinner or going to the movies. We never really talked about it. Then I went to a performance of the Gay Men's Chorus, and there he was, singing baritone. At first I was afraid to congratulate him on a wonderful concert, but then I realized that that's a very public sort of thing, to get up there on stage. I mean, Carnegie Hall, that's pretty public. And so I told him I enjoyed the concert, and since then we've been friendly."

The distinction between personal and company time is further eroded in those exceptional institutions that establish no such boundaries. Most organizations permit some segregation of professional and personal lives, however vague or shifting the boundary. It is a different matter, however, when the "total" quality of an organization precludes such distinctions. "My boss has this view of officers as representatives, twenty-four hours per day, of the company," says Jeff. As evidence of this he cites a story he heard about the director of human resources, a man named Greg, shortly after he joined the company. "I've never asked Greg whether this is true or not, but somebody told me that the president of the company told Greg that he didn't want him seen coming out of the all-male theater, the Tom Cat bookstore. Apparently Greg had been seen going in there a couple of times."

Tip complains that he has no personal time. As a surgical resident he is accustomed to long hours and frequent nights on call. Even when not at the hospital, he is at the beck and call of the hospital—practically and symbolically affirmed by the pager he wears. "My boss doesn't like you to take vacations," he says, "even though it's allowed. He feels you're wasting your time. If you come in with a tan, he'll give you grief about the fact that you weren't at home reading." Other organizations, like churches and the military, argue that their members are always on the job, that one simply *is* a soldier or priest. In dismissing thousands of lesbian and gay men, the military has argued that their sexual behavior falls within its broad jurisdiction, even when it takes place off site and after hours.

But such organizations are unusual. In most cases the question is not if but *where* the boundary between the public and private shall be placed. The asexual imperative, having insisted that such a divide is possible, ensures that work and sex will be on opposite sides of it. The imperative is neither unconditional nor universally imposed (or self-imposed); indeed, it varies in strength from one setting to the next, even within the same organization. Yet virtually all gay men articulate it—and quite often defend it—in one form or another.

It is easy to see why the asexual imperative might appeal to gay men. Describing it, they are sometimes emotional, often passionate. They adopt a tone of voice reserved for sensitive subjects, and it is clear that they have used these same words before. In their comments one often hears what appear to be contradictions, as they articulate their wishes (the hortatory "Sexuality *shouldn't* matter") in the form of observations or statements of fact (the declarative "Sexuality *doesn't* matter"). Yet the repeated insistence—that sexuality *doesn't* matter, *doesn't* belong in the workplace, *is* a private matter—scarcely conceals the men's recognition that it is not always so.

The asexual imperative insists that workers be judged on the quality of their work, that professional interactions be stripped of their sexual component. For men whose sexuality has been stigmatized, criminalized, medicalized, morally condemned, and subjected to interpersonal penalties of all sorts, this is a powerful idea. Seen in this way, the invocation of the imperative is an appeal for fairness; it demands that "work" be defined narrowly, that it not be confused with the social or sexual characteristics of the individual doing it. "It's not a perfect world," says Terry. "Sexuality should have no impact on the people you work with, on clients, or on business development and all of that." But Terry knows that this isn't the case. "I know some people in town who have that situation, but there are damn few."

The imperative is appealing for another reason. By demanding that workers be asexual, it permits gay men to rationalize the painful efforts they sometimes make to misrepresent themselves at work. As they worry about the necessity of misleading coworkers, as they speak to them of imaginary lovers or take pains to disguise actual ones, they often believe that they are acting on principle. Strict beliefs about privacy and professionalism are comforting; they supply a justification, other than self-protection, for sexual secrecy. "Even if coming out were easier, if you weren't worried about losing your job or something, I don't think I would do it," says Glen. "Even if gay people were in the majority, I would want a certain amount of privacy. I don't think I'd want everyone at work to know my business." But beneath his statement of principle lies another motive. "It would be nice," he adds, "to have the choice."

NOTES

1. David F. Greenberg, *The Construction of Homosexuality* (Chicago: University of Chicago Press, 1988), pp. 437–38. See also pp. 434–54.

2. *New York Times*, June 13, 1991, p. D1.

3. Andrea Warfield, "Co-Worker Romances: Impact on the Work Group and on Career-Oriented Women," *Personnel*, May 1987, pp. 22–35.

4. Ibid., p. 30.

5. "Romance in the Workplace: Corporate Rules for the Game of Love," *Business Week*, June 18, 1984, pp. 70–71.

6. Letitia Baldrige, *Letitia Baldrige's Complete Guide to Executive Manners* (New York: Rawson, 1985), p. 53.

7. Barbara Gutek, "Sexuality in the Workplace: Key Issues in Research and Organizational Practice, in Hearn et al., *The Sexuality of Organization*, p. 57.

8. Woods, James D. "Self-Disclosure at Work." Results of a questionnaire distributed in *Out/Look*, vol. 16 (Spring 1992), pp. 87–88.

9. Woods, "Self-Disclosure at Work," pp. 87–88.

32

The Social Structure of Managerial Work

Robert Jackall

Robert Jackall is Willmott Family Professor of Sociology and Social Thought at Williams College. This reading is from his 1988 book, *Moral Mazes: The World of Corporate Managers*. Jackall is currently writing a book on detective work and its ways of knowing.

I

The hierarchical authority structure that is the linchpin of bureaucracy dominates the way managers think about their world and about themselves.

Managers do not see or experience authority in any abstract way; instead, authority is embodied in their personal relationships with their immediate bosses and in their perceptions of similar links between other managers up and down the hierarchy. When managers describe their work to an outsider, they almost always first say: "I work for [Bill James]" or "I report to [Harry Mills]" or "I'm in [Joe Bell's] group," and only then proceed to describe their actual work functions. Such a personalized statement of authority relationships seems to contradict classical notions of how bureaucracies function but it exactly reflects the way authority is structured, exercised, and experienced in corporate hierarchies.

American businesses typically both centralize and decentralize authority. Power is concentrated at the top in the person of the chief executive officer (CEO) and is simultaneously decentralized; that is, responsibility for decisions and profits is pushed as far down the organizational line as possible. For example, Alchemy Inc. is one of several operating companies of Covenant Corporation. When I began my research, Alchemy employed 11,000 people; Covenant had over 50,000 employees and now has over 100,000. Like the other operating companies, Alchemy has its own president, executive vice-presidents, vice-presidents, other executive officers, business area managers, staff divisions, and more than eighty manufacturing plants scattered throughout the country and indeed the world producing a wide range of specialty and commodity chemicals. Each operating company is, at least theoretically, an autonomous, self-sufficient organization, though they are all monitored and coordinated by a central corporate staff, and each president reports directly to the corporate CEO. Weft Corporation has its corporate headquarters and manufacturing facilities in the South; its marketing and sales offices, along with some key executive personnel, are in New York City. Weft employs 20,000 people, concentrated in the firm's three textile divisions that have always been and remain its core business. The Apparel Division produces seven million yards a week of raw, unfinished cloth in several greige (colloquially gray) mills, mostly for sale to garment manufacturers; the Consumer Division produces some cloth of its own in several greige mills and also finishes—that is, bleaches, dyes, prints, and sews—twelve million yards of

raw cloth a month into purchasable items like sheets, pillowcases, and tablecloths for department stores and chain stores; and the Retail Division operates an import-export business, specializing in the quick turnaround of the fast-moving cloths desired by Seventh Avenue designers. Each division has a president who reports to one of several executive vice-presidents, who in turn report to the corporate CEO. The divisional structure is typically less elaborate in its hierarchical ladder than the framework of independent operating companies; it is also somewhat more dependent on corporate staff for essential services. However, the basic principle of simultaneous centralization and decentralization prevails and both Covenant and Weft consider their companies or divisions, as the case may be, "profit centers." Even Images Inc., while much smaller than the industrial concerns and organized like most service businesses according to shifting groupings of client accounts supervised by senior vice-presidents, uses the notion of profit centers.

The key interlocking mechanism of this structure is its reporting system. Each manager gathers up the profit targets or other objectives of his or her subordinates and, with these, formulates his commitments to his boss; this boss takes these commitments and those of his other subordinates, and in turn makes a commitment to his boss. At the top of the line, the president of each company or division, or, at Images Inc., the senior vice-president for a group of accounts, makes his commitment to the CEO. This may be done directly, or sometimes, as at Weft Corporation, through a corporate executive vice-president. In any event, the commitments made to top management depend on the pyramid of stated objectives given to superiors up the line. At each level of the structure, there is typically "topside" pressure to achieve higher goals and, of course, the CEO frames and paces the whole process by applying pressure for attainment of his own objectives. Meanwhile, bosses and subordinates down the line engage in a series of intricate negotiations—managers often call these "conspiracies"—to keep their commitments respectable but achievable.

This "management-by-objective" system, as it is usually called, creates a chain of commitments from the CEO down to the lowliest product manager or account executive. In practice, it also shapes a patrimonial authority arrangement that is crucial to defining both the immediate experiences and the long-run career chances of individual managers. In this world, a subordinate owes fealty principally to his immediate boss. This means that a subordinate must not overcommit his boss, lest his boss "get on the hook" for promises that cannot be kept. He must keep his boss from making mistakes, particularly public ones; he must keep his boss informed, lest his boss get "blindsided." If one has a mistake-prone boss, there is, of course, always the temptation to let him make a fool of himself, but the wise subordinate knows that this carries two dangers—he himself may get done in by his boss's errors, and, perhaps more important, other managers will view with the gravest suspicion a subordinate who withholds crucial information from his boss even if they think the boss is a nincompoop. A subordinate must also not circumvent his boss nor ever give the appearance of doing so. He must never contradict his boss's judgment in public. To violate the last admonition is thought to constitute a kind of death wish in business, and one who does so should practice what one executive calls "flexibility drills," an exercise "where you put your head between your legs and kiss your ass goodbye." On a social level, even though an easy, breezy, first-name informality is the prevalent style of American business, a concession perhaps to our democratic heritage and egalitarian rhetoric, the subordinate must extend to the boss a certain ritual deference. For instance, he must follow the boss's lead in conversation, must not speak out of turn at meetings, must laugh at his boss's jokes while not making jokes of his own that upstage his boss, must not rib the boss for his foibles. The shrewd subordinate learns to efface himself, so that his boss's face might shine more clearly.

In short, the subordinate must symbolically reinforce at every turn his own subordination and his willing acceptance of the obligations of fealty. In return, he can hope for those perquisites that are in his boss's gift—the better, more attractive secretaries, or the nudging of a movable panel to enlarge his office, and perhaps a couch to fill the added space, one of the real distinctions in corporate bureaucracies. He can hope to be elevated when and if the boss is elevated, though other important criteria intervene here. He can also expect protection for mistakes made, up to a point. However, that point is never exactly defined and depends on the complicated politics of each situation. The general rule is that bosses are expected to protect those in their bailiwicks. Not to do so, or to be unable to do so, is taken as a sign of untrustworthiness or weakness. If, however, subordinates make mistakes that are thought to be dumb, or especially if they violate fealty obligations—for example, going around their boss—then abandonment of them to the vagaries of organizational forces is quite acceptable.

Overlaying and intertwined with this formal monocratic system of authority, with its patrimonial resonance, are patron-client relationships. Patrons are usually powerful figures in the higher echelons of management. The patron might be a manager's direct boss, or his boss's boss, or someone several levels higher in the chain of command. In either case, the manager is still bound by the immediate, formal authority and fealty patterns of his position but he also acquires new, though more ambiguous, fealty relationships with his highest ranking patron. Patrons play a crucial role in advancement, a point that I shall discuss later.

It is characteristic of this authority system that details are pushed down and credit is pulled up. Superiors do not like to give detailed instructions to subordinates. The official reason for this is to maximize subordinates' autonomy. The underlying reason is, first, to get rid of tedious details. Most hierarchically organized occupations follow this pattern; one of the privileges of authority is the divestment of humdrum intricacies. This also insulates higher bosses from the peculiar pressures that accompany managerial work at the middle levels and below: the lack of economy over one's time because of continual interruption from one's subordinates, telephone calls from customers and clients, and necessary meetings with colleagues; the piecemeal fragmentation of issues both because of the discontinuity of events and because of the way subordinates filter news; and the difficulty of minding the store while sorting out sometimes unpleasant personnel issues. Perhaps more important, pushing details down protects the privilege of authority to declare that a mistake has been made. A high-level executive in Alchemy Inc. explains:

> If I tell someone what to do—like do A, B, or C—the inference and implication is that he will succeed in accomplishing the objective. Now, if he doesn't succeed, that means that I have invested part of myself in his work and I lose any right I have to chew his ass out if he doesn't succeed. If I tell you what to do, I can't bawl you out if things don't work. And this is why a lot of bosses don't give explicit directions. They just give a statement of objectives, and then they can criticize subordinates who fail to make their goals.

Moreover, pushing down details relieves superiors of the burden of too much knowledge, particularly guilty knowledge. A superior will say to a subordinate, for instance: "Give me your best thinking on the problem with [X]." When the subordinate makes his report, he is often told: "I think you can do better than that," until the subordinate has worked out all the details of the boss's predetermined solution, without the boss being specifically aware of "all the eggs that have to be broken." It is also not at all uncommon for very bald and extremely general edicts to emerge from on high. For example, "Sell the plant in [St. Louis]; let me know when you've struck a deal," or "We need to get higher prices for [fabric X]; see what you can work out," or "Tom, I want you to go down there and meet with those guys and make a deal and I don't want you to come back until you've got one." This pushing down of details has important consequences.

First, because they are unfamiliar with—indeed deliberately distance themselves from—entangling details, corporate higher echelons tend to expect successful results without messy complications. This is central to top executives' well-known aversion to bad news and to the resulting tendency to kill the messenger who bears the news.

Second, the pushing down of details creates great pressure on middle managers not only to transmit good news but, precisely because they know the details, to act to protect their corporations, their bosses, and themselves in the process. They become the "point men" of a given strategy and the potential "fall guys" when things go wrong. From an organizational standpoint, overly conscientious managers are particularly useful at the middle levels of the structure. Upwardly mobile men and women, especially those from working-class origins who find themselves in higher status milieux, seem to have the requisite level of anxiety, and perhaps tightly controlled anger and hostility, that fuels an obsession with detail. Of course, such conscientiousness is not necessarily, and is certainly not systematically, rewarded; the real organizational premiums are placed on other, more flexible, behavior.

Credit flows up in this structure and is usually appropriated by the highest ranking officer involved in a successful decision or resolution of a problem. There is, for instance, a tremendous competition for ideas in the corporate world; authority provides a license to steal ideas, even in front of those who originated them. Chairmen routinely appropriate the useful suggestions made by members of their committees or task forces; research directors build their reputations for scientific wizardry on the bricks laid down by junior researchers and directors of departments. Presidents of whole divisions as well are always on the lookout for "fresh ideas" and "creative approaches" that they can claim as their own in order to put themselves "out in front" of their peers. A subordinate whose ideas are appropriated is expected to be a good sport about the matter; not to balk at so being used is one attribute of the good team player. The person who appropriates credit redistributes it as he chooses, bound essentially and only by a sensitivity to public perceptions of his fairness. One gives credit, therefore, not necessarily where it is due, although one always invokes this old saw, but where prudence dictates. Customarily, people who had nothing to do with the success of a project can be allocated credit for their exemplary efforts. At the middle levels, therefore, credit for a particular idea or success is always a type of refracted social honor; one cannot claim credit even if it is earned. Credit has to be given, and acceptance of the gift implicitly involves a reaffirmation and strengthening of fealty. A superior may share some credit with subordinates in order to deepen fealty relationships and induce greater efforts on his behalf. Of course, a different system obtains in the allocation of blame.

Because of the interlocking character of the commitment system, a CEO carries enormous influence in his corporation. If, for a moment, one thinks of the presidents of operating companies or divisions as barons, then the CEO of the corporation is the king. His word is law; even the CEO's wishes and whims are taken as commands by close subordinates on the corporate staff, who turn them into policies and directives. A typical example occurred in Weft Corporation a few years ago when the CEO, new at the time, expressed mild concern about the rising operating costs of the company's fleet of rented cars. The following day, a stringent system for monitoring mileage replaced the previous casual practice. Managers have a myriad of aphorisms that refer to how the power of CEOs, magnified through the zealous efforts of subordinates, affects them. These range from the trite "When he sneezes, we all catch colds" to the more colorful "When he says 'Go to the bathroom,' we all get the shits."

Great efforts are made to please the CEO. For example, when the CEO of Covenant Corporation visits a plant, the most significant order of business for local management is a fresh paint job, even when, as in several cases, the cost of paint alone exceeds $100,000. If a paint job has already been scheduled at a plant, it is deferred along with all other cosmetic maintenance until just before the CEO arrives; keeping up appearances without recognition for one's efforts is pointless. I am told that similar anecdotes from other corporations have been in circulation since 1910, which suggests a certain historical continuity of behavior toward top bosses.

The second order of business for the plant management is to produce a book fully describing the plant and its operations, replete with photographs and illustrations, for presentation to the CEO; such a book costs about $10,000 for the single copy. By any standards of budgetary stringency, such expenditures are irrational. But by the social standards of the corporation, they make perfect sense. It is far more important to please the king today than to worry about the future economic state of one's fief, since, if one does not please the king, there may not be a fief to worry about or indeed vassals to do the worrying.

By the same token, all of this leads to an intense interest in everything the CEO does and says. In all the companies that I studied, the most common topic of conversation among managers up and down the line is speculation about their respective CEO's plans, intentions, strategies, actions, style, public image, and ideological leanings of the moment. Even the metaphorical temper of a CEO's language finds its way down the hierarchy to the lower reaches of an organization. In the early stages of my fieldwork at Covenant Corporation, for example, I was puzzled by the inordinately widespread usage of nautical terminology, especially in a corporation located in a landlocked site. As it happens, the CEO is devoted to sailboats and prefers that his aides call him "Skipper." Moreover, in every corporation that I studied, stories and rumors circulate constantly about the social world of the CEO and his immediate subordinates—who, for instance, seems to have the CEO's ear at the moment; whose style seems to have gained approbation; who, in short, seems to be in the CEO's grace and who seems to have fallen out of favor. In the smaller and more intimate setting of Images Inc., the circulation of favor takes an interesting, if unusual, tack. There, the CEO is known for attaching younger people to himself as confidants. He solicits their advice, tells them secrets, gets their assessments of developments further down in the hierarchy, gleans the rumors and gossip making the rounds about himself. For the younger people selected for such attention, this is a rare, if fleeting, opportunity to have a place in the sun and to share the illusion if not the substance of power. In time, of course, the CEO tires of or becomes disappointed with

particular individuals and turns his attention to others. "Being discarded," however, is not an obstacle to regaining favor. In larger organizations, impermeable structural barriers between top circles and junior people prevent this kind of intimate interchange and circulation of authoritative regard. Within a CEO's circle, however, the same currying and granting of favor prevails, always amidst conjectures from below about who has edged close to the throne.

But such speculation about the CEO and his leanings of the moment is more than idle gossip, and the courtlike atmosphere that I am describing more than stylized diversion. Because he stands at the apex of the corporation's bureaucratic and patrimonial structures and locks the intricate system of commitments between bosses and subordinates into place, it is the CEO who ultimately decides whether those commitments have been satisfactorily met. The CEO becomes the actual and the symbolic keystone of the hierarchy that constitutes the defining point of the managerial experience. Moreover, the CEO and his trusted associates determine the fate of whole business areas of a corporation.

Within the general ambiance established by a CEO, presidents of individual operating companies or of divisions carry similar, though correspondingly reduced, influence within their own baronies. Adroit and well-placed subordinates can, for instance, borrow a president's prestige and power to exert great leverage. Even chance encounters or the occasional meeting or lunch with the president can, if advertised casually and subtly, cause notice and the respect among other managers that comes from uncertainty. Knowledge of more clearly established relationships, of course, always sways behavior. A middle manager in one company, widely known to be a very close personal friend of the president, flagged her copious memoranda to other managers with large green paperclips, ensuring prompt attention to her requests. More generally, each major division of the core textile group in Weft Corporation is widely thought to reflect the personality of its leader—one hard-driving, intense, and openly competitive; one cool, precise, urbane, and proper; and one gregarious, talkative, and self-promotional. Actually, market exigencies play a large role in shaping each division's tone and tempo. Still, the popular conception of the dominance of presidential personalities not only points to the crucial issue of style in business, a topic to be explored in depth later, but it underlines the general tendency to personalize authority in corporate bureaucracies.

Managers draw elaborate cognitive maps to guide them through the thickets of their organizations. Because they see and experience authority in such personal terms, the singular feature of these maps is their biographical emphasis. Managers carry around in their heads thumbnail sketches of the occupational history of virtually every other manager of their own rank or higher in their particular organization. These maps begin with a knowledge of others' occupational expertise and specific work experience, but focus especially on previous and present reporting relationships, patronage relationships, and alliances. Cognitive maps incorporate memories of social slights, of public embarrassments, of battles won and lost, and of people's behavior under pressure. They include as well general estimates of the abilities and career trajectories of their colleagues. I should mention that these latter estimates are not necessarily accurate or fair; they are, in fact, often based on the flimsiest of evidence. For instance, a general manager at Alchemy Inc. describes the ephemeral nature of such opinions:

It's a feeling about the guy's perceived ability to run a business—like he's not a good people man, or he's not a good numbers man. This is not a quantitative thing. It's a gut feeling that a guy can't be put in one spot, but he might be put in another spot. These kinds of informal opinions about others are the lifeblood of an organization's advancement system. Oh, for the record, we've got the formal evaluations; but the real opinions—the ones that really count in determining people's fates—are those which are traded back and forth in meetings, private conferences, chance encounters, and so on.

Managers trade estimates of others' chances within their circles and often color them to suit their own purposes. This is one reason why it is crucial for the aspiring young manager to project the right image to the right people who can influence others' sketches of him. Whatever the accuracy of these vocabularies of description, managers' penchant for biographical detail and personal histories contrasts sharply with their disinclination for details in general or for other kinds of history. Details, as I have mentioned, get pushed down the ladder; and a concern with history, even of the short-run, let alone long-term, structural shifts in one's own organization, constrains the forward orientation and cheerful optimism highly valued in most corporations. Biographical detail, however, constitutes crucial knowledge because managers know that, in the rough-and-tumble politics of the corporate world, individual fates are made and broken not necessarily by one's accomplishments but by other people. . . .

III

. . . Here I want to highlight a few basic structures and experiences of managerial work, those that seem to form its essential framework. First of all, at the psychological level, managers have an acute sense of organizational contingency. Because of the interlocking ties between people, they know that a shake-up at or near the top of a hierarchy can trigger a widespread upheaval, bringing in its wake startling reversals of fortune, good and bad, throughout the structure. Managers' cryptic aphorism, "Well, you never know . . . ," repeated often and regularly, captures the sense of uncertainty created by the constant potential for social reversal. Managers know too, and take for granted, that the personnel changes brought about by upheavals are to a great extent arbitrary and depend more than anything else on one's social relationships with key individuals and with groups of managers. Periods of organizational quiescence and stability still managers' wariness in this regard, but the foreboding sense of contingency never entirely disappears. Managers' awareness of the complex levels of conflict in their world, built into the very structure of bureaucratic organizations, constantly reminds them that things can very quickly fall apart.

The political struggles at Covenant Corporation, for instance, suggest some immediately observable levels of conflict and tension.

First, occupational groups emerging from the segmented structure of bureaucratic work, each with different expertise and emphasis, constantly vie with one another for ascendancy of their ideas, of their products or services, and of themselves. It is, for instance, an axiom of corporate life that the greatest satisfaction of production people is to see products go out the door; of salesmen, to make a deal regardless of price; of marketers, to control salesmen and squeeze profits out of their deals; and of financial specialists, to make sure that everybody meets budget. Despite the larger interdependence of such work, the necessarily fragmented functions performed day-to-day by managers in one area often put them at cross purposes with

managers in another. Nor do competitiveness and conflict result only from the broad segmentation of functions. Sustained work in a product or service area not only shapes crucial social affiliations but also symbolic identifications, say, with particular products or technical services, that mark managers in their corporate arenas. Such symbolic markings make it imperative for managers to push their particular products or services as part of their overall self-promotion. This fuels the constant scramble for authoritative enthusiasm for one product or service rather than another and the subsequent allocation or reallocation of organizational resources.

Second, line and staff managers, each group with different responsibilities, different pressures, and different bailiwicks to protect, fight over organizational resources and over the rules that govern work. The very definition of staff depends entirely on one's vantage point in the organization. As one manager points out: "From the perspective of the guy who actually pushes the button to make the machine go, everyone else is staff." However, the working definition that managers use is that anyone whose decisions directly affect profit and loss is in the line; all others in an advisory capacity of some sort are staff. As a general rule, line managers' attitudes toward staff vary directly with the independence granted staff by higher management. The more freedom staff have to intervene in the line, as with the environmental staff at Alchemy or Covenant's corporate staff, the more they are feared and resented by line management. For line managers, independent staff represent either the intrusion of an unwelcome "rules and procedures mentality" into situations where line managers feel that they have to be alert to the exigencies of the market or, alternatively, as power threats to vested interests backed by some authority. In the "decentralized" organizations prevalent today in the corporate world, however, most staff are entirely dependent on the line and must market their technical, legal, or organizational skills to line managers exactly as an outside firm must do. The continual necessity for staff to sell their technical expertise helps keep them in check since line managers, pleading budgetary stringency or any number of other acceptable rationales, can thwart or ignore proffered assistance. Staff's dependent position often produces jealous respect for line management tinged with the resentment that talented people relegated to do "pine time" (sit on the bench) feel for those in the center of action. For instance, an environmental manager at Weft Corporation comments on his marginal status and on how he sees it depriving him of the recognition he feels his work deserves:

> I also want recognition. And usually the only way you get that is having a boss near you who sees what you do. It rubs me raw in fact. . . . For instance, you know they run these news releases when some corporate guy gets promoted and all? Well, when I do something, nothing ever gets said. When I publish papers, or get promoted, and so on, you never see any public announcement. Oh, they like me to publish papers and I guess someone reads them, but that's all that's ever said or done. . . . I can get recognition in a variety of arenas, like professional associations, but if they're going to recognize the plant manager, why not me? If we walked off, would the plants operate? They couldn't. We're *essential*.

This kind of ambivalent resentment sometimes becomes vindictiveness when a top boss uses staff as a hammer.

Staff can also become effective pitchmen; line managers' anxious search for rational solutions to largely irrational problems, in fact, encourages staff continually to invent and disseminate new tactics and schemes. Alternatively, social upheavals that produce rapid shifts in public opinion—such as occurred in the personnel or environmental areas in the aftermath of the 1960s—may encourage proliferation of staff. In either circumstance, staff tend to increase in an organization until an ideological cycle of "organizational leanness" comes around and staff, at least those of lower rank, get decimated.

Third, powerful managers in Alchemy Inc., each controlling considerable resources and the organizational fates of many men and women, battle fiercely with one another to position themselves, their products, and their allies favorably in the eyes of their president and of the CEO. At the same time, high-ranking executives "go to the mat" with one another striving for the CEO's approval and a coveted shot at the top. Bureaucratic hierarchies, simply by offering ascertainable rewards for certain behavior, fuel the ambition of those men and women ready to subject themselves to the discipline of external exigencies and of their organization's institutional logic, the socially constructed, shared understanding of how their world works. However, since rewards are always scarce, bureaucracies necessarily pit people against each other and inevitably thwart the ambitions of some. The rules of such combat vary from organization to organization and depend largely on what top management countenances either openly or tacitly.

Nor are formal positions and perquisites the only objects of personal struggle between managers. Even more important on a day-to-day basis is the ongoing competition between talented and aggressive people to see whose will prevails, who can get things done their way. The two areas are, of course, related since one's chances in an organization depend largely on one's "credibility," that is, on the widespread belief that one can act effectively. One must therefore prevail regularly, though not always, in small things to have any hope of positioning oneself for big issues. The hidden agenda of seemingly petty disputes may be a struggle over long-term organizational fates.

At the same time, all of these struggles take place within the peculiar tempo and framework each CEO establishes for an organization. Under an ideology of thorough decentralization—the gift of authority with responsibility—the CEO at Covenant actually centralizes his power enormously because fear of derailing personal ambitions prevents managers below him from acting without his approval. A top official at Alchemy comments:

> What we have now, despite rhetoric to the contrary, is a very centralized system. It's [the CEO] who sets the style, tone, tempo of all the companies. He says: "Manage for cash," and we manage for cash. The original idea . . . was to set up free-standing companies with a minimum of corporate staff. But . . . we're moving toward a system that is really beyond what we used to have, let alone modeled on a small corporate staff and autonomous divisions. What we used to have was separate divisions reporting to a corporate staff. I think we're moving away from that idea too. I think what's coming is a bunch of separate businesses reporting to the corporation. It's a kind of portfolio management. This accords perfectly with [the CEO's] temperament. He's a financial type guy who is oriented to the bottom line numbers. He doesn't want or need intermediaries between him and his businesses.

In effect, the CEO of Covenant, who seems to enjoy constant turmoil, pits himself and his ego against the whole corporation even while he holds it in vassalage. Other CEOs establish different frameworks and different tempos, depending on self-image and temperament. The only firm rule seems to be that articulated by a middle-level Covenant

manager: "Every big organization is set up for the benefit of those who control it; the boss gets what he wants."

Except during times of upheaval, the ongoing conflicts that I have described are usually hidden behind the comfortable and benign social ambiance that most American corporations fashion for their white-collar personnel. Plush carpets, potted trees, burnished oak wall paneling, fine reproductions and sometimes originals of great art, mahogany desks, polished glass tables and ornaments, rich leather upholstery, perfectly coiffured, attractive and poised receptionists, and private, subsidized cafeterias are only a few of the pleasant features that grace the corporate headquarters of any major company. In addition, the corporations that I studied provide their employees with an amazing range and variety of services, information, and social contacts. Covenant Corporation, for instance, through its daily newsletter and a variety of other internal media, offers information about domestic and international vacation packages; free travelers' checks; discounted tickets for the ballet, tennis matches, or art exhibits; home remedies for the common cold, traveling clinics for diagnosing high blood pressure, and advice on how to save one's sight; simple tests for gauging automotive driving habits; tips on home vegetable gardening; advice on baby-sitters; descriptions of business courses at a local college; warning articles on open fireplaces and home security; and directions for income tax filing. The newsletter also offers an internal market for the sale, rental, or exchange of a myriad of items ranging from a Jamaican villa, to a set of barbells, to back issues of *Fantasy* magazine. Covenant offers as well intracompany trapshooting contests, round-robin tennis and golf tournaments, running clinics, and executive fitness programs. Weft Corporation's bulletin is even more elaborate, with photographic features on the "Great Faces" of Weft employees; regular reports on the company's 25- and 50-year clubs; personal notes on all retirees from the company; stories about the company's sponsorship of art exhibits; human-interest stories about employees and their families—from a child struggling against liver cancer to the heroics of a Weft employee in foiling a plane hijacker; and, of course, a steady drumbeat of corporate ideology about the necessity for textile import quotas and the desirability of "buying American."

My point here is that corporations are not presented nor are they seen simply as places to work for a living. Rather the men and women in them come to fashion an entire social ambiance that overlays the antagonisms created by company politics; this makes the nuances of corporate conflict difficult to discern. A few managers, in fact, mistake the first-name informality, the social congeniality, and the plush exterior appointments for the entire reality of their collective life and are surprised when hard structural jolts turn their world upside down. Even battle-scarred veterans evince, at times, an ambivalent half-belief in the litany of rhetorics of unity and cohesive legitimating appeals. The latter are sometimes accompanied by gala events to underline the appeal. For instance, not long after the "big purge" at Covenant Corporation when 600 people were fired, the CEO spent $1 million for a "Family Day" to "bring everyone together." The massive party was attended by over 14,000 people and featured clowns, sports idols, and booths complete with bean bag and ring tosses, foot and bus races, computer games, dice rolls, and, perhaps appropriately, mazes. In his letter to his "Fellow Employees" following the event, the CEO said:

> I think Family Day made a very strong statement about the [Covenant] "family" of employees at [Corporate Headquarters]. And that is that we can accomplish whatever we set out to do if we work together; if we share the effort, we will share the rewards. The "New World of [Covenant]" has no boundaries only frontiers, and each and everyone can play a role, for we need what *you* have to contribute.

The very necessity for active involvement in such rituals often prompts semicredulity. But wise and ambitious managers resist the lulling platitudes of unity, though they invoke them with fervor, and look for the inevitable clash of interests beneath the bouncy, cheerful surface of corporate life. They understand implicitly that the suppression of open conflict simply puts a premium on the mastery of the socially accepted modes of waging combat.

The continuous uncertainty and ambiguity of managerial hierarchies, exacerbated over time by masked conflict, causes managers to turn toward each other for cues for behavior. They try to learn from each other and to master the shared assumptions, the complex rules, the normative codes, the underlying institutional logic that governs their world. They thus try to control the construction of their everyday reality. Normally, of course, one learns to master the managerial code in the course of repeated, long-term social interaction with other managers, particularly in the course of shaping the multiple and complex alliances essential to organizational survival and success.

Alliances are ties of quasiprimal loyalty shaped especially by common work, by common experiences with the same problems, the same friends, or the same enemies, and by favors traded over time. Although alliances are rooted in fealty and patronage relationships, they are not limited by such relationships since fealty shifts with changing work assignments or with organizational upheavals.

Making an alliance may mean, for instance, joining or, more exactly, being included in one or several of the many networks of managerial associates that crisscross an organization. Conceptually, networks are usually thought of as open-ended webs of association with a low degree of formal organization and no distinct criteria of membership. One becomes known, for instance, as a trusted friend of a friend; thought of as a person to whom one can safely refer a thorny problem; considered a "sensible" or "reasonable" or, especially, a "flexible" person, not a "renegade" or a "loose cannon rolling around the lawn"; known to be a discreet person attuned to the nuances of corporate etiquette, one who can keep one's mouth shut or who can look away and pretend to notice nothing; or considered a person with sharp ideas that break deadlocks but who does not object to the ideas being appropriated by superiors.

Alliances are also fashioned in social coteries. These are more clublike groups of friends that, in Weft Corporation, forge ties at the cocktail hour over the back fence on Racquet Drive, the road next to the company's tennis courts where all important and socially ambitious executives live; or in Friday night poker sessions that provide a bluff and hearty setting where managers can display their own and unobtrusively observe others' mastery of public faces, a clue to many managerial virtues. In other companies, coteries consist of "tennis pals" who share an easy camaraderie over salad and yogurt lunches following hard squash games or two-mile jogs at noon. They are also made up of posthours cronies who, in midtown watering holes, weld private understandings with ironic bantering, broad satire, or macabre humor, the closest some managers ever get to open discussion of their work with their fellows; or gatherings of the smart social set where business circles intersect with cliques from intellectual and artistic worlds and

where glittering, poised, and precisely vacuous social conversation can mark one as a social lion. In one company, a group of "buddies" intertwine their private lives with their organizational fates in the most complete way by, for example, persuading an ambitious younger colleague to provide a woodsy cabin retreat and local girls for a collegial evening's entertainment while on a business trip. At the managerial and professional levels, the road between work and life is usually open because it is difficult to refuse to use one's influence, patronage, or power on behalf of another regular member of one's social coterie. It therefore becomes important to choose one's social colleagues with some care and, of course, know how to drop them should they fall out of organizational favor.

Alliances are also made wholly on the basis of specific self-interests. The paradigmatic case here is that of the power clique of established, well-placed managers who put aside differences and join forces for a "higher cause," namely their own advancement or protection. Normally, though not always, as Brown's case at Covenant shows, one must be "plugged into" important networks and an active participant in key coteries in order to have achieved an organizational position where one's influence is actively counted. But the authority and power of a position matter in and of themselves. Once one has gained power, one can use one's influence in the organization to shape social ties. Such alliances often cut across rival networks and coteries and can, in fact, temporarily unite them. Managers in a power clique map out desired organizational tacks and trade off the resources in their control. They assess the strengths and weaknesses of their opponents; they plan coups and rehearse the appropriate rationales to legitimate them. And, on the other hand, they erect requisite barriers to squelch attempted usurpations of their power. Cliques also introduce managers to new, somewhat more exclusive networks and coteries. Especially at the top of a pyramid, these social ties extend over the boundaries of one's own corporation and mesh one's work and life with those of top managers in other organizations.

I shall refer to all the social contexts that breed alliances, fealty relationships, networks, coteries, or cliques, as circles of affiliation, or simply managerial circles. Now, the notion of "circles," as it has been used in sociological literature as well as colloquially, has some drawbacks for accurately delineating the important features of the web of managerial interaction. Specifically, a circle suggests a quasiclosed social group made up of members of relatively equal status without defined leadership and without formal criteria for membership or inclusion. In a bureaucratic hierarchy, nuances of status are, of course, extremely important. Moreover, since business cannot be conducted without formal authorization by appropriate authorities, one's formal rank always matters even though there is ample scope for more informal charismatic leadership. Finally, the most crucial feature of managerial circles of affiliation is precisely their establishment of informal criteria for admission, criteria that are, it

is true, ambiguously defined and subject to constant, often arbitrary, revision. Nonetheless, they are criteria that managers must master. At bottom, all of the social contexts of the managerial world seek to discover if one "can feel comfortable" with another manager, if he is someone who "can be trusted," if he is "our kind of guy," or, in short, if he is "one of the gang." The notion of gang, in fact, insofar as it suggests the importance of leadership, hierarchy, and probationary mechanisms in a bounded but somewhat amorphous group, may more accurately describe relationships in the corporation than the more genteel, and therefore preferable, word "circle." In any event, just as managers must continually please their boss, their boss's boss, their patrons, their president, and their CEO, so must they prove themselves again and again to each other. Work becomes an endless round of what might be called probationary crucibles. Together with the uncertainty and sense of contingency that mark managerial work, this constant state of probation produces a profound anxiety in managers, perhaps the key experience of managerial work. It also breeds, selects, or elicits certain traits in ambitious managers that are crucial to getting ahead.

33

The Marginalization of Black Executives
Sharon M. Collins

Sharon Collins is associate professor of sociology at the University of Illinois, Chicago. Collins has published extensively on black managers' experiences in predominantly white corporations. In 1997, she published *Black Corporate Executives: The Making and Breaking of a Black Middle Class.*

. . . In the wake of the United States civil rights movement, some scholars and policy makers speculate that class now plays a larger role than race in the ability of blacks to get good jobs (e.g., Fairmont Papers 1981, Gershman 1980, Wilson 1987). Wilson (1978) specifically notes that changes in urban economies in conjunction with affirmative action efforts have eroded racial barriers for talented blacks. Moreover, the growth of service industries—with jobs requiring high educational prerequisites—compound the employment problems of poor blacks in inner cities. Against this backdrop, an emergent view is that government intrudes unnecessarily to protect employment opportunities for better-educated blacks. At the same time, the most pressing problem of blacks— social and economic dislocation in inner cities—stands outside the reach of affirmative action (Loury 1985, Sowell 1983). This paper challenges the notion that underpins the class perspective, namely, that blacks are assimilating. I argue that the convergence of economic trends and employment policies that exclude the underclass also creates an administratively marginal black middle class. It is a middle class that is politically-constructed and occupies a useful but expedient position in urban labor markets. In short, I believe that employers' response to civil rights pressures created a highly visible but economically vulnerable black elite.

This argument is similar to that in a previous paper (Collins 1983) in which I used census data and occupational trends to look at job opportunities for middle class blacks. To follow up that analysis I used a qualitative approach, interviewing top-ranking black executives in major white corporations. I found that the upward mobility of these executives was a result of the political pressures that distinguish the civil rights movement. For example, in Chicago, where I interviewed, Jesse Jackson placed pressure on companies; the National Association for the Advancement of Colored People (NAACP), precursors to the Southern Christian Leadership Conference (SCLC), and various grass roots coalitions similarly confronted corporations nationwide.

Further, I found that blacks' status in management is based in new jobs created in affirmative action and urban affairs that led to dead-end careers. These findings contradict the notion that market demands in tandem with affirmative action mitigated employment barriers faced by highly talented blacks. Even within the black managerial elite, upward mobility is channeled by race-conscious systems. Moreover, this system of attainment has created a less obvious version of employment inequality. In short, I found that the mobility of a black elite within management is interlaced with politically mediated and race-conscious phenomena. These features contribute to their segregation within corporate job structures and build a race-linked element of vulnerability into their job gains. . . .

Methods

I opted to study top black executives since their presence in white corporations indicates blacks' greater access to traditionally closed avenues of economic advancement (see Freeman 1976a). When researchers and policy makers stress the new capacity of blacks to compete in the labor market, these are some of the people they are talking about.

I considered blacks to be "top executives" if their major job responsibilities involved decision making around company policy (e.g., establishing fundamental directions, goals or orientations of the company) or first line planning, managing or supervising the implementation of policy once it is set. This conception was operationalized by selecting respondents if: 1) they were employed in a banking institution and had a title of comptroller, trust officer, vice president (excluding "assistant" vice president), president or chief officer; or 2) they were employed in a non-financial institution with a title of department manager, director, vice president, or chief officer.

Locating this elite was a relatively straightforward process. First, I identified 52 of the largest corporations in Chicago using the *Chicago Reporter* (1983, 1986) listings of industrials, utilities, retail companies, transportation companies, and banks. Second, I asked knowledgeable informants familiar with the corporate community in Chicago to identify black officers in these firms. These informants also referred "in-house" people (people employed in each targeted company). Third, in-house informants identified blacks at the selected levels of management who would fit the research criteria. Fourth, I asked black executives who participated in the study to identify other top blacks in the selected Chicago firms.

Every respondent was in a targeted firm although not every firm targeted is represented by a respondent. Managers worked in 37 of the original 52 identified firms. Eighty-seven managers were identified and 76 managers were interviewed between May 1986 and January 1987. Only two of the remaining 11 referrals did not respond or declined to participate in the study. Others were not included because of logistical problems. Using vitae that respondents had forwarded, I focused the interviews on the jobs people held over the course of their careers.

Because of their high average rank in the companies, the respondents are not representative of black managers in Chicago's corporations or of black managers in general. The people in this study are, however, the total population of Chicago's corporate black elite in 1986. Almost all of the senior level black executives employed in major Chicago companies participated in this study. Fifty-six people (74%) had the title of director, or above, in a major white corporation including two chief officers, 30 vice presidents, and 24 unit directors. (The total includes three people with the title of "manager" whose rank within the organization was equivalent to vice president or director.) Moreover, participants in this study were among the highest ranking executives in the country and the only executives in the country at select levels. Thirty-two of 76 (42%) were the highest ranking black in a company's nationwide management structure. The careers of these managers demonstrate how far blacks have come under supportive civil rights conditions.

Old Forms of Job Segregation

Employment opportunities for college educated blacks were considerably restricted in
the decades before the modern civil rights era
(Broom and Glenn 1965:112; Freeman 1976a,
1976b). Prior to the 1960s, professional opportunities for middle class blacks were relegated
to a separate and marginalized economy
(Pitts 1982:153). That is, the occupational
structure of the black middle class essentially
was tied to the black business and professional opportunities that sprang up to serve
black ghettos. Evidence of this employment
pattern typically is associated with qualita-
tive/descriptive studies (e.g., Drake and
Cayton 1962, Frazier 1957), and the exact degree to which black businessmen and professionals were supported by black consumer
markets is not quantified by strict measures.
Research does show, however, that only token
numbers of blacks were employed in expanding industries (Newman et. al. 1978, Urban
League 1961). Rather, blacks principally were
relegated to the segregated professions as
preachers, physicians, dentists, lawyers, em-
balmers, and proprietors of small retail and
personal service businesses. This narrow
range of opportunity was augmented somewhat by black employment within the public
sector as teachers, social workers, and employees of other public funded social service
agencies. But many government funded jobs
further reflected racial limitations because
black professionals were located within organizations that distributed services primarily
to blacks, not to the total community.

Seen against this backdrop, it is significant that fewer than one-half of the 29 people
I interviewed who entered the labor market
before 1965 worked initially in the white private sector (see Figure 1a). Rather, they
worked primarily in government, black
businesses, and community agencies. The
experience of a vice president for sales for a
Fortune 500 retailer is typical. After searching
for management trainee positions in Chicago

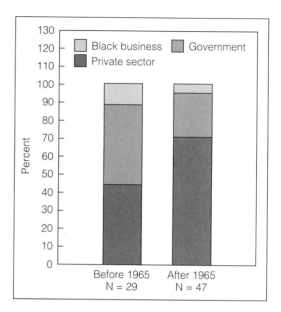

FIGURE 1a   First Employment Sector of
People Who Entered the Labor Force Before
and After 1965

corporations and being told by potential employers that jobs were "non-existent" in
1960, he accepted work in government. His
experience was that "white companies did
not respond . . . to black resumes." Although
this man is now one of the highest ranking
black executives in the United States, he began his career, perforce, as a caseworker for
the Chicago Housing Authority.

Respondents did enter the white private
sector before 1965 but found they had limited access both to high paying white collar
occupations and to jobs in which they interacted with white clients and customers. They
performed low-status clerical and administrative support functions or worked in sales
jobs assigned to black, not mainstream, consumer markets. Thus people were channeled
into the low-paying, "back room" and segregated jobs in companies (see Figure 1b). A
vice president and marketing manager
within the wholesale food industry reported
that in 1957 he expected to work with a major chemical company since he had a bache-

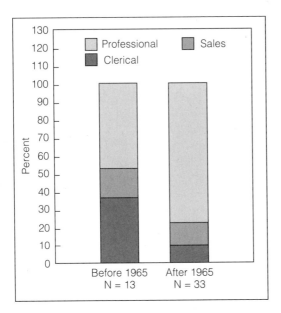

FIGURE 1b First Occupation of People Who Entered the Labor Force in the White Private Sector Before and After 1965

lor's degree in chemistry. Instead, he emphasized, "... it was *tremendously* difficult to find that kind of job ... I had *huge* difficulties getting work. My first job was as a stock clerk." It should be kept in mind that his job search occurred during a time when chemicals were a fast growth industry in the United States.

In the 1950s and early 1960s blacks in sales fields were not in mainstream markets. When hired by white companies, respondents served black consumer sectors. A senior vice president within the beverage industry recounted the limitations that blacks faced in sales:

> We were all special markets, or black skewed, or involved in black activities, in the black consumer market. . . . I was the only black at [the first employer] and [at the second employer] there were three other blacks [all in black territories].

Respondents did break into the professional mainstream, but opportunities there were heavily skewed toward the most highly

educated people I interviewed, those holding advanced degrees. Further, job opportunities were racially delineated even for this educationally elite group. Almost exclusively these "good" job offers came from companies that were sensitive to government oversight. The following quotation from an executive with an MBA in finance from a prestigious "white" university indicates that in 1962 large government contractors were induced by federal government contract compliance laws to hire highly educated blacks:

> I wanted to be in the investment banking community, but there was no opportunity there at all. I finally settled on a job as an accountant at [an aerospace firm]. [The] company stacked the roster; they wanted lots of graduate degrees and they wanted minorities, despite the fact that there were not the obvious or blatant kind of [affirmative action] regulations [at that time]. . . . And I was not doing work [at] the level of an MBA.

This executive began his career as an over qualified but under utilized accountant. In 1986 he was the only black CEO of a major insurance company, a subsidiary of a *Fortune* 500 service company.

In summary, until the broadening of employment policies associated with the mid-1960s, a potential black elite was excluded from the occupations that provide the incomes and lifestyles available to the U.S. white middle class. Had it not been for changes that occurred in the labor market in the 1960s, the people whom I interviewed probably would have replicated a tradition of depressed employment patterns.

Black Integration into Primary Labor Markets

In the 1960s and throughout the 1970s, the proportion of blacks decreased in the professions where they traditionally had been represented (i.e., the segregated professions serving black clients). In contrast, blacks increased their visibility in job markets that had been "traditionally closed" to them. The term "traditionally closed" is borrowed from Richard Freeman (1976b:146) to characterize a particular change in the job structure of blacks. This change consists of intertwined phenomena where blacks increased their proportions in the business-related professions because they found increased job opportunities in white-owned-and-oriented economic structures. The juncture of blacks' entry into new jobs and into new job settings delineates new job markets for blacks. During the 1960s and 1970s in the business world a new elite of blacks began to emerge as professionals and managers both in government and in major white corporations (see Figure 2).

The access of blacks to the mainstream middle class increased after 1965 in part because their ability to get higher paying white collar jobs in the central economy increased. Government obviously retained major importance as an employer during the 1960s and 1970s as indicated in Figure 2 (see also Collins 1983). But professional and managerial job opportunities for blacks expanded within the private for-profit sector as well, accelerating particularly in the 1970s. Although they had been excluded from these jobs previously, blacks were able to make inroads into high paying occupations because of different recruitment procedures implemented by major corporations. Freeman (1976a:35) documents, for instance, that the number of white corporations conducting employee searches at predominantly black colleges jumped dramatically after 1965. Recruitment activity rose from almost no campus visits from white corporations in 1960 and about 30 visits in 1965 to an average of almost 300 recruiters from various firms per campus in 1970. The occupational structure supporting the black middle class was transformed during the 1960s and particularly the 1970s due

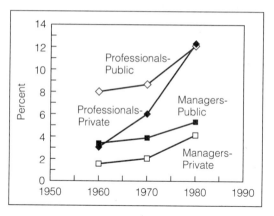

FIGURE 2   Black Percent of Total Employed Managers and Professionals in the Public and Private Sector, 1960, 1970, 1980.

Note: Data for 1960 and 1970 are for non-whites; 1980, for blacks.

Source: U.S. Census, 1963, table 21 & 22: 1973, table 43 & 44: 1984, table 279.

to the unique emergence of blacks in the professional-managerial strata of jobs within major white corporations.

In this social context, once again, my interview data illustrate the positive shift in the nature of job opportunities afforded people entering the labor market after 1965. For instance, a technical director of research for a Chicago communications company reported that in 1971 a firm in New York was so interested in him they offered him nine different jobs. That company even offered to send him back to law school so he could work on their discrimination suits, although he had just completed his doctorate in engineering. The initial employment opportunities for people whom I interviewed were greatly enhanced after 1965 and reflect a much broader market demand.

Respondents' first jobs were derived much more from the private sector than from government and black businesses. The rate of entry into the professional-managerial strata of private sector jobs also jumped dramatically. About twice the proportion of post-1965 entrants as pre-1965 entrants had access to

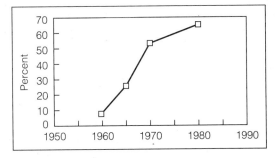

FIGURE 3a Percent of First Jobs Performed Face to Face with a White Public[a]

Note: a. Excludes all jobs not interacting with an internal or external public, e.g. most technical and some clerical/administrative support jobs, N=49.

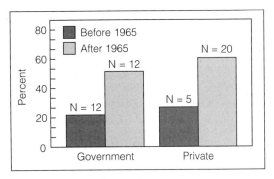

FIGURE 3b Percent of First Jobs Performed Face to Face with a White Public, by Sector

the white private sector via these jobs. Supplementing the conventional indicators cited above, Figures 3a and 3b illustrate a previously untapped measure of black assimilation and market change.

Using detailed job descriptions, I coded first jobs of respondents according to: 1) whether representing the company to internal labor or an external public was integral to their work role; and 2) whether this role engaged them most with whites or blacks. Public relations, retail sales, and clerical jobs such as secretary/receptionist represent a company to an external public, albeit for different purposes. Managers and supervisors represent a company via authority over internal labor. Non-interactive roles in technical, clerical, and administrative support areas (e.g., non-supervisory chemists, clerk typists, and billing clerks) are excluded. During the 1960s and 1970s respondents increasingly were hired into higher-paying and highly visible jobs that brought them face to face with a white public.

Eleven of the 12 people (92%) who entered labor markets before 1961 were in jobs that interacted primarily with blacks; only one person interacted with whites. In contrast, eight of the 12 people (66%) who entered labor markets after 1971 interacted with whites, four with blacks. Over the two

decades, government jobs for blacks were tied less to segregated teaching and social work slots and more to management and administrative positions that required these black employees to interact with white employees and institutions. In the private sector, respondents were hired into sales tied to total consumer sectors rather than to black sectors and into slots that required them to supervise whites. Overall, these alterations in the pattern of black employment are consistent with, but substantively expand, the findings of other research. The economic status of the black middle class was elevated because blacks were hired to fill radically different work roles from those filled in their previous history.

Politically and Market Mediated Demand Factors

Why did employers in the white private sector alter their hiring practices? Explanations include improved quality of schooling for blacks (Smith and Welch 1986) and lucrative employment opportunities for both college educated whites and blacks due to the expansion of U.S. private industry (Levitan, Johnson, and Taggart 1975). Despite improvements in the quality of schooling and an expanding economy, however, my study points to the fact that blacks still depended upon job opportunities created by government contract compliance efforts and other political interventions (also see Freeman 1976a, Leonard 1984). The new black middle class grounded in jobs in private industry was not created merely by tight markets and supply factors, such as educational attainment. Given the pre- and post-1965 employment data presented earlier, I suggest that the black middle class ascended within professions because private hiring practices were altered to temper black activists' demands and to meet government regulations.

Demand for labor can be conceptualized as being either economically or politically induced. Economic demands for labor occur in response to consumer preferences and buying patterns as they are mediated through the marketplace. Political demands for labor occur in response to black protest and pressures, especially as they are mediated through governmental intervention. In what follows, I show that the forces expanding blacks' economic opportunities were protest related, and that the emergence of a new black middle class was at least in part politically mediated.

The executives I interviewed entered private enterprise at a time when the service economy and the need for skilled labor were expanding. They also moved into the private sector at a time when it was responding to employment pressures exerted by government and the black community. For example, as pressures from the Equal Employment Opportunity Commission (EEOC) and the Office of Federal Contract Compliance Programs (OFCCP) increased, a greater proportion of initial employers were reported to have had formal Equal Employment Opportunity (EEO) policies. Among people entering before 1965 only one first employer was reported to have had a written EEO hiring policy. Seventeen percent of first employers between 1965 to 1969 had written EEO policies and 78 percent of first employers after 1970 had them. When professional/managerial opportunities in the white private sector

were scarce so were government hiring requirements. Black opportunities multiplied in tandem with federal intervention. Over 70 percent of these managers (54 of 76 people) were first hired by white companies between 1965 and 1974 when civil rights momentum was greatest. The vast majority of these people were the first black or in the first group of black recruits hired into a professional or managerial job by a white company. Aside from meeting production requirements, blacks' increased visibility within corporate structures helped to keep government off corporations' backs. If nothing else, the presence of blacks symbolized that, indeed, there were opportunities.

Black activism and civil disturbances also contributed to the expansion of job opportunities. For instance, people entering managerial fields in the white private sector reported that organized black protest and civil disturbances were instrumental in creating access to these jobs. A manager of community affairs explains his opportunity to move into corporate management in the following way. First, the employer, a Chicago-based consumer goods company, foresaw the emergence of People United to Save Humanity (PUSH) boycotts and recognized the vulnerability of the corporation to such actions. Second, the company was unprepared, administratively, to respond to grass roots demands, in particular, to contacts from the Black Panther party. Third, the company was being pressured by internal coalitions of black staff to be socially sensitive to the needs of the black community. The manager said,

> Those were things [that] were in the works at that time [and] the leadership [of the company] looks around here and it's all white men that you see. There wasn't a black face in any one of these [Chicago corporate] offices. They had a few blacks in some cubical . . . but no one that was to be a manager. So here

was a tremendous opportunity to make this nigger a manager. [You?] Sure.

In 1970 the respondent was the first black to be hired into the company's corporate offices with the title "manager"; he became the manager of community relations.

Two areas of vulnerability, in addition to government, that companies responded to are the loss of profits and bad public relations due to black protest, and the destruction of physical assets such as company plants located in volatile black neighborhoods. For example, a director of community affairs/district personnel manager described his management trainee position in 1966 as a response to Jesse Jackson's threats of a black consumer boycott against a chain of food stores in Chicago, a threat that created "at least 20 to 25" new positions:

> The store had about 32 operations in the black community and nobody in management. . . . They had a big black consumer base. So Jesse came in and got a [hiring] covenant. I got hired as a part of that covenant. . . . Blacks started coming into the business structure at that time. I would say [the store] put at least 20 to 25 blacks into management training at that time.

The same story emerged from a respondent who worked in the New York clothing industry. A vice president, whose first job was assistant manager in a clothing store in 1966, was hired when the NAACP organized black consumers to take action against the retailer. Until that confrontation, blacks were absent within the management structure of the company. He explains,

> Managers were, you know, the guy would be the manager of the porters, . . . or the elevator starters . . . or the kitchen. But there were no front line blacks . . . in buying . . . or merchandising responsibilities. And black people

spent a lot of money in [the store]. So that's how I got in . . . because of the pressures of the NAACP picketing.

Similar dynamics occurred in Ohio. A director of human resources for sales operations explained that he was the first black college graduate recruited in 1967 as a management trainee in a Cincinnati based consumer goods company: "Some of the companies were being boycotted . . . by SCLC and a coalition of ministers in the Cincinnati area. [They had gone after] companies like Kroeger and [Proctor & Gamble] and other highly visible consumer companies." These comments illustrate that retail business is sensitive to its market share and, therefore, its consumer base. Blacks constituted a sizable proportion of sales; for this reason, top management responded by making blacks visible in management.

In 1969, for example, a vice president of sales was the first black ever hired into management in a particular retail company. Significantly, he was hired immediately following a period of rioting in East Cleveland during which the store of a nearby competitor burned down:

> Our store was not far from East Cleveland. . . . All of a sudden [headquarters called and] said, "We want [you] for the [management] job." . . . The store I was put in . . . was 50 percent black . . . So then it became very clear. [That your employment was connected to the rioting?] That's right.

In short, increasing black visibility in management was a forced-fed public relations effort to stave off the destruction of assets. A black manager of community affairs for a public utility who was hired following riots in Chicago joked:

> I'm not too sure that if we could we wouldn't . . . [have taken] the cable out of the ground and off the poles [in] . . .

north Lawndale, which is black, and south Lawndale, which is mainly Hispanic. Some of [the employment programs were] motivat[ed by] a desire to do good . . . but some of it was to develop [good public relations as] a buffer around the assets that the company has in [those neighborhoods].

Two-thirds of 35 informants entering the white private sector in managerial fields after 1965 described the vulnerability of their company to black consumer boycotts and the vulnerability of company property to urban upheaval. Three-quarters of the people entering managerial fields (27 of 36) also reported that their employment was a result of a company effort specifically to hire blacks. A senior investment analyst, whose first job in a white company was as personnel supervisor, describes the hiring environment this way:

I was at an NAACP convention . . . and [the company] offered me a job right there on the spot [in 1966]. Over the next 3 or 4 years they hired 25 to 30 people like that. If you were black and walked by . . . they'd just about grab you . . . off the streets.

In short, political pressures affected corporate hiring policy. While the economy was expanding, black activism and government action helped transform race, for some, into a preferential status. Preferential status increased the demand for black talent in the private sector, playing a crucial role in the growth of a black managerial class.

Some scholars suggest that the gains by blacks within prestigious occupations are an indication that race is losing influence over employment opportunities. My analysis of black mobility disputes this notion; entry into the white private sector is heavily linked with race-conscious pressures. Further, the link between employment growth and political pressure underscores an obvious, but thus far neglected, possibility. The decline of

pressure could erode the tendency to employ blacks in managerial jobs, thus undermining black advance into corporate positions. In the next section, I illustrate that black executive mobility in white corporations is tied to an expedient structure of jobs created to implement company policies associated with black protest and civil rights legislation.

Racialized and Mainstream Labor

To explore whether the market response to political initiatives created a fragile structure of jobs, I separated "racialized" and "mainstream" labor based on job descriptions provided by respondents. "Racialized" labor performs white institutional functions that have a manifest or symbolic connection to black constituents or black issues. "Mainstream" labor performs jobs that lack these racial implications. For example, I viewed labor as racialized when respondents were selling or supervising a sales force in predominantly black consumer territories. Labor performed in sales territories not dominated by blacks was coded mainstream. In operations or production areas, I viewed labor as racialized when respondents held authority over a work force that was made up disproportionately of blacks or when they mediated black-white worker relationships in racially volatile employment settings. In public service areas, such as public relations, urban affairs, and corporate contribution programs, labor was racialized when blacks acted as representatives of white institutions in jobs that interacted heavily with and advocated the needs of black communities. In personnel specialties, labor was racialized when it created or implemented personnel functions primarily to recruit blacks, to train blacks, or to otherwise ease the entry and promotion of blacks within white-dominated institutions. Mainstream labor was neither tied to nor symbolically associated with black constituents and issues. Figure 4 shows sample

Type of Labor		
	Racialized	Mainstream
Political	Mediates the social pressures related to black protest for civil rights, i.e., affirmative action or urban affairs manager.	Mediates public perception and legal initiatives which influence corporate strategy and profit, i.e., government affairs manager, Political Action Committees (PACs).
Market	Develops and exploits the black cosumer market, i.e., special market sales and advertising.	Supports production and sales to the total (predominately white) consumer market, i.e., sales and production managers.

Type of Demand labels the rows.

FIGURE 4   Characteristics of Racialized and Mainstream Labor, by Demand

characteristics of racialized and mainstream labor in relationship to political and market demands.

Although the people I interviewed made gains in management, a sizeable majority occupied politically induced jobs and performed racialized labor for major corporations at some point in their careers. That is, the majority moved into, stayed in, or moved through a structure of jobs that was created to help corporations respond to pressures for civil rights. Sixty-six percent (51 of 76) of the people I interviewed were tracked into jobs created in national corporations to handle "black problems" with reference to civil rights (see Figure 5).

The career of a senior vice president for a fast foods company illustrates this phenomenon. He was recruited to become an urban affairs manager in 1971 after seven years on a mainstream sales track in a white corporation. Urban affairs was a new job in the company, created because of black protests demanding that the company allocate black-owned franchises in their Detroit neighborhoods. As a consequence, this manager was shifted into the public relations department to create a minority business set-aside program and to recruit and assist blacks in buying franchises. After two years the manager re-entered the sales field, but as racialized labor. He was assigned to prob-lematic stores in volatile urban areas in Detroit and Washington, DC where he was the company's token representative to heavily black communities. His career became one in which he moved up the corporate ladder by moving in and out of these race-sensitive assignments.

One-half (26 of 51) of the managers who had these jobs moved in, and stayed in, racialized slots throughout their corporate careers. This second group of managers ascended the corporate ladder almost entirely within a politically constructed niche of jobs. One example is a director of affirmative action who is the second highest ranking black manager in a Chicago-based *Fortune* 500 retail company. His career with the company began in 1966 when he was hired as a management trainee operating in various phases of mainstream sales management. In 1969 he shifted from sales into the field of personnel management to begin a career grounded in the affirmative action area. Between 1969 and 1986 he was promoted within management in newly created jobs implementing equal employment policies. Aside from his initial four years of experience in sales, this manager's mobility in the white private sector was entirely through jobs mediating blacks' employment demands and the attending requirements of federal legislation. The data indicate that blacks were hired into higher-paying and highly visible

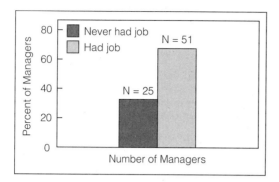

FIGURE 5   Managers Who Had Racialized Jobs Dealing with Civil Rights

jobs in which they came face to face with a white public. But data also indicate that during the post-entry period blacks were shifted into corporate roles to help white institutions deal with the problem of blacks.

Given the political climate, the fact that blacks were tracked as racial labor is not surprising. The federal government and black communities demanded accommodation, and incentives were great for companies to have blacks in key departments. In public relations, for instance, corporate giving programs needed broadened initiatives because of increasing pressures from black communities and from changing urban environments. Even more distinctively, personnel departments underwent dramatic transitions to address hiring priorities established by the government. Pressures on corporations were great and companies exerted effort in channeling blacks into these areas. Forty-five of 76 managers specifically had jobs in affirmative action and urban affairs. Twenty-two of these 45 managers (49%) were working in mainstream areas and were approached by company management to take these jobs. Twelve of these 22 approached managers (55%) were personally solicited for these jobs by senior level white management, for example, senior vice presidents and chief executive officers,

not their immediate supervisors. Nine of these 22 managers (41%) turned these jobs down, and were approached a second time by top management. Eleven of the 22 approached managers (50%) were given salary increases, more prestigious job titles, and promises of future rewards.

The response of companies was to track blacks into affirmative action and urban relations functions even when their background was not relevant to these areas. For instance, even managers experienced in technical functions reported they were offered positive inducements to fill these jobs. Ten of 17 (59%) managers with highly technical skills, such as accountants, engineers, and chemists, were recruited to fill these jobs. The pull on black professionals to fill racial roles in companies cut across personal preference and previous work experience. As one respondent commented,

> Whether or not they used my talents to the best of their ability or my ability, that's a different story. . . It was during the early 1970s, and there weren't very many people around that could do anything for minorities . . . I mean, they were really, all the companies were really scrambling. . . . All you saw was minorities functioning in that . . . and it doesn't take much brain power to figure out that that's where most of us were going to end up.

Another manager, who had a master's degree and four years of experience in engineering when he shifted into the affirmative action role in 1968, offers this assessment:

> When they would send me to some of these conferences about affirmative action . . . you'd walk in and there would be a room full of blacks. . . . And I met titles . . . directors, and you name it, of equal employment opportunity . . . It was a terrible misuse at that time of

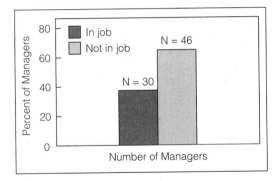

FIGURE 6 Managers Holding Racialized Jobs in Most Recent White Private Sector Employment

some black talent. There were some black people in those jobs that were rather skilled, much like myself.

Racially oriented jobs in personnel and public relations fields were the last job held in the white private sector for 39 percent of 76 managers I interviewed (see Figure 6).

This race conscious system of upward mobility built impermanence into the position blacks currently hold in management. Affirmative action and urban affairs jobs once flourished as a fast track for black mobility into middle and upper staff management. Now, blacks who followed this track are uniquely vulnerable. Black entry into these specialties during the 1960s and 1970s occurred in an atmosphere of economic expansion and intense social upheaval. In the 1980s, upheaval has been quelled, and competition for market share has intensified; racial functions especially have lost their value. In an era of corporate mergers and acquisitions, heavily leveraged debt will be reduced by reducing the cost of management. The lack of a strong push by government on the one hand and the need to reduce staff costs on the other will eradicate these positions. Moreover, the specialized political skills of people that performed racial jobs have limited exploitability

in mainstream areas. A director of affirmative action in his mid-40s, feeling that he had reached the end of his corporate career ladder, expressed this regret: "Nobody ever told me . . . that if you stay in [this] job you'd be in [this] job for-ever. You don't move to Vice President of Personnel from Manager of EEO."

Conclusions

There is a link between government policy and black occupational advance, but my study demonstrates that the intent of this policy was not fully adopted by the market. I have focused upon a group of people who have been highly successful within non-traditional jobs and who have had the greatest potential to assimilate into mainstream labor. Then I have shown their marginality. Occupational advancement for many of them occurred in a distinctive and peripheral way. Private employers channeled the variety of black talent into race-oriented jobs during the 1960s and 1970s and, consequently, diminished the pool of blacks who, a decade or two later, could compete to manage mainstream production units. Since talent was funnelled into race oriented positions, the gains blacks have made over the last two decades are less likely to be translated into powerful production and planning jobs.

Middle class blacks were beneficiaries of affirmative action policies. However, their gains are not necessarily indicative of greater market equality. Despite occupational gains, some forms of job segregation have been maintained and even facilitated. I have shown that jobs that were both politically induced and racialized are important mechanisms for mobility among blacks in management. In other words, race is influential in determining the role of blacks in corporations, notwithstanding black gains within managerial positions.

If government efforts abate in areas that have supported the black middle class, the ability of blacks to maintain and to continue their gains in mainstream enterprise may also erode. Entry conditions were supported by government policy; weakened commitment to affirmative action would diminish the mobility of blacks in this sector of the marketplace. In the current climate of political and economic conservatism, black gains may already be in jeopardy. The racialized holding cells for blacks in personnel and community relations fields are losing their value. As corporations compete to capture the market and to maximize profits, black advocacy programs and racial priorities are being diluted. Twenty years of federal pressure does not necessarily mean that blacks can replicate and/or increase the gains of the past decades. But the fault is not with federal policy; fault lies with market implementation. Attainments in management will not be consolidated until black ability to gain power in core corporate areas is a frequent, not an occasional, phenomenon.

REFERENCES

Broom, Leonard and Norval Glenn. 1965. *Transformation of the American Negro.* New York: Harper and Row.

Chicago Reporter. 1983."Annual corporate survey." December:2-6.

———. 1986. "Annual corporate survey." January:3, 7-10.

Collins, Sharon M. 1983."The making of the black middle class." *Social Problems* 30:369-82.

Drake, St. Clair and Horace R. Cayton. 1962. *Black Metropolis,* Vol. 2. New York: Harper and Row.

Fairmont Papers: Black Alternatives Conference. 1981.Proceedings of conference sponsored by the Institute for Contemporary Studies. December, 1980, San Francisco, CA.

Frazier, E. Franklin. 1957. *The Black Bourgeoisie: The Rise of a New Middle Class.* New York: The Free Press.

Freeman, Richard B. 1976a. *The Black Elite.* New York: McGraw Hill.

———. 1976b. *The Over-Educated American.* New York: Academic Press.

Gershman, Carl. 1980. "A matter of class." *New York Times Sunday Supplement* October 5:22.

Leonard, Jonathan S. 1984."The impact of affirmative action on employment." *Journal of Labor Economics* 2:439-64.

Levitan, Sar, William B. Johnson, and Robert Taggart 1975. *Still a Dream: The Changing Status of Blacks Since 1960.* Cambridge, MA: Harvard University Press.

Loury, Glenn C. 1985. "The moral quandary of the black community." *The Public Interest* 79:9-22.

Newman, Dorothy K, Nancy J. Amidei, Barbara L. Carter, Dawn Day, William J. Kruvant, and Jack S. Russell. 1978. *Protest, Politics and Prosperity: Black Americans and White Institutions, 1940-1975.* New York: Pantheon Books.

Pitts, James P. 1982. "The Afro-American experience: changing models of integration and race consciousness." Pp. 141-67 in Anthony Gary Dworkin and Rosalind J. Dworkin (eds.), *The Minority Report: An Introduction to Racial, Ethnic, and Gender Relations.* 2d ed. New York: CBS College Publishing.

Smith, James P. and Finis R. Welch. 1986. *Closing the Gap: Forty Years of Economic Progress for Blacks.* Santa Monica, CA: RAND Corporation.

Sowell, Thomas. 1983."The economics and politics of race." Transcript of *The Firing Line* program. Taped in New York City on November 1983.

United States Bureau of Census. 1963. *Subject Reports.* Occupational Characteristics Series PC (2)-7A. Washington, DC: Government Printing Office.

———. 1973. *Subject Reports.* Occupational Characteristics Series PC (2)-7A. Washington, DC: Government Printing Office.

———. 1984. *Detailed Population Characteristics. Characteristics of the Population.* Part 1. Section A. PC80-1-D1-A. Washington, DC: Government Printing Office.

Urban League. 1961. *Equal Rights—Greater Responsibility: The Challenge to Community Leadership in 1961.* Chicago: Urban League Research Department.

Wilson, William J. 1978. *The Declining Significance of Race.* Chicago: University of Chicago Press.

———. 1987. *The Truly Disadvantaged: The Inner City, the Underclass, and Public Policy.* Chicago: University of Chicago Press.

PART V

Work and Family

In her 1977 monograph on work and family in the United States, Kanter observed, "If any one statement can be said to define the most prevalent sociological position on work and family, it is the 'myth' of separate worlds" (p. 8). Kanter identifies the elements of this myth, the most important being the idea that work and family "constitute two separate and non-overlapping worlds, with their own functions, territories, and behavioral rules" (Kanter 1977). Needless to say, sociologists have become increasingly critical of this conception of work-family relations and have profoundly rejected the myth of separate worlds. In its place they have begun to explore the interconnections between work and family life and the consequences of these relations for workers, families, employers, and society.

Constructing Work-Family Relations

How should we characterize relations between work and family? How do relations between work and family vary by gender, social class, race, ethnicity, sexual orientation, and other demographic, job, or family characteristics? These questions have inspired many attempts to theorize about and model work-family relations. In recent years, however, efforts to put forward a single dominant conception of work-family relations have been abandoned in favor of attempts to explore these relations in particular, historically specific contexts. The three readings in this section demonstrate some of the variability in work-family relations in the late twentieth century.

Hochschild (1989) uses the term *second shift* to refer to the time women spend performing unpaid household work in addition to their time working in the paid labor force. In her 1989 book on this topic, Hochschild (p. 7) quotes from a woman she interviewed: "You're on duty at work. You come home, you're on duty. Then you go back to work and you're on duty." The second shift is a pertinent issue for women in dual-earner households. Because women's entrance into the labor force has not been accompanied by any significant corresponding change in their male partners' participation in family work, balancing the demands of work and family falls heavily on women.

In recent years, the number of dual-earner families has risen substantially. The work-family relations of this group are the focus of Reading 34 by Arlie Hochschild. In "The Second Shift: Working Parents and the Revolution at Home," Hochschild describes how one couple, Nancy and Evan Holt, manages to combine paid work and family responsibilities. Hochschild shows that, despite Nancy Holt's desire for an egalitarian relationship, she has more household responsibilities than her husband. By exploring how Nancy and Evan define their roles in the relationship and the gender ideologies that underlie each view, Hochschild reveals the complexity of meanings attached to contemporary work and family relations.

The geographic separation of work and home is more true for some than others, however. Doing paid work at home represents another way that work and family can overlap. When performed by women, this arrangement is often a response to women's continuing responsibilities for childcare. For example, in Reading 35, M. Patricia Fernández-Kelly and Anna M. García describe Mexican and Cuban women's participation in the flourishing informal economies of Miami and Los Angeles. The authors show that the boundary between home and work is quite fluid for these Hispanic women. Employed by the garment and electronics industries to do piecework at home, these women avoid child-care costs yet work long hours for minimal pay. As Fernández-Kelly and García note, however, women's experiences of homework differed depending on their ethnic background and the characteristics of their communities.

Whereas some perform paid work at home, others bring family life into the workplace. Nicole Biggart explores this type of work-family connection in her reading on family and gender in direct selling organizations. Biggart argues that, in contrast to more traditional employers who often seek to prevent the spillover of family life to the workplace, direct selling organizations actively encourage these connections. Based on her study of such direct selling organizations as Mary Kay Cosmetics, Tupperware, and Amway, Biggart shows how these companies' strategic use of family metaphors and relationships has produced a highly distinctive and successful organizational form.

Perspectives and Policies on Work-Family Relations

The latter half of the twentieth century has witnessed profound changes in the organization and meaning of *work* and *family*. Economic shifts that have transformed the United States from an industrial to a post-industrial society, and the changes in women's employment patterns that accompanied this transformation, are key parts of the explanation for new forms and conceptions of work and family. For example, women's

labor force participation saw a sharp increase in the decades following World War II, with most women filling predominantly female jobs in service industries. As Urquhart notes, "the primary source of new employees in the services sector was the employment of women who had previously not held jobs" (1984, p. 21). Although service jobs are diverse, many involve tasks that have been performed historically by women in the home. Hence, as jobs such as food preparation, child care, and care for the elderly have been shifted from unpaid to paid work, many women have also moved from the status of homemaker to worker. The increasing availability of services, in turn, makes families less dependent on women's unpaid work in the home, enabling women with families to seek paid employment. Among all racial groups, families with two wage earners have become more prevalent than families with two adults and only one wage earner. Changes in families thus can be seen as both cause and consequence of broader changes in the economy and women's employment.

These trends begin to illustrate the changing nature of work and family life in post-industrial American society. Regardless of what one identifies as the *sources* of change in work-family relations, most agree that these changes pose profound challenges for employers and workers. The three readings in this section explore these challenges, offering solutions, analyses, and perspectives.

The first reading, "Management Women and the New Facts of Life," by Felice Schwartz, presents one of the more controversial perspectives on changing work-family relations and their implications for employers. Schwartz urges employers to distinguish between "career-primary" and "career-and-family" women. The former, she argues, should have the same opportunities to succeed and move up as men, whereas the latter should expect restricted career growth but receive generous accommodations for family concerns. By creating a "mommy track" for women who are committed to careers but want to devote equal time and energy to family life, Schwartz believes, employers and women workers will both be better off.

The remaining two readings offer somewhat less programmatic perspectives on changing work-family relations. In Reading 38, Arlie Hochschild introduces the concept of *emotional culture* to convey the ways that people feel about the domains of work and family and the meanings they assign to each sphere. Hochschild makes the provocative claim that "instead of the model of the *family* as haven from work, more of us fit the model of *work* as haven from home" (1996, p. 28). Her efforts to understand why this shift has occurred and to explain the forces that sustain it yield important insights about work-family trends at the end of the twentieth century.

"What Do Men Want?" is the topic of the final reading in this section, by Michael S. Kimmel. Kimmel reminds us that it is not only women whose work and family lives have been transformed in recent years. Men's lives are also changing in ways that are increasingly at odds with corporate definitions of masculinity. Thus, in contrast to Schwartz, who recommends that employers' work and family policies focus primarily on women, Kimmel argues that men's changing needs, desires, and identities should also be accommodated by employers.

REFERENCES

Hochschild, Arlie with Anne Machung. 1989. *The Second Shift: Working Parents and the Revolution at Home*. New York: Viking.

Kanter, Rosabeth Moss. 1977. *Work and Family in the United States: A Critical Review and Agenda for Research and Policy*. New York: Russell Sage Foundation.

Urquhart, Michael. 1984. "The Employment Shift to Services: Where Did It Come From?" *Monthly Labor Review* 107: 15–22.

CONSTRUCTING WORK-FAMILY RELATIONS

34

The Second Shift
Working Parents and the Revolution at Home

Arlie Hochschild with Anne Machung

Arlie Hochschild is professor of sociology at the University of California, Berkeley. She has written extensively on the topic of gender, work, and family life. She is the author of *The Managed Heart: The Commercialization of Human Feeling* (1978) and *The Second Shift: Working Parents and the Revolution at Home* (1989).

Nancy Holt arrives home from work, her son, Joey, in one hand and a bag of groceries in the other. As she puts down the groceries and opens the front door, she sees a spill of mail on the hall floor, Joey's half-eaten piece of cinnamon toast on the hall table, and the phone machine's winking red light: a still-life reminder of the morning's frantic rush to distribute the family to the world outside. Nancy, for seven years a social worker, is a short, lithe blond woman of thirty who talks and moves rapidly. She scoops the mail onto the hall table and heads for the kitchen, unbuttoning her coat as she goes. Joey sticks close behind her, intently explaining to her how dump trucks dump things. Joey is a fat-cheeked, lively four-year-old who chuckles easily at things that please him.

Having parked their red station wagon, Evan, her husband, comes in and hangs up

his coat. He has picked her up at work and they've arrived home together. Apparently unready to face the kitchen commotion but not quite entitled to relax with the newspaper in the living room, he slowly studies the mail. Also thirty, Evan, a warehouse furniture salesman, has thinning pale blond hair, a stocky build, and a tendency to lean on one foot. In his manner there is something both affable and hesitant.

From the beginning, Nancy describes herself as an "ardent feminist," an egalitarian (she wants a similar balance of spheres and equal power). Nancy began her marriage hoping that she and Evan would base their identities in both their parenthood and their careers, but clearly tilted toward parenthood. Evan felt it was fine for Nancy to have a career, if she could handle the family too.

As I observe in their home on this evening, I notice a small ripple on the surface of family waters. From the commotion of the kitchen, Nancy calls, "Eva-an, will you *please* set the table?" The word *please* is thick with irritation. Scurrying between refrigerator, sink, and oven, with Joey at her feet, Nancy wants Evan to help; she has asked him, but reluctantly. She seems to resent having to ask. (Later she tells me, "I *hate* to ask; why should I ask? It's begging.") Evan looks up from the mail and flashes an irritated glance toward the kitchen, stung, perhaps, to be asked in a way so barren of appreciation and respect. He begins setting out knives and forks, asks if she will need spoons, then answers the doorbell. A neighbor's child. No, Joey can't play right now. The moment of irritation has passed.

Later as I interview Nancy and Evan separately, they describe their family life as unusually happy—except for Joey's "problem." Joey has great difficulty getting to sleep. They start trying to put him to bed at 8:00. Evan tries but Joey rebuffs him; Nancy has better luck. By 8:30 they have him *on* the bed but not *in* it; he crawls and bounds playfully. After 9:00 he still calls out for water or toys, and sneaks out of bed to switch on the light. This continues past 9:30, then 10:00 and 10:30. At about 11:00 Joey complains that his bed is "scary," that he can only go to sleep in his parents' bedroom. Worn down, Nancy accepts this proposition. And it is part of their current arrangement that putting Joey to bed is "Nancy's job." Nancy and Evan can't get into bed until midnight or later, when Evan is tired and Nancy exhausted. She used to enjoy their lovemaking, Nancy tells me, but now sex seems like "more work." The Holts consider their fatigue and impoverished sex life as results of Joey's Problem.

The official history of Joey's Problem— the interpretation Nancy and Evan give me—begins with Joey's fierce attachment to Nancy, and Nancy's strong attachment to him. On·an afternoon walk through Golden Gate Park, Nancy devotes herself to Joey's every move. Now Joey sees a squirrel; Nancy tells me she must remember to bring nuts next time. Now Joey is going up the slide; she notices that his pants are too short—she must take them down tonight.

The two enjoy each other. (Off the official record, neighbors and Joey's baby-sitter say that Nancy is a wonderful mother, but privately they add how much she is "also like a single mother.")

For his part, Evan sees little of Joey. He has his evening routine, working with his tools in the basement, and Joey always seems happy to be with Nancy. In fact, Joey shows little interest in Evan, and Evan hesitates to see that as a problem. "Little kids need their moms more than they need their dads," he explains philosophically; "All boys go through an oedipal phase."

Perfectly normal things happen. After a long day, mother, father, and son sit down to dinner. Evan and Nancy get the first chance all day to talk to each other, but both turn anxiously to Joey, expecting his mood to deteriorate. Nancy asks him if he wants celery with peanut butter on it. Joey says yes. "Are you sure that's how you want it?" "Yes." Then the fidgeting begins. "I don't like the strings on my celery." "Celery is made up of strings." "The celery is too big." Nancy grimly slices the celery. A certain tension mounts. Every time one parent begins a conversation with the other, Joey interrupts. "I don't have anything to drink." Nancy gets him juice. And finally, "Feed me." By the end of the meal, no one has obstructed Joey's victory. He has his mother's reluctant attention and his father is reaching for a beer. But talking about it later, they say, "This is normal when you have kids."

Sometimes when Evan knocks on the baby-sitter's door to pick up Joey, the boy looks past his father, searching for a face behind him: "Where's Mommy?" Sometimes he outright refuses to go home with his father. Eventually Joey even swats at his father, once quite hard, on the face for "no reason at all." This makes it hard to keep imagining Joey's relation to Evan as "perfectly normal." Evan and Nancy begin to talk seriously about a "swatting problem."

Evan decides to seek ways to compensate for his emotional distance from Joey. He brings Joey a surprise every week or so—a Tonka truck, a Tootsie Roll. He turns weekends into father-and-son times. One Saturday, Evan proposes the zoo, and hesitantly, Joey agrees. Father and son have their coats on and are nearing the front door. Suddenly Nancy decides she wants to join them, and as she walks down the steps with Joey in her arms, she explains to Evan, "I want to help things out."

Evan gets few signs of love from Joey and feels helpless to do much about it. "I just don't feel good about me and Joey," he tells me one evening, "that's all I can say." Evan loves Joey. He feels proud of him, this bright, good-looking, happy child. But Evan also seems to feel that being a father is vaguely hurtful and hard to talk about.

The official history of Joey's problem was that Joey felt the "normal" oedipal attachment of a male child to his mother. Joey was having the emotional problems of growing up that any parent can expect. But Evan and Nancy add the point that Joey's problems are exacerbated by Evan's difficulties being an active father, which stem, they feel, from the way Evan's own father, an emotionally remote self-made businessman, had treated him. Evan tells me, "When Joey gets older, we're going to play baseball together and go fishing."

As I recorded this official version of Joey's Problem through interviews and observation, I began to feel doubts about it. For one thing, clues to another interpretation appeared in the simple pattern of footsteps on a typical evening. There was the steady pacing of Nancy, preparing dinner in the kitchen, moving in zigzags from counter to refrigerator to counter to stove. There were the lighter, faster steps of Joey, running in large figure eights through the house, dashing from his Tonka truck to his motorcycle man, reclaiming his sense of belonging in this house, among his things. After dinner, Nancy and Evan

mingled footsteps in the kitchen, as they cleaned up. Then Nancy's steps began again: click, click, click, down to the basement for laundry, then thuck, thuck, thuck up the carpeted stairs to the first floor. Then to the bathroom where she runs Joey's bath, then into Joey's room, then back to the bath with Joey. Evan moved less—from the living room chair to Nancy in the kitchen, then back to the living room. He moved to the dining room to eat dinner and to the kitchen to help clean up. After dinner he went down to his hobby shop in the basement to sort out his tools; later he came up for a beer, then went back down. The footsteps suggest what is going on: Nancy was at work on her second shift.

Behind the Footsteps

Between 8:05 A.M. and 6:05 P.M., both Nancy and Evan are away from home, working a "first shift" at full-time jobs. The rest of the time they deal with the varied tasks of the second shift: shopping, cooking, paying bills; taking care of the car, the garden, and yard; keeping harmony with Evan's mother who drops over quite a bit, "concerned" about Joey, with neighbors, their voluble baby-sitter, and each other. And Nancy's talk reflects a series of second-shift thoughts: "We're out of barbecue sauce. . . . Joey needs a Halloween costume. . . . The car needs a wash. . . ." and so on. She reflects a certain "second-shift sensibility," a continual attunement to the task of striking and re-striking the right emotional balance between child, spouse, home, and outside job.

When I first met the Holts, Nancy was absorbing far more of the second shift than Evan. She said she was doing 80 percent of the housework and 90 percent of the childcare. Evan said she did 60 percent of the housework, 70 percent of the childcare. Joey said, "I vacuum the rug, and fold the dinner napkins," finally concluding, "Mom and I do it all." A neighbor agreed with Joey. Clearly, between Nancy and Evan, there was a "leisure gap": Evan had more than Nancy. I asked both of them, in separate interviews, to explain to me how they had dealt with housework and childcare since their marriage began.

One evening in the fifth year of their marriage, Nancy told me, when Joey was two months old and almost four years before I met the Holts, she first seriously raised the issue with Evan. "I told him: 'Look, Evan, it's not working. I do the housework, I take the major care of Joey, *and* I work a full-time job. I get pissed. This is *your* house too. Joey is *your* child too. It's not all *my* job to care for them.' When I cooled down I put to him, 'Look, how about this: I'll cook Mondays, Wednesdays, and Fridays. You cook Tuesdays, Thursdays, and Saturdays. And we'll share or go out Sundays.' "

According to Nancy, Evan said he didn't like "rigid schedules." He said he didn't necessarily agree with her standards of housekeeping, and didn't like that standard "imposed" on him, especially if she was "sluffing off" tasks on him, which from time to time he felt she was. But he went along with the idea in principle. Nancy said the first week of the new plan went as follows. On Monday, she cooked. For Tuesday, Evan planned a meal that required shopping for a few ingredients, but on his way home he forgot to shop for them. He came home, saw nothing he could use in the refrigerator or in the cupboard, and suggested to Nancy that they go out for Chinese food. On Wednesday, Nancy cooked. On Thursday morning, Nancy reminded Evan, "Tonight it's your turn." That night Evan fixed hamburgers and french fries and Nancy was quick to praise him. On Friday, Nancy cooked. On Saturday, Evan forgot again.

As this pattern continued, Nancy's reminders became sharper. The sharper they became, the more actively Evan forgot—perhaps anticipating even sharper reprimands if he resisted more directly. This cycle of passive refusal followed by disappointment and anger gradually tightened, and before long the struggle had spread to the task of doing the laundry. Nancy said it was only fair that Evan share the laundry. He agreed in principle, but anxious that Evan would not share, Nancy wanted a clear, explicit agreement. "You ought to wash and fold every other load," she had told him. Evan experienced this "plan" as a yoke around his neck. On many weekdays, at this point, a huge pile of laundry sat like a disheveled guest on the living-room couch.

In her frustration, Nancy began to make subtle emotional jabs at Evan. "I don't know *what's* for dinner," she would say with a sigh. Or "I can't cook now, I've got to deal with this pile of laundry." She tensed at the slightest criticism about household disorder; if Evan wouldn't do the housework, he had absolutely *no* right to criticize how she did it. She would burst out angrily at Evan. She recalled telling him: "After work *my* feet are just as tired as *your* feet. I'm just as wound up as you are. I come home. I cook dinner. I wash and I clean. Here we are, planning a second child, and I can't cope with the one we have."

About two years after I first began visiting the Holts, I began to see their problem in a certain light: as a conflict between their two gender ideologies. Nancy wanted to be the sort of woman who was needed and appreciated both at home and at work—like Lacey, she told me, on the television show "Cagney and Lacey." She wanted Evan to appreciate her for being a caring social worker, a committed wife, and a wonderful mother. But she cared just as much that she be able to appreciate *Evan* for what *he* contributed at home, not just for how he supported the family. She would feel proud to explain to women friends that she was married to one of these rare "new men."

A gender ideology is often rooted in early experience, and fueled by motives formed early on and such motives can often be traced to some cautionary tale in early life. So it was for Nancy. Nancy described her mother:

> My mom was wonderful, a real aristocrat, but she was also terribly depressed being a housewife. My dad treated her like a doormat. She didn't have any self-confidence. And growing up, I can remember her being really depressed. I grew up bound and determined not to be like her and not to marry a man like my father. As long as Evan doesn't do the housework, I feel it means he's going to be like my father—coming home, putting his feet up, and hollering at my mom to serve him. That's my biggest fear. I've had *bad* dreams about that.

Nancy thought that women friends her age, also in traditional marriages, had come to similarly bad ends. She described a high school friend: "Martha barely made it through City College. She had no interest in learning anything. She spent nine years trailing around behind her husband [a salesman]. It's a miserable marriage. She hand washes all his shirts. The high point of her life was when she was eighteen and the two of us were running around Miami Beach in a Mustang convertible. She's gained seventy pounds and she hates her life." To Nancy, Martha was a younger version of her mother, depressed, lacking in self-esteem, a cautionary tale whose moral was "if you want to be happy, develop a career and get your husband to share at home." Asking Evan to help again and again felt like "hard work" but it was essential to establishing her role as a career woman.

For his own reasons, Evan imagined things very differently. He loved Nancy and if Nancy loved being a social worker, he was happy and proud to support her in it. He knew that because she took her caseload so seriously, it was draining work. But at the same time, he did not see why, just because she chose this demanding career, *he* had to change *his own* life. Why should her personal decision to work outside the home require him to do more inside it? Nancy earned about two-thirds as much as Evan, and her salary was a big help, but as Nancy confided, "If push came to shove, we could do without it." Nancy was a social worker because she loved it. Doing daily chores at home was thankless work, and certainly not something Evan needed her to appreciate about him. Equality in the second shift meant a loss in his standard of living, and despite all the high-flown talk, he felt he hadn't *really* bargained for it. He was happy to help Nancy at home if she needed help; that was fine. That was only decent. But it was too sticky a matter "committing" himself to sharing.

Two other beliefs probably fueled his resistance as well. The first was his suspicion that if he shared the second shift with Nancy, she would "dominate him." Nancy would ask him to do this, ask him to do that. It felt to Evan as if Nancy had won so many small victories that he had to draw the line somewhere. Nancy had a declarative personality; and as Nancy said, "Evan's mother sat me down and told me once that I was too forceful, that Evan needed to take more authority." Both Nancy and Evan agreed that Evan's sense of career and self was in fact shakier than Nancy's. He had been unemployed. She never had. He had had some bouts of drinking in the past. Drinking was foreign to her. Evan thought that sharing housework would upset a certain balance of power that felt culturally "right." He held the purse strings and made the major decisions about large purchases (like their house) because he "knew more about finances" and because he'd chipped in more inheritance than she when they married. His job difficulties had lowered his self-respect, and now as a couple they had achieved some ineffable "balance"—tilted in his favor, she thought—which, if corrected to equalize the burden of chores, would result in his giving in "too much." A certain driving anxiety behind Nancy's strategy of actively renegotiating roles had made Evan see agreement as "giving in." When he wasn't feeling good about work, he dreaded the idea of being under his wife's thumb at home.

Underneath these feelings, Evan perhaps also feared that Nancy was avoiding taking care of *him.* His own mother, a mild-mannered alcoholic, had by imperceptible steps phased herself out of a mother's role, leaving him very much on his own. Perhaps a personal motive to prevent that happening in his marriage—a guess on my part, and unarticulated on his—underlay his strategy of passive resistance. And he wasn't altogether wrong to fear this. Meanwhile, he felt he was "offering" Nancy the chance to stay home, or cut back her hours, and that she was refusing his "gift," while Nancy felt that, given her feelings about work, this offer was hardly a gift.

In the sixth year of her marriage, when Nancy again intensified her pressure on Evan to commit himself to equal sharing, Evan recalled saying, "Nancy, why don't you cut back to half time, that way you can fit everything in." At first Nancy was baffled: "We've been married all this time, and you *still* don't get it. Work is important to me. I worked *hard* to get my MSW. Why *should* I give it up?" Nancy also explained to Evan and later to me, "I think my degree and my job has been my way of reassuring myself that I won't end up like my mother." Yet she'd received little emotional support in getting her degree from either her parents or in-laws. (Her mother had avoided asking about her thesis, and her in-laws, though invited, did not attend her graduation, later claiming they'd never been invited.)

In addition, Nancy was more excited about seeing her elderly clients in tenderloin hotels than Evan was about selling couches to furniture salesmen with greased-back hair. Why shouldn't Evan make as many compromises with his career ambitions and his leisure as she'd made with hers? She couldn't see it Evan's way, and Evan couldn't see it hers.

In years of alternating struggle and compromise, Nancy had seen only fleeting mirages of cooperation, visions that appeared when she got sick or withdrew, and disappeared when she got better or came forward.

After seven years of loving marriage, Nancy and Evan had finally come to a terrible impasse. Their emotional standard of living had drastically declined: they began to snap at each other, to criticize, to carp. Each felt taken advantage of: Evan, because his offering of a good arrangement was deemed unacceptable, and Nancy, because Evan wouldn't do what she deeply felt was "fair."

This struggle made its way into their sexual life—first through Nancy directly, and then through Joey. Nancy had always disdained any form of feminine wiliness or manipulation. Her family saw her as "a flaming feminist" and that was how she saw herself. As such, she felt above the underhanded ways traditional women used to get around men. She mused, "When I was a teen-ager, I vowed I would *never* use sex to get my way with a man. It is not self-respecting; it's demeaning. But when Evan refused to carry his load at home, I did, I used sex. I said, 'Look, Evan, I would not be this exhausted and asexual every night if I didn't have so much to face every morning.'" She felt reduced to an old "strategy," and her modern ideas made her ashamed of it. At the same time, she'd run out of other, modern ways.

The idea of a separation arose, and they became frightened. Nancy looked at the deteriorating marriages and fresh divorces of couples with young children around them. One unhappy husband they knew had become so uninvolved in family life (they didn't know whether his unhappiness made him uninvolved, or whether his lack of involvement had caused his wife to be unhappy) that his wife left him. In another case, Nancy felt the wife had "nagged" her husband so much that he abandoned her for another woman. In both cases, the couple was less happy after the divorce than before, and both wives took the children and struggled desperately to survive financially. Nancy took stock. She asked herself, "Why wreck a marriage over a dirty frying pan?" Is it really worth it?

Upstairs-Downstairs: A Family Myth as "Solution"

Not long after this crisis in the Holts' marriage, there was a dramatic lessening of tension over the issue of the second shift. It was as if the issue was closed. Evan had won. Nancy would do the second shift. Evan expressed vague guilt but beyond that he had nothing say. Nancy had wearied of continually raising the topic, wearied of the lack of resolution. Now in the exhaustion of defeat, she wanted the struggle to be over too. Evan was "so good" in *other* ways, why debilitate their marriage by continual quarreling. Besides, she told me, "Women always adjust more, don't they?"

One day, when I asked Nancy to tell me who did which tasks from a long list of household chores, she interrupted me with a broad wave of her hand and said, "I do the upstairs, Evan does the downstairs." What does that mean? I asked. Matter-of-factly, she explained that the upstairs included the living room, the dining room, the kitchen, two bedrooms, and two baths. The downstairs meant the garage, a place for storage

and hobbies—Evan's hobbies. She explained this as a "sharing" arrangement, without humor or irony—just as Evan did later. Both said they had agreed it was the best solution to their dispute. Evan would take care of the car, the garage, and Max, the family dog. As Nancy explained, "The dog is all Evan's problem. I don't have to deal with the dog." Nancy took care of the rest.

For purposes of accommodating the second shift, then, the Holts' garage was elevated to the full moral and practical equivalent of the rest of the house. For Nancy and Evan, "upstairs and downstairs," "inside and outside," was vaguely described like "half and half," a fair division of labor based on a natural division of their house.

The Holts presented their upstairs-downstairs agreement as a perfectly equitable solution to a problem they "once had." This belief is what we might call a "family myth," even a modest delusional system. Why did they believe it? I think they believed it because they needed to believe it, because it solved a terrible problem. It allowed Nancy to continue thinking of herself as the sort of woman whose husband didn't abuse her—a self-conception that mattered a great deal to her. And it avoided the hard truth that, in his stolid, passive way, Evan had refused to share. It avoided the truth, too, that in their showdown, Nancy was more afraid of divorce than Evan was. This outer cover to their family life, this family myth, was jointly devised. It was an attempt to agree that there was no conflict over the second shift, no tension between their versions of manhood and womanhood, and that the powerful crisis that had arisen was temporary and minor.

The wish to avoid such a conflict is natural enough. But their avoidance was tacitly supported by the surrounding culture, especially the image of the woman with the flying hair. After all, this admirable woman also proudly does the "upstairs" each day without a husband's help and without conflict.

After Nancy and Evan reached their up-stairs-downstairs agreement, their confrontations ended. They were nearly forgotten. Yet, as she described their daily life months after the agreement, Nancy's resentment still seemed alive and well. For example, she said:

Evan and I eventually divided the labor so that I do the upstairs and Evan does the downstairs and the dog. So the dog is my husband's problem. But when I was getting the dog outside and getting Joey ready for childcare, and cleaning up the mess of feeding the cat, and getting the lunches together, and having my son wipe his nose on my outfit so I would have to change—then I was pissed! I felt that I was doing *everything*. All Evan was doing was getting up, having coffee, reading the paper, and saying, "Well, I have to go now," and often forgetting the lunch I'd bothered to make.

She also mentioned that she had fallen into the habit of putting Joey to bed in a certain way: he asked to be swung around by the arms, dropped on the bed, nuzzled and hugged, whispered to in his ear. Joey waited for her attention. He didn't go to sleep without it. But, increasingly, when Nancy tried it at eight or nine, the ritual didn't put Joey to sleep. On the contrary, it woke him up. It was then that Joey began to say he could only go to sleep in his parents' bed, that he began to sleep in their bed and to encroach on their sexual life.

Near the end of my visits, it struck me that Nancy was putting Joey to bed in an "exciting" way, later and later at night, in order to tell Evan something important: "You win, I'll go on doing all the work at home, but I'm angry about it and I'll make you pay." Evan had won the battle but lost the war. According to the family myth, all was well: the struggle had been resolved by the upstairs-downstairs agreement. But sup-pressed in one area of their marriage, this struggle lived on in another—as Joey's Problem, and as theirs.

Nancy's "Program" to Sustain the Myth

There was a moment, I believe, when Nancy seemed to *decide* to give up on this one. She decided to try not to resent Evan. Whether or not other women face a moment just like this, at the very least they face the need to deal with all the feelings that naturally arise from a clash between a treasured ideal and an incompatible reality. In the age of a stalled revolution, it is a problem a great many women face.

Emotionally, Nancy's compromise from time to time slipped; she would forget and grow resentful again. Her new resolve needed maintenance. Only half aware that she was doing so, Nancy went to extraordinary lengths to maintain it. She could tell me now, a year or so after her "decision," in a matter-of-fact and noncritical way: "Evan likes to come home to a hot meal. He doesn't like to clear the table. He doesn't like to do the dishes. He likes to go watch TV. He likes to play with his son when he feels like it and not feel like he should be with him more." She seemed resigned.

Everything was "fine." But it had taken an extraordinary amount of complex "emotion work"—the work of *trying* to feel the "right" feeling, the feeling she wanted to feel—to make and keep everything "fine." Across the nation at this particular time in history, this emotion work is often all that stands between the stalled revolution on the one hand, and broken marriages on the other.

It would have been easier for Nancy Holt to do what some other women did: indignantly cling to her goal of sharing the second shift. Or she could have cynically renounced all forms of feminism as misguided, could have cleared away any ideological supports to her indignation, so as to smooth her troubled bond with Evan. Or, like her mother, she could have sunk into quiet depression, disguised perhaps by overbusyness, drinking, overeating. She did none of these things. Instead, she did something more complicated. She became *benignly* accommodating.

How did Nancy manage to accommodate graciously? How did she really live with it? In the most general terms, she had to bring herself to *believe* the myth that the upstairs-downstairs division of housework was fair, and that it had resolved her struggle with Evan. She had to decide to accept an arrangement which in her heart of hearts she had felt was unfair. At the same time, she did not relinquish her deep beliefs about fairness.

Instead, she did something more complicated. Intuitively, Nancy seemed to *avoid* all the mental associations that reminded her of this sore point: the connections between Evan's care of the dog and her care of their child and house, between her share of family work and equality in their marriage; and between equality and love. In short, Nancy refused to consciously recognize the entire chain of associations that made her feel that something was wrong. The maintenance program she designed to avoid thinking about these things and to avoid the connections between them, was, in one way, a matter of denial. But in another way, it was a matter of intuitive genius.

First, it involved dissociating the inequity in the second shift from the inequity in their marriage, and in marriages in general. Nancy continued to care about sharing the work at home, about having an "equal marriage" and about other people having them too. For reasons that went back to her depressed "doormat" mother, and to her consequent determination to forge an independent identity as an educated, middle-class woman for whom ca-

reer opportunities had opened up in the early 1980s, Nancy cared about these things. Egalitarianism as an ideology made sense of her biography, her circumstances, and the way she had forged the two. How could she *not* care? But to ensure that her concern for equality did not make her resentful in her marriage to a man remarkably resistant to change, she "rezoned" this anger-inducing territory. She made that territory much smaller: only if Evan did not take care of the dog would she be indignant. Now she wouldn't need to be upset about the double day *in general*. She could still be a feminist, still believe in fifty-fifty with housework, and still believe that working toward equality was an expression of respect and respect the basis of love. But this chain of associations was now anchored more safely to a more minor matter: how lovingly Evan groomed, fed, and walked the dog.

For Evan, also, the dog came to symbolize the entire second shift: it became a fetish. Other men, I found, had second-shift fetishes too. When I asked one man what he did to share the work of the home, he answered, "I make all the pies we eat." He didn't have to share much responsibility for the home; "pies" did it for him. Another man grilled fish. Another baked bread. In their pies, their fish, and their bread, such men converted a single act into a substitute for a multitude of chores in the second shift, a token. Evan took care of the dog.

Another way in which Nancy encapsulated her anger was to think about her work in a different way. Feeling unable to cope at home, she had with some difficulty finally arranged a half-time schedule with her boss at work. This eased her load, but it did not resolve the more elusive moral problem: within their marriage, her work and her time "mattered less" than Evan's. What Evan did with his time corresponded to what he wanted her to depend on him for, to appreciate him for; what she did with her time did not. To deal with this, she devised the idea of dividing all of her own work in the new schedule into "shifts." As she explained: "I've been resentful, yes. I was feeling mistreated, and I became a bitch to live with. Now that I've gone part-time, I figure that when I'm at the office from eight to one, and when I come home and take care of Joey and make dinner at five—all that time from eight to six is my shift. So I don't mind making dinner every night *since it's on my shift.* Before, I had to make dinner on time I considered to be *after* my shift and I resented always having to do it."

Another plank in Nancy's maintenance program was to suppress any comparison between her hours of leisure and Evan's. In this effort she had Evan's cooperation, for they both clung hard to the notion that they enjoyed an equal marriage. What they did was to deny any connection between this equal marriage and equal access to leisure. They agreed it couldn't be meaningfully claimed that Evan had more leisure than Nancy or that his fatigue mattered more, or that he enjoyed more discretion over his time, or that he lived his life more as he preferred. Such comparisons could suggest that they were both treating Evan as if he were *worth more* than Nancy, and for Nancy, from that point on, it would be a quick fall down a slippery slope to the idea that Evan did not love and honor her as much as she honored and loved him.

For Nancy, the leisure gap between Evan and herself had never seemed to her a simple, practical matter of her greater fatigue. Had it been just that, she would have felt tired but not indignant. Had it been only that, working part time for a while would have been a wonderful solution, as many other women have said, "the best of both worlds." What troubled Nancy was the matter of her worth. As she told me one day: "It's not that I mind taking care of Joey. I

love doing that. I don't even mind cooking or doing laundry. It's that I feel sometimes that Evan thinks his work, his time, is worth more than mine. He'll wait for me to get the phone. It's like his time is more sacred."

As Nancy explained: "Evan and I look for different signs of love. Evan feels loved when we make love. Sexual expression is very important to him. I feel loved when he makes dinner for me or cleans up. He knows I like that, and he does it sometimes." For Nancy, feeling loved was connected to feeling her husband was being considerate of her needs, and honoring her ideal of sharing and equity. To Evan, "fairness" and respect seemed impersonal moral concepts, abstractions rudely imposed on love. He thought he expressed his respect for Nancy by listening carefully to her opinions on the elderly, on welfare, on all sorts of topics, and by consulting her on major purchases. But who did the dishes had to do with a person's role in the family, not with fairness and certainly not with love. In my interviews, a surprising number of women spoke of their fathers helping their mothers "out of love" or consideration. As one woman said, "My dad helped around a lot. He really loved my mom." But in describing their fathers, not one man I interviewed made this link between help at home and love.

Suppressing the Politics of Comparison

In the past, Nancy had compared her responsibilities at home, her identity, and her life to Evan's, and had compared Evan to other men they knew. Now, to avoid resentment, she seemed to compare herself more to *other working mothers*—how organized, energetic, and successful she was compared to them. By this standard, she was doing great: Joey was blooming, her marriage was fine, her job was all she could expect.

Nancy also compared herself to single women who had moved further ahead in their careers, but they fit another mental category. There were two kinds of women, she thought—married and single. "A single woman could move ahead in her career but a married woman has to do a wife's work and mother's work as well." She did not make this distinction for men.

When Nancy decided to stop comparing Evan to men who helped more around the house, she had to suppress an important issue that she had often discussed with Evan: How *unusually* helpful was Evan? How unusually lucky was she? Did he do more or less than men in general? Than middle-class, educated men? What was the "going rate"?

Before she made her decision, Nancy had claimed that Bill Beaumont, who lived two doors down the street, did half the housework without being reminded. Evan gave her Bill Beaumont, but said Bill was an exception. Compared to *most men,* Evan said, he did more. This was true if "most men" meant Evan's old friends. Nancy felt "upwardly mobile" compared to the wives of those men, and she believed that they looked upon Evan as a model for their own husbands, just as she used to look up to women whose husbands did more than Evan. She also noted how much the dangerous "unionizer" she had appeared to a male friend of theirs:

One of our friends is a traditional Irish cop whose wife doesn't work. But the way they wrote that marriage, even when she had the kid and worked full time, she did everything. He couldn't understand our arrangement where my husband would help out and cook part time and do the dishes once in a while and help out with the laundry [an arrangement that didn't last]. We were *banned* from his house for a while because he told Evan, "Every time your

wife comes over and talks to my wife, I get in trouble." I was considered a flaming liberal.

When the wife of Joe Collins, a neighbor on the other side, complained that Joe didn't take equal responsibility, Joe in turn would look down the invisible chain of sharing, half-sharing, and nonsharing males to someone low on his wife's list of helpful husbands and say, "At least I do a hell of a lot more than *he* does." In reply, Joe's wife would name a husband she knew who took fully half the responsibility of caring for the child and the home. Joe would answer that this man was either imaginary or independently wealthy, and then cite the example of another male friend who, though a great humorist and fisherman, did far less at home.

I began to imagine the same evening argument extending down the street of this middle-class Irish neighborhood, across the city to other cities, states, regions . . . wives pointing to husbands who did more, husbands pointing to men who did less. Comparisons like these—between Evan and other men, between Nancy and other women—reflect a semiconscious sense of *the going rates for a desirable attitude or behavior in an available member of the same and opposite sex.* If most of the men in their middle-class circle of friends had been given to drinking heavily, beating their wives, and having affairs, Nancy would have considered herself "lucky" to have Evan because he didn't do those things. But most of the men they knew weren't like that either, so Nancy didn't consider Evan "above the going rate" in this way. Most of those men only halfheartedly encouraged their wives to advance at work, so Nancy felt lucky to have Evan's enthusiastic encouragement.

This idea of a "going rate" indicated the market value, so to speak, of a man's behavior or attitudes. If a man was really "rare," his wife intuitively felt grateful, or at least both of them felt she ought to. How far the whole culture, and their particular corner of it had gotten through the feminist agenda— criminalizing wife battery, disapproving of a woman's need for her husband's "permission" to work, and so on—became the cultural foundation of the judgment about how rare and desirable a man was.

The "going rate" was a tool in the marital struggle, useful in this case mainly on the male side. If Evan could convince Nancy that he did as much or more than "most men," she couldn't as seriously expect him to do more. Like most other men who didn't share, Evan felt the male norm was evidence on his side: men "out there" did less. Nancy was lucky he did as much as he did.

Nancy thought men "out there" did more at home but were embarrassed to say so. Given her view of "men out there," Nancy felt less lucky than seemed right to Evan, given his picture of things. Besides that, Nancy felt that sheer rarity was not the only or best measure. She felt that Evan's share of the work at home should be assessed, not by comparing it to the real inequalities in other people's lives, but by comparing it to the ideal of sharing.

Comparisons between Evan and the going rate of male helpfulness was one basis on which to appraise Evan's offerings to their marriage and the credit and gratitude due him for those offerings. The more rare, the more credit. Their ideals of manhood and womanhood formed another basis. The closer to the ideal, the more credit. And the harder it was to live up to the ideal, the more pride-swallowing it took, or the more effort shown, the more credit. Since Evan and Nancy didn't see this going rate the same way, since they differed in their ideals, and since Evan hadn't actually shown much effort in changing, Nancy had not been as grateful to Evan as he felt she should have been. Not only had she not been grateful, she'd resented him.

But now, under the new "maintenance program" to support the necessary myth of equality in her marriage, Nancy set aside the tangles in the give and take of credit. She thought now in a more "segregated" way. She compared women to women, and men to men, and based her sense of gratitude on that way of thinking. Since the going rate was unfavorable to women, Nancy felt she should feel more grateful for what Evan gave her (because it was so rare in the world) than Evan should feel for what she gave him (which was more common). Nancy did not have to feel grateful because Evan had compromised his own views on manhood; actually he had made few concessions. But she did feel she owed him gratitude for supporting her work so wholeheartedly; that was unusual.

For his part, Evan didn't talk much about feeling grateful to Nancy. He actually felt she wasn't doing enough around the house. But he said this in a curious way that avoided an Evan-Nancy comparison. He erased the distinction between Nancy and himself: his "I" disappeared into "we," leaving no "me" to compare to "you." For example, when I asked him if he felt that he did enough around the house, he laughed, surprised to be asked point-blank, and replied mildly: "No, I don't think so. No. I would have to admit that we probably could do more." Then using "we" in an apparently different way, he went on: "But I also have to say that I think we could do more in terms of the household chores than we really do. See, we let a lot more slide than we should."

Nancy made no more comparisons to Bill Beaumont, no more unfavorable comparisons to the "going rate." Without these frames of reference, the deal with Evan seemed "fair." This did not mean that Nancy ceased to care about equality between the sexes. On the contrary, she cut out magazine articles about how males rose faster in social welfare than females, and she complained about the condescending way male psychiatrists treat female social workers. She pushed her feminism "out" into the world of work, a safe distance away from the upstairs-downstairs arrangement at home.

Nancy now blamed her fatigue on "everything she had to do." When she occasionally spoke of conflict, it was conflict between her job and Joey, or between Joey and housework. Evan slid out of the equation. As Nancy spoke of him now, he had no part in the conflict.

Since Nancy and Evan no longer conceived of themselves as comparable, Nancy let it pass when Evan spoke of housework in a "male" way, as something he "would do" or "would not do," or something he did when he got around to it. Like most women, when Nancy spoke of housework, she spoke simply of what had to be done. The difference in the way she and Evan talked seemed to emphasize that their viewpoints were "naturally" different and again helped push the problem out of mind.

Many couples traded off tasks as the need arose; whoever came home first started dinner. In the past, Evan had used flexibility in the second shift to camouflage his retreat from it; he hadn't liked "rigid schedules." He had once explained to me: "We don't really keep count of who does what. Whoever gets home first is likely to start dinner. Whoever has the time deals with Joey or cleans up." He had disparaged a female neighbor who kept strict track of tasks as "uptight" and "compulsive." A couple, he had felt, ought to be "open to the flow." Dinner, he had said, could be anytime. The very notion of a leisure gap disappeared into Evan's celebration of happy, spontaneous anarchy. But now that the struggle was over, Evan didn't talk of dinner at "anytime." Dinner was at six.

Nancy's program to keep up her gracious resignation included another tactic: she would focus on the *advantages* of losing the struggle. She wasn't *stuck* with the upstairs. Now, as she talked she seemed to preside over it as her dominion. She would do the housework, but the house would feel like "hers." The new living-room couch, the kitchen cabinet, she referred to as "mine." She took up "supermom-speak" and began referring to *my* kitchen, *my* living-room curtains, and, even in Evan's presence, to *my* son. She talked of machines that helped *her,* and of the work-family conflict itself as *hers.* Why shouldn't she? She felt she'd earned that right. The living room reflected Nancy's preference for beige. The upbringing of Joey reflected Nancy's ideas about fostering creativity by giving a child controlled choice. What remained of the house was Evan's domain. As she remarked: "I never touch the garage, not ever. Evan sweeps it and straightens it and arranges it and plays with tools and figures out where the equipment goes—in fact, that's one of his hobbies. In the evening, after Joey has settled down, he goes down there and putzes around; he has a TV down there, and he figures out his fishing equipment and he just plays around. The washer and dryer are down there, but that's the only part of the garage that's my domain."

Nancy could see herself as the "winner"—the one who got her way, the one whose kitchen, living room, house, and child these really were. She could see her arrangement with Evan as *more* than fair—from a certain point of view.

As a couple, Nancy and Evan together explained their division of the second shift in ways that disguised their struggle. Now they rationalized that it was a result of their two *personalities.* For Evan, especially, there was no problem of a leisure gap; there was only the continual, fascinating interaction of two personalities. "I'm lazy," he explained. "I like to do what I want to do in my own time. Nancy isn't as lazy as I am. She's compulsive and very well organized." The comparisons of his work to hers, his fatigue to hers, his leisure time to hers—comparisons that used to point to a problem—were melted into freestanding personal characteristics, his laziness, her compulsiveness.

Nancy now agreed with Evan's assessment of her, and described herself as "an energetic person" who was amazingly "well organized." When I asked her whether she felt any conflict between work and family life, she demurred: "I work real well overnight. I pulled overnights all through undergraduate and graduate school, so I'm not too terribly uncomfortable playing with my family all evening, then putting them to bed, making coffee, and staying up all night [to write up reports on her welfare cases] and then working the next day—though I only do that when I'm down to the wire. I go into overdrive. I don't feel any conflict between the job and the child that way at all."

Evan was well organized and energetic on his job. But as Nancy talked of Evan's life at home, he neither had these virtues nor lacked them; they were irrelevant. This double standard of virtue reinforced the idea that men and women cannot be compared, being "naturally" so different.

Evan's orientation to domestic tasks, as they both described it now, had been engraved in childhood, and how could one change a whole childhood? As Nancy often reminded me, "I was brought up to do the housework. Evan wasn't." Many other men, who had also done little housework when they were boys, did not talk so fatalistically about "upbringing," because they were doing a lot of it now. But the idea of a fate sealed so very early was oddly *useful* in Nancy's program of benign resignation. She needed it, because if the die had been cast in the dawn of life, it was inevitable that she should work the extra month a year.

This, then, was the set of mental tricks that helped Nancy resign herself to what

had at one time seemed like a "bad deal." This was how she reconciled believing one thing and living with another.

How Many Holts?

In one key way the Holts were typical of the vast majority of two-job couples: their family life had become the shock absorber for a stalled revolution whose origin lay far outside it—in economic and cultural trends that bear very differently on men and women. Nancy was reading books, newspaper articles, and watching TV programs on the changing role of women. Evan wasn't. Nancy felt benefited by these changes; Evan didn't. In her ideals and in reality, Nancy was more different from her mother than Evan was from his father, for the culture and economy were in general pressing change faster upon women like her than upon men like Evan. Nancy had gone to college; her mother hadn't. Nancy had a professional job; her mother never had. Nancy had the idea that she should be equal with her husband; her mother hadn't been much exposed to that idea in her day. Nancy felt she should share the job of earning money, and that Evan should share the work at home; her mother hadn't imagined that was possible. Evan went to college, his father (and the other boys in his family, though not the girls) had gone too. Work was important to Evan's identity as a man as it had been for his father before him. Indeed, Evan felt the same way about family roles as his father had felt in his day. The new job opportunities and the feminist movement of the 1960s and '70s had transformed Nancy but left Evan pretty much the same. And the friction created by this difference between them moved to the issue of second shift as metal to a magnet. By the end, Evan did less housework and childcare than most men married to working women—but not much less. Evan and Nancy were also typical of nearly forty percent of the marriages I studied in their clash of gender ideologies and their corresponding difference in notion about what constituted a "sacrifice" and what did not. By far the most common form of mismatch was like that between Nancy, an egalitarian, and Evan, a transitional.

But for most couples, the tensions between strategies did not move so quickly and powerfully to issues of housework and childcare. Nancy pushed harder than most women to get her husband to share the work at home, and she also lost more overwhelmingly than the few other women who fought that hard. Evan pursued his strategy of passive resistance with more quiet tenacity than most men, and he allowed himself to become far more marginal to his son's life than most other fathers. The myth of the Holts' "equal" arrangement seemed slightly more odd than other family myths that encapsulated equally powerful conflicts.

Beyond their upstairs-downstairs myth, the Holts tell us a great deal about the subtle ways a couple can encapsulate the tension caused by a struggle over the second shift without resolving the problem or divorcing. Like Nancy Holt, many women struggle to avoid, suppress, obscure, or mystify a frightening conflict over the second shift. They do not struggle like this because they started off wanting to, or because such struggle is inevitable or because women inevitably lose, but because they are forced to choose between equality and marriage. And they choose marriage. When asked about "ideal" relations between men and women in general, about what they want for their daughters, about what "ideally" they'd like in their own marriage, most working mothers "wished" their men would share the work at home.

But many "wish" it instead of "want" it. Other goals—like keeping peace at home—

come first. Nancy Holt did some extraordinary behind-the-scenes emotion work to prevent her ideals from clashing with her marriage. In the end, she had confined and miniaturized her ideas of equality successfully enough to do two things she badly wanted to do: feel like a feminist, and live at peace with a man who was not. Her program had "worked." Evan won on the reality of the situation, because Nancy did the second shift. Nancy won on the cover story; they would talk about it as if they shared.

Nancy wore the upstairs-downstairs myth as an ideological cloak to protect her from the contradictions in her marriage and from the cultural and economic forces that press upon it. Nancy and Evan Holt were caught on opposite sides of the gender revolution occurring all around them. Through the 1960s, 1970s, and 1980s masses of women entered the public world of work—but went only so far up the occupational ladder. They tried for "equal" marriages, but got only so far in achieving it. They married men who liked them to work at the office but who wouldn't share the extra month a year at home. When confusion about the identity of the working woman created a cultural vacuum in the 1970s and 1980s, the image of the supermom quietly glided in. She made the "stall" seem normal and happy. But beneath the happy image of the woman with the flying hair are modern marriages like the Holts', reflecting intricate webs of tension, and the huge, hidden emotional cost to women, men, and children of having to "manage" inequality. Yet on the surface, all we might see would be Nancy Holt bounding confidently out the door at 8:30 A.M., briefcase in one hand, Joey in the other. All we might hear would be Nancy's and Evan's talk about their marriage as happy, normal, even "equal"—because equality was so important to Nancy.

35

Hispanic Women and Homework
Women in the Informal Economy of Miami and Los Angeles

M. Patricia Fernández-Kelly • Anna M. García

M. Patricia Fernández-Kelly is associate professor of sociology and a research scientist at the Institute for Policy Studies at the Johns Hopkins University. She is the author of *For We Are Sold, I and My People: Woman and Industry in Mexico's Frontier* and has published extensively on questions regarding international development, women's employment in export processing zones, and the informal economy.

Anna M. García is a research associate at the Center for U.S.-Mexican Studies at the University of California at San Diego. She has participated in several projects focusing on the health of Mexican immigrants and their access to public services. Her current work focuses on the impact of immigration reform upon the employment patterns of California businesses. She has co-authored several articles with M. Patricia Fernández-Kelly.

In the latter part of the twentieth century, underground economies are expanding in industrial regions like the United States and western Europe. The proliferation of sweat shops, unlicensed industrial operations, and homework seems incongruous in information-based societies in which multinational corporations rely upon advanced technology. Nevertheless, a growing body of quantitative and qualitative evidence points to economic informalization as a distinctive and ongoing process in advanced industrial nations.[1] Low-tech industries like apparel and high-tech industries like electronics share this feature.

A considerable degree of internal variation characterizes informal economies. An understanding of this differentiation should entail the study of labor market conditions and of the household structures to which informal workers and employers belong. It is within the household that the constraints of class and gender mesh, resulting in various modes of adaptation to the surrounding economic system and in differing patterns of employment. A comparison between Miami and Los Angeles provides an invaluable opportunity to illustrate this point. Homework involving Hispanic women, particularly immigrants and refugees, is widespread in the two locations, especially in the garment industry. On the surface, the two cases seem to be similar outcomes resulting from identical economic processes. However, as we will see, in Miami the existence of an ethnic enclave formed by Cuban entrepreneurs, most of them political exiles, enabled women from the same families and community to transform homework into a strategy for maximizing earnings and for reconciling cultural and economic demands.

Theirs is a position of qualified vulnerability when judged against the totality of economic and political interactions. By contrast, in Los Angeles the high degree of proletarianization of Mexican women (partly resulting from their working class background, undocumented immigrant status, and particular household characteristics) has accentuated their vulnerability in the labor market. For many of these women, industrial homework and even the purchase of small assembly shops are measures of last resort; they are strategies to stay a step above poverty.

The comparison proposed in this chapter not only illuminates diversity within the informal economy but also suggests that the meaning of homework varies with the economic, political, and social context of women's lives. This is true even among Hispanic women, who are usually regarded as an undifferentiated whole. Class, ethnicity, and household composition intersect with regional economic structures to define the function of homework. Thus, home assembly cannot be fully understood without regard for the economic significance to the household; the articulation between domestic labor and wage employment shapes and is shaped by the informal economy.

Two hypotheses guide this comparative analysis. (1) Proletarianization—that is, dependence on the larger mechanisms of the wage labor market—reduces the possibility of upholding patriarchal norms of reciprocity between men and women. This, in turn, translates into high levels of economic and political vulnerability. (2) Conversely, the existence of an ethnic entrepreneurial class predicated upon patriarchal notions of reciprocity can improve the bargaining ability of women in the labor market and raise the political strength of the group as a whole. The first proposition applies to Mexican women employed in garment and electronics manufacture in southern California. The second refers to Cuban garment workers in southern Florida.

A Social Portrait of Hispanic Women in Wage Labor

Although Hispanics are often portrayed as a uniform population, their employment and social profiles show differences as well as similarities when national backgrounds, educational levels, citizen status, and length of residence in the U.S. are considered. For example, Mexicans comprised more than half of all Hispanics between eighteen and sixty-four years of age living in the U.S. in 1976. Of these, approximately 70 percent had been born in this country. Average levels of education were low; less than 50 percent graduated from high school. About 60 percent of working-age Mexicans were under thirty-five years of age compared with less than 50 percent of working-age, non-Hispanic white workers. Cubans, on the other hand, represented less than 7 percent of the Hispanic population. They were mostly foreign born and had a mean age of thirty-nine years. They also had a higher level of education than Mexicans. Fifty-eight percent of Cubans had twelve or more years of formal schooling in 1976.[2]

On the other hand, Cubans and Mexicans share similar marital profiles and household compositions. Intact marriages as well as a relatively low percentage of households headed by women are distinguishing features in both groups. Seventeen percent of Cuban and 16 percent of Mexican households are headed by females, compared to about 8 percent of white domestic units in the same situation. Sixty-seven percent of Mexican and 64 percent of Cuban women were married and living with their spouses in 1976. Sixty-five percent of Mexican men and 70 percent of Cuban males lived in stable marital unions. Finally, about 74 percent of Mexican women had children living with them. The equivalent figure for Cubans was 62 percent.[3]

Both Cuban and Mexican women have had a prominent representation as remunerated workers in the United States. Their labor force participation rates dispel the widespread notion that work outside the home is a rare experience among Hispanic women. For instance, 50 percent of native-born and 45 percent of foreign-born Mexican women were employed outside the home in 1976. The equivalent figure for foreign-born Cubans was 65 percent (despite the fact that their labor participation rate prior to their arrival in the United States was about 30 percent). Thus, current levels of employment among Mexican and Cuban women in the U.S. approximate or surpass the labor force participation of non-Hispanic white women, of whom 57 percent work outside the home. Moreover, while other ethnic groups in the United States have diminished their participation in blue collar employment, Hispanic women have increased their relative share in it, particularly in the production of nondurable goods.[4]

The importance of minority women's employment in assembly is readily apparent in southern California, where 67 percent of working women classified as "operators, fabricators, and laborers" belong to ethnic minority groups. Fifty-one percent of those are Hispanic. These findings contradict the assumption that Hispanic women's participation in the labor force is confined to the service sector. Census figures for Los Angeles County further confirm the significance of Hispanic women's employment in manufacturing: 73.7 percent of all female "operators, fabricators, and laborers" (136,937 persons) are members of ethnic minorities. Almost 60 percent of that subgroup (105,621 individuals) are Hispanic. Even more revealing is the composition of workers classified as "textile, apparel, and furnishings machine operators."

Approximately 46,219 women are employed in that occupation in Los Angeles. Almost 91 percent of those are minorities; 71.76 percent, Hispanic. Equivalent data for New York and Miami (the two other areas with the fastest growing Hispanic populations) indicate that we are looking at a substantial percentage of the manufacturing labor force.[5] However, census material may underestimate the actual involvement of Hispanic women in wage labor: many are part of the underground economy; they are found in small unregulated assembly shops or doing piece work and industrial homework.

The preceding summary is useful for comparative purposes. However, some features vary when observations are limited to certain industries, their correspondent labor market incorporation patterns, and household characteristics prevalent among their workers. For example, in both southern California and southern Florida most direct production workers in the garment industry are Hispanic. In Los Angeles and Miami apparel firms approximately 75 percent of the operatives are Mexican; 85 percent, Cuban. In contrast to the characteristics of the population at large, among Los Angeles garment workers approximately 29 percent are female-headed households, a figure much larger than that for Mexicans living in the United States in general (16 percent). By contrast, there is little variation when comparing the number of female-headed households in the Florida needle trade industry with the population as a whole. About 17 percent of Cuban households are headed by females; the equivalent figure for the Florida garment industry is 19 percent.[6]

The large number of female-headed households in the Los Angeles garment industry calls for an explanation. Because Cubans and Mexicans share many cultural characteristics, that explanation cannot rely exclusively on differences regarding values and attitudes about family life or sex roles.

Instead, it must take into consideration the differential modes of incorporation of the two ethnic groups into their receiving economic milieu. Before addressing this question, we provide a description of apparel manufacturing in the two locations under study.

Structures of the Garment Industry in California and Florida

For many generations, garment production has provided a locus in which immigrant women, including Hispanics of various national backgrounds, have found entry-level jobs. But the development and nature of the industry has varied over time and by region, affecting the incorporation of immigrant labor and the use of homeworkers. To understand the current position of Mexican and Cuban homeworkers, we must first compare garment manufacture in Los Angeles and Miami.

The two sites differ in the timing of the industry, its evolution, maturity, and restructuring. In Los Angeles, garment production is not only older, developing first in the late nineteenth century with the gold rush and waves of Chinese immigrants. It is also rooted in specific events such as the Great Depression, changing conditions of assembly and unionization in New York, emphasis on new definitions of casual wear, and, finally, continued reorganization during the seventies and eighties as a response to the impact of foreign imports. Restructuring in the Los Angeles garment industry has led to a decreasing number of large firms and a proliferation of small, subcontracted shops, many of which fall partly or totally outside government supervision. Sixty-two percent of the 2,717 apparel and textile manufacturers in Los Angeles County in 1984 employed between one and nineteen workers.

Several studies show that the predominance of small, productive establishments in a given industry raises the probability of informal activities such as tax and licensing evasions and violations of the labor code. The prevalence of small shops accounts, to a large extent, for the survival of the garment industry in Los Angeles. Thus, contrary to a widespread impression, garment production in the area is actually growing quickly, due to the expansion of the informal sector. Between 30 and 50 percent of the $3.5 billion in 1983 Los Angeles garment industry sales may have originated in home production or unregulated shops, the majority of which are small.[7]

Apparel production in Miami has had a shorter history and a less diversified experience. In the early sixties Miami's industry was highly seasonal, employed fewer than 7,000 workers, and depended on New York entrepreneurs feeding U.S. and European luxury markets in belts, gloves, and purses. As retired manufacturers from New York living in Miami saw the advantages of opening new businesses and hiring large numbers of freshly arrived Cubans, Miami expanded by 1973 to employ more than 24,000 people, the vast majority of whom were Cuban women. This same process led to the predominance of Cuban males among contractors. From its inception, then, apparel manufacturing in Miami illustrated gender and ethnic stratification: 70 percent of the manufacturers were Jewish; 90 percent of the contractors, Cuban men; and 95 percent of the work force, Cuban females. As in Los Angeles in the early eighties, many of the 716 firms in Miami employed fewer than thirty workers, and a substantial proportion of the industry (at least one third) originated in unregulated shops and homes.

However, unlike Los Angeles, since the late seventies Florida has suffered labor shortages caused by the relatively advanced age (over forty) of the work force and the absence of a new labor supply. The decreasing availability of Cuban women's labor has contributed, as we shall see, to the expansion of homework in Miami.[8]

The two locations also differ in the availability of a favored labor supply. The growth of the Los Angeles clothing industry resulted from capitalists' ability to rely on steady waves of Mexican immigrants, many of whom were undocumented. Over the last century this continuous migration has ensured a permanent supply of workers. From the twenties, Mexican women dominated the work force; the majority were below the age of thirty, two-thirds were born in the United States, and nine-tenths were unmarried. By 1944, when the number of garment manufacturers had grown to 900, 75 percent of their 28,000 employees were Mexican women and girls.[9] By contrast, garment production in Miami expanded because of an unprecedented influx of exiles ejected by a unique political event. Cubans working in the Florida apparel industry arrived in the United States as refugees, protected and relatively privileged. Their exile was filled with uncertainty and the possibility of dislocation but not, as in the case of undocumented Mexican aliens, with the probability of harassment, detention, and deportation.

Implicit in the previous point is a differentiation in social class between the two groups of newcomers. For more than a century, the majority of Mexican immigrants have had a markedly proletarian background. Until the seventies, the majority had rural roots; in more recent times the number of urban immigrants has grown.[10] In sharp contrast, Cuban waves of migration have included a larger proportion of professionals, mid-level service providers, and various types of entrepreneurs ranging from those with previous experience in large companies to those able to start small family enterprises. Research has shown that entrepreneurial experience among Cubans and reliance on their own ethnic network accounts, to a large extent, for their success in business formation and appropriation in Miami.[11] Thus, while Mexican migration has

been characterized by a relative homogeneity regarding class background, Cuban exile resulted in the transposition of an almost intact class structure containing investors and professionals as well as unskilled, semi-skilled and skilled workers.

In addition to disparate class compositions, the two groups differ in the degree of their homogeneity by place of birth. Besides the sizable undocumented contingent, the Los Angeles garment industry also employs U.S.-born citizens of Mexican heritage. Although no systematic studies have been done on the subject, first-hand reports and anecdotal evidence indicate a fragmentation between "Chicanas" and "Mexicans," with the latter occupying the lower rungs in the labor hierarchy. Differences in citizenship status, length of residence in the United States, and skill often result in open or latent conflict among the two groups. Recently arrived Mexican immigrants point to discrimination and prejudice from workers with whom they share a common ethnic background. Cubans, on the other hand, were a highly cohesive population until recently, when the arrival of the Port of Mariel refugees resulted in a potentially damaging fragmentation of the community.

Perhaps the most important difference between Mexicans in Los Angeles and Cubans in Florida is related to their distinctive patterns of labor market insertion. Historically, Mexicans have arrived in the U.S. labor market in a highly individuated and dispersed manner. As a result, they have been extremely dependent on labor supply and demand—forces beyond their control. Their working-class background and the stigma attached to their frequent undocumented status has accentuated even further their vulnerability vis-à-vis employers. By contrast, Cubans have been able to consolidate an economic enclave containing immigrant businesses which hire workers of a common culture and national background.[12]

This economic enclave operates as a buffer zone, separating and often shielding members of the same ethnic group from the market forces at work in the larger society. The existence of an economic enclave does not preclude exploitation on the basis of class; indeed, it is predicated upon the existence of a highly diversified immigrant class structure. However, the quantitative and qualitative evidence suggests that commonalities of culture, national background, and language between immigrant employers and workers can become a mechanism for collective improvement of income levels and standards of living. As a result, differences in labor market insertion patterns among Mexicans and Cubans have led to varying social profiles and a dissimilar potential for socioeconomic attainment.

Household Organization and the Politics of Home and Work

Neither proletarian atomization among Mexicans nor participation in an economic enclave among Cubans can be explained without consideration of the role played by households and families in the allocation of workers to different segments of the labor market. Both Mexican and Cuban women have sought homework as one way to reconcile the responsibilities of family and domestic care with the need to earn a wage. Employers, in turn, have found in homework a vehicle to lower the wage bill, evade government regulations, and maintain competitiveness in the market. While these two aspects have remained constant, the circumstances surrounding homework in southern California and southern Florida highlight the varying impact that class has on household composition and that class-defined households have on various types of labor force participation. Differences in class background and household composition

have led to the contrasting experiences of Mexican and Cuban homeworkers.

Both Cubans and Mexicans prize the idealized family—long-term, stable unions in which men act as main providers and women as principal caretakers of children. However, the possibility of forming such family units over extended periods of time varies in consonance with several factors including class background. Stable nuclear families and clearly defined sex roles are often found among the middle and upper classes; the poor must often live in highly flexible households in which resources and services flow constantly but adherence to the norms of the patriarchal family are unattainable. As we will illustrate below, the large number of female-headed households in the Los Angeles garment industry can be partly explained as an outcome of proletarianization and the absence of an ethnic enclave in which the injuries of class are mitigated.

The experience of Petra R., a thirty-two-year-old native from Torreón, Coahuila (Mexico), exemplifies the conditions surrounding many recently arrived Mexican immigrants:[13] "I've worked in several garment shops since I came to California five years ago. At first I lived with my aunt and uncle and another Mexican family with whom we shared an apartment. None of us had papers, but that didn't matter so much. The problem was the language—how to make yourself understood when looking for a job. So I ended up sewing . . . then I got pregnant. I didn't want to live with relatives then, so I had to work at home. Fortunately, the old man [her employer] gives me enough so that I don't have to go to the shop."

The employment history of Amelia Ruiz, a U.S.-born woman of Mexican ancestry, more fully illustrates the ways that economic uncertainty, cultural expectations, and household stability lead women to homework. She was born into a family of six children in El Cerrito, Los Angeles County. Her mother, a descendant of Native American Indians, married at a young age the son of Mexican immigrants. Among Amelia's memories are the fragmentary stories of her paternal grandparents working in fields and, occasionally, in canneries. On the other hand, her father was not a stoop laborer but a trained upholsterer. Her mother was always a homemaker. Amelia grew up with a distinct sense of the contradictions that plague the relationships between men and women: "All the while I was a child, I had this feeling that my parents weren't happy. My mother was smart but she could never make much of herself. Her parents taught her that the fate of woman is to be a wife and mother; they advised her to find a good man and marry him. And that she did. My father was dependable, and I think he was faithful, but he was also distant; he lived in his own world. He would come home and expect to be served hand on foot. My mother would wait on him, but she was always angry about it."

After getting her high school diploma, Amelia took up odd jobs in all the predictable places: as a counter clerk in a dress shop, as a cashier in a fast food establishment, and as a waitress in two restaurants. When she was twenty, she met Miguel. He was a consummate survivor, having worked in the construction field, as a truck driver, and even as an ESL (English as a Second Language) instructor. At the age of twenty-one and despite her misgivings, Amelia was married: "For a while I kept my job, but when I became pregnant, Miguel didn't want me to work anymore. Two more children followed and then, little by little, Miguel became abusive. He wanted to have total authority over me and the children. He said a man should know how to take care of a family and get respect, but it was hard to take him seriously when he kept changing jobs and when the money he brought home was barely enough to keep ends together."

After the birth of her second child, Amelia started work at Shirley's, a women's wear factory in the area. Miguel was opposed to the idea. For Amelia, work outside the home was an evident need prompted by financial stress. At first, it was also a means to escape growing disillusion: "I saw myself turning into my mother, and I started thinking that to be free of men was best for women. Maybe if Miguel had had a better job, maybe if he had kept the one he had, things would have been different. . . . We started drifting apart."

She had worked at Shirley's for almost a year when one late afternoon, after collecting the three children from her parents' house, she returned to an empty home. She knew, as soon as she stepped inside, that something was amiss. In muted shock she confirmed the obvious: Miguel had left, taking with him all personal possessions; even the wedding picture in the living room had been removed. No explanations had been left behind. Amelia was then twenty-eight years of age, alone, and the mother of three small children.

Under the circumstances, employment became even more desirable, but the difficulty of reconciling home responsibilities with wage work persisted. Amelia was well regarded at Shirley's and her condition struck a cord of sympathy among other factory women. In a casual conversation, her supervisor described how other women were leasing industrial sewing machines from the local Singer distributor and doing piece work at home. By combining factory work and home assembly, she could earn more money without further neglecting her children. Mr. Driscoll, Shirley's owner and general manager, made regular use of homeworkers, most of whom were former employees. That had allowed him to retain a stable core of about twenty employees and to depend on approximately ten homeworkers during peak seasons.

Between 1979, the year of her desertion, and 1985 when we met her, Amelia had struggled hard, working most of the time and making some progress. Her combined earnings before taxes fluctuated between $950 and $1,150. In 1985 almost half of her income went to rent for the two-bedroom apartment which she shared with the children. She was in debt and used to working at least twelve hours a day. On the other hand, she had bought a double-needle sewing machine and was thinking of leasing another one to enable a neighbor to help with additional sewing. She had high hopes: "Maybe some day I'll have my own business; I'll be a liberated woman. . . . I won't have to take orders from a man. Maybe Miguel did me a favor when he left after all."

Although there are individual variations, Amelia's life history is shared by many garment workers in southern California. Two aspects are worth noting in this experience. First, marriage and a stable family life are seen as desirable objectives which are, nonetheless, fraught with ambivalent feelings and responsibilities. Second, tensions surrounding home life express a contradiction between the intent to fulfill sexual roles defined according to a shared culture and the absence of the economic base necessary for their implementation. Male unemployment and women's need to become breadwinners militate against the maintenance of patriarchal standards. Male desertion adds to the vulnerability of women. Mexican garment workers, especially those who are heads of households, face great disadvantages in the labor market. They are targeted as a preferred labor force for jobs which offer the lowest wages paid to industrial workers in the United States; they also have among the lowest unionization rates in the country. Ironically, household atomization, partly caused by proletarianization and the ensuing breakdown of patriarchal norms, has not been followed by the elimination of similar patriarchal standards in the labor market.

Although our focus is on women employed in the garment industry, it is worth noting some commonalities in electronics production. Mexican women working in southern California's booming electronics industry reflect similar reasons for homework; like their counterparts in garments, they provide a large labor pool attractive to entrepreneurs who find in them the flexibility needed in highly competitive sectors of the economy. When activity peaks, some employees take batches of components to their own homes, where they assemble them at piece rates (as low as seven cents per unit), often aided by friends and family members. Several aspects are striking in this case. The public image of high-tech industries appears antithetical to practices such as the putting out of assembly work among Hispanic and Indo-Chinese workers in southern California. However, for a large number of electronics firms, this is a customary practice. In Kearny Mesa, an area in San Diego County where there is a large concentration of electronics producers, 75 percent of firms make regular use of homeworkers. Maribel Guzman, who has worked at one electronics firm for two years, thinks homework is a good idea: "I'm always looking for ways to earn a little more. . . . I have worked in all sorts of jobs. But with a family to look after, and the cost of child care what it is, I can use the extra money. Sometimes, my neighbor helps and I give her part of what I get. She can't leave home because she has a baby and doesn't speak a word of English, but she too needs the money."

Tales like the ones related above can be found among Cuban and Central American women in Miami. However, a larger proportion have had a different trajectory than Mexicans in Los Angeles. Among the first waves of refugees were many who worked hard to bring the standards of living of their families to the same level or higher than those they had been familiar with in their countries of origin. The consolidation of an ethnic enclave allowed many Cuban men to become successful entrepreneurs. While their wives toiled in garment factories, they entered the world of business. Eventually, they purchased homes, put their children through school, and achieved comfortable styles of life. At that point, many Cuban men pressed their wives to stop working outside the home. They had only allowed them to work in the first place out of economic necessity. In the words of a prominent manufacturer in the area:

> You have to understand that Cuban workers were willing to do anything to survive. When they became prosperous, the women saw the advantage of staying at home and still earning additional income. Because they had the skill, owners couldn't take them for granted. Eventually, owners couldn't get operators anymore. The most skilled would tell a manager, "My husband doesn't let me work out of the home." This was a worker's initiative based on the values of the culture. I would put ads in the paper and forty people would call and everyone would say, "I only do homework." That's how we got this problem of labor shortages.

This testimony partly shows that decisions made at the level of the household can remove workers highly desired by employers from the marketplace, thus endangering certain types of production. In those cases, loyalty to familial values can act against the interests of capitalist firms. Interviews with Cuban women involved in homework confirm this general interpretation. By capitalizing on their skill and experience, many of these women became subcontractors, employing their own neighbors and transforming so-called "Florida rooms" (the covered porches in their houses) into sewing shops.

In one of those improvised sewing shops we interviewed Elvira Gómez. She was thirty-four when she arrived in Miami with her four children, ages three to twelve, in 1961.

> Leaving Havana was the most painful thing that ever happened to us. We loved our country, we would have never left willingly. Cuba was not like Mexico: we didn't have immigrants in large numbers. But Castro betrayed us and we had to join the exodus. We became exiles. My husband left Cuba three months before I did, and there were moments where I doubted I would ever see him again. Then after we got together, we realized we would have to forge ahead without looking back.

> We lost everything. Even my mother's china had to be left behind. We arrived in this country as they say, "covering our nakedness with our bare hands" (una mano delante y otra detrás). My husband had had a good position in a bank. To think that he would take any old job in Miami was more than I could take; a man of his stature having to beg for a job in a hotel or a factory? It wasn't right!

Before her marriage Elvira had worked briefly as a secretary. As a middle-class wife and mother she was used to hiring at least one maid. Coming to the United States changed all that: "Something had to be done to keep the family together. So I looked around and finally found a job in a shirt factory in Hialeah. Manolo [her husband] joined a childhood friend and got a loan to start an export-import firm. All the time they were building the business, I was sewing. There were times when we wouldn't have been able to pay the bills without the money I brought in."

In her case, working outside the home was justified as a way to maintain the integrity of her family and as a means to support her husband's early incursions into the business world:

> For six long years I worked in the factory, but when things got better financially, Manolo asked me to quit the job. He felt bad that I couldn't be at home all the time with the children. But it had to be done. There's no reason for women not to earn a living when necessary. But I tell my daughters that the strength of a family rests on the intelligence and work of women. It is foolish to give up your place as a mother and a wife only to take orders from men who aren't even part of the family. What's so liberated about that? It is better to see your husband succeed and to know you have supported one another.

Several points are worth noting in the experience of Cuban garment workers. Exile, for example, did not transform sexual roles; rather, it extended them in surprising ways. The high labor-force participation rates of Cuban women in the U.S. have been mentioned earlier. However, prior to their migration, only a small number of Cuban women had worked outside the home for any length of time. It was the need to maintain the integrity of their families and to achieve class-related ambitions that precipitated their entrance into the labor force of a foreign country.

As with Mexicans in southern California, Cuban women in Miami earned low wages in unskilled and semiskilled jobs. They too worked in environments devoid of union benefits. However, their membership in an economic enclave allowed them to see industrial homework as an expression of relative prosperity and as a means to achieve a supplementary income while minding domestic responsibilities.

Conclusions

The comparison between different experiences among Hispanic women in two distinct geographical locations shows that involvement in informal production can have entirely dissimilar meanings, depending on the type of incorporation into the broader economic context and on the interplay between sexual politics and household composition. In the case of Mexicans in southern California, proletarianization is related to a high number of female-headed households in which the earnings provided by women are indispensable for maintaining standards of modest subsistence. In the Cuban case, women's employment was a strategy for coping with the receiving environment and raising standards of living. This contrasting experience involving the relationships between households and labor markets occurred despite shared values regarding the family among Mexicans and Cubans. Both groups partake of similar mores regarding the roles of men and women; nevertheless, their actual experience has differed significantly.

This comparison of Mexican and Cuban experiences also shows that the meaning of women's participation in the labor force remains plagued by paradox. On the one hand, paid employment expands the potential for greater personal autonomy and financial independence. This should have a favorable impact upon women's capacity to negotiate an equitable position within the home and labor market. On the other hand, women's search for paid employment is frequently the consequence of severe economic need; it expresses vulnerability, not strength, within homes and in the marketplace. Under certain conditions, women's entry into the labor force also parallels the collapse of reciprocal exchanges between men and women.

While homework is perceived as a problem by observers and policy makers, our study suggests that an apparently identical outcome can have radically disparate meanings when actual processes are examined. This should lead to a reassessment of industrial homework as a highly diversified phenomenon rather than a secondary outcome resulting from the interaction of abstract economic factors.

NOTES

This chapter is based on findings from the research project titled "A Collaborative Study of Hispanic Women in Garment and Electronics Industries." Fieldwork in Southern California (Los Angeles, Orange and San Diego Counties) took place between 1984 and 1986. Preliminary research in Miami-Dade County, Florida, took place during the winters of 1985 and 1986. Funds for research in Southern California were provided by the Programs in Human Rights and Governance and in Urban Poverty at the Ford Foundation, and by the Tinker Foundation. Special thanks are due to Dr. William Diaz and Ms. Patricia Biggers for their faith and encouragement.

1. *Informalization* is understood in this chapter as a process leading to the expansion of industrial and service operations which do not comply with legislation regarding taxes, working conditions, licensing, wages, and other labor code requirements. For recent findings regarding the growth of the informal sector of underground economy in the United States see A. Portes and Saskia Sassen-Koob, "Making it Underground: Comparative Material on the Informal Sector in Western Market Economics," *American Journal of Sociology* 93 (July 1987): 30–61; see also Jonathan I. Gershuny, "The Informal Economy: Its Role in An Industrial Society," *Futures* 11 (February 1979): 3–16.

2. George J. Borgas and Marta Tienda, ed., *Hispanics in the U.S. Economy* (New York: Academic Press, 1985).

3. Ibid.

4. Figures abstracted from the U.S. Bureau of the Census, *1980 Census of Population* (Washington, D.C.: GPO, 1983).

5. Ibid.

6. Ibid. . . .

7. P. S. Taylor, "Mexican Women in Los Angeles Industry in 1928," *Aztlan: International Journal of Hispanic Research,* 11, no. 1 (Spring 1980): 99–129; M. Perlmutter, *The Rag Business* (Los Angeles, 1944); Commission on California State Government, Organization, and Economy, *Review of Selected Taxing and Enforcing Agencies' Programs to Control the Underground Economy* (Los Angeles: Commission on California State Government, Organization, and Economy, 1985).

8. School of Business Administration, University of Florida at Gainesville, *Florida Statistical Abstract, 1985.*

9. Perlmutter, *The Rag Business,* pp. 40–53; Taylor, "Mexican Women in Los Angeles Industry in 1928," pp. 91–129.

10. Alejandro Portes and Robert Bach, *Latin Journey* (Berkeley: University of California Press, 1985), p. 135.

11. Alejandro Portes, "The Social Origins of the Cuban Enclave Economy in Miami," *Sociological Perspectives* 30 (October 1987): 340–72

12. Ibid.

13. In the following ethnographic accounts we have altered the names of firms and individuals for reasons of confidentiality. However, the situations are real.

36

Family, Gender, and Business in Direct Selling Organizations
Nicole Woolsey Biggart

Nicole Woolsey Biggart is professor of management and sociology at the University of California, Davis. Her research and writing focus on issues in economic and organizational sociology. This reading draws from Biggart's 1989 book, *Charismatic Capitalism: Direct Selling Organizations in America.*

An Amway distributor described the usual separation between people's work lives and their family lives and the problem he saw with that arrangement:

> In today's structure, the man goes to work here, and the woman goes to work there, and they come home at night and they're tired. It's been a long day, and a lot of the time they can't even share what's going on in each other's day because it's so different. There comes to be a separation between the husband and wife.

His network DSO [Direct Selling Organization], on the other hand, promises an alternative relationship between work and family.

> With the Amway business you have continuity, and both people can work together to achieve a goal that's going to benefit them and their family. And the kids too. They like to come around and serve cookies at the meetings, or clean the products on the shelf. So there's a real strong moral attitude in this business that everyone [in the family] should become involved.

Most businesses today, as this distributor described, exclude workers' families from the place and process of work. People in the United States now generally accept that bringing one's personal life into the office is improper and disrupts the efficient conduct of business. Moreover, firms often have nepotism rules about employing members of the same family. Corporations fear that selection and promotion on merit might be compromised if employees are related to each other. Businesses can also lose control of important processes: members of a family can favor each other or band together in decision making. The impersonal, economically efficient running of firms is predicated on the separation of work from family—if not absolutely, then as an ideal.

This separation of the public sphere of work from the private sphere of domestic life is a strategy for managing the tension between two powerful, commitment-seeking units. Although work organizations cannot make employees give up all outside commitments (as a convent or military organization can), they can require that employees leave their families behind when they walk through the door at work. Rosabeth Kanter describes the compromise that modern business organizations exact from workers: "While you are here, you will *act as though* you have no other loyalties, no other life."[1]

Network DSOs, however, though they have no less need for members' loyalty than firms do, employ a radically different strategy for controlling the tension between work and family: *they manage the family*, making its powerful emotions and social unity serve organizational ends or actively manipulating the pull of family ties. The affective bonds and authority relations of the family are directed toward profit-making ends. . . .

A Family Business

The preoccupation with "family" among network DSOs is nothing less than extraordinary when compared with the whole of American business. All the DSOs I studied expressed concern with the effect of work on family. Many of them have an ideology of family participation that permeates their literature and public meetings. An A. L. Williams distributor told me that "as a company, there's no question that A. L. Williams is absolutely committed to producing more successful families than any other company in the history of the world," not only through product sales, but through organization.

Many network DSOs integrate the family into the business of selling, using its powerful emotions and authority structure to serve economic ends, not unlike the factories of the 1800s. In some instances DSOs manage the obstacle that competing family ties present. Unlike most firms, network DSOs recognize the power of the family and attempt to harness or actively divert it. Not all DSOs stress the work/family linkage to the same extent, and they vary in how they solicit family participation or acceptance, but four family-management strategies are common in the industry.

1. *Network DSOs encourage the recruitment of family members.* The "family tree" of a DSO line is often filled with actual relatives who have sponsored each other into the business.

Nephews, sisters, brothers, and cousins are prime targets for sponsorship. There are many mother and daughter units in Mary Kay Cosmetics. In DSOs where both men and women sell, such as Amway and Shaklee, there is very strong pressure for spouses to build an organization together. Recognition awards and promotion through status levels are often given to couples, not individuals. Attendance at meetings by only one spouse raises eyebrows in some lines. The Amway and Shaklee house organs are filled with pictures of couples who have achieved success together. An A. L. Williams distributor described his preferred recruits:

> Although we have some very successful single people, we try to stay away from single people. A lot of times, if they want to become involved, they do so. If we're going to pick and choose, we will pick people who are married and have similar lives, families.

A Shaklee distributor, a divorcee, described her status in that organization:

> [As a single person] I'm looked at as kind of rare. In fact, the home office has called me and had me talk to a group about what it is like to build a Shaklee business as a single person.

Recruiting people with whom there is an existing social bond, such as relatives, creates a good basis for business relations in direct selling. When mothers encourage daughters and cousins support each other in their selling, the act reproduces their non-business relations. Support in selling appears to spring from a long-term foundation of caring, and the financial self-interest of sponsors is obscured. In fact, for distributors who are committed to the ideology of direct selling, there is no separation between the interest of the loved one and self-interest: they truly want to share their commitment with those they love.

Recruiting spouses utilizes the emotions and authority relations of marriage for business purposes, as I discuss further below. However, even in DSOs where only women sell, husbands are sometimes a co-optive target of the organization. In Mary Kay Cosmetics, for example, gaining husbands' support is an explicit corporate goal. Husbands are invited to attend Seminar, the annual meeting for beauty consultants, and are given a parallel three-day schedule of activities. They are briefed by the company's executives, paid a visit by Mary Kay Ash, and treated to a recreation program that may include a top sports figure such as Arnold Palmer. Winners of the sports competitions, including a bowling tournament with pink bowling pins, are given recognition at a ceremony not unlike those for beauty consultants. One distributor described the purpose of including husbands in Seminar:

> They are treated so royally and so wonderfully that they want their wives to belong to this organization. So that is kind of a psychology on Mary Kay's part. These men are really treated with kid gloves. I mean, you couldn't imagine how it must make them feel for Mary Kay to say how wonderful they are.

Husbands who do not attend Seminar are not neglected. Mary Kay Ash sends a telegram to the husband of each participating woman thanking him for, as one beauty consultant put it, "eating scrambled eggs and frozen dinners" and taking care of the children.

The president of another DSO said it is crucial to gain the husband's acceptance of his wife's work and is an important management strategy in direct selling.

> A lot of [our talk to husbands] is very casual, but it's very direct. It starts with top management, and [then] our regional managers see how we han-

dle the husbands. So when they start recruiting people, one of the first things they do is bring the husbands in. They take them to dinner. They bring them to sales meetings and make them a part of it. At a high-level convention or meeting with top-level awards, we call both husband and wife up, and we let [the audience] know that this woman could not be successful without his support and backing.

This same company uses the husbands of successful distributors to explain to the husbands of new recruits how they can assist their wives. The subliminal message is that other "real men" accept their wives' selling. "And so they begin to realize, 'Well, gosh, that's no big deal if I baby-sit and fix dinner. Sure, I can do it.'"

Husbands' approval is critical in companies such as Mary Kay and Tupperware. Much selling takes place at night, and husbands must handle child care alone and accept the absence of their wives.

2. *Network DSOs espouse an ideology that claims family is more important than work.* For many people who feel guilty because their work leads them to neglect spouses and children, an industry that encourages the subordination of work to family seems worthy of commitment. Mary Kay Cosmetics, Home Interiors and Gifts, A. L. Williams, and a number of other DSOs support the aphorism "God first, family second, career third." This phrase was recited frequently in interviews. For example:

> I want to succeed financially. That's not the most important thing in my life. My God's first, and my family is second. My wife knows that I could quit A. L. Williams in a minute if it meant losing her and my family.

DSOs' professed support of this formula for organizing one's life is comforting to people who believe its tenets. The reality does not always match the formula, however.

> There was a time there when I was going crazy with Mary Kay. That's all I thought about. I ate it, I drank it, I slept it. Everything, OK? And things were getting just crazy for me. I was feeling guilty. I was feeling like I was taking time away from my family.

> Sometimes it is hard to put Mary Kay third, sometimes the others get shoved down the line a bit. . . . It is just a continuing effort remembering to put it third instead of first.

It is not clear that distributors, especially committed ones, organize their lives differently than they would if they had other attractive occupations. Direct selling is seductive, and for some distributors it becomes the center of their lives. That revered founders such as Mary Kay Ash and Art Williams profess commitment to families, however, is comforting to distributors struggling to reconcile work and home.

3. *Network DSOs argue that a commitment to direct selling can strengthen marriages.* The promise of a closer marital bond is an important recruiting point in some DSOs, including Amway. What direct selling can do for a marriage is "a big carrot," as one distributor put it. "The greatest marriages, the most absolutely blissful relationships I have ever witnessed, have been in this business." DSOs hold out the possibility of a shared enterprise that will bring not only riches, but emotional closeness.

Even DSOs where only women sell promote direct selling as healthful for marriages. Women who become entrepreneurs are described as more interesting to their husbands. These wives have another way to strengthen the marriage bond. A number of women, in fact, said their husbands took an interest in their businesses. One woman described how her Mary Kay business gave her some influence with her husband:

> We have a new line of communication. We got to talking the other night about customer service and were just sitting there really going at it. I have a little more clout. If I had talked to him about customer service five years ago, I didn't have a lot of clout because where was I coming from? You know, I might have been on the tennis court all day long.

The breakdown of the good provider role has left many families struggling both with the problem of generating new income and with maintaining the "face" of husbands whose paychecks are insufficient for family needs. This problem is widespread, but most corporations treat it as a private concern. A number of DSOs, however, deal with this emotional issue quite openly, although they vary in how they manage it. Some urge recognition of pressure on husbands to recruit wives into selling. Direct selling becomes a way of expressing wifely love.

> Mary Kay says there's a lot of men out there who are going to go to their graves earlier because they have to work so hard. What's wrong with helping your husband out and sharing? In this day and age most women work, so why not work and get the most out of it, plus have time for your family?

Some companies, particularly those that recruit women largely from blue-collar families, such as Tupperware, downplay the "career" character of direct selling. Selling is presented as a way to make money that does not threaten the essential position of the husband as head of household.

Yet others actively attempt to preserve the good provider role for families that fear its loss. These companies, including to varying degrees Amway, A. L Williams, and Shaklee, maintain an image of the family as one with the husband in control and the wife as a submissive helper. A sexual division of labor is encouraged within the couple's direct selling business: men go out to demonstrate the business opportunity to prospects, while women do the inside work of managing product sales and demonstrations. Women are supposed to encourage their husbands to greater efforts, to help them be "winners." Stephen Butterfield, a former distributor, described an Amway leadership seminar that included separate lectures for husbands and wives trying to build successful businesses:

> The male leader told the husbands to be gentle and considerate in their sexual approaches to their wives; the lady should be wooed with furs, jewelry and candlelight dinners in expensive restaurants. The female leader told the wives to submit to their husbands cheerfully, even if they thought it was unpleasant sometimes, because a man needed to feel like a winner in the bedroom as well as out in that livingroom showing the Plan. The year was 1980. I wondered if I had been caught in some time-[warp].[2]

As Butterfield describes it, some DSOs attempt to stop the clock of social change at a familiar, reassuring time while maintaining the modern rhetoric of economic partnership.

Direct selling organizations are aggressive in attempting to manage families, but they are not always successful. Those with women distributors routinely fail at co-opting husbands, according to my interviews. A Tupperware distributor, a Mary Kay sponsor, and an industry executive spoke of how husbands posed significant hurdles to achieving business goals:

> My husband, the only way he supports me is baby-sitting and helping me spend the money. Otherwise I get no support from him at all. That's a real drain. I'm always just running, trying to get every-

thing done so he doesn't have anything to complain about when I leave. I don't know if I'm going to get to go to Jubilee [Tupperware's annual meeting], because if he throws too big a stink about it, it's just not worth the fight.

> The consultants who are doing well, they're either single and don't have a husband, or if you're married, you've got to hope that your husband is supportive. It's that middle husband, the one who is insecure himself, the one who has to have dinner on the table at five and never wants to baby-sit [who is a problem]. There are a lot of men who are like that, and there are women who cater to that.

> If a husband is the type where his ego needs the glory, the applause, and he has to be center stage with the spotlight on him, it won't work. Because all those [downline recruits] are there because of her, not him. What will work is if the guy is smart enough to realize that he has to keep her in the spotlight. She's the number one, and he sits back and gives her tips.

A wife's absences from home and her business success are sometimes tolerated by otherwise recalcitrant husbands because of the income she earns. Mary Kay Ash has a much-repeated saying for beauty consultants: "If you want to keep your husband excited, stay thin and make bank deposits."

4. *Children are a fourth way DSOs solicit distributors' commitment.* All stress that flexible work arrangements allow parents to put their children's schedules before work. Some distributors like being able to work with their children present—for example, when they deliver products, or solicit business. One Mary Kay beauty consultant approaches women with her young son:

> My little boy, he got so used to me approaching women at the shopping

mall that he would ask the ladies first, "Do you use Mary Kay cosmetics?" He was only four years old at the time. Of course I would bring my card out and I would say, "Could I have your name and number?" And he would say, "Address, too." I had to calm him down a bit.

Women, especially, cite the ease of integrating their roles as mother and worker as a reason for doing direct sales. For some, particularly blue-collar women who treat direct selling as a sideline and not a "real job," they can have the happy combination of making money and being an "at home" mother. One Tupperware dealer put it this way:

I was driving my son and four friends to a birthday party, and I heard them talking in the back about their moms working. And one of the kids says, "Say, does your mommy work?" And he goes, "No." That's what I want. I don't want them to think I work. They don't even think that I have a job because I'm not gone from eight to five.

Network DSOs that recruit husband-and-wife teams usually try to integrate the children into the business in some way. Children sometimes attend meetings held in parents' homes and are occasionally included at conventions and other events. Many children of Amway and Shaklee distributors are paid to deliver products, take telephone orders, and otherwise participate in their parents' business. The ideology of a family business is realized in some homes, with all members participating in some fashion.

In DSOs with strong entrepreneurial ideologies, the parents' continuing commitment is often sustained because of their belief in the importance of teaching their children the moral principles of capitalist enterprise. This is not unlike parents' going to church because it sets a good example for their children. A father and a mother spoke

about the influence of direct selling on their children's development:

I have a ten-year-old son. He's my partner. Most of our social life revolves around either his school or A. L. Williams. He's very, very supportive. As a matter of fact, for a ten-year-old, he's one of my best recruiters. He'll talk to his friends about asking if their parents could use extra money. . . . It's teaching him how to set his goals and what he wants out of life.

I have bought a division under Avacare for my daughter and have it on ice because she's only twenty. But I figured when she gets older she will have that division. I have sponsored my son into another multilevel marketing company, and I'm helping him develop that business. . . . What I'm doing with my children is much more than earning money [for them]. It's teaching them. They will be totally self-sufficient by the time they get married. They will never go on welfare. That would just break my heart.

Some DSOs actively encourage parents to see their selling as a critical part of their children's moral education. One Amway tape, for example, encourages children to be their parents' paid helpers and to view unearned allowances as "welfare for children."

The inclusion of children in the business is sometimes more illusory than real, however. Although children may perform some business-related work at home, by its very nature direct selling requires parents to be away from home a lot. Direct selling is also hard work, and active distributors find it demanding. Some parents spoke of this problem:

I'm not there all the time—I can't be. I've got to work harder now than I've ever worked in my life. But when I do take off I spend quality time. I don't go home and watch television like I used to do five years ago. I can afford to do some things and spend time that the kids are going to remember.

A lot of beauty consultants have kids. . . . I sort of have this uncomfortable feeling. . . . I don't know. There is sort of that superwoman consciousness about it all. You can do it. You can look beautiful and sell products and work full time and get home on time.

Children are actively co-opted by some DSOs. Amway, for instance, encourages parents to let children choose an item from their product catalog as a "goal." The picture of the item is taped to the refrigerator, along with a calendar. Each night that their father goes out to show the business plan to a prospective recruit, the children check off a space. When enough spaces are checked, they receive the item. The parent's absence is made to serve children's material interests. As an Amway distributor put it, eventually "there will be freedom for us from jobs, and we'll be able to be together as a family,'" but in the meantime "there are rewards for them."

Direct selling's flexible schedule does make it possible for family needs to be accommodated. As more wives and mothers enter the labor force, part-time jobs, flextime, temporary work, and other new work arrangements are appearing. Corporate America is beginning to recognize and make some adjustment to the nonwork lives of its employees. Most firms, though, offer these new arrangements not so that the barrier between family and work can be lowered, but so that it can remain high.

Direct selling uses a very different strategy. It begins by recognizing the pull of family obligations and certifying them as real and important. In some instances it uses those ties to serve business purposes, for example, by encouraging the recruitment of relatives and sustaining commitment for the children's

sake. The industry even uses the desire to be with loved ones to urge work outside the home. The contradiction inherent in this ploy may be blatant, but the appeal is effective precisely because of the strong commitment people feel to their families. In an industry that cannot rely on bureaucratic controls, harnessing the emotions, aspirations, and fears of families is an important business strategy.

The Metaphorical Family

By integrating the family into business activity, direct selling organizations use existing social ties for economic purposes. The industry also does the reverse, making the economic ties of sponsorship the basis for familylike social relations. DSOs are "metaphorical families." The result of both strategies is to create a double-stranded bond far stronger than either one alone. Moreover, pecuniary self-interest and affective interest in the other are indistinguishable.

Metaphorical expressions of kinship, what anthropologists call "fictive relations," are widely employed in network DSOs. The expressions vary by individual and by organization, but distributors commonly understand themselves as "family" or, in Tupperware, as "close friends." For example, Mary Kay Cosmetics is a "sisterhood."

Whereas individuals employed by firms tend to describe their positions in the organization by function or level, such as "accountant" or "supervisor," in DSOs people use kinship terms to describe their place. Lines in companies such as Amway and Shaklee are often spoken of as branches on a "family tree." People trace their "genealogies" by identifying their upline sponsors. Amway lines have "family reunions." Women in Mary Kay are "sisters," but Tupperware distributors are "daughter dealers" to their "mother managers." In Cameo Coutures, a recruit's sponsor is likewise her "mother," and the mother's sponsor is the recruit's "grandmother." When a Mary Kay distributor has enough recruits to form her own unit, she becomes the "offspring" of her director. Movement up the director ranks is measured in part by the number of offspring a woman gives birth to.

The overlay of a metaphorical family on top of blood ties and marital bonds creates some interesting organizational relations. For example, one Mary Kay beauty consultant's real sister is her "offspring." Her mother remains in her unit as a consultant. Thus all three are "sisters" in the larger enterprise.

Family metaphors also describe organizational activities. In Amway and a number of other DSOs, recruiting people to set up their own business is called "duplication." Duplication means doing exactly as the upline does, but it also refers to an organizational growth strategy reminiscent of biological asexual reproduction. Tupperware uses the terminology of courtship to describe securing appointments for home parties: these are "dates." "Dating" future hostesses is understood to be a crucial job at a party. In Shaklee and some other DSOs, a distributor whose line becomes inactive is known as an "orphan." There are "adoption" rules that regulate the incorporation of orphans into active lines.

Family metaphors refer not only to positional relations and activities, but also to the *content* of ties between distributors. "Family" establishes an ideal of loving, nurturing relations between distributors; the metaphor establishes normative expectations. For example, distributors assume familylike obligations toward each other in their conduct of business. The obligations typically extend beyond the economic sphere, too. Amway and Mary Kay distributors described this situation:

I found a family I had never had. There was a tremendous amount of support to

achieve. I went through a divorce about five years after I got into the business, and I took five years off from actively building my organization. In that time period I was never forgotten. I would get postcards once in a while, and it made me feel like I was still part of something. There was a tremendous amount of love and acceptance, support in growing.

There is a sisterhood charisma between all the consultants. I have been stranded at airports and know for a fact [it's true]. One time I was stranded two days in Denver because of a storm. All I did was look in the phone book under "Mary Kay Cosmetics," and the [local] director came over to have lunch with me. I know that anywhere I go I can call up a sister consultant and I'll be taken to her home.

"Family" provides a powerful model for intraorganizational relations. It is a satisfying conceptualization for distributors who are welcomed into a network of emotional ties and not seen merely as "workers" or financially significant "recruits." There is a preservation of personhood in some DSOs that is conspicuously absent in many corporations. "Family" also provides a well-understood model for interpersonal relations, especially useful to people without significant paid work experience. Direct selling puts them in familiar interactional territory by importing the logic of one institution—the family—for use in another—business.

"Family" has distinctive management advantages. In an industry that cannot oversee intraorganizational relations very effectively, the metaphor provides a flexible guide to relations for distributors. For example, while all distributors are formally competitors for sales to consumers and all believe in free enterprise and competition, the notion of "family" mutes destructive competitive practices. "Mothers" do not compete with "daughters." Internecine warfare is thwarted by distributors' embracing family norms. Caring relations are typically interpreted to mean helping each other to be successful—that is, generating profit for the individual and the company.

The management of Mary Kay Cosmetics discovered the force with which the family metaphor is held when it completed a leveraged buy-out. Mary Kay Ash and her son Richard Rogers, cofounders of the company, bought back all publicly owned stock in 1985, returning the company to family ownership. The company had faced a decline in the period just before the buy-out, and management was concerned with the beauty consultants' interpretation of the financial transaction, hoping they would not understand it as an act of weakness. One executive described how the family metaphor provided a useful interpretive vehicle for the sales force:

> The word "family" in Mary Kay means something. People consider themselves part of the family. All of a sudden they're asking, "What does this buy-out mean?" [They've come up with the answer]: "Everything's back and owned by the family." All of a sudden they feel like—I don't know what's going through their minds—"We weren't family before, but now we're back?" "All of those outsiders had stock, we got rid of them?" If I've heard it once, I've heard it a thousand times, "It's great to be family again."

A family strategy, in both its "real" and its metaphorical forms, utilizes strong emotional bonds and social patterns to inspire and channel economic activity. It also sustains an interactional character within the industry that is wholly distinctive. . . .

Does Direct Selling Empower Women?

Is an organization that accords so well with women's experiences and abilities feminist? Does it lead to more power for women as individuals and as a class? The answer that comes from this study of the direct selling industry is clearly mixed. My interviews suggest that network DSOs empower women as individuals in significant ways. They also suggest that the industry does not challenge, and sometimes reinforces, the patriarchal structure of society.

Women distributors spoke of at least three ways direct selling gives them influence. First, they describe the power that an independent income gives them in marriage. This sort of power is not granted exclusively by direct selling, of course, but women who would not or could not do other types of work find DSOs a possible route to economic strength. As a Tupperware dealer put it, "My husband has this claw on the checkbook, and he doesn't like to share it. So having my own income gives me a little bit more freedom." She established her own checking account, an act of independence, at the encouragement of her "mother manager."

Although most women do direct selling part time and earn very modest amounts, it does provide a route to a good, even substantial income for very hard-working women with a talent for this form of business. The fifty-nine national sales directors in Mary Kay Cosmetics earn over $100,000 each—some two or three times that figure—and there are women in other established DSOs who have large incomes. The nurturing skills these women used to achieve success in direct selling would not have been valued in corporate settings.

Distributors spoke, second, of how their work in direct selling is a source of influence with their children. Many believe that direct selling allows them to be more than "just a mom" in a society that values economic achievement and allows them to be role models to their daughters. As one woman said, "[my daughter] sees me in a very independent role, yet whenever she needs me I'm always there."

Third, and perhaps most important, direct selling gives women the *experience* of being powerful. Women who have been in subordinate positions all their lives and, further, had seen other women only as dependents, spoke of the pleasure of being thought of as skilled and able. For many, direct selling gave them their first glimpse of their own sex in the role of competent adult. A Mary Kay beauty consultant described her first direct selling function:

> I couldn't believe it. [These women] were just bubbling. I had never been around a bunch of women who were not talking about their kids, not talking about so-and-so running around with so-and-so, you know, all the negative things and about household chores. You see, that's what I had been around because I had been home for a while. Housewifey things. These women were talking about *business*.

The entrance to the Mary Kay Cosmetics headquarters in Dallas, Texas, is an impressive sight for the thousands of women who visit each year. The vestibule has the requisite oil painting of the founders, Mary Kay Ash and Richard Rogers, in a prominent place. Where one would expect to find pictures of pinstriped male executives or corporate directors, there are large paintings of the national sales directors, the industrious women who sustain the sales force. The display of fifty-nine images of hugely successful women is jarring because it so thoroughly violates expectations. Women who see other women succeed begin to imagine the possibility for themselves.

Women's DSOs, such as Mary Kay Cosmetics, Home Interiors and Gifts, and Tupperware, celebrate women's abilities in business. They are unabashedly women's worlds where pink Cadillacs, fur coats, and warm hugs are as much a part of the organizational culture as aggressive individualism is part of a firm's. While they differ from one other, they all have the character of sororities: women's spheres where women enjoy each other and act "naturally." In DSOs where men also sell, the atmosphere is different but still familylike and expressive.

Although women distributors have been empowered personally and economically by direct selling, and though women's DSOs celebrate women's abilities as a whole, direct selling does not challenge existing social arrangements in which women are subordinate. In particular, the model of the family that DSOs embrace includes a submissive wife.

The submissive wife role is expressed most overtly in DSOs that recruit husband-and-wife teams. For example, A. L. Williams recruits the whole family, but the expectation is that only the husband will sell insurance. The wife will do her part by giving her husband moral support and encouragement and by not complaining when he is out at night trying to bolster their income. A. L. Williams has a Partners' Organization run by Williams's wife Angela. Angela Williams is, like her husband, a gifted orator and tells a very moving story about how her support of Art's business was critical to his success against great odds. She urges the "partners" in rally audiences to do the same and, further, to participate in her auxiliary organization. There are women A. L. Williams agents, but the model the organization supports is clearly that of the traditional family.

> [Angela Williams] runs a great Partners' Organization, which is the wives' side of things. And we have some male partners, too. They get together for monthly meetings on how to support us. Next week they're doing a pep rally. They're going all out—they make costumes, pom-poms. So my wife is just loving the business too.
>
> [My wife doesn't sell insurance], definitely not. She's not licensed. Some wives get licensed, just so they can talk

about it a little more, but they don't have to be licensed. That doesn't mean they can't go out and actively crusade our concepts. They can recruit people. They can talk about what we do a little bit, and then refer them to us. But my wife's taking an active role in building up the Partners' Organization.

Amway, Shaklee, and United Science of America distributors similarly follow a sexual division of labor. The husband shows the business plan while women sell vitamins or cosmetics to their friends and keep the books.

More than one woman said her husband paid no attention to her business at first, but after she began to make a good income he became involved. A Shaklee wife said it was not uncommon for retired husbands to take over the businesses their wives had built.

In fact, Tupperware has institutionalized this practice. Only women are dealers, the beginning level of distributor. Managers, the next level, may be single women or husband-and-wife teams. Such teams, in which a husband quits any other job, are called Total Tupper families and are regarded favorably by the company. The next level, a distributorship, for a long time could be assigned *only* to a husband-and-wife team. A woman's mobility was thus constrained by her husband's career choice. Although there have been exceptions to this practice in recent years, according to informants it remains the rule.

Occasionally, too, the Tupperware headquarters fills executive positions by recruiting from among the distributors. The husband always becomes the employee, although the wife may consider herself part of the team and travel with him at company expense. The paycheck, though, has only the husband's name on it. According to former Tupperware president Joe Hara, "We have to pay it to somebody. What we are trying to do is decide what is in the interest of good marital relations. . . . I know of no situations that involve

a gal who doesn't want more free time."[3]

Even women's DSOs assume that a wife's duty is first to support her husband's needs and only then to care for her business. For example, Mary Crowley's book of aphorisms includes, "Don't marry a man you aren't willing to adjust to" and "Let the husband be the HEAD of the household and the wife be the neck. You never saw a head turn without the neck."[4] Mary Kay Ash's advice to beauty consultants is less religious and more witty. She is a sort of Erma Bombeck to working women, convinced of women's extraordinary abilities but urging women to coddle their way to autonomy. Her autobiography is filled with tidbits on how to gain a husband's support and manage a direct selling business so as to interfere as little as possible with a man's life at home. For example, she says she sometimes fooled her husband by putting a frozen dinner on a plate and heating it in the microwave oven: "Mel used to brag that I never served him a TV dinner, but I did sometimes—on a plate!"[5]

Mary Kay beauty consultants are urged to gain a husband's permission for a new recruit to begin work. A beauty consultant described how she did this:

> Because it's a family business, there is no way I want to recruit a lady without talking to her husband. Because eventually she is going to have to go to him for money or guidance and there'll be customers calling and coming, so he's going to have to get involved. I ask her, "Do you feel I need to sit down and talk with your husband?" If so, we will stop the interview right there and set another time so I can go and talk with them.

In truth, Mary Kay urges women to recognize that social realities such as divorce and the husbands' early death can leave women financially and socially on their own. She prompts women to learn to take care of themselves, but first to secure their husbands' support for such an undertaking. As one former beauty consultant put it, "Everything [Mary Kay] says, even listening to her inspirational tapes, is all directed to women. It has an undertone of 'we are capable, but we still have our place.'"

Traditional marital ties are also used to support profits in DSOs. Romantic love as the ideal bond between spouses emerged with the rise of industrial capitalism and the separation of spheres. No longer tied by shared activities, husbands and wives were cemented by a new romantic model of mutual affection. Love is the critical social glue that holds the family together under the conditions of modern capitalism. There is an implicit exchange model in romantic love: women provide affection and sex, and men give their wives money and status. Butterfield argues that the Amway line he belonged to exploited this exchange relationship and that sexual impulses, alternately suppressed and titillated, fueled economic activity:

> Despite their unintentional parody of Bible school sexual ethics, a great deal of subliminal—and perverted—sexuality goes on at Amway functions. Audiences are led in mass denunciations of soap operas dealing with the theme of adultery, husbands and wives are instructed from the stage to kiss and hold hands. Dexter Yager jokingly refers to the "other woman" in his life, who turns out to be his daughter; the wife of a prominent Diamond[-level distributor] calls the ladies to Christ by describing Jesus as a wonderful "hunk" of a man. But just beneath these comfortably square plugs for the monogamous "Christian" nuclear family lurks the tail of the serpent: the men strutting in their suits, leaving business cards on the chairs like dogs peeing on fire hydrants to mark their territories; the women arrayed in alluring and

expensive costumes, turning heads as they pass; the equation of attractiveness with pin level ("I'm so glad my man is a *Winner*"); [and] the salacious play on the word "excited" (Are you *excited?* Show me how *excited* you are!)[6]

According to Butterfield, Amway distributors are encouraged to read books about preserving love in marriage.

Historians and sociologists who study the development of the family over time have debated whether the separation of spheres served women's interests. Many agree that, at the least, the domestic sphere did create a world in which women could develop expertise and exercise a degree of independence and authority. It was a world in which women's values and culture were preserved. This arrangement, while to an extent liberating, did not threaten the essentially patriarchal character of the economy or the husband as head of the family.

I think this judgment fits the direct selling industry too. Network DSOs give women a sphere in which they can develop competence, a degree of economic independence, and the opportunity to interact in ways that do not do violence to their sense of themselves as women. But DSOs, even one led by such an obvious booster of women as Mary Kay Ash, do not challenge the prevailing sociopolitical arrangements of society. In fact, it is probably the compromise direct selling represents that has made it attractive to so many women. They can be personally empowered—*feel* liberated and modern—without upsetting the traditional premises of their lives.

Whether a women's organization is feminist depends not only on its grounding in women's culture, but on its political and ideological bases. Women's DSOs might be characterized as *prefeminist*, celebrating womanly abilities and values but not challenging dominant social structures.[7] It is also clear that creating economic organizations that emulate the domestic sphere can be used not only to empower women, as women's organizers hope, but to maintain their submission.

A quick look at network DSOs might lead an observer to conclude that they are an anachronism, a throwback to a preindustrial model of social organization where husbands, wives, and children worked and played together. In fact, direct selling organizations are a product of today. They are a response to families' desire to be together in an economy that keeps them apart and to a world of work that disadvantages women in several ways. Network direct selling organizations are one industry's opportunistic response to the segmented and gender-divided arrangements of postindustrial society.

NOTES

1. Kanter (1977: 15).
2. Butterfield (1985: 116).
3. Quoted by Wedemeyer (1975). This interesting article explores the congruence of women's gender and working-class culture in Tupperware.
4. Crowley (1974: 46–47).
5. Ash (1981: 75).
6. Butterfield (1985: 117).
7. This is a term suggested by Estelle Freedman (1979: 527). A prefeminist organization may become feminist if "the group experience leads to insights about male domination" and if the group is relatively autonomous from control by men. My study suggests that the former condition holds in some women's DSOs but the latter does not.

REFERENCES

Ash, Mary Kay. 1981. *Mary Kay.* New York: Harper and Row.

Butterfield, Stephen. 1985. *Amway: The Cult of Free Enterprise.* Boston: South End Press.

Crowley, Mary C. 1974. *Be Somebody . . . God Doesn't Take Time to Make a Nobody.* Dallas: Crescendo.

Freedman, Estelle. 1979. "Separatism as Strategy: Female Institution Building and American Feminism, 1870–1930." *Feminist Studies* 5 (3): 512–29.

Kanter, Rosabeth Moss. 1977. *Work and Family in the United States: A Critical Review and Agenda for Research and Policy.* New York: Russell Sage Foundation.

Wedemeyer, Dee. 1975. "There's a Tupperware Party Starting Every Ten Seconds." *Ms.* 4(2).

PERSPECTIVES AND POLICIES ON WORK AND FAMILY

37

Management Women and the New Facts of Life

Felice N. Schwartz

Felice Schwartz was the founder of Catalyst, a national organization dedicated to
the advancement of women in the workplace. Catalyst was founded in 1962 and
Schwartz was the organization's President for thirty years, retiring in 1993.
Schwartz is the author of several books and articles on women, work, and family.
She died in 1996 at the age of 71.

. . . Women in the corporation are about to move from a buyer's to a seller's market. The sudden, startling recognition that 80% of new entrants in the work force over the next decade will be women, minorities, and immigrants has stimulated a mushrooming incentive to "value diversity."

Women are no longer simply an enticing pool of occasional creative talent, a thorn in the side of the EEO officer, or a source of frustration to corporate leaders truly puzzled by the slowness of their upward trickle into executive positions. A real demographic change is taking place. The era of sudden population growth of the 1950s and 1960s is over. The birth rate has dropped about 40%, from a high of 25.3 live births per 1,000 population in 1957, at the peak of the baby boom, to a stable low of a little more than 15 per 1,000 over the last 16 years, and there is no indication of a return to a higher rate. The tidal wave of baby boomers that

swelled the recruitment pool to overflowing seems to have been a one-time phenomenon. For 20 years, employers had the pick of a very large crop and were able to choose males almost exclusively for the executive track. But if future population remains fairly stable while the economy continues to expand, and if the new information society simultaneously creates a greater need for creative, educated managers, then the gap between supply and demand will grow dramatically and, with it, the competition for managerial talent.

The decrease in numbers has even greater implications if we look at the traditional source of corporate recruitment for leadership positions—white males from the top 10% of the country's best universities. Over the past decade, the increase in the number of women graduating from leading universities has been much greater than the increase in the total number of graduates, and these women are well represented in the top 10% of their classes.

The trend extends into business and professional programs as well. In the old days, virtually all MBAs were male. I remember addressing a meeting at the Harvard Business School as recently as the mid-1970s and looking out at a sea of exclusively male faces. Today, about 25% of that audience would be women. The pool of male MBAs from which corporations have traditionally drawn their leaders has shrunk significantly.

Of course, this reduction does not have to mean a shortage of talent. The top 10% is at least as smart as it always was—smarter, probably, since it's now drawn from a broader segment of the population. But it now consists increasingly of women. Companies that are determined to recruit the same number of men as before will have to dig much deeper into the male pool, while their competitors will have the opportunity to pick the best people from both the male and female graduates.

Under these circumstances, there is no question that the management ranks of business will include increasing numbers of women. There remains, however, the question of how these women will succeed—how long they will stay, how high they will climb, how completely they will fulfill their promise and potential, and what kind of return the corporation will realize on its investment in their training and development.

There is ample business reason for finding ways to make sure that as many of these women as possible will succeed. The first step in this process is to recognize that women are not all alike. Like men, they are individuals with differing talents, priorities, and motivations. For the sake of simplicity, let me focus on . . . what I call the career-primary woman and the career-and-family woman.

Like many men, some women put their careers first. They are ready to make the same trade-offs traditionally made by the men who seek leadership positions. They make a career decision to put in extra hours, to make sacrifices in their personal lives, to make the most of every opportunity for professional development. For women, of course, this decision also requires that they remain single or at least childless or, if they do have children, that they be satisfied to have others raise them. Some 90% of executive men but only 35% of executive women have children by the age of 40. The *automatic* association of all women with babies is clearly unjustified.

The secret to dealing with such women is to recognize them early, accept them, and clear artificial barriers from their path to the top. After all, the best of these women are among the best managerial talent you will ever see. And career-primary women have another important value to the company that men and other women lack. They can act as role models and mentors to younger women who put their careers first. Since upwardly mobile career-primary women still have few role models to motivate and inspire them, a company with women in its top echelon has a significant advantage in the competition for executive talent.

Men at the top of the organization—most of them over 55, with wives who tend to be traditional—often find career women "masculine" and difficult to accept as colleagues. Such men miss the point, which is not that these women are just like men but that they are just like the *best* men in the organization. And there is such a shortage of the best people that gender cannot be allowed to matter. It is clearly counterproductive to disparage in a woman with executive talent the very qualities that are most critical to the business and that might carry a man to the CEO's office.

Clearing a path to the top for career-primary women has four requirements:

1. Identify them early.
2. Give them the same opportunity you give to talented men to grow and develop and contribute to company profitability. Give them client and customer responsibility. Expect them to travel and relocate, to make

the same commitment to the company as men aspiring to leadership positions.

3. Accept them as valued members of your management team. Include them in every kind of communication. Listen to them.
4. Recognize that the business environment is more difficult and stressful for them than for their male peers. They are always a minority, often the only woman. The male perception of talented, ambitious women is at best ambivalent, a mixture of admiration, resentment, confusion, competitiveness, attraction, skepticism, anxiety, pride, and animosity. Women can never feel secure about how they should dress and act, whether they should speak out or grin and bear it when they encounter discrimination, stereotyping, sexual harassment, and paternalism. Social interaction and travel with male colleagues and with male clients can be charged. As they move up, the normal increase in pressure and responsibility is compounded for women because they are women.

Stereotypical language and sexist day-to-day behavior do take their toll on women's career development. Few male executives realize how common it is to call women by their first names while men in the same group are greeted with surnames, how frequently female executives are assumed by men to be secretaries, how often women are excluded from all-male social events where business is being transacted. With notable exceptions, men are still generally more comfortable with other men, and as a result women miss many of the career and business opportunities that arise over lunch, on the golf course, or in the locker room.

The majority of women, however, are what I call career-and-family women, women who want to pursue serious careers while participating actively in the rearing of children. These women are a precious re-source that has yet to be mined. Many of them are talented and creative. Most of them are willing to trade some career growth and compensation for freedom from the constant pressure to work long hours and weekends.

Most companies today are ambivalent at best about the career-and-family women in their management ranks. They would prefer that all employees were willing to give their all to the company. They believe it is in their best interests for all managers to compete for the top positions so the company will have the largest possible pool from which to draw its leaders.

"If you have both talent and motivation," many employers seem to say, "we want to move you up. If you haven't got that motivation, if you want less pressure and greater flexibility, then you can leave and make room for a new generation." These companies lose on two counts. First, they fail to amortize the investment they made in the early training and experience of management women who find themselves committed to family as well as to career. Second, they fail to recognize what these women could do for their middle management.

The ranks of middle managers are filled with people on their way up and people who have stalled. Many of them have simply reached their limits, achieved career growth commensurate with or exceeding their capabilities, and they cause problems because their performance is mediocre but they still want to move ahead. The career-and-family woman is willing to trade off the pressures and demands that go with promotion for the freedom to spend more time with her children. She's very smart, she's talented, she's committed to her career, and she's satisfied to stay at the middle level, at least during the early child-rearing years. Compare her with some of the people you have there now.

Consider a typical example, a woman who decides in college on a business career and enters management at age 22. For nine years, the company invests in her career as she gains experience and skills and steadily improves her performance. But at 31, just as the investment begins to pay off in earnest, she decides to have a baby. Can the company afford to let her go home, take another job, or go into business for herself? The common perception now is yes, the corporation can afford to lose her unless, after six or eight weeks or even three months of disability and maternity leave, she returns to work on a full-time schedule with the same vigor, commitment, and ambition that she showed before.

But what if she doesn't? What if she wants or needs to go on leave for six months or a year or, heaven forbid, five years? In this worst-case scenario, she works full-time from age 22 to 31 and from 36 to 65—a total of 38 years as opposed to the typical male's 43 years. That's not a huge difference. Moreover, my typical example is willing to work part-time while her children are young, if only her employer will give her the opportunity. There are two rewards for companies responsive to this need: higher retention of their best people and greatly improved performance and satisfaction in their middle management.

The high-performing career-and-family woman can be a major player in your company. She can give you a significant business advantage as the competition for able people escalates. Sometimes too, if you can hold on to her, she will switch gears in mid-life and reenter the competition for the top. The price you must pay to retain these women is threefold: you must plan for and manage maternity, you must provide the flexibility that will allow them to be maximally productive, and you must take an active role in helping to make family supports and high-quality, affordable child care available to all women. . . .

For all the women who want to combine career and family—the women who want to participate actively in the rearing of their children and who also want to pursue their careers seriously—the key to retention is to provide the flexibility and family supports they need in order to function effectively.

Time spent in the office increases productivity if it is time well spent, but the fact that most women continue to take the primary responsibility for child care is a cause of distraction, diversion, anxiety, and absenteeism—to say nothing of the persistent guilt experienced by all working mothers. A great many women, perhaps most of all women who have always performed at the highest levels, are also frustrated by a sense that while their children are babies they cannot function at their best either at home or at work.

In its simplest form, flexibility is the freedom to take time off—a couple of hours, a day, a week—or to do some work at home and some at the office, an arrangement that communication technology makes increasingly feasible. At the complex end of the spectrum are alternative work schedules that permit the woman to work less than full-time and her employer to reap the benefits of her experience and, with careful planning, the top level of her abilities.

Part-time employment is the single greatest inducement to getting women back on the job expeditiously and the provision women themselves most desire. A part-time return to work enables them to maintain responsibility for critical aspects of their jobs, keeps them in touch with the changes constantly occurring at the workplace and in the job itself, reduces stress and fatigue, often eliminates the need for paid maternity leave by permitting a return to the office as soon as disability leave is over, and, not least, can greatly enhance company loyalty. The part-time solution works particularly well when a work load can be reduced for one individual in a department or when a full-time job can be broken down by skill levels and apportioned to two individuals at different levels of skill and pay.

I believe, however, that shared employment is the most promising and will be the most widespread form of flexible scheduling in the future. It is feasible at every level of the corporation except at the pinnacle, for both the short and the long term. It involves two people taking responsibility for one job.

Two red lights flash on as soon as most executives hear the words "job sharing": continuity and client-customer contact. The answer to the continuity question is to place responsibility entirely on the two individuals sharing the job to discuss everything that transpires—thoroughly, daily, and on their own time. The answer to the problem of client-customer contact is yes, job sharing requires reeducation and a period of adjustment. But as both client and supervisor will quickly come to appreciate, two contacts means that the customer has continuous access to the company's representative, without interruptions for vacation, travel, or sick leave. The two people holding the job can simply cover for each other, and the uninterrupted, full-time coverage they provide together can be a stipulation of their arrangement.

Flexibility is costly in numerous ways. It requires more supervisory time to coordinate and manage, more office space, and somewhat greater benefits costs (though these can be contained with flexible benefits plans, prorated benefits, and, in two-paycheck families, elimination of duplicate benefits). But the advantages of reduced turnover and the greater productivity that results from higher energy levels and greater focus can outweigh the costs. . . .

The woman who is eager to get home to her child has a powerful incentive to use her time effectively at the office and to carry with her reading and other work that can be done at home. The talented professional who wants to have it all can be a high performer by carefully ordering her priorities and by focusing on objectives rather than on the legendary 15-hour day. By the time professional women have their first babies—at an average age of 31—they have already had nine years to work long hours at a desk, to travel, and to relocate. In the case of high performers, the need for flexibility coincides with what has gradually become the goal-oriented nature of responsibility.

Family supports—in addition to maternity leave and flexibility—include the provision of parental leave for men, support for two-career and single-parent families during relocation, and flexible benefits. But the primary ingredient is child care. The capacity of working mothers to function effectively and without interruption depends on the availability of good, affordable child care. Now that women make up almost half the work force and the growing percentage of managers, the decision to become involved in the personal lives of employees is no longer a philosophical question but a practical one. To make matters worse, the quality of child care has almost no relation to technology, inventiveness, or profitability but is more or less a pure function of the quality of child care personnel and the ratio of adults to children. These costs are irreducible. Only by joining hands with government and the public sector can corporations hope to create the vast quantity and variety of child care that their employees need.

Until quite recently, the response of corporations to women has been largely symbolic and cosmetic, motivated in large part by the will to avoid litigation and legal penalties. In some cases, companies were also moved by a genuine sense of fairness and a vague discomfort and frustration at the absence of women above the middle of the corporate pyramid. The actions they took were mostly quick, easy, and highly visible—child care information services, a three-month parental leave available to men as well as women, a woman appointed to the board of directors.

When I first began to discuss these issues 26 years ago, I was sometimes able to get an appointment with the assistant to the assistant in personnel, but it was only a courtesy. Over the past decade, I have met with the CEOs of many large corporations, and I've watched them become involved with ideas they had never previously thought much about. Until recently, however, the shelf life of that enhanced awareness was always short. Given pressing, short-term concerns, women were not a front-burner issue. In the past few months, I have seen yet another change. Some CEOs and top management groups now take the initiative. They call and ask us to show them how to shift gears from a responsive to a proactive approach to recruiting, developing, and retaining women.

I think this change is more probably a response to business needs—to concern for the quality of future profits and managerial talent—than to uneasiness about legal requirements, sympathy with the demands of women and minorities, or the desire to do what is right and fair. The nature of such business motivation varies. Some companies want to move women to higher positions as role models for those below them and as beacons for talented young recruits. Some want to achieve a favorable image with employees, customers, clients, and stockholders. These are all legitimate motives. But I think the companies that stand to gain most are motivated as well by a desire to capture competitive advantage in an era when talent and competence will be in increasingly short supply. These companies are now ready to stop being defensive about their experience with women and to ask incisive questions without preconceptions.

Even so, incredibly, I don't know of more than one or two companies that have looked into their own records to study the absolutely critical issue of maternity leave—how many

women took it, when and whether they returned, and how this behavior correlated with their rank, tenure, age, and performance. The unique drawback to the employment of women is the physical reality of maternity and the particular socializing influence maternity has had. Yet to make women equal to men in the workplace we have chosen on the whole not to discuss this single most significant difference between them. Unless we do, we cannot evaluate the cost of recruiting, developing, and moving women up.

Now that interest is replacing indifference, there are four steps every company can take to examine its own experience with women:

1. Gather quantitative data on the company's experience with management-level women regarding turnover rates, occurrence of and return from maternity leave, and organizational level attained in relation to tenure and performance.
2. Correlate this data with factors such as age, marital status, and presence and age of children, and attempt to identify and analyze why women respond the way they do.
3. Gather qualitative data on the experience of women in your company and on how women are perceived by both sexes.
4. Conduct a cost-benefit analysis of the return on your investment in high-performing women. Factor in the cost to the company of women's negative reactions to negative experience, as well as the probable cost of corrective measures and policies. If women's value to your company is greater than the cost to recruit, train, and develop them—and of course I believe it will be—then you will want to do everything you can to retain them.

We have come a tremendous distance since the days when the prevailing male wisdom saw women as lacking the kind of intelligence that would allow them to succeed in business. For decades, even women themselves have harbored an unspoken belief that they couldn't make it because they couldn't be just like men, and nothing else would do. But now that women have shown themselves the equal of men in every area of organizational activity, now that they have demonstrated that they can be stars in every field of endeavor, now we can all venture to examine the fact that women and men are different.

On balance, employing women is more costly than employing men. Women can acknowledge this fact today because they know that their value to employers exceeds the additional cost and because they know that changing attitudes can reduce the additional cost dramatically. Women in management are no longer an idiosyncrasy of the arts and education. They have always matched men in natural ability. Within a very few years, they will equal men in numbers as well in every area of economic activity.

The demographic motivation to recruit and develop women is compelling. But an older question remains: Is society better for the change? Women's exit from the home and entry into the work force has certainly created problems—an urgent need for good, affordable child care; troubling questions about the kind of parenting children need; the costs and difficulties of diversity in the workplace; the stress and fatigue of combining work and family responsibilities. Wouldn't we all be happier if we could turn back the clock to an age when men were in the workplace and women in the home, when male and female roles were clearly differentiated and complementary?

Nostalgia, anxiety, and discouragement will urge many to say yes, but my answer is emphatically no. Two fundamental benefits that were unattainable in the past are now within our reach. For the individual, freedom of choice—in this case the freedom to choose career, family, or a combination of the two. For the corporation, access to the most gifted individuals in the country. These benefits are neither self-indulgent nor insubstantial. Freedom of choice and self-realization are too deeply American to be cast aside for some wistful vision of the past. And access to our most talented human resources is not a luxury in this age of explosive international competition but rather the barest minimum that prudence and national self-preservation require.

38

The Emotional Geography of Work and Family Life

Arlie Russell Hochschild

Arlie Hochschild is professor of sociology at the University of California, Berkeley. She has written extensively on the topic of gender, work, and family life. She is the author of *The Managed Heart: The Commercialization of Human Feeling* (1978) and *The Second Shift: Working Parents and the Revolution at Home* (1989).

Over the last two decades, American workers have increasingly divided into a majority who work too many hours and a minority with no work at all. This split hurts families at both extremes, but I focus here on the growing scarcity of time among the long-hours majority. For many of them, a speed-up at the office and factory has marginalized life at home, so that the very term "work–family balance" seems to them a bland slogan with little bearing on real life. In this chapter, I describe the speed-up and review a range of cultural responses to it, including "family-friendly reforms" such as flextime, job sharing, part time work and parental leave. Why, I ask, do people not resist the speed-up more than they do? When offered these reforms, why don't more take advantage of them? Drawing upon my ongoing research in an American Fortune 500 company, I argue that a company's "family-friendly" policy goes only as deep as the "emotional geography" of the workplace and home, the drawn and redrawn boundaries between the sacred and the profane. I show how ways of talking about time (for example,

separating "quality" from "quantity" time) become code words to describe that emotional geography. . . .

A Work–Family Speed-Up

Three factors are creating the current speed-up in work and family life in the United States. (By the term "family", I refer to committed unmarried couples, same-sex couples, single mothers, two-job couples and wage-earner–housewife couples. My focus is on all families who raise children.) First of all, increasing numbers of mothers now work outside the home. In 1950, 22 per cent of American mothers of children eighteen and under worked for pay; in 1991, 67 per cent did. Half of the mothers of children age one year and younger work for pay.

Second, they work in jobs which generally lack flexibility. The very model of "a job" and "career" has been based, for the most part, on the model of a traditional man whose wife cared for the children at home. Third, over the last 20 years, both women and men have increased their hours of work. In her book, *The Overworked American* the economist, Juliet Schor, argues that over the last two decades American workers have added an extra 164 hours to their year's work—an extra month of work a year (Schor, 1992, p. 26). Compared to 20 years ago, workers take fewer unpaid absences, and even fewer *paid* ones. Over the last decade, vacations have shortened by 14 per cent (Schor, 1992, pp. 12–13). The number of families eating evening meals together has dropped by 10 per cent (Blyton, 1985; Fuchs, 1991). Counting overtime and commuting time, a 1992 national sample of men averaged 48.8 hours of work, and women, 41.7 (Galinsky *et al.*, 1993, p. 9). Among young parents, close to half now work more than 8 hours a day. Compared to the 1970s, mothers take less time off for the birth of a child and are more likely to work through the summer. They are more likely to work continuously until they retire at age 65. Thus, whether they have children or not, women increasingly fit the profile of year-round, life-long paid workers, a profile that has long characterized men. Meanwhile, male workers have not reduced their hours but, instead, expanded them.

Not all working parents with more free time will spend it at home tending children or elderly relatives. Nor, needless to say, if parents do spend time at home, will all their children find them kind, helpful and fun. But without a chance for more time at home, the issue of using it well does not arise at all.

Cool Modern, Traditional, Warm Modern Stances toward the Speed-Up

Do the speed-up people think the speed-up is a problem? Does anybody else? If so, what cultural stances toward gender equity, family life and capitalism underlie the practical solutions they favor? If we explore recent writing on the hurried life of a working parent, we can discern three stances toward it.

One is a *cool modern* stance, according to which the speed-up has become "normal," even fashionable. Decline in time at home does not "marginalize" family life, proponents say, it makes it different, even better. Like many other popular self-help books ad-

dressed to the busy working mother, *The Superwoman Syndrome,* by Marjorie Schaevitz offers busy mothers tips on how to fend off appeals for help from neighbors, relatives, friends, how to stop feeling guilty about their mothering. It instructs the mother how to frugally measure out minutes of "quality time" for her children and abandons as hopeless the project of getting men more involved at home (Schaevitz, 1984). Such books call for no changes in the workplace, no changes in the culture and no change in men. **The solution to rationalization at work is rationalization at home.** Tacitly such books accept the corrosive effects of global capitalism on family life and on the very notion of what people need to be happy and fulfilled. (Hochschild, 1994).

A second stance toward the work–family speed-up is **traditional** in that it calls for women's return to the home, or **quasi-traditional** in that it acquiesces to a secondary role, a lower rank "mommy track," for women at work (Schwartz, 1989). Those who take this sort of stance acknowledge the speed-up as a problem but deny the fact that most women now have to work, want to work, and embrace the concept of gender equity. They essentialize different male and female "natures," and notions of time, for men and women—"industrial" time for men, and "family" time for women (Hareven, 1975).

A third **warm modern** stance is both humane (the speed-up is a problem) and egalitarian (equity at home and work is a goal). Those who take this approach question the terms of employment—both through a nationwide program of worksharing, (as in Germany), a shorter working week, and through company-based family friendly reforms. What are these family-friendly reforms?

- flextime; a workday with flexible starting and quitting times, but usually 40 hours of work and the opportunity to "bank" hours at one time and reclaim them later;

- flexplace; home-based work, such as telecommuting.

- regular or permanent part-time; less than full-time work with full- or pro-rated benefits and promotional opportunities in proportion to one's skill and contribution;

- job sharing; two people voluntarily sharing one job with benefits and salary pro-rated;

- compressed working week; four 10-hour days with 3 days off, or three 12-hour days with 4 days off;

- paid parental leave;

- family obligations as a consideration in the allocation of shift work and required overtime.

Together, worksharing and this range of family-friendly reforms could spread work, increase worker control over hours, and create a "warm modern" world for women to be equal within. As political goals in America over the last 50 years, worksharing and a shorter working week have "died and gone to heaven" where they live on as Utopian ideals. In the 1990s, family-friendly reforms are the lesser offering on the capitalist bargaining table. But are companies in fact offering these reforms? Are working parents pressing for them?

The news is good and bad. Recent nationwide studies suggest that more and more American companies offer their workers family-friendly alternative work schedules. According to one recent study, 88 per cent of 188 companies surveyed offer part-time work, 77 per cent offer flextime of some sort, 48 per cent offer job-sharing, 35 per cent offer some form of flexplace, and 20 per cent offer a compressed working week (Galinsky *et al.*, 1991). (But in most companies, the interested worker must seek and receive the ap-

proval of a supervisor or department head. Moreover, most policies do not apply to lower-level workers whose conditions of work are covered by union contracts.)

But even if offered, regardless of need, few workers actually take advantage of the reforms. One study of 384 companies noted that only nine companies reported even one father who took an official unpaid leave at the birth of his child (Friedman, 1992, p. 50). Few are on temporary or permanent part-time. Still fewer share a job. Of workers with children ages 12 and under, only 4 per cent of men and 13 per cent of women worked less than 40 hours a week (Galinsky *et al.*, 1991, p. 123).

Inside a Fortune 500 Company

Why, when the opportunity presents itself, do so few working parents take it? To find out, I set about interviewing managers, and clerical and factory workers in a large manufacturing company in the northeastern United States—which I shall call, simply, the Company. I chose to study this Company because of its reputation as an especially progressive company. Over the last 15 years, for example, the Company devoted millions of dollars to informing workers of its family-friendly policies, hiring staff to train managers to implement them, making showcase promotions of workers who take extended maternity leaves or who work part-time. If change is to occur anywhere, I reasoned, it was likely to be within this Company.

But the first thing I discovered was that even in this enlightened Company, few young parents or workers tending elderly relatives took advantage of the chance to work more flexible or shorter hours. Among the 26 000 employees, the average working week ranged from 45 to 55 hours. Managers and factory workers often worked 50 or 60 hours a week while clerical workers tended to work a more normal, 40-hour, week. Everyone agreed the Company was a "pretty workaholic place". Moreover, for the last 5 years, hours of work had increased.

Explanations That Don't Work

Perhaps workers shy away from applying for leaves or shortening their hours because they can't afford to earn less. This certainly explains why many young parents continue to work long hours. But it doesn't explain why the wealthiest workers, the managers and professionals, are among the **least** interested in additional time off. Even among the Company's factory workers, who in 1993 averaged between eleven and twelve dollars an hour, and who routinely competed for optional overtime, two 40-hour-a-week paychecks with no overtime work were quite enough to support the family. A substantial number said they could get by on one paycheck if they sold one of their cars, put in a vegetable garden and cut down on "extras". Yet, the overwhelming majority did not want to.

Perhaps, then, employees shied away from using flexible or shorter hour schedules because they were afraid of having their names higher on the list of workers who might be laid off in a period of economic downturn. Through the 1980s, a third of America's largest companies experienced some layoffs, though this did not happen to managers or clerical workers at this company.

By union contract, production workers were assured that layoffs, should they occur, would be made according to seniority and not according to any other criteria—such as how many hours an employee had worked. Yet, the workaholism went on. Employees in the most profitable sectors of the Company showed no greater tendency to ask for shorter or more flexible hours for family reasons than employees in the least profitable sectors.

Is it, then, that workers who could afford shorter hours didn't *know* about the Company's family-friendly policies? No. All of the 130 working parents I spoke with had heard about alternative schedules and knew where they could find out more.

Perhaps the explanation lies not with the workers but with their managers. Managers responsible for implementing family-friendly policies may be openly or covertly undermining them. Even though Company policy allowed flexibility, the head of a division could, for reasons of production, openly refuse a worker permission to go part-time or to job-share, which some did. For example when asked about his views on flextime, the head of the engineering division of the Company replied flatly, "My policy on flextime is that there is no flextime". Other apparently permissive division heads had supervisors who were tough on this issue "for them". Thus, there seemed to be some truth to this explanation for why so few workers stepped forward.

But even managers known to be cooperative had few employees asking for alternative schedules. Perhaps, then, workers ask for time off, but do so "off the books". To some extent, this "off the books" hypothesis did hold, especially for new fathers who may take a few days to a week of sick leave for the birth of a baby instead of filing for "parental leave", which they feared would mark them as unserious workers.

Even counting informal leaves, most women managers returned to full-time 40- to 55-hour work schedules fairly soon after their 6 weeks of paid maternity leave. Across ranks, most women secretaries returned after 6 months; most women production workers returned after 6 weeks. Most new fathers took a few days off at most. Thus, even "off the books", working parents used very little of the opportunity to spend more time at home.

Far more important than all these factors seemed to be a company "speed-up" in response to global competition. In the early years of the 1990s, workers each year spoke of working longer hours than they had the year before, a trend seen nationwide. When asked why, they explained that the Company was trying to "reduce costs", in part by asking employees to do more than they were doing before.

But the sheer existence of a company speed-up doesn't explain why employees weren't trying to actively resist it, why there wasn't much backtalk. Parents were eager to tell me how their families came first, how they were clear about that. (National polls show that next to a belief in God, Americans most strongly believe in "the family".) But, practices that might express this belief—such as sharing breakfast and dinner—were shifting in the opposite direction. In the minds of many parents of young children, warm modern intentions seemed curiously, casually, fused with cool modern ideas and practices. In some ways, those within the work–family speed-up don't seem to want to slow down. . . .

Work and Family as Emotional Cultures

Through its family-friendly reforms, the Company had earned a national reputation as a desirable family-friendly employer. But at the same time, it wasn't inconvenienced by having to arrange alternate schedules for very many employees. One can understand how this might benefit a company. But how about the working parents?

For the answer, we may need a better grasp of the emotional cultures, and the relative "draw" of work and family. Instead of thinking of the workplace or the family as unyielding thing-like structures, Giddens suggests that we see structures as fluid and changeable. "Structuration", Anthony Giddens tells us, is the "dynamic process whereby structures come into being" (Giddens, 1976, pp. 121, 157). For structures to change, there must be changes in what people do. But in doing what they do, people unconsciously draw on resources, and depend on larger conditions to develop the skills they use to change what they do (*ibid.,* p. 157).

With this starting point, then, let us note that structures come with—and also "are"—emotional cultures. A change in structure requires a change in emotional culture. What we lack, so far, is a vocabulary for describing this culture, and what follows is a crude attempt to create one. An emotional culture is a set of rituals, beliefs about feelings and rules governing feeling which induce emotional focus, and even a sense of the "sacred". This sense of the sacred selects and favors some social bonds over others. It selects and reselects relationships into a core or periphery of family life.

Thus, families have a more or less *sacred core* of private rituals and shared meanings. In some families what is most sacred is sexuality and marital communication (back rubs, pillow talk, sex), and in other families the "sacred" is reserved for parental bonds (bedtime cuddles with children, bathtime, meals, parental talk about children). In addition, families have secondary zones of less important daily, weekly, seasonal rituals which back up the core rituals. They also have a profane outer layer, in which members might describe themselves as "doing nothing in particular"—doing chores, watching television, sleeping. The character and boundaries of the sacred and profane aspects of family life are in the eye of the beholder. "Strong families" with "thick ties" can base their sense of the sacred on very different animating ideas and practices. Families also differ widely on how much one member's sense of the sacred matches another's and on how much it is the occasion for expressing harmony or conflict.

Furthermore, families creatively adapt to new circumstances by ritualizing new activities—for example, couples in commuter marriages may "ritualize" the phone call or the daily e-mail exchange. Couples with "too much time together" may de-ritualize meals, sex, or family events. Furthermore, families have different structures of sacredness. Some have thick actual cores and thin peripheries, others have a porous core and extensive peripheral time in which people just "hang out". But in each case, emotional culture shapes the experience of family life.

Emotional cultures stand back-to-back with ideas about time. In the context of the work–family speed-up, many people speak of actively "managing time, finding time, making time, guarding time, or fighting for time". Less do they speak of simply "having" or "not having" time. In their attempt to take a more active grip on their schedules, many working parents turn a telephone answering machine on at dinner, turn down work assignments and social engagements, and actively fight to defend "family time".

One's talk about time is itself a verbal practice that does or doesn't reaffirm the ritual core of family life. In the core of family life, we may speak more of living in the moment. Because a sacred activity is an end in itself, and not a means to an end, the topic of time is less likely to arise. If it does, one speaks of "enjoying time", or "devoting time". With the work–family speed-up, the term "quality time" has arisen, as in "I need more quality time with my daughter", a term referring to freedom from distraction, time spent in an attitude of intense focus. In general, we try to "make" time for core family life because we feel it matters more.

In the intermediate and peripheral zones of family life, we may speak of "having time on our hands, wasting or killing time". In the new lexicon, we speak of "quantity time". In general, we feel we can give up peripheral time, because it matters less. More hotly contested is the time to participate in a child's school events, help at the school auction, buy a birthday gift for a babysitter, or call an elderly neighbor.

With a decline in this periphery, the threads of reciprocity in the community and neighborhood grow weaker. By forcing families to cut out what is "least important", the speed-up thins out and weakens ties that bind it to society. Thus, under the press of the "speed-up", families are forced to give up their periphery ties with neighbors, distant relatives, bonds sustained by "extra time". **The speed-up privatizes the family.** The "neighborhood goes to work", where it serves the emotional interests of the workplace. Where are one's friends? At work.

Although the family in modern society is separated from the workplace, its emotional culture is ecologically linked to and drawn from it. Both the family and workplace are also linked to supportive realms. For the family, this often includes the neighborhood, the church, the school. For the workplace, this includes the pub, the golf club, the commuter-van friendship network. A loss of supportive structure around the family may result in a gain for the workplace, and vice versa. Insofar as the "periphery" of family life protected its ritual core, to a certain degree for working parents these ties are not so peripheral at all.

A gender pattern is clear. Because most women now must and for the most part want to work outside the home, they are performing family rituals less. At the same time, men are not doing them very much more. Together, these two facts result in a net loss in ritual life at home.

At the same time, at some workplaces, an alternative cultural magnet is drawing on the human need for a center, a ritual core. As family life becomes de-ritualized, in certain sectors of the economy, the engineers of corporate cultures are re-ritualizing the workplace. Thus, the contraction of emotional culture at home is linked to a socially engineered expansion of emotional culture at work.

Work Like a Family, and Family, for Some, Like Work

At a certain point, change in enough personal stories can be described as a change in culture, and I believe many families at the Company are coming to this turning-point now. Pulled toward work by one set of forces and propelled from the family by another set of forces, a growing number of workers are unwittingly altering the twin cultures of work and family (Kanter, 1977; Lash, 1977). As the cultural shield surrounding work has grown stronger, the supportive cultural shield surrounding the family has weakened. Fewer neighborhood "consultants" talk to one when trouble arises at home, and for some, they are more to help out with problems at work.

These twin processes apply unevenly; the pull toward work is stronger at the top of the occupational ladder, and marginalization of family life, more pronounced at the bottom. Indeed, the picture I shall draw is one in a *wide array* of work and family "structurations" resulting from various combinations of social forces.

The Model of Family as a Haven in a Heartless World

When I entered the field, I assumed that working parents would *want* more time at home. I imagined that they experienced home as a place where they could relax, feel emotionally sheltered and appreciated for who they "really are". I imagined home to feel to the weary worker like the place where he or she could take off a uniform, put on a bathrobe, have a beer, exhale—a picture summed up in the image of the worker coming in the door saying, "Hi honey, I'm home!". To be sure, home life has its emergencies and strains but I imagined that home was the place people thought about when they thought about rest, safety and appreciation. Given this, they would want to maximize time at home, especially time with their children. I also assumed that these working parents would not feel particularly relaxed, safe or appreciated at work, at least not more so than at home, and especially not factory workers.

When I interviewed workers at the Company, however, a picture emerged which partly belied this model of family life. For example, one 30-year-old factory shift supervisor, a remarried mother of two, described her return home after work in this way:

> I walk in the door and the minute I turn the key in the lock my oldest daughter is there. Granted she needs somebody to talk to about her day. The baby is still up . . . she should have been in bed two hours ago and that upsets me. The oldest comes right up to the door and complains about anything her father said or did during the evening. She talks about her job. My husband is in the other room hollering to my daughter, "Tracy, I don't ever get no time to talk to your mother because you're always monopolizing her time first before I even get a chance!" They all come at me at once.

The un-arbitrated quarrels, the dirty dishes, and the urgency of other people's demands she finds at home contrast with her account of going to work:

> I usually come to work early just to get away from the house. I go to be there at a quarter after the hour and people are there waiting. We sit. We talk. We joke. I let them know what is going on, who has to be where, what changes I have

made for the shift that day. We sit there and chitchat for five or ten minutes. There is laughing. There is joking. There is fun. They aren't putting me down for any reason. Everything is done in humour and fun from beginning to end. It can get stressful, though, when a machine malfunctions and you can't get the production out.

Another 38-year-old working mother of two, also a factory worker, had this to say:

My husband is a great help (with caring for their son). But as far as doing housework, or even taking the baby when I'm at home, no. When I'm home, our son becomes my job. He figures he works five days a week, he's not going to come home and clean. But he doesn't stop to think that I work seven days a week . . . Why should I have to come home and do the housework without help from anybody else? My husband and I have been through this over and over again. Even if he would pack up the kitchen table and stack the dishes for me when I'm at work, that would make a big difference. He does nothing. On his weekends off, I have to provide a sitter for the baby so he can go fishing. When I have my day off, I have the baby all day long. He'll help out if I'm not here . . . the minute I'm here he lets me do the work.

To this working mother, her family was not a haven, a zone of relief and relaxation. It was a workplace. More than that, she could only get relief from this domestic workplace by going to the factory. As she continued:

I take a lot of overtime. The more I get out of the house, the better I am. It's a terrible thing to say, but that's the way I feel!

I assumed that work would feel to workers like a place in which one could be fired at the whim of a profit-hungry employer, while in the family, for all its hassles, one was safe. Based as it is on the impersonal mechanism of supply and demand, profit and loss, work would feel insecure, like being in "a jungle". In fact, many workers I interviewed had worked for the Company for 20 years or more. But they were on their second or third marriages. To these employed, *work* was their rock, their major source of security, while they were receiving their "pink slips" at home.

To be sure, most workers *wanted* to base their sense of stability at home, and many did. But I was also struck by the loyalty many felt toward the Company and a loyalty *they felt* coming from it, despite what might seem like evidence to the contrary— the speed-up, the restructuring. When problems arose at work, many workers felt they could go to their supervisors or to a human resources worker and resolve it. If one division of the Company was doing poorly, the Company might "de-hire" workers within that division and rehire in a more prosperous division. This happened to one female engineer, very much upsetting her, but her response to it was telling:

I have done very well in the Company for twelve years, and I thought my boss thought very highly of me. He'd said as much. So when our division went down and several of us were de-hired, we were told to look for another position within the Company *or* outside. I thought, "Oh my God, *outside!*" I was stunned! Later, in the new division it was like a remarriage . . . I wondered if I could love again.

Work was not always "there for you", but increasingly "home", as they had known it, wasn't either. As one woman recounted, "One day my husband came home and told me, 'I've fallen in love with a woman at work . . . I want a divorce.' "

Finally, the model of family-as-haven led me to assume that the individual would feel most known and appreciated at home and least so at work. Work might be where they felt unappreciated, "a cog in the machine",—an image brought to mind by the Charlie Chaplin classic film on factory life, *Modern Times.* But the factory is no longer the archetypical workplace and, sadly, many workers felt more appreciated for what they were doing at work than for what they were doing at home. For example, when I asked one 40-year-old technician whether he felt more appreciated at home or at work, he said:

> I love my family. I put my family first . . . but I'm not sure I feel more appreciated by them (laughs). My 14-year-old son doesn't talk too much to anyone when he gets home from school. He's a brooder. I don't know how good I've been as a father . . . we fix cars together on Saturday. My wife works opposite shifts to what I work, so we don't see each other except on weekends. We need more time together—need to get out to the lake more. I don't know . . .

This worker seemed to feel better about his skill repairing machines in the factory than his way of relating to his son. This is not as unusual as it might seem. In a large-scale study, Arthur Emlen found that 59 per cent of employees rated their family performance "good or unusually good" while 86 per cent gave a similar rating to their performance on the job (Friedman, 1988, p. 16).

This overall cultural shift may account for why many workers are going along with the work–family speed-up and not joining the resistance against it. A 1993 nationally representative study of 3400 workers conducted by The Families and Work Institute reflects two quite contradictory findings. On one hand, the study reports that 80 per cent of workers feel their jobs require "working very hard" and 42 per cent "often feel used up by the end of the work day". On the other hand, when workers are asked to compare how much

time and energy they *actually* devoted to their family, their job or career and themselves, with how much time they would *like* to devote to each, there was little difference (Galinsky *et al.* 1993, pp. 1, 98). Workers estimate that they actually spend 43 per cent of their time and energy on family and friends, 37 per cent on job or career, and 20 per cent on themselves. But they *want* to spend just about what they *are* spending—47 per cent on family and friends, 30 per cent on the job, and 23 per cent on themselves (Galinsky *et al.* 1993, p. 98). Thus, the workers I spoke to who were "giving" in to the work–family speed-up may be typical of a wider trend.

Causal Mechanisms

Three sets of factors may exacerbate this reversal of family and work cultures; trends in the family, trends at work, and a cultural consumerism which reinforces trends in the family and work.

First, half of marriages in America end in divorce—the highest divorce rate in the world. Because of the greater complexity of family life, the emotional skills of parenting, woefully underestimated to begin with, are more important than ever before. Many workers spoke with feeling about strained relationships with step-children and ex-wives or husbands (White and Riesmann, 1992). New in scope, too, are the numbers of working wives who work "two shifts", one at home and one at work, and face their husband's resistance to helping fully with the load at home—a strain that often leaves both spouses feeling unappreciated (Hochschild, 1989).

Second, another set of factors apply at work. Many corporations have emotionally engineered for top and upper middle managers a world of friendly ritual and positive reinforcement. New corporate cultures call for "valuing the individual" and honoring the "internal customer" (so that requests made by employees within the Company are honored as highly as those by customers outside the Company). Human relations employees give seminars on human problems at work. High-performance teams, based on co-operation between relative equals who "manage themselves", tend to foster intense relations at work. The Company frequently gives out awards for outstanding work at award ceremonies. Compliments run freely. The halls are hung with new plaques praising one or another worker on recent accomplishments. Recognition luncheons, department gatherings and informal birthday remembrances are common. Career planning sessions with one's supervisor, team meetings to talk over "modeling, work relations, and mentoring" with co-workers all verge on, even as they borrow from, psychotherapy. For all its aggravation and tensions, the workplace is where quite a few workers feel appreciated, honored, and where they have real friends. By contrast, at home there are fewer "award ceremonies" and little helpful feedback about mistakes.

In addition, courtship and mate selection, earlier more or less confined to the home-based community, may be moving into the sphere of work. The later age for marriage, the higher proportion of unmarried people, and the high divorce rate all create an ever-replenishing courtship pool at work. The gender desegregation of the workplace, and the lengthened working day also provide opportunity for people to meet and develop romantic or quasi-romantic ties. At the factory, romance may develop in the lunchroom, pub, or parking lot; and for upper management levels, at conferences, in "fantasy settings" in hotels and dimly lit restaurants (Kanter, 1989, p. 281).

In a previous era, an undetermined number of men escaped the house for the pub, the fishing hole, and often the office. A common pattern, to quote from the title of an article by Jean Duncombe and Dennis Marsden, was that of "workaholic men" and "whining women" (Duncombe and Marsden, 1993). Now that women compose 45 per cent of the American labor force and come home to a "second shift" of work at home, some women are escaping into work too—and as they do so, altering the cultures of work and home.

Forces pulling workers out of family life and into the workplace are set into perpetual motion by consumerism. Consumerism acts as a mechanism which maintains the emotional reversal of work and family (Schor, 1992). Exposed to advertisements, workers expand their material "needs". To buy what they now "need", they need money. To earn money, they work longer hours. Being away from home so many hours, they make up for their absence at home with gifts which cost money. They "materialize" love. And so the cycle continues.

Once work begins to become a more compelling arena of appreciation than home, a self-fulfilling prophecy takes hold. For, if workers flee into work from the tensions at home, tensions at home often grow worse. The worse the tensions at home, the firmer the grip of the workplace on the worker's human needs, and hence the escalation of the entire syndrome.

If more workers conceive of work as a haven, it is overwhelmingly in some sense *against their wishes.* Most workers in this and other studies say they value family life above all. Work is what they do. Family is why they live. So, I believe the logic I have described proceeds despite, not because of, the powerful intentions and deepest wishes of those in its grip.

Models of Family and Work in the Flight Plan of Capitalism

To sum up, for some people work may be becoming more like family, and family life more like work. Instead of the model of the *family* as haven from work, more of us fit the model of *work* as haven from home. In this model, the tired parent leaves a world of unresolved quarrels, unwashed laundry and dirty dishes for the atmosphere of engineered cheer, appreciation and harmony at work. It is at work that one drops the job of *working* on relating to a brooding adolescent, an obstreperous toddler, rivaling siblings or a retreating spouse. At last, beyond the emotional shield of work, one says not, "Hi honey, I'm home", but "Hi fellas, I'm here!" For those who fit this model, the ritual core of family life is not simply smaller, it is less of a ritual core.

How extensive is this trend? I suspect it is a slight tendency in the lives of many working parents, and the basic reality for a small but growing minority. This trend holds for some people more than others and in some parts of society more than in others. Certain trends—such as the growth of the contingency labor force—may increase the importance of the family, and tend toward reinstalling the model of family as haven, and work as "heartless world". A growing rate of unemployment might be associated with yet a third "double-negative" model according to which neither home nor work are emotional bases, but rather the gang at the pub, or on the street.

But the sense of sacred that we presume to be reliably attached to home may be more vulnerable than we might wish.

Most working parents more deeply want, or want to want, a fourth, "double-positive" model of work–family balance. In the end, these four patterns are unevenly spread over the class structure—the "haven in a heartless world" more at the top, the "double-negative" more at the bottom, the "reverse-haven" emerging in the middle.

Each pattern of work and family life is to be seen somewhere in the flight plan of late capitalism. For, capitalist competition is not simply a matter of market expansion around the globe, but of local geographies of emotion at home. The challenge, as I see it, is to understand the close links between economic trends, emotional geographies, and pockets of cultural resistance. For it is in those pockets that we can look for "warm modern" answers.

REFERENCES

Duncombe, Jean and Marsden, Dennis (1993), "Workaholics and Whining Women, Theorizing Intimacy and Emotion Work: The Last Frontier of Gender Inequality?", unpublished paper, Department of Sociology, University of Essex, England.

Fuchs, V. (1991), "Are Americans Underinvesting in their Children?", *Society,* Sept/Oct, pp. 14–22.

Galinsky, Ellen, Friedman, Dana E. and Hernandez, Carol A. (1991), *The Corporate Reference Guide to Work Family Programs* (New York: Families and Work Institute).

Galinsky, Ellen, Bond, James and Friedman, Dana (1993), *The Changing Workforce: Highlights of the National Study* (New York: Family and Work Institute).

Giddens, Anthony (1976), *New Rules of Sociological Method* (New York: Basic Books).

Giddens, Anthony (1991), *Modernity and Self-Identity* (Stanford, CA: Stanford University Press).

Hochschild, Arlie (1983), *The Managed Heart: The Commercialization of Human Feeling* (Berkeley, CA: University of California Press).

Hochschild, Arlie (1994),"The Commercial Spirit of Intimate Life and the Abduction of Feminism: Signs from Women's Advice Books", *Theory, Culture & Society,* vol. II (May), pp. 1–24.

Hochschild, Arlie with Anne Machung (1989), *The Second Shift: Working Parents and the Revolution at Home* (New York: Viking Press).

Kanter, Rosabeth Moss (1997), *Work and Family in the United States: A Critical Review and Agenda for Research and Policy* (New York: Russell Sage Foundation).

Kanter, Rosabeth Moss (1983), *The Change Masters* (New York: Simon & Schuster).

Popenoe, David (1989), *Disturbing the Nest: Family Change and Decline in Modern Societies* (New York: Aldine De Gruyter).

Schaevitz, Marjorie Hansen (1984), *The Superwoman Syndrome* (New York: Warner Books).

Schor, Juliet B. (1992), *The Overworked American: The Unexpected Decline of Leisure* (New York: Basic Books).

Schwartz, Felice N. (1989), "Management Women and the New Facts of Life", *Harvard Business Review,* 1, January–February, pp. 65–76.

Skolnick, Arlene (1991), *Embattled Paradise* (New York: Basic Books).

White, Lynn K. and Riesmarnn, Agnes (1992), "When the Brady Bunch Grows Up: Step-,

Half- and Full-Sibling Relationships in Adulthood", *Journal of Marriage and the Family,* vol. 54 (February), pp. 197–208.

Zedek, Sheldon, Maslach, Christina, Mosier, Kathleen, and Skitka, Linda (1992), "Affective Response to Work and Quality of Family Life: Employee and Spouse Perspectives", in Goldsmith, Elizabeth (ed.), *Work and Family: Theory, Research and Applications* (London: Sage Publishers).

39

What Do Men Want?

Michael S. Kimmel

Michael S. Kimmel teaches sociology at State University of New York, Stony Brook, and edits the scholarly journal, *masculinities.* Professor Kimmel writes, "All my life I've worked with words. I started out in junior high school with a newspaper route. In college, I worked in a book bindery. I loved music and played banjo in a bluegrass band, so I wrote music reviews for the campus paper (which I still do). In graduate school, I began writing book reviews for local newspapers (which I still do). As a working writer, I've been active in the National Writers' Union, which organizes freelance journalists—among the working world's most unorganized and disorganized people! In my scholarship, I try and write so that real people can understand what I'm thinking. My books include *Manhood in America: A Cultural History* (1996), *The Politics of Manhood* (1995), *Men Confront Pornography* (1990), and *Men's Lives* (1989; 4th edition, 1997)."

Freud's famous cry of resignation—"Women, what do they want?"—has been a feminist touchstone for nearly a century. By contrast, the good doctor and countless other social commentators always assumed they knew what men wanted, especially in the realm of work. After all, a

man's profession and his ability to bring home a paycheck have traditionally defined who that man was. With wives to manage the domestic scene, working men of the past had little reason to question a system designed by and for them.

But unlike the man in the gray flannel suit of the 1950s or the fast-tracker of the 1970s and 1980s, today's organization man faces a contracting economy in which corporations are restructuring, downsizing, and laying off thousands of employees. Though many wives of male chief executives still stay at home, spouses of most other men now work. These two trends—the recent economic downturn and women's entry into the workplace—are forcing men to redefine themselves. In order to do so, men of the 1990s must reevaluate what it means to be a success, both on the job and in the home.

Not all men want the same thing, of course. Some still resist efforts to change the old rules for masculine behavior. But in the professional ranks, a new organization man has indeed emerged, one who wants to be an involved father with no loss of income, prestige, and corporate support—and no diminished sense of manhood. Like working women, we want it all. Yet in today's insecure corporate world, we're even less sure of how to get it.

Few 1990s men fit the traditional picture of distant father, patriarchal husband, and work-obsessed breadwinner; fewer still have dropped out of the working world completely into full-time daddydom and house-husbandhood. Rather than a suburban conformist or high-flying single yuppie, today's organization man carries a briefcase while pushing a baby carriage. He's in his late thirties or forties, balding, perhaps a bit paunchy since there's no time these days for the health club; he no longer wears power ties, and his shirts are rumpled. While he considers his career important, he doesn't want to sacrifice time with his family. His wife may have a demanding job, which he supports; but he may wonder if she thinks he's less of a man than her father, and he may resent her for the time she spends away from home.

Given that most American men grew up believing in the traditional symbols of manhood—wealth, power, status—there are clear emotional and financial costs involved in making other choices. Since many companies still deem dedication to career the sole marker of professional success, the new organization man may believe he has to hide his participation at home. Instead of taking advantage of his company's formal parental-leave policies,

for instance, he's more likely to use sick days to watch over a new baby. Even if his boss knows this man is caring for a child and not really sick, the time off is viewed as an exception rather than a threat to the status quo.

With the costs of redefining the male role, however, come the benefits that are driving men to change: as a number of the books reviewed here will show, men who call themselves involved fathers often report that their lives are more meaningful. Some have chosen careers that provide more intrinsic satisfaction, like social work or teaching. Other involved fathers build a sense of who they are outside of work, essentially opting for less demanding jobs or "daddy tracks" that allow for more time with their kids.

But what about those who want both a challenging career and involved fatherhood? Not surprisingly, the compromises made by the new organization man bear a striking resemblance to those of the new organization woman. Because the male experience has been viewed as the norm, many more research studies have been conducted on women's efforts to balance work and family. Yet even if the evidence supporting the changing needs of corporate men is primarily anecdotal, based as it is on interviews and clinical case studies, companies would do well to consider what the new breed of organization man says he wants.

Just as many senior managers now recognize they'll lose their most ambitious women if they don't develop strategies to accommodate family needs, I believe corporations will also lose their best and brightest men if they don't address the needs of the 1990s man.

Who Was the Old Organization Man?

The conventional image of the man in the gray flannel suit emerged in the early 1950s, after the tumult of the Great Depression and World War II. According to the business writer William H. Whyte, Jr., the organization man wanted a settled, stable, suburban existence. Individual expression was cut as short as suburban lawns; these were company men. In Whyte's best-selling and now classic *The Organization Man,* published in 1956, he complained that the rugged individualist had vanished. In his place were workers motivated more by a "passive ambition," those who were "obtrusive in no particular, excessive in no zeal." The future of these organization men would be "a life in which they will all be moved hither and yon and subject to so many forces outside their control."

Whyte's goal in *The Organization Man* was to promote the need for individualism within the context of collective life. For Whyte, increasing collectivization was not a temporary fad but had its roots in the Industrial Revolution and the rise of large corporations and mass production. In addition, the organization man's need to belong derived from one aspect of the U.S. national character: what De Tocqueville called the "special genius" of Americans for cooperative action.

But such belongingness also conflicts with "the public worship of individualism," in Whyte's words, the other side of the American coin. Unquestioning allegiance to the company, then, doesn't jibe with the work ethic of the first U.S. entrepreneurs. And a corporate environment that places emphasis on the primacy of compromise and "group think" certainly doesn't promote the entrepreneurial virtues of hard work and self-reliance.

By the early 1970s, of course, Whyte's organization man no longer matched the economic or social times. Mack Hanan heralded a new arrival in "Make Way for the New Organization Man" (*Harvard Business Review,* July-August 1971). Rejecting the comforts of corporate conformity, this new man ran on the fast track. Preoccupied with success, he used the company for his own

career advancement as much as the company used him. He was more interested in attaining power than in fitting in.

In this light, the new organization man was back in control of his career, no longer moved "hither and yon" by the inevitable organizational forces described by Whyte. According to Hanan, this new man belonged to himself first and only afterward to his profession, while "corporate belonging often runs . . . a distant fourth, after his sense of social belonging."

During the high-flying 1980s, the image of the career-oriented professional took a back seat to that of the greedy Wall-Streeter popularized by Hollywood. But Hanan's new organization man, having cut his teeth on the political and social movements of the 1960s, was by no means amoral or uncommitted to community. Rather, this man believed in the importance of questioning authority and "that intelligent, consistent dialogue can accelerate institutional change." He fully expected to have more than one career and was most excited by entrepreneurial opportunities within his corporation, such as subsidized start-ups of new businesses. These "corporateurs" didn't necessarily want to start their own companies, but they certainly wanted "to share in the personal benefits of leadership."

Hanan urged companies to take advantage of this new definition of male success by expanding board representation, equity participation, and decentralized decision making; by providing opportunities for collaborative leadership; and by creating an executive fast track that allowed for self-fulfillment through career advancement.

Many U.S. companies have done just that in the name of business necessity and increased productivity. The fast and furious environment of high-tech companies, exemplified by Microsoft, Apple, and Sun Microsystems, has reinforced the image of male business success that is popular today.

Whether a programming nerd or a shirt-sleeved manager, he lives and breathes his job because he loves it, even if that means eating takeout in front of his computer every night.

But just as the fast-tracker of the 1970s rode roughshod over the conventional organization man Whyte portrayed, today's men are now rebelling against the career expectations that Hanan described. In part, that's because many of the young male professionals of the 1970s and 1980s now have children. While Hanan's men believed in the need for institutional change, his article never questions a system in which only men have careers. Yet today wives work too, and they may be fast-trackers themselves. Most important, given the economic fallout of the 1980s, organization men can no longer count on their careers as an unquestioned source of self-fulfillment—or even as a clear path to financial success.

Manhood Today and the Marketplace

In an expanding economy, hitching one's manhood to a career may make some sense. In a recession, it's a recipe for feelings of failure. A 30-year-old man in 1949 would see his real earnings rise by 63% by the time he turned 40; the same man in 1973 would see his income decline by 1% by his fortieth birthday. Men who are now 30 to 50 years old are the first U.S. generation to be less successful than their fathers were at the same age. As one of the major trends of the past two decades, this economic decline has caused many men to reevaluate work in a harsh new light.

In *The Male Ego*, psychiatrist Willard Gaylin discusses the current erosion of American manhood in three roles: protector, procreator, and, especially, provider. He notes that "nothing is more important to a man's pride, self-respect, status, and man-

hood than work. Nothing. Sexual impotence, like sudden loss of ambulation or physical strength, may shatter his self-confidence. But . . . pride is built on work and achievement, and the success that accrues from that work. Yet today men often seem confused and contradictory in their attitudes about work."

Gaylin accurately captures the ambivalence and frustration of many men. He says, for example, that "I have never met a man—among my patients or friends—who in his heart of hearts considers himself a success." He satirizes the executive's need for "little pink roses," those pink message slips that tell a man that he's wanted. But when that chairman of the board or CEO finally retires, he suddenly learns he's lost all value. "He becomes a non-person," in Gaylin's words, shocked and overwhelmed by the fact that "he never was someone to be cherished for his own sake but only as an instrument of power and a conduit of goods."

Such strong words sound a bit sweeping; but they do resonate emotionally with the experiences of men who have recently lost their jobs. Indeed, depression is often the result, and as a number of recent studies show, the rate of various forms of depressive illness is on the rise for American men.[1] Gaylin describes self-loathing as one of the hallmarks of depression, a state in which a man tells himself, "I am not dependable; I am a fragile reed. Indeed, I must depend on you." As Gaylin indicates, a man's success is often defined by those around him rather than his own sense of how well he's done. Consider, then, the shaky ground that men are on once they've been laid off. No longer able to provide for their families (or perhaps even themselves), they've lost both their own sense of purpose and their value in society's eyes.

Even men, who have achieved success as traditionally defined—such as high-paying executives who can fully provide for their families—may feel that something is missing. Few of the "well-functioning" 80 executives sociologist Robert S. Weiss chose to interview for *Staying the Course,* his insightful if overly celebratory 1990 study, defined themselves by vaulting ambition; most seemed to be content with a kind of grounded stability—being what they called good fathers, good providers, good men. But all of them reported stress and irritability; half had trouble sleeping; most had few close friends, choosing instead to compartmentalize their lives to get through the day.

While they claimed to be devoted fathers and husbands, none of these executives shared housework or child care equally with their wives. Most continued to see their children in economic terms, as "a commitment, an investment, an obligation." Weiss's executives clearly demonstrate how twentieth-century fathers have come to nurture through financial support, a notion that still underpins the prevailing definition of manhood, especially in the corporate arena.

Yet that hasn't always been the case. Historian Robert L. Griswold's impressive 1993 book, *Fatherhood in America,* charts how involved fatherhood has waxed and waned throughout U.S. history. Some middle class eighteenth- and nineteenth-century fathers, for instance, were deeply involved in their children's lives—or at least in the education of their sons. In the early nineteenth century, advice manuals to parents about how to raise their children were addressed primarily to fathers, not mothers.

Although these fathers didn't shoulder domestic responsibilities as their wives did, they were sources of intellectual support. Affectionate bonds were especially strong between fathers and sons; before and during the Civil War, for example, letters from sons were primarily addressed to fathers. But after the war, letters written home were increasingly directed to mothers, as fathers became more remote, enveloped by the rise of the modern corporation and the financial rewards of American Big Business.

But now the terms have changed again, Griswold argues. The economic need for the two-income couple and women's desires to enter or remain in the labor force bring men face-to-face with their children in unprecedented ways. And by necessity, men may find a new sense of purpose through close bonds with their children. One of Griswold's "daddy-trackers," a man who left a top corporate job to start his own consulting firm comments: "I don't want to make out like I'm a super father or the perfect husband because that's not true. But I know I see the kids more now. I coach baseball in the spring and soccer in the fall because I've got the flexibility in my schedule. . . . I feel a little sorry for men whose only definition of success is what it says on their business cards."

Given increasing job insecurity, it's no surprise that men are now searching for ways to control their lives outside of work. But the daddy-tracker quoted above is still able to provide for his family. What about men who have lost their jobs or don't have the option of starting their own business? What about the disillusioned yuppies of the go-go 1980s who are still childless? What about gay men who are breaking out of stereotypically gay professions? If Hanan's corporateurs searched for a sense of empowerment on the job, today's men are looking for a personal potency that doesn't reside in the nature of corporate life itself. But simply switching one's allegiance to the domestic sphere has its own costs for men. At the very least, it's easier said than done.

Housework: The Final Frontier?

In some respects, William Whyte's organization man *did* have it all; in the 1950s, it was men who had the careers and families but only so long as their wives did virtually all of the housework and child care. Whyte's very use of organization man reflects his assumption that the world of work was almost exclusively male, an assumption Hanan carries through in the hard-driving, careerist language of the 1970s. Yet such descriptions, even if they linger in popular culture, hardly match reality today. The entry of women into the workplace is the other major trend pushing men to redefine themselves, whether they want to or not.

Just because so many U.S. women now work doesn't mean that women as a whole care less about nurturing family intimacy. Women not only want both work and family but seem to need both. A number of researchers have discovered that, contrary to conventional wisdom, women who are both employees and mothers often have better self-esteem and experience less stress than those who spend all their time at home with children. But ironically, the very fact of women in the workplace has thrown men's lives into disarray. Now men too face some painful choices. "I want the best of both worlds," says one man to sociologist Kathleen Gerson, author of the significant new book *No Man's Land: Men's Changing Commitments to Family and Work.* "I want to make a lot of money and spend time with my daughter, but obviously I can't have both."

It's not that men don't say they want to change. A 1989 *New York Times* article is typical of the many work-family surveys conducted in recent years: in it, two-fifths of the fathers interviewed said they would quit their jobs if they could spend more time with their children.[2] But the desire to change is often more rhetorical than real; few men would actually switch places with their nonworking wives if given the opportunity. In reality, taking on an increasing share of domestic responsibilities usually represents a trade-off. Of the executives Robert Weiss interviewed, those who had won custody of their children took on the parental work of mothers, such as cooking, shopping for clothes, giving baths. Yet Weiss implies that

for the few men in his study who were single fathers, their careers suffered. Indeed, in corporations that view family involvement as a blight on performance, a male professional may well believe that investing more energy into the home is a form of treason.

"Housework remains the last frontier that men want to settle," writes Kathleen Gerson. But in this case, "need" may be a better word than "want." No one wants to do housework, but like Mt. Everest, that mountain of unwashed clothing still has to be laundered. Unfortunately, for most male executives, conquering the crabgrass frontier doesn't begin to compare with blazing a trail through the corporate jungle. And there are few social supports available for men's equal participation in domestic life. Male friends don't nod approvingly when men say that they have household chores to finish.

In fact, men's share of housework and child care has significantly increased since 1965—from 20% to 30%. But for most men who say they're involved fathers, a sense of domestic purpose begins in the nursery, not in the kitchen or laundry room. Men "make use of various employer policies to accommodate their work role to their family obligations to a far greater degree than is generally realized," reports psychologist Joseph H. Pleck in Jane C. Hood's *Men, Work, and Family,* a useful collection of cutting-edge empirical research on men's shifting priorities on the job and on the domestic front.

As Pleck notes, however, in the absence of corporate or peer-group support, men often do so through less formal channels. For example, a man may take vacation or sick leave to attend to births and the rigors of a young baby. This professional may tell his boss that he's having some tests run and will be in the hospital for a week—wink, wink. Even committed family men may steer clear of parental-leave policies that are essentially intended by top management for women. In addition, while many more men use a company's options for flexible scheduling than paternity leave, they often say it's for another reason besides child care.

Such dissembling is one indication of how little the conception of success on the job has changed—and why men still avoid the domestic responsibilities many say they want. For one thing, housework is not an exciting frontier to conquer but a necessary task to be taken care of. For another, men—and their managers—don't look upon competent homemaking as a badge of masculinity. Last but certainly not least, while current economic and social trends are forcing changes on the home front, the source of meaning in men's lives is open to individual interpretation.

Male Demons and the Search for Meaning

Clearly, the new male ideal is not "Mr. Mom," a simple flip of conventional male and female roles. In fact, rather than accepting the age-old notion that the good man is a family man—and giving it a politically correct 1990s twist—some men may actively rebel against such expectations. The search for meaning outside of family *or* work is by no means new. Despite the ubiquity of the gray flannel suit, 1950s men struggled with the cultural ambivalence created by two male demons: the free loner without obligations and the faceless sheep of the corporation. The demon of defiant nonconformity, personified by Marlon Brando in *The Wild One*, didn't have the self-control necessary to become a responsible adult. Yet the demon of overconformity also haunted male professionals, as organization men of the past worried about losing their individuality and their sense of personal purpose.

Men still struggle with the same desire to break free, to leave the "rat race," to jump off the fast track. In *No Man's Land*, Kathleen Gerson finds that the 138 men she interviewed fall into three categories: breadwinners (36%), autonomous men (30%), and involved fathers (33%). Gerson concludes that, in a recession, becoming an involved father may help redeem a troubled manhood. This new ideal combines both family responsibility and the quest for individuality—the middle ground between undisciplined nonconformity and today's version of the corporate "clone." But it's clear from Gerson's interviews that many men still resist the middle ground.

Gerson's first two groups loosely match the two demons of male identity: overconformers and loners. The first group clings tenaciously to the traditional breadwinner ethic in order to maintain stability and control. Gerson notes that some look back nostalgically "to a time when male advantages were uncontested and supporting a family was an easier task." One of her breadwinners is typical in his assessment of why such an arrangement is fair: "My wife cooks, shops, cleans. I provide the money. To me, to run a home and raise children is a full-time job. If you do more, that's where you lose your children and you lose control."

Gerson's second group of "autonomous" men eschew family obligations altogether, either by remaining single or childless. Wary of intimate attachments, these men consume high-end consumer goods and leisure time. Some have failed in the sexual marketplace, others continue to play the field as contemporary versions of the 1950s playboy. Consider these comments from a 40-year-old computer consultant: "Nobody has a hold on me. I do as I wish, and if tomorrow I don't want to, I don't have to. It's very important that I never feel trapped, locked in."

Many of these men are divorced fathers who no longer contribute to either the financial or emotional support of their children, the "deadbeat dads" of the Clinton era. As Robert Griswold cites in *Fatherhood in America*, nearly two-thirds of all divorced fathers contribute nothing at all to the financial support of their children. Although Gerson calls these men autonomous, they seem more pitiful than free; a deadbeat dad is hardly the archetype of male autonomy.

Some of Gerson's "autonomous" men, being relatively affluent, are indulging in American men's time-honored coping strategy for dealing with conflict in their lives: escape. It's one thing to leave the rat race and find another source of work that's fulfilling; it's quite another to run for the sake of running from family commitments. But in past centuries and decades, American men have left wives and children to go west, to sea, to war, or to any other unblemished arena where a man could find himself and prove his masculine prowess.

At the turn of the century, this search for manhood and autonomy brought American men to fraternal lodges (one in five were members in 1897, according to one observer),[3] while they sent their sons to the Boy Scouts or YMCA as a way to avoid the feminine influence of mothers and wives. Today they're likely to be heading off to the woods with Robert Bly, there to drum, chant, and bond with other men in an evocation of the "deep masculine."

Yet real autonomy isn't the same as escape or disconnection. A truly autonomous man is one who feels in control of what he's doing—be that a high-powered career, a bohemian existence, family life, or some combination of the above. As it turns out, neither Gerson's breadwinners nor "autonomous" men feel especially powerful. One 35-year-old said, "I think it's a tough world to live in. I personally find I'm struggling to do it; why am I going to bring somebody into the world to struggle?" These men feel they've backed into responsibilities reluctantly, either because they became parents against their will or through drifting passively atop an anomic sea of emotional detachment. Neither group believes they actively chose their lives. Theirs

is not the life of "quiet desperation" that Thoreau abjured; it's more a life of wistful resignation, of roads not taken.

Not so for the involved fathers, the third group of men Gerson identifies. Most of these men are part of dual-career families. What's more, they have renounced workplace success as the measure of their manhood. One man who had custody of his two children chose to take advantage of his company's early retirement plan because "there's only so far you can go in a corporation, and I reached that level and realized I can't go past it. I realized I paid too high a price for what I got in return. What I got cannot get me back the time with the kids." Those who do stay in high-pressure workplaces often feel out of step, as this one accountant notes: "I'm a different person at work than I am outside work. When I'm in an environment that somehow nurtures, that somehow is cooperative rather than competitive, it enables me to be a different person, to be myself."

These men most closely fit the image of the new man of the 1990s, both in their embrace of a life outside their jobs and in the difficulties they encounter. Rather than defining themselves rigidly as breadwinners or loners, these men are searching for coherence, for a way to combine the many aspects of their lives. Many of Gerson's involved fathers have left the pitfalls of corporate life altogether, starting their own businesses or going into professions that allow for more flexibility. Through such choices, they avoid putting their manhood on the line when it comes to how their job performance is perceived. But in this respect, the new man isn't an organization man at all. And by placing less emphasis on the importance of work success, these men present a dilemma for corporations that want to retain the best professionals.

The demons of defiance and overconformity continue to haunt men for good reason; in most companies, a man's options seem limited to rebelling or not bucking the system.

Before the current economic downturn, the rewards for focusing primarily on career were clear enough, while the benefits of other choices for men often seemed mixed. Although fathers today are most obviously affected by an outmoded image of manhood and professional success, men without children who want other involvements besides a career face similar obstacles. Whether gay or straight, involved fathers or public-service volunteers, male professionals still confront resistance to change on the job, much of it from top management itself.

Resistance to Change: Corporate Inflexibility

The definition of masculinity has proved remarkably inelastic—or, depending on your perspective, amazingly resilient—under its current siege. Except for a few involved fathers, it binds men as tightly as ever to success in the public sphere, in the world of other men, as the markers of manhood and success. "I'm not secure enough, I guess, to stay home and be a househusband," confesses one man, himself an involved father, to Kathleen Gerson.

The traditional definitions of masculinity leave today's new man stranded without social support or a set of viable options. But the real problem, Gerson argues, is institutional. It's corporate inflexibility that reinforces rigid gender definitions. In this, company policies toward family leave exemplify the unconscious assumptions top managers make about what men want—or are supposed to want. A 1989 survey, cited in Joseph Pleck's chapter of *Men, Work, and Family,* found that only 1% of U.S. male employees had access to paid paternity leave, while another 18% had access to unpaid leave. Nine of ten companies made no attempt to inform employees that such leaves were available to new fathers. As a result, we currently have "more reasons to be optimistic about men's desire to nurture children than their opportunity to do so," claims Gerson.

Child care is not simply a women's issue in the workplace anymore; it's a *parents'* issue. Yet the difficulties Gerson's involved fathers face in redefining themselves suggest that companies must do more than provide child care options. Even in Sweden, with its paid parental-leave policies and an official stance on gender equality, men spend more time at work than women do. In another chapter of *Men, Work, and Family,* sociologist Linda Haas reports on whether gender roles in Sweden and other progressive Scandinavian countries differ markedly from those in the United States. To some extent, they do: the participation of Swedish men and women in the labor market is almost identical. But while 43% of Swedish women work part-time, only 7% of the men do. In addition, after government efforts in the late 1980s to increase fathers' participation in family life, the number of Swedish men who took formal parental leave rose to 44%; but again, fathers stayed home with their children for a much shorter time compared with mothers—an average of 43 days rather than 260.

Most telling, some studies have found that Swedish occupations are among the most sex-segregated in the world. Men and women do very different kinds of work at different levels of pay: two-thirds of public-sector employees are women, while only one-third of the private sector are women. Only 3% of Swedish senior executives are women. And in general, an earnings gap of 10% to 30% between men and women exists. As Haas notes of Swedish policymakers, "There is no sign that they realize that the benefits to be gained by restructuring work in nongendered ways might outweigh the personal costs to male stakeholders." In other words, business interests still cling to a traditional view of the world, one in which the primacy of men in the corporation remains unchallenged.

In the United States, men now work alongside an increasing number of female colleagues, which has dramatically altered the traditionally all-male arena of the corporation. Such a shift in the workplace has helped to change some old prejudices; but it has also produced a new tension between the sexes, as some men complain that women are competing for "their" jobs. Gerson's breadwinners, for example, resent women's entry into the workplace, holding fast to the solace of the all-male public arena before it was "invaded" by women. In this context, sexual harassment will continue to be a significant problem for working women. Such harassment is a way for men to remind women that they are, after all, "just" women who happen to be in the workplace but don't really belong there.

The cause of such bitterness and uncertainty, however, lies not in the supposed new power of women but in the rapid changes taking place in today's corporations. In fact, the Corporate America originally designed by men doesn't work anymore for most of us. The tension and low morale now found in many large companies reflect the clash between the need for organizational change and the old ideology. On the one hand, companies furiously restructure and reengineer work to match a new information economy and more diverse labor force; on the other hand, the perceived costs of being an involved father—loss of income, male comradeship, and manhood—remain real because the traditional view of what makes a professional successful hasn't changed.

Make Way for the New Employee

For obvious reasons, men who believe their lives are meaningful are likely to have the strongest sense of self-esteem. Compared with Gerson's so-called "autonomous" men, many of whom expressed frustration about their claustrophobic jobs and irritating coworkers, the involved men had a much clearer sense of why they had made the choices they did. And according to Gerson and other researchers, these men say they're more productive workers, better managers, and more creative team players. Gerson reports that the involved fathers she interviewed tended to be the most egalitarian, especially when it came to the right of women to pursue their own careers. Thus these men are the most respectful of female colleagues in the workplace. Since involved fathers and husbands appear to be the most emotionally flexible employees, they're in the best position to make the kinds of changes corporations now require.

Given the prevailing atmosphere of job insecurity, companies need to become increasingly creative in developing ways for their employees to feel good about themselves and their work. As Joseph Pleck notes, Malcolm Forbes' 1986 declaration "new daddies need paternity leave like they need a hole in the head"—seems as false for today's employers as it is for today's employees. Still, it's not enough for senior managers to put enlightened parental-leave and flexible-scheduling policies on the books. If Gerson's involved fathers are to stay in the organization, they must feel comfortable using those policies. And they must believe their job performance is evaluated fairly, not based on old conceptions of the male breadwinner.

Perhaps a professional's willingness to move to another city, for instance, isn't the best demonstration of his or her motivation. Basing promotions on how many weeks an employee spends working 16-hour days may lead to burnout rather than increased productivity, let alone creativity. In addition, not every male professional wants to be on a management track, though most still believe the work they do defines an important part of who they are. Certainly, some men and some women may always be more career-oriented than others are. Indeed, companies may require a certain number of fast-trackers to get the job done. But whether those people should be men or women is still based more on outmoded gender stereotypes than economic sense.

At the very least, companies can encourage a new kind of male-female comradeship at work, as does Silicon Valley's Organizational Development Network. As the current flood of diversity training attests, there are undoubtedly new difficulties in the workplace as male employees wrestle with both job insecurity and the increasing presence of female colleagues. But even if top managers bring in diversity trainers to help people work together, many still fail to examine their own attitudes about what it means to be a success. And it's in changing the larger framework for viewing employee loyalty and commitment that managers will bring about the biggest changes.

When Mack Hanan announced the arrival of the new organization man in 1971, he was right to call forth a new vision of the empowered corporateur: a professional who wanted to control his own career, who would be motivated by equity participation and the opportunity to take creative leaps, not just the stability of a monthly paycheck. Today's professionals still want much of what Hanan suggested corporations give them. Many certainly want the chance to run on a fast track, at least at some point in their working lives. By necessity, most of them are learning to live with economic insecurity, as long as companies reward their performance adequately.

Yet in Hanan's hierarchy of belonging, family didn't figure at all; in fact, he never even mentions the word in his article. In the 1990s, companies can no longer take for granted that family life is the exclusive domain of women. For the new man—that is, the new employee—family and career often receive equal weight. Freud himself suggested a similar prescription for the healthy person: "Lieben und arbeiten." Love and work.

But Hanan's sense of "social belonging" also has its place in the new mix. Rather than simply retreating into family life as a way to avoid the disappointments of the current workplace, today's men can find meaning through involvement with the larger world as well. A balance of career, family, and community suggests more than a hierarchy in which one occupation takes precedence over everything else; a life focused on more than just work—or family—can provide a stable foundation for every man's personal definition of success.

NOTES

1. Cross-National Collaborative Group, "The Changing Rate of Major Depression: Cross-National Comparisons," *Journal of the American Medical Association,* December 2, 1992, pp. 3098–3105; Gerald L. Klerman and Myrna M. Weissman, "Increasing Rates of Depression," JAMA, April 21, 1989, pp. 2229–2235; and Priya J. Wickramaratne, Myrna M. Weissman, Philip J. Leap, and Theodore R. Holford, "Age, Period, and Cohort Effects on the Risk of Major Depression: Results from Five United States Communities," *Journal of Clinical Epidemiology,* Vol. 42, No. 4, 1989, pp. 333–343.
2. Lisa Belkin, "Bars to Equality of Sexes Seen as Eroding, Slowly," *New York Times,* August 20, 1989, p. A1, A26.
3. W. Harwood, "Secret Societies in America," *North American Review,* 1897. This article and others are also discussed in Mark Carnes's *Fraternal Ritual and Manhood in Victorian America,* Yale University Press, 1989.

REFERENCES

The Organization Man, by William H. Whyte, Jr. New York: Simon and Schuster, 1956.
"Make Way for the New Organization Man," by Mack Hanan. *Harvard Business Review,* July-August 1971.
The Male Ego, by Willard Gaylin. New York: Viking, 1992.

Staying the Course: The Emotional and Social Lives of Men Who Do Well at Work, by Robert S. Weiss. New York: The Free Press, 1990.

Fatherhood in America: A History, by Robert L. Griswold. New York: BasicBooks, 1993.

No Man's Land: Men's Changing Commitments to Family and Work, by Kathleen Gerson. New York: BasicBooks, 1993.

Men, Work, and Family, edited by Jane C. Hood. Newbury Park: Sage Publications, 1993.

"Are 'Family-Supportive' Employer Policies Relevant to Men?," by Joseph H. Pleck, in Hood (above).

"Nurturing Fathers and Working Mothers: Changing Gender Roles in Sweden," by Linda Haas, in Hood (above).

PART VI

Work and Society in the Twenty-First Century

It is much easier to understand the past and present than it is to anticipate the future. What will the workplace look like in the twenty-first century? Will the views of classical sociology—spawned by the industrial revolution—be replaced by newer perspectives on work and society? The two concluding sections may help us begin to answer these questions.

Corporate Restructuring and New Forms of Work

Change is an inevitable and ongoing feature of work. The occupations employing the most workers at the beginning of the twentieth century were much different than those most prominent at the century's end. Some occupations, such as farming, have virtually disappeared, whereas others, such as systems analysis, emerged only recently. In addition, other changes have transformed the conditions under which many occupations are performed. Some jobs have been so altered by technological change that only their names remain the same. Technology, however, is not the only force transforming the occupational landscape. Corporate restructuring, aimed at creating a more flexible workplace, is also reshaping the conditions under which work is performed. In addition, the changing demographics of workers, fueled in part by high levels of immigration, are reshaping the workplace. The readings in this section examine these forces that are transforming the occupational world.

A major trend affecting work organization is the growth of contingent, or tempo-

rary, work. In their desire to cut costs and increase flexibility, employers in many industries have begun to shrink their permanent workforces and rely on workers subcontracted from a temporary agency. Robert E. Parker's book, *Flesh Peddlers and Warm Bodies* (1994), is among the first sociological studies of the temporary help industry. In Reading 40, Parker describes the experiences of temporary clerical workers. Because over half of all temporary help assignments are for clerical positions, temporary clerical work plays an important role in the growing contingent economy.

A somewhat less pessimistic view of current changes is provided by Vicki Smith in her case study of white-collar service workers. Smith suggests that the move toward flexible, more decentralized work may have some positive consequences for lower-level workers. Involvement in employee participation programs can empower workers by teaching the types of interpersonal skills valued in higher level jobs. Smith reminds us that change produces intended and unintended consequences. Sociologists of work should thus not assume that conceptual frameworks and assumptions drawn from the past will operate the same in workplaces of the future.

In their report, *Workforce 2000: Work and Workers for the Twenty-First Century,* Johnston and Packer (1987, p. xx) conclude that, during the next few years, "Immigrants will represent the largest share of the increase in the population and the workforce since the first World War." Immigrants are becoming an important sector of the labor force, especially in the South and West. Karen Hossfeld explores the work experiences of immigrant women in California's "Silicon Valley." Immigrant women represent a cheap source of labor for microelectronics firms, and, Hossfeld argues, managers foster divisions by gender, race, and immigrant status to prevent workers from organizing collectively to contest their employment conditions. Labor unions in the twenty-first century thus face both the challenge and potential of a demographically diverse workforce.

The Future of Work

The last two readings move away from the workplace to offer a broader perspective on the future. In the first reading in the section, Juliet Schor offers a modest proposal for positive change: reducing work time. Schor shows how the respective values of work time and leisure time have changed in response to the economic imperatives of a consumer society. She weighs the costs and benefits of increased leisure and concludes that less work would benefit workers, employers, and society.

The final reading speculates on the structure of occupational life in the twenty-first century. Andrew Abbott questions the "classical agenda" that has guided the study of work in the past and urges us to consider new questions that are more relevant to current realities. Among Abbott's suggestions is for sociologists of work to devote more attention to consumption and to consider it as a form of work. Hence, like Schor, Abbott recognizes the ways in which consumerism has become increasingly linked to the patterns of work. Whether the future will emerge as Abbott predicts remains to be seen. In any case, he reminds us that the workplace is changing, and the sociology of work must change with it.

REFERENCE

Johnston, William B. and Arnold E. Packer. 1987. *Workforce 2000: Work and Workers for the Twenty-First Century.* Indianapolis, IN: The Hudson Institute.

CORPORATE RESTRUCTURING AND NEW FORMS OF WORK

40

Temporary Clerical Workers

Robert E. Parker

Robert E. Parker is associate professor of sociology at the University of Nevada, Las Vegas. Professor Parker writes, "Work runs through most of my writing. I believe my academic interest in work was partly the product of having a father who was a first-line manager at a very traditionally run Midwestern chemical company. His position placed him just one rung above the rest of the workers but at the very bottom of the managerial hierarchy. The company had a strong union in the 1950s and they were on strike the day I was born, so my father missed my birth due to industrial strife. Another personal note: My grandfather, a railroad worker, was an on-the-job fatality . . . in short, the significance of work in an every day sense was revealed to me at a young age."

"I think my first real interest in temp work emerged because I knew a woman in college who was temping (like my Dad, I had a permanent job in a chemical company) where I worked. She was very good, productive, but was summarily dismissed one day . . . she may have been outside of the company's culture, but she needed the job. I attempted to go to bat for her but no luck. I was a sociology major but this vignette didn't evolve into a paper until 1982 (a few years later). At that point, the temporary help industry was really growing rapidly and few seemed to be paying attention. The confluence of my memories about work and my friend, coupled with the need for a Ph.D. topic, led me to pursue studying temp work systematically. Although I look at things somewhat more broadly now (in terms of how temp and related forms of work are undermining economy and the performance of many companies—it really isn't in their long-term interest), my original impetus to study temps was because I saw them as superexploited members of the working class. In addition, for four years I was a temp professor; for three of those years, my maximum potential earnings were approximately $6,000, yet I was performing the same work as those that made four to five times as much . . . again the blatant exploitation (by a public employer) drove home to me how fast and wide the phenomenon was growing. I created a course at UNLV so I could focus students' attention for one semester on this aspect of work . . . not only is temp work a continuing trend, but outsourcing and subcontracting have become an ever more common 'human resource' strategy."

Temporary clerical workers are central to the economic success of the temporary help industry. These workers are hired by employers more frequently than any other occupational category. In 1990 a little more than 63 percent of all temporary help assignments were for clerical-related positions.[1] According to NATS, more than 90 percent of companies with automated office equipment use temporary clerical workers at some point. Although other categories of temporary help (such as home health care workers) have been growing faster, clerical positions continue to provide the majority of the employment opportunities for temporary workers.

Why do workers take clerical jobs for employers on a temporary basis? How do employees feel about being a temporary secretary, data-entry operator, clerk, or receptionist? What are workplace conditions like for temporary clerical workers? These are some of the basic questions guiding this chapter. In large measure the answer to these inquiries stem from my experience working as a temporary clerical employee, from in-depth interviews with temporary clerical workers, and from interviews with the managers of temporary help firms.

Choice versus Economic Coercion

One prominent aspect of working as a temporary clerical employee is its largely involuntary character. Few workers prefer to be employed on any kind of contingent basis; most workers want year-round, full-time jobs. Workers choose temporary work to survive. Most employees of temporary companies share much in common with involuntary part-time workers (those who express a preference for full-time work but who accept

part-time work for "economic reasons"). Among the clerical workers I interviewed, the preference for permanent employment was unambiguous. Furthermore, managers of temporary firms corroborated the fact that their employees were mainly frustrated workers searching for full-time jobs. In fact, only one of eleven managers said that the percentage of full-time job seekers might be as small as 50 percent. According to this manager, the other 50 percent are "housewives looking to supplement the family income." Representative of the belief found in most temporary firms was the comment offered by one manager that "almost all of the clerical workers are looking for full-time jobs."

Despite workers' clear preference for full-time employment, the temporary help industry has propagated a different image about the typical temporary worker. Through industry efforts a number of self-serving myths have been created and perpetuated surrounding employees of the temporary help industry. Often they are characterized as housewives with a weak labor force attachment or workers who value leisure time more than permanent employment. The following is how the leading private spokesperson for the temporary industry, Manpower's CEO Mitchell Fromstein, expressed this view:

As housewives become aware of the labor market value of their former office skills, they cautiously seek possible work opportunities and skill measurements as the preliminary step to worklife re-entry. These women are unsure of their marketability and their real desire to work. They are inhibited in their willingness to seek or accept normal office positions but are curious at the possibility. They could best be described as job market "probers" rather than job seekers. . . . In many cases, their skills need improvement and assurance that they still have the ability to be productive and will be accepted into the workforce. They fear the classic job interview. . . . The temporary help firm offers a suitable "half-way house" to these job seekers.[2]

In these comments, Fromstein overemphasized the role of free choice in working on a temporary basis while neglecting economic coercion as a factor causing many to rely on contingent work. Additionally, he implied that the typical woman worker is weak of character and deficient, requiring extra assistance to enter or reenter the world of work.

In a similar vein the industry publication *Modern Office Procedures* identified every type of person in its litany of temporary employees except full-time job seekers. According to this publication's account, temporary workers are "students home on vacation, retirees who would like to work occasionally to relieve boredom and supplement their income, housewives who are through raising their children and are just beginning to get back into the swing of things, and even artists and freelancers of various sorts."[3] Sam Sacco, speaking for NATS, added to the leisure-seeker mythology, claiming that "many temporary service operators . . . have noticed the emergence of a new type of employee—a career temporary—who enjoys the diversity of working in different office environments, likes picking his or her own hours, and can live on the salaries."[4] Finally, Barbara Johnson gave much weight to the role of voluntariness in working as a temporary employee. In her view, temps are employees who have "elected to be without company ties so that they can work when they want to, can consider other jobs any time they want to, and can be free to enter or leave the temporary work force."[5]

The idea that most clerical temporary workers are either leisure seekers or workers with a primary attachment to family life was not borne out by either the workers or the managers I interviewed. Most of the managers said the leisure or reluctant housewife types were 10 percent or less of their entire pool of temporary workers. All the managers were aware of the industry-propagated image of temporary workers as laid-back leisure seekers, but the majority dismissed it, describing that kind of employee as a nonexistent or vanishing breed.

Observations, interviews, and other corroborating evidence did suggest, however, that a strong, positive association exists between a voluntary choice of temporary work and skill level. The greater the skill level, the more likely the worker will be able to work regularly for a temporary help firm. Thus higher-skilled workers exercise greater discretion and autonomy about their temporary work lives. But lesser-skilled temporary workers cannot afford to be choosy and are forced by economic necessity to accept any and all assignments offered. Martin Gannon, using a mail survey completed by 1,101 temporary employees of health care companies, confirmed this relationship between skill level and the free choice of temporary employment. He found that two groups of higher-skilled workers (registered nurses and licensed practical nurses) were less likely to desire a five-day (or more) workweek than were two lesser-skilled groups (nurses' aides and homemakers). Similarly, the higher-skilled groups were much more likely than the lesser-skilled workers to cite "freedom to schedule work flexibly" as the most important reason for becoming a temporary help employee. Thus, there is some truth to the notion that temps choose such arrangements freely, but those workers are in the minority. Why do most temporary employees want full-time, rather than intermittent, working schedules? Not surprisingly most temporary employees offer the same reasons cited by permanent full-time workers. The major reasons include the desire for economic security, job stability, better pay, and fringe benefits. In fact, several workers said a part-time job is better than working as a temporary employee because of greater job security.

Moving from Permanent to Temporary Work

Most of the temporary employees interviewed for this [chapter] who wanted full-time work had had previous full-time working experience. As such, they were in an insightful position to evaluate differences between permanent, full-time jobs and contingent work. Before joining the ranks of the temporary workforce, most of the clerical workers had been full-time clerical workers or educators. Fairly typical of the workers who agreed to in-depth interviews was a woman with two and one-half years of teaching experience and one and one-half years of full-time secretarial experience. One worker had been a full-time elementary schoolteacher for the previous six years. In each of the years before the interview, she had been able to find a full-time job for the summer to supplement her income. Now unable to find other, more stable employment, she was relying on temporary firms to make ends meet.

The majority of temporary clerical workers in this study arrived at temporary help as a result of one of three sets of circumstances. Some were recent arrivals to the community and had been unable to find permanent work. Others were entering the labor market on a full-time basis for the first time and could not find full-time work. And still others were accustomed to full-time positions but were in between jobs because of resignations, layoffs, or terminations. So in my sample clerical employees worked for temporary firms largely on an involuntary basis. This was a "choice" they had made after exhausting other, more preferable working options.

Of course, some temporary employees do work on an intermittent basis without feeling economically coerced. Among the clerical

workers, the ability to continue an education while earning income was the most common reason cited for preferring a temporary working arrangement. Nevertheless, among the employees who did not prefer full-time work, none cited reasons that were consistent with the industry's public-relations image. For example, none of the workers mentioned having a primary orientation to home life or wanting more leisure time.

Logistically the clerical employees who arrive at a temporary help firm after exhausting more desirable alternatives do so in a number of ways. Some prospective clerical temps got the idea to work on a temporary basis after reading help-wanted ads in a local newspaper. Another handful applied to a temporary firm after having the idea suggested to them by an acquaintance, friend, or spouse. Others applied after seeing openings for temporary work listed alongside full-time advertisements, such as those posted with state employment offices. Some found temporary offices listed in the yellow pages under "employment services." And still others began to work as temporary employees after visiting a temporary firm while searching for permanent full-time work. One clerical worker explained that she had first applied for temporary assignments as "an accident." She thought the firm was a full-service full-time employment agency. When she learned of her mistake, she decided to give the agency a try because it was "free" and "some work was better than none." . . .

Working Conditions

Employment Uncertainty

From the workers' perspective, there is an important flip side to the "human resource flexibility" being aggressively implemented by corporate America and championed by the temporary help industry. Workers tend to experience flexible work arrangements differently; what employers see as flexibility, temporary workers often perceive as uncertainty. Indeed, uncertainty is a key distinguishing feature of all types of contingent employment. And for many it is the most salient and pervasive characteristic of temporary work. The timing and length of temporary work assignments are perhaps the most obvious aspects of this ubiquitous uncertainty. Even among workers who reported receiving an adequate amount of work, considerable suspense remained concerning when work would be assigned and, conversely, when an extended period of idleness might ensue. One employee succinctly expressed the issue in terms of "never knowing when you're going to work and then not knowing how much work there will be."

Uncertainty surrounding the workday, then, frequently begins at the outset of each new day—with no knowledge if any assignments are available. If workers want to stay employed with a temporary firm, they must remain on-call without interruption. In this way the uncertainty of temporary work intrudes into a person's leisure time as well, blurring the boundaries between personal time and working time.

Among the clerical workers I interviewed, most said they worked an adequate amount of hours during most weeks. There was, however, a distinct minority that said they were not satisfied with the amount of work assigned. On average these workers were receiving between 5 percent and 20 percent of the amount of work they preferred. Again, manager comments corroborated the workers' assertions about the lack of certainty in obtaining adequate amounts of work. The consensus view among managers was that most temporary clerical employees had to remain active and available before they could reasonably expect to obtain an adequate amount of work.

A worker's skill level plays an important role in the receipt of adequate workweeks. As several managers indicated, there is a strong positive association between skill level and the ability of workers to garner as many assignments as desired. For example, among clerical workers general office clerks have a harder time finding regular employment than do more highly qualified full-service secretaries. Also, the ability to operate automated word processing systems helps ensure that clerical temps will receive adequate hours. In contrast, a clerk whose skills are largely limited to filing and typing is likely to have many shortened workweeks.

Among the clerical workers who reported receiving an adequate amount of work, most usually worked nearly forty hours. The rest were working an average of between twenty and thirty-five hours weekly. Despite the adequacy of hours reported by the majority of clerical temporary employees, many noted that great uncertainty persisted about the availability of working opportunities. For example, one clerical employee who had completed several forty-hour workweeks over a six-month period, and who reported being generally satisfied with the amount of hours worked, remarked that "you never really know when or how much you're going to work. One week when I really needed to have a full paycheck, I had only one assignment—four hours on Wednesday."

Moreover, even when a temporary employee is provided a working opportunity, uncertainty continues concerning the duration of the assignment. An example of this type of uncertainty arose while I was working at one of my first clerical assignments. Near the end of my first day performing clerical work with a public housing authority, there was much discussion and confusion among the other three temporary employees in my work group about whether we would be asked back for the following day. Although we were scheduled to check out at 5:00 P.M., at

4:20 our supervisor was uncertain whether there was an ongoing need for our labor. Shortly later the supervisor returned and asked us to stay "until 8:30 or so." Having arrived shortly after 7:30 A.M., I declined but offered to return the following day. The supervisor indicated that was agreeable but said she needed only two, not three, of us to stay or return. At that point one clerical temp opted not to return. A similar vignette unfolded at the end of the second day, and during a slow period on the third day, I offered to leave.

Uncertainty about the duration of assignments was a frequently mentioned source of dissatisfaction among the workers I interviewed. In most of my experiences as a temp, the employer asked me to return for additional days. But the obverse also occurs routinely. Several workers complained about being sent out on work assignments that were supposed to last two weeks only to have them cut short by several days or more. Temporary firms tell workers how long the assignment is expected to last, but most employees soon learn such information is an educated estimate at best. . . .

Wages

Wages can vary considerably for employees in the temporary help industry. In my experience working clerical assignments, the pay ranged from $4.00 and $10.00 per hour. In a majority of the assignments, I earned $4.50 or less. Wages in the range of $4.00–$5.00 per hour were common among the temporary workers with whom I spoke. In fact, of those who agreed to in-depth interviews, the majority reported that the most frequent pay range was $4.00–$5.00 per hour. Only a handful reported earning, on average, $5.00 or more per hour. The relatively low pay for clerical assignments was a frequent complaint voiced by temporary workers. One young employee who was still living with

her parents asked rhetorically, "What would I have done if I had to live on this?" One of the better-paid clerical workers declared, "People work to make money, but there's no way you can make money doing this; it's a rook." Several other clerical employees questioned whether temporary assignments were "worth it" after taxes and commuting expenses were calculated.

Managers of temporary firms reported a similar pay range, although they tended to emphasize the upper end of the pay scale that highly qualified secretarial employees sometimes earn. The pay for clerical workers did not vary much among different temporary firms. The highest-paying company among the nine I surveyed claimed to maintain a minimum wage of $4.75 for clerical workers. Apologists for the temporary help industry frequently assert that temporary workers earn as much, if not more, than full-time employees. For example, Teresia Ostrach, director of temporary operations with Dunhill Temporary Systems, said, "In many cases, working temporary pays as well, if not better, than full-time employment."[6] Both the primary and secondary sources of evidence presented in this book strongly suggest such assertions regarding pay are part of an industry-created and -perpetuated mythology.

The myth of well-paid temporary clerical employees has emerged for a number of reasons. First, it is true that some temporary employees are highly compensated, but most of these are technical or administrative workers. Second, some temporary companies have adopted the bait-and-switch marketing techniques (or other forms of deceptive advertising) long associated with the retail industry. Some unscrupulous temporary help operators advertise for highly paid clerical temps, but when workers apply, they are told that all the high-paying jobs are currently filled. Then the firm switches the applicants to less remunerative assignments.[7]

Third, the image of the well-paid temporary clerical worker is reinforced by firms whose managers boast of "paying temporary employees a wage comparable to a permanent employee in the same position." Even when true, the permanent employee receives fringe benefits generally unavailable to temporary workers.

Of the managers who agreed to in-depth interviews, none could recall an instance in which a temporary clerical worker was paid more than a full-time employee in the same position. Most stressed that temporary employees were paid on a comparable basis with full-time entry-level workers. Usually that meant temporary workers earned at least $.50 less per hour than their permanent clerical counterparts.

Benefits

There is one area of temporary work life that is not riddled with uncertainty: fringe benefits. Temporary workers do not receive any of the perks typically earned by full-time workers, including health insurance, paid days off, and pensions. The barrier is not simply the unavailability of benefits. Many temporary firms advertise that they offer fringe benefits. Rather, few workers stay at this work long enough or consistently enough to satisfy the criteria temporary firms set to qualify for benefits. Only one clerical worker interviewed for this book indicated receiving any kind of fringe benefit. This solitary worker was employed by the temporary employment division of a major research university and after six months of continual experience earned benefits comparable to those received by permanent employees.

The policies of most temporary help firms dictate that workers complete the equivalent or near-equivalent of a full-time working schedule over an extended period to qualify for benefits. This makes it very difficult to ever earn benefits because even

among clerical employees who said they were receiving an adequate amount of work, many were not working forty hours a week. To receive pay for a major holiday, one firm requires that an employee work both the day before and after the holiday, and six hundred hours within the previous six months. Another company offers vacation pay to employees who have worked fifteen hundred hours within the calendar year; in a hypothetical second year, they are eligible for eighty hours of vacation pay after completing one thousand eight hundred hours. Generally, these requirements are simply unrealistic and unattainable for temporary clerical workers. . . .

The managers of firms I interviewed confirmed that temporary workers seldom receive benefits. Indeed, when I asked one manager about workers receiving benefits, he appeared surprised and shot back, "What benefits?" If most are unable to earn fringe benefits, what alternatives do temporary workers have? According to Johnson, "Temporary employees should set up their own retirement accounts and take out full insurance coverage for medical care and accidents."[8] However, it is highly unrealistic, given the prevailing low wages, that temporary workers could pursue this course. Later in her book Johnson acknowledged how ludicrous her own advice was when she noted, "Insurance premiums are sometimes the determining factor in turning temporary employees into permanent employees when they wish to receive company-paid benefit packages."[9] Aside from an occasional referral bonus, it would be presumptuous for temporary workers to expect to receive any fringe benefits. As Jamie Laughridge summarized, "For the most part, temps give up benefits, pensions, sick days and paid vacations. Some well-established services do have benefit programs, but they're generally offered only to those for whom temping is, in fact, a permanent job."[10]

Opportunities for Full-Time Employment

One benefit that may stem from being employed as a temporary worker is the opportunity to find full-time employment. The extent to which this occurs, however, is significantly overstated by the temporary help industry. For example, Kate Tomlin and Ron Kapche reported that 30 percent of temporary workers find permanent positions through temporary assignments.[11] An even more optimistic appraisal was offered by Roberts. To temporary employees seeking full-time jobs, she advised:

> As the time for your temporary placement draws to a close you will probably be asked directly whether or not you wish to remain with the organization. All the experts concur in the belief that if you've been on the job every day, have diligently performed your duties, shown initiative, been resourceful and achieved something, the company almost inevitably will evince a strong desire to recruit you to its permanent workforce.[12]

Among the temporary clerical workers interviewed for this [study], only one reported being offered a full-time job, and she accepted.

The practice of temporary workers moving from contingent to permanent status is formally and informally discouraged. For example, virtually all temporary companies charge their clients a fee (usually $1,500) if the employer hires one of the company's temporary workers within ninety days of the initial assignment. As Edward Lenz noted, the purpose of charging "liquidated damages is to discourage customers from using the temporary help company as an employment agency—and a free one to boot."[13] An alternative arrangement that discourages temporary employees from becoming permanent workers is the requirement that employees remain on the temporary firm's account for a designated period (often thirteen weeks) after the date the worker has accepted the client's offer of employment. In addition, some temporary firms now require their employees to sign contracts with restrictive covenants. These agreements prohibit the employee from working for customers or competitors for a fixed period of time following the termination of employment. Perhaps of more profound importance than these formal obstacles is the resistance from employers, which is great because most are using temporary firms in an expanded way to avoid a commitment to additional full-time workers. As a Midwest management support supervisor stated in *The Office*, "We like the idea of temporary services, but we don't like it when temporaries begin feeling as if we should hire them after they have worked on several different long term assignments. Temporaries sometimes forget there are no obligations on our part to hire them full-time."[14]

The formal organizational structure of the temporary help industry does not facilitate or encourage its employees to make the transition from temporary to full-time work. Managers disagreed sharply over the frequency with which temporary workers moved into permanent employment. One manager said that as many as 30 to 40 percent of the firm's clerical employees eventually got full-time jobs with an employer for which they had worked previously as a temporary worker. A more commonly cited figure was 20 percent, and even that was an exaggeration. Most managers did not think in terms of all the temporary workers in their pool of available employees, just those working on a regular basis. Thus, the actual number of temporary workers moving from temporary to permanent employment appears to be quite negligible. . . .

Interaction with Permanent Workers

The presence or absence of permanent coworkers and the quality of interaction between the two are other aspects of temporary work life colored by uncertainty. For example, I always included "working with other workers" as a preference on my employment application. Despite that request, a majority of my clerical assignments involved isolated work settings. Most of the clerical employees I interviewed reported very little workplace interaction. Adjectives such as "polite" crept up frequently to characterize the interaction that did exist. The following comments from clerical workers were typical concerning workplace interaction:

- "When you're there for a long period, you really get to know them and feel like you're part of the team. . . . On the other hand, if you are only there for a day or two, you don't feel like you really make much of a difference."

- "There was hardly any interaction at all. Most of it was indifferent, just supervisors giving out instructions. . . . They tell you what to do and when to take breaks."

- "People treat you nice and polite, but they also treat you differently. . . . There is no feeling of attachment, and sometimes attitudes are condescending."

- "Overall, there was not much interaction. Most of the full-time people see a lot of faces come and go. They are interested in you getting the work done but don't want to know you personally. The emphasis is on casual relationships."

- "Most of the interaction is characterized by uneasiness and ambiguity. . . . No one seems sure how to treat each other. I try to make an impression, but no one seems to care."

- "Many people have been warm and extended themselves to me. But other assignments have been different. In some cases, the permanent workers seem to be threatened by the temps."

- "The counselor at the service where I worked specifically told me never to talk with full-time employees."

This frequent lack of regular interaction with permanent workers has apparently contributed to the growing success of temporary help firms. In a brief review of the temporary help industry, the assistant editor of *Management World* stressed that "a temporary worker comes in fresh, alert, and ready to work, and is not socially or politically involved with other workers."[15]

Advantages of Temporary Employment

The temporary help industry aggressively markets a variety of alleged advantages of temporary work, including skill upgrading and flexible work schedules. During National Temporaries Week (an industry-sponsored promotional event), for example, the Canadian Federation of Temporary Help Services sponsors an essay contest for temporary employees to encourage them to write about their (positive) experiences as a temporary employee. According to *Temporary Topics*, "essay after essay told us that working temp provided needed employment (often as an entry or re-entry to the work force), helped develop skills, provided experience, allowed flexibility, and was an enjoyable change from routine."[16] One of the winners in the essay contest had high praise for temporary work. The essayist compared her "being in a rut" life in a permanent job to working as "a temp—a sort of rolling stone of the secretarial work force, not content to stay in one position gathering moss for more than a few weeks at a time." Of her learning experiences, this temporary clerical worker wrote, "I have learned how to make coffee in almost every coffee machine on the market. I can use manual, electric, and even electronic typewriters."[17]

Johnson identified several advantages that temporary employees may enjoy, including discretion over when and where to work, job satisfaction derived from working where they know they are really needed, fast pay for emergencies, prospects for finding permanent employment, opportunities to learn new skills, a chance to explore different types of jobs, and the likelihood of meeting new people.[18] Again, the evidence gathered for this book suggests that these advantages are difficult for workers to realize.

One survey of temporary workers conducted by Adia Temporary Services found that 44 percent listed the opportunity to broaden work experiences as the aspect of temporary employment they liked best. The canvass, which covered two thousand workers worldwide, also found that 44 percent considered variety of work and working hours as important advantages of temporary employment and that 42 percent identified flexibility as a major advantage.[19]

Gannon, in a mail survey of 1,101 temporary workers, found that only 16.6 percent cited variety as the most important reason for working as a temporary employee. In contrast, more than 60 percent chose freedom to schedule work in a flexible manner as the most important reason for electing a contingent work arrangement.[20] In my interviews, these advantages were mentioned, but typically they had a different spin. Here is how a few of the clerical employees expressed the advantages of temporary work:

- "I like meeting different people."
- "The flexibility, not having to work every day . . . getting away from the monotonous drag of everyday work."
- "You can sort of be irresponsible in that if they call you for a job, you don't have to go, only if you feel like it."
- "The idea that you could work whenever you want and be off whenever you want."
- "Getting paid on a weekly basis."

- "You can quit anytime you want; you don't feel obligated to any single employer."
- "The opportunities for leisure . . . You can leave a job you hate . . . The variety of work experiences."
- "I didn't like anything about being a temp; it was just a way to pay bills."

Several themes emerge in these and similar comments made by temporary clerical workers. The first is that the flexibility touted by the temporary help industry is a double-edged sword: flexibility accrues advantages for temporary firms and employers but fails to consistently benefit temporary workers. Clearly, employers and the temporary help industry gain inordinately from a flexible workforce. As Karen Nussbaum of the National Association of Working Women (9 to 5) suggested, the benefit of flexibility is extended on management's terms.[21] For temporary employees the chance to schedule work in a flexible manner is a limited benefit at best.

Another theme revealed in these comments is that flexibility, variety, and the other advantages cited by workers are frequently couched in a kind of tentative, hesitant language. Indeed, many workers seemed to have had a difficult time identifying any advantages. When conducting in-depth interviews, I probed on flexibility and variety (the advantages most frequently cited by industry and worker surveys). Despite the probes, neither feature emerged as a significant theme in the workers' comments concerning advantages. Indeed, few workers openly identified variety and flexibility as advantages of temporary work. Other workers cast the advantages in plainly negative terms. To illustrate, consider the worker who said, "You can quit anytime you want." This employee is intimating something quite different about temporary work from one who says that working as a temporary employee offers variety and the opportunity to learn new things. Similarly, the statement that "you can leave a job you hate" is not conveying anything positive about temporary employment. It is merely expressing the somewhat dubious benefit of being able to choose between idling oneself indefinitely or being subjected to unpleasant working conditions. It is the kind of advantage that is mentioned only after other, more common advantages, such as adequate pay and job security, have been eliminated.

Few temporary clerical workers identified advantages of temporary work that could be labeled outwardly and explicitly positive. Among temporary workers the prevailing sentiment was that it was advantageous to work for a temporary help firm because they could quickly leave disagreeable working conditions. In this sense temporary work becomes an advantageous arrangement because it means a worker can leave offensive workplaces without permanent termination.

Managers emphasized more conventional connotations surrounding flexibility as a major advantage for temporary workers. According to firm executives, workers desire flexibility in order to have a family life and a work life or to continue an education. Additionally, managers frequently cited variety and the opportunity to earn cash quickly as advantages. Several were candid in acknowledging that there were few genuine advantages associated with a temporary working arrangement. One executive prefaced her remarks about the advantages of working as a temporary employee this way:

> Temporary work is not good for everyone and is not to be recommended to just anyone. It's no way to make a living because even if you sign up with every outfit in town, there will be days without work. Then there is the lack of benefits. So the advantages here are for those individuals who have self-

selected themselves for this kind of schedule.

Another manager said a major advantage is that because of ever-changing work sites, a temporary worker is "less likely to get bored or burnt out." Contained here is a highly qualified view of the advantages of temporary work. The managers' views do not overtly convey anything intrinsically positive about temporary work. Rather, the benefits can be more accurately characterized as workers' rational reactions to the dead-end, demoralizing character of so much full-time employment in the U.S. economy.

There is, however, an important alternative interpretation of the advantages identified by temporary employees. It could be argued that temporary workers are reasserting control over their working lives through the use of temporary help companies. When workers turn down an offer of employment, they are sending a signal about the perceived quality of the work. Temporary help firms offer an unusual opportunity for (regularly employed) temporary workers to determine an important aspect of their working lives: when and how often they will work.

Nonetheless, the attempt to recover a portion of their alienated labor may be of only marginal significance. When temporary workers do decide to begin accepting assignments again, they are relegated to the bottom of the occupational hierarchy. Furthermore, when temporary employees remain idle, they are seldom eligible for unemployment compensation or paid days off. Full-time workers, in contrast, can occasionally take off for a "mental health day" at their employer's expense.

The benefits of being employed as a temporary worker are limited. To workers they are advantages because the world of full-time employment seems even more dreary, monotonous, and dismal. These peculiarly qualified advantages reflect the alienation that both permanent and temporary workers experience under U.S. capitalism. Perhaps to justify working under an arrangement that offers so few visible benefits, some temporary workers "find" advantages in their jobs even where few exist.

Disadvantages of Temporary Employment

According to both workers and managers of temporary firms, the disadvantages of being employed as a temporary clerical worker far outdistance the benefits. As this chapter closes, I return to the fundamental issue of the uncertainty that burdens temporary workers. Nearly all the temporary workers identified insecurity as the underlying problem of being employed on a temporary basis. Temporary workers routinely face uncertainty regarding when they will work, the length of their assignments, and the quality of co-worker and supervisory interaction, not to mention the numerous daily nuances in organizational procedures.

Beyond this insecurity and uncertainty (called flexibility by employers and the temporary help industry), temporary employees mentioned other aspects of temporary employment they disliked. The following excerpted comments are representative of the disadvantages typically voiced by temporary clerical workers:

- "doing the same thing all the time . . . it's bad and boring work."
- "When you are sent out to a job, a lot of people look down on you. They think that temporaries are very unskilled or poor people. . . . It's not always true."
- "The constant adjustment to new faces and the untried job routine. Being held in low esteem because of temporary status is a big problem . . . the perception that 'temporary' is a category that is okay to discriminate against."
- "I didn't like the often antagonistic attitude of the regular workers toward me and the other temps. We were looked down upon because we were 'just temps.'"
- "My problem was the gap between the projected image of the service and the reality of the assignments. They made it sound as if you could work any time you wanted . . . They also made it sound like there was a lot of different work to do. But it looks like it's all dead-end work you couldn't stand to do for more than one day."
- "The uncertainty . . . never knowing when and how much work there will be."
- "You only get paid if you work . . . no holiday or vacation pay. I didn't like getting an assignment for one week and then being asked to leave before the time was up. I also didn't like the hectic pace of much of the work."
- "It's stifling work, completely without content. One big problem is that you never get to complete a job; you've got several bosses and they are always switching you around."

Several central issues surrounding temporary employment emerge in these comments. One distinct problem is the absence of varied and interesting assignments. This disadvantage stands in direct contrast to the industry's position that temporary work offers employees a great diversity of occupations to fill. Actually, workers are employed in many different industries, but as several employees suggested, this means "doing the same thing all of the time." If a worker performs data-entry work, the tasks are quite similar despite dissimilar industrial contexts. And again these comments raise the issue of everyday uncertainty. One worker referred to the "constant adjustment to new faces"; another echoed a common complaint about "never knowing when you're going to work."

Beyond these negative aspects, a prominent issue was the stigma associated with working as a temporary employee. Temporary workers repeatedly expressed the feeling of being shunned because they were not permanent workers. The popular phrase workers used to describe themselves and other temporary workers was "warm bodies." In similar fashion the workers labeled the temporary companies "flesh peddlers." Temps found they were not treated like other workers; because of their contingent status, they did not command the same level of respect as full-time workers. There were, of course, some temporary clerical workers who expressed no complaints. Said one, "Nothing bothered me. . . . I didn't need the income, so pay wasn't an issue." But overall, with little probing, the majority expressed a profound underside connected with temporary employment.

This devalued view of temporary workers is held by many co-workers. That many accept the impression that these workers are *"just* temps" appears to stem from the occupations they most commonly occupy. Temporary workers serve many different roles, labor at a wide range of jobs, but usually make major sacrifices in every important occupational dimension related to job satisfaction. They are paid less; receive few, if any, fringe benefits; and are assigned the most mundane jobs within organizations. For managers and full-time co-workers, temporary and other contingent employees represent a new substratum of workers.

NOTES

1. Bob Whalen and Susan Dennis, "The Temporary Help Industry: An Annual Update," pp. 1–4, reprint from *Contemporary Times* (Spring 1991).

2. Mitchell Fromstein, *The Socio-Economic Roles of the Temporary Help Service in the United States Labor Market.* (Washington, D.C.: GPO, 1977) pp. 16–17.

3. "Temporary Help to the Rescue!" *Modern Office Procedures (May 1979):96.*

4. Deborah Churchman, "High-Tech Training Gives 'Temps' New Professional Status," *Christian Science Monitor,* December 29, 1983.

5. Barbara Johnson, *Working Whenever You Want* (Englewood Cliffs, N.J.: Prentice-Hall, (1983)), p. 7.

6. Teresia R. Ostrach, "A Second Look at Temporaries," *Personnel Journal* (June, 1981):441.

7. Howard Rudnitsky, "A Cushion for Business," *Forbes,* February 5, 1979, pp. 78–80.

8. Johnson *Working Whenever You Want, p. 34.*

9. Ibid., p. 35.

10. Jamie Laughridge, "Temporary Work: How to Make It Work for You," *Harper's Bazaar* (April 1982): 236.

11. Tomlin and Kapche.

12. Sandra Roberts, "From Part-Time to Full-Time," *Black Enterprise* (July 1983):62.

13. Edward A. Lenz, "The Ties That Bind," *Contemporary Times* 4 (13) (1985):16.

14. "Why and How Business Uses Temporary Help," *The Office* (6) (1980):101.

15. Joseph McKendrick, "Temporary Help: Profile of a Growing Industry," *Management World* (June 1981):18.

16. "National Temporaries Week," *Temporary Topics* 1 (1) (1985):7.

17. Ibid.

18. Johnson, *Working Whenever You Want,* pp. 25–30.

19. Karen E. Debats, "Temporary Services Flourish," *Personnel Journal* (October, 1983):781–782.

20. Gannon, "Preferences of Temporary Workers," pp. 26–27.

21. 9 to 5, National Association of Working Women *Working at the Margins: Part-Time and Temporary Workers in the United States* (Cleveland: National Association of Working Women 1986).

41

Employee Involvement, Involved Employees
Participative Work Arrangements in a White-Collar Service Occupation

Vicki Smith

Vicki Smith is associate professor in the department of sociology at the University of California, Davis. She studies production and staffing flexibility and has published articles on this research in *Social Problems* and *Work and Occupations*. Professor Smith observes, "My interest in work stems from a job in a bagel bakery that I held to support myself while in undergraduate school. Working both as a worker and a manager fueled my sociological ambitions to study power and consent in the workplace. I no longer bake bagels but I do continue to believe that the workplace is one of the most important and fruitful arenas for sociological investigation."

Throughout the U.S. economy, employers and managers are promoting a new ethos of participation for their workers. The spread of a paradigm of participation—comprised of extensive discussion about the merits of worker involvement as well as actual transformation of production methods and staffing practices—may indeed be one of the most significant trends sweeping across postindustrial, late twentieth-century workplaces (Appelbaum and Batt 1994; Harrison 1994; Heckscher 1988; Hodson 1995; U.S. Department of Labor 1994). As Appelbaum and Batt (1994:5) note in their exhaustive study of emergent U.S. work systems, "In the 1990s, a new *vision* of what constitutes an effective production system appears to dominate management's views, if not yet its actions."

Sociologists, industrial relations researchers, organizational scientists, and policymakers who have studied this trend agree that leaders and managers of U.S. companies are climbing aboard the bandwagon of worker participation in their urgent attempts to maintain competitiveness under changing economic circumstances. Employers believe that when workers participate in making decisions, when they gain opportunities to apply their tacit knowledge to problem solving, and when they acquire responsibility for designing and directing production processes, they feed into an infrastructure enabling firms to respond to shifting market and product demands in a rapid and timely way.

The introduction of management-initiated employee involvement programs (EIPs) has inspired a significant body of research by sociologists who study work, the labor process, organizations, and industrial relations. By and large, these researchers have been skeptical about workers' commitments and consent to such participative programs, suggesting that demands for participation thinly veil a reality of harder work with fewer resources, leaving workers themselves suspicious of such reform (Hodson 1995). Yet, as I will discuss, most research has focused on

Abridgment of "Employee Involvement, Involved Employees: Participative Work Arrangements in a White-Collar Service Occupation" by Vicki Smith, reprinted from *Social Problems*, Vol. 43, No. 2, May 1996, by permission. © 1996 by the Society for the Study of Social Problems, Inc.

participative arrangements that are subject to collective bargaining in unionized, industrial work settings that employ a homogeneous and declining fraction of the U.S. labor force. As a result, our knowledge about the causes of, negotiations over, and outcomes associated with EIPs does not extend to the white-collar service work settings in which a vast number of Americans are employed in the late twentieth-century postindustrial U.S. . . .

Employee Involvement Programs in the U.S. Economy

The data on employee involvement or participation programs in the United States are overlapping, murky, sometimes contradictory, occasionally reported to be scientific but generally believed not to be entirely reliable. Thus, estimates vary about how extensively employers have adopted such programs, ranging from claims that the proportion of Fortune 1000 companies with at least one employee involvement practice had reached about 85 percent in 1990 (Appelbaum and Batt 1994:60), to more cautious projections that a smaller number (37 percent) have "*significant* (my emphasis) involvement . . . (in which) a majority of core employees (are) covered by two or more forms of workplace innovation" (U.S. Department of Labor 1994:34-35).

As Fantasia, Clawson, and Graham (1988:469) point out, "Everything from a suggestion box to a worker-controlled economy has been included under the rubric" of worker participation. Despite the wide-ranging nature of these data, few sociologists who study work dispute that at the very least a *discourse* of involvement, but very often its practice, has become a common approach to work in the postindustrial workplace.

Part of the difficulty in pinning down precisely what employee involvement is and how far it has entered the corporate workplace is that many different participative

schemes are included in the definition. Nevertheless, it is possible to categorize these schemes into two clusters, one geared toward the macro-level, power structure of the firm, and one geared toward micro-level work systems, toward improving and changing the way goods and services are produced.

In the first cluster of EIPs, workers negotiate and shape firm-level policies. Including representation on boards of directors (Stern 1988), joint labor/management committees (Bate and Murphy 1981), and ownership by workers (Tucker, Nock, and Toscano 1989), these organizational modes of participation are formal, structured, and nearly completely pertain to goods-producing, manufacturing workers who are represented by unions.

The second cluster contains participative approaches, varied in their depth, duration, and transformative potential, that oversee, coordinate, direct, and manage work systems. Some *consultative* practices, such as intermittently organized quality circles, or daily, weekly or monthly problem-solving and communicational meetings involving workers and managers, exist apart from everyday work routines.

Other participative innovations are comparatively more integrated into the labor process, enabling workers to participate on a permanent rather than sporadic, consultative basis. In theory, they reorganize how workers produce goods and services. They create opportunities for workers to learn new skills, acquire greater amounts of organizational/production information, use their judgement, provide meaningful input, and to make on-the-spot decisions. Particular innovations include job rotation, job enrichment, and self-managed teams and can be found across the occupational and industrial spectrum.

This paper addresses the latter cluster of EIPs—involvement at the point of production—but looks at a work setting that is different from those typically studied. Although all evidence suggests that these programs can be found across the spectrum of occupations and industries, to date we know much more about how they work in unionized, goods-producing firms (Applebaum and Batt 1994; Fantasia, Clawson, and Graham 1988; Harrison 1994; Heckscher 1988; Hodson et al. 1993; Kochan, Katz, and McKersie 1986; Wells 1987). This limited framework universalizes the experiences of a relatively small proportion of the U.S. workforce, and implicitly suggests that innovations reshaping unionized, blue-collar workplaces are a harbinger of things to come for all U.S. workers.

Because we lack a well-developed body of research about participative forms in white-collar, service, non-union firms, our model of worker participation in the U.S. economy, and our knowledge about control, skill, and autonomy, is incomplete. Moreover, our explanation for why workers' responses to EIPs range from "cynicism and active resistance to grudging acceptance and even enthusiasm" (Hodson 1995:101) is partial. Most studies focus on the cynicism, resistance, or grudging acceptance that follows when workers feel they have no choice but to participate. They either have to comply with management's request for worker involvement and intensified effort or they lose their jobs and perhaps their plant. Sociologists and industrial relations researchers have well documented U.S. workers' weakened bargaining power as employers have shipped their jobs overseas, have downsized and laid off workers, forcing workers to accept management's terms for greater involvement. Such disadvantageous conditions can well explain why much of the labor movement has resisted or only grudgingly gone along with the new participatory agenda.

But those conclusions apply to a limited set of historically specific institutional work settings. Firms that are restructuring both entrenched production processes and industrial relations systems presumably will vary significantly from firms in which labor processes

have not been as firmly institutionalized and bound by rules, which have never been characterized by adversarial labor/management relations, and whose workers demographically are comparatively new to core-sector, white-collar employment. We must ask whether, under the latter set of conditions, workers might be less likely to resist and will perhaps even embrace work reforms. And, if they embrace them, is it because they are uncritical dupes of managerial control, or is their endorsement linked in some fundamental way to the demands, constraints, and opportunities presented in their work? One purpose of the following analysis is to demonstrate that production workers' "enthusiastic effort" was explained by their belief that EI gave them new competencies in simultaneously handling and deflecting stressful work relations.

A secondary claim here is that endorsement was conditioned by the prevailing class, gender, and race hierarchy in the postindustrial United States. What we *do* know about why workers have appropriated or struggled over participation programs is limited to the experiences of male, primarily white workers, workers who have held historically secure positions in the labor market and who make up the overwhelming majority of the industrial, unionized workforce. Their institutionalized interests in regulating work, their definition of advantages gained and privileges lost, their willingness to adopt a new ethos of production, will most likely differ from the interests of relatively new workforce entrants, white women, and men and women of color who have struggled recently to make strides in an expanding, white-collar service economy.

Case Study Participants and Methods

The data analyzed here, drawn from interviews with and observations of white-collar service workers, were gathered in the course of studying an employee involvement program in a division of a large U.S. service firm: Reproco, a pseudonym for a company that manufactures photocopy and computer equipment and sells copying and other business services. These data illuminate the subjective side of a structural innovation as experienced by nonmanagerial employees.

I observed (in 10 of 40 worksites in this division), used company and business publications to do archival research, and conducted 26 in-depth, semistructured interviews (ranging from 1 to 2 ½ hours) with 10 supervisors and managers and 16 nonmanagerial employees. Of the managers and supervisors, 5 were men and 5 were women (8 white women and men, 2 women of color); of the nonmanagerial employees 11 were women and 5 were men (6 white, 10 nonwhite [African American and Hispanic]).

I interviewed Reproco employees about the programmatic aspects of employee involvement and explored their work biographies, job requirements, and experiences with the program. In particular, I explored their interpretations of employee involvement and their organizational interests in participation. Interview data were then coded to mine the subjective experiences of corporate workers at different organizational levels. This paper focuses on an unsolicited, serendipitous finding, in which workers delved at length into personal transformations that they felt had occurred as a result of training and participation. Finally, I distributed a survey to everyone I interviewed that collected data on salary, job experience, educational background, age, and family status.

The Jobs and the Workers: Skill, Compensation, Training

Reproco's employee involvement scheme was introduced to white-collar service work-

ers who labored in an unpredictable, continually changing, low-status, and socially variegated job environment. To understand the meaning of employee involvement to workers, then, requires understanding the work conditions, job rewards, and human capital of the job holders; and how the EIP attempted to smooth possible friction between these features.

First, this division of Reproco had successfully marketed a flexible service by subcontracting out business-service workers to perform photocopy work in "facilities" on the premises of other companies. Taking advantage of an economic climate in which an increasing number of U.S. firms are downsizing the total number of their permanent employees and hiring others to work for a delimited period of time (Callaghan and Hartmann 1992; Harrison 1994), Reproco subcontracted the photocopy function to companies that no longer wished to organize and manage this service themselves. Reproco employees set up photocopy rooms in other companies, staffing them with two to five machine operators; company managers trained the photocopiers and provided, in Reproco's own centralized office, backup staff and machines to accommodate changing, unpredictable photocopy loads.

This arrangement meant that while employed by Reproco, machine operators performed their work in diverse organizational settings; they were "organizational boundary spanning" workers (Wharton 1993) who continually and simultaneously had to be cognizant of their own employers' demands (Reproco) and those of the employing company in which they physically worked. They were accountable to diverse sets of "corporate clients" (who differed with respect to professional and industry status, and race and gender) as well as to their offsite supervisors.

They moved from one type of organizational setting to another over time, receiving little forewarning about when and where they would work when a contract expired. They could perform quite routine photocopy work (photocopying 8.5" × 11" documents day in and day out for an insurance company) or they could perform highly complex photocopy work, quality production of which could be urgent (photocopying plant blueprints for trouble-shooting engineers in a nuclear power facility, for example). They learned the specifications for each organization on the job.

During any given day, the machine operators' work load was unpredictable and potentially stressful: "Corporate clients," those employees bringing jobs to the machine operators, rarely knew in advance when they would need something photocopied, and they felt no compunction to try and coordinate with or subordinate their needs to the needs of others, often demanding immediate turnaround for their job. The machine operators had to use their own judgement continually, whether about scheduling copy jobs, deciding upon specifications they could provide for a client, or sending jobs they couldn't accommodate to the divisional center.

The tone of these "unscriptable" interactions could be problematic because corporate clients often viewed Reproco machine operators as low-status workers: "just button pushers," or "just copiers" (epithets reported by copiers). In this highly uncertain, social-relationally complex environment, machine operators had no official supervisor or managers, a lead operator, designated as head worker without formal managerial status or compensation, took informal responsibility for coordinating the group as a whole. This reflected Reproco's agenda to cut back layers of management (typical of many large firms [Smith 1990]); supervisors and managers from the division's center periodically visited the facilities to gather information and evaluate work performance. In significant ways, corporate clients were as much agents of control as were Reproco managers.

The job carried with it a bundle of characteristics typical of white-collar service sector jobs in the U.S. postindustrial occupational structure (Sullivan 1989). Like other white-collar working-class jobs, it offered modest pay (the typical income category checked off by machine operators on a survey was the $15,000–$19,000 category), low status in the organizational hierarchy, required only a high school degree (only one machine operator of the 16 I interviewed possessed a college degree), offered limited mobility to management, and did not demand or develop complex technical skills. But it also had characteristics of a white-collar middle-class job: Job holders developed social-relational skills and unique kinds of organizational knowledge, the work was unpredictable rather than routine, and semiautonomous rather than directed by others.

The machine operator position was highly race stratified although surprisingly gender balanced. Nearly 40 percent of the machine operators were African American and Hispanic, and these aggregate company statistics covered up much deeper regional stratification—in urban facilities there was much higher representation of men and women of color. Most men in machine operator positions were African American and Hispanic, while white men were found primarily in supervisory and management positions.

Like many other U.S. companies, Reproco's top management had formulated a new work system to increase the ability of its workforce to handle both the complexities of decentralized production and occupationally and demographically diverse work relations. To level its own organizational hierarchy, to iron out disparate work conditions and the potential tensions that might occur at their intersection, corporate-level management had implemented an employee involvement program. Reproco was attempting to manage the unpredictable work environment and to equip new workers to accommodate this unpredictability.

Reproco's EIP taught an in-depth approach to understanding the social relations of work, couched in conventional individualistic and psychologistic terms. Employees learned new communication techniques, taking turns, for example, playing different roles, simulating attack and defend situations, and learning to identify different kinds of statements and types of dialogues. They learned how to respond to aggressive and/or hostile individuals in an "appropriate" manner, in a way that supported the adage that "the customer is always right" but that allowed the worker to remain self-possessed.

The communications skills tied into the techniques they learned for determining the production of services independently of management. Employees were trained to initiate and lead problem-solving groups, for example, using their newfound communications skills to facilitate them. They learned group process procedures, such as running the meetings, identifying, describing, analyzing, and solving problems. Roundrobin techniques, which gave everyone a chance to talk and which enabled the suppression of constant talkers, formally opened up the opportunity for all to participate.

Communications, problem solving, and group process techniques were used for myriad purposes. Workers and managers used them, casually and more formally, to figure out how to work more cost effectively, to open up bottlenecks in production processes, and adjudicate conflicts between fellow employees, or between Reproco employees and clients. The whole package of techniques was designed to enhance flexibility at work, to

give company employees a chance to act on their own accumulated knowledge about the best way to conduct work tasks, to depend on co-workers to get them through difficult and unanticipated situations in the absence of formal management: in other words, to self-manage through the often choppy waters of flexible work life. Thus, despite the low level of these jobs in the overall hierarchy, there was a structural basis for involvement, for autonomous decision making, job planning, and limited self-management albeit under conditions clearly established by management.

Participating in Participation: Workers' Perceptions

Machine operators were expected to accommodate to shifting work loads and organizational contexts and to assume responsibility for basic supervisorial tasks without the formal recognition and compensation for being a manager. I anticipated, when I started interviewing the service workers in these settings, to find significant evidence of stress, noncompliance, or at least, cynicism about the conditions under which they worked. But I found instead something quite unanticipated: workers' expression of what Hodson (1991) calls "enthusiastic effort," wherein workers not only were willing to fine tune their efforts to unpredictable work loads, but they routinely praised the EIP, articulating their perceptions of benefits they received from their preparation and training for EI.

I argue that white-collar business-service workers in Reproco endorsed employee involvement because they saw it as providing a set of interpretive skills that enabled them to negotiate complex social relations in a decentralized organizational context. Working autonomously, building and using tacit knowledge, and working across the boundaries of multiple organizations implicated them in exacting and stressful work encounters. The EIP, according to my informants, had offered a means for reflecting on these encounters and to interpret them, thus increasing workers' feelings of efficacy in controlling them. In other words, workers viewed the EIP as critical to on-the-job survival.

Their interpretations of these advantages are situated within a larger context of class and race stratification. Most people hired as machine operators had limited educational backgrounds and occupational histories and had experienced rocky transitions into even this low level of the corporate work world. Their chances for upward mobility into professional and managerial occupations were statistically narrow. I argue that their responses to Reproco's EIP were thus conditioned by the prevailing institutional sources of race, class, and gender inequality constraining their labor market choices. The EIP training and skills positioned them with a new cultural capital (Lamont and Lareau 1988), a body of knowledge about and awareness of interactions in the corporate world; workers believed this would help them succeed in their current position but also with long-term professional goals.

It is impossible to say with certainty that what workers identify as a new set of skills would genuinely lead to new opportunity, or that their perceptions of control translate into real control over interactions; nevertheless their impression of opportunity and advantage is an important ingredient in their willingness to accommodate themselves to the chaotic job of machine operator.

Building the Self, Learning Interaction

Machine operators repeatedly emphasized the sharpening of four skills: interpreting others' actions and meaning; taking the role of others; "depersonalizing" or transcending particular conflicts; and gaining confidence to participate to a greater degree.

Anita, a pseudonym for a 33-year-old African American woman who had worked for Reproco as a machine operator in various sites for 11 years, described her experiences and thoughts in painstaking terms that were echoed by many of the machine operators. Anita started working for Reproco as a temporary worker when, after a year of college, she was told that she would not be allowed to return due to poor grades.

Reproco's EIP had required her to participate in meetings and problem-solving groups for the first time in her life, a process that appeared to have been personally difficult. She said she had had to become involved:

> One step at a time. Its', ah, 'cause I don't want to get out there and fall flat on my face. But people are like taking numbers. "Oh god, there she is. She was never here before. What's she doing back there?" 'Cause you're seen, you know, you become more focused, you know, they can see it. "Gosh, she's in view."

Even though major life experiences such as having children and raising them as a single parent had forced her to be a "leader" (her word) in her family, it was only recently, in the course of participating in a few problem-solving groups, that she felt other people had "brought her into focus," recognizing about her, "Oh, she *does* have a mouth, and, oh, she *does* have thought."

When I asked Anita how EI might be useful to her in the way she performed her job—serving professional "clients" in a facility in a large architectural firm—she reflected that:

There's a way that you want to be perceived. There's a way that you want people to respond to you. You don't want people snapping at you. You don't want people, ah, just tuning you out. You want people to try and understand what's going on with you and where you're coming from.

I have to try and understand what the other person's point is. And to understand the other person's point you have to step out of your shoes for a moment and step in theirs. What they want. What they require . . . I come to work, put myself in the customer's position. Well, you don't want nobody snapping at you. Because if you snap at someone too much, it's a snap back attitude. But you have to remove yourself and think about the other person. So, yes, I've taken it and put it into everyday life.

Learning to detect and gaining the ability to deflect the "snap back attitude" of other people had been eye opening for Anita; she spoke of becoming "voiced" her word, and visible in her facility work group when she gained the ability to interpret the needs of clients and co-workers, and to more successfully manage perceptions of herself.

The notion of stepping into someone else's shoes was echoed by Sally, a white re-entry woman in her fifties, who commented that she had learned new tools to

. . . look at their [her clients'] perspective as well as your own and how you're trying to solve the problem. So, I try to . . . get their perspective of it and see if I can work around it.

This growing awareness of interpersonal dynamics and their implications for work was reported by men as well, who noted similar processes that had occurred in both training and in on-the-job deployment of new communications skills at Reproco. Ralph, for example, emphasized how he felt his ability to interpret others' behavior, to gain some control over interactions with others, had grown and that he felt mentally better equipped to control his reactions to others' behavior.

Ralph was an ex-Marine and Vietnam veteran, one of 10 children raised in a Hispanic family in the Bronx who had moved through a series of working-class, white-collar jobs, and had unsuccessfully tried to establish a small business, before working for Reproco. He emphasized that he had never had professional role models in his family and that he ultimately wished to run his own small business (a goal he felt he was getting closer to because of his experience with Reproco as a machine operator in the engineering division of a nuclear power plant facility). When I asked Ralph whether EIP had assisted him in any way he answered:

Yeah, the communicative skills impressed me. They showed me how I could get information from the customer in a clear way, *taught me how to read body language.* I used to say "Here's your copies, now get out of here." Now I have to make sure I'm communicating, *to understand their needs.* The customer is important and I have to figure out what they need and I'm trying to have more sensitivity to their needs.

In Ralph's eyes, the ability to interpret others' needs and to avoid overreacting to people had enabled him to master his ability to avoid and/or manage crisis, an ability he claimed was newfound. He spoke of avoiding "chain reactions and repetition of problems" (referring to business misfortunes in the past), and how the problem identifying and solving process had "organized his problem solving" ability (as did a number of other respondents, he elaborated in some detail how he used this in church and family affairs). In his thinking, these skills had very tangible outcomes: he saw them as necessary for eventually having his own business. He remarked:

> I don't want to reach the point where I'll have multiples of problems. I don't want to make the mistakes others have made. I want to he able to identify and solve before problems turn into a big crisis. I always wanted to have my own business but I've always been insecure *about my knowledge of people,* customers.

Having dropped out of Howard University and then community college for financial reasons, and having worked at two temporary clerical positions before joining Reproco, James, a 29-year-old African American man, was understandably committed to the company: The job security, the benefits package, the training he had undergone, and prospects for diverse job opportunities, were attractive even if limited. He started as a machine operator and at the time of our interview was working as a lead operator, coordinating seven operators. James's facility was one of the few that was not located inside another company; it was in a regional center and accepted copy jobs from firms in the area. This entailed a more complex set of negotiations with people from a range of diverse organizations.

He felt that training in group process and communications had changed his work life and his ability to effectively work in a job that was de facto a supervisorial job. Moreover, he emphasized that he had imported the tools and insights into other realms of his life, a claim mentioned by nearly all of my respondents. He spontaneously described his feeling that clear and undefensive communication enabled him to coordinate the work of

the machine operators and deal with clients more authoritatively:

> . . . like I said, what I've learned here and dealing with people, I've taken outside. And I transfer what I learned and put it into my daily life and it helped me to, I learned how to, like I said before, *how to listen, and how to make sure that I understand exactly what someone is telling me* . . . just to listen and see if I'm able to do as someone is instructing me to do or if I'm able to do that . . .

Using the technique of getting people to clarify their statements, confusion about which could evoke the wrath of customers (and had, on occasion), enabled him to

> . . . test my understanding, make sure I understand exactly what someone was telling me. (I get them) to repeat it, to clarify it. That way, you won't cause any problems at the end because I . . . if I asked you again to repeat it, to clarify, then we won't have any problems at the end. I find that it helps me to avoid conflict, helps me to resolve conflict . . . I find I help a lot of other people resolve conflicts and issues in their lives . . . It gives me a way of helping them see things from another perspective and in a nonthreatening way, it's kinda weird.

New to him, learning to pay attention to the dynamics of conversation and interaction added to his belief that he was better able to organize and accomplish complex jobs. In one recent job for which he could take credit, a leading chemical company had contracted the services of this facility to photocopy volumes of material for a federal investigation. James had not only had to organize the entire production process, but he also had to coordinate dozens of temporary workers brought in solely for this purpose and negotiate extensively with Reproco divisional-level management and with representatives of the federal government.

Being trained in communication and involvement, acquiring knowledge about work relations, I argue, built workers' perception of greater efficacy in interaction. The formal techniques of EI also provided openings for people to experience validation of different kinds of verbal participation by the organization. Gaining the confidence to talk, and thus not feeling completely at the mercy of others who could monopolize interaction, was another outcome of the EIP identified by nearly all my respondents.

For example, linguistic competence itself can be an important barrier for individuals who wish to deal effectively with co-workers and clients. For one Hispanic woman—for whom English was her second, extremely well-spoken language—differences in language competency translated, in her mind, to inferior thought itself.

Hilda's experience shows how one of the techniques followed in EI groups—the round-robin approach, wherein everyone around the room has to verbally contribute—helped her overcome genuine terror over language inadequacies and to place her own insights and contributions on a par with those she perceived as being "smarter," "more impressive" (who happened to be experienced male co-workers). She described her introduction to an EI group in the following way:

> I remember when we were first trained in leadership through quality, that you do the meetings and we were learning the lingo—seeking information, giving information—normally in a crowd full of people I would not talk because I'd figure—I would feel—the barrier of language would come up, the barriers of, *well, these are men that have been doing this for years,* maybe they know better than I do so let me shut up and not get involved . . .

They were more impressive. And then once the employee involvement makes everybody get involved and the best thing about it, which I loved was that nobody is—when you're brainstorming, no one is allowed to criticize your idea. Even if it's weird, even if it's the worst idea you could ever make and you know it and it sorta comes out of your lips—nobody is allowed to make a comment because that's what brainstorming is. *Free ideas without an evaluation on them.* So the facilitator was, "No, no, no, you can't make a comment" (Author's note: Her facilitator stopped people from interrupting her). And he makes you feel better because you can say anything and you don't feel like, intimidated by the boys network.

Her insights about how public involvement and visibility rattled her were vivid in equating language mastery with competency itself:

> . . . in meetings, as soon as you said a meeting—I would have a fit. My palms would sweat. I would start sweating and I would be like, "Please God, don't let them ask me anything." *Because my accent would automatically get very heavy and my brain was not translating at the pace that it normally does.* So my thoughts were coming in two languages . . . You know that I had a stomach ache. But I had to think real good because I wanted to say something that was intelligent. But it made me say something and it made me open up a little bit more in meetings and things like that.

These insights and experiences were seconded by others. Hillary, a 48-year-old African American woman, identified the importance of understanding hidden principles of communication, which she learned in her in-depth training session, for independently organizing cooperative relations in the course of working. She appreciated the participative approach to problem solving because it meant that groups had to "acknowledge that a person has made a proposal instead of *just ignoring it and going on,*" a kind of silencing process in which she felt herself to have been on the receiving end.

Speaking especially of one communication technique (learning how to clarify statements and requests) she pointed out the virtues of using this technique for helping people better understand cultural complexity and smoothing out tensions incurred in the process of accomplishing work tasks:

> These are all behaviors that this training helped us to identify, and that's part of the first step of being able to change anybody's behavior, *is to recognize it.* And once you are aware of it then you can begin to change it, address it. One of the areas that they taught and I was unaware of this until this training so this is very key for me, was the—what they call, clarifying, the clarifying behavior. To ask a clarifying question as opposed to making an assumption that is wrong. Because our language can be very, ah, ah, *can have many meanings,* depending on voice inflection and ah, you know, a person can say something and they can mean something totally different from what you understand.

Pondering meaning, interpreting action, and taking the perspective of others; using the communication tools and an interpretive framework to strengthen one's voice and efficacy in a complex work setting; to become more involved in group processes and decision making, were themes raised over and over and spontaneously in interviews with machine operators. The perceived benefits that service workers identified cemented their commitments to Reproco, even when it

was questionable whether these benefits lent themselves to meaningful upward mobility or wage improvement. In these informants' minds, new interactional insights and skills were meaningful if intangible assets.

"Procedural Resistance": Using Employee Involvement Techniques to Resist Clients

Workers' beliefs about how they benefited were bolstered in additional and comparatively concrete ways by the EI training. The EIP provided the techniques for "procedural resistance," a means for machine operators to coopt unreasonably insistent, contemptuous and otherwise difficult corporate clients, many of them professionals who could be a more immediate, intense, and stressful source of control than off-site supervisors or managers. Machine operators appropriated these simple techniques to enlist clients themselves as partners in the participative agenda and to set limits on their demands.

Machine operators reported having talked clients into helping finish copy jobs that operators couldn't complete themselves (for example, collating particularly complex documents); drawing clients into the process of planning the work flow; getting clients to take joint responsibility for decisions about working overtime to complete urgently needed jobs; and using simple surveys to solicit feedback about machine operators' job performance as well as ideas about improving the service.

Using communications skills with the goal of sharing information with clients, encouraging them to participate in brainstorming about techniques for completing work, and eliciting feedback about service production and improvement of service delivery gave machine operators a way to negotiate competing demands and defuse potentially hostile client-operator interactions within the terms of the new participative program.

This ability to use authorized procedures as tools of resistance, to establish parameters on their work loads, was an important defense mechanism for the operators. Importantly, workers didn't resist new techniques themselves, but they used the techniques to resist and co-opt negative, antagonistic clients.

Conclusion

In many ways, Reproco's EIP is a stunning example of how contemporary managers draw on prevailing popular ideologies about participation to extract greater effort from workers. The machine operators in this study willingly directed their own work efforts day in and day out, engaged in group decision making, took risks in using their own judgement for production decisions, and represented the interests of Reproco by absorbing conflict and dispute in relations with corporate clients. In other words, this program coordinated workers' and management's goals, a participative system of control (Dickson 1981) highly successful in "securing yet obscuring" (Burawoy 1979:30) workers' consent.

Living up to the gravest concerns that observers have about EIP in U.S. workplaces, Reproco's system has intensified everyday work life for poorly compensated workers. The findings presented here confirm one pessimistic claim that has been made by those studying EIP: that these innovations may strengthen management's capacity to extract additional effort from workers by concealing job speedups and work intensification behind the language of enrichment (cf. O'Reilly 1994).

But what this research makes clear is that some workers have compelling reasons to participate in new systems and may consent to the conditions described throughout this paper because they perceive unanticipated payoffs and opportunities. For one thing, low-level, white-collar service workers endorsed Reproco's EIP precisely because the program and its micro-level techniques, in their eyes, heightened their sense of greater efficacy in managing those conditions. Their endorsement, then, was conditioned by the structural arrangements and the social relations of their jobs.

For another, workers saw these new skills as part of a process of career building. They envisioned taking these skills and applying them to their own small businesses, to different positions in other large corporations, and to higher level positions inside Reproco. Thus, while Reproco's participative arrangements entailed significant intensity of work effort and commitment, they also created a context for workers to develop new skills, seen by workers as relevant to future opportunity. They were not technological skills, much emphasized by the literature on involvement and worker participation; rather they were social-relational skills that were potentially transferable to other white-collar, service contexts, and perhaps to low levels of supervision and management. Participation in participation, then, ostensibly represented a new step on a constrained mobility ladder.

Broadly, the acquisition of these skills is important for workers who have historically been excluded from core-sector, permanent job opportunities. Much research has been done on the difficulty African American and Hispanic youth, for example, have in making the transition from school to paid work (see Powers, forthcoming, for an overview of this transition). Neckerman and Kirshenman's (1991) important article on the way racist assumptions circumscribe employers' recruitment, selection, and hiring practices similarly underscores the achievement of those African Americans and Hispanics who have made it into the secure, albeit lowest employed, ranks of large, urban, white-collar firms. Neckerman and Kirschenman emphasize the significance of the very skills, identified by my informants, that employers use to screen out many people of color in the hiring process: Employers look for "appropriate interaction and conversational style—in short, shared culture" (1991:442); "job applicants must be sensitive to verbal and nonverbal cues and to the hidden agenda underlying interviewers' questions" (1991:442). These "social skills and cultural compatibility" are used to make future promotion decisions.

These conclusions are echoed by Moss and Tilly (1995), who analyze the way employers discriminate against African American men in their hiring practices. Employers feel that African American men lack the appropriate "soft" skills (communication and people skills, teamwork skills, demeanor and so forth) that are crucial to successful outcomes in the post-industrial workplace.

My respondents have made it past this screening process, laden with negative assumptions about race and class, and are now struggling to survive—to do their jobs on terms acceptable to the corporation, to achieve some degree of personal and occupational efficacy in order to work with others. They have found success in Reproco's white-collar ranks, doing work that is unskilled technically, but that builds white-collar interpersonal skills that can be transferred to other corporate contexts; in a position that pays low wages but offers a benefits package and secure employment; working in demographically and occupationally heterogeneous settings that build their interactional skill set.

Even if these new skills don't lead directly to upward mobility, even if structural reorganization flattens hierarchies and runs counter to the expansion of vertical opportunities (a structural trend affecting workers across the occupational spectrum [Smith 1993]), lower-level workers can compete for new lateral opportunities and learn to more effectively manipulate their work environments to defend their own interests and existing status, an important skill noted recently by sociologists studying other work settings (Paules 1991). They can learn to better negotiate the day-to-day operations of workplaces and to exercise authority in relations with co-workers. Although a beginning, such individual paths of change may have the long-term effect of transforming the workplace hierarchies that have consolidated around race, gender, and class.

REFERENCES

Appelbaum, Eileen, and Rosemary Batt. 1994. *The New American Workplace*. Ithaca: ILR Press.

Bate. S. P., and J. Murphy. 1981. "Can joint consultation become employee participation?" *Journal of Management Studies* 18:389–409.

Burawoy, Michael. 1979. *Manufacturing Consent*. Chicago: University of Chicago Press.

Callaghan, Polly, and Heidi Hartmann. 1992. *Contingent Work: A Chart Book on Parttime and Temporary Employment*. Washington, D.C.: Institute for Women's Policy Research/Economic Policy Institute.

Dickson, John. 1981. "Participation as a means of organizational control." *Journal of Management Studies* 18:159–176.

Edwards, Richards. 1979. *Contested Terrain*. New York: Basic Books.

Fantasia, Rick, Dan Clawson, and Gregory Graham. 1988. "A critical view of worker participation in American industry." *Work and Occupations* 15:468–488.

Harrison, Bennett. 1994. *Lean and Mean*. New York: Basic Books.

Heckscher, Charles. 1988. *The New Unionism*. New York: Basic Books.

Hodson, Randy. 1991. "The active worker: Compliance and autonomy at the workplace." *Journal of Contemporary Ethnography* 20:47–78.

———. 1995. "Worker resistance: An underdeveloped concept in the sociology of work." *Economic and Industrial Democracy* 16:79–110.

Hodson, Randy, Sean Creighton, Cheryl Jamison, Sabine Rieble, and Sandy Welsh. 1993. "Is worker solidarity undermined by autonomy and participation? Patterns from the ethnographic literature." *American Sociological Review* 58:398–416.

Kochan, Thomas, Harry Katz, and Robert McKersie. 1986. *The Transformation of American Industrial Relations*. New York: Basic Books.

Lamont, Michelle, and Annette Lareau. 1988. "Cultural capital: Allusions, gaps, and glissandos in recent theoretical developments." *Sociological Theory* 6:153–168.

Leidner, Robin. 1993. *Fast Food, Fast Talk.* Berkeley: University of Caliornia Press.

Moss, Philip, and Chris Tilly. 1995. "'Soft' skills and race: An investigation of Black men's employment problems." *Russell Sage Foundation Working Paper #80.*

Neckerman, Kathryn, and Joleen Kirschenman. 1991. "Hiring strategies, racial bias, and inner-city workers." *Social Problems* 38:433–447.

O'Reilly, Jacqueline. 1994. *Banking on Flexibility.* Aldershot: Avebury.

Paules, Greta. 1991. *Dishing it Out.* Philadelphia: Temple University Press.

Powers, Brian. Forthcoming. *Shadowed Passages: Remaking Inequality from High School to the Workplace.*

Smith, Vicki. 1990. *Managing in the Corporate Interest.* Berkeley: University of California Press.

———. 1993. "Flexibility in work and employment: The Impact on women." *Research in the Sociology of Organizations* 11:195–216.

Stern, Robert. 1988. "Participation by representation: Workers on boards of directors in the United States and abroad." *Work and Occupations* 15:396–422.

Sullivan, Teresa. 1989. "Women and minority workers in the new economy." *Work and Occupations* 16:393–415.

Tausky, Curt, and Anthony Chelte. 1988. "Workers' participation." *Work and Occupations* 15:363–373.

Tucker, James, Steven Nock, and David Toscano. 1989. "Employee ownership and perceptions of work: The effect of an employee stock ownership plan." *Work and Occupations* 16:26–42.

U.S. Department of Labor. 1994. *Fact Finding Report: Commission on the Future of Worker-Management Relations.*

Wells, Donald. 1987. *Empty Promises: Quality of Working Life Programs and the Labor Movement.* New York: Monthly Review Press.

Wharton, Amy. 1993. "The affective consequences of service work: Managing emotions on the job." *Work and Occupations* 20:205–232.

42

"Their Logic Against Them"
Contradictions in Sex, Race, and Class in Silicon Valley

Karen J. Hossfeld

Karen J. Hossfeld is associate professor of sociology at San Francisco State University. The research described in this reading is part of a larger study Hossfeld conducted on immigrant women workers in Silicon Valley.

The bosses here have this type of reasoning like a seesaw. One day it's "you're paid less because women are different than men," or "immigrants

From "'Their Logic Against Them': Contradictions in Sex, Race, and Class in Silicon Valley" by Karen J. Hossfeld in *Women Workers and Global Restructuring,* edited by Kathryn Ward. Used by permission of the publisher, Cornell University Press.

need less to get by." The next day it's "you're all just workers here—no special treatment just because you're female or foreigners."

Well, they think they're pretty clever with their doubletalk, and that we're just a bunch of dumb aliens. But it takes two to use a seesaw. What we're gradually figuring out here is how to use their own logic against them.

—FILIPINA CIRCUIT BOARD ASSEMBLER IN SILICON VALLEY (EMPHASIS ADDED)

This chapter examines how contradictory ideologies about sex, race, class, and nationality are used as forms of both labor control and labor resistance in the capitalist workplace today. Specifically, I look at the workplace relationships between Third World immigrant women production workers and their predominantly white male managers in high-tech manufacturing industry in Silicon Valley, California. My findings indicate that in workplaces where managers and workers are divided by sex and race, class struggle can and does take gender- and race-specific forms. Managers encourage women immigrant workers to identify with their gender, racial, and national identities when the managers want to "distract" the workers from their *class* concerns about working conditions. Similarly, when workers have workplace needs that actually *are* defined by gender, nationality, or race, managers tend to deny these identities and to stress the workers' generic class position. Immigrant women workers have learned to redeploy their managers' gender and racial tactics to their own advantage, however, in order to gain more control over their jobs. As the Filipina worker quoted at the beginning of the chapter so aptly said, they have learned to use managers' "own logic against them." . . .

This chapter draws from a larger study of the articulation of sex, race, class, and nationality in the lives of immigrant women high-tech workers (Hossfeld 1988b). Empirical data draw on more than two hundred interviews conducted between 1982 and 1986 with Silicon Valley workers; their family members, employers, and managers; and labor and community organizers. Extensive in-depth interviews were conducted with eighty-four immigrant women, representing twenty-one Third World nationalities, and with forty-one employers and managers, who represented twenty-three firms. All but

five of these management representatives were U.S.-born white males. All of the workers and managers were employed in Santa Clara County, California, firms that engaged in some aspect of semiconductor "chip" manufacturing. I observed production at nineteen of these firms. . . .

Silicon Valley

The Prototype

"Silicon Valley" refers to the microelectronics-based high-tech industrial region located just south of San Francisco in Santa Clara County, California. The area has been heralded as an economic panacea and as a regional prototype for localities around the globe that seek rapid economic growth and incorporation into the international market. Representatives from more than two thousand local and national governments, from People's Republic of China delegations to the queen of England, have visited the valley in search of a model for their own industrial revitalization. They have been awed by the sparkling, clean-looking facilities and the exuberant young executives who claim to have made riches overnight. But the much-fetishized Silicon Valley "model" that so many seek to emulate implies more than just the potential promise of jobs, revenue, growth, and participation in the technological "revolution." . . .

Class Structure and the Division of Labor

Close to 200,000 people—one out of every four employees in the San Jose Metropolitan Statistical Area labor force—work in Silicon Valley's microelectronics industry. There are more than 800 manufacturing firms that hire ten or more people each, including 120 "large" firms that each count over 250 employees. An even larger number of small firms hire fewer than ten employees apiece. Approximately half of this high-tech labor force—100,000 employees—works in production-related work: at least half of these workers—an estimated 50,000 to 70,000—are in low-paying, semiskilled operative jobs (Siegel and Borock 1982; *Annual Planning Information* 1983).

The division of labor within the industry is dramatically skewed according to gender and race. Although women account for close to half of the total paid labor force in Santa Clara County both inside and outside the industry, only 18 percent of the managers, 17 percent of the professional employees, and 25 percent of the technicians are female. Conversely, women hold at least 68 percent and by some reports as many as 85 to 90 percent of the valley's high-tech operative jobs. In the companies examined in my study, women made up an average of 90 percent of the assembly and operative workers. Only rarely do they work as production managers or supervisors, the management area that works most closely with the operatives.

Similar disparities exist vis-à-vis minority employment. According to the 1980 census, 26.51 percent of the civilian work force of Santa Clara County was composed of racial minorities. Fifteen percent were Hispanic (all races); 7.5 percent were Asian–Pacific Islanders; 3 percent were Black; 0.5 percent were Native-American; and 0.2 percent were listed as "other races—not Hispanic" (*Annual Planning Information* 1983:96–97). Over 75 percent of the Hispanics were of Mexican descent. Of the 102,000 Asian–Pacific Islanders counted in the 1980 census as living in the area, roughly 28 percent were Filipino or of Filipino descent; 22 percent each were Japanese and Chinese; 11 percent were Vietnamese; 6 percent were Korean; 5 percent were Asian Indian; and less than 2 percent

each were of other national origins (*Annual Planning Information* 1983:64).

Since the census was taken, influxes of refugees from Indochina have quadrupled the number of Vietnamese, Laotians, and Cambodians in the area: as of early 1984, there were an estimated forty-five thousand Southeast Asian refugees in Santa Clara County, as well as a smaller but growing number of refugees from other regions such as Central America. I have talked with Silicon Valley production workers from at least thirty Third World nations. In addition to the largest groups, whose members are from Mexico, Vietnam, the Philippines, and Korea, workers hail from China, Cambodia, Laos, Thailand, Malaysia, Indonesia, India, Pakistan, Iran, Ethiopia, Haiti, Cuba, El Salvador, Nicaragua, Guatemala, and Venezuela. There are also small groups from southern Europe, particularly Portugal and Greece.

Within the microelectronics industry, 12 percent of the managers, 16 percent of the professionals, and 18 percent of the technicians are minorities—although they are concentrated at the lower-paying and less powerful ends of these categories. An estimated 50 to 75 percent of the operative jobs are thought to be held by minorities.[1] My study suggests that the figure may be closer to 80 percent.

Both employers and workers interviewed in this study agreed that the lower the skill and pay level of the job, the higher the percentage of Third World immigrant women who were employed. Thus assembly work, which is the least skilled and lowest-paid production job, tends to be done predominantly by Third World women. Entry-level production workers, who work in job categories such as semiconductor processing and assembly, earn an average of $4.50 to $5.50 an hour; experienced workers in these jobs earn from $5.50 to $8.50. At the subcontracting assembly plants I observed, immigrant women accounted for 75 to 100 percent of the production labor force. At only one of these plants did white males account for more than 2 percent of the production workers. More than 90 percent of the managers and owners at these businesses were white males, however.

This occupational structure is typical of the industry's division of labor nationwide. The percentage of women of color in operative jobs is fairly standardized throughout various high-tech centers; what varies is *which* minority groups are employed, not the job categories in which they are employed.

Obviously, there is tremendous cultural and historical variation both between and within the diverse national groups that my informants represent. Here I emphasize their commonalities. Their collective experience is based on their jobs, present class status, recent uprooting, and immigration. Many are racial and ethnic minorities for the first time. Finally, they have in common their gender and their membership in family households.

Labor Control on the Shop Floor

Gender and Racial Logic

In Silicon Valley production shops, the ideological battleground is an important arena of class struggle for labor control. Management frequently calls upon ideologies and arrangements concerning sex and race, as well as class, to manipulate worker consciousness and to legitimate the hierarchical division of labor. Management taps both traditional popular stereotypes about the presumed lack of status and limited abilities of women, minorities, and immigrants and the workers' own fears, concerns, and sense of priorities as immigrant women.

But despite management's success in disempowering and devaluing labor, immigrant women workers have co-opted some of these ideologies and have developed others of their own, playing on management's prejudices to the workers' own advantage. In so doing, the workers turn the "logic" of capital against managers, as they do the intertwining logics of patriarchy and racism. . . .

From interviews with Silicon Valley managers and employers, it is evident that high-tech firms find immigrant women particularly appealing workers not only because they are "cheap" and considered easily "expendable" but also because management can draw on and further exploit preexisting patriarchal and racist ideologies and arrangements that have affected these women's consciousness and realities. In their dealings with the women, managers fragment the women's multifaceted identities into falsely separated categories of "worker," "ethnic," and "woman." The effect is to increase and play off the workers' vulnerabilities and splinter their consciousness. But I also found limited examples of the women drawing strength from their multifaceted experiences and developing a unified consciousness with which to confront their oppressions. These instances of how the workers have manipulated management's ideology are important not only in their own right but as models. To date, though, management holds the balance of power in this ideological struggle.

I label management's tactics "gender-specific" and "racial-specific" forms of labor control and struggle, or gender and racial "logic". I use the term *capital logic* to refer to strategies by capitalists to increase profit maximization. Enforcement by employers of a highly stratified class division of labor as a form of labor control is one such strategy. Similarly, I use the terms *gender logic* and *racial logic* to refer to strategies to promote gender and racial hierarchies. Here I am concerned primarily with the ways in which employers and managers devise and incorporate gender and racial logic in the interests of capital logic. Attempts to legitimate inequality form my main examples.

I focus primarily on managers' "gender-specific" tactics because management uses race-specific (il)logic much less directly in dealing with workers. Management clearly draws on racist assumptions in hiring and dealing with its work force, but usually it makes an effort to conceal its racism from workers. Management recognizes, to varying degrees, that the appearance of blatant racism against workers is not acceptable, mainly because immigrants have not sufficiently internalized racism to respond to it positively. Off the shop floor, however, the managers' brutal and open racism toward workers was apparent during "private" interviews. Managers' comments demonstrate that racism is a leading factor in capital logic but that management typically disguises racist logic by using the more socially acceptable "immigrant logic." Both American and immigrant workers tend to accept capital's relegation of immigrants to secondary status in the labor market.

Conversely, "gender logic" is much less disguised: management uses it freely and directly to control workers. Patriarchal and sexist ideology is *not* considered inappropriate. Because women workers themselves have already internalized patriarchal ideology, they are more likely to "agree" with or at least accept it than they are racist assumptions. This chapter documents a wide range of sexist assumptions that management employs in order to control and divide workers. . . .

The Logic of "Secondary" Work

Central to gender-specific capital logic is the assumption that women's paid work is both secondary and temporary. More than 70 percent of the employers and 80 percent of the

women workers I interviewed stated that a woman's primary jobs are those of wife, mother, and homemaker, even when she works full time in the paid labor force. Because employers view women's primary job as in the home, and they assume that, prototypically, every woman is connected to a man who is bringing in a larger paycheck, they claim that women do not need to earn a full living wage. Employers repeatedly asserted that they believed the low-level jobs were filled only by women because men could not afford to or would not work for such low wages.

Indeed, many of the women would not survive on what they earned unless they pooled resources. For some, especially the nonimmigrants, low wages did mean dependency on men—or at least on family networks and household units. None of the women I interviewed—immigrant or nonimmigrant—lived alone. Yet most of them would be financially better off without their menfolk. For most of the immigrant women, their low wages were the most substantial and steady source of their family's income. *Eighty percent of the immigrant women workers in my study were the largest per annum earners in their households.*

Even when their wages were primary—the main or only family income—the women still considered men to be the major breadwinners. The women considered their waged work as secondary, both in economic value and as a source of identity. Although most agreed that women and men who do exactly the same jobs should be paid the same, they had little expectation that as women they would be eligible for higher-paying "male" jobs. While some of these women—particularly the Asians—believed they could overcome racial and class barriers in the capitalist division of labor, few viewed gender as a division that could be changed. While they may believe that hard work can overcome many obstacles and raise their *families'* socioeconomic class standing, they do not feel that their position in the gender division of labor will change. Many, of course, expect or hope for better jobs for themselves—and others expect or hope to leave the paid labor force altogether—but few wish to enter traditional male jobs or to have jobs that are higher in status or earnings than the men in their families.

The majority of women who are earning more than their male family members view their situation negatively and hope it will change soon. They do not want to earn less than they currently do; rather, they want their menfolk to earn more. This was true of women in all the ethnic groups. The exceptions—a vocal minority—were mainly Mexicanas. Lupe, a high-tech worker in her twenties, explained:

> Some of the girls I work with are ridiculous—they think if they earn more than their husbands it will hurt the men's pride. They play up to the machismo. . . . I guess it's not entirely ridiculous, because some of them regularly come in with black eyes and bruises, so the men are something they have to reckon with. But, my God, if I had a man like that I would leave. . . .
>
> My boyfriend's smart enough to realize that we need my paycheck to feed us and my kids. He usually brings home less than I do, and we're both damn grateful for every cent that either of us makes. When I got a raise he was very happy—I think he feels more relieved, not more resentful. But then, he's not a very typical man, no? Anyway, he'd probably change if we got married and had kids of his own—that's when they start wanting to be the king of their castle.

A Korean immigrant woman in her thirties told how her husband was so adamant that she not earn more than he and that the men in the household be the family's main supporters that each time she cashed her paycheck she gave some of her earnings to her teenaged son to turn over to the father as part of the earnings from his part-time job. She was upset about putting her son in a position of being deceitful to his father, but both mother and son agreed it was the only alternative to the father's otherwise dangerous, violent outbursts.

As in the rest of America, in most cases, the men earned more in those households where both the women and men worked regularly. In many of the families, however, the men tended to work less regularly than the women and to have higher unemployment rates. While most of the families vocally blamed very real socioeconomic conditions for the unemployment, such as declines in "male" industrial sector jobs, many women also felt that their husbands took out their resentment on their families. A young Mexicana, who went to a shelter for battered women after her husband repeatedly beat her, described her extreme situation:

> He knows it's not his fault or my fault that he lost his job: they laid off almost his whole shift. But he acts like I keep my job just to spite him, and it's gotten so I'm so scared of him. Sometimes I think he'd rather kill me or have us starve than watch me go to work and bring home pay. He doesn't want to hurt me, but he is so hurt inside because he feels he has failed as a man.

Certainly not all laid-off married men go to the extreme of beating their wives, but the majority of married women workers whose husbands had gone through periods of unemployment said that the men treated other family members significantly worse when they were out of work. When capitalism rejects male workers, they often use patriarchal channels to vent their anxieties. In a world where men are defined by their control over their environment, losing control in one arena, such as that of the work world, may lead them to tighten control in another arena in which they still have power—the family. This classic cycle is not unique to Third World immigrant communities, but as male unemployment increases in these communities, so may the cycle of male violence.

Even some of the women who recognize the importance of their economic role feel that their status and identity as wage earners are less important than those of men. Many of the women feel that men work not only for income but for respect and dignity. They see their own work as less noble. Although some said they derive satisfaction from their ability to hold a job, none of the women considered her job to be a primary part of her identity or a source of self-esteem. These women see themselves as responsible primarily for the welfare of their families: their main identity is as mother, wife, sister, and daughter, not as worker. Their waged work is seen as an extension of caring for their families. It is not a question of *choosing* to work—they do so out of economic necessity.

When I asked whether their husbands' and fathers' waged work could also be viewed as an extension of familial duties, the women indicated that they definitely perceived a difference. Men's paid labor outside the home was seen as integral both to the men's self-definition and to their responsibility vis-à-vis the family; conversely, women's labor force participation was seen as contradictory both to the women's self-image and to their definitions of female responsibility.

Many immigrant women see their wage contribution to the family's economic survival not only as secondary but as *temporary,* even when they have held their jobs for several years. They expect to quit their production jobs after they have saved enough money to go to school, stay home full time,

or open a family business. In actuality, however, most of them barely earn enough to live on, let alone to save, and women who think they are signing on for a brief stint may end up staying in the industry for years.

That these workers view their jobs as temporary has important ramifications for both employers and unions, as well as for the workers themselves. When workers believe they are on board a company for a short time, they are more likely to put up with poor working conditions, because they see them as short term. A Mexican woman who used to work in wafer fabrication reflected on the consequences of such rationalization:

> I worked in that place for four years, and it was really bad—the chemicals knocked you out, and the pay was very low. My friends and me, though, we never made a big deal about it, because we kept thinking we were going to quit soon anyway, so why bother. . . . We didn't really think of it as our career or anything—just as something we had to do until our fortune changed. It's not exactly the kind of work a girl dreams of herself doing.
>
> My friend was engaged when we started working there, and she thought she was going to get married any day, and then she'd quit. Then, after she was married, she thought she'd quit as soon as she got pregnant. . . . She has two kids now, and she's still there. Now she's saying she'll quit real soon, because her husband's going to get a better job any time now, and she'll finally get to stay home, like she wants.

Ironically, these women's jobs may turn out to be only temporary, but for different reasons and with different consequences than they planned. Industry analysts predict that within the next decade the majority of

Silicon Valley production jobs may well be automated out of existence (Carey 1984). Certainly for some of the immigrant women, their dreams of setting aside money for occupational training or children's schooling or to open a family business or finance relatives' immigration expenses do come true, but not for most. Nonetheless, almost without exception, the women production workers I interviewed—both immigrant and nonimmigrant—saw their present jobs as temporary.

Employers are thus at an advantage in hiring these women at low wages and with little job security. They can play on the women's *own* consciousness as wives and mothers whose primary identities are defined by home and familial roles. While the division of labor prompts the workers to believe that women's waged work is less valuable than men's, the women workers themselves arrive in Silicon Valley with this ideology already internalized.

A young Filipina woman, who was hired at a walk-in interview at an electronics production facility, experienced a striking example of the contradictions confronting immigrant women workers in the valley. Neither she nor her husband, who was hired the same day, had any previous related work experience or degrees. Yet her husband was offered an entry-level job as a technician, while she was offered an assembly job paying three dollars per hour less. The personnel manager told her husband that he would "find [the technician job] more interesting than assembly work." The woman had said in the interview that she wanted to be considered for a higher-paying job because she had two children to support. The manager refused to consider her for a different job, she said, and told her that "it will work out fine for you, though, because with your husband's job, and you *helping out* [emphasis added] you'll have a nice little family income."

The same manager told me on a separate occasion that the company preferred to hire members of the same families because it meant that workers' relatives would be more supportive about their working and the combined incomes would put less financial strain on individual workers. This concern over workers and their families dissipated, however, when the Filipino couple split up, leaving the wife with only the "helping-out" pay instead of the "nice little family income." When the woman requested a higher-paying job so she could support her family, the same manager told her that "family concerns were out of place at work" and did not promote her.

This incident suggests that a woman's family identity is considered important when it is advantageous to employers and irrelevant when it is disadvantageous. Similarly, managers encourage women workers to identify themselves primarily as workers or as women, depending on the circumstances. At one plant where I interviewed both managers and workers, males and females were openly separated by the company's hiring policy: entry-level jobs for females were in assembly, and entry-level jobs for males were as technicians. As at the plant where the Filipino couple worked, neither the "male" nor the "female" entry-level jobs required previous experience or training, but the "male" job paid significantly more.

Apparently, the employers at this plant *did* see differences between male and female workers, despite their claims to the contrary. Yet, when the women workers asked for "special treatment" because of these differences, the employers' attitudes rapidly changed. When the first quality circle was introduced in one production unit at this plant, the workers, all of whom were women, were told to suggest ways to improve the quality of work. The most frequently mentioned concern of all the women production workers I met was the lack of decent child-care facilities. The company replied that child care was not a quality of work–related issue but a "special women's concern" that was none of the company's business.

A Portuguese worker succinctly described the tendency among employers to play on and then deny such gender logic:

> The boss tells us not to bring our "women's problems" with us to work if we want to be treated equal. What does he mean by that? I am working here *because* of my "women's problems"— because I am a woman. Working here *creates* my "women's problems." I need this job because I am a woman and have children to feed. And I'll probably get fired because I am a woman and need to spend more time with my children. I am only one person—and I bring my whole self to work with me. So what does he mean, don't bring my "women's problems" here?

As this woman's words so vividly illustrate, divisions of labor and of lives are intricately interwoven. Any attempts to organize the women workers of Silicon Valley—by unions, communities, political or social groups and by the women themselves— must deal with the articulation of gender, race, and class inequalities in their lives. . . .

Racial and Ethnic Logic

Typically, high-tech firms in Silicon Valley hire production workers from a wide spectrum of national groups. If their lack of a common language (both linguistically and culturally) serves to fragment the labor force, capital benefits. Conversely, management may find it more difficult to control workers with whom it cannot communicate precisely. Several workers said they have feigned a language barrier in order to avoid taking instructions; they have also called forth cultural taboos—both real and feigned—to avoid undesirable situations. One Haitian woman, who took a lot of kidding from her employer about voodoo and black magic, insisted that she could not work the night shift because evil spirits were out then. Because she was a good worker, the employer let her switch to days. When I tried to establish whether she believed the evil spirits were real or imagined, she laughed and said, "Does it matter? The result is the same: I can be home at night with my kids."

Management in several plants believed that racial and national diversity minimized solidarity. According to one supervisor, workers were forbidden from sitting next to people of their own nationality (i.e., language group) in order to "cut down on the chatting." Workers quickly found two ways to reverse this decision, using management's own class, racial, and gender logic. Chinese women workers told the supervisor that if they were not "chaperoned" by other Chinese women, their families would not let them continue to work there. Vietnamese women told him that the younger Vietnamese women would not work hard unless they were under the eyes of the older workers and that a group of newly hired Vietnamese workers would not learn to do the job right unless they had someone who spoke their language to explain it them. Both of these arguments could also be interpreted as examples of older workers wanting to control younger ones in a generational hierarchy, but this was not the case. Afterwards both the Chinese and the Vietnamese women laughed among themselves at their cleverness. Nor did they forget the support needs of workers from other ethnic groups: they argued with the supervisor that the same customs and needs held true for many of the language groups represented, and the restriction was rescinded.

Another example of a large-scale demonstration of interethnic solidarity on the shop floor involved workers playing off supervisors' stereotypes regarding the superior work of Asians over Mexicans. The incident was precipitated when a young Mexicana, newly assigned to an assembly unit in which a new circuit board was being assembled, fell behind in her quota. The supervisor berated her with racial slurs about Mexicans' "laziness" and "stupidity" and told her to sit next to and "watch the Orientals." As a group, the Asian women she was stationed next to slowed down their production, thereby setting the average quota on the new boards at a slower than usual pace. The women were in fits of laughter after work because the supervisor had assumed that the speed set by the Asians was the fastest possible, since they were the "best" workers.

Hispanic workers also turn management's anti-Mexican prejudices against them, as a Salvadorean woman explained:

First of all, the bosses think everyone from Latin America is Mexican, and they think all Mexicans are dumb. So, whenever they try to speed up production, or give us something we don't want to do, we just act dumb. It's not as if you act smart and you get a promotion or a bonus anyway.

A Mexicana operative confided, "They [management] assume we don't understand much English, but we understand when we want to."

A Chinese woman, who was under five feet tall and who identified her age by saying she was a "grandmother," laughingly told how she had her white male supervisor "wrapped around [her] finger." She consciously played into his stereotype that Asian women are small, timid, and obedient by frequently smiling at and bowing to him and doing her job carefully. But when she had a special need, to take a day or a few hours off,

for example, she would put on her best guileless, ingratiating look and, full of apologies, usually obtained it. She also served as a voice for co-workers whom the supervisor considered more abrasive. On one occasion, when three white women in her unit complained about poor lighting and headaches, the supervisor became irritated and did not respond to their complaint. Later that week the Chinese "grandmother" approached him, saying that she was concerned that poor lighting was limiting the workers' productivity. The lighting was quickly improved. This incident illustrates that managers can and do respond to workers' demand when they result in increased productivity.

Some workers see strategies to improve and control their work processes and environments as contradictory and as "Uncle Tomming." Two friends, both Filipinas, debated this issue. One argued that "acting like a China doll" only reinforced white employers' stereotypes, while the other said that countering the stereotype would not change their situation, so they might as well use the stereotype to their advantage. The same analysis applies to women workers who consciously encourage male managers to view women as different from men in their abilities and characteristics. For women and minority workers, the need for short-term gains and benefits and for long-term equal treatment is a constant contradiction. And for the majority of workers, short-term tactics are unlikely to result in long-term equality.

Potential for Organizing

Obviously, the lesson here for organizing is contradictory. Testimonies such as the ones given in these pages clearly document that immigrant women are not docile, servile people who always follow orders, as many employers interviewed for this study claimed. Orchestrating major actions such as family migration so that they could take control of and better their lives has helped these women develop leadership and survival skills. Because of these qualities, many of the women I interviewed struck me as potentially effective labor and community organizers and rank-and-file leaders. Yet almost none of them were interested in collective organizing, because of time limitations and family constraints and because of their lack of confidence in labor unions, the feminist movement, and community organizations. Many were simply too worn out from trying to make ends meet and caring for their families. And for some, the level of inequality and exploitation on the shop floor did not seem that bad, compared to their past experiences. A Salvadorean woman I interviewed exemplified this predicament. Her job as a solderer required her to work with a microscope all day, causing her to develop severe eye and back strain. Although she was losing her eyesight and went home exhausted after working overtime, she told me she was still very happy to be in the United States and very grateful to her employer. "I have nothing to complain about," she told me. "It is such a luxury to know that when I go home all of my children will still be alive." After losing two sons to government-backed terrorist death squads in El Salvador, her work life in Silicon Valley was indeed an improvement.

Nonetheless, their past torment does not reduce the job insecurity, poor working conditions, pay inequality, and discrimination so many immigrant workers in Silicon Valley experience in their jobs. In fact, as informants' testimonies suggest, in many cases, past hardships have rendered them less likely to organize collectively. At the same time, individual acts of resistance do not succeed on their own in changing the structured inequality of the division of labor. Most of these actions remain at the agitation level and lack the coordination needed to give workers real bargaining power. And, as mentioned, individual strate-

gies that workers have devised can be contradictory. Simultaneous to winning short-run victories, they can also reinforce both gender and racial stereotypes in the long run. Further, because many of these victories are isolated and individual, they can often be divisive. For workers to gain both greater workplace control *and* combat sexism and racism, organized *collective* strategies hold greater possibilities.

Neither organized labor nor feminist or immigrant community organizations have prioritized the needs of the Silicon Valley's immigrant women workers.[2] As of 1989, for example, not a single full-time paid labor union organizer was assigned to the local high-tech industry. Given that Silicon Valley is the center of the largest and fastest-growing manufacturing industry in the country, this is, as one long-time local organizer, Mike Eisenscher, put it, "a frightening condemnation of the labor movement" (1987). That union leadership has also failed to mark for attention a work force that is dominated by women of color is equally disheartening.

My findings indicate that Silicon Valley's immigrant women workers have a great deal to gain from organizing, but also a great deal to contribute. They have their numeric strength, but also a wealth of creativity, insight, and experience that could be a shot in the arm to the stagnating national labor movement. They also have a great deal to teach—and learn from—feminist and ethnic community movements. But until these or new alternative movements learn to speak and listen to these women, the women will continue to struggle on their own, individually and in small groups. In their struggle for better jobs and better lives, one of the most effective tactics they have is their own resourcefulness in manipulating management's "own logic against them."

NOTES

1. "Minority" is the term used by the California Employment Development Department and

the U.S. Department of Labor publications in reference to people of color. The statistics do not distinguish between immigrants and nonimmigrants within racial and ethnic groupings.

2. One of the few organizations that *has* included immigrant women workers and that addresses their needs is the Silicon Valley Toxics Coalition. This group effectively addresses itself to improving residential and occupational health and safety hazards posed by the highly toxic local high-tech industry.

REFERENCES

Annual Planning Information: San Jose Standard Metropolitan Statistical Area, 1983–1984. 1983. Sacramento: California Department of Employment Development.

Carey, Pete. 1984. "Tomorrow's Robots: A Revolution at Work." *San Jose Mercury News,* February 8–11.

Eisenscher, Mike. 1987. "Organizing the Shop in Electronics." Paper presented at the West Coast Marxist Scholars Conference, November 14, Berkeley, California.

Hossfeld, Karen. 1988a. "Divisions of Labor, Divisions of Lives: Immigrant Women Workers in Silicon Valley." Ph.D. diss., University of California, Santa Cruz.

———. 1988b. "The Triple Shift: Immigrant Women Workers and the Household Division of Labor in Silicon Valley." Paper presented at the annual meetings of the American Sociological Association, Atlanta.

Siegel, Lenny, and Herb Borock. 1982. *Background Report on Silicon Valley.* Prepared for the U.S. Commission on Civil Rights. Mountain View, Calif.: Pacific Studies Center.

THE FUTURE OF WORK

43

Exiting the Squirrel Cage

Juliet B. Schor

Juliet Schor is a university professor, author, and frequent lecturer on the topics of worktime, consumerism, and alternative economic visions. Professor Schor is critical of the current directions of U.S. society, and argues instead for a future with shorter hours of work, less accumulation of consumer goods, and more time for family and community. Her new book, *The Overspent Society*, is an examination of how the pressures to keep up with an escalating American dream are leading millions of Americans to save too little, take on too much debt, and live with a persistent sense of dissatisfaction.

Schor is active in politics and is a supporter of the New Party, a grass-roots third party seeking to transform the political process in the United States. Her New Party pamphlet, *A Sustainable Economy for the 21st Century*, lays out her vision of a better economic future.

Schor is the mother of two young children and is trying, in her own life, to achieve a balance between the pressures of work, family, and consumerism that she writes about. She finds that her research "leads" her life—she usually gets into topics for academic or political reasons, and as she writes about them they begin to transform her life. First, she cut her work hours, then her spending. What's next, she asks?

I t is often said that an economist is a person who knows the price of everything and the value of nothing. On the question of time, we may all have become economists. We are keenly aware of the price of time—the extra income earned with a second job, the wage and a half for an hour of

overtime. In the process, we may have forgotten the real worth of time.

The origins of modern time consciousness lie in the development of a capitalist economy. Precapitalist Europe was largely "timeless"— or, in historian Jacques Le Goff's words, "free of haste and careless of exactitude." As capitalism raised the "price" of time, people began to think of time as a scarce resource. Indeed, the ideology of the emerging market economy was filled with metaphors of time: saving time, using time wisely, admonitions against "passing" time. The work ethic itself was in some sense a time ethic. When Benjamin

Franklin preached that time is money, he meant that time should be used productively. Eventually capitalism did more than make time valuable. Time and money began to substitute for each other. Franklin's aphorism took on new meaning, not only as prescription, but as an actual description. Money buys time, and time buys money. *Time itself had become a commodity.*[1] . . .

Establishing a right to free time may sound utopian—but the principle of limiting exchange has already been established. It is not legal to sell oneself into slavery. It is not legal to sell one's vote. It is not legal to sell children. Even the principle of limiting the exchange of time is well established. The state has regulated working hours since the colonial period. The right to free time has been legislated in some forms, such as legal holidays. Most important of all is the social security system, which assumes that workers have a right to leisure for a period at the end of their lives. What I am arguing for is the extension of this right—so that everyone can enjoy free time while they are still young and throughout their lives.

Breaking the Work-and-Spend Cycle

To gain this right—to reduce the reliance on long hours—it will be necessary to break the work-and-spend cycle. Changes must be made on a number of fronts: altering employers' incentives; improving wages for the lowest-paid; creating gender equality; preempting the automatic spiraling of consumption; and throughout, establishing time's value independent of its price, so that it can no longer be readily substituted for money.

New Incentives for Employers

The employer's bias toward excessive hours is strongest for salaried workers. Effective change will therefore lay the burden of extra hours on the employer. What a firm now re-

ceives courtesy of its salaried workforce, it should have to pay for. Therefore, I propose that every salaried job be formally (and legally) attached to a standard schedule. Along with annual pay, every position would also have an explicit standard of hours—for example, a nine-to-six schedule—and a specified number of holidays, vacation and personal days, and sick time. Thus, if an employee actually works longer than the standard, the hours would be counted as extra, and the firm must pay for them. Ideally, the firm would designate an annual total of hours and allow flexible scheduling within it. Of course, many, and probably most, salaried positions already have official weekly hours even if they're not adhered to. And paid time off is almost always specified in advance. But standard hours would be a departure in many of the longest-hour fields, such as finance, consulting, upper administration and management, and law. (It should be noted that I am advocating not that limits be set on the amount of standard hours but that the government require firms to set some standard.)

This system would not be a cure-all for the excessive hours of some occupations. Employers could still set very high standard hours and thereby considerably negate the benefits of standardizing hours. A replication of Japanese practices is even possible, where employees are subtly (or not so subtly) pressured to ignore any standard. Salaried employees may fail to claim extra hours, or forgo vacations, in order to advance their careers—as happened in a California firm where a quarter of management came to work without pay.[2] In the most competitive environments, it is almost impossible to prevent the long-hour bias without a transformation of the corporate culture. But clearly defined schedules would both place a useful limitation on employers and give employees the right to be paid for their overtime. And competition for personnel may discourage the setting of excessively long days. If a prospective trainee at Salomon Brothers were asked to guarantee eighty hours and Goldman, Sachs sets seventy, the former would be at a disadvantage. For those employees who *want* their time, the standardization of hours could be effective.

As for paying for extra hours, my second proposal is that the company should pay back time with time, rather than with money. The idea is to transform overtime into "comp" time—and make it voluntary. Every job—salaried, hourly, or piece rate—would have a standard workday, workweek, and workyear. Companies could request—although not demand—extra hours, which would be recompensed in time off. An extra hour worked today would yield an extra hour of paid time off in the future. Workers would be able to bank their overtime hours and accumulate them. They could save up for longer vacations, take sabbaticals, or go to part-time at full-time pay. The shift from overtime to comp time would not only reduce the total number of hours worked, it would also make jobs much more flexible. It would become far easier to go to school, be a parent, or do volunteer work and, at the same time, carry on a full-time job. Of course, there may be limitations on the scheduling of time off. Existing practices involving comp time or programs of voluntary work reduction usually have some restrictions such as prior notification and management approval. But in situations where both sides have shown flexibility and goodwill, these limitations have not been onerous.

Expanding the use of comp time represents a big step toward eroding the substitution of time and money—and would encounter significant opposition. Employers would like some things about the proposal and not others. Payment by comp time means that workers are remunerated for extra hours at their regular wage rate (which is all they are paid for time off), rather than time and a half. Employers will like this. But it also means that they will have to find

more employees to fill in for the additional time off. They will not be happy about this, in part because of the fringe benefits. But I suspect employers will be most averse to the idea of associating standard hours with all salaried jobs. Despite the flexibility built into the proposal (they can choose any level of standard hours and adjust it frequently), they will complain that it is an unnecessary intrusion on their prerogatives.

Many hourly workers, especially men, would be bitterly opposed to the elimination of overtime pay, at least at the beginning. Overtime is the only way many can earn high or even "livable" rates of pay—a circumstance that has turned more than a few into slaves to their jobs. One union steward noted:

> The people I represent in the union want to work *more* hours, not less. Working overtime is the only way to make decent money, so they're always looking for ways to stretch the work out, or find something that needs to be done over the weekend or into the evening. When I talk to them about working shorter hours, they just laugh like it's a joke. Maybe for some yuppie who already makes enough in twenty or thirty hours, or even forty—but not us. But I know how tired and bored they are after fifty or sixty hours on the line. After sixty hours your mind is still doing that job after you're asleep and dreaming, and then it's up at six and back to the job. It's not that they want to work those hours. There's just no other way to break even.[3]

But the idea that jobs pay more where overtime is available is to some extent an illusion. A recent study shows that workers who get overtime receive lower hourly wages, as firms "undo" some of the effect of the overtime premium.[4] If this research is correct, it is likely that hourly wages would rise in response to the elimination of overtime. Even so, there would be significant resistance to this proposal. In some unionized shops, workers with seniority have opposed work sharing as an alternative to layoffs, preferring to have some workers laid off rather than having all workers' hours reduced.

A much-needed change is to make part-time work more feasible. At the moment, the great majority of part-time positions are low-pay, low-mobility, and largely without benefits. Yet growing numbers of people are expressing interest in reducing their hours. The impediments for professionals and managers are especially powerful. In many places, part-time is tantamount to career suicide. A California study of professionals who opted for shorter hours catalogued the difficulties. When one state employee went to her supervisor with a proposal to work fewer hours, his reaction was typical: "My gawd . . . do you realize what this means to your career?" The private sector is even more discriminatory. A manager in a private public relations firm went on part-time with the birth of her child. After more than a decade of excellent performance, the firm still will not put her on the list for promotion—not until she's willing to return to work full-time.[5] And, despite new thinking by some employers, many still won't give the opportunity to cut back:

> When I asked for six months off from my job after I had a new baby, they treated me like I was lazy. They just turned me down flat. Then I tried asking to come back earlier part-time. And they still said no. The thinking was that if I was serious about my career, that just meant working full-time or nothing. And so I did it. I'd rather give up the money than some of the time with my family, but they just wouldn't offer me that choice.[6]

There are some simple reforms that would enhance the feasibility of part-time work. A first, crucial step is to eliminate the "fringe benefits" penalty. Part-time workers would receive a share of health insurance, pension benefits, and other fringes, prorated by their hours of work. They would also get the option to go to full coverage at their own expense. There are already many full-time workers who would prefer part-time work but don't take it because of the loss of benefits. This provision would allow them to scale back. (A superior solution is universal, government-guaranteed health insurance for all, regardless of employment status. I offer my suggestion in the absence of such a program. Furthermore, granting full employer-paid benefits to part-timers, however desirable, would create a powerful incentive for firms to refuse to offer part-time positions.) A second option is to institute job sharing, in which two people split one position's fringe benefits, responsibility, work, and pay. Each of these changes would reduce existing biases toward long-hour jobs.

The major remaining incentive toward long hours is that associated with the sale of labor by the hour. . . . [A]dditional hours increase the employment rent and thereby raise productivity. Although there is no simple "institutional" trick for eliminating this bias, there are effective productivity-raising substitutes for long hours. Examples include giving workers more participation and decision-making power on the job, narrowing wage differentials, and humanizing the work environment. A large number of studies show that these reforms raise satisfaction and productivity. The more prevalent they become, the less costly it would be for companies to shorten hours. Other measures can also be effective. One straightforward reform, long overdue, is to outlaw the practice of mandatory overtime. Workers should not be forced, as many currently are, to work more than their normal workweek in order to keep their jobs.

Giving Up Future Income for Time Off

To sever the work-consumption link, we must exploit the psychological difference between income that is already being spent and income that is merely expected. People cling tenaciously to their current paycheck, unwilling or unable to trade it for time, but polls indicate strong sentiment for using future income to fund additional time off. Suppose that companies were required by law to give people this choice. What if, as we take the "productivity challenge" in coming decades, there is no bias toward money?

The company would announce the percentage pay increase it plans to give to each group of employees. Then it would calculate equivalent hours of time off. The employee could decide among the alternatives—from the extremes of all pay or all time, to half and half, or three-quarter/one-quarter splits. The company could offer different forms of time off (reductions in daily hours, part-time schedules, or additional vacation or personal days). Free time could be accumulated from year to year. Administratively, this option could be added on to existing personnel routines. Many firms already allow employees to choose their health coverage, whether to participate in the company savings plan, or how much company-sponsored life insurance to carry. The money/time tradeoff is just one more benefit option.

Exactly how would this choice work out if it were available today? There are two key parameters: the amount of income a company is willing to give, and the fraction of it workers designate toward free time. Let's assume the former is 2 percent plus an adjustment for inflation, and the latter is 100 percent. Then, about a decade from now—in the year 2002, say—the average workyear will have fallen by 340 hours—from 1,960 hours to 1,600 hours per year (see table 1). That's enough for an additional two months of vacation or a 6 ½-hour day. At lower rates of real income growth, the leisure gain is lower. Higher rates produce rapid gains. If a person's real income were to rise by 4 percent a year, and all of it was channeled into time off, after ten years the annual workyear would be near 1,300

TABLE 1 Potential Gains in Leisure Annual Hours if 2 Percent Productivity Growth Is Transformed into Leisure

Year	Hours	Year	Hours
1991	2000	2002	1608
1992	1961	2003	1577
1993	1922	2004	1546
1994	1885	2005	1516
1995	1848	2006	1486
1996	1811	2007	1457
1997	1776	2008	1428
1998	1741	2009	1400
1999	1707	2010	1373
2000	1673	2020	1126
2001	1641		

hours—a total gain in free time of over 600 hours. This person could go to school one semester a year, take a four-month vacation, or follow a five-hour daily schedule year-round.

If it sounds too good to be true, remember that in my example purchasing power is completely stagnant. The person who goes 100 percent toward free time for ten years will experience no increase whatsoever in his or her material standard of living. Purchasing power will keep up with inflation, but not go beyond it. The appeal of such a scheme is that what you don't know can't hurt you. As shopping addicts tend to discover, dissatisfaction with their possessions vanish once they stop going into stores and exposing themselves to the newest items. If you can be content tomorrow with the amount you consume today, then trading off future income can be a blessing.

How many people would actually choose to forgo future income? A few voluntary worktime reduction plans for government employees already exist, going by the name of V-Time (the *V* stands for "voluntary"). Participation in these plans is small—typically below even 5 percent. But it would be wrong to read too much into these programs. They require individuals to reduce *current* income, as we already know they are very reluctant to do. Only future-oriented V-time is relevant; and to my knowledge, no such plans exist. But survey data give some idea of how people would respond to them. In the 1978 survey, 84 percent of workers said they would choose to trade off *some* future income—with almost half opting for a 100-percent tradeoff. A 1989 poll asked people which of two career paths they would choose: "one enabling you to schedule your own full-time work hours, and give more attention to your family, but with slower career advancement; and the other with rigid work hours and less attention to your family, but faster career advancement." Nearly eight out of ten preferred the path with more free time. Indeed, large majorities of both men and women (74 percent and 82 percent) chose this option. Fifty-five percent also said they would not be "likely to accept a promotion involving greater responsibility if it meant spending less time with family," compared with 34 percent who said they would. Of course, these are hypothetical questions, with no guarantee that people would actually act in this way. But even if the participation were considerably lower—say, at two-thirds or half—the program would have to be deemed very popular and would eventually have a major impact on worktime.[7]

There would be hard-core resisters. This country has plenty of workaholics—people for whom work is an escape, an obsession, or, if they have nothing better to do, the default option, who will not be interested in my proposal. There are others for whom money is everything, who will avail themselves of almost any opportunity to make a few more bucks. Or those who sell their souls to the highest-paying job they can find—regardless of its working hours, stress level, effect on their family life, or social implications. And half the population has a special problem, as a forty-five-year-old machinist explains: "Being a man means being willing to put all your waking hours into working to support your family. If you ask for time off, or if you turn down overtime, it means you're lazy or you're a wimp."[8] Men are ensnared not only in the traditional breadwinner role but also by the tendency of our culture to equate self-worth with job and pay.

Hard-core resistance to giving up money for time would, I hope, give way in the face of the positive experience of many, such as this group of overtime-loving workers in a British shoe factory:

> It was easy to find volunteers for Sundays as well. I'm sure that there were times when you could have asked them to work seven days out of seven for a whole year; they'd have done it, if they'd been pushed. . . . And there were people who worked after hours as well, cash in hand, as well as their split shift, either through alienation, or sometimes from necessity. You see, when you were working forty-eight hours a week, cash really became the thing you were after. . . . A friend said to me, jokingly (but jokes always have a serious side): "Me, when I'm not working, I don't know what to do, I'm bored stiff, I'm better off at work." Your factory is your life. . . . You have a bit more money, you'll buy as much electrical gadgetry as you can. You'll chase after money, but it won't do you much good in the end.

When hard times hit, the plant went into worksharing:

> Then bit by bit, there was an unbelievable phenomenon of physical recuperation. The idea of money really lost its intensity. I don't mean it had disappeared but eventually even the blokes with families to look after said, "It's better now than before." It's true that we

lost a good deal of money [25 percent of former income] . . . but, quite soon, only one or two of the blokes minded.

It was about now that . . . friendships began: we were now able to go beyond political conversation, and we managed to talk about love, impotence, jealousy, family life. . . . It was also at this time that we realized the full horror of working in the factory on Saturday afternoons or evenings. Before, the blokes had put up with it, but now we were once again learning the meaning of the word living. . . . Similarly for Sundays or Bank Holidays, which were paid at triple time, management admitted to us that they had difficulty finding people. . . . There had been a change of attitude, they weren't able to buy workers as easily as before.[9]

Inequalities of Time

Of course the wages of many Americans are so low, or their conditions of employment so precarious, that they cannot afford to give up any income—present or future. And their numbers are rising. Nearly one-third of all U.S. workers currently earn wages which, on a full-time schedule, are insufficient to lift them out of poverty. As I have stressed, millions can make ends meet only through overtime, moonlighting, and multi-earner families. And many are unable to make ends meet at all.

The danger of increasing leisure time voluntarily is that it could replace one inequity with another—as inequality of income creates inequality of time. The poorest third would work just as many hours as ever—or more, as more work became available—while the top two-thirds would gradually become a leisured class. The people who would gain free time would be those who already had the financial resources that

make it possible—education, homes, and a bank account. They would be mainly white and mainly upper and middle class.

To redress these imbalances, I also advocate mandatory increases in free time. The United States stands out among rich countries in its failure to ensure basic rights to vacation or parental leaves. What about government-mandated four-week paid vacations for all employees, independent of length of service? Or six-month paid parental leaves, financed through the social security system? These would be a start in the right direction.

Ultimately, inequality of time must be solved by redressing the underlying inequality of income. Only when the poorest make a living wage can their right to free time be realized. And barring an economic miracle, part of it will have to come from the people at the top. In the 1980s, the rich grabbed a fantastic amount from those below them. Now it's time to give it back.

Raising low incomes is not a simple matter, but at least two strategies will help. First, companies should begin to equalize the large differences in wages and salaries which exist among their employees, by paying more to those at the bottom and less to those at the top. The United States has high levels of wage inequality in comparison with other industrialized nations. Second, the federal minimum wage should be raised and indexed to the economy's average wage. While only a limited fraction of workers receive the minimum, when it rises, it creates upward pressure on those wages which are somewhat higher. Therefore, raising the minimum can be an effective strategy for improving the living standards of many low-wage workers.

Finally, as should be clear from my earlier discussion, the problem of worktime cannot be solved without an equalization of the distribution of work itself. This means we must find a durable solution for the crisis of unemployment and underemployment plaguing this economy. Such a solution will require an ongoing commitment from the federal government to ensure a more equal allocation of total work hours.

My proposals also run the risk of reproducing inequalities of gender. The suggestions themselves—such as making part-time work more desirable or allowing people to trade off income for time—are gender-neutral. Without change in underlying gender roles, however, women will be more likely to take advantage of them. If this occurs, it will reproduce women's current responsibility for housework and child care. Therefore, ongoing feminist efforts to equalize the division of labor within the family are crucial to the larger success of my proposed reforms. If men take considerably more responsibility for children and housework—as many now say they want to—then they too will want to opt for working patterns that are compatible with family duties. In that event, the effect of the proposals will be quite different. They will, as I intend, help undermine rigid gender roles, by making shared parenting and two-career families more feasible. These transformations, however, require that the culture of U.S. workplaces must change, in order to be more accommodating to society's needs for child care, care of the sick and elderly, and other domestic labor. And the change must happen for both men and women.

We must also confront the legacy of inefficiency in household technology, in order to reverse the built-in backwardness of the American home. Architects and product designers should be encouraged to invent new, truly labor-saving household technologies, emphasizing low maintenance and ease of cleaning. Progress against wage discrimination on the basis of sex will also help, by eliminating one source of the bias which devalues women's time. Ultimately, we need a serious public debate on household labor, which addresses both who should do it and how it should be done. . . .

Overcoming Consumerism

Economic feasibility is an important condition for gaining leisure. So is breaking the automatic translation of productivity into income. But for many Americans escaping the trap of overwork will also entail stepping off the consumer treadmill, which requires altering a way of life and a way of thinking. The transformation must be not only economic and social but cultural and psychological.

The first step is practical—to put oneself in a financial position where a fixed or smaller income is sufficient. For example, one California environmental planner spent three years preparing to cut back his work hours. He had to "grind down the charge cards," pay off his car, and convince his partner that life with less money would be okay: "There are two ways to get through. You either have to make the money which will buy you the kind of life that you think you have to have, or you can change those expectations and you don't need the money anymore. And that's what I've done."[10]

Being able to change expectations depends on understanding the psychological and cultural functions that material goods fulfill. They can be the means to an identity or a way to create self-esteem. Things fill up empty spaces in our lives. Many couples concentrate on owning a house or filling it with nice furnishings, when what they really crave is an emotional construction—home. Some women turn to fashion to create a fantasy self that compensates for what they are consciously or unconsciously missing. Materialism can even be an altruistic vice. Men pursue the pot of gold to give it to their wives or children—to provide the "best that life can offer" or "what I never had." But in the process everyone is cheated: "I thought I was doing the right thing making money at work all the time. But I was never home." Realization often comes too late: "Now that I'm older, I can see . . . what I was missing."[11]

Involuntary reductions in income caused by a company shutdown or an inability to work can be painful, often devastating. But those who willingly reject the quest for affluence can find themselves perfectly satisfied. One public employee, currently on a four-fifths schedule, swears that only a financial disaster could get her back to full-time: "The extra twenty percent just isn't worth it." Even at the California company where employees were forced to take a ten-percent reduction in pay and hours, reactions were positive: only 22 percent of the workforce rated the program negatively, and half were positive about it.[12]

For many, opting out of the rat race has transformed their lives: "In the last four years, I went from upper middle class to poor, but I am a lot richer than most people, and I'm happier too." A divorced father raising three young children rejected the long hours, high-income route. He's at home with his children in the evenings, and has learned that "less is more." A career woman gave up her job, and along with it designer clothes, hair and nail appointments, lunching out and a second car: "I adopted a whole new set of values and put aside pride, envy, competitiveness and the need for recognition."[13]

The Value of Leisure Time

Some people are skeptical of Americans' need for leisure time. Work may be bad, but perhaps leisure isn't all it's cracked up to be either. According to economist Gary Burtless, "Most Americans who complain they enjoy too little leisure are struggling to find a few extra minutes to watch Oprah Winfrey and 'L.A. Law.'"[14] Will free time be "wasted," in front of the tube or at the mall? What will we do with all that leisure? Won't people just acquire second jobs? These are serious questions, embodying two main assumptions. The first is that people prefer work or, if they don't, they should. The sec-

ond is that leisure time is wasted time that is neither valued nor valuable.

One possibility is that work is irrepressible. The Akron rubber workers immediately come to mind. After they won the six-hour day, many of the men who worked at Firestone started driving cabs, cutting hair, and selling insurance. While no one knows exactly what percentage of the workers took on extra jobs, during the 1950s it was thought to be between one in five and one in seven.[15] Some observers concluded from this experience that American workers do not want, or cannot handle, leisure time. If they are right, so be it. My aim is not to force leisure on an unwilling population but to provide the possibility of a real choice. If the chance to work shorter hours—when fairly presented—is not appealing, then people will not take it. But before we take the Akron experience as definitive, let's ask a few more questions.

Why did so many take a second job? The male rubber workers were reasonably well paid by the blue-collar standards of the day, and many of their wives worked. They did not labor out of sheer economic necessity. I suspect that their behavior was dictated more by a cultural imperative—the same imperative that drove the operatives in the shoe factory, or the colleagues of the machinist quoted earlier. The imperative that says that men with leisure are lazy. It is significant that women rubber workers did not seek a second paycheck.

Today there are signs that this cultural imperative is becoming less compelling. Perhaps most important is the transformation of sex roles. Women have taken up responsibility for breadwinning. And men are more at home around the house. Increasing numbers of fathers want to parent. In a recent poll of men between the ages of eighteen and twenty-four, nearly half said they would like to stay home and raise their children. The ethos of "male sacrifice" is disappearing: a declining portion of the population believes that being a "real man" entails self-denial and being the family provider.[16]

The traditional work ethic is also undergoing transformation. Commitment to hard work retains its grip on the American psyche. But young people are moving away from "the frenzied work ethic of the 1980s to more traditional values." In addition, ideas of what work is and what it is for are being altered. The late 1960s and 1970s witnessed the rise of what some have called "post-materialist values"—desires for personal fulfillment, self-expression, and meaning. Throughout the industrialized world, a culture shift occurred as young people especially began demanding satisfying work. Although there was a burst of old-style materialism during the 1980s, it did not permanently dislodge what now looks more and more like a long-term trend. People are expecting more from work than a paycheck and more from life than what 1950s culture offered.[17]

People *will* work on their time off. They will work hard and long in what is formally designated as leisure time. But where the Akron example leads us astray is the quest for the second paycheck. Americans need time for unpaid work, for work they call their own. They need the time to give to others. Much of what will be done was the regular routine in the days when married women were full-time housewives. And it is largely caring work—caring for children, caring for sick relatives and friends, caring for the house. Today many haven't got the time to care. If we could carve the time out from our jobs, we could prevent the current squeeze on caring labor. And this time around, the men should share the load. The likelihood is good that unpaid work would occupy a significant fraction of any "leisure" gained in the market. At the California company that gave its employees two days off a month, nearly as much time was devoted to household and volunteer work as to leisure itself.

Predictably, women did more of this labor. But times are changing.[18]

Other productive activities would take up uncommitted time as well. Many people would like to devote more time to their churches, get involved in their children's schools, coach a sports team, or help out at a soup kitchen. But the time squeeze has taken a toll on volunteer activities, which have fallen considerably since the rise in hours began. Time out of work would also be used for schooling. Education remains a primary factor in economic success. And continual training and retraining are projected to be increasingly important in the economy of the twenty-first century, as job skills become obsolete more rapidly. A survey at two large Boston corporations found that over 20 percent of full-time employees were also enrolled in school.[19]

The unpaid work—at home and in the community—that will fill free time is vital to us as individuals and as a society—as should be clear from the mounting social problems attendant upon its decline. Still, if we were to gain free time only to fill it up again with work, the battle will be only half won. There is also a pressing need for more true leisure. For the first time in fifteen years, people have cited leisure time as the "more important" thing in their lives than work.[20] The nation needs to slow down, unwind, and recover from its ordeal of labor. But can we handle leisure time?

The skeptics, who cite heavy television viewing or excessive shopping, have a point. It may be, however, that work itself has been eroding the ability to benefit from leisure time. Perhaps people are just too tired after work to engage in active leisure. Evidence from the Gallup Poll suggests this may be the case. Today, the most popular ways to spend an evening are all low-energy choices: television, resting, relaxing, and reading. Although it certainly isn't proof, it is suggestive that the globe's only other rich, industrialized country with longer hours than the United States—namely, Japan—is also the only nation to watch more television.[21]

The issue goes beyond the physical capacity to use free time. It is also true that the ability to use leisure is not a "natural" talent, but one that must be cultivated. If we veer too much toward work, our "leisure skills" will atrophy. At the extremes are workaholics like Sheila Mohammed. After sixteen-hour days—two full-time shifts—as a drug rehabilitation counselor, Sheila finds herself adrift outside the job: "I'm so used to . . . working and then when I have the time off, what do I do, where do I go?"[22] But even those with moderate working habits are subject to a milder version of this syndrome. Many potentially satisfying leisure activities are off limits because they take too much time: participating in community theater, seriously taking up a sport or a musical instrument, getting involved with a church or community organization. In the leisure time available to us, there's less of interest to do. To derive the full benefits of free time, we just may need more of it.

A final impediment to using leisure is the growing connection between free time and spending money. Private corporations have dominated the leisure "market," encouraging us to think of free time as a consumption opportunity. Vacations, hobbies, popular entertainment, eating out, and shopping itself are all costly forms of leisure. How many of us, if asked to describe an ideal weekend, would choose activities that cost nothing? How resourceful are we about doing things without spending money? A successful movement to enhance free time will have to address this dynamic head on. Governments and communities will need to subsidize more affordable leisure activities, from the arts to parks to adult education. We need a conscious effort to reverse "the commodification of leisure."

Whatever the potential problems associated with increasing leisure time, I do not

think they are insurmountable. A significant reduction in working hours will by itself alleviate some of the difficulties. And if we can take positive steps to enhance the value of leisure time, we will be well rewarded. The experience of the Kellogg workers calls for optimism: "The visitor sees . . . a lot of gardening and community beautification . . . athletics and hobbies were booming . . . libraries well patronized . . . and the mental background of these fortunate workers. . . becoming richer."[23]

Reclaiming Leisure

While leisure holds great appeal, it is difficult to be confident that the next century will bring us more of it. It is possible that the future holds yet another episode in the nation's saga of work-and-spend. Of course, some observers continue to believe that work will disappear, as robots, computers, and micro-electronic technology replace human labor. Others see a more sinister side to leisure, in which the little work that remains is monopolized by a fraction of the population. Society will split into two great classes—those with jobs (and income) and those without. Economic inequality, already on the rise, will mount.

Then there are those, as we have seen, who think America *needs* more work, to compete against the Japanese. But having already gone through two decades of rising hours, this "Japanese solution" is truly daunting. If current U.S. trends in work continue for another twenty years, the average person would be on the job sixty hours a week, fifty weeks a year—for an annual total of three thousand hours. If it sounds like Dickens's England, that's because it would be. If hours rise again, how can we solve the parenting deficit, marital problems, or the adverse health effects of stress and overwork? And then there's the ecology: another round of work, produce, and spend may put the human habitat beyond the point of no return.

I have already chronicled the many barriers to becoming a more leisured society. Corporations remain the most significant obstacle. Most will be vociferous opponents to my ideas. At last count, the Conference Board reports that fewer than fifty firms nationwide have comprehensive programs for work and family issues. But, as always, enlightened, forward-looking companies do exist. Wells Fargo gives personal-growth leaves, Xerox offers social-service sabbaticals. Job sharing is possible at a growing number of companies, including Hewlett Packard, Black & Decker, TRW Vidar, and Levi-Strauss. Control Data has a vibrant part-time program which includes benefits. Anna Roddick, founder of the rapidly expanding Body Shop, gives her employees a half-day off each week with pay to engage in volunteer activities. While the number of innovative corporations is still small, it is growing. And apparently awareness of time-related personnel problems is increasing as well. In the last few years, at least some corporate executives have been waking up to the realities of their employees' lives.

None of this is to say that increased leisure is impossible. Certainly not. It is only to remind ourselves that it will not come about through automatic market forces, the munificence of technology, or as a natural consequence of postindustrial society. Long hours are a hallmark of the market; labor-saving technology frequently does not save labor; and it is capitalism, not industry, that has been responsible for expanding work schedules. There will be more leisure only when people become convinced that they must have it.

On some parts of the landscape, the signs are hopeful. There is growing public awareness of the need for change. For the first time since such surveys have been systematically conducted, a majority of Americans report that they are willing to relin-

quish even current income to gain more family and personal time. In a 1989 poll, almost two-thirds said they would prefer to give up some of their salary, by an average amount of 13 percent; fewer than one quarter were unwilling to give up any money at all.[24] Despite this survey's limited scope and its variance with previous results, its findings are intriguing. Have we entered a new era, in which Americans have begun to rebel against their demanding worklives?

Other trends in public opinion also bode well for leisure. The "greening" of public consciousness is forcing us to take stock of the American life style. The crisis of the family—the problem of child care and the strains of marriage—is also intruding onto the social agenda. Both men and women, particularly young ones, are adopting new expectations about family and career. They are overturning the assumptions that men are responsible for breadwinning and women must take the second shift—trends that point in the direction of more balance between work and family. Although still only a trickle, the stream of "downshifters"—those who reject high-powered, demanding jobs in order to gain more control over their lives—may be the latest trendsetters. But as I have stressed throughout this book, public opinion on its own is not an effective force for change. To organize and mobilize it, we will need to look to environmental and women's organizations, the children's lobby, and even the trade-union movement. The few labor organizations that have been expanding in recent years—public and service sector unions with heavily female membership—are already in the forefront on work and family issues. And government will need to play a major role, as should be clear from the failures of the market in this area.

If we are to have a chance at leisure, we'll need to resurrect the public debate that ended in the 1920s. For despite the major transformations our nation has gone through since then, the basic alternatives remain surprisingly the same. On the one hand, commitment to an expanding material standard of living for everyone—or what Galbraith has called the "vested interest in output"—entails our continuing confinement in the "squirrel cage" of work and holds the potential for ecological disaster.[25] Or, we can redirect our concern with material goods toward redressing the inequalities of their distribution—and realize the promise of free time which lies before us. This time, let's make the choice for leisure.

NOTES

1. Jacques Le Goff, "The Crisis of Labor Time," in *Time, Work and Culture in the Middle Ages* (Chicago: Chicago University Press, 1980), 44. . . .

2. Victor Fuchs and Joyce P. Jacobsen, "Employee Response to Compulsory Short-Time Work," National Bureau of Economic Research Working Paper 2089, December 1986, 10, table 2.

3. Laurie Sheridan survey, "Interviews on Working Hours," unpublished mimeo.

4. Stephen J. Trejo, "Compensating Differentials and Overtime Pay Regulation," Working Paper 2–89, Department of Economics, University of California at Santa Barbara, January 1989.

5. Ann Harriman, *The Work/Leisure Trade Off: Reduced Work Time for Managers and Professionals* (New York: Praeger, 1982), 78, 98–99.

6. Sheridan, "Interviews."

7. Barbara Moorman and Barney Olmsted, "V-Time: A New Way to Work" (San Francisco: New Ways to Work, 1985). . . .

8. Sheridan, "Interviews."

9. Cited in André Gorz, *A Critique of Economic Reason* (London: Verso, 1989), 117–18.

10. Quoted in Harriman, *Work/Leisure Tradeoff*, 107–8.

11. Sheridan, "Interviews."

12. Quoted in Harriman, *Work/Leisure Tradeoff*, 109.

13. All quotes from Ann Landers, *Boston Globe*, 26 February 1990, 37.

14. Gary Burtless, "Are We All Working Too Hard? It's Better Than Watching Oprah," *Wall Street Journal*, 4 January 1990.

15. Harvey Swados, "Less Work—Less Leisure," *The Nation* (22 February 1958): 153–58.

16. Dana Kennedy, "Sexes Agree: Women Face Too Much Pressure," *Boston Globe*, 26 October 1990. Results are from a *Time* magazine/Yankelovich Clancy Shulman poll.

On "real men," see Daniel Yankelovitch, The World at Work (New York: Octagon Books, 1985), 139.

17. "Frenzied work ethic" conclusion is from the *Time* magazine/Yankelovich Clancy Shulman poll cited in note 16. See Kennedy, "Sexes Agree," 62. . . .

18. Fuchs and Jacobsen, "Employee Response," 10, table 2.

19. Bureau of Labor Statistics News Release, "Thirty-Eight Million Persons Do Volunteer Work," 29 March 1990. The rate of volunteering fell from 24 percent in 1974 to 20 percent in 1989. An increase in leisure will almost certainly result in a rise of volunteering, given that workers on part-time schedules have much higher rates of volunteering than any other group.

Boston study is Dianne S. Burden and Bradley Googins, *Boston University Balancing Job and Homelife Study*, mimeo, Boston University, 1987, p. 55.

20. "The Public Perspective: A Roper Center Review of Public Opinion Polling," 1, 4 (May/June 1990): 118.

21. Choices from *The Gallup Report*, 248, May 1986, p. 8. . . .

22. Mohammed was interviewed by Katie Abel for a Boston documentary, "Overworked and Out of Time," which aired on "Our Times," WHDH-TV Boston, 14 April 1990.

23. Quote from Henry Goddard Leach, editor of *The Forum and Century*, cited in Hunnicutt, "Kellogg," p. 47.

24. Robert Half International, "Family Time," pp. 2, 4. The use of the word salary may have been problematic. Although the poll did not explicitly target salaried, rather than hourly workers, the wording of the question may have imparted a bias to the answers.

25. John Kenneth Galbraith, *The Affluent Society*, 4th ed. (Boston: Houghton Mifflin, 1984), chap. 12.

44

The New Occupational Structure
What Are the Questions?

Andrew Abbott

Andrew Abbott is professor of sociology and master of the social science collegiate division at the University of Chicago. He has written widely on occupations, professions, and the sociology of work. Abbott also served as editor of the journal, *Work and Occupations.*

The early theorists of sociology found few subjects more important than the division of labor. We too make it a central topic. Yet modern societies confute traditional formulations of the problem. The merging of occupation and organization in the great professions, the flow of diverse people through varying types of work, the endless arabesques of specialization all make this problem one of far greater complexity for us than for our predecessors.

Historically, our contemporary occupational structure is young; the early modern economy was organized more in occupations than in organizations. While the product division of labor did imply some worker specialization, the relatively simple task division of labor made most products the work of one person. Organized in guilds, specialized workers were directly identified with their form of work. By contrast, the modern economy is structured in the Chinese boxes of organizational structure. The corporation, a fictive person, has re-

placed the company of equals as the legal scaffolding of work.

Early writers confronted the change from occupation to organization while it yet proceeded. Thence came their passions: Smith's wonder at efficiency, Marx's wistfulness about artisanal labor, Durkheim's faith in the feudal *compagnonnages*. But for us the modern economy is an accomplished fact; we must study the occupational structure for what it has now become. This means discarding the agenda of the classics and again asking ourselves, as they asked themselves, what are the important questions about occupations.

Like many concepts, "occupation" has a number of senses. Sometimes we oppose occupations to guilds, construing occupations as a simpler form of identification with work. Sometimes we oppose occupations in the broad sense to professions, which specialize in certain kinds of expert work, and to crafts, which specialize in expert physical skills. Sometimes we think of occupations as grouped around common organizational positions, as in the occupation of foreman; sometimes we imagine them in terms of common physical capital, as in the occupation of drill press operator. Indeed, when we once begin to face the concept, it comes apart in our hands. What exactly is required for us to call a group of workers "an occupation"?

Excerpted from "The New Occupational Structure" by Andrew Abbott, *Work and Occupations,* Vol. 16, No. 3, August 1989. Copyright © 1989 by Sage Publications, Inc. Reprinted by permission of Sage Publications, Inc.

If we take such questions seriously, they imply considering the problem of occupations within a broader framework, that of the social organization of work in general. In some societies, the structures generating and supporting occupations have been stable enough to justify treating occupations as isolable phenomena. In our own, the changes in that structural context are too many and too far-reaching. We cannot study occupations without invoking the entire theory of work.

There are four fundamental aspects to the modern social organization of work: the division of labor, the structure of occupations, the structure of work organizations, and the pattern of staffing. These were combined in the earlier system. There, the division of products was isomorphic with the relatively permanent partitioning of persons into occupations. Occupations themselves provided whatever social structure was required for work, and, since the division of products was a division of people, staffing was itself isomorphic with the division of products. In our world, all of these identities are broken. The division of tasks implies the separation of occupation and organization, while the decline of ascription, aided by the immense division of tasks, has made staffing—the direct mapping of types of persons into types of work—a central problem for us. In our current work system, these four structures must be considered both independently and in dynamic interrelation.

The social organization of work begins with the division of labor. As the classical writers recognized, the division of labor itself has two aspects: the division of products and the division of tasks. It is the latter, of course, that kindled Smith's admiration and Marx's ire. And it is the latter that has drawn explanation, usually attributing it to efficiency, if an author shares Smith's politics, or Marx's power. Although the distinction between the two forms is actually a relative one, it raises some important questions. In capitalist societies, the division of products is largely mediated by systems of market exchange, while the division of tasks is mediated by formal organization. Why this elective affinity exists, why certain matters are subject to one division of labor and others to the other, how markets and organizations trade off with each other are all questions that have received but need more substantial study.

Links between parts of the division of labor arise in two general ways. There are external links—links between separate units—through traditional, coercive, and market exchange. There are also internal links that agglomerate units into larger units. The shift of these internal links from occupation-based to organization-based, which is the central development of modern work history, makes occupations and organizations the second and third central social structures of work after the division of labor itself.

Even so simple a concept as occupation presents major difficulties. While occupations may easily be defined as "social groups made up of people who do the same kind of work," such a definition simply buries the problems. To say occupations are social groups is implicitly to assert that their members are in interaction; a category of workers is not an occupation, although it may become one. "Occupationness" resembles class consciousness; it results from social and cultural structuring of merely implicit links. And this structuring alone answers the other conundrum of the definition: what is meant by "the same kind of work?" In early modern society, such structuring was very complete; "the same kind of work" could then be easily discerned. The early division of labor first separated household and family work from artisanal work. The artisanal division of labor then divided persons into occupations whose internal structure was completely regulated by general and local law as well as by occupational custom and tradition. Between these structured occupations, both relations of market exchange and traditional or legal status precedence provided a linking structure. The society of orders gave each *metier* its place and each man his *metier*.

With the coming of new organizational forms, however, this early modern occupational structure broke down. Organizations provided the new internal links within the division of labor. The story is old and familiar. Commercial corporations and administrative bureaucracies subdivided traditional tasks, transferring skill from workers to organization charts and relegating simple, repetitive, and laborious tasks to machines. Since the traditional division of products was now crosscut by a division of tasks, people "doing the same kind of work" were now located in different organizations producing different products. Relations between these new organizations were largely governed by market exchange and state regulation; traditional and occupational regulation rapidly disappeared.

Organizations' increasing supremacy in the work world thus directly undermined the bases of occupational solidarity; more than a century of unionism witnesses the not-always-successful attempts to regain it. With the waning of occupational solidarity, the mapping of categories of individuals into categories of work has become a major social problem. This problem—the staffing problem—has occupied much of what is misleadingly called occupational research. Speaking for increasingly self-conscious social categories, social scientists have considered how various age, gender, racial, ethnic, and socioeconomic status groups fare in type of work or extent of work rewards. The structures articulating these non-occupational groups with types of work may be called staffing structures. The decline of occupational regulation and the increase of age, gender, and similar solidarities has made these staffing structures—among which education and certification are clearly the most important—the fourth central social structure of the work system.

We know less of staffing structures than perhaps any other work structure. In early modern times occupation was strongly hereditary. The sectoral differences of occupations *were* the major categorical differences in society; other categorical differences—of age and ethnicity, for example—had effects subordinate to them. The staffing problem in the modern sense, then, did not exist. But the breakdown of occupational heredity joined with growing organizational dominance to produce the modern staffing problem. The staffing structures that address this problem are either well-defended hangovers from early modern times (apprenticeship in the trades) or new structures pioneered by upwardly mobile, highly organized groups (advanced education in the professions). Meritocratic arguments from the ideology of professionalism, egalitarian demands by successive categorical groups, and organizational needs for social control of the labor force have combined to construct a staffing system of great complexity. A number of its correlates can be quickly remarked. First, categorical staffing (i.e., serving one occupation with only one kind of person) is now culturally perceived in the United States and some other nations as a moral delict. Second, types of work (some of them organized into occupations) fall into a widely accepted status hierarchy by which individual "achievement" is scored, both by social scientists and others. Third, meritocracy within the occupational status hierarchy implies a declining range of ability within given types of work. As people move competitively to jobs at particular levels, rather than being ascriptively channeled into occupations, whole types of work lose their "meritorious" practitioners to others, resulting in less merit overlap across types of work.

Durkheim and the other classical writers did not foresee the importance of staffing structures vis-à-vis the twentieth-century division of labor, although Marx and Weber clearly saw that organizations would overwhelm occupations as its most important linking structures. (Both actually saw this too clearly, underrating the new professionalism and other anti-organizational manifestations.) Recent writers on occupations, leaving the high plane of such issues, have generally asked more mundane questions. Hughes and his school have emphasized processes of occupational change as well as the biographical experience of work. The positivist tradition has dissected the mobility of categorical groups within census-derived occupational categories. Theoretical analysis does continue among scholars influenced by Marx, who have retained his focus on the destruction of skill and the alienation of labor through organizational change. And numerous writers have analyzed credentialing systems, although few have merged those analyses with realistic discussions of the work system itself. It is indeed time to create a new list of theoretical problems. In our time, questions about the occupational system concern four basic structures: the division of labor, the organizations and occupations that structure and fight over it, and the staffing structures that channel non-occupational social groups into them. What are the central questions about these various structures?

A Regional Theory of the Division of Labor

My own work falls within a first area of inquiry: Does the division of labor operate in the same way throughout the work system? If not, how are the regions of the division of labor established? How do their boundaries fluctuate? What are the respective roles of occupations and organizations in shaping this regionalization?

As an example of a regional theory of the division of labor, consider my analysis of the division of labor among experts, or, as we usually call them, professionals (Abbott, 1988). The division of labor between professions is established by conflict between professions over work. There is a body of "problems amenable to professional-type work" and a body of professions eager to do that work. Through cultural practices usually involving abstract knowledge, professions construct the problems into jurisdictions (e.g., problems with the body become diseases, disputes between people become legal cases). On the basis of their successful construction of problems, professions claim certain rights—from others in the workplace, from the public, from clients, and from the state. These other actors may then ratify, limit, or contest a profession's claims of jurisdiction, thereby creating a social structure for jurisdictions whose cultural structure arises in the original practices of the professions. At any given time, the system of professions comprises the problems professions work with, the professions themselves, and the links of jurisdiction—social and cultural—that bind one to the other. These links may be stronger or weaker depending on aspects of the professions' own cultural practices, on the constellation of competitors for the work, on the social organization and power of the professions, and so on. . . .

. . . Abstract knowledge is not, however, the general currency of the division of labor. The professions constitute a region of the division of labor, one whose operation differs from that of other regions. To be sure, some assert that there is no real distinction between doctors and plumbers, and so on. But divisions of labor in different areas of the work world are clearly established by different processes. No one studying divisions of labor in manufacturing industries discusses competition through abstract knowledge. On the contrary, writers in the Braverman (1976) tradition attribute the factory division of labor to the bureaucratic aim of centralized control over the labor force; the contest between management and workers is far more important than any competition between more or less free competitors. In other regions of the division of labor—for example, in the various building trades—the process has been one of negotiation and competition, as in the professions, but the currency of the competition is not abstract knowledge.

Setting out a regional theory of the division of labor means unmasking the simple opposition of deskilling and efficiency bequeathed to us by Marx and Smith. Nor is Durkheim's attribution of the division of labor to fear of competition any more useful than this standard opposition; it too makes the division of labor more a political than an analytic problem. We must take a new approach to the division of labor, specifying the various processes by which actual divisions of labor are established. I have discussed competition through abstract knowledge among the professions. The Braverman tradition has analyzed bureaucratically imposed subdivision within large organizations. Direct negotiation and competition using other means than abstract knowledge have also seen some study. To these we must add the imposition of divisions of labor by the state, a common feature of the Old Regime, and the division of labor through tradition, a mechanism easily overlooked in modern society. Furthermore, these various processes can be nested inside one another, for we presently have professions proliferating subordinated, bureaucratically structured divisions of labor under their own direction (hospitals, law, accounting, and architectural firms), and we also have extensive competition and negotiation within the presumably Bravermanian

rigidities of large organizations. A regional theory must recognize these complexities.

After analyzing the various ways of establishing divisions of labor, we must then discover the conditions of their succession. There is little mistaking the emergence of bureaucratic, Bravermanian deskilling in the larger professions in the last 50 years. Does this mean that the production of expertise, like most other modern production, will hereafter be institutionalized in organizations rather than in individuals, that professionalism—the very notion of institutionalizing expertise in individuals—is dead? Under what conditions can professionalism recoup against the subdivision and bureaucratization of professional work? What kinds of external authorities are invoked to support the various mechanisms of the division of labor? When? . . .

The Problem of Occupational Coalescence

Recognizing that organization has prevailed over occupation in the last 200 years entails a set of questions about occupations. The most obvious is whether occupations exist, or indeed really ever have existed in the majority of the labor force. This is by no means a silly question. We know that even among professionals out-migration is extremely high. Electrical and chemical engineers, operations researchers, accountants, clergy, and college teachers all face probabilities of more than 50% of leaving by age 40 the census categories in which they began their careers. If this is the case among professionals, how much greater is it among other workers! Yet we have remarkably little information about job patterns over the life course, and remarkably little knowledge of real occupational commitment.

Retrospectively, too, there are doubts as to the reality of occupational identification.

Nineteenth-century data does show some workers persistently remaining within particular industries and workplaces (their data is more likely to survive), but also shows other workers whose fluid careers span a dozen or more occupations. The modern problem of turnover in types of work does indeed question the ontological status of occupations. We cannot simply assume occupations exist because census categories exist, and because older arguments about the division of labor assumed that occupations exist. We must uncover the real patterns of membership in and allegiance to occupations in both past and present, and we must link these patterns within life histories to understand the changing role of occupation in individual lives and, conversely, the patterns of individual lives within occupations.

In part, the real question is what it means to say that occupations exist. We face this question more squarely as organizations increasingly control definitions of work and define career ladders within themselves. A host of writers describe professionals' deserting of professionalism for bureaucratic advancement; this is an old theme about engineers; and nineteenth-century data shows American railroads operating a system in which one advanced from shop laborer to yard laborer to brakeman to freight conductor to passenger conductor and so on. How long, then, must individuals remain in an occupation for that occupation to develop a group consciousness and a social structure? These are familiar questions about class membership, but not about occupational membership. What kinds of occupational structure are possible under different kinds of employment systems? How real are our images of occupations in the past? . . . One can immediately see, in all of these questions, an interaction of occupational change with increasingly explicit staffing structures; deskilling often involves replacing the older and more skilled with the younger (cheaper) and less skilled. Age is thus articulated directly with the occupational system through the organizational revolution.

Very much the same concerns, therefore, lie behind my questions about occupations as lie behind my questions about the division of labor. We need a regional theory of occupations. For the professions and, to some extent, for crafts and operatives, we have had such theories. But these theories have had little to say to one another. Moreover, there is no general analysis of the different types of occupational coalescence and the conditions, particularly the biographical and career conditions, under which the varying types are possible. We need more models for occupational consciousness than simply unionism and professionalism. We need to understand the interaction between the forces affecting occupational coalescence and the structures embodying staffing patterns; for it is through their control of staffing that organizations have ultimately undermined occupations' ability to come together. We need to further analyze deskilling to see whether and how deskilling undermined both old and new forms of occupational coalescence. Only such a comprehensive analysis of the actual social structuring of occupations can tell us the new position of occupations in the world of work.

The Cultural Structure of Work

Echoing these largely social questions about occupational coalescence are a set of cultural questions about our usual view of occupational life. Is not the idea that most people in the labor force "are members of occupations" rather than simply "have jobs" basically a creation of progressive reforms in vocational guidance and education? The vocational guidance movement took up the image of lifetime career from the professions and the crafts—the two groups that had preserved it in face of the organizational revolution. It attempted to impose that image on the entire labor force, working through the school, which was rapidly becoming the central staffing structure of the new work system. Persisting to this day in high school guidance departments, the vocational guidance "career model" hides from us the profound conceptual differences between the work systems of today and of two centuries ago.

Doubtless, too, the excellence of recent materialist work blinds theorists to work as a *cultural* category. Yet our cultural critique of work must be as thoroughgoing as the materialist has been, examining not only the cultural forces shaping the work system we observe but also those determining the categories and terms with which we observe it. As I have implied, this critique must begin with the cultural structure of occupations themselves; the common language terms and images we have for occupational life. I have argued that these came in large measure from progressive reformers. Where did the progressive reformers get their ideas? Were these ideas peculiar to the culture of work in America, reflecting the lack of a guild tradition that elsewhere provided a vocabulary for rethinking work after the organizational revolution? What were the common, everyday senses of "occupation," "career," and "vocation," in the nineteenth and early twentieth centuries? A few writers (e.g., Rodgers, 1978) have studied the misalignments of these cultural categories with the realities they describe. We need more such work.

Among the cultural models for occupations, the concepts of profession and union have had pride of place. By mid-century, the two had become an antithetical pair, consistently used to analyze American labor structures. Was this vocabulary characteristic of all modern labor systems, or did it fare differently in France, say, where professions had joined other workers in the great wave of syndicalism in the late nineteenth century? We also need studies of other cultural

models for occupations, even of those that, like the small proprietorship, have nearly vanished in modern systems.

Not only must we study cultural forces in the work world, we must also consciously criticize the categories we use to analyze that world. Consider the system of occupational and labor statistics. The classifying and counting of occupations has a distinct history, one that parallels and reinforces the larger triumph of organizational forces in the division of labor. Societies that count occupations in census categories view the nature of occupations in a manner both distinctive and reductionistic. Yet our research on occupations generally takes this view for granted. We must rather ask how the current system of counting occupations began and how it has influenced perception of occupation, both within and beyond social science. There has been some work in this area (e.g., Coxon et al., 1986), but we need more.

Dominating our conception of occupations in America is the notion of a status hierarchy of occupations, observed years ago by social scientists and gradually reified by the culture into a scale of social success. Indeed, some have argued that such a ladder is culturally universal. While historical and cross-cultural analysis prove its particularity, the ladder concept is still centrally important in the current occupational system. It matters less for its role in the actual relations of occupations—these being mostly established by the division of labor within organizations—than for its culturally authoritative position in the staffing structures. Students ignorant of the daily work of lawyers and doctors nonetheless diligently pursue these occupations because they stand at the top of occupational status rankings. When did this pattern begin? Does it, as seems apparent at first glance, simply reflect the professions' emergence as the upper middle-class evasion of organizational employment? Or is it a symptom of a more general role for reified occupational status—as a measure of personal achievement, a means of autobiographical understanding, and so on?

We need also to analyze the cultural portrayal of organizational employment. The cultural myths of entrepreneurship have seen some study (e.g., Sutton et al., 1962), as have some images of working-class employment (e.g., Rodgers, 1978). But there is less on the portraits of organizational advancement that would ultimately lead to the gray flannel man. Was the triumph of organization over occupation merely one of social structure and material power, or did the new form of work exercise a cultural authority as well? Was the cultural triumph of organization easier, for example, in societies without the intense individualism of the United States?

Even more general questions arise concerning the global ideologies of the modern work world, such as the notion that economic growth is inherently good or the idea that work is a necessary evil on the way to the real end and true business of living—the consumption of goods and services. These ideas, too, must be analyzed in relation to the modern occupational system. To write of them is inevitably to write politics. Yet we cannot avoid them. They are the framework on which the current work system is legitimated. When such legitimations change, work suddenly looks very different. They have done so before, and understanding why they did will help us see why we find certain structures of work preferable to others despite their manifest flaws. Serious comparative study, particularly of cultures with substantially different work beliefs (e.g., Japan) is thus the more necessary.

The Organization of Consumption as Work

Lying both inside and outside the world of work is the activity of consumption that takes products and services back into households and other consuming units. Another central question about the modern work world concerns the relation of consumption to the division of labor. To what degree has consumption become a position in the division of labor, another form of "work," a part-time occupation? (I set aside here the fact that part of people's work in organizations is to buy goods and services for organizational use; such work represents a large fraction of final consumption in modern economies.) In one sense, of course, the idea that consumption is work is absurd, denied a priori by our cultural definitions of work and leisure. In another sense, the notion is not absurd at all. Consumption is as necessary a part of the division of labor as is production; in particular, certain forms and extents of consumption are necessary to organizational dominance of the division of labor. The organizations dominating the modern division of labor have a great interest in overproduction, which has led them to work hard to develop an "occupation" of consumers. That this occupation is unpaid does not impugn its existence, for the fact is that consumption in modern societies can be hard work, whether one is waiting in line in the Soviet Union or struggling through traffic in the United States.

One facet of this occupation-building derives from the restructuring of mass distribution. Chandler (1977) has shown the gradual replacement of local distribution in America first by wholesale jobbers, then by department stores and mail-order houses, and finally by chain stores. It is striking that the jobbers, who sold through country stores and similar small outlets, and the mail-order houses, who sold directly to consumers at home, both lost ground to the department and chain stores. For while both the latter lowered consumer prices, both required consumers to provide more of the final transportation of the goods. Consumers were willing to pay these costs—the carfare to get to a central city department store or automobile costs to reach a suburban chain store—merely because of the lowered prices, there being little immediate increase in the available variety of goods. The new distribution forms made consumers do some of the work previously incumbent on the corporation or its agents. Fast food chains, supermarkets, and self-service gas stations merely take the process a step further.

Very much as in Burawoy's (1979) analysis of shop floor practices, the consumer is induced to work for the organization by means of a game. In order to "make out" as consumers—to acquire goods and services at lessened expense—purchasers pay some of the final costs of transporting the merchandise. To the same end, they are also willing to spend much time in shopping, to read pages of mendacious advertisements, and to gossip unendingly about restaurants, floor polishers, beers, and so on. While these seem to some consumers like pleasant pastimes, one could label such an attitude as so much false consciousness. For in fact consumers work actively for the firms' marketing departments as well. The gradual increase in articles of clothing (and other consumer goods) that carry identifiable manufacturer's labels—a practice long standard on jeans, but more recently standard for leisure apparel generally, has culminated in T-shirts and hats that carry advertisements for breweries, clothing merchandisers, seed houses, and so on. I recently counted such articles of clothing on an average Saturday at an average airport and found 45% of the population wearing at least one item containing a direct or indirect advertisement. It doesn't matter that these markings serve a manifest personal function of status assertion; they serve the undoubtedly more important latent function of maintaining organizational dominance of the division of labor.

Even consumers, then, have become part of the modern division of labor. How this has occurred—how consumption has been turned from something like a consummatory activity into something rather like work—seems an essential question. There is, thankfully, a great new interest in historical studies of consumption (e.g., McKendrick et al., 1982); we need corresponding analyses of the contemporary scene. Central questions, too, arise from the relation of consumption to staffing processes. The early twentieth-century consumption structure rested heavily on married women as its central consumers. As those women enter the "real" labor market, the work of consumption must be spread more effectively. Among the many questions about the staffing of consumption, then, are its increasing organization around the categorical solidarities (like age groups and genders) noted earlier and the processes of education that produce effective consumers. All of these are just as surely questions about "occupation" as are traditional questions about the division of labor. A great deal is in fact known about them—not among academic social scientists, but among the market researchers who work so hard to train consumers. Learning their knowledge would tell us a great deal.

The Interrelation of Work Structures

Hidden behind all these questions is the more general one of the relation between the division of labor, occupation, organization, and staffing; a relation that changes from society to society and from time to time within given societies. Undoubtedly the most important general question about work concerns the forces that affect this balance. For cross-national variation in the balance itself is great. In the United States, occupations are largely on the defensive. Union membership, even membership in professional associations, has fallen significantly. In Japan, although the overall unionization rate is slightly higher than in America, the structure of unions is dictated by the structure of the organizations. Unions do not represent comparable occupations at all. In England, where by contrast large organizations emerged well after a substantial labor movement began, unionization still stands at about half the labor force and reflects occupational structure directly. Now while union membership is a very indirect measure of occupational identification, it serves to indicate the variety of modern occupational structures and in turn the various relations between the four central features of the work world. A number of factors affecting that balance require substantial study.

In a way, the most surprising of these is the long stable relation between the occupational world and the division of labor in the household. The modern occupational system took its initial structure from the separation of work and home in the nineteenth century. That separation dictated the gender structure of many occupations and limited the economic functions of the household to distribution and consumption. But now the welfare state has stripped the household of the welfare functions that it retained from feudal times, functions that fell on it with increased force during the heyday of laissez-faire capitalism in the mid- to late nineteenth century. In the more advanced welfare states, extensive social support systems have facilitated the entry of married women into the labor force, a process that proceeds in other advanced economies even without that support. The impact of these changes on consumption, the lone remaining economic function of the household, has already been mentioned. But the entry of women into the labor force has clearly affected the relation of organization and occupation as well. In America, at least, women have predominantly entered parts of the service sector with new and ill-defined occupational structures, thereby favoring organizational dominance. Married women re-entering the labor force have, to some extent, bypassed the staffing structures that process those going directly from school to work. The shifting position of the family, and in particular the shifts in gender roles permitted and fostered by the welfare state, clearly need substantial research, not only in their own right, but in their larger effects on the ability of organizations to dominate the social structure of work.

Much of the relation between organizations and occupations, staffing and the division of labor, is determined by the state, a force that modifies and supplements the effects of the changing division of household labor. For example, by giving workers an entirely new set of political stakes, state welfare policies have removed workers' attention from the politics of work (Zussman, 1985). Some have seen in this change a declining political significance of the division of labor. The state also directs staffing policies, although the extent of this direction varies widely. In the United States, the state has undertaken endless rearrangements of the organizational side of the staffing structures through negative sanctions, incentive systems, and formal regulation. These rearrangements reflect the demands of categorical groups seeking recognition. In Great Britain, the state has now protected occupations' interests, now organizations'. In France, many of the staffing structures are themselves the creation of state efforts to articulate population and work; under state leadership the partnership between industry and education has been strong since the mid-nineteenth century.

Varied questions can be asked about state involvement. Do states favor organizational dominance? Does the willingness of the state to listen to categorical groups provide a new counterweight to organizational dominance, replacing the lost authority of occupations? How and why do states utilize and control staffing structures? Here cross-cultural comparison will provide important answers. The Japanese educational system, many argue (e.g., Rohlen, 1983), is ideally suited to training participants in large organizational structures. Absolutely uniform in the early years, it uses individual competition to determine location in highly stratified systems at the high school and college level. Instruction remains factory-like throughout, and produces workers who, in Thomas Rohlen's words, are used to "hard, efficient work in organizations, effective information processing, [and] orderly private behavior" (1983: 305). The contrast with American staffing structures—largely controlled by local jurisdictions burdened with other obligations and by faculties enamored of individualism—could not be more marked. The 12 years spent in school by most citizens in modern countries clearly provide the implicit model for later industrial relations. That within student bodies there is no real analogue for occupations—indeed for the division of labor itself—may explain why occupations have weakened in modern, "educated" labor forces.

Education is the main girder supporting modern staffing structures; therefore understanding its relation to occupations is essential. I have already mentioned the issue of vocational education and guidance. Even more important is the nature and relevance of educational content. I have argued elsewhere (Abbott, 1988: 67) that the vast majority of education professionals receive in universities is irrelevant to their future practice. Practicing doctors have little need for biochemistry, and practicing lawyers seldom see constitutional law. This practice does vary; professional education proceeds largely out-

side the universities in Britain, for example, and its content is much more practical. But in general, even professional education seems as much a winnowing tactic as a teaching of necessary materials. The general college curriculum is even more clearly a winnowing tactic. Although an educated populace may seem an enlightenment ideal, the majority of college students in the United States (and their equivalents in the secondary school systems of most other first-world nations) will have no use at work for the skills or facts they are learning in college. They will be taught what is necessary on the job, much as professionals are. Nothing makes this clearer than the stunning fact that the American corporate sector now spends on education an amount equal to 70% of the entire higher education budget.

Rigorous training for work has not, of course, been the only reason for educational systems. They have also existed to train effective citizens, to provide esoteric knowledge to elites, and to spread acquaintance with cultural classics to a broader public. But mass media have usurped many of these traditional functions. Aside from elite universities and colleges, which continue along paths set long ago, modern educational systems have come largely to serve the staffing functions of allocating and assorting social groups into the world of work, where they will then be trained and directed by large organizations. How this has happened, how it varies from society to society, and how the change has affected other staffing structures are important questions about the modern structure of work.

Yet the condition of the household division of labor, the policies of the state, and the alternative functions of education do not exhaust the factors shaping the balance of the four fundamental structures of work. I have only touched on a few issues of outstanding importance. The question of the new occupational structure, I have suggested throughout, has less to do with the history of occupations than with the history of work in general. The central theme of that history in the recent past has been the replacement of occupations by organizations as the central linking structures of the division of labor. That change produced a need for direct mediation between organizations and society, a mediation provided by the staffing structures. If we can understand the forces producing these large-scale changes, an understanding of most changes internal to the occupational structure will follow from them.

My aim has been to replace the classical agenda of questions about occupations. The old agenda saw the division of labor as driven either by efficiency or by management dominance. It took industrial labor as paradigmatic. It accepted as given the idea of occupations and indeed our whole cultural construction of work. It ignored the management of consumption, taking for granted a model of consumption far more appropriate to nineteenth-century economies of scarcity than to twentieth-century economies of excess.

Ultimately, this old agenda produces a sociology of work that can tell us little about our future occupational structure. Research on categorical group achievement on reified occupational rating scales may be useful political ammunition for the government or for the groups involved. But it constitutes rather than studies the world of work; citizens think so-called occupational achievement important because social scientists tell them it is, having themselves unthinkingly accepted census descriptions as realities. Correlatively, the old agenda wallows in romanticism about free artisanal labor, undoubtedly because most social scientists are artisans producing research for elite customers. The blunt fact is that such labor was scarce in early modern times, is even more

so today, and shows every likelihood of becoming yet scarcer in the future.

Can we predict the future of occupations? Certainly there are some obvious predictions one might make for the 1990s. Service will increase as a labor force sector in advanced economies, and in particular commercial occupations like retail sales and credit will expand rapidly toward the American model, particularly in Europe with the unification of 1992. Larger and deeper divisions of labor will appear in most professions, particularly in those dealing with large-scale problems like design and information. Artificial intelligence will reshuffle the social structures of numerous occupations and present monumental deskilling threats in others. Computerized worker control and surveillance will increase in the workplace, but decentralization may offset traditional worker control, through work at home and flexible hours. These predictions require little more than an educated glance at the *Statistical Abstract;* they are extrapolations of current trends.

However, to make such predictions is by no means to know what they mean, what larger trends they have a place in, what strange and different futures may grow, naturally but unpredictably, out of these developments after the turn of the century. Only substantial theoretical inquiry can tell us that, and as I have argued throughout, our past agenda of problems and issues has kept us from that inquiry. If we can understand how different divisions of labor proceed, whether and how occupations become real, how we and others imagine work, how consumption has become work, and how the various forces of the work world trade off with one another, we may be able to understand the future of occupations and of work generally. But understanding will not produce prediction. People are too creative for that. Understanding will produce reinterpretation and action. When we finally understand the new economy, we will have created it.

REFERENCES

Burawoy, M. (1979) *Manufacturing Consent.* Chicago: Univ. of Chicago Press.

Chandler, A. D. (1977) *The Visible Hand.* Cambridge, MA: Harvard Univ. Press.

Coxon, A. P. M., P. M. Davies, and C. L. Jones (1986) *Images of Occupational Stratification.* Beverly Hills, CA: Sage.

McKendrick, N., J. Brewer, and J. H. Plumb (1982) *The Birth of a Consumer Society.* Bloomington: Indiana Univ. Press.

Rodgers, D. T. (1978) *The Work Ethic in America.* Chicago: Univ. of Chicago Press.

Rohlen, T. (1993) *Japanese High Schools.* Berkeley: Univ. of California Press.

Sutton, F. X., S. E. Harris, C. Kaysen, and J. Tobin (1962) *The American Business Creed.* New York: Schocken.

Zussman, R. (1985) *Mechanics of the Middle Class.* Berkeley: Univ. of California Press.